Doing Business 2009

258067674

COMPARING REGULATION IN 181 ECONOMIES

A copublication of the World Bank, the International Finance Corporation, and Palgrave Macmillan

© 2008 The International Bank for Reconstruction and Development / The World Bank
1818 H Street NW
Washington, DC 20433
Telephone 202-473-1000
Internet www.worldbank.org
E-mail feedback@worldbank.org

1 2 3 4 5 6 10 09 08

A publication of the World Bank and the International Finance Corporation.

Additional copies of *Doing Business 2009, Doing Business 2008, Doing Business 2007: How to Reform, Doing Business in 2006: Creating Jobs, Doing Business in 2005: Removing Obstacles to Growth* and *Doing Business in 2004: Understanding Regulations* may be purchased at www.doingbusiness.org.

ISBN: 978-0-8213-7609-6
E-ISBN: 978-0-8213-7610-2
DOI: 10.1596/978-0-8213-7609-6
ISSN: 1729-2638

Library of Congress Cataloging-in-Publication data has been applied for.

Contents

Doing Business 2009 is the sixth in a series of annual reports investigating the regulations that enhance business activity and those that constrain it. *Doing Business* presents quantitative indicators on business regulations and the protection of property rights that can be compared across 181 economies—from Afghanistan to Zimbabwe—and over time.

Regulations affecting 10 stages of the life of a business are measured: starting a business, dealing with construction permits, employing workers, registering property, getting credit, protecting investors, paying taxes, trading across borders, enforcing contracts and closing a business. Data in *Doing Business 2009* are current as of June 1, 2008. The indicators are used to analyze economic outcomes and identify what reforms have worked, where and why.

The methodology for the legal rights of lenders and borrowers, part of the getting credit indicators, changed for *Doing Business 2009*. See Data notes for details.

Current features
News on the *Doing Business* project
http://www.doingbusiness.org

Rankings
How economies rank—from 1 to 181
http://www.doingbusiness.org/economyrankings

Reformers
Short summaries of DB2009 reforms, lists of reformers since DB2004 and a ranking simulation tool
http://www.doingbusiness.org/reformers

Data time series
Customized data sets since DB2004
http://www.doingbusiness.org/customquery

Methodology and research
The methodologies and research papers underlying *Doing Business*
http://www.doingbusiness.org/MethodologySurveys

Blog
Online journal focusing on business regulation reform
http://blog.doingbusiness.org

Downloads
Doing Business reports as well as subnational, country and regional reports and case studies
http://www.doingbusiness.org/downloads

Subnational projects
Differences in business regulations at the subnational level
http://www.doingbusiness.org/subnational

Law library
Online collection of business laws and regulations
http://www.doingbusiness.org/lawlibrary

Local partners
More than 6,700 specialists in 181 economies who participate in *Doing Business*
http://www.doingbusiness.org/LocalPartners

Reformers' Club
Celebrating the top 10 *Doing Business* reformers
http://www.reformersclub.org

Business Planet
Interactive map on the ease of doing business
http://www.doingbusiness.org/map

About Doing Business

In 1664 William Petty, an adviser to England's Charles II, compiled the first known national accounts. He made 4 entries. On the expense side, "food, housing, clothes and all other necessaries" were estimated at £40 million. National income was split among 3 sources: £8 million from land, £7 million from other personal estates and £25 million from labor income.

In later centuries estimates of country income, expenditure and material inputs and outputs became more abundant. But it was not until the 1940s that a systematic framework was developed for measuring national income and expenditure, under the direction of British economist John Maynard Keynes. As the methodology became an international standard, comparisons of countries' financial positions became possible. Today the macroeconomic indicators in national accounts are standard in every country.

Governments committed to the economic health of their country and opportunities for its citizens now focus on more than macroeconomic conditions. They also pay attention to the laws, regulations and institutional arrangements that shape daily economic activity.

Until very recently, however, there were no globally available indicator sets for monitoring these microeconomic factors and analyzing their relevance. The first efforts, in the 1980s, drew on perceptions data from expert or business surveys. Such surveys are useful gauges of economic and policy conditions. But their reliance on perceptions and their incomplete coverage of poor countries limit their usefulness for analysis.

The *Doing Business* project, launched 7 years ago, goes one step further. It looks at domestic small and medium-size companies and measures the regulations applying to them through their life cycle. *Doing Business* and the standard cost model initially developed and applied in the Netherlands are, for the present, the only standard tools used across a broad range of jurisdictions to measure the impact of government rule-making on business activity.[1]

The first *Doing Business* report, published in 2003, covered 5 indicator sets in 133 economies. This year's report covers 10 indicator sets in 181 economies. The project has benefited from feedback from governments, academics, practitioners and reviewers.[2] The initial goal remains: to provide an objective basis for understanding and improving the regulatory environment for business.

WHAT *DOING BUSINESS* COVERS

Doing Business provides a quantitative measure of regulations for starting a business, dealing with construction permits, employing workers, registering property, getting credit, protecting investors, paying taxes, trading across borders, enforcing contracts and closing a business—as they apply to domestic small and medium-size enterprises.

A fundamental premise of *Doing Business* is that economic activity requires good rules. These include rules that establish and clarify property rights and reduce the costs of resolving disputes, rules that increase the predictability of economic interactions and rules that provide contractual partners with core protections against abuse. The objective: regulations designed to be efficient, to be accessible to all who need to use them and to be simple in their implementation. Accordingly, some *Doing Business* indicators give a higher score for more regulation, such as stricter disclosure requirements in related-party transactions. Some give a higher score for a simplified way of implementing existing regulation, such as completing business start-up formalities in a one-stop shop.

The *Doing Business* project encompasses 2 types of data. The first come from readings of laws and regulations. The second are time and motion indicators that measure the efficiency in achieving a regulatory goal (such as granting the legal identity of a business). Within the time and motion indicators, cost estimates are recorded from official fee schedules where applicable. Here, *Doing Business* builds on Hernando de Soto's pioneering work in applying the time and motion approach first used by Frederick Taylor to revolutionize the production of the Model T Ford. De Soto used the approach in the 1980s to show the obstacles to setting up a garment factory on the outskirts of Lima.[3]

WHAT *DOING BUSINESS* DOES NOT COVER

Just as important as knowing what *Doing Business* does is to know what it does not do—to understand what limitations must be kept in mind in interpreting the data.

LIMITED IN SCOPE

Doing Business focuses on 10 topics, with the specific aim of measuring the regulation and red tape relevant to the life cycle of a domestic small to medium-size firm. Accordingly:

- *Doing Business* does not measure all aspects of the business environment that matter to firms or investors—or all factors that affect competitiveness. It does not, for example, measure security, macroeconomic stability, corruption, the labor skills of the population, the underlying strength of institutions or the quality of infrastructure.[4] Nor does it focus on regulations specific to foreign investment.

- *Doing Business* does not cover all regulations, or all regulatory goals, in any economy. As economies and technology advance, more areas of economic activity are being regulated. For example, the European Union's body of laws (*acquis*) has now grown to no fewer than 14,500 rule sets. *Doing Business* measures regulation affecting just 10 phases of a company's life cycle, through 10 specific sets of indicators.

BASED ON STANDARDIZED CASE SCENARIOS

Doing Business indicators are built on the basis of standardized case scenarios with specific assumptions, such as the business being located in the largest business city of the economy. Economic indicators commonly make limiting assumptions of this kind. Inflation statistics, for example, are often based on prices of consumer goods in a few urban areas.

Such assumptions allow global coverage and enhance comparability. But they come at the expense of generality. Business regulation and its enforcement differ across an economy, particularly in federal states and large economies. And of course the challenges and opportunities of the largest business city—whether Mumbai or São Paulo, Nuku'alofa or Nassau—vary greatly across economies. Recognizing governments' interest in such variation, *Doing Business* has complemented its global indicators with subnational studies in such economies as Brazil, China, Mexico, Nigeria, the Philippines and the Russian Federation.[5] *Doing Business* has also begun a work program focusing on small island states.[6]

In areas where regulation is complex and highly differentiated, the standardized case used to construct the *Doing Business* indicator needs to be carefully defined. Where relevant, the standardized case assumes a limited liability company. This choice is in part empirical: private, limited liability companies are the most prevalent business form in most economies around the world. The choice also reflects one focus of *Doing*

Business: expanding opportunities for entrepreneurship. Investors are encouraged to venture into business when potential losses are limited to their capital participation.

FOCUSED ON THE FORMAL SECTOR

In constructing the indicators, *Doing Business* assumes that entrepreneurs are knowledgeable about all regulations in place and comply with them. In practice, entrepreneurs may spend considerable time finding out where to go and what documents to submit. Or they may avoid legally required procedures altogether—by not registering for social security, for example.

Where regulation is particularly onerous, levels of informality are higher. Informality comes at a cost: firms in the informal sector typically grow more slowly, have poorer access to credit and employ fewer workers—and their workers remain outside the protections of labor law.[7] *Doing Business* measures one set of factors that help explain the occurrence of informality and give policy makers insights into potential areas of reform. Gaining a fuller understanding of the broader business environment, and a broader perspective on policy challenges, requires combining insights from *Doing Business* with data from other sources, such as the World Bank Enterprise Surveys.[8]

WHY THIS FOCUS

Doing Business functions as a kind of cholesterol test for the regulatory environment for domestic businesses. A cholesterol test does not tell us everything about the state of our health. But it does measure something important for our health. And it puts us on watch to change behaviors in ways that will improve not only our cholesterol rating but also our overall health.

One way to test whether *Doing Business* serves as a proxy for the broader business environment and for competitiveness is to look at correlations between the *Doing Business* rankings and

other major economic benchmarks. The indicator set closest to *Doing Business* in what it measures is the Organisation for Economic Co-operation and Development's indicators of product market regulation; the correlation here is 0.80. The World Economic Forum's Global Competitiveness Index and IMD's *World Competitiveness Yearbook* are broader in scope, but these too are strongly correlated with *Doing Business* (0.80 and 0.76, respectively). These correlations suggest that where peace and macroeconomic stability are present, domestic business regulation makes an important difference in economic competitiveness.

A bigger question is whether the issues on which *Doing Business* focuses matter for development and poverty reduction. The World Bank study *Voices of the Poor* asked 60,000 poor people around the world how they thought they might escape poverty.[9] The answers were unequivocal: women and men alike pin their hopes on income from their own business or wages earned in employment. Enabling growth—and ensuring that poor people can participate in its benefits—requires an environment where new entrants with drive and good ideas, regardless of their gender or ethnic origin, can get started in business and where firms can invest and grow, generating more jobs.

Small and medium-size enterprises are key drivers of competition, growth and job creation, particularly in developing countries. But in these economies up to 80% of economic activity takes place in the informal sector. Firms may be prevented from entering the formal sector by excessive bureaucracy and regulation.

Where regulation is burdensome and competition limited, success tends to depend more on whom you know than on what you can do. But where regulation is transparent, efficient and implemented in a simple way, it becomes easier for any aspiring entrepreneurs, regardless of their connections, to operate within the rule of law and to benefit from the opportunities and protections that the law provides.

In this sense *Doing Business* values

good rules as a key to social inclusion. It also provides a basis for studying effects of regulations and their application. For example, *Doing Business 2004* found that faster contract enforcement was associated with perceptions of greater judicial fairness—suggesting that justice delayed is justice denied.[10] Other examples are provided in the chapters that follow.

DOING BUSINESS AS A BENCHMARKING EXERCISE

Doing Business, in capturing some key dimensions of regulatory regimes, has been found useful for benchmarking. Any benchmarking—for individuals, firms or states—is necessarily partial: it is valid and useful if it helps sharpen judgment, less so if it substitutes for judgment.

Doing Business provides 2 takes on the data it collects: it presents "absolute" indicators for each economy for each of the 10 regulatory topics it addresses, and it provides rankings of economies, both by indicator and in aggregate. Judgment is required in interpreting these measures for any economy and in determining a sensible and politically feasible path for reform.

Reviewing the *Doing Business* rankings in isolation may show unexpected results. Some economies may rank unexpectedly high on some indicators. And some that have had rapid growth or attracted a great deal of investment may rank lower than others that appear to be less dynamic.

Still, a higher ranking in *Doing Business* tends to be associated with better outcomes over time. Economies that rank among the top 20 are those with high per capita income and productivity and highly developed regulatory systems.

But for reform-minded governments, how much their indicators improve matters more than their absolute ranking. As economies develop, they strengthen and add to regulations to protect investor and property rights. Meanwhile, they find more efficient ways to implement existing regulations and

cut outdated ones. One finding of *Doing Business:* dynamic and growing economies continually reform and update their regulations and their way of implementing them, while many poor economies still work with regulatory systems dating to the late 1800s.

DOING BUSINESS— A USER'S GUIDE

Quantitative data and benchmarking can be useful in stimulating debate about policy, both by exposing potential challenges and by identifying where policy makers might look for lessons and good practices. These data also provide a basis for analyzing how different policy approaches—and different policy reforms—contribute to desired outcomes such as competitiveness, growth and greater employment and incomes.

Six years of *Doing Business* data have enabled a growing body of research on how performance on *Doing Business* indicators—and reforms relevant to those indicators—relate to desired social and economic outcomes. Some 325 articles have been published in peer-reviewed academic journals, and about 742 working papers are available through Google Scholar.[11] Among the findings:

- Lower barriers to start-up are associated with a smaller informal sector.[12]
- Lower costs of entry can encourage entrepreneurship and reduce corruption.[13]
- Simpler start-up can translate into greater employment opportunities.[14]

How do governments use *Doing Business?* A common first reaction is to doubt the quality and relevance of the *Doing Business* data. Yet the debate typically proceeds to a deeper discussion exploring the relevance of the data to the economy and areas where reform might make sense.

Most reformers start out by seeking examples, and *Doing Business* helps in this. For example, Saudi Arabia used the company law of France as a model for re-

vising its own. Many economies in Africa look to Mauritius—the region's strongest performer on *Doing Business* indicators—as a source of good practices for reform. In the words of Dr. Mahmoud Mohieldin, Egypt's minister of investment:

What I like about Doing Business… *is that it creates a forum for exchanging knowledge. It's no exaggeration when I say I checked the top 10 in every indicator and we just asked them, "What did you do?" If there is any advantage to starting late in anything, it's that you can learn from others.*

Over the past 6 years there has been much activity by governments in reforming the regulatory environment for domestic businesses. Most reforms relating to *Doing Business* topics were nested in broader programs of reform aimed at enhancing economic competitiveness. In structuring their reform programs, governments use multiple data sources and indicators. And reformers respond to many stakeholders and interest groups, all of whom bring important issues and concerns into the reform debate.

World Bank Group support to these reform processes is designed to encourage critical use of the data, sharpening judgment and avoiding a narrow focus on improving *Doing Business* rankings.

METHODOLOGY AND DATA

Doing Business covers 181 economies—including small economies and some of the poorest ones, for which little or no data are available in other data sets. The *Doing Business* data are based on domestic laws and regulations as well as administrative requirements. (For a detailed explanation of the *Doing Business* methodology, see Data notes.)

INFORMATION SOURCES FOR THE DATA
Most of the indicators are based on laws and regulations. In addition, most of the cost indicators are backed by official fee schedules. *Doing Business* contributors both fill out written surveys and provide

references to the relevant laws, regulations and fee schedules, aiding data checking and quality assurance.

For some indicators part of the cost component (where fee schedules are lacking) and the time component are based on actual practice rather than the law on the books. This introduces a degree of subjectivity. The *Doing Business* approach has therefore been to work with legal practitioners or professionals who regularly undertake the transactions involved. Following the standard methodological approach for time and motion studies, *Doing Business* breaks down each process or transaction, such as starting and legally operating a business, into separate steps to ensure a better estimate of time. The time estimate for each step is given by practitioners with significant and routine experience in the transaction.

Over the past 6 years more than 10,000 professionals in 181 economies have assisted in providing the data that inform the *Doing Business* indicators. This year's report draws on the inputs of more than 6,700 professionals. The *Doing Business* website indicates the number of respondents per economy and per indicator (see table 12.1 in Data notes for the number of respondents per indicator set). Because of the focus on legal and regulatory arrangements, most of the respondents are lawyers. The credit information survey is answered by officials of the credit registry or bureau. Freight forwarders, accountants, architects and other professionals answer the surveys related to trading across borders, taxes and construction permits.

The *Doing Business* approach to data collection contrasts with that of perception surveys, which capture often one-time perceptions and experiences of businesses. A corporate lawyer registering 100–150 businesses a year will be more familiar with the process than an entrepreneur, who will register a business only once or maybe twice. A bankruptcy judge deciding dozens of cases a year will have more insight into bankruptcy than a company that may undergo the process.

DEVELOPMENT OF THE METHODOLOGY

The methodology for calculating each indicator is transparent, objective and easily replicable. Leading academics collaborate in the development of the indicators, ensuring academic rigor. Six of the background papers underlying the indicators have been published in leading economic journals. Another 2 are at an advanced stage of publication in such journals.

Doing Business uses a simple averaging approach for weighting subindicators and calculating rankings. Other approaches were explored, including using principal components and unobserved components.[15] The principal components and unobserved components approaches turn out to yield results nearly identical to those of simple averaging. The tests show that each set of indicators provides new information. The simple averaging approach is therefore robust to such tests.

IMPROVEMENTS TO THE METHODOLOGY AND DATA REVISIONS

The methodology has undergone continual improvement over the years. Changes have been made mainly in response to suggestions from economies in the *Doing Business* sample. For enforcing contracts, for example, the amount of the disputed claim in the case scenario was increased from 50% to 200% of income per capita after the first year, as it became clear that smaller claims were unlikely to go to court.

Another change relates to starting a business. The minimum capital requirement can be an obstacle for potential entrepreneurs. Initially, *Doing Business* measured the required minimum capital regardless of whether it had to be paid up front or not. In many economies only part of the minimum capital has to be paid up front. To reflect the actual potential barrier to entry, the paid-in minimum capital has been used since 2004.

This year's report includes one change in the core methodology, to the strength of legal rights index, which is part of the getting credit indicator set.

All changes in methodology are explained in the report as well as on the *Doing Business* website. In addition, data time series for each indicator and economy are available on the website, beginning with the first year the indicator or economy was included in the report. To provide a comparable time series for research, the data set is back-calculated to adjust for changes in methodology and any revisions in data due to corrections. The website also makes available all original data sets used for background papers.

Information on data corrections is provided on the website (also see Data notes). A transparent complaint procedure allows anyone to challenge the data. If errors are confirmed after a data verification process, they are expeditiously corrected.

NOTES

1. The standard cost model is a quantitative methodology for determining the administrative burdens that regulation imposes on businesses. The method can be used to measure the effect of a single law or of selected areas of legislation or to perform a baseline measurement of all legislation in a country.
2. In the past year this has included a review by the World Bank Group Independent Evaluation Group (2008).
3. De Soto (2000).
4. The indicators related to trading across borders and dealing with construction permits take into account limited aspects of an economy's infrastructure, including the inland transport of goods and utility connections for businesses.
5. http://www.doingbusiness.org/subnational.
6. http://www.doingbusiness.org.
7. Schneider (2005).
8. http://www.enterprisesurveys.org.
9. Narayan and others (2000).
10. World Bank (2003).
11. http://scholar.google.com.
12. For example, Masatlioglu and Rigolini (2008), Kaplan, Piedra and Seira (2008) and Djankov, Ganser, McLiesh, Ramalho and Shleifer (2008).

13. For example, Alesina and others (2005), Perotti and Volpin (2004), Klapper, Laeven and Rajan (2006), Fisman and Sarria-Allende (2004), Antunes and Cavalcanti (2007), Barseghyan (2008) and Djankov, Ganser, McLiesh, Ramalho and Shleifer (2008).

14. For example, Freund and Bolaky (forthcoming), Chang, Kaltani and Loayza (forthcoming) and Helpman, Melitz and Rubinstein (2008).

15. See Djankov and others (2005).

Overview

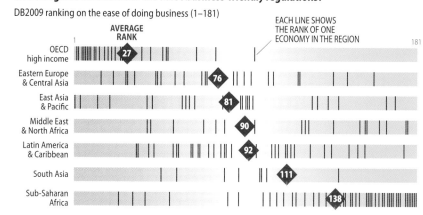

FIGURE 1.1

Which regions have some of the most business-friendly regulations?

DB2009 ranking on the ease of doing business (1–181)

Source: Doing Business database.

For the fifth year in a row Eastern Europe and Central Asia led the world in *Doing Business* reforms. Twenty-six of the region's 28 economies implemented a total of 69 reforms. Since 2004 *Doing Business* has been tracking reforms aimed at simplifying business regulations, strengthening property rights, opening up access to credit and enforcing contracts by measuring their impact on 10 indicator sets.[1] Nearly 1,000 reforms with an impact on these indicators have been captured. Eastern Europe and Central Asia has accounted for a third of them.

The region surpassed East Asia and Pacific in the average ease of doing business in 2007—and maintained its place this year (figure 1.1). Four of its

economies—Georgia, Estonia, Lithuania and Latvia—are among the top 30 in the overall *Doing Business* ranking.

Rankings on the ease of doing business do not tell the whole story about an economy's business environment. The indicator does not account for all factors important for doing business—for example, macroeconomic conditions, infrastructure, workforce skills or security. But improvement in an economy's ranking does indicate that its government is creating a regulatory environment more conducive to operating a business. In Eastern Europe and Central Asia many economies continue to do so—and economies in the region once again dominate the list of top *Doing Business* reformers

in 2007/08. New this year: reforms in the region are moving eastward as 4 newcomers join the top 10 list of reformers: Azerbaijan, Albania, the Kyrgyz Republic and Belarus (table 1.1).

Many others reformed as well. Worldwide, 113 economies implemented 239 reforms making it easier to do business between June 2007 and June 2008. That is the most reforms recorded in a single year since the *Doing Business* project started. In the past year reformers focused on easing business start-up, lightening the tax burden, simplifying import and export regulation and improving credit information systems.

Across regions, East Asia had the biggest pickup in the pace of reform.

TABLE 1.1

The top 10 reformers in 2007/08

Economy	Starting a business	Dealing with construction permits	Employing workers	Registering property	Getting credit	Protecting investors	Paying taxes	Trading across borders	Enforcing contracts	Closing a business
Azerbaijan	✔		✔	✔	✔	✔	✔		✔	
Albania	✔			✔	✔	✔				
Kyrgyz Republic	✔	✔			✔					
Belarus	✔	✔		✔	✔		✔	✔		
Senegal	✔			✔				✔		
Burkina Faso		✔	✔	✔			✔			
Botswana	✔					✔		✔		
Colombia	✔	✔					✔	✔		✔
Dominican Republic	✔			✔			✔	✔		
Egypt	✔	✔		✔	✔	✔		✔		

Note: Economies are ranked on the number and impact of reforms. First, *Doing Business* selects the economies that implemented reforms making it easier to do business in 3 or more of the *Doing Business* topics. Second, it ranks these economies on the increase in rank on the ease of doing business from the previous year. The larger the improvement, the higher the ranking as a reformer.

Source: Doing Business database.

FIGURE 1.2
Eastern European and Central Asian economies— leaders in *Doing Business* reforms

Share of economies with at least 1 reform making it easier to do business in past 5 years (%)
by *Doing Business* report year

Eastern Europe & Central Asia
(28 economies)

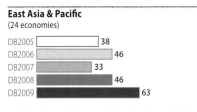

DB2005	82
DB2006	93
DB2007	89
DB2008	82
DB2009	93

East Asia & Pacific
(24 economies)

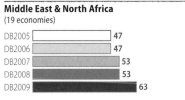

DB2005	38
DB2006	46
DB2007	33
DB2008	46
DB2009	63

Middle East & North Africa
(19 economies)

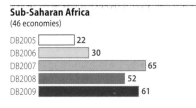

DB2005	47
DB2006	47
DB2007	53
DB2008	53
DB2009	63

Sub-Saharan Africa
(46 economies)

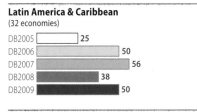

DB2005	22
DB2006	30
DB2007	65
DB2008	52
DB2009	61

Latin America & Caribbean
(32 economies)

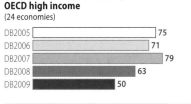

DB2005	25
DB2006	50
DB2007	56
DB2008	38
DB2009	50

OECD high income
(24 economies)

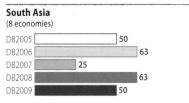

DB2005	75
DB2006	71
DB2007	79
DB2008	63
DB2009	50

South Asia
(8 economies)

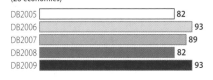

DB2005	50
DB2006	63
DB2007	25
DB2008	63
DB2009	50

Source: Doing Business database.

Two-thirds of its economies reformed, up from less than half last year (figure 1.2). The Middle East and North Africa continued its upward trend, with two-thirds of its economies reforming. In a region once known for prohibitive entry barriers, 2 countries—Tunisia and Yemen—eliminated the minimum capital requirement for starting a business, while Jordan reduced it from 30,000 Jordanian dinars to 1,000.

Sub-Saharan Africa continued its upward trend in reform too: 28 economies implemented 58 reforms, more than in any year since *Doing Business* began tracking reforms. Two West African countries led the way, Senegal and Burkina Faso. In Latin America, Colombia and the Dominican Republic were the most active. OECD high-income economies saw a slowdown in reform. So did South Asia.

Azerbaijan is the top reformer for 2007/08. A one-stop shop for business start-up began operating in January 2008, halving the time, cost and number of procedures to start a business. Business registrations increased by 40% in the first 6 months. Amendments to the labor code made employment regulation more flexible by allowing the use of fixed-term contracts for permanent tasks, easing restrictions on working hours and eliminating the need for reassignment in case of redundancy dismissals. And property transfers can now be completed in 11 days—down from 61 before—thanks to a unified property registry for land and real estate transactions.

That's not all. Azerbaijan eliminated the minimum loan cutoff of $1,100 at the credit registry, more than doubling the number of borrowers covered. Minority shareholders enjoy greater protection, thanks to amendments to the civil code and a new regulation on related-party transactions. Such transactions now are subject to stricter requirements for disclosure to the supervisory board and in annual reports. Moreover, interested parties involved in a related-party transaction harmful to the company must cover the damages and pay back

personal profits.

Taxpayers in Azerbaijan now take advantage of online filing and payment of taxes, saving more than 500 hours a year on average in dealing with paperwork. And a new economic court in Baku helped speed contract enforcement. With the number of judges looking at commercial cases increasing from 5 to 9, the average time to resolve a case declined by 30 days.

Albania is the runner-up, with reforms in 4 of the areas measured by *Doing Business*. A new company law strengthened the protection of minority shareholder rights. The law tightened approval and disclosure requirements for related-party transactions and, for the first time, defined directors' duties. It also introduced greater remedies to pursue if a related-party transaction is harmful to the company. Albania made start-up easier by taking commercial registration out of the court and creating a one-stop shop. Companies can now start a business in 8 days—it used to take more than a month. The country's first credit registry opened for business. And tax reforms halved the corporate income tax rate to 10%.

AFRICA—MORE REFORM THAN EVER BEFORE

Economies in Africa implemented more *Doing Business* reforms in 2007/08 than in any previous year covered. And 3 of the top 10 reformers are African: Senegal, Burkina Faso and Botswana. Three postconflict countries—Liberia, Rwanda and Sierra Leone—are reforming fast too (figure 1.3). Mauritius, the country with the region's most favorable business regulations, continues to reform, and this year joins the top 25 on the ease of doing business.

This focus on reform comes after several years of record economic growth in Africa. Annual growth has averaged nearly 6% in the past decade, thanks to better macroeconomic conditions and greater peace on the continent. With more economic opportunities, regulatory

FIGURE 1.3
Who reformed the most in Africa in 2007/08?
Improvement in the ranking on the ease of doing business, DB2008–DB2009

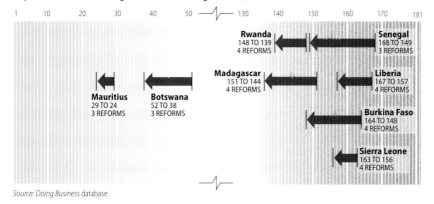

Source: Doing Business database.

constraints on businesses have become more pressing. Governments increasingly focus on reducing these constraints. And reformers recognize that bringing more economic activity to the formal sector through business and job creation is the most promising way to reduce poverty.[2]

Rwanda is one example of the dividends of peace and good macroeconomic policies. The country has been among the most active reformers of business regulation worldwide this decade. In 2001 it introduced a new labor law as part of the national reconstruction program. In 2002 it started property titling reform. In 2004 reformers simplified customs, improved the credit registry and undertook court reforms. In 2007 Rwanda continued with property registration and customs. Some reforms took longer to implement. For example, judicial reforms were initiated in 2001, but it was not until 2008 that the necessary laws were passed and new commercial courts started functioning.[3]

Most African reformers focused on easing start-up and reducing the cost of importing and exporting. There is room to do more. Entrepreneurs in Africa still face greater regulatory and administrative burdens, and less protection of property and investor rights, than entrepreneurs in any other region. The upside: reform in such circumstances can send a strong signal of governments' commitment to sound institutions and policies, catalyzing investor interest.

EASING ENTRY—ONCE AGAIN THE MOST POPULAR REFORM

Making it easier to start a business continued to be the most popular *Doing Business* reform in 2007/08. Forty-nine economies simplified start-up and reduced the cost (figure 1.4). These are among the 115 economies—more than half the world's total—that have reformed in this area over the past 5 years. The second most popular were reforms to simplify taxes and their administration. Third were reforms to ease trade. In all 3 areas much can be achieved with administrative reforms.

Reforms in other areas can be harder, particularly if they require legal changes or involve difficult political tradeoffs. Only 12 economies reformed their judicial system. Seven amended collateral or secured transactions laws. Six amended labor regulations to make them more flexible; 9 opted for more rigidity.

The 3 boldest reforms driving the biggest improvements in the *Doing Business* indicators (table 1.2):

• Albania's increase in investor protections
• Yemen's easing of business start-up
• The Dominican Republic's tax reform.

REFORM CONTINUES AMONG BEST PERFORMERS

Singapore continues to rank at the top on the ease of doing business, followed by New Zealand, the United States and Hong Kong (China) (table 1.3). And reform continues. Five of the top 10 economies implemented reforms that had an impact on the *Doing Business* indicators in 2007/08. Singapore further simplified its online business start-up service. New Zealand introduced a single online procedure for business start-up, lowered the corporate income tax and implemented a new insolvency act. Hong Kong (China) streamlined construction permitting as part of a broader reform of its licensing regime. Denmark implemented tax reforms. And entrepreneurs in Toronto, Canada, can now start a business with just one procedure.

This continuing reform is not surprising. Many high-income economies have institutionalized regulatory reform, setting up programs to systematically target red tape. Examples include the "Be the Smart Regulator" program in Hong Kong (China), Simplex in Portugal, the Better Regulation Executive in the United Kingdom, Actal in the Netherlands and Kafka in Belgium. To identify priorities, these governments routinely ask businesses what needs reform. Belgium reformed business registration after 2,600 businesses identified it as a major problem in 2003. Starting a business there used to take 7 procedures and nearly 2 months. Today it takes 3

TABLE 1.2
Top reformers in 2007/08 by indicator set

Starting a business	Yemen
Dealing with construction permits	Kyrgyz Republic
Employing workers	Burkina Faso
Registering property	Belarus
Getting credit	Cambodia
Protecting investors	Albania
Paying taxes	Dominican Republic
Trading across borders	Senegal
Enforcing contracts	Mozambique
Closing a business	Poland

Source: Doing Business database.

FIGURE 1.4

239 reforms in 2007/08 made it easier to do business—26 made it more difficult

	49	**18**	**6**	**24**	**32**
Reforms making it easier to do business	Albania				
	Angola				Albania
	Azerbaijan				Azerbaijan
	Bangladesh				Belarus
	Belarus				Cambodia
	Botswana				Cameroon
	Bulgaria				Central African Republic
	Canada				Chad
	Colombia				China
	Costa Rica			Azerbaijan	Congo, Rep.
	Czech Republic			Bangladesh	Egypt
	Dominican Republic			Belarus	Equatorial Guinea
	Egypt			Bosnia and Herzegovina	Finland
	El Salvador			Burkina Faso	Gabon
	Georgia			Congo, Rep.	Georgia
	Ghana			Dominican Republic	Guatemala
	Greece	Angola		Egypt	Indonesia
	Hungary	Armenia		Georgia	Kazakhstan
	Italy	Belarus		Hungary	Liberia
	Jordan	Bosnia and Herzegovina		Jamaica	Macedonia, former Yugoslav Republic of
	Kenya	Burkina Faso		Kazakhstan	Mauritius
	Kyrgyz Republic	Colombia		Latvia	Moldova
	Lebanon	Croatia		Lithuania	Montenegro
	Lesotho	Egypt		Macedonia, former Yugoslav Republic of	Morocco
	Liberia	Hong Kong, China		Madagascar	Sri Lanka
	Macedonia, former Yugoslav Republic of	Jamaica	Argentina	Mauritius	Taiwan, China
	Madagascar	Kyrgyz Republic	Azerbaijan	Rwanda	Tunisia
	Malaysia	Liberia	Burkina Faso	Saudi Arabia	Ukraine
	Mauritania	Mauritania	Czech Republic	Senegal	United Arab Emirates
	Mauritius	Portugal	Mozambique	Serbia	Uzbekistan
	Moldova	Rwanda	Slovenia	Sierra Leone	Vanuatu
	Namibia	Sierra Leone		Thailand	Vietnam
	New Zealand	Singapore		Zambia	West Bank and Gaza
	Oman	Tonga			
	Panama				
	Saudi Arabia				
	Senegal				
	Sierra Leone				
	Singapore				
	Slovakia				
	Slovenia				
	South Africa				
	Syria				
	Tonga				
	Tunisia				
	Uruguay				
	West Bank and Gaza				
	Yemen				
	Zambia				
	Starting a business	**Dealing with construction permits**	**Employing workers**	**Registering property**	**Getting credit**
Reforms making it more difficult to do business	Indonesia	Benin	Cape Verde		
	Switzerland	Bulgaria	China		
		Fiji	Fiji		
		Montenegro	The Gambia		
		Serbia	Italy		
		Tajikistan	Kazakhstan		
		Ukraine	Korea		
		West Bank and Gaza	Sweden		
		Zimbabwe	United Kingdom		

Source: Doing Business database.

Protecting investors

12
- Albania
- Azerbaijan
- Botswana
- Egypt
- Greece
- Kyrgyz Republic
- Saudi Arabia
- Slovenia
- Tajikistan
- Thailand
- Tunisia
- Turkey

Paying taxes

36
- Albania
- Antigua and Barbuda
- Azerbaijan
- Belarus
- Bosnia and Herzegovina
- Bulgaria
- Burkina Faso
- Canada
- China
- Colombia
- Côte d'Ivoire
- Czech Republic
- Denmark
- Dominican Republic
- France
- Georgia
- Germany
- Greece
- Honduras
- Italy
- Macedonia, former Yugoslav Republic of
- Madagascar
- Malaysia
- Mexico
- Mongolia
- Morocco
- Mozambique
- New Zealand
- Samoa
- South Africa
- St. Vincent and the Grenadines
- Thailand
- Tunisia
- Ukraine
- Uruguay
- Zambia

Botswana
Venezuela

Trading across borders

34
- Belarus
- Benin
- Botswana
- Brazil
- Colombia
- Croatia
- Djibouti
- Dominican Republic
- Ecuador
- Egypt
- El Salvador
- Eritrea
- France
- Haiti
- Honduras
- India
- Kenya
- Korea
- Liberia
- Macedonia, former Yugoslav Republic of
- Madagascar
- Mali
- Mongolia
- Morocco
- Nigeria
- Palau
- Philippines
- Rwanda
- Senegal
- Sierra Leone
- Syria
- Thailand
- Ukraine
- Uruguay

Equatorial Guinea
Gabon
Tunisia

Enforcing contracts

12
- Armenia
- Austria
- Azerbaijan
- Belgium
- Bhutan
- Bulgaria
- China
- Macedonia, former Yugoslav Republic of
- Mozambique
- Portugal
- Romania
- Rwanda

Closing a business

16
- Bosnia and Herzegovina
- Bulgaria
- Cambodia
- Colombia
- Czech Republic
- Finland
- Germany
- Greece
- Hong Kong, China
- Latvia
- Mexico
- New Zealand
- Poland
- Portugal
- Saudi Arabia
- St. Vincent and the Grenadines

Bolivia

TABLE 1.3
Rankings on the ease of doing business

2009 RANK	2008 RANK	ECONOMY	2009 RANK	2008 RANK	ECONOMY	2009 RANK	2008 RANK	ECONOMY
1	1	Singapore	62	53	Peru	122	120	India
2	2	New Zealand	63	62	Jamaica	123	119	Lesotho
3	3	United States	64	56	Samoa	124	122	Bhutan
4	4	Hong Kong, China	65	59	Italy	125	126	Brazil
5	5	Denmark	66	61	St. Vincent and the Grenadines	126	121	Micronesia
6	6	United Kingdom	67	63	St. Kitts and Nevis	127	124	Tanzania
7	7	Ireland	68	99	Kyrgyz Republic	128	129	Morocco
8	8	Canada	69	68	Maldives	129	127	Indonesia
9	10	Australia	70	80	Kazakhstan	130	128	Gambia, The
10	9	Norway	71	79	Macedonia, former Yugoslav Republic of	131	132	West Bank and Gaza
11	11	Iceland				132	130	Algeria
12	12	Japan	72	77	El Salvador	133	134	Honduras
13	19	Thailand	73	81	Tunisia	134	131	Malawi
14	13	Finland	74	70	Dominica	135	150	Cambodia
15	21	Georgia	75	65	Czech Republic	136	133	Ecuador
16	24	Saudi Arabia	76	72	Poland	137	140	Syria
17	14	Sweden	77	74	Pakistan	138	145	Uzbekistan
18	17	Bahrain	78	69	Belize	139	148	Rwanda
19	16	Belgium	79	75	Kiribati	140	136	Philippines
20	25	Malaysia	80	71	Trinidad and Tobago	141	139	Mozambique
21	15	Switzerland	81	76	Panama	142	138	Iran
22	18	Estonia	82	78	Kenya	143	137	Cape Verde
23	22	Korea	83	90	China	144	151	Madagascar
24	29	Mauritius	84	73	Grenada	145	144	Ukraine
25	20	Germany	85	115	Belarus	146	141	Suriname
26	27	Netherlands	86	135	Albania	147	142	Sudan
27	23	Austria	87	82	Ghana	148	164	Burkina Faso
28	28	Lithuania	88	83	Brunei	149	168	Senegal
29	26	Latvia	89	85	Solomon Islands	150	149	Bolivia
30	30	Israel	90	84	Montenegro	151	143	Gabon
31	32	France	91	88	Palau	152	146	Iraq
32	35	South Africa	92	87	Vietnam	153	153	Djibouti
33	97	Azerbaijan	93	86	Marshall Islands	154	147	Haiti
34	33	St. Lucia	94	91	Serbia	155	152	Comoros
35	31	Puerto Rico	95	89	Papua New Guinea	156	163	Sierra Leone
36	37	Slovakia	96	106	Greece	157	167	Liberia
37	38	Qatar	97	110	Dominican Republic	158	154	Zimbabwe
38	52	Botswana	98	123	Yemen	159	156	Tajikistan
39	34	Fiji	99	98	Lebanon	160	166	Mauritania
40	36	Chile	100	101	Zambia	161	155	Côte d'Ivoire
41	50	Hungary	101	94	Jordan	162	161	Afghanistan
42	40	Antigua and Barbuda	102	103	Sri Lanka	163	159	Togo
43	39	Tonga	103	92	Moldova	164	158	Cameroon
44	41	Armenia	104	93	Seychelles	165	162	Lao PDR
45	44	Bulgaria	105	95	Guyana	166	160	Mali
46	54	United Arab Emirates	106	107	Croatia	167	165	Equatorial Guinea
47	47	Romania	107	96	Nicaragua	168	169	Angola
48	43	Portugal	108	100	Swaziland	169	157	Benin
49	46	Spain	109	113	Uruguay	170	170	Timor-Leste
50	45	Luxembourg	110	104	Bangladesh	171	172	Guinea
51	48	Namibia	111	105	Uganda	172	171	Niger
52	49	Kuwait	112	116	Guatemala	173	173	Eritrea
53	66	Colombia	113	102	Argentina	174	175	Venezuela
54	64	Slovenia	114	125	Egypt	175	176	Chad
55	51	Bahamas, The	115	108	Paraguay	176	177	São Tomé and Principe
56	42	Mexico	116	109	Ethiopia	177	174	Burundi
57	57	Oman	117	118	Costa Rica	178	178	Congo, Rep.
58	55	Mongolia	118	114	Nigeria	179	179	Guinea-Bissau
59	60	Turkey	119	117	Bosnia and Herzegovina	180	180	Central African Republic
60	67	Vanuatu	120	112	Russian Federation	181	181	Congo, Dem. Rep.
61	58	Taiwan, China	121	111	Nepal			

Note: The rankings for all economies are benchmarked to June 2008 and reported in the country tables. Rankings on the ease of doing business are the average of the economy's rankings on the 10 topics covered in *Doing Business 2009*. Last year's rankings are presented in italics. These are adjusted for changes in the methodology, data corrections and the addition of 3 new economies.

Source: Doing Business database.

procedures and 4 days. New business registrations increased by 30% in 2 years. In Portugal 86 of the 257 initiatives of the Simplex program came from discussions with businesses.

Simplifying regulation helps businesses and governments alike. In Portugal the "on the spot" registration reform saved entrepreneurs 230,000 days a year in waiting time.[4] And the government saves money. The United Kingdom estimated an annual administrative burden for businesses of £13.7 billion in 2005. Easing such burdens would allow businesses to expand faster and generate savings that governments could use to enhance public services.

FIVE YEARS OF *DOING BUSINESS* REFORM

The key to regulatory reform? Commitment. For many economies the reforms captured in *Doing Business* reflect a broader, sustained commitment to improving their competitiveness. Among these systematic reformers: Azerbaijan, Georgia and the former Yugoslav Republic of Macedonia in Eastern Europe and Central Asia. France and Portugal among the OECD high-income economies. Egypt and Saudi Arabia in the Middle East and North Africa. India in South Asia. China and Vietnam in East Asia. Colombia, Guatemala and Mexico in Latin America. And Burkina Faso, Ghana, Mauritius, Mozambique and Rwanda in Africa. Each of these countries has reformed in at least 5 of the areas covered by *Doing Business*, implementing up to 22 reforms in one country over the past 5 years.

Several reformers were motivated by growing competitive pressure related to joining common markets or trade agreements, such as the European Union (the former Yugoslav Republic of Macedonia) or the U.S.–Central America Free Trade Agreement (Guatemala). Others saw a need to facilitate local entrepreneurship (Azerbaijan, Colombia, Egypt) or diversify their economy (Mauritius, Saudi Arabia). And others faced the daunting task of reconstructing their economy after years of conflict (Rwanda).

Many of the reformers started by learning from others. Egypt looked to India for information technology solutions. Colombia took Ireland as an example. As the country's trade minister, Luis Guillermo Plata, put it, "It's not like baking a cake where you follow the recipe. No. We are all different. But we can take certain things, certain key lessons, and apply those lessons and see how they work in our environment."

Several now serve as examples to others. The Azerbaijan reformers visited Georgia and Latvia. Angola has requested legal and technical assistance based on the Portuguese model of business start-up.

The most active reformers did not shy away from broad reform programs. Since 2005 Georgia has introduced a new company law and customs code, a new property registry that replaced a confusing system requiring duplicate approvals by multiple agencies, the country's first credit information bureau and large-scale judicial reforms. Egypt has implemented one-stop shops for import and export and business start-up, undertaken sweeping tax reforms, continually improved its credit information systems and modified the listing rules of the Cairo Stock Exchange. Colombia has strengthened investor protections through stricter disclosure rules, amended insolvency laws and reformed customs. And its one-stop shop for business start-up has served as an inspiration to others in the region.

Among emerging market reformers, India has focused on technology, implementing electronic registration of new businesses, an electronic collateral registry and online submission of customs forms and payments. China has focused on easing access to credit. In 2006 a new credit registry allowed more than 340 million citizens to have credit histories for the first time. A new company law lowered the minimum capital requirement and strengthened investor protections. And in 2007 a new property law expanded the range of assets that can be used as collateral. Mexico has focused on strengthening investor protections through a new securities law while continually reducing bureaucracy at the state level.

REGULATORY REFORM— WHAT ARE THE BENEFITS?

Of Egypt's estimated 25 million urban properties, only 7% were formally registered in 2005. Six months after reforms of its property registry, title registration increased and revenue rose by 39%.[5] After reforms of the property registry in Tegucigalpa, Honduras, the registry received 65% more registration applications between July and December of 2007 than in the same period of 2006.

Similarly, a reduction in the minimum capital requirement was followed by an increase in new company registrations of 55% in Georgia and 81% in Saudi Arabia. Georgia now has 15 registered businesses per 100 people—comparable to numbers in such economies as Malaysia and Singapore.

Initial results like these show that reforms are leading to change on the ground. Confirming this are the findings of an increasing number of studies using the *Doing Business* data to analyze the effect of regulatory burdens on such outcomes as informality, job creation, productivity, economic growth and poverty reduction.[6]

Research generally finds that countries with burdensome regulation have larger informal sectors, higher unemployment rates and slower economic growth. More recent research gives first insights into the impact of reforms. One study reports some of the payoffs of reforms in Mexico: the number of registered businesses rose by nearly 6%, employment increased by 2.6%, and prices fell by 1% thanks to competition from new entrants.[7] Another study finds that increasing the flexibility of labor regulations in India would reduce job informality in the retail sector by a third.[8]

But nothing says more than the experience of the people affected. Janet, who runs a business producing baskets

in Kigali, Rwanda, says, "I have sur-
vivors, I have widows, I have women
whose husbands are in prison. To see
them sitting under one roof weaving
and doing business together is a huge
achievement . . . these women are now
together earning an income."[9]

NOTES

1. *Doing Business* records only reforms
   relevant to the 10 indicator sets. Legal
   changes are counted once the respective
   legislation and implementing decrees, if
   applicable, are effective. Administrative
   reforms such as the introduction of time
   limits must be fully implemented.

2. Narayan and others (2000).

3. Hertveldt (2008).

4. Ramos (2008).

5. Haidar (2008).

6. The data on the regulation of entry, for
   example, have been used in 168 articles
   published in refereed journals and more
   than 200 research working papers. The
   data on the efficiency of court proceedings have been used in 54 articles and
   86 working papers. Altogether, the data
   generated by the *Doing Business* project
   have been used in 325 published articles
   and 742 working papers.

7. Bruhn (2008).

8. Amin (forthcoming).

9. This example is from the World Bank's
   Doing Business: Women in Africa (2008a),
   a collection of case studies of African
   entrepreneurs.

Starting a business

Overview

Dealing with construction permits

Employing workers

Registering property

Getting credit

Protecting investors

Paying taxes

Trading across borders

Enforcing contracts

Closing a business

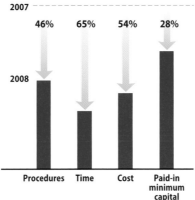

FIGURE 2.1

Top 10 reformers in starting a business

Average improvement

1. *Yemen*
2. *Slovenia*
3. *Senegal*
4. *Albania*
5. *Liberia*
6. *Azerbaijan*
7. *Syria*
8. *Hungary*
9. *Oman*
10. *Sierra Leone*

Source: Doing Business database.

Julian started out working for her brothers. But she was saving to start her own business. She began trading, traveling from Uganda to neighboring Kenya to buy goods for resale. "I would take the overnight bus and stand up the whole way to get the 50% discount," she recalls. "My aim was to start a juice processing business, a real factory."

Once she had saved enough money, Julian began production. Unable to afford transport, she had to take her products by foot to the government chemist for testing. "My only means of transport was my wheelbarrow, and I was the whole company."

Julian also remembers how arduous it was to register her business. "There was so much to do and so many different places I had to go—for business registration and taxpayer identification

numbers, different licenses from different authorities, a declaration that had to be made before a commissioner of oaths, a company seal to get, inspections of my premises from municipal and health authorities. I remember paying a lawyer what seemed to me a gigantic fee of USh 500,000 [$279]."[1]

Entrepreneurs like Julian now have it easier. Reforms in Uganda and in many other economies have streamlined business start-up in the past 5 years. Look at Azerbaijan. In 2004 its government set a preliminary time limit for the registration process. In 2005 it introduced a silence-is-consent rule for tax registration. A year later it further tightened the time limit for business registration. In 2007 it abolished the need for a company seal. And in 2007/08 it set up a one-stop shop. Starting a business used to take 122 days. Now it takes only 16 (figure 2.3).

Formal incorporation of companies has several benefits. Legal entities outlive their founders. Resources are often pooled as shareholders join forces to start a company. And companies have access to services and institutions ranging from courts to commercial banks.

But many economies make starting and legally running a business as measured by *Doing Business* so cumbersome that entrepreneurs opt out and operate in the informal sector.

Simpler entry encourages the creation of new companies. Take Senegal, which reformed business registration in

July 2007. By May 2008 entrepreneurs had registered 3,060 new firms, 80% more than in the previous year. Studies in Mexico, India, Brazil and the Russian Federation all conclude that simpler entry regimes are associated with more new firms being registered. The study in Mexico analyzes the effect of making it simpler to get a municipal license, 1 of several procedures required to start a business. The finding: easing business entry increased new start-ups by about 4%.[2]

Easier start-up is also correlated with higher productivity among existing firms. A recent study, in an analysis of 97 countries, finds that reducing entry costs by 80% of income per capita increases total factor productivity by an estimated 22%. Analyzing 157 countries, it finds that the same reduction in entry costs raises output per worker by an estimated

TABLE 2.1

Where is it easy to start a business—and where not?

Easiest	RANK	Most difficult	RANK
New Zealand	1	Cameroon	172
Canada	2	Djibouti	173
Australia	3	Equatorial Guinea	174
Georgia	4	Iraq	175
Ireland	5	Haiti	176
United States	6	Guinea	177
Mauritius	7	Eritrea	178
United Kingdom	8	Togo	179
Puerto Rico	9	Chad	180
Singapore	10	Guinea-Bissau	181

Note: Rankings are the average of the economy rankings on the procedures, time, cost and paid-in minimum capital for starting a business. See Data notes for details.
Source: Doing Business database.

FIGURE 2.2

Rankings on starting a business are based on 4 subindicators

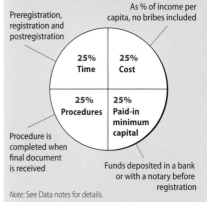

Note: See Data notes for details.

FIGURE 2.3
Starting a business in Azerbaijan gets faster and cheaper
Time and cost to start a business

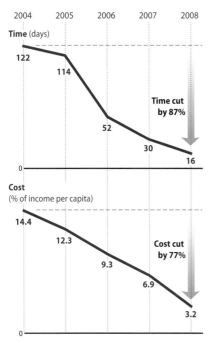

Source: Doing Business database.

29%.[3] One reason for these large effects may be that reducing entry costs increases entry pressure, pushing firms with lower productivity out of the market. Indeed, a study on business entry in Mexico finds that competition from new entrants lowered prices by 1% and reduced the income of incumbent businesses by 3.5%.[4]

Simpler and faster business entry makes it easier for workers and capital to move across sectors when economies experience economic shocks. A recent study of 28 sectors in 55 countries compares sectoral employment reallocation in the 1980s and 1990s. The finding: reallocation is smoother in countries where it takes fewer days to start a business.[5] This finding is confirmed by many studies on the effect of entry regulation in economies opening their product markets to trade.[6] The explanation is simple: with high fixed costs of entry, firms cannot easily move into the industries benefiting the most from trade openness. This friction reduces the value of greater openness.

Recognizing such benefits, economies around the world have been devel-

oping innovative solutions to ease the entry of new firms into the market. As one company registrar put it, "At the end of the day, we all have the same goal."

Yet as *Doing Business* shows, company registration is often only one piece of the puzzle. In many economies entrepreneurs have to visit at least 7 agencies before they can get down to business. The most efficient economies focus on creating a single interface between government and entrepreneur to take care of all necessary registrations and notifications, mainly commercial and tax registration. Entrepreneurs in New Zealand, for example, have to file all necessary information only once—because agencies are linked through a unified database. There is no minimum capital requirement. And no judge has to approve the creation of a company.

WHO REFORMED IN 2007/08?

In 2007/08, 49 economies made it easier to start a business—more reforms than in any previous year (table 2.2). One highlight of the reforms: entrepreneurs in Canada and New Zealand can now start a business with a single online procedure.

Yemen reformed business start-up the most. In 2007 it had the second largest minimum capital requirement in the world at $15,225 (2,003% of income per

capita). This is now gone, reduced to zero. That's not all. Yemen also activated its one-stop shop, making it possible to complete all steps—from reserving the company name to obtaining a license for incorporation to announcing the company's formation—in a single location. It made it easier to obtain a license from the municipality and to register with the chamber of commerce and the tax office. And it publicized the fact that a company seal is not mandatory. The reforms reduced the number of procedures to start a business by 5, and the time by 50 days.

Slovenia was the runner-up in business start-up reforms. It simplified business registration by introducing a single access point, making company information available online and eliminating court fees and the requirement to register at the statistical office. The changes reduced the procedures by 4, the time by 41 days and the cost by 8.4% of income per capita.

Senegal is among the 14 economies that made Africa the leading region in start-up reforms. Senegal's one-stop shop became fully operational, merging 7 start-up procedures into 1. Start-up time fell from 58 days to 8. Liberia too streamlined business registration, cutting 3 months from the time. Businesses can now start in less than 1 month. Liberia also made the process more affordable, making the use of lawyers optional.

TABLE 2.2
Simplifying registration formalities—the most popular reform feature in 2007/08

Simplified other registration formalities (seal, publication, notary, inspection, other requirements)	Bangladesh, Botswana, Bulgaria, Costa Rica, El Salvador, Georgia, Ghana, Hungary, Kenya, Kyrgyz Republic, Liberia, former Yugoslav Republic of Macedonia, Moldova, Namibia, Saudi Arabia, Syria, Yemen
Created or improved one-stop shop	Albania, Angola, Azerbaijan, Belarus, Bulgaria, Czech Republic, Italy, Lebanon, Lesotho, former Yugoslav Republic of Macedonia, Oman, Senegal, Slovakia, Slovenia, Yemen, Zambia
Introduced or improved online registration procedures	Bulgaria, Canada, Colombia, Dominican Republic, Hungary, Italy, former Yugoslav Republic of Macedonia, Malaysia, Mauritius, New Zealand, Panama, Senegal, Singapore
Abolished or reduced minimum capital requirement	Belarus, Egypt, El Salvador, Georgia, Greece, Hungary, Jordan, Tunisia, Uruguay, Yemen
Cut or simplified postregistration procedures	Colombia, Madagascar, Mauritania, Sierra Leone, South Africa, Tonga, West Bank and Gaza

Source: Doing Business database.

The cost is a fourth of what it used to be. Madagascar also focused on cost, abolishing the professional tax.

Sierra Leone and South Africa made the use of lawyers optional. South Africa also introduced electronic means of certifying and publishing company documents. In Botswana and Namibia entrepreneurs now benefit from computerized registration systems. Zambia revamped the company registry and created a one-stop shop. So did Lesotho, reducing start-up time by 33 days. Burkina Faso continued reforms at its one-stop shop, CEFORE. Ghana officially eliminated the requirement for a company seal. Angola, Kenya, Mauritania and Mauritius also reformed.

Eastern Europe and Central Asia saw reform in 10 economies. Six reduced the running-around time for entrepreneurs by creating one-stop shops. Albania took registration out of the courts and merged company, social security, labor and tax registrations. Before, entrepreneurs had to wait more than a month to start doing business; now it's just 8 days. Azerbaijan's one-stop shop reduced delays by 2 weeks, Slovenia's by 6. Bulgaria, the Kyrgyz Republic and the former Yugoslav Republic of Macedonia undertook reforms similar to Azerbaijan's. And while Czech entrepreneurs still have to obtain multiple documents, the new "Project Czech Point" allows them to do so at one place.

Belarus activated a unified registration database and cut the minimum capital requirement by half. Georgia eliminated the minimum capital requirement altogether. It also cut the requirement for a company seal and made the use of notaries optional. Moldova introduced 2 new laws, on limited liability companies and company registration, and tightened time limits. In contrast, Bosnia and Herzegovina increased the time to start a business by tightening notarization requirements.

The Middle East and North Africa made big strides in reform. Syria was the second biggest reformer in the region, behind Yemen. A new company law and

TABLE 2.3

Who regulates business start-up the least—and who the most?

Procedures (number)			
Fewest		**Most**	
Canada	1	Greece	15
New Zealand	1	Montenegro	15
Australia	2	Philippines	15
Belgium	3	Venezuela	16
Finland	3	Guinea-Bissau	17
Georgia	3	Brazil	18
Sweden	3	Brunei	18
Bulgaria	4	Uganda	18
Denmark	4	Chad	19
Singapore	4	Equatorial Guinea	20

Time (days)			
Fastest		**Slowest**	
New Zealand	1	Lao PDR	103
Australia	2	Brunei	116
Georgia	3	Equatorial Guinea	136
Belgium	4	Venezuela	141
Singapore	4	São Tomé and Principe	144
Canada	5	Brazil	152
Hungary	5	Congo, Dem. Rep.	155
Iceland	5	Haiti	195
Denmark	6	Guinea-Bissau	233
Mauritius	6	Suriname	694

Cost (% of income per capita)			
Least		**Most**	
Denmark	0.0	Benin	196.0
Slovenia	0.1	Angola	196.8
Ireland	0.3	Djibouti	200.2
New Zealand	0.4	Burundi	215.0
Canada	0.5	Central African Republic	232.3
Bahrain	0.6	Togo	251.3
Sweden	0.6	Gambia, The	254.9
United States	0.7	Guinea-Bissau	257.7
Singapore	0.7	Zimbabwe	432.7
United Kingdom	0.8	Congo, Dem. Rep.	435.4

Paid-in minimum capital		
Most	% of income per capita	US$
Burkina Faso	459	1,973
Oman	461	51,282
Guinea	477	1,907
Central African Republic	514	1,953
Djibouti	514	5,602
Togo	560	2,016
Ethiopia	694	1,526
Niger	702	1,966
Guinea-Bissau	1,015	2,030
Syria	4,354	76,627

Note: Sixty-nine economies have no paid-in minimum capital requirement.
Source: Doing Business database.

FIGURE 2.4

Eastern Europe & Central Asia leads reforms, Africa runner-up

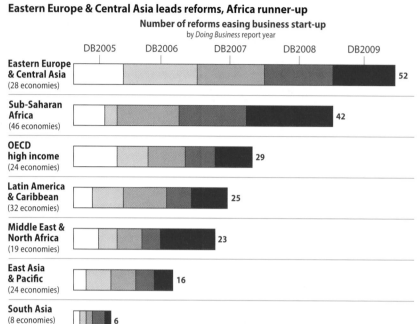

Number of reforms easing business start-up
by *Doing Business* report year

Note: A reform is counted as 1 reform per reforming economy per year.
Source: Doing Business database.

commercial code took registration out of the court and introduced statutory time limits. Using lawyers became optional. But along with the reforms making it easier to start a business came a reform making it more difficult—a 33% increase in paid-in minimum capital.

Lebanon and Oman improved the efficiency of their one-stop shops. What used to take 46 days in Lebanon now takes 11. Tunisia, having already reduced its minimum capital requirement, abolished it altogether. Jordan reduced its minimum capital requirement by more than 96%. Following on the previous year's reforms, Egypt further reduced registration costs and paid-in minimum capital. Saudi Arabia continued to simplify commercial registration formalities and reduced fees by 80%. Computerization of the registry in West Bank and Gaza reduced the time to register.

Among OECD high-income economies there were 6 reformers. Canada and New Zealand made it possible to start a business with a single procedure. Entrepreneurs in Toronto, Canada, can incorporate their company online and automatically receive a business number

within 5 days. Those in New Zealand can now register for taxes while incorporating their company online. Greece and Hungary reduced minimum capital requirements by about 80%. Hungary also introduced online filing and publication and made the use of notaries optional. Italy reformed its electronic registration system, enabling businesses to complete all procedures at once. Slovakia's one-stop shop merged 4 procedures into 1 and reduced costs. Entrepreneurs in Switzerland were less fortunate: they now must deposit twice as much capital in the bank (nearly $20,000) before registering a company.

El Salvador led reform efforts in Latin America and the Caribbean, reforming for the third year in a row. A new commercial code reduced the minimum capital requirement, simplified the legalization of accounting books and eased publication requirements. Uruguay abolished the minimum capital requirement. Colombia focused on administrative changes, substantially reducing costs and simplifying requirements for accounting books. Computerization was another trend: Costa Rica

cut 17 days by computerizing tax registration. Panama simplified licensing procedures. The Dominican Republic reduced start-up cost and introduced online name verification.

In East Asia, Malaysia cut the time by 11 days by introducing an online registration system. Singapore merged the name search with online business registration. Tonga saved on time and cost by reforming business licensing. Indonesia reduced the time to start a business from 105 days to 76, but almost doubled the minimum capital requirement.

In South Asia only Bangladesh reformed. It made involving lawyers in company registration optional.

WHAT ARE THE REFORM TRENDS?

In the past 5 years 115 economies around the world have simplified business start-up through 193 reforms (figure 2.4). Many opted for low-cost administrative reforms requiring little or no change in regulation. Others went further, introducing or amending legislation. Here are some of the most prevalent reforms along with some of the lessons learned on the way (figure 2.5).

FIGURE 2.5

**Top 5 reform features
in starting a business**

Reforms including feature since DB2005 (%)

20%	Created or improved one-stop shop
12%	Simplified other registration formalities
11%	Abolished or reduced minimum capital requirement
11%	Introduced or improved online procedures
7%	Cut or simplified postregistration procedures

Note: A reform may include several reform features.
Source: Doing Business database.

CREATING A ONE-STOP SHOP

Thirty-nine economies have created or improved a one-stop shop in the past 5 years: 16 in Eastern Europe and Central Asia, 7 in Africa, 6 in the OECD high-income group, 5 in Latin America and 5 in the Middle East and North Africa. One-stop shops can be a quick way to build momentum for reform. Azerbaijan, El Salvador, Guatemala and Morocco created theirs in less than 6 months. And introducing a one-stop shop has had promising results. In Oman business registrations increased from an average 733 a month in 2006 to 1,306 a month in 2007. In Azerbaijan registrations grew by 40% between January 1 and May 2008. Croatia saw company formation in Zagreb and Split increase by more than 300% over 3 years.

But creating a one-stop shop is no magic bullet. Often entrepreneurs must still deal with formalities elsewhere as well (figure 2.6). In Guatemala, for example, the one-stop shop can organize commercial, tax and social security registration in 2–3 days. But before the registrar can finalize the registration, a notice must be published for 8 days during which third parties can raise objections. Despite the one-stop shop, 11 procedures and 26 days are still required. Reformers also run the risk of creating "one-more-stop shops" or "mailboxes" that merely receive applications and forward them to ministries for approval. Delays continue.

ABOLISHING THE MINIMUM CAPITAL REQUIREMENT

Sixty-nine economies allow entrepreneurs to start a company without putting up a fixed amount of capital before registration. They allow entrepreneurs to determine what is appropriate for the business based on its type and capital structure. Twenty-two economies have reduced or abolished their minimum capital requirement in the past 5 years, including Egypt, Finland, France, Georgia, Hungary, Japan, Jordan, Uruguay and Yemen. This group has seen some of the biggest spikes in new company registrations. After Madagascar reduced its

FIGURE 2.6

One-stop shops—same name, different results
Time and procedures to start a business

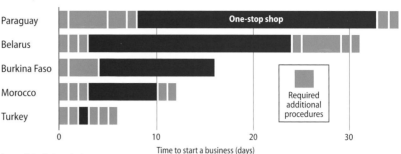

Source: Doing Business database.

minimum capital requirement by more than 80% in 2006, the rate of new registrations jumped from 13% to 26%. After Tunisia reduced its requirement, new registrations increased by 30% between 2002 and 2006.[7] That encouraged the country to abolish it altogether in 2007/08.

USING TECHNOLOGY

Making registration electronic is among the most effective ways to speed company formation. Seven of the economies with the fastest business start-up offer electronic registration—Australia, Canada, Denmark, Estonia, New Zealand, Portugal and Singapore. More than 20 economies have introduced electronic registration in the past 5 years. Customers are not the only ones saving on time and cost. When Belgium implemented its paperless registration and filing system, it reduced annual administrative costs by €1.7 billion.

Electronic registration is possible in more than 80% of rich economies but only about 30% of developing ones. That is not surprising, of course, given the differences in internet access and costs.[8]

And electronic registration is more complicated than it looks. In Sweden applications for company, tax and labor registrations can be completed online. But most forms still must be printed out and signed by hand. The Philippines allows entrepreneurs to reserve the company name and register online, but still requires payment in person. Belgium allows electronic filing—but only through a notary or lawyer. In Argentina corporate managers have to get a fiscal code before using the online tax system and obtaining a tax identification number. Countries also have to make sure that the legislation needed to allow electronic transactions is in place.

But much can be gained already—in time and cost and also in safety—by computerizing files at the registry or offering some online services such as name checking. And everyone has to start somewhere. It was only 13 years ago that one of the company registries in the United States stored all files in a warehouse so big that employees were using roller skates to get to the documents. Obtaining documents took about a month. Thankfully there was no fire.

NOTES

1. This example is from the World Bank's *Doing Business: Women in Africa* (2008a), a collection of case studies of African entrepreneurs.

2. Kaplan, Piedra and Seira (2008) on Mexico, Chari (2008) on India, Monteiro and Assunção (2008) on Brazil and Yakovlev and Zhuravskaya (2008) on the Russian Federation.

3. Barseghyan (2008).

4. Bruhn (2008).

5. Ciccone and Papaioannou (2007).

6. Freund and Bolaky (forthcoming), Chang, Kaltani and Loayza (forthcoming), Cunat and Melitz (2007), Helpman and Itskhoki (2007) and Helpman, Melitz and Rubinstein (2008).

7. Klapper and others (2008).

8. World Bank Group Entrepreneurship Database, 2008.

Dealing with construction permits

FIGURE 3.1

**Top 10 reformers
in dealing with construction permits**

Average improvement

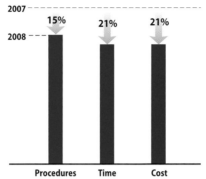

1. *Kyrgyz Republic*
2. *Burkina Faso*
3. *Hong Kong, China*
4. *Rwanda*
5. *Armenia*
6. *Belarus*
7. *Jamaica*
8. *Croatia*
9. *Bosnia and Herzegovina*
10. *Angola*

Source: Doing Business database.

In 2007 the municipality of Niamey, Niger, issued only 300 building permits. But you wouldn't know it by looking around the city, where buildings are sprouting fast. "Building permit? Who needs that? Just hire a contractor, tell him what you want, and out of the ground it comes," says a local developer.

This approach to building has resulted in a city at odds with the original zoning plans: water pipes zigzag in every direction, and houses extend beyond their assigned land parcels. The reason: obtaining all building-related approvals and connecting to utilities can take entrepreneurs almost 9 months, at a cost of 2,694% of income per capita.

The situation may soon change. Niger adopted a new building law in March 2008, following the collapse of 2

buildings in the center of Niamey.

In Almaty, Kazakhstan, builders suffer the burden of overregulation. Undertaking the construction of a simple warehouse requires navigating a labyrinth of 38 procedures and 18 agencies—and spending 231 days in the process.

Striking the right balance is a challenge when it comes to construction regulations. Good regulations ensure the safety standards that protect the public while making the permitting process efficient, transparent and affordable for both building authorities and the private professionals who use it. If procedures are overly complicated or costly, builders build without a permit.

In an effort to achieve this balance between safety and cost, Bavaria introduced a differentiated permitting approach in 1994. Low-risk projects require that the designing architects show proof of their qualifications and assume liability for the construction. Medium-risk ones require that an independent certified appraiser approve the plans. Only high-risk, complex projects are fully reviewed by building authorities.[1] By 2002 builders had saved an estimated €154 million in building permit fees, and building authorities had 270 fewer employees on their payroll. The approach has spread to the rest of Germany.

Economies that score well on the ease of dealing with construction permits tend to have rigorous yet expeditious and transparent permitting processes (table

3.1). Speed matters. A recent study in the United States shows that accelerating permit approvals by 3 months in a 22-month project cycle could increase property tax revenue by 16.15% and construction spending for local governments by 5.7%.[2] Yet in 80 of the 181 economies studied in *Doing Business*, compliance with construction formalities takes longer than the standardized 30-week construction project itself.

Singapore's Building and Construction Authority provides easy access to the information needed for obtaining a construction permit. Its website lists all the forms that must be filled out, provides downloadable copies and enables users to submit all paperwork electronically. Developers in Austria, Denmark, Iceland, Malaysia and the United States also complete their applications online.

TABLE 3.1

Where is dealing with construction permits easy—and where not?

Easiest	RANK	Most difficult	RANK
St. Vincent and the Grenadines	1	Tanzania	172
Singapore	2	Burundi	173
New Zealand	3	Zimbabwe	174
Belize	4	Kazakhstan	175
Marshall Islands	5	China	176
St. Kitts and Nevis	6	Liberia	177
Denmark	7	Tajikistan	178
Maldives	8	Ukraine	179
Kenya	9	Russian Federation	180
Georgia	10	Eritrea	181

Note: Rankings are the average of the economy rankings on the procedures, time and cost to comply with formalities to build a warehouse. See Data notes for details.
Source: Doing Business database.

FIGURE 3.2

Rankings on dealing with construction permits are based on 3 subindicators

Days to build a warehouse in main city

As % of income per capita, no bribes included

33.3% Time
33.3% Cost
33.3% Procedures

Procedure is completed when final document is received; construction permits, inspections and utility connections included

Note: See Data notes for details.

Twenty-seven economies, including France and Hong Kong (China), ensure timely approvals for building permits through silence-is-consent rules, with time limits ranging from 2 to 4 weeks.

Finland and Singapore—both among the 10 fastest in dealing with construction permits—hold the architect or another qualified professional accountable for supervising the construction and ensuring its quality.

WHO REFORMED IN 2007/08?

Eighteen economies made it easier for businesses to comply with construction-related formalities in 2007/08 (table 3.2). Africa had the most reforms, with 6 economies—Angola, Burkina Faso, Liberia, Mauritania, Rwanda and Sierra Leone—making it easier to deal with construction permits. Eastern Europe and Central Asia followed, with reforms in Armenia, Belarus, Bosnia and Herzegovina, Croatia and the Kyrgyz Republic.

In East Asia and Pacific, Hong Kong (China), Singapore and Tonga streamlined procedures. In Latin America and the Caribbean, Colombia and Jamaica reduced the time to process building permit applications. Among OECD high-income economies, Portugal was the only reformer. In the Middle East and North Africa, Egypt was the only one. South Asia recorded no major reforms.

The Kyrgyz Republic was the top reformer in dealing with construction permits in 2007/08. A new one-stop shop was launched for issuing architectural planning terms and construction permits. Regulations left over from Soviet times had required builders to obtain separate preapprovals from each utility authority. Now all approvals are handled in the one-stop shop.

Kyrgyz reformers didn't stop there. A presidential decree eliminated the location permit, which had required the signature of Bishkek's mayor and took 60 days to obtain. "It used to be a nightmare. You never knew what additional papers would be required," says Bekbolot, owner of a medium-size construction company. The mayor's office no longer handles occupancy permits either. "It took me 6 months before the reforms, and I still could not obtain the mayor's signature. After the reforms, it took me just over a week to get my occupancy permit signed and sealed."

After cutting 9 procedures and 173 days, the government is now focusing on reducing the cost—still high at more than 405% of income per capita.

Burkina Faso, once among the bottom 10 on the ease of dealing with construction permits, was the second fastest reformer. A multifaceted reform program cut 12 days and reduced the cost by 25%. To start, a government decree limited the number of on-site inspections by the National Laboratory for Buildings and Public Works. That eliminated the biweekly random inspections that used to plague builders in Ouagadougou. "We can still expect inspections at certain critical stages, but this is a far cry from the up to 15 or so we could receive before," says one architect. In May 2008 the government launched a one-stop shop. This has already shown results. It cut fees for soil exams in half and reduced those for municipal approvals and fire safety studies. And it allows applicants for building permits to make all payments at a single place.

Reformers were active in Africa. In Liberia the Ministry of Public Works committed to delivering building permits in just 30 days, down from 90. The ministry advertised the 30-day statutory time limit and designed a user-friendly checklist of all the documents required.

It also eliminated the need for the minister's signature on building permits for simpler projects by delegating approval to mid-level staff.

Liberia's deputy minister of public works cut building permit fees in half, from $1,400 to $700, to encourage more legal building in Monrovia. "I thought people were going underground because costs were too high, so I decided to cut fees." In a country where obtaining a building permit used to cost 10 times income per capita and other costs of construction permitting remain high, this makes sense (table 3.3).

Sierra Leone revamped its inspection regime. Existing regulations provided for inspections after each stage of construction. But inspectors would come at random once or even twice a week. Starting in 2007, the Ministry of Lands, Housing, Country Planning and Environment recruited a new cadre of professional inspectors and began enforcing the regulations.

Rwanda streamlined project clearances for the second year in a row by combining the applications for a location clearance and building permit in a single form. And businesses now need to submit only one application form for water, sewerage and electricity connections. Angola incorporated the applications for electricity and water connections into the building permit process, cutting procedures from 14 to 12.

Mauritania introduced its first building code. This simplifies the requirements for small construction projects and lays the groundwork for a one-

TABLE 3.2

Streamlining permitting procedures—a popular reform feature in 2007/08

Streamlined construction permit procedures	Angola, Colombia, Croatia, Hong Kong (China), Jamaica, Kyrgyz Republic, Rwanda, Tonga
Reduced permit processing times	Belarus, Bosnia and Herzegovina, Colombia, Jamaica, Liberia, Singapore
Adopted new building regulations	Croatia, Egypt, Mauritania, Portugal, Tonga
Reduced fees	Armenia, Bosnia and Herzegovina, Burkina Faso, Hong Kong (China), Liberia
Improved inspection regime for construction projects	Burkina Faso, Hong Kong (China), Sierra Leone

Source: Doing Business database.

TABLE 3.3
Who regulates construction permits the least—and who the most?

Procedures *(number)*

Fewest		Most	
Denmark	6	Azerbaijan	31
New Zealand	7	Hungary	31
Vanuatu	7	Brunei	32
Sweden	8	Guinea	32
Chad	9	Tajikistan	32
Maldives	9	El Salvador	34
St. Lucia	9	Czech Republic	36
Grenada	10	China	37
Jamaica	10	Kazakhstan	38
Kenya	10	Russian Federation	54

Time *(days)*

Fastest		Slowest	
Korea	34	Cameroon	426
Finland	38	Suriname	431
Singapore	38	Ukraine	471
United States	40	Lesotho	601
Vanuatu	51	Côte d'Ivoire	628
Marshall Islands	55	Iran	670
Bahrain	56	Russian Federation	704
Solomon Islands	62	Cambodia	709
New Zealand	65	Haiti	1,179
Belize	66	Zimbabwe	1,426

Cost *(% of income per capita)*

Least		Most	
Qatar	0.8	Ukraine	1,902
United Arab Emirates	1.5	Tanzania	2,087
St. Kitts and Nevis	5.1	Serbia	2,178
Brunei	5.3	Russian Federation	2,613
Trinidad and Tobago	5.5	Guinea-Bissau	2,629
Palau	5.9	Niger	2,694
Malaysia	7.9	Burundi	8,516
St. Vincent and the Grenadines	8.4	Afghanistan	14,919
Thailand	9.4	Zimbabwe	16,369
Hungary	10.3	Liberia	60,989

Source: Doing Business database.

stop shop for building permits.

In Zimbabwe and Benin, obtaining building permits became more difficult. In Zimbabwe's capital, Harare, employees have been leaving the construction administration. With fewer trained professionals to review applications, getting a building plan approved by the city council can now take a year.

In Cotonou, Benin, it now takes about 180 days to obtain a building permit—3 months longer than it used to—because of administrative backlogs. A new regulation released in June 2007

sets statutory time limits of 120 days for building permits. But these time limits have yet to be enforced.

Eastern Europe and Central Asia saw many reforms, though only half of them easing the regulatory burden. In Croatia a new building code eliminated the need for a building permit for smaller projects and eased the requirements for larger ones. Now midsize commercial construction projects no longer need clearances from the fire department, water and sewerage authorities, telephone company, labor inspec-

torate and sanitary authority—cutting 5 procedures.

In Bosnia and Herzegovina administrative improvements made it easier to obtain cadastre excerpts, required for building permits, and to register new buildings in the cadastre and land book registry. That cut the time from 467 days to 296. In Belarus new statutory time limits for pre-permitting procedures and building permits reduced the time by 140 days. In Armenia companies no longer have to pay "charitable contribution" fees to obtain the designing right. That cut the cost by 383.3% of income per capita.

Several economies went the other way. In Serbia the wait for building permits increased by an average 75 days. In Ukraine a regulation introduced in 2007 requires businesses to pay a "contribution" to infrastructure development that amounts to 15% of construction costs. Now builders in Kiev can expect to pay 1,902% of income per capita to deal with construction-related formalities.

In East Asia, Hong Kong (China) pursued a broad program that eliminated 8 procedures and cut the time for construction permits by more than 5 weeks, ranking it among the top reformers globally. In 2006 the government, working with the private sector, created a cross-sector consultation team to identify ways to improve permitting procedures. Working groups started with agencies and companies operating in the construction sector found redundant procedures, improved communication and coordination schemes and identified regulatory "easy fixes" that could improve efficiency. "This is a very clever and pragmatic approach—something very much in touch with our culture," comments the owner of a local construction company.

Singapore reduced the time for dealing with construction permits by two-thirds in 2007/08—more than any other economy in the world. The agencies responsible for approvals cut their internal time limits by half. To save more time, the Building and Construction Authority's new data management system makes processing smarter and more user friendly. Today builders regularly receive updates on the status of their permit applications by e-mail and text messaging.

Latin America and the Caribbean also saw important reforms. In Colombia the magistrates responsible for issuing building permits started using a single form. Builders no longer need to obtain the names and contact information of all neighbors before submitting a permit application. A decree implementing a decade-old silence-is-consent rule kicked in, reducing the time to obtain a building permit from 3 months to 2. In Jamaica the government began implementing a 90-day statutory time limit. That cut the time to obtain a building permit from 210 days to 130—much better, though still short of the target.

Elsewhere, economies continued to revamp their building codes. Tonga implemented its 2005 building code in late 2007. The new code incorporates zoning and health and fire safety approvals into the building permit process, cutting 3 procedures and reducing the time by 12 days. Portugal's new building regulations introduced electronic processing of documents. Egypt's new building code aims to reduce the time to obtain a building permit by establishing a single window and enforcing a 30-day statutory time limit. The new code also introduces a single certificate for obtaining all utility connections. Before, each utility connection required 3 separate letters from the municipality.

WHAT ARE THE REFORM TRENDS?

In the past 4 years, with 20 reforms, Eastern Europe and Central Asia has had the most reforms making it easier to deal with construction permits (figure 3.3). Africa follows, with 13. OECD high-income economies have had 9, East Asia and Pacific 8, Latin America and the Caribbean 6, the Middle East and North Africa 4 and South Asia 0.

Of the 60 reforms easing construction permitting, 35 have been legal and

FIGURE 3.3

Reforms in Sub-Saharan Africa picking up

Number of reforms making it easier to deal with construction permits

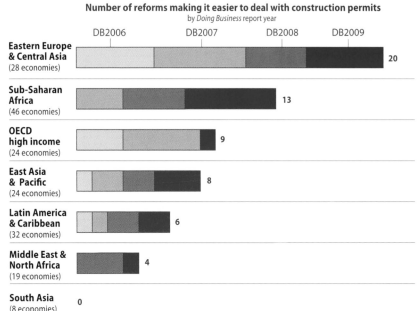

Note: A reform is counted as 1 reform per reforming economy per year.
Source: Doing Business database.

25 administrative. Legal reforms deal with new building codes, regulations and bylaws that change the standards and organization of construction permitting. Administrative reforms include streamlining project clearances and introducing time limits and online processes. Reforming building codes can be a long, complex exercise, requiring input from many stakeholders. A new building code enacted in 2007 in the Czech Republic was 18 years in the making.

The focus in Eastern Europe and Central Asia, while initially on legal reforms, is shifting to administrative changes. Georgia is a good example. After 3 years of reform it claimed a place in the top 10 on the ease of dealing with construction permits. But long delays remain in the rest of the region—where the process takes 260 days on average, over 100 days more than the average of 154 in OECD high-income economies.

Reformers in Africa started with administrative reforms. They began in earnest in 2006, cutting 4 procedures and reducing delays by 15 days on average. Meanwhile, delays in the rest of the region increased by 26 days. In Nigeria

administrative reforms have cut superfluous procedures and inspections. But builders in Africa still face outdated construction codes or new ones not yet fully implemented. Kenya overhauled all its building regulations. Today it is the only African economy to rank among the top 10 on the ease of dealing with construction permits.

FIGURE 3.4

Top 5 reform features in dealing with construction permits

Reforms including feature since DB2006 (%)

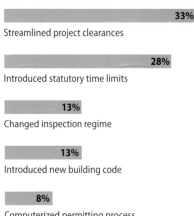

Note: A reform may include several reform features.
Source: Doing Business database.

STREAMLINING PROJECT CLEARANCES

The most popular reform feature globally has been to streamline project clearances (figure 3.4). Because building approvals require the technical oversight of multiple agencies, an obvious choice has been to set up a one-stop shop. But this is no easy fix. One-stop shops are designed to integrate services through a single point of contact between building authorities and entrepreneurs. Their success depends on coordination between these authorities and on sound overarching legislation.

Take the experience of Bangladesh. In August 2007 Dhaka's municipal building authority introduced a one-stop shop for building permits. Almost a year later builders still had to visit each agency responsible for approvals, mainly because of inconsistent fire safety regulations. By law, only buildings with more than 10 floors should require fire safety clearance. The fire department insists that the cutoff should be 6 floors, as in the old regulations. Builders can spend 6 months shuttling between agencies, trying to make sense of the inconsistent rules.

SETTING TIME LIMITS

The second most popular reform feature has been to introduce statutory time limits or silence-is-consent rules. Many economies write time limits into the law in the hope of ending administrative delays. Algeria put a 2-month time limit on issuing building permits in 2006. But obtaining a building permit still takes an average 150 days because of lack of administrative resources. Builders wait, out of fear that their buildings will be demolished if they proceed without a permit.

In Colombia a law introduced a silence-is-consent rule in 1997. Ten years later an implementing regulation and a far-reaching public awareness campaign finally made it possible for builders to take control of the process. "Now we can begin construction after 45 working days without any fear. As long as every requirement is complied with, we know the law protects us," says one Colombian architect.

RATIONALIZING INSPECTIONS

The third most popular reform feature has been to shift from random inspections toward a more risk-based approach, with inspections only at critical stages of construction. Building authorities have traditionally relied on random inspections to ensure compliance. Today only 41 economies—most in Africa, Latin America and the Caribbean and the Middle East and North Africa—still use them. Building authorities have learned that random inspections strain their limited resources and are an inefficient way to ensure building safety (figure 3.5).

Eleven of the top 15 economies on the ease of dealing with construction permits have gone beyond risk-based inspections. Instead, they allow certified professionals or independent agencies to perform inspections during construction. Building authorities usually inspect buildings only after they are complete. Singapore, one of the top performers, delegates control and supervision of the entire construction process to licensed engineers and architects. In Japan more flexible licensing regulations for private inspection companies have increased their numbers and made contracting with them faster and cheaper for builders.

FIGURE 3.5
Private and risk-based inspections—greater efficiency
Average delay for inspections (days)

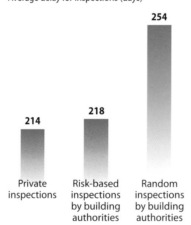

Source: Doing Business database.

Most EU economies have shifted at least part of inspections to the private domain. Their experience shows that private inspections work best when supported by strong professional associations with well-regulated accreditation mechanisms. A mature insurance industry also helps. In 2007 the Czech Republic introduced a new profession of authorized inspectors. Two professional chambers of architects and engineers and technicians provide a strong base.[3]

NOTES

1. Bayerisches Staatsministerium des Innern (2002).
2. PricewaterhouseCoopers (2005).
3. Geginat and Malinska (2008).

Employing workers

FIGURE 4.1
Economies with rigid labor regulations have fewer business start-ups

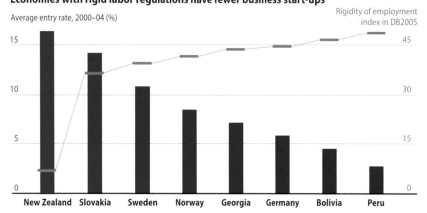

Source: Doing Business database; Djankov, Ganser, McLiesh, Ramalho and Shleifer (2008).

Aissa, a successful designer, owns a business exporting traditional Senegalese handwoven fabrics to upscale international brands like Hermès and Christian Lacroix. Demand is growing, so much so that Aissa would have to quadruple production to meet it. But that would mean hiring more workers—and that seems too risky.[1] What if demand should decline? It would be difficult to downsize again. "People can sue you and say you have fired them illegally," Aissa explains. "You have to give them a letter and then a long process begins."

That process would involve multiple letters to the labor inspector, all requiring a formal response. Aissa would have to give specific reasons for dismissing workers and prove that she had tried other solutions. She could not choose which workers to dismiss; she would have to follow a particular order of seniority. And she would have to prove that her industry is suffering a slowdown. This is nearly impossible, since Senegal lacks reliable statistics on industrywide trends. Besides, there are no formal criteria on what constitutes a slowdown. The labor inspector decides.

Senegal's restrictive labor laws make it difficult to adjust to demand. Besides the burdensome dismissal requirements, employers face tight restrictions on working hours and a ban on using fixed-term contracts for permanent tasks. All this leads to another problem for Aissa: many of her competitors circumvent labor regulations altogether by operating in the informal sector.

Aissa is not alone. A study of 1,948 retail stores in large Indian cities finds that 27% see labor regulations as a problem.[2] The study also finds that making labor laws more flexible could increase employment in stores by 22% on average. This is substantial: the retail sector is India's second largest employer, providing jobs to 9.4% of workers. Similarly, a study in Brazil finds that enforcement of rigid labor regulations limits firm size and reduces employment.[3]

Employment regulations are needed to allow efficient contracting between employers and workers and to protect workers from discriminatory or unfair treatment by employers. In its indicators on employing workers, *Doing Business*

measures flexibility in the regulation of hiring, working hours and dismissal in a manner consistent with the conventions of the International Labour Organization (ILO). An economy can have the most flexible labor regulations as measured by *Doing Business* while ratifying and complying with all conventions directly relevant to the factors measured by *Doing Business*[4] and with the ILO core labor standards. No economy can achieve a better score by failing to comply with these conventions.

Doing Business supports the ILO core labor standards—the 8 conventions covering the right to collective bargaining, the elimination of forced labor, the abolition of child labor and equitable treatment in employment practices. Respect for these standards helps create an environment in which business can

TABLE 4.1
Where is it easy to employ workers—and where not?

Easiest	RANK	Most difficult	RANK
United States	1	Panama	172
Singapore	2	Sierra Leone	173
Marshall Islands	3	Angola	174
Maldives	4	Congo, Dem. Rep.	175
Georgia	5	Guinea-Bissau	176
Brunei	6	Paraguay	177
Tonga	7	Equatorial Guinea	178
Australia	8	São Tomé and Principe	179
Palau	9	Bolivia	180
Denmark	10	Venezuela	181

Note: Rankings are the average of the economy rankings on the difficulty of hiring, rigidity of hours, difficulty of firing and firing cost indices. See Data notes for details.
Source: Doing Business database.

FIGURE 4.2
Rankings on employing workers are based on 4 subindicators

Note: See Data notes for details.

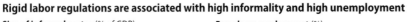

FIGURE 4.3

Rigid labor regulations are associated with high informality and high unemployment

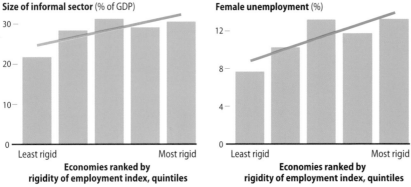

Size of informal sector (% of GDP)

Female unemployment (%)

Least rigid   Most rigid
**Economies ranked by
rigidity of employment index, quintiles**

Least rigid   Most rigid
**Economies ranked by
rigidity of employment index, quintiles**

Note: Relationships are significant at the 1% level for size of the informal sector and at the 10% level for female unemployment, and remain significant when controlling for income per capita.
Source: Doing Business database; WEF (2007); World Bank, World Development Indicators database.

develop. *Doing Business* does not measure compliance with them, however, and these 8 conventions are not reflected in the employing workers indicators. This year's report shows which of the 8 conventions have been ratified by each of the 181 economies it includes (see table on ratification status of the 8 ILO conventions regarding core labor standards, page 147). Ratification of the core labor standards is not necessarily a good indicator of compliance. A measure of compliance is being developed under the *Doing Business* project for future inclusion in the employing workers indicators.

Governments all over the world face the challenge of finding the right balance between worker protection and labor market flexibility. Denmark, for example, seeks to reconcile job flexibility with employment security through "flexicurity." Employers face no regulations against laying off workers for economic reasons. They only provide advance notice. More than 80% of workers belong to a voluntary unemployment insurance scheme.[5] Workers benefit from the flexible regulations, which give them the opportunity for a job in the formal sector and easy transitions from one job to another. Indeed, more than 70% of Danes think it is good to change jobs frequently.[6]

But in developing countries especially, regulators often err to one extreme—pushing employers and workers into the informal sector. Across developing economies, overly rigid labor regula-

tions are associated with a larger informal sector[7] (figure 4.3). This pattern is evident in Venezuela and Bolivia. Both have laws that ban dismissing workers on economic grounds and are among the economies with the most rigid employment regulations (table 4.1). And both are among the 5 economies with the largest informal sectors (41% of GDP in Venezuela, 43% in Bolivia).[8]

In the end, workers in the informal sector lose out the most. They are generally paid lower wages and enjoy no legal protections or social benefits. The most vulnerable groups, women and young workers, are often at the greatest disadvantage. A study in Indonesia finds that if it had enjoyed the same flexibility in labor regulations as Finland, for example, its unemployment rate might have been 2.1 percentage points lower and, among young people, 5.8 percentage points lower.[9]

Finding the right balance can be difficult, but the quest is worth it. Another recent study looks at the effects of labor regulation in Latin America, using survey data for 10,396 firms in 14 countries.[10] Firms were asked how many permanent workers they would hire and how many they would dismiss if labor regulations were made more flexible. The analysis suggests that the result would be an average net increase of 2.1% in total jobs. Firms with fewer than 20 employees benefit the most, with average gains of 4.2%.

Flexible labor regulations also en-

courage entrepreneurship. Two recent studies suggest that flexible regulations increase the probability of start-ups by about 30%.[11] The researchers offer 2 explanations. For employees, lower job security makes starting their own business attractive. For entrepreneurs, the greater flexibility in running a business makes business ownership more attractive.

Reforms making labor regulations more flexible also may increase industrial production and reduce urban unemployment. In the Indian states of Andhra Pradesh and Tamil Nadu such reforms increased manufacturing output by 15%. In West Bengal, by contrast, reforms making labor regulations more rigid cut output by 20%.[12] The estimated result: 1.8 million more urban poor in West Bengal.[13]

WHO REFORMED IN 2007/08?

Fifteen economies made significant changes to their labor regulations in 2007/08. Six economies increased flexibility; 9 reduced it. Eastern Europe and Central Asia introduced the most reforms increasing flexibility, followed by Africa and Latin America and the Caribbean (table 4.2).

Burkina Faso was the most active reformer, adopting a new labor code that replaced its 2004 code. Employees and employers can now determine the weekly rest day without having to seek the approval of the authorities. And employers may be encouraged to take greater risks in hiring new workers thanks to increased flexibility in using fixed-term contracts and less rigid dismissal procedures. For example, strict priority rules, including seniority, no longer apply in dismissing workers for redundancy.

Azerbaijan was the second most active reformer. Working hours became more flexible, with restrictions on night work now applying only where labor conditions are hard or hazardous. Before the reform, an employer could dismiss a worker for economic reasons only if the worker could not be reassigned to another position. That requirement is

TABLE 4.2
Easing restrictions on fixed-term contracts—a popular reform feature in 2007/08

Eased restrictions on fixed-term contracts	Azerbaijan, Burkina Faso, Mozambique, Slovenia
Made working hours more flexible	Azerbaijan, Burkina Faso, Czech Republic
Reduced dismissal costs	Argentina, Mozambique, Slovenia
Removed requirements for dismissal	Azerbaijan, Burkina Faso
Made dismissal more difficult	Cape Verde, China, Fiji, The Gambia, Italy, Kazakhstan
Increased restrictions on fixed-term employment	Korea, Sweden
Increased paid annual leave	United Kingdom

Source: Doing Business database.

gone. Specific notification and approval requirements for redundancy were also eased. And as in Burkina Faso, fixed-term contracts can now be used for any task. On the basis of the new labor code, Azerbaijan now ranks among the 10 economies with the least rigid employment regulations as measured by *Doing Business* (table 4.3).

Mozambique's new labor law also increased flexibility in the use of fixed-term contracts. It reduced the notice period for dismissals, from 90 days to 30. And it introduced phased reductions in severance pay.

In Eastern Europe, Slovenia and the Czech Republic provided for greater flexibility in using employment contracts. Slovenia now permits employers to extend fixed-term contracts from the statutory 24 months to the duration of a project. It also reduced the notice period for dismissals from 75 days to 60. The Czech Republic introduced flexibility in overtime hours, probationary periods and length of the workweek. In addition, its amended labor code simplified the working hours account, allowing choice in the distribution of working hours over a 4-week period.

Continuing the trend toward greater flexibility in Eastern Europe, the former Yugoslav Republic of Macedonia is in the final stages of passing a new labor relations law that will increase flexibility in working hours and reduce dismissal costs for redundancies. The new provisions will allow flexible use of fixed-term contracts, increasing their maximum duration from 4 years to 5. It will also

eliminate restrictions on weekend work and ease constraints on the dismissal of redundant workers.

In Latin America, Argentina reduced the severance payment for a worker with 20 years of seniority from 30 months to 20. After its unemployment rate fell below 10%, a 2007 decree abolished the 50% increase in severance payments that had been part of the 2002 "emergency laws."

Reforms in East Asia and Pacific were a mix, both increasing flexibility and reducing it. China introduced new priority

rules for group redundancy dismissals, making it more difficult for employers to adjust during economic downturns. In Fiji new legislation strengthened protections against discrimination in employment and shifted dispute resolution from litigation to mediation. But it also introduced new notification requirements for dismissals and reduced the flexibility of working hours by imposing a limit of 48 hours in a 6-day workweek.

Among OECD high-income economies, Korea introduced important provisions on equality of opportunity and nondiscrimination in hiring and promotion. It also limited fixed-term contracts to 24 months.

Several economies made employment regulations more rigid. Kazakhstan now requires employers to first transfer an employee to another job when considering redundancy. Italy increased the notice period for dismissal of workers from 2 weeks to 75 days, The Gambia from 2 months to 6 and Cape Verde from 30 days to 45. Sweden reduced the maximum

TABLE 4.3
Who makes employing workers easy—and who does not?

Rigidity of employment index (0–100)			
Least		**Most**	
Hong Kong, China	0	São Tomé and Principe	63
United States	0	Angola	66
Singapore	0	Equatorial Guinea	66
Maldives	0	Guinea-Bissau	66
Marshall Islands	0	Panama	66
Australia	3	Congo, Rep.	69
Azerbaijan	3	Niger	70
Uganda	3	Congo, Dem. Rep.	74
Canada	4	Bolivia	79
Jamaica	4	Venezuela	79
Firing cost (weeks of salary)			
Least		**Most**	
Denmark	0	Equatorial Guinea	133
New Zealand	0	Mozambique	134
United States	0	Ecuador	135
Puerto Rico	0	Sri Lanka	169
Afghanistan	0	Ghana	178
Iraq	0	Zambia	178
Marshall Islands	0	Sierra Leone	189
Micronesia	0	Zimbabwe	446
Palau	0	Bolivia	NOT POSSIBLE
Tonga	0	Venezuela	NOT POSSIBLE

Note: The rigidity of employment index is the average of the difficulty of hiring index, rigidity of hours index and difficulty of firing index.
Source: Doing Business database.

duration of fixed-term contracts from 3 years to 2. The United Kingdom increased the paid annual leave to which workers are entitled from 20 working days to 24.

WHAT ARE THE REFORM TRENDS?

Across the world, *Doing Business* has recorded only 77 reforms affecting the employing workers indicators since 2004. Of the 77 reforms, 47 made labor regulations more flexible; 30 made them more rigid. Labor reforms are rare. This is unsurprising. Governments work on such reforms for years, and there are many stakeholders involved. Labor reforms normally imply a tripartite consultation—between government, employers' representatives and workers' representatives. Finding the right balance of interests is a challenging and important exercise.

MOVING TOWARD MORE FLEXIBLE REGULATIONS

Governments in Eastern Europe and Central Asia have been the most active reformers in the past 5 years, introducing 19 reforms increasing the flexibility of labor regulations (figure 4.4). OECD

high-income economies follow with 16, with Australia, Germany and Switzerland all reforming more than once.

In Africa, Uganda (in 2006), Mozambique (in 2007) and Burkina Faso (in 2008) enacted new labor laws, introducing worker protections while increasing the flexibility of labor regulations. Namibia (in 2004) eased restrictions on working hours. Yet among regions, Africa continues to have the most rigid labor regulations. Dismissal costs for a worker with 20 years of employment amount to more than 3 years of salary in Sierra Leone and more than 8 years in Zimbabwe. Africa is also home to the countries with the largest numbers of mandatory paid annual leave days: Eritrea with 34, Ethiopia with 33 and Cameroon with 32.

Three reformers stand out in Eastern Europe and Central Asia. Slovakia (in 2004) and Azerbaijan (in 2008) introduced flexibility in the use of fixed-term contracts, in work schedules and in redundancy requirements. Georgia made big changes in those areas in 2005 and 2006 and also introduced changes in notice periods and severance payments.

Reform was widespread: 8 of the 10 countries in the region that have joined the European Union have reformed their labor laws. Several, including Lithuania and Romania, did so to harmonize their laws with EU legislation.

In South Asia 2 economies have reformed. Bhutan went far, implementing its first labor code in 2007. The new labor code established protective measures for workers without imposing heavy burdens on employers. The protections created incentives for workers to join the private sector—and employers now have a larger pool of candidates to choose from. The better working conditions have led to higher productivity.[14]

In Latin America, Colombia and Argentina made labor regulations more flexible. Both made redundancy dismissals easier—Colombia in 2004 and Argentina in 2005. Argentina also reduced dismissal costs in 2007. In East Asia and Pacific, Vietnam eased restrictions on fixed-term contracts, and Taiwan (China) on working hours. Except for Israel, no economies in the Middle East and North Africa made labor regulations more flexible.

FIGURE 4.4

Most reforms in Eastern Europe & Central Asia

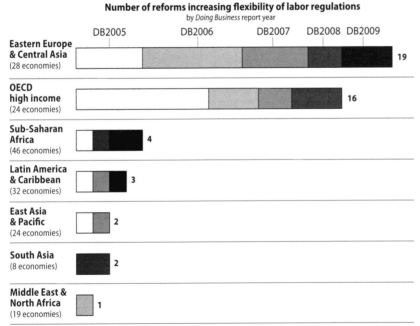

Number of reforms increasing flexibility of labor regulations
by *Doing Business* report year

Note: A reform is counted as 1 reform per reforming economy per year.
Source: Doing Business database.

FIGURE 4.5

Top 4 reform features in employing workers

Reforms including feature since DB2005 (%)

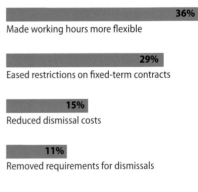

36%
Made working hours more flexible

29%
Eased restrictions on fixed-term contracts

15%
Reduced dismissal costs

11%
Removed requirements for dismissals

Note: A reform may include several reform features.
Source: Doing Business database.

INCREASING FLEXIBILITY IN SETTING HOURS AND USING CONTRACTS

Over the past 5 years 36 reforms have been aimed at increasing flexibility in working hours and the use of fixed-term contracts (figure 4.5). Five reforms have made scheduling working hours more difficult. Nine have restricted the use of fixed-term contracts.

Most of the reforms aimed at increasing flexibility in working hours took place in Eastern Europe and Central Asia. These reforms, concentrated in 2004 and 2005, allowed more flexible arrangements for overtime and permitted businesses to shift working hours from the low to the high season. In Latvia and Poland working hours must balance out within 4 months; in Hungary, within a year. Overtime hours have become more predictable for employees, and employers can more easily adjust to cyclical demand. Elsewhere in the world, Pakistan eased limits on overtime, while Uganda allowed employers and employees to freely set the legally required rest day. Bhutan eased restrictions on night work.

Sixteen economies allowed greater flexibility in the use of fixed-term contracts. In Azerbaijan and Burkina Faso, for example, fixed-term contracts can now be used for permanent tasks. Latvia and Togo extended their maximum duration. That makes it easier for both employers and employees to adapt work arrangements to their needs.

REDUCING DISMISSAL COSTS

Ten economies granted businesses more flexibility in dismissals during economic downturns. But 15 economies (including Bolivia, Fiji, Kazakhstan and Zimbabwe) made such dismissals costlier or more difficult. In Bolivia and Venezuela an employer cannot let workers go for economic reasons without their consent. Under these circumstances employers might think twice before hiring a new worker.

High dismissal costs can deter employers from creating jobs in the formal sector. That argues for reducing dismissal burdens. But excessive flexibility leads to another problem: concern among existing employees about losing their jobs and being left without a safety net.

One solution is to offer unemployment insurance rather than severance pay. In Austria employers contribute to a fund from which they may withdraw if a worker is made redundant after 3 years of employment. In St. Kitts and Nevis severance payments are made from a government-administered fund that employers pay into over time. In Italy employers deposit a portion of each employee's salary into a designated fund over the course of the employment relationship. In Korea employers adopting the new defined contribution plan will contribute 1 month's salary annually to each employee's private pension account.

Chile adopted a successful unemployment insurance system in 2002. The reform introduced individual savings accounts to which both employee and employer contribute. It also reduced severance pay from 30 working days to 24 for each year worked. Unemployed Chilean workers receive benefits from their individual savings accounts for 5 months.

NOTES

1. This example is from the World Bank's *Doing Business: Women in Africa* (2008a), a collection of case studies of African entrepreneurs.
2. Amin (forthcoming).
3. Almeida and Carneiro (forthcoming).
4. ILO Convention 14 on weekly rest (industry), ILO Convention 171 on night work, ILO Convention 132 on holidays with pay and ILO Convention 158 on termination of employment.
5. Data on the share of the labor force covered by unemployment insurance, from Clasen and Viebrock (2008), are for 2002.
6. Eurobarometer (2006).
7. Djankov and Ramalho (2008). A 10-point increase in the rigidity of employment index is associated with an increase of 0.9% of GDP in the size of the informal sector.
8. Djankov and Ramalho (2008).
9. Feldmann (2008).
10. Kaplan (forthcoming). The study uses data from the World Bank Enterprise Surveys, available at http://www.enterprisesurveys.org.
11. Van Stel, Storey and Thurik (2007) and Ardagna and Lusardi (2008).
12. Aghion and others (forthcoming).
13. Besley and Burgess (2004).
14. Wangda (forthcoming).

Registering property

FIGURE 5.1

Top 10 reformers in registering property

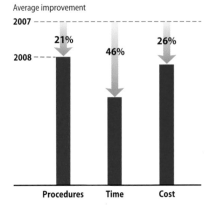

Average improvement

1.	*Belarus*
2.	*Rwanda*
3.	*Azerbaijan*
4.	*Kazakhstan*
5.	*Hungary*
6.	*Zambia*
7.	*Mauritius*
8.	*Burkina Faso*
9.	*Madagascar*
10.	*Egypt*

Source: Doing Business database.

Ida, a Gambian entrepreneur, wants to sell her plot of land to expand her manufacturing business. She has found an interested buyer. But she has also learned that transferring property in The Gambia requires the consent of the Department of Lands and Surveys—and getting that takes about a year. There is another option: hire a lawyer with connections at the department and obtain the consent in a day. But Ida cannot afford the cost, about 3% of the value of her property. Ida decides to wait for the department's consent, putting on hold her plans to expand her business.

Besides The Gambia, 11 other economies still require a ministerial consent to transfer property: Lesotho, Madagascar, Malawi, Nigeria, Papua New Guinea, Senegal, Solomon Islands, Tanzania, Tonga, Uganda and Zambia. Côte d'Ivoire

TABLE 5.1

Where is registering property easy—and where not?

Easiest	RANK	Most difficult	RANK
Saudi Arabia	1	Liberia	172
Georgia	2	Angola	173
New Zealand	3	Afghanistan	174
Lithuania	4	Bangladesh	175
Armenia	5	Nigeria	176
Thailand	6	Brunei	177
Slovakia	7	Maldives	178
Norway	8	Marshall Islands	179
Azerbaijan	9	Micronesia	180
Sweden	10	Timor-Leste	181

Note: Rankings are the average of the economy rankings on the procedures, time and cost to register property. See Data notes for details.
Source: Doing Business database.

used to be another. But in 2005 it eliminated the requirement for approval by the Ministry of Urban Planning. That slashed the time required to register property from 397 days to 62—and the number of property transfers in Abidjan almost quadrupled, from 500 in 2005 to 1,968 in 2007.[1]

Formal property titles help promote the transfer of land, encourage investment and give entrepreneurs access to formal credit markets.[2] But a large share of property in developing countries is not formally registered. Informal titles cannot be used as security in obtaining loans, which limits financing opportunities for businesses. Many governments have recognized this and started extensive property titling programs. But bringing assets into the formal sector is only part of the story. The more difficult and costly it is to formally transfer property, the greater the chances that formalized titles will quickly become informal again. Eliminating unnecessary obstacles to registering and transferring property is therefore important for economic development.

Economies that score well on the ease of registering property tend to have simple procedures, low transfer taxes, fixed registration fees, online registries and time limits for administrative procedures. They also make the use of notaries and lawyers optional. Saudi Arabia computerized procedures in 2007, making it possible to register property in 2 proce-

dures and 2 days. In Georgia and Lithuania, which recently simplified procedures, it takes 3 days to register property. In New Zealand, number 3 on the ease of registering property, online registration is straightforward. In Slovakia, which replaced a percentage-based fee with a fixed fee, the cost to register property is only 0.05% of the property value.

WHO REFORMED IN 2007/08?

Twenty-four economies made it easier to register property in 2007/08 (table 5.2). The most popular reform feature: lowering the cost of registration by reducing the property transfer tax, registration fees or stamp duty. Five economies—Burkina Faso, the Dominican Republic, Jamaica, Serbia and Thailand—reduced the transfer tax. The Republic of Congo

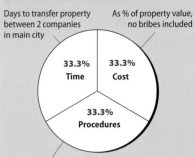

FIGURE 5.2

Rankings on registering property are based on 3 subindicators

Days to transfer property between 2 companies in main city

As % of property value, no bribes included

33.3% Time

33.3% Cost

33.3% Procedures

Steps for encumbrance checking, deed and title transfer until property can be sold again or used as collateral

Note: See Data notes for details.

TABLE 5.2
Reducing the cost to register property—the most popular reform feature in 2007/08

Reduced taxes or fees	Burkina Faso, Republic of Congo, Dominican Republic, Jamaica, Madagascar, Rwanda, Serbia, Thailand
Combined and reduced procedures	Azerbaijan, Belarus, Georgia, Kazakhstan, Latvia, Lithuania, Mauritius
Computerized procedures	Belarus, Bosnia and Herzegovina, Georgia, Madagascar, Saudi Arabia, Zambia
Sped procedures in the registry	Bangladesh, Egypt, former Yugoslav Republic of Macedonia, Madagascar, Sierra Leone
Introduced time limits	Belarus, Egypt, Senegal
Introduced fast-track procedures	Azerbaijan, Hungary
Allowed private valuers to complete valuations	Republic of Congo

Source: Doing Business database.

and Rwanda reduced registration fees. Madagascar eliminated the stamp duty.

Belarus was the top reformer in property registration. The government had initiated the creation of a one-stop shop in March 2004. In early 2006 the legal changes necessary for the one-stop shop to become operational took effect. To complete its implementation and to address remaining bottlenecks at the Land Registry, the government launched a broad administrative simplification program in November 2007. The program introduced strict time limits, computerized the registry and digitized property records. The government's ambitious reform agenda paid off: the time to register property in Minsk fell from 231 days to 21. Belarus now ranks among the top 25 economies on the ease of registering property.

"Comparing the registry a few years

back and today is like night and day. From waiting in long lines taking up to a few months, we went to a modern, efficient one-stop shop. They even have a webcam in the one-stop shop to check the waiting line," says Alexander, a seasoned entrepreneur in Minsk.

Rwanda was the runner-up reformer. A presidential decree in January 2008 replaced a 6% registration fee with a flat rate of 20,000 Rwanda francs (about $34), regardless of the property value. Before, the 6% registration fee applied to every property transaction, and the Rwanda Revenue Authority had to value the property, which took 35 days on average. Registering property in Kigali now requires only 4 procedures and less than 1% of the property value (figure 5.3). Yet with the process still taking almost a year on average, there is room for improvement.

Eastern Europe and Central Asia

had the most reforms in property registration. Azerbaijan introduced a one-stop shop and gave the State Registry of Real Estate sole responsibility for all property registrations in the country. That required amending the civil code in April 2006. Before, entrepreneurs had to register land and buildings separately. This meant going through 7 lengthy procedures, including getting clearances from 2 agencies and an updated inventory file from the Bureau of Technical Inventory listing the property's boundaries and technical features. Those requirements are gone. With the new option of expediting 2 of the 4 remaining procedures, it is now possible to register property in only 11 days.

Kazakhstan followed a similar path. By launching public service centers—local one-stop shops—Kazakhstan simplified property registration in its major cities. Georgia, a repeat reformer for 4 years in a row, launched an electronic database. Registrars can now obtain a business registry extract, nonencumbrance certificate and cadastral sketch online. Before, these documents could be obtained only by visiting several different agencies.

Bosnia and Herzegovina was another notable reformer. The time needed to register a title in Sarajevo fell by 203 days, from 331 to 128. Once the registry is fully computerized (80% of its files were as of mid-2008), the time is expected to drop even more. The former Yugoslav Republic of Macedonia sped

TABLE 5.3
Who regulates property registration the least—and who the most?

Procedures *(number)*				**Time** *(days)*				**Cost** *(% of property value)*			
Fewest		Most		Fastest		Slowest		Least		Most	
Norway	1	Greece	11	New Zealand	2	Bangladesh	245	Saudi Arabia	0.00	Congo, Rep.	16.48
Sweden	1	Swaziland	11	Saudi Arabia	2	Afghanistan	250	Bhutan	0.01	Cameroon	17.79
Bahrain	2	Eritrea	12	Sweden	2	Togo	295	Georgia	0.03	Central African Republic	18.55
Georgia	2	Uzbekistan	12	Thailand	2	Solomon Islands	297	Belarus	0.04	Mali	20.31
Lithuania	2	Ethiopia	13	Georgia	3	Rwanda	315	Slovakia	0.05	Senegal	20.61
Netherlands	2	Liberia	13	Lithuania	3	Angola	334	Kiribati	0.06	Comoros	20.82
New Zealand	2	Uganda	13	Norway	3	Gambia, The	371	Kazakhstan	0.08	Nigeria	21.93
Oman	2	Algeria	14	Armenia	4	Slovenia	391	New Zealand	0.09	Chad	22.72
Saudi Arabia	2	Brazil	14	Iceland	4	Haiti	405	Russian Federation	0.20	Zimbabwe	25.01
Thailand	2	Nigeria	14	Australia	5	Kiribati	513	Qatar	0.25	Syria	28.05

Source: Doing Business database.

FIGURE 5.3
Easing property registration in Rwanda
Reduction in time and cost, 2007–08

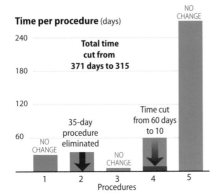

Time per procedure (days)

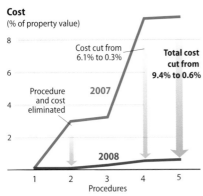

Cost
(% of property value)

Source: Doing Business database.

the process at the cadastre by adding staff. Lithuania cut a procedure by introducing special software that allows notaries to obtain the real estate transaction certificate from their office. Before, the buyer had to pick up this certificate at the registry.

Africa saw the second largest number of reforms. The Republic of Congo adopted a new law on May 11, 2007, that cut the registration fee by 10 percentage points. Transferring property used to take 137 days and cost 27% of the property value. Now it takes 116 days and costs about 17% of the property value. Senegal introduced time limits at the Land Registry to speed the delivery of certificates and the registration of property transactions. That reduced the time to register property from 145 days to 124.

Zambia computerized its land registry and set up a customer service center to eliminate the backlog of registration requests. The time to register property fell from 70 days to 39.

Madagascar was another reformer in the region. A new financial law abolished the mandatory stamp duty and 2 taxes, reducing the cost of transferring property from 11.6% of the property value to 7.5%. Madagascar did not stop there. It reorganized its registry by expanding the number of offices, purchasing new computers and hiring more staff. Transferring property in Antananarivo now takes 8 weeks less than it did a year before. Burkina Faso abolished the requirement to obtain the municipality's approval for property transactions, cutting the time by 46 days, from 182 to 136.

In the Middle East and North Africa, Egypt and Saudi Arabia reformed. Egypt simplified administrative procedures and introduced time limits. That cut the time to register property by 4 months, from 193 days to 72. Saudi Arabia introduced a comprehensive electronic system to register title deeds at the First Notary Public Department in Riyadh, making it possible to transfer property in 2 procedures and 2 days.

Here is how the process works: A notary public at the First Notary Public Department, in the presence of the legal representatives of the buyer and seller, first verifies that all documents are complete. The notary public then transfers them electronically to the Records Department, which prepares a new title deed showing the buyer as the owner of the property. The new title deed is immediately added to the electronic records of all title deeds in Riyadh. After a few hours the representatives of the buyer and seller appear a second time before the notary public, who prints a copy of the new title deed and asks the representatives and 2 witnesses to sign the sale agreement, which is a standard form. The signed sale agreement is scanned and saved in the electronic records, while the original is kept in the notary public's files.

In South Asia, Bangladesh halved the time to apply for registration at the Municipal Deed Registry Office, from 360 days to 180. The total time to register property dropped from 425 days to 245.

In Latin America and the Carib-

bean, Jamaica introduced a new law in May 2008 reducing the transfer tax from 7.5% of the property value to 6%, and the stamp duty from 5.5% to 4.5%. The cost to transfer property dropped from 13.5% of the property value to 11%. The Dominican Republic reduced the transfer tax from 4.3% to 3%. Transferring property now costs 3.8% of the property value, down from 5.1%.

In East Asia and Pacific, Thailand reduced the transfer fee from 2% to 0.01% and the specific business tax from 3.3% to 0.11%, cutting the overall cost to transfer property from 6.3% of the property value to 1.13%. Thailand now ranks among the top 10 economies on the ease of registering property. The cost reductions are provisional and valid for one year from March 2008, to allow the Thai government to assess the results of the reform in April 2009.

WHAT ARE THE REFORM TRENDS?

Almost 60% of all property registration reforms recorded by *Doing Business* in the past 4 years took place in 2 regions: Africa and Eastern Europe and Central Asia (figure 5.4). In 2005 Eastern Europe and Central Asia had the most reforms. In 2006 and 2007 Africa took the lead. In 2007/08 Eastern Europe and Central Asia led with 9 reforms, closely followed by Africa with 8.

LOWERING COSTS

Across regions, the most popular reform feature has been reducing property transfer taxes and fees—registration fees, notary fees and stamp duties (figure 5.5). In 2005 and 2006 such reductions were made by 7 of 10 reforming economies. Big cuts were made in Africa. In 2004 the region had the highest average cost for property transfer, at around 13% of the property value. Today the average cost is 10.5% of the property value—much lower, though still higher than the 6% in Latin America, the region with the second highest cost.

Many economies have reduced the cost of property registration by estab-

FIGURE 5.4
Africa has reformed the most

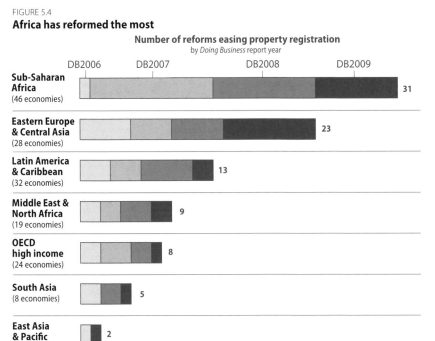

Number of reforms easing property registration
by *Doing Business* report year

Note: A reform is counted as 1 reform per reforming economy per year.
Source: Doing Business database.

FIGURE 5.5
**Top 5 reform features
in registering property**
Reforms including feature since DB2006 (%)

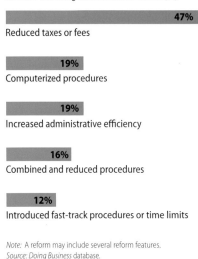

Note: A reform may include several reform features.
Source: Doing Business database.

lishing a low fixed registration fee rather than charging entrepreneurs a percentage of their property value. In 2005 Slovakia abolished its 3% real estate transfer tax and set a low fixed fee for expedited registration at 8,000 koruny ($286). In 2007 Egypt and Poland adopted similar reforms. And in 2007/08 Rwanda followed suit. This reform tends to reduce fraud in reporting the market value of property and increase tax revenue. Six months after Egypt replaced its 3% registration fee with a fixed fee of 2,000 Egyptian pounds ($323), revenues rose by 39%.[3]

COMPUTERIZING THE REGISTRY

One of the most popular reform features has been computerizing the registry and introducing online procedures that aid interaction between the notary and the registry. Computerization can be costly, so it is not surprising that more than half of such reforms have been in Eastern Europe and Central Asia and OECD high-income economies.

Computerizing registries has proved to be highly effective. The economies that have done so since 2005 have seen the time to register property drop by 45% on average. In El Salvador, which computerized its registry in 2006, the time to register property fell from 52 days to 33. Portugal computerized the Lisbon real estate registries in 2007, reducing the time from 81 days to 42. Computerizing records not only facilitates registration but also improves the preservation of the records and, as a result, the security of titles.

Digitizing the property registry's records and facilitating electronic access can improve things, but this alone is often not enough. In 2005 Honduras launched a reform aimed at allowing every entrepreneur online access to the registry's information. But online access did not resolve the many inconsistencies in information between the registry and the cadastre. To do this, the 2 agencies must be coordinated, and the cadastre updated regularly.[4] Comayagua, 80 kilometers northwest of Tegucigalpa, is the only city in Honduras that has completely digitized its property registry's records, thanks to an updated digital cadastre.

HOW TO REFORM

Some reforms to ease property registration, such as eliminating unnecessary procedures or reducing the number of approvals required, can be done quickly—once everyone is convinced of the benefits. Such reforms usually require no drastic changes in the legislation and can be executed administratively. In previous years such economies as Côte d'Ivoire, Georgia and Ghana have reduced the time required to register property by eliminating long and unnecessary procedures.

Inspiration can sometimes be found at home. *Doing Business* subnational studies have shown that local authorities, federal and municipal, learn from one another to improve registration processes, even if they share the same legal and regulatory framework. This process was at work in Mexico, where Aguascalientes followed Yucatán's experience in simplifying the registration process and reducing fees at the land registry. In 2007/08 San Luis Potosí and Chiapas followed Aguascalientes's example of introducing a bar code to allow computerized tracking of property records.[5]

Other reforms, such as overhauls of the entire property registration system, can take years. Consider the top reformer in property registration for 2007/08. Belarus passed the law establishing its one-stop shop in March 2004. Making the one-stop shop operational took another 3.5 years and several presidential decrees. The previous year's top reformer, Ghana, has been working for more than 4 years to complete the transition from a deeds registration to a title registration system. Entrepreneurs in Accra can now register a title in 34 days. In other parts of the country the same process still takes months.[6]

Shifting from a deeds system to a title system is also taking time in Hong Kong (China), which launched this reform in July 2004. The reform is still under way as the government continues to work on such legal issues as how it will indemnify users for errors and how the system will deal with third-party claims.

NOTES

1. Data on property transfers in Abidjan are from Côte d'Ivoire, Direction du Domaine, de la Conservation Foncière, de l'Enregistrement et du Timbre.
2. Miceli and Kieyah (2003).
3. Haidar (2008).
4. Coma-Cunill and Delion (2008).
5. Cruz-Osorio and Enrigue (2008).
6. Hacibeyoglu (2008).

FIGURE 6.1

Cambodia leads in legal rights reform, Albania and the United Arab Emirates top reform in credit information

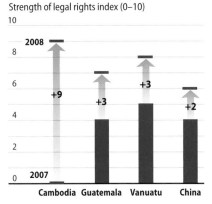

Strength of legal rights index (0–10)

Depth of credit information index (0–6)

Source: Doing Business database.

Sibongile was meant to fly. "I grew up near an Air Force base and always had a love for planes," she says, remembering a childhood spent waving at jets at South Africa's Hoedspruit base.

After a successful 7-year career in human resources, Sibongile seized the opportunity presented by the passage of South Africa's Black Economic Empowerment Act in 2003: she started her own business, SRS Aviation. Opportunities for government contracts came quickly, but getting financing was difficult. "I took the government tender to the bankers," says Sibongile. "Forget it, they said. Because the amount of money was too large and the collateral too small."

Sibongile ended up using her family's savings, along with her mother's and aunt's retirement funds, to finance the first deal: leasing a plane from the Russian Federation. "I remember waiting for days at the airport for the plane to arrive, panicking that after paying so much money and risking people's savings it may not arrive." But all went well in the end, and Sibongile's business took off.[1]

Where collateral laws are effective and credit registries are present, banks are more likely to extend loans. Hong Kong (China), Singapore and Kenya facilitate access to credit through laws that allow all types of assets to be used as collateral and do not require a specific description of the collateral or obligation. They also have unified collateral registries and allow out-of-court enforcement of security rights.

In Canada, El Salvador, Georgia, Korea, Peru, Saudi Arabia and the United States credit registries record and make available historical credit information on all bank loans—as well as credit from utilities and retailers—for both individuals and companies. The registries also make available both positive information (such as loan amounts and on-time payment patterns) and negative information (such as late payments and defaults). And they allow borrowers to inspect and dispute their information.

Doing Business measures the legal rights of borrowers and lenders and the scope and quality of credit information systems. The first set of indicators describes how well collateral and bankruptcy laws facilitate lending. The second set measures the coverage, scope, qual-

ity and accessibility of credit information available through public and private credit registries (figure 6.2).

Both creditor protection through the legal system and credit registries are associated with higher ratios of private credit to GDP. For example, an increase of 1 in the creditors' rights index is associated with a 6.5 percentage point increase in the average annual growth rate of the private-credit-to-GDP ratio in the 3 years after the reform relative to the 3 years before.[2]

Research shows that introducing a credit registry is associated with an increase of 4.2 percentage points in firms' reliance on credit.[3] This is in part because introducing registries increases the repayment rate: borrowers become less willing to default, since defaults can prevent future loans. In developing econo-

TABLE 6.1

Where is getting credit easy— and where not?

Easiest	RANK	Most difficult	RANK
Malaysia	1	Bhutan	172
Hong Kong, China	2	Djibouti	173
South Africa	3	Eritrea	174
United Kingdom	4	Madagascar	175
Australia	5	Tajikistan	176
Bulgaria	6	Yemen	177
Israel	7	Afghanistan	178
New Zealand	8	Syria	179
Singapore	9	Timor-Leste	180
United States	10	Palau	181

Note: Rankings on the ease of getting credit are based on the sum of the strength of legal rights index and the depth of credit information index. See Data notes for details.
Source: Doing Business database.

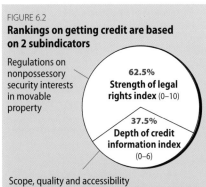

FIGURE 6.2

Rankings on getting credit are based on 2 subindicators

Regulations on nonpossessory security interests in movable property

62.5%
Strength of legal rights index (0–10)

37.5%
Depth of credit information index (0–6)

Scope, quality and accessibility of credit information through public and private credit registries

Note: Private bureau coverage and public registry coverage do not count for the rankings. See Data notes for details.

mies the repayment rate can increase by up to 80% when a credit registry starts operation. Small firms benefit the most: in transition economies that introduced new credit registries, their access to credit grew twice as fast as that of large firms.[4]

Strengthening the legal rights of borrowers and lenders allows businesses to invest more in new technologies. One recent study finds that economies that score higher on creditor protections have newer airplanes.[5] Beyond that, their airlines invest in better safety and communication technologies. Why? Part of the reason is that where strong protections are lacking, creditors offer only leasing, not loans. So in economies with weak creditor protections, most planes are leased, and airline owners have less incentive to upgrade their safety features.

New evidence suggests that establishing strong legal rights and new credit registries may also reduce income inequality.[6] One possible explanation is that these changes allow more entrepreneurs to expand their business. Borrowing money from the bank becomes more about their creditworthiness—and less about whom they know.

WHO REFORMED IN 2007/08?

Cambodia's new secured transactions law made it the top reformer in getting credit in 2007/08. Albania was the runner-up reformer. It created a new public credit registry with full information on loans of all sizes, for individuals and for firms.

Before the new law took effect in Cambodia, business owners could use only immovable property as collateral. With little land under private ownership, getting a loan was an unreachable dream for most small to medium-size businesses. The new law changed that. Cambodian entrepreneurs can now use a broad range of movable assets to secure a loan. That includes revolving assets such as inventory and accounts receivable. A general description of collateral suffices in loan agreements, permitting such wording as "all assets" or "all movable property" of the borrower. Thanks to these and other provisions of the law, Cambodia's score on the strength of legal rights index shot up from 0 to 9.

Three other economies in East Asia and Pacific—Vanuatu, China and Taiwan (China)—also made it easier for businesses to use movable property as collateral. Vanuatu passed a new secured transactions law, the Personal Property Securities Act. China revised its property law to allow borrowers to use a variety of revolving assets and a combined set of assets (such as raw material, production equipment and finished goods) as collateral. The new law is expected to put into circulation more than $2 trillion worth of movable assets.[7] Taiwan (China) amended its civil code to allow parties to a pledge agreement to set the loan amount as a maximum line of credit.

In South Asia, Sri Lanka exempted secured creditors from automatic suspension of enforcement procedures in court during bankruptcy.

Georgia amended its civil code in June 2007 to allow parties to agree that collateral can be sold without court intervention. Guatemala passed a law in October 2007 establishing a special regime for registering security interests in movable property. The law went into effect in January 2008.

Twenty-seven economies reformed their credit information systems in 2007/08, improving the quality and scope of information collected and distributed by credit registries and bureaus (table 6.2). Uzbekistan created both a public credit registry and a private credit bureau. Albania, Liberia and Montenegro launched new public credit registries— and in Montenegro the coverage of borrowers went from 0 to 26% of the adult population. Ukraine and the United Arab Emirates each set up a private credit bureau. Zambia is doing so.

Six more economies in Eastern Europe and Central Asia introduced credit information reforms, bringing the total to 10, the most of any region. Georgia now distributes a full range of information, including on-time repayment patterns and outstanding loan amounts. Coverage has increased 20 times. Kazakhstan's private credit bureau is adding new suppliers of information at a rate of 2 a month. Prominent among them are nonbank institutions such as retailers and utility companies. Coverage has shot up by 80%. Moldova passed a new law to

TABLE 6.2

More credit information, more access—popular reform features in 2007/08

Provided online access to credit registry	Cameroon, Central African Republic, Chad, Republic of Congo, Equatorial Guinea, Gabon, Sri Lanka, West Bank and Gaza
Expanded set of information collected in credit registry	Azerbaijan, Belarus, Georgia, Kazakhstan, Mauritius, Sri Lanka, Tunisia, Vietnam
Introduced regulations guaranteeing that borrowers can inspect data in credit registry	Belarus, Egypt, Georgia, Indonesia, former Yugoslav Republic of Macedonia, Morocco, Tunisia
Established new credit registry or bureau	Albania, Liberia, Montenegro, Ukraine, United Arab Emirates, Uzbekistan
Expanded range of revolving movable assets that can be used as collateral	Cambodia, China, Guatemala, Vanuatu
Allowed out-of-court enforcement of collateral	Georgia, Guatemala, Vanuatu
Allowed maximum rather than specific amounts in debt agreements	Cambodia, Taiwan (China)
Gave priority to secured creditors' claims outside and inside bankruptcy procedures	Cambodia, Vanuatu
Exempted secured creditors' claims from an automatic stay in reorganization	Cambodia, Sri Lanka
Created a unified registry for movable property	Cambodia

Source: Doing Business database.

FIGURE 6.3
Private credit bureaus provide more comprehensive services to lenders

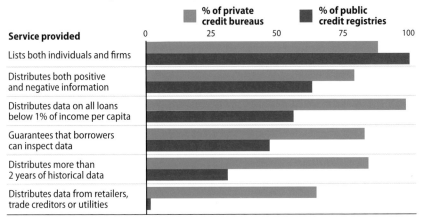

Source: Doing Business database.

facilitate the creation of a private credit bureau. Azerbaijan, Belarus and the former Yugoslav Republic of Macedonia also reformed.

The most popular credit information reform feature was providing online access to members. The regional public credit registry of the Central African Monetary Union made information accessible to banks online. That led to exponential growth in coverage in Cameroon, Chad, the Republic of Congo and Gabon. Sri Lanka's credit bureau and West Bank and Gaza's public credit registry set up systems allowing banks to update information and obtain credit reports online.

Many economies issued regulations guaranteeing borrowers access to their credit information. Egypt issued such regulations for the private credit bureau. Georgia amended its civil code with the same purpose. In the former Yugoslav Republic of Macedonia a new law on personal data protection guarantees that borrowers can review their data in the new public credit registry. In Belarus and Tunisia new laws allow individuals and firms to inspect their credit data in all central bank offices. Morocco published new circulars guaranteeing that borrowers can review their data in credit registries—and laying the groundwork for new private bureaus.

Other economies eliminated the minimum threshold for loans recorded in credit registries. Sri Lanka's private bureau started using a new online system to collect data on all loans, regardless of value. Coverage grew threefold, to around 1.3 million individuals and firms. Azerbaijan saw coverage more than double after eliminating its minimum loan cutoff of $1,100. So did Belarus, after abolishing its $10,000 cutoff. Mauritius too eliminated its cutoff, of $3,000.

Tunisia now collects and distributes more detailed information—both positive and negative—on borrowers. Sri Lanka extended the length of time information is recorded from 1 year to 2—and distributes positive information for 5 years. Indonesia now distributes 2 years of historical information. Vietnam extended the period that data are distributed from 2 years to 5. That helps explain its 49% increase in coverage, to more than 8 million individuals and firms. Finland passed a new credit information law that regulates the use of corporate credit data.

Two economies saw developments that reduced the efficacy of their credit information systems. Indonesia's private credit bureau closed, unable to compete with the public registry (figure 6.3). And Burundi was forced to double the minimum cutoff for loans registered in the database to around $900, to cope with technical limitations and a sudden increase in loan transactions.

TABLE 6.3
Who has the most credit information and the most legal rights for borrowers and lenders—and who the least?

Legal rights for borrowers and lenders (strength of legal rights index, 0–10)			
Most		**Least**	
Hong Kong, China	10	Burundi	2
Kenya	10	Madagascar	2
Malaysia	10	Rwanda	2
Singapore	10	Afghanistan	1
Australia	9	Bolivia	1
Bahamas, The	9	Djibouti	1
Cambodia	9	Syria	1
Denmark	9	Timor-Leste	1
New Zealand	9	Palau	0
United Kingdom	9	West Bank and Gaza	0

Borrowers covered by credit registries (% of adults)			
Most		**Least**	
Argentina	100	Nepal	0.24
Australia	100	Algeria	0.20
Canada	100	Djibouti	0.18
Iceland	100	Mauritania	0.17
Ireland	100	Ethiopia	0.13
New Zealand	100	Madagascar	0.07
Norway	100	Yemen	0.07
Sweden	100	Nigeria	0.06
United Kingdom	100	Zambia	0.05
United States	100	Guinea	0.02

Note: The rankings on borrower coverage reflected in the table include only economies with public or private credit registries (129 in total). Another 52 economies have no credit registry and therefore no coverage. See Data notes for details.
Source: Doing Business database.

FIGURE 6.4
Collateral reform—East Asia & Pacific rapidly moving forward

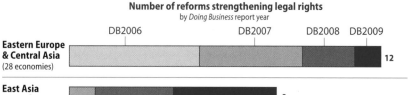

Number of reforms strengthening legal rights
by *Doing Business* report year

Note: A reform is counted as 1 reform per reforming economy per year.
Source: *Doing Business* database.

FIGURE 6.5
Top 5 reform features in legal rights
Reforms including feature since DB2006 (%)

53%
Allowed out-of-court enforcement of collateral

47%
Expanded range of revolving movable assets
that can be used as collateral

35%
Created a unified registry for movable property

21%
Gave priority to secured creditors' claims
outside and inside bankruptcy procedures

9%
Exempted secured creditors' claims
from an automatic stay in reorganization

Note: A reform may include several reform features.
Source: *Doing Business* database.

WHAT ARE THE REFORM TRENDS?

In the past 4 years 34 reforms have strengthened the legal rights of borrowers and lenders in 27 economies around the world—while 88 reforms have improved credit information systems in 61 economies.

Eastern Europe and Central Asia has had the most reforms strengthening the legal rights of borrowers and lenders in the past 4 years, with a total of 12 (figure 6.4). Large emerging market economies, with the exception of the Russian Federation, also figure prominently on the list of reformers. China was a repeat reformer in the past 2 years, broadening the range of movable assets that can be used as collateral. India reformed in 2 successive years starting in 2006, establishing an online collateral registry and expanding the availability of out-of-court enforcement. Ukraine improved the standing of secured creditors in bankruptcy by giving their claims priority over labor and state tax claims. Vietnam made it easier for entrepreneurs to get a loan by expanding the range of assets that can be used as collateral and by allowing out-of-court enforcement.

Allowing parties to agree to pursue out-of-court enforcement if the debtor defaults has been the most popular reform feature strengthening the legal rights of borrowers and lenders (figure 6.5). The ability to make such an agreement can persuade lenders wary of long court procedures to make a loan in the first place. Beyond India and Vietnam, economies that have allowed such agreements include Croatia, France, Ghana, Honduras, the Kyrgyz Republic and Peru.

Establishing a geographically unified collateral registry that covers substantially all movable property has been another popular reform feature. Such a registry allows potential lenders to find out easily and with certainty whether there are competing claims on the collateral. India stands out among those that have taken such a step. Its huge geographic area and large population make its creation of an online, unified national database of security rights in movable assets a notable achievement.

Many economies passed new secured transactions laws. Three of this year's top reformers—Cambodia, Guatemala and Vanuatu—did just that. Peru introduced a new bill on guarantees based on movable property in 2006. Now almost any type of movable asset—tangible or intangible, present or future—can secure a loan, and assets no longer have to be described specifically. More than 20 different types of pledges were consolidated into 1. The country's 17 collateral registries have been combined as well.[8]

The 88 reforms improving credit information in the past 4 years have shown clear results: worldwide, coverage by credit registries more than doubled, to around 1.8 billion individuals and firms. The fastest reforming region was Eastern Europe and Central Asia (figure 6.6). Its average score on the depth of credit information index has more than doubled in the past 4 years—from 2.1 points to 4.4 out of a maximum of 6—and its coverage of borrowers has increased by a factor of almost 5. That propelled the region past Latin America and the Caribbean, and it now ranks behind only the OECD high-income economies.

More than a quarter of the reforms in credit information involved setting up

FIGURE 6.6

A third of credit information reforms in Eastern Europe & Central Asia

Number of reforms easing credit information sharing
by *Doing Business* report year

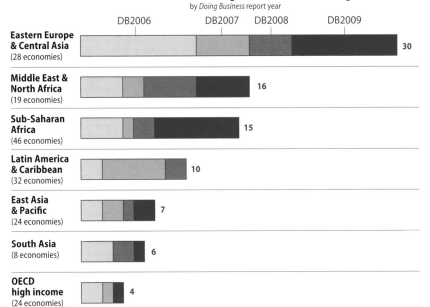

Note: A reform is counted as 1 reform per reforming economy per year.
Source: *Doing Business* database.

FIGURE 6.7

Top 5 reform features in credit information

Reforms including feature since DB2006 (%)

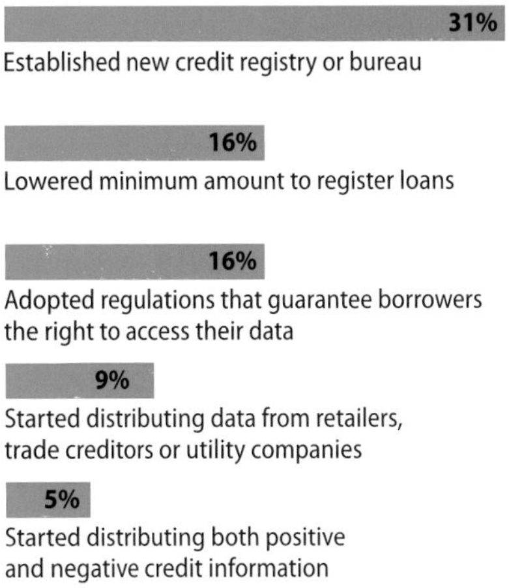

31%
Established new credit registry or bureau

16%
Lowered minimum amount to register loans

16%
Adopted regulations that guarantee borrowers the right to access their data

9%
Started distributing data from retailers, trade creditors or utility companies

5%
Started distributing both positive and negative credit information

Note: A reform may include several reform features.
Source: *Doing Business* database.

new registries: 19 economies saw the creation of private credit bureaus; 8 others set up new public credit registries (figure 6.7). The biggest gains were in Eastern Europe and Central Asia, where nearly half the economies established either a public credit registry or a private credit bureau, followed by the Middle East and North Africa.

In 20 economies reforms expanded the range of credit information collected and distributed by public or private credit registries. In 13 of these, the public registry eliminated the minimum cutoff for recording loans, more than quadrupling coverage on average. What made this reform possible in many cases was developing the information infrastructure and shifting from a paper-based to an online system.

In the 8 economies private credit bureaus expanded the sources of credit information to nonfinancial institutions such as utilities (like mobile phone companies) or retailers (like supermarkets and furniture stores). Such changes took place in Bulgaria, Georgia, Kazakhstan, Kenya, Kuwait, Nicaragua, Saudi Arabia and Trinidad and Tobago. Now people with a cell phone but no bank loans can still build a credit history—particularly important in poor economies.

NOTES

1. This example is from the World Bank's *Doing Business: Women in Africa* (2008a), a collection of case studies on African entrepreneurs.
2. Djankov, McLeish and Shleifer (2007).
3. Brown, Jappelli and Pagano (2008).
4. Brown and Zehnder (2007).
5. Benmelech and Bergman (2008).
6. Claessens and Perotti (2007).
7. World Bank (2007c).
8. Marechal and Shahid-Saless (2008).

Protecting investors

FIGURE 7.1

More investor protections associated with greater access for firms to equity markets and faster stock turnover

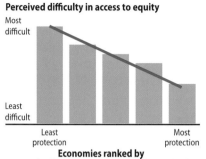

Perceived difficulty in access to equity

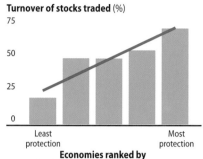

Turnover of stocks traded (%)

Note: Relationships remain significant at the 5% level when controlling for income per capita. Economies are ranked on the perceived difficulty in access to equity, with 131 being the most difficult. See Data notes for details.
Source: Doing Business database; WEF (2007); World Bank, World Development Indicators database.

Investing in Costa Rica can be a risky business. Diego, a Costa Rican entrepreneur, is well aware of that: "Why would I buy shares in a company if I know its management can approve large transactions between interested parties without ever disclosing them to its shareholders?" In Costa Rica, as in many other countries around the world, minority investors are not protected against self-dealing—the use by company insiders of corporate assets for personal gain.

Companies grow by raising capital —either through a bank loan or by attracting equity investors. Selling shares allows companies to expand without the need to provide collateral and repay bank loans. But investors worry about getting their money back—and look for laws that protect them. A recent study finds that the presence of legal and regulatory

protections for investors explains up to 73% of the decision to invest. In contrast, company characteristics explain only between 4% and 22%.[1] Thus both governments and businesses have an interest in reforms strengthening investor protections.

Without investor protections, equity markets fail to develop and banks become the only source of finance. The result: businesses fail to reach efficient size for lack of financing, and economic growth is held back. Research in 22 emerging market economies shows that where investors have little recourse against actions that damage the company, they invest in a few companies in which they take majority stakes.[2] In contrast, good protections for minority shareholders are associated with larger and more active stock markets.

Vibrant stock markets are not the only reason to introduce stronger investor protections. Tanzania started reforms of investor protections as part of a larger initiative to reduce corruption and create an environment that inspires the trust needed to do business.[3] Such an environment strengthens investor confidence in local businesses and government alike.

Economies that rank high on the strength of investor protection index have extensive disclosure requirements and give shareholders broad access to information both before and during trials to determine director liability. New Zealand and Singapore, which top the

rankings on the index with 29 and 28 of 30 possible points, both require immediate disclosure of a related-party transaction and of the conflict of interest (table 7.1). They require prior approval of the transaction by the other shareholders. They enable the shareholders to hold the directors liable and to have the transaction voided if it damages the company. And in New Zealand shareholders can inspect all internal documents before deciding whether to sue.

Vietnam shows the benefits of reforms to strengthen investor protections. In 2005, before Vietnam adopted clear legislation, its unregulated stock market saw 60–100 daily trades with a value of $10,000–16,000. That was 3–6 times the trading volume of the regulated Ho Chi Minh Stock Exchange.[4] After reform of the Law on Securities and the Law on

TABLE 7.1

Where are investors protected—and where not?

Most protected	RANK	Least protected	RANK
New Zealand	1	Micronesia	172
Singapore	2	Palau	173
Hong Kong, China	3	Rwanda	174
Malaysia	4	Venezuela	175
Canada	5	Vietnam	176
Ireland	6	Djibouti	177
Israel	7	Suriname	178
United States	8	Swaziland	179
South Africa	9	Lao PDR	180
United Kingdom	10	Afghanistan	181

Note: Rankings are based on the strength of investor protection index. See Data notes for details.
Source: Doing Business database.

FIGURE 7.2

Rankings on protecting investors are based on 3 subindicators

Requirements on approval and disclosure of related-party transactions

Liability of CEO and board of directors in related-party transactions

33.3% Extent of disclosure index

33.3% Extent of director liability index

33.3% Ease of shareholder suits index

Type of evidence that can be collected before and during the trial

Note: See Data notes for details.

Enterprises, the number of listed firms climbed from 41 in 2005 to 193 today—and 107 of these are listed on the Ho Chi Minh Stock Exchange. Despite the recent difficulties in the Vietnamese securities markets, market capitalization increased from less than $1 billion in 2005 to more than $13 billion today.

Across regions, Latin America regulates related-party transactions the least, imposing the weakest requirements for disclosure and approval. Many Latin American economies have commercial laws that have not been reformed since the 1920s. Economies in Eastern Europe and Central Asia have stronger requirements for disclosure and approval. But once a transaction is approved and disclosed, the company directors are not liable for any damage resulting from it.

Economies in the Middle East and North Africa, such as Djibouti and Oman, limit access to information. That makes it difficult for minority shareholders to obtain the evidence needed to prove their case in court.

WHO REFORMED IN 2007/08?

Twelve economies strengthened investor protections in 2007/08 (table 7.2). Albania was the top reformer. It adopted the Law on Entrepreneurs and Commercial Companies, which regulates conflicts of interest by requiring shareholder approval of related-party transactions involving more than 5% of company assets. The law also provides for extensive disclosure requirements and makes it easier for minority investors to sue directors. And minority shareholders can now request compensation from directors for harm resulting from a related-party transaction, including repayment of all profits from the transaction. With the new law, Albanian company directors have strong incentives to be responsive to investor interests.

The runner-up reformer was Thailand. After being the top reformer in protecting investors 3 years ago, Thailand made new efforts to strengthen minority shareholder rights, particularly in

TABLE 7.2
Greater disclosure—the most popular reform feature in 2007/08

Increased disclosure requirements	Albania, Azerbaijan, Egypt, Saudi Arabia, Tajikistan
Made it easier to sue directors	Albania, Botswana, Kyrgyz Republic, Thailand
Allowed derivative or direct suits	Greece, Kyrgyz Republic, Slovenia
Regulated approval of related-party transactions	Albania, Azerbaijan, Tajikistan
Passed a new company law	Albania, Botswana, Tajikistan
Required an external body to review related-party transactions before they take place	Egypt, Turkey
Allowed rescission of prejudicial related-party transactions	Tunisia

Source: Doing Business database.

the area of director liability. Directors damaging the company's interests can no longer rely on having obtained shareholder approval of a transaction to avoid liability. If they are held liable, sanctions will be harsh. They will have to compensate the company for all damages, pay back all profits made from the transaction and pay fines to the state. They even risk jail time.

Central Asian economies also strengthened minority shareholder rights. Tajikistan, Azerbaijan and the Kyrgyz Republic brought their company laws into line with modern regulations and corporate governance principles.

Tajikistan adopted a new joint stock companies act. The law defines "interested parties" and requires shareholder approval of transactions between such parties. It also requires interested parties to immediately disclose conflicts of interest to the board of directors. In addition, derivative suits are now possible: shareholders with at least 10% of shares can file a lawsuit on behalf of the company against company directors.

Azerbaijan reformed its civil code, and its State Securities Commission adopted new rules regulating related-party transactions. The new law defines what is meant by "related transactions between interested parties" and requires shareholder approval when such transactions exceed 5% of company assets. However, interested parties are allowed to vote at the shareholders meeting. The law also includes requirements for disclosure

both to the market regulator and through the company's annual reports. As in Albania, minority shareholders can now request compensation for damages to the company resulting from related-party transactions.

The Kyrgyz Republic reformed its joint stock companies act. From now on, shareholders can sue in their own name the directors who damaged shareholders' interests and request compensation from them.

Botswana defined related-party transactions and clarified disclosure provisions in its Companies Act of 2004, which came into force in July 2007. Establishing the liability of directors is now easier: shareholders can file suit against them if the transaction proves prejudicial to the company. If directors are held liable, they not only have to cover damages but also have to pay back all profits made—a good reason to think twice before attempting to misuse company assets.

The Egyptian Capital Market Authority made improving disclosure requirements a priority when it amended the listing rules of the Cairo Stock Exchange. The amendments are aimed at increasing transparency both before and after related-party transactions are concluded. Such transactions now have to be assessed by an independent financial adviser before they take place, ensuring that shareholders will be better informed. The amendments also clarify requirements for disclosure through companies' annual reports. In March 2008 Turkey

TABLE 7.3
Where are investor protections strong—and where not?

Extent of disclosure index (0–10)			
Most		Least	
Bulgaria	10	Ukraine	1
China	10	Afghanistan	0
France	10	Lao PDR	0
Hong Kong, China	10	Maldives	0
Ireland	10	Micronesia	0
Malaysia	10	Palau	0
New Zealand	10	Sudan	0
Singapore	10	Swaziland	0
Thailand	10	Switzerland	0
United Kingdom	10	Tunisia	0

Extent of director liability index (0–10)			
Most		Least	
Albania	9	Tajikistan	1
Cambodia	9	Togo	1
Canada	9	Zimbabwe	1
Israel	9	Afghanistan	0
Malaysia	9	Dominican Republic	0
New Zealand	9	Marshall Islands	0
Singapore	9	Micronesia	0
Slovenia	9	Palau	0
Trinidad and Tobago	9	Suriname	0
United States	9	Vietnam	0

Ease of shareholder suits index (0–10)			
Easiest		Most difficult	
Kenya	10	Lao PDR	2
New Zealand	10	Syria	2
Colombia	9	United Arab Emirates	2
Hong Kong, China	9	Venezuela	2
Ireland	9	Yemen	2
Israel	9	Guinea	1
Mauritius	9	Morocco	1
Poland	9	Rwanda	1
Singapore	9	Djibouti	0
United States	9	Iran	0

Source: Doing Business database.

undertook similar reforms. The listing rules of the Istanbul Stock Exchange now require an independent body to assess all related-party transactions before they are approved.

Saudi Arabia amended provisions of its company law. Interested directors may no longer vote at a shareholders meeting to approve related-party transactions. And just as in Albania, Botswana and Thailand, directors found liable for damage to a company due to a related-party transaction will have to repay all profits made from it.

Greece adopted a new company law

that lowers the threshold for derivative suits. Now shareholders need to have only 10% of the company's shares, down from 33% before. Slovenia changed its laws to allow minority investors with at least 10% of shares to bring derivative suits before the court.

Tunisia adopted a law giving shareholders the right to directly access internal company documents and to ask for the appointment of an independent inspector. That will make it easier to gather evidence to support a court claim. The new law also gives 10% shareholders the right to request a judge to rescind

prejudicial related-party transactions.

Reforms of corporate governance and, in particular, of company laws took place worldwide—from Syria to Sri Lanka, from Indonesia to Vietnam. Argentina further strengthened corporate governance principles by introducing a comprehensive set of "comply or explain" rules for listed companies.

Ongoing reforms to implement the European Union Transparency Directives are taking place in several EU member countries, such as Austria and Luxembourg, and in candidate member countries, such as Croatia. Implementing these EU directives often requires amending the company and securities laws. Bulgaria and Romania amended their company laws in the past 2 years, and both countries are now implementing these amendments.

WHAT ARE THE REFORM TRENDS?

Experience over the past 4 years shows that economies can successfully enhance the protections they provide to minority shareholders. It often takes time, even when the necessary political will exists. But economies like Albania, Azerbaijan and the Kyrgyz Republic demonstrate that it can be done in months, not years.

Sometimes the private sector opposes reforms that are designed to protect minority investors, especially in economies with a high concentration of ownership. One possible reason is that complying with extensive disclosure requirements can represent a financial burden for companies, particularly in developing economies. In Mexico, for example, the most vocal opponent of reform was one of the country's wealthiest businessmen.[5] In Georgia it was one of the largest commercial banks.

Such opposition has not prevented reform: *Doing Business* has recorded more than 50 reforms to strengthen investor protections in 41 economies over the past 4 years. Eastern Europe and Central Asia and the OECD high-income economies have had the most reforms, with 12 each (figure 7.3).

FIGURE 7.3
Accelerating reforms in Eastern Europe & Central Asia

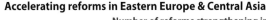
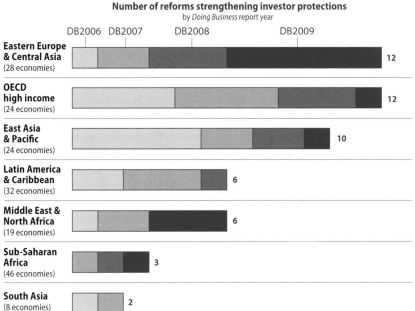

Number of reforms strengthening investor protections
by Doing Business report year

DB2006 DB2007 DB2008 DB2009

Eastern Europe & Central Asia (28 economies) — 12

OECD high income (24 economies) — 12

East Asia & Pacific (24 economies) — 10

Latin America & Caribbean (32 economies) — 6

Middle East & North Africa (19 economies) — 6

Sub-Saharan Africa (46 economies) — 3

South Asia (8 economies) — 2

Note: A reform is counted as 1 reform per reforming economy per year.
Source: Doing Business database.

FIGURE 7.4
**Top 4 reform features
in protecting investors**
Reforms including feature since DB2006 (%)

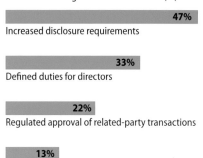

47% — Increased disclosure requirements

33% — Defined duties for directors

22% — Regulated approval of related-party transactions

13% — Allowed shareholder access to corporate documents

Note: A reform may include several reform features.
Source: Doing Business database.

In Eastern Europe and Central Asia the main driver of the reforms was accession to the European Union. Economies such as Poland, Romania and Slovenia updated company and securities laws to EU standards. These reforms focused on developing regulations requiring more transparency in the day-to-day management of companies. The reforms raised the region's average score on the extent of disclosure index from 4.7 in 2005 to 5.8 today.

OECD high-income economies protect minority investors the most. Why would they continually reform? There is a logical reason: sophisticated and active financial markets must respond rapidly to challenges that are constantly evolving, such as fraud. Among the repeat reformers are Hong Kong (China) and the United Kingdom—both in the top 10 on the strength of investor protection index. Both economies reformed twice during the past 3 years, by strengthening disclosure requirements and expanding shareholder access to internal corporate documents.

Fewer reforms have taken place in Latin America and the Caribbean, Africa and South Asia. In 2007/08 only one reform was recorded in these regions—in Botswana. But in previous years reforms strengthened investor protections in such economies as Colombia and Mexico in Latin America and Mozambique and Tanzania in Africa.

GOING FOR MORE DISCLOSURE

Across regions, the most popular reform feature has been to require greater disclosure of related-party transactions (figure 7.4). The results of a 2002 global survey on corporate governance provide one explanation: around 90% of the investors surveyed want more transparency in the day-to-day management of companies.[6] What do they mean by more transparency? Unified accounting standards, immediate disclosure of major transactions and more involvement of minority investors in major decisions and transactions.

Requirements for greater disclosure, while popular, are unlikely to succeed everywhere. Extensive disclosure standards require the necessary infrastructure to communicate the information effectively and, more importantly, people such as

lawyers and accountants to comply with the standards. Many poor countries lack both. They may have stock exchanges—but no website to post the information on. And they may have certified accountants—but in such small numbers that complying with disclosure requirements is virtually impossible. Take Vietnam. Its securities law has significant disclosure and reporting requirements, but the country still lacks the systems to store and monitor the information electronically.[7]

FINDING INSPIRATION FOR REFORM

Crisis can be an important engine of reform. The East Asian financial crisis and corporate scandals such as those involving Enron, Parmalat and WorldCom triggered regulatory reforms around the world. These crises exposed weaknesses in markets previously considered models of sound regulation. Countries affected by the crises reformed their laws. So did other countries, using the experiences to avoid the same mistakes. Mexico, for example, used the U.S. experience to create impetus for its regulatory reforms.

Countries that want to reform can

FIGURE 7.5
Top reformers in 2005–08 in protecting investors

Average improvement (index 0–10)

Source: *Doing Business* database.

choose to amend existing regulations or start from scratch, depending on how up-to-date their current legislation is. In 2007 Georgia amended its securities legislation by adding provisions regulating disclosure and approval of transactions between interested parties. Belarus, Colombia and Thailand did the same. Other countries, such as Mozambique and Slovenia, started from scratch. Adopting an entirely new law offers an opportunity to reform other areas—such as business registration, directors' duties, disclosure rules and issuance of shares.

Reformers often find inspiration in economies with a similar legal origin or in their main commercial partners. Mexico's securities law reform took into account aspects of a U.S. law—the Public Company Accounting Reform and Investor Protection Act of 2002, commonly known as the Sarbanes-Oxley Act. Botswana and Mozambique followed the South African model. As a reformer from Mozambique explains, "Our previous code was inherited from Portugal. Today our main commercial partner is South Africa, and we are surrounded by countries that have the same model. We prefer to adopt legislation that would enable us to attract more investment from South Africa and make life easier for our main investors."

Even the best regulations will make little difference if the court system is weak. Bangladesh and Montenegro have laws setting out strong disclosure requirements and extensive obligations for directors. But with the most basic commercial disputes taking more than 1,000 days to resolve in Bangladesh and more than 500 in Montenegro, these laws may not have the desired effect.

NOTES

1. Doidge, Karolyi and Stulz (2007).
2. Dahya, Dimitrov and McConnell (2008).
3. Sitta (2005).
4. World Bank (2006c).
5. See Johns and Lobet (2007).
6. McKinsey & Company (2002, p. 8).
7. Lobet (2008).

Paying taxes

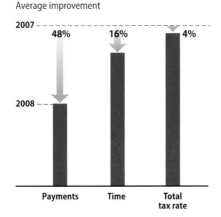

FIGURE 8.1

Top 10 reformers in paying taxes

Average improvement

1.	**Dominican Republic**
2.	**Malaysia**
3.	**Azerbaijan**
4.	**South Africa**
5.	**China**
6.	**Greece**
7.	**Colombia**
8.	**France**
9.	**Honduras**
10.	**Thailand**

Source: Doing Business database.

For Kah, the owner of a Cameroon-based management consulting business, having a simple tax system with standardized rates and payment channels is fundamental to the ease of doing business. Yet in Cameroon, which ranks among the most difficult economies in which to pay taxes, complying with tax regulations takes more than 1,000 hours and 41 tax payments a year.[1]

To file a tax return for her company, Kah often spends hours waiting in the tax office for information from tax inspectors. Because she refuses to pay extra, she regularly endures long, costly court procedures. And because the tax system lacks transparency, results are often arbitrary.

Kah feels that tax officers see her as an easy target. She is not the only one. A recent study in Uganda shows that enterprises headed by women perceive a greater regulatory burden—and more harassment from public officials—than those headed by men.[2]

Taxes are essential. Without them there would be no funds for the basic public services vital to a well-functioning economy and an inclusive society. Yet firms in 90% of the countries covered by the World Bank Enterprise Surveys rank tax rates and tax administration among the top 5 obstacles to doing business.[3] Businesses prefer lower tax rates that are applied in a straightforward way. Or, if rates are high, businesses want good services in return.

Where taxes are high and commensurate gains seem low, many businesses simply choose to stay informal. A recent study finds that higher tax rates are associated with less private investment, fewer formal businesses per capita and lower rates of business entry. The analysis suggests, for example, that a 10% increase in the effective corporate tax rate reduces the investment-to-GDP ratio by 2 percentage points.[4]

Economies that rank high on the ease of paying taxes tend to have lower and less complex business taxes (table 8.1). They also have simple administrative processes for paying the taxes and filing tax returns. For businesses, it's not just the tax rates that matter. The administrative processes do too.

Fast and efficient administration means less hassle for businesses—and often higher revenue for governments. In Mauritius in 2007/08, the government collected 4 billion Mauritian rupees ($150 million) more in revenue than had been projected. Reforming the tax system was a key part of the government's agenda over the past 3 years. The focus: creating an enabling environment for businesses through low and simple taxes coupled with fast and efficient administration. The strategy paid off.

WHO REFORMED IN 2007/08?

Thirty-six economies made it easier to pay taxes in 2007/08. As in previous years, the most popular reform feature was reducing the profit tax rate, done in no fewer than 21 economies. The second most popular was introducing and improving electronic filing and pay-

TABLE 8.1

Where is it easy to pay taxes—and where not?

Easiest	RANK	Most difficult	RANK
Maldives	1	Panama	172
Qatar	2	Jamaica	173
Hong Kong, China	3	Mauritania	174
United Arab Emirates	4	Gambia, The	175
Singapore	5	Bolivia	176
Ireland	6	Venezuela	177
Saudi Arabia	7	Central African Republic	178
Oman	8	Congo, Rep.	179
Kuwait	9	Ukraine	180
Kiribati	10	Belarus	181

Note: Rankings are the average of the economy rankings on the number of payments, time and total tax rate. See Data notes for details.
Source: Doing Business database.

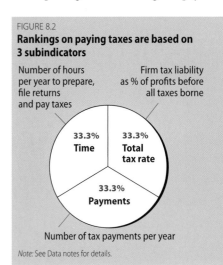

FIGURE 8.2

Rankings on paying taxes are based on 3 subindicators

Number of hours per year to prepare, file returns and pay taxes

Firm tax liability as % of profits before all taxes borne

33.3% Time

33.3% Total tax rate

33.3% Payments

Number of tax payments per year

Note: See Data notes for details.

ment systems. This reform, done in 12 economies, reduced the frequency of payments and the time spent paying taxes and filing returns. Eight economies reduced the number of taxes paid by businesses by eliminating smaller taxes such as stamp duties. The top 10 reformers for paying taxes this year reduced the number of payments by almost half. Bosnia and Herzegovina, Bulgaria, Morocco, Mozambique and Zambia revised their tax codes (table 8.2).

Two economies introduced new taxes: Botswana and Venezuela. That increases not only the costs but also the administrative burden for businesses.

The Dominican Republic was the top reformer in 2007/08. It lowered the corporate income tax from 30% to 25%, abolished several taxes (including the stamp duty) and reduced the property transfer tax. In addition, in 2007 it fully implemented online filing and payment, piloted in 2006.

Malaysia was the runner-up reformer. It reduced the corporate income tax for 2009 to 25%—part of a gradual reduction that has seen the rate decline to 27% in 2007 and 26% in 2008. The reform also introduced a single-tier tax system, in which profits are taxed only after dividend payments are exempted. The capital gains tax was abolished in 2007 to spur investment in the real

FIGURE 8.3

Profit taxes lowest, but overall tax burden still high in Eastern Europe & Central Asia

Total tax rate (% of profit)

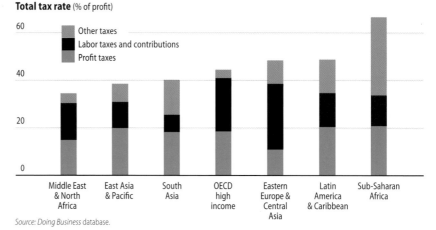

Source: *Doing Business* database.

property and financial market sectors. And electronic payment systems were improved, increasing online filing and payments.

Among regions, Eastern Europe and Central Asia had the most reforms in 2007/08. Nine economies reformed, mainly continuing the trend of reducing the profit tax rate, already among the lowest in the world (figure 8.3). Albania, Bosnia and Herzegovina and the former Yugoslav Republic of Macedonia all reduced their profit tax to 10%. Georgia reduced the corporate income tax from 20% to 15% and abolished the social tax. The Czech Republic reduced its corporate income tax rate to 21%.

Azerbaijan and Ukraine made it simpler to file and pay taxes by introducing electronic systems and online payment capabilities. That significantly reduced the time spent preparing, filing and paying taxes in the region. Belarus reduced the tax and administrative burden on businesses by abolishing some taxes and reducing the frequency of payments. Bulgaria reduced labor taxes and contributions.

Following closely with 7 reforms each are the OECD high-income economies and Latin America and the Caribbean. Five OECD high-income economies reduced corporate income tax rates. Canada is gradually reducing the corporate income tax to 15% by 2012 as part of ambitious reforms in its tax system. The reforms also include abolishing the 1.12% surtax and introducing accelerated depreciation for buildings (10%) and computers (50%). Also reducing the corporate tax rate were Denmark (from 28% to 25%), Germany (from 25% to 15%), Italy (from 33% to 27.5%) and New Zealand (from 33% to 30%).

France and Greece made filing and paying taxes faster by implementing mandatory electronic filing for labor taxes and contributions.

In Latin America and the Caribbean, besides the reforms in the Dominican Republic, Antigua and Barbuda reduced the corporate income tax rate from 30% to 25%. St. Vincent and the Grenadines introduced a new value added tax that replaced several existing taxes, includ-

TABLE 8.2

Reducing tax rates—the most common reform feature in 2007/08

Reduced profit tax rates	Albania, Antigua and Barbuda, Bosnia and Herzegovina, Burkina Faso, Canada, China, Côte d'Ivoire, Czech Republic, Denmark, Dominican Republic, Georgia, Germany, Italy, former Yugoslav Republic of Macedonia, Madagascar, Malaysia, Morocco, New Zealand, Samoa, St. Vincent and the Grenadines, Thailand
Simplified process of paying taxes	Azerbaijan, Belarus, China, Colombia, Dominican Republic, France, Greece, Honduras, Malaysia, Mozambique, Tunisia, Ukraine
Eliminated taxes	Belarus, Dominican Republic, Georgia, Madagascar, Malaysia, Mexico, South Africa, Uruguay
Revised tax code	Bosnia and Herzegovina, Bulgaria, Morocco, Mozambique, Zambia
Reduced labor tax or contribution rates	France, Mongolia, Ukraine

Source: *Doing Business* database.

ing the hotel tax, entertainment tax, consumption duty, stamp duty on receipts and domestic and international telecommunications surcharge. Uruguay abolished a tax on consumption. Mexico abolished its asset tax. Colombia and Honduras made paying taxes easier by implementing and improving online filing and payment systems. That cut the time spent filing and paying taxes, especially in Honduras.

In Africa 6 economies reformed. Three reduced their corporate income tax rate (table 8.3). Burkina Faso reduced its corporate income tax rate from 35% to 30%, its dividend tax rate from 15% to 12.5% and its property transfer tax rate from 10% to 8%. Côte d'Ivoire reduced the corporate income tax rate from 27% to 25%. Madagascar reduced that rate from 30% to 25% and abolished 9 taxes, including the stamp duty and dividend tax. In Africa taxes other than the profit tax—such as stamp duties, property taxes and labor taxes—account for the largest share of the total tax rate. This is reflected in the large number of

FIGURE 8.4
Most time in Latin America & Caribbean

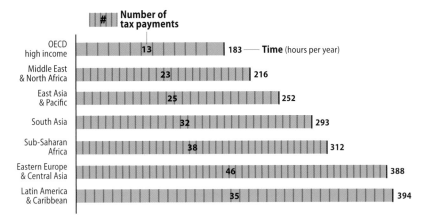

Source: Doing Business database.

tax payments African businesses must make each year (figure 8.4).

Mozambique eased the filing and paying of taxes by introducing electronic systems. It also revised its tax code to make necessary updates, remove ambiguities and strengthen tax compliance and collection. Zambia did the same. These changes should increase the effectiveness of tax administration.

In East Asia and Pacific 5 economies

reformed. Aside from Malaysia, China made notable reforms, reducing the corporate income tax from 33.3% to 25% and unifying accounting methods and criteria for tax deductions and exemptions. Meanwhile, online filing became more prevalent. Thailand introduced corporate income tax exemptions for small companies, reduced the corporate income tax rate to 25% for newly listed companies and reduced several property taxes by sizable rates. It also made online filing and payments easier. Samoa lowered its corporate income tax from 29% to 27%. Mongolia reduced social security contributions paid by employers from 19% to 11% of gross salaries.

In the Middle East and North Africa only 2 economies reformed. Morocco lowered the standard corporate tax rate from 35% to 30%. Tunisia made filing and paying taxes easier by expanding electronic options. Although companies have been able to file and pay taxes online since 2005, many have been reluctant to pay their taxes this way. To address their concerns while easing the administrative burden, Tunisian authorities introduced an option for filing tax returns online while paying the taxes in person at a tax office. This is a practical intermediate step toward a full online system.

South Asia recorded no significant reforms.

TABLE 8.3
Major cuts in corporate income tax rates in 2007/08

Region	Reduction in corporate income tax rate (%)
OECD high income	Canada from 22.1 to 19.5
	Czech Republic from 24 to 21
	Denmark from 28 to 25
	Germany from 25 to 15
	Italy from 33 to 27.5
	New Zealand from 33 to 30
East Asia & Pacific	China from 33.3 to 25
	Malaysia from 27 to 25
	Samoa from 29 to 27
	Thailand from 30 to 25
Eastern Europe & Central Asia	Albania from 20 to 10
	Bosnia and Herzegovina from 30 to 10
	Georgia from 20 to 15
	Macedonia, former Yugoslav Republic of, from 12 to 10
Latin America & Caribbean	Antigua and Barbuda from 30 to 25
	Dominican Republic from 30 to 25
	St. Vincent and the Grenadines from 40 to 37.5
Sub-Saharan Africa	Burkina Faso from 35 to 30
	Côte d'Ivoire from 27 to 25
	Madagascar from 30 to 25
Middle East & North Africa	Morocco from 35 to 30

Source: Doing Business database.

WHAT ARE THE REFORM TRENDS?

Revenue authorities around the world are making great efforts to streamline administrative processes and modernize payment systems. In the past 4 years *Doing Business* has recorded 126 reforms aimed at reducing tax rates or the time or cost to comply with tax laws.

The trend across all regions has been to lower the total tax rate paid by businesses. In 2004 the average total tax rate was 50.6% of commercial profits. By 2007 it had fallen to 49.3%. Meanwhile, the time to comply with tax laws dropped by 16 hours a year on average.

About 50% of economies have implemented reforms making it easier to pay taxes in the past 4 years. Among regions, Eastern Europe and Central Asia has had the most reforms, followed by Africa (figure 8.5). South Asia has had the fewest.

CUTTING RATES

Reducing corporate income tax rates has been the most popular reform feature (figure 8.6). More than 60 economies have done this. Countries can increase tax revenue by lowering rates and persuading more businesses to comply with the more favorable rules.

Look at the Russian Federation's large tax cuts in 2001. Corporate tax rates fell from 25% to 24%, and a simplified tax scheme lowered rates for small business. Yet tax revenue increased—by an annual average of 14% over the next 3 years. One study shows that the new revenue was due to greater compliance.[5]

GOING ELECTRONIC

Introducing electronic filing has been a popular and effective way to make it easier to pay taxes. Businesses can enter financial information online and file it with one click—with no calculations and no interaction with tax officials. Errors can be identified instantly, and returns processed quickly. In Hong Kong (China) businesses file an electronic corporate tax return and pay corporate income tax annually. Complying with tax requirements takes just 80 hours a year. Sixty economies—from Azerbaijan to Colombia and Lesotho—have made e-filing possible, and the list is growing.

These reforms can ease the adminis-trative burden of paying taxes. But it can take time for them to make a real difference. In Argentina and Tunisia it took almost 3 years before smaller firms felt the impact. The reason is that small firms often lack the software needed for electronic filing and payments. Moreover, taxpayers often distrust online systems when it comes to dealing with sensitive financial information.

Businesses in Azerbaijan are benefiting from an ambitious tax modernization reform started by the government 3 years ago. Electronic payment and filing systems have been in place since March 2007. The goal is to have 100% online filing. Tax authorities have been actively promoting online filing among businesses paying value added tax. The efforts have had results: 95% of these businesses are using the service, completing more than 200,000 online transactions in the first 3 months of 2008 alone—and saving an average 577 hours a year. Online filing is also available for corporate income tax.

Reforms introducing electronic payment and filing systems often need to provide public education and training.

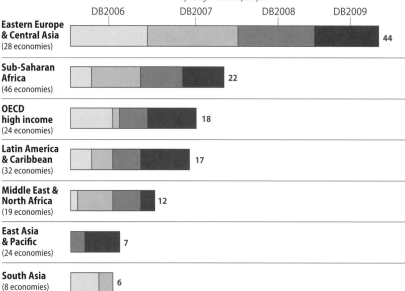

FIGURE 8.5
A third of reforms in Eastern Europe & Central Asia

Number of reforms easing payment of taxes
by *Doing Business* report year

DB2006   DB2007   DB2008   DB2009

Eastern Europe & Central Asia (28 economies)	44
Sub-Saharan Africa (46 economies)	22
OECD high income (24 economies)	18
Latin America & Caribbean (32 economies)	17
Middle East & North Africa (19 economies)	12
East Asia & Pacific (24 economies)	7
South Asia (8 economies)	6

Note: A reform is counted as 1 reform per reforming economy per year.
Source: Doing Business database.

FIGURE 8.6
Top 5 reform features in paying taxes
Reforms including feature since DB2006 (%)

Reduced profit tax	71%
Simplified process of paying taxes	22%
Revised tax code	19%
Eliminated taxes	17%
Reduced labor taxes or contributions	14%

Note: A reform may include several reform features.
Source: Doing Business database.

Azerbaijan provided free software to taxpayers 6 months before implementing its new system, giving them time to become familiar with it. Distributing the tax software early paid off in more than one way: users also suggested improvements simplifying the design of the software's interface.

To make the new online system more effective, Azerbaijan's government also introduced advanced accounting software to help in computing tax payments. This has especially benefited medium-size companies, which make up a sizable share of the users. For smaller enterprises, more likely to lack access to the internet, the Ministry of Taxes is installing computer stations around the country that are linked to the central database.

Kenyan and Mozambican taxpayers too are enjoying the benefits of electronic tax systems. Companies in Kenya can complete and submit social security forms online. Complying with labor tax obligations used to take them 72 hours a year; now it takes about 20% less time. Their Mozambican counterparts can complete social security forms electronically and are looking forward to being able to submit them online, which will further simplify the task.

NOTES

1. This example is from the World Bank's *Doing Business: Women in Africa* (2008a), a collection of case studies of African entrepreneurs.
2. Ellis, Manuel and Blackden (2006).
3. World Bank Enterprise Surveys (http://www.enterprisesurveys.org).
4. Djankov, Ganser, McLiesh, Ramalho and Shleifer (2008).
5. Ivanova, Keen and Klemm (2005).

TABLE 8.4

Who makes paying taxes easy—and who does not?

Payments *(number per year)*

Fewest		Most	
Maldives	1	Côte d'Ivoire	66
Qatar	1	Serbia	66
Sweden	2	Venezuela	70
Hong Kong, China	4	Jamaica	72
Norway	4	Kyrgyz Republic	75
Singapore	5	Montenegro	89
Kiribati	7	Ukraine	99
Latvia	7	Uzbekistan	106
Mauritius	7	Belarus	112
Afghanistan	8	Romania	113

Time *(hours per year)*

Fastest		Slowest	
Maldives	0	Ukraine	848
United Arab Emirates	12	Venezuela	864
Bahrain	36	Czech Republic	930
Qatar	36	Nigeria	938
Bahamas, The	58	Armenia	958
Luxembourg	59	Vietnam	1,050
St. Lucia	61	Bolivia	1,080
Oman	62	Belarus	1,188
Switzerland	63	Cameroon	1,400
New Zealand	70	Brazil	2,600

Total tax rate *(% of profit)*

Lowest		Highest	
Vanuatu	8.4	Tajikistan	85.5
Maldives	9.1	Uzbekistan	90.6
Qatar	11.3	Mauritania	98.7
United Arab Emirates	14.4	Argentina	108.1
Kuwait	14.4	Belarus	117.5
Saudi Arabia	14.5	Central African Republic	203.8
Bahrain	15.0	Congo, Dem. Rep.	229.8
Zambia	16.1	Sierra Leone	233.5
West Bank and Gaza	16.8	Burundi	278.7
Botswana	17.1	Gambia, The	292.4

Source: Doing Business database.

Trading across borders

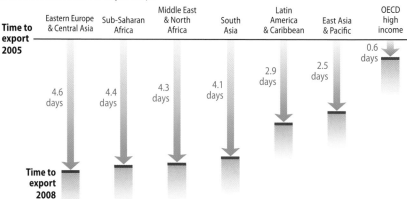

FIGURE 9.1

Speeding trade—especially in Eastern Europe & Central Asia

Reduction in the time to export (days)

Source: Doing Business database.

Cáñamo, a Venezuelan company exporting handicrafts, is eager to supply larger clients—preferably, large U.S. department stores. It has the capacity to fill orders within 2 weeks. But there is one problem: bureaucracy. "I need to get a labor compliance certificate from the Ministry of Labor, but before issuing the certificate the ministry demands 4 other documents from municipal authorities. For each export consignment I need to inform the authorities of my intention to export, confirm the exports and get a letter confirming that I have refunded the foreign exchange earned to the central bank," says Bruno, the company's owner.

Getting through all the paperwork can take 2–6 months on average. Faced with this long and unpredictable export process, Cáñamo has little chance of entering the U.S. market.

TABLE 9.1

Where is trading easy—and where not?

Easiest	RANK	Most difficult	RANK
Singapore	1	Angola	172
Hong Kong, China	2	Burkina Faso	173
Denmark	3	Azerbaijan	174
Finland	4	Central African Republic	175
Estonia	5	Congo, Rep.	176
Sweden	6	Tajikistan	177
Norway	7	Iraq	178
Panama	8	Afghanistan	179
Israel	9	Kazakhstan	180
Thailand	10	Kyrgyz Republic	181

Note: Rankings are the average of the economy rankings on the documents, time and cost required to export and import. See Data notes for details.
Source: Doing Business database.

Exporters in landlocked Rwanda have a better chance, thanks to ongoing reforms. Indeed, baskets from Gahaya Links, a Kigali-based business run by sisters Janet and Joy, are already available to U.S. households in Macy's department stores.[1] It wasn't easy at first, with high shipping costs and inadequate roads to the port city of Mombasa, Kenya. But the government has reformed 2 years in a row, and exporting is becoming easier.

Doing Business measures the procedural requirements, including the number of necessary documents and the associated time and cost (excluding trade tariffs) for exporting and importing.

The more time consuming the export or import process, the less likely that a trader will be able to reach markets in a timely fashion. This affects the ability to expand businesses and create jobs. Recognizing this, many economies have worked to introduce practices that reduce the time and costs associated with trade. These include providing electronic filing of trade documents (through electronic data interchange systems), allowing shippers to declare manifests online, reducing document requirements and using risk-based inspections. Another good approach is to provide a single window for obtaining different permits and authorizations, which reduces the time spent preparing documents. An efficient banking system also helps, by speeding the processing of trade financing instruments such as letters of credit.

Implementing these practices has reduced the time to trade. The average time to export has fallen by 3 days since 2005. The biggest decline was in Eastern Europe and Central Asia—almost 5 days (figure 9.1). The time to export dropped by 4 days in Africa, the Middle East and North Africa and South Asia. It declined by less than 3 days in East Asia and Pacific and Latin America. The longest average export delays are in Central Asia (58 days) and Central Africa (48 days), where most countries are landlocked.

The top performers on the ease of trading across borders continually consult export businesses on how to make trading easier (table 9.1). In Denmark, for example, 3 main trade documents (bill of lading, commercial invoice and customs declaration) suffice to cover most trade transactions. And these are

FIGURE 9.2

Rankings on trading across borders are based on 3 subindicators

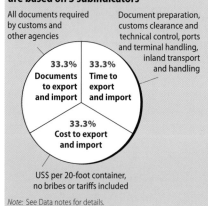

All documents required by customs and other agencies

Document preparation, customs clearance and technical control, ports and terminal handling, inland transport and handling

33.3% Documents to export and import

33.3% Time to export and import

33.3% Cost to export and import

US$ per 20-foot container, no bribes or tariffs included

Note: See Data notes for details.

TABLE 9.2

Electronic data interchange—the most popular reform feature in 2007/08

Introduced or improved electronic data interchange system	Botswana, Brazil, Colombia, Dominican Republic, El Salvador, France, India, Kenya, Madagascar, Mali, Mongolia, Morocco, Palau, Philippines, Rwanda, Senegal, Syria, Thailand, Uruguay
Introduced or improved risk-based inspections	Brazil, Colombia, Dominican Republic, El Salvador, Haiti, Kenya, former Yugoslav Republic of Macedonia, Madagascar, Mali, Mongolia, Philippines, Rwanda, Senegal
Improved procedures at ports	Benin, Croatia, Djibouti, Ecuador, Egypt, El Salvador, Eritrea, Kenya, Liberia, Madagascar, Nigeria, Ukraine
Reduced number of trade documents	Djibouti, Ecuador, El Salvador, France, Honduras, former Yugoslav Republic of Macedonia, Senegal, Sierra Leone, Thailand
Improved customs administration	Belarus, Botswana, Egypt, Kenya, Liberia, former Yugoslav Republic of Macedonia, Rwanda, Senegal, Thailand
Introduced or improved single window	El Salvador, Korea, Madagascar, Mongolia, Senegal
Implemented border cooperation agreements	Botswana, Mali

Source: Doing Business database.

transmitted online. Traders can begin the clearance process before goods arrive at the port. Because risk-based inspections apply, only about 2% of cargo is physically inspected. It takes only 5 days for goods to leave the factory, clear customs and be on a vessel heading to its destination.

Other countries might take note. A recent study of 126 economies calculates the loss from export delays at around 1% of trade for each extra day. For perishable agricultural products the cost is nearly 3% of the volume of trade for each day's delay.[2] Some nonagricultural products are time-sensitive too, such as fashion apparel and consumer electronics.

Another study finds that each extra signature an exporter has to collect reduces trade by 4.2%. For high-end exports the reduction is nearly 5%.[3] High trade costs constrain participation in global trade for many countries, particularly in Africa. One study finds that preferences under the tariff-free regimes for the U.S. market (under the African Growth and Opportunity Act) and the European Union (under the Cotonou agreement) are significantly underused.[4]

Delays and cumbersome procedures in importing hurt economies too. Many exports are part of global supply chains. To be part of these chains, producers depend on timely delivery of imported inputs. Imported materials account for a third of China's export value for electronic products, for example. They account for 55% of export value for Ireland, 65% for Thailand.[5] Economies that reduce delays can integrate more rapidly in global trade.

WHO REFORMED IN 2007/08?

Thirty-four economies made it easier to trade in 2007/08. Making it possible to submit customs documents electronically was the most popular reform feature, done in 19 economies (table 9.2).

Africa had the most reforms in easing trade. Senegal was the top reformer, easing the administrative requirements for trading across borders. One big change: linking those involved in the clearance process—customs, customs brokers, banks, the treasury, traders and several government ministries—through an electronic single-window system. Traders no longer need to visit each of these entities to obtain the required clearances. Instead, they can fill out a single form. In addition, customs has implemented a risk-based inspection regime and extended its operating schedule by 4 hours.

Reforms to ease trade were extended to neighboring countries. Senegal signed a border cooperation agreement with Mali, harmonizing trade documents between the 2 countries. Once goods are cleared at Dakar, Malian traders need no additional documents. And the number of checkpoints between Dakar and Bamako has dropped from 25 to 4. Trips that used to take 7–10 days now take only 1 or 2. Recognizing this, Malian traders increasingly use the port of Dakar rather than Abidjan. Mali also abolished a requirement for an official escort to the border for all cargo trucks carrying exports—something that had inevitably meant big delays.

In Madagascar traders can now submit customs declarations and payments online, thanks to the Madagascar Community Network (figure 9.3). Sierra Leone abolished the requirement for an export license for coffee. Rwanda extended the end of customs operating hours at its borders from 6:00 p.m to 10:00 p.m. Now fewer trucks stay at the border overnight.

Botswana licensed more customs brokers, spurring competition and leading to lower customs brokerage fees. Liberia cut the customs administrative fee from 3% of the cargo value to 1.5%. Kenya extended ports' operating schedule to 24 hours. In addition, postclearance audits allow some traders to fast-track their cargo for clearance. Nigeria is beginning to reap the rewards from concessioning its container terminals to private operators: clearing goods at the port of Apapa now takes 2 days less.

In Latin America, El Salvador made it easier to trade for the second year running. It set up a single window between customs, government ministries and tax and social security authorities. That cut the number of documents traders need to submit by 2. Guatemala reduced the share of goods that are physically inspected from 54% to 33%, thanks to ongoing implementation of its risk man-

FIGURE 9.3
Madagascar speeds imports
Time to import (days)

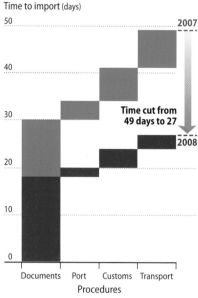

Source: *Doing Business* database.

agement system. Uruguay completed its automated customs system. Now traders can send documents to customs from their own office. Brazil introduced an electronic manifest system, allowing customs clearance to begin before the cargo arrives.

In East Asia and Pacific, Korea and Thailand carried out the most comprehensive reforms. Both introduced internet-based electronic data interchange systems and online issuance of trade documents. Traders can submit customs declarations from anywhere. Singapore, already the leader in trade facilitation, is going a step further. It is upgrading its system to a 3-dimensional trade platform allowing traders to interface with government agencies as well as local and international businesses.

In Indonesia a single window started operating in December 2007 in the port of Jakarta. The Philippines introduced new scanners, reducing the level of physical inspection at the ports. In addition, traders can submit customs declarations electronically through value added service providers. In Palau and Tonga traders can file customs declarations on a USB drive. Customs no longer needs to reenter the data, saving time.

In the Middle East and North Africa,

Egypt continued to reform. It now allows customs clearance on companies' premises. It also monitors the performance of border agencies to enhance service delivery. Djibouti cut the documents required to trade from 8 to 5. Saudi Arabia cut port fees by 50%. Morocco is bringing together different border agencies through a port community network to speed the clearance of goods.

Eastern Europe and Central Asia kept up the pace of reform. Georgia implemented a risk management system, reducing the share of merchandise inspected to 10%. Belarus introduced legislative changes that cut the maximum time allowed for customs clearance from 10 days to 1. The former Yugoslav Republic of Macedonia purchased 4 mobile scanners, reducing the number of physical inspections carried out.

OECD high-income economies also carried out reforms. In France traders can now submit documents electronically. Fast-track clearance procedures were also put into place. Belgium introduced a paperless customs clearance system. Denmark improved its online customs system. In Austria it is now possible to use an electronic letter of credit.

Reforms in some countries made things more complicated. In Equatorial Guinea traders used to take their consignments from the ports while completing customs formalities. This is no longer possible. In Burkina Faso the threshold value triggering inspections has been lowered, even though prices are on the rise. Now more consignments need to be inspected, slowing the process. The Gambia reinstated compulsory scanning fees. Traders complain that they have to pay the scanning fee even when their cargo is not scanned.

WHAT ARE THE REFORM TRENDS?

The number of economies implementing new reforms to facilitate trade has been on the increase globally. In 2005 there were 25 reformers. In 2007/08 there were 34. Africa increasingly took the lead (figure 9.4). In 2005, 5 African

economies reformed. In 2007/08, 11 did. Ghana, Kenya, Mauritius, Rwanda and Tanzania reformed in multiple years. In the Middle East and North Africa on average, 4 economies reformed each year. In Latin America and the Caribbean reforms ranged from 3 to 8.

SPEEDING CLEARANCE

The most popular reform feature in facilitating trade has been to implement an electronic data interchange system (figure 9.5). Electronic transmission of documents not only speeds the clearance of goods; it often reduces the possibilities for paying bribes. "There is an old saying—don't pay me a salary, put me in customs," remarks a Honduran freight forwarder. That changed with the advent of electronic data processing. But to avoid a dual electronic and manual customs clearance process, the new systems must be complemented by supporting legislation authorizing electronic transactions.

Economies implementing an electronic data interchange system saw the time to clear goods cut by 3 days on average. The reform also helps increase predictability in clearance times. Before Pakistan implemented its electronic system, only 4.3% of goods were cleared within a day; for a quarter of the goods, clearance took a week. Now 93% of goods are cleared within a day.[6]

Where electronic data interchange systems are in place, it is easier to apply risk management to customs clearance, another popular reform. Thirteen economies, including Colombia, Madagascar and Mongolia, have introduced risk-based inspections alongside electronic transmission of documents. In economies that use risk-based inspections, 19% of containers are inspected on average; in economies that do not, 53% are.

LOOKING BEYOND CUSTOMS

While customs reform remains most important to trading across borders, several other reforms also play a part. Indeed, in the *Doing Business* sample, customs clearance accounts for less than 20% of the time to export, from the time

FIGURE 9.4
Africa has reformed the most

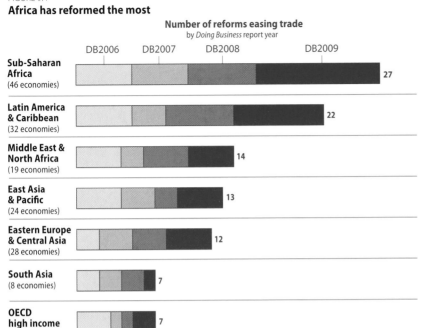

Note: A reform is counted as 1 reform per reforming economy per year.
Source: Doing Business database.

FIGURE 9.5
Top 5 reform features in trading across borders
Reforms including feature since DB2006 (%)

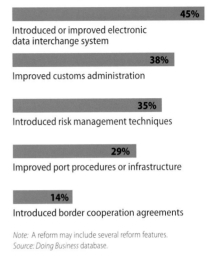

Note: A reform may include several reform features.
Source: Doing Business database.

the export contract is concluded to the time the goods leave the port. Approvals from ministries, health authorities, security agencies, inspection agencies, port authorities, banks and immigration authorities account for most delays.

Countries increasingly recognize the importance of a comprehensive approach to trade facilitation. Korea has brought together 69 government agencies as well as private participants through its single-window system. Senegal has brought together 15 agencies. El Salvador has linked 3 government departments and continues to expand this network.

FINDING INEXPENSIVE REFORMS

Some needed trade reforms are expensive, such as building roads or port infrastructure. But much can be done without heavy spending. Clarifying the rules is an important start. "Sometimes they demand this document, and other times they don't. We are at the mercy of the officials," says a trader in Uzbekistan. "We had to go back to South Africa to retrieve the right form before we could get permission for the truck to leave the

border," complains a clearing agent in Botswana.

More publicity, training and regular meetings with exporters on the clearance process can also make a difference. In Jamaica, where such efforts are in place, customs brokers with low error rates are rewarded with access to fast-track clearance procedures, while those with high error rates face more scrutiny. "Because I want my goods cleared quickly, I do not accept all documents sent to me by my clients. I sometimes ask them to bring a clearer invoice," says Loraine, a customs broker in Jamaica.

Payment of customs duties need not delay the release of cargo. Why not introduce a bond or financial guarantee, allowing goods to be released pending completion of the paperwork? Many economies, such as Malaysia, have done just that.

Countries save costs by synchronizing documents and procedures at the border. Thanks to a border cooperation agreement with Sweden and Finland, Norway is estimated to have avoided more than $9 million a year in costs to customs

authorities and $48 million a year in costs to economic operators.[7]

In some regions trade is hindered by bureaucratic hurdles at borders. In Africa and Central Asia border crossings account for significant delays in trade. But change has begun. South Africa and Mozambique are creating a one-stop border post at the Lebombo–Ressano Garcia crossing. Indeed, regional approaches to trade facilitation may yield the biggest benefits in both regions.

NOTES

1. This example is from the World Bank's *Doing Business: Women in Africa* (2008a), a collection of case studies on African entrepreneurs.
2. Djankov, Freund and Pham (forthcoming).
3. Sadikov (2007).
4. Bureau, Chakir and Gallezot (2007).
5. Nordas, Pinali and Geloso-Grosso (2006).
6. Ahmad (2008).
7. WTO (2005).

TABLE 9.3

Who makes exporting easy—and who does not?				Who makes importing easy—and who does not?			

Documents *(number)*				**Documents** *(number)*			
Fewest		Most		Fewest		Most	
France	2	Namibia	11	France	2	Burkina Faso	11
Estonia	3	Mauritania	11	Denmark	3	Afghanistan	11
Panama	3	Burkina Faso	11	Sweden	3	Congo, Rep.	12
Canada	3	Congo, Rep.	11	Thailand	3	Fiji	13
Micronesia	3	Kazakhstan	11	Singapore	4	Russian Federation	13
Singapore	4	Malawi	12	Hong Kong, China	4	Eritrea	13
Hong Kong, China	4	Angola	12	Estonia	4	Kazakhstan	13
Denmark	4	Afghanistan	12	Norway	4	Kyrgyz Republic	13
Finland	4	Fiji	13	Panama	4	Azerbaijan	14
Sweden	4	Kyrgyz Republic	13	Israel	4	Central African Republic	18

Time *(days)*				**Time** *(days)*			
Fastest		Slowest		Fastest		Slowest	
Singapore	5	Central African Republic	57	Singapore	3	Venezuela	71
Denmark	5	Niger	59	Hong Kong, China	5	Burundi	71
Estonia	5	Kyrgyz Republic	64	Denmark	5	Zimbabwe	73
Hong Kong, China	6	Angola	68	Estonia	5	Kyrgyz Republic	75
Netherlands	6	Afghanistan	74	United States	5	Kazakhstan	76
United States	6	Chad	78	Sweden	6	Afghanistan	77
Luxembourg	6	Uzbekistan	80	Netherlands	6	Tajikistan	83
Norway	7	Tajikistan	82	Luxembourg	6	Iraq	101
Germany	7	Kazakhstan	89	Norway	7	Chad	102
Ireland	7	Iraq	102	Germany	7	Uzbekistan	104

Cost *(US$ per container)*				**Cost** *(US$ per container)*			
Least		Most		Least		Most	
Malaysia	450	Kazakhstan	3,005	Singapore	439	Niger	3,545
Singapore	456	Azerbaijan	3,075	Malaysia	450	Burkina Faso	3,630
China	460	Uganda	3,090	China	545	Burundi	3,705
Finland	495	Uzbekistan	3,100	Finland	575	Iraq	3,900
Pakistan	611	Tajikistan	3,150	São Tomé and Principe	577	Zimbabwe	3,999
United Arab Emirates	618	Rwanda	3,275	United Arab Emirates	587	Tajikistan	4,550
Hong Kong, China	625	Niger	3,545	Israel	605	Uzbekistan	4,600
Thailand	625	Iraq	3,900	Fiji	630	Rwanda	5,070
Brunei	630	Central African Republic	5,121	Hong Kong, China	633	Central African Republic	5,074
Tonga	650	Chad	5,367	Qatar	657	Chad	6,020

Source: Doing Business database.

Enforcing contracts

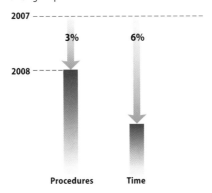

FIGURE 10.1

Top 10 reformers in enforcing contracts

Average improvement

1. *Mozambique*
2. *Macedonia, former Yugoslav Republic of*
3. *Bulgaria*
4. *Romania*
5. *Armenia*
6. *China*
7. *Bhutan*
8. *Belgium*
9. *Azerbaijan*
10. *Portugal*

Source: Doing Business database.

Tan, a litigation lawyer in Singapore, does not mind waiting at the supreme court until his case is called. A computer screen shows the expected wait time for each case. And a text message on his cell phone will alert him when the judge is ready to hear his. Meanwhile, he reviews his oral arguments and enjoys a nice lunch at Academy Bistro, located in the supreme court building.

Tan and his clients can afford to relax, because they know their cases will be resolved expeditiously. In Singapore it takes only 150 days to resolve a commercial dispute—faster than anywhere else in the world.

Not everyone bringing a commercial dispute to court can expect similar efficiency. One common obstacle to doing business in developing countries is the weakness of courts. The problem is

especially severe in Africa, where 80% of the people turn to informal institutions when seeking justice.[1]

Justice delayed is often justice denied. And in many countries only the rich can afford to go to court. For the rest, justice is out of reach. In the absence of efficient courts, firms undertake fewer investments and business transactions. And they prefer to involve only a small group of people who know each other from previous dealings.

Inefficient courts impose big costs. A recent study on Eastern Europe finds that in countries with slower courts, firms on average have less bank financing for new investment. Reforms in other areas, such as creditors' rights, help increase bank lending only if contracts can be enforced before the courts.[2] A second study, on 41 developing countries, finds that for each 10% improvement in the efficiency of commercial dispute resolution, the informal sector's share in overall economic activity falls by 2.3%.[3]

Courts serve business best when they are fast, affordable and fair. Worldwide, only 35% of businesses covered by the World Bank Enterprise Surveys believe that the courts in their country are fair, impartial and uncorrupt.[4]

Doing Business measures the efficiency of the judicial system in resolving a commercial dispute. It looks at the time, cost and procedures to enforce a contract through the courts (figure 10.2).

Economies that score well on the

ease of enforcing contracts keep courts efficient by introducing case management, strict procedural time limits and specialized commercial courts or e-courts; by streamlining appeals; and by making enforcement of judgments faster and cheaper (table 10.1).

In Singapore court documents can be filed electronically, and each case is monitored from the moment the action is filed until the moment it is finally decided. Using case management also makes it possible to measure the performance of judges. The right to appeal to the high court exists only for cases above S$50,000 ($35,500). Cases below this threshold need prior leave to go to appeal.

Hong Kong (China) speeds the enforcement of judgments by allowing the process to start based on the essentials

TABLE 10.1

Where is enforcing contracts easy—and where not?

Easiest	RANK	Most difficult	RANK
Hong Kong, China	1	Cameroon	172
Luxembourg	2	Congo, Dem. Rep.	173
Iceland	3	Syria	174
Latvia	4	Benin	175
Finland	5	Honduras	176
United States	6	Suriname	177
Norway	7	Bangladesh	178
Korea	8	Angola	179
Germany	9	India	180
France	10	Timor-Leste	181

Note: Rankings are the average of the economy rankings on the procedures, time and cost to resolve a commercial dispute through the courts. See Data notes for details.
Source: Doing Business database.

FIGURE 10.2

Rankings on enforcing contracts are based on 3 subindicators

Days to resolve commercial sale dispute before courts

Attorney, court and enforcement costs as % of claim value

33.3% Time
33.3% Cost
33.3% Procedures

Steps to file claim, obtain and enforce judgment

Note: See Data notes for details.

TABLE 10.2

Where is enforcing contracts the most efficient—and where the least?

Procedures (number of steps)			
Fewest		**Most**	
Ireland	20	Guinea	50
Singapore	21	Kuwait	50
Hong Kong, China	24	United Arab Emirates	50
Rwanda	24	Belize	51
Austria	25	Iraq	51
Belgium	25	Oman	51
Netherlands	25	Timor-Leste	51
Iceland	26	Sudan	53
Luxembourg	26	Syria	55
Czech Republic	27	Brunei	58

Time (days)			
Fastest		**Slowest**	
Singapore	150	Sri Lanka	1,318
Kyrgyz Republic	177	Trinidad and Tobago	1,340
Uzbekistan	195	Colombia	1,346
Lithuania	210	Slovenia	1,350
Hong Kong, China	211	India	1,420
New Zealand	216	Bangladesh	1,442
Belarus	225	Guatemala	1,459
Bhutan	225	Afghanistan	1,642
Kazakhstan	230	Suriname	1,715
Korea	230	Timor-Leste	1,800

Cost (% of claim)			
Least		**Most**	
Bhutan	0.1	Comoros	89.4
Iceland	6.2	Cambodia	102.7
Luxembourg	8.8	Burkina Faso	107.4
United States	9.4	Papua New Guinea	110.3
Norway	9.9	Indonesia	122.7
Korea	10.3	Malawi	142.4
Finland	10.4	Mozambique	142.5
China	11.1	Sierra Leone	149.5
Poland	12.0	Congo, Dem. Rep.	151.8
Hungary	13.0	Timor-Leste	163.2

Source: Doing Business database.

of the court decision. Fully motivated, written court decisions are not needed. The 10 economies with the fastest average times to enforce a contract tend to have specialized commercial courts or specialized commercial sections within existing courts and limits on the number and length of adjournments once a case has started.

Reducing entry barriers in the market for legal services helps. Allowing women to enter the legal profession, for example, can increase competition among lawyers and reduce attorneys'

fees. Saudi Arabia saw its first female law graduates—170 of them—in June 2008. The Saudi government is sending the top 4 to graduate programs abroad, to prepare them to return as the country's first female law professors. Some countries still prohibit women from serving as judges. Others have recently started allowing women on the bench. Bahrain, which did so in 2003, now has 3 female judges. And the first female federal judge was appointed in Abu Dhabi in late March 2008.

WHO REFORMED IN 2007/08?

Twelve economies reformed contract enforcement in 2007/08 (table 10.3). The reforms reduced the time, cost or number of steps in court proceedings by introducing specialized commercial courts and case management, simplifying rules for small cases, streamlining appeals and making enforcement of judgments more efficient.

Most reforms took place in Eastern Europe and Central Asia—in Armenia, Azerbaijan, Bulgaria, the former Yugoslav Republic of Macedonia and Romania. Among OECD high-income economies, Austria, Belgium and Portugal reformed. In Africa, Mozambique and Rwanda did. In South Asia, Bhutan was the only economy that improved its courts in 2007/08. In East Asia, China was the only reformer. The Middle East and North Africa had no reforms.

Mozambique, the top reformer in enforcing contracts, reduced the average time to resolve a commercial dispute from 1,010 days to 730. The newly established commercial courts have started to produce results. Since March 2008 the country has also gained 22 new judges— a 10% increase. Besides hiring more judges, Mozambique introduced performance measures for them. And court administrators now take care of administrative tasks that judges used to handle, such as paying creditors after a public auction of a debtor's assets.

In the former Yugoslav Republic of Macedonia, the runner-up reformer, a commercial division of the Skopje civil court started operating in November 2007, after initial difficulties with allocating judges were resolved. Starting in January 2008, all cases have been electronically recorded. The Skopje commercial division will soon have 15 additional computers to begin electronic registration of cases.

In Rwanda specialized commercial courts started operating in May 2008. Three lower commercial courts—in Kigali and in the Northern and Southern Provinces—cover commercial disputes

TABLE 10.3
Increasing procedural efficiency—the most popular reform feature in 2007/08

Increased procedural efficiency at main trial court	Armenia, Belgium, Bulgaria, former Yugoslav Republic of Macedonia, Mozambique
Introduced or expanded specialized commercial courts	Azerbaijan, former Yugoslav Republic of Macedonia, Rwanda
Made enforcement of judgment more efficient	China, Romania
Simplified rules for small claims	Bhutan, Portugal
Established e-courts	Austria
Streamlined appeals	Bulgaria

Source: Doing Business database.

with a value below about $37,000. A fourth commercial court, attached to the high court, handles cases above that value in addition to appeals of decisions from the 3 lower courts. Commercial courts not only resolve disputes faster; they also bring the needed expertise to commercial cases.

Bulgaria shortened trial times by requiring judges to refuse incomplete court filings rather than allow multiple extensions. To ensure compliance with deadlines, disciplinary sanctions now apply to judges who systematically violate them. Bulgaria also reformed its appeals process. Appeals are now possible only on the basis of newly discovered facts and only against judgments exceeding lev 1,000 (about $800). And final appeals before the supreme court have been limited to substantive issues.

Romania simplified the enforcement of judgments by eliminating the need for an enforcement order and allowing the attachment of credit balances and accounts receivable. The reform reduced the time to enforce a judgment by a month, from 120 days to 95.

In Armenia procedural rules that became effective in January 2008 introduced a new principle: all court decisions become enforceable 1 month after being issued. In addition, a May 2007 law established specialized criminal and administrative jurisdictions and a new civil court that will deal with the financially most important cases.

Azerbaijan reduced the average time to enforce a contract from 267 days to 237 by establishing a second specialized

commercial court in Baku and increasing the number of commercial court judges from 5 to 9.

In Western Europe, Austria made electronic filing mandatory in the civil courts. All filings from lawyers in civil litigation and enforcement proceedings now go through an electronic data channel operated by the Ministry of Justice. And judgments are delivered by e-mail rather than by the old hard-copy notification process.

Belgium adopted a law in 2007 to speed court procedures. The law introduced a mandatory procedural calendar that includes binding time limits to submit written pleadings. The agenda is fixed by the parties or, if they fail to agree, by the judge. If judges fail to render a judgment within a month after hearing a case, they are subject to disciplinary sanctions. A separate law aims to encourage experts to produce their reports more quickly by having the court control the payment of their fees.

Portugal expanded the scope of its simplified proceedings to include all cases with a value up to €30,000.

China adopted a new set of procedural rules. The focus was on speeding the enforcement of judgments. In East Asia enforcement accounts for 34% on average of the time needed to resolve a commercial dispute—the largest share among all regions. In China, enforcing a judgment takes up almost half the total time to resolve a commercial dispute.

To reduce the time for enforcement, China's new rules require parties to disclose their assets at the beginning of the

court procedure. Those refusing to do so may be fined. Enforcement officers can take measures to prevent parties from concealing or transferring their assets during or immediately after court proceedings. And courts can prohibit parties from leaving the country if they are suspected of trying to escape the enforcement of a decision.

In South Asia, Bhutan transferred all land disputes—which account for about 30% of cases before the Thimphu district court—to a specialized land commission. The measure freed up more of the court's time to handle commercial cases. The result: the Thimphu district court reduced the average time to resolve commercial disputes from 275 days to 225.

WHAT ARE THE REFORM TRENDS?

Reformers considering ways to improve the regulatory environment for businesses often shy away from tackling court reforms. This is not surprising. The success rate of court reforms is low: on average, only 1 in 4 attempted reforms succeed in reducing costs and delays. Even successful reforms often take years to produce visible results.

As a general rule, economies that rank high on the ease of enforcing contracts continually reform their courts to adjust to changing business realities. Denmark is an example. In 2006 it introduced special rules for cases below about $8,600. That reduced the number of cases before the general courts in Copenhagen by 38%. Reformers did not stop there. In March 2008 a new law introduced mediation after a successful pilot showed that two-thirds of all cases referred to mediation in 2003–05 resulted in an amicable settlement. The message: stay focused on improvement, even if you are already doing well.

INTRODUCING COMMERCIAL COURTS IN AFRICA

The most popular reform feature in Africa over the past 5 years has been introducing specialized commercial courts or commercial sections within

FIGURE 10.3

Few reforms in the Middle East & North Africa and in South Asia

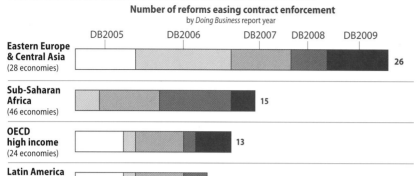

Number of reforms easing contract enforcement
by *Doing Business* report year

| | DB2005 | DB2006 | DB2007 | DB2008 | DB2009 |

Eastern Europe & Central Asia (28 economies) — 26

Sub-Saharan Africa (46 economies) — 15

OECD high income (24 economies) — 13

Latin America & Caribbean (32 economies) — 11

East Asia & Pacific (24 economies) — 7

South Asia (8 economies) — 1

Middle East & North Africa (19 economies) — 1

Note: A reform is counted as 1 reform per reforming economy per year.
Source: Doing Business database.

FIGURE 10.4

Top 5 reform features in enforcing contracts

Reforms including feature since DB2005 (%)

43%
Increased procedural efficiency

18%
Established or expanded commercial courts

12%
Made enforcement of judgment cheaper or more efficient

9%
Streamlined appeals

8%
Simplified rules for small claims

Note: A reform may include several reform features.
Source: Doing Business database.

existing courts. Some African countries have a longer track record with specialized courts or divisions—including Kenya, Madagascar, Tanzania, Uganda and Zambia.

In 7 African countries that introduced commercial courts or sections in the past 5 years—Burkina Faso, the Democratic Republic of Congo, Ghana, Mauritania, Mozambique, Nigeria and Rwanda—the average time to resolve a commercial dispute dropped by about 19%, from 604 days to 492 (figure 10.5). Because judges must be hired and trained, rules adjusted and funding ensured, achieving such reductions in time usually takes years. In Ghana, for example, a commercial division began operating in its high court in March 2005. *Doing Business 2008* records a drop in time from 552 days to 487—more than 2 years later.

Specialized commercial courts are often criticized because they deal only with the financially most important cases. Those in Tanzania, for example, accept only cases with a value 66 times income per capita. In Zambia it is 15 times income per capita. Minimum thresholds can be justified as a way to avoid overloading

newly established specialized courts. But a balance must be struck between access to justice and a reasonable caseload for the new courts. A pragmatic approach is to lower minimum thresholds as courts are gradually able to accept more cases. This is better than having courts inundated with cases from the start.

MOVING TO ORAL PROCEEDINGS IN LATIN AMERICA

Countries in Latin America have sped criminal cases by using oral proceedings rather than an exchange of written documents. Argentina and Chile started this trend in the 1990s. Colombia, Gua-

temala, Honduras and Mexico are now working on similar reforms. And Colombia plans to extend oral proceedings to commercial cases over the next 4 years.

In El Salvador the legislature is close to adopting a bill to make court cases, including commercial cases, oral. Now everything takes place in writing between the parties, with little intervention from the judge. In the future there will be a preliminary hearing during which the judge will first try to reconcile the parties. Failing that, the judge will determine the facts and evidence to be presented in the case. At a second and final hearing the parties, witnesses and

FIGURE 10.5

Specialized commercial courts in Africa help to reduce delays in enforcing contracts

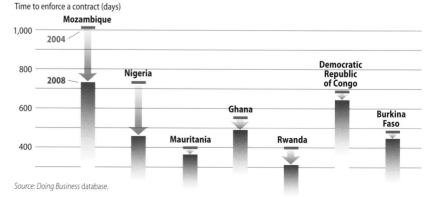

Time to enforce a contract (days)

Source: Doing Business database.

experts will be questioned. Under the new rules the judge must issue a written judgment within 15 days after the second hearing.

While oral proceedings are a recent trend in Latin America, countries in other regions have a longer history with them. Take Luxembourg, which ranks second on the ease of enforcing contracts. There, parties do not exchange long, written pleadings in commercial cases. Instead, they exchange only the written evidence they intend to rely on during oral arguments before the judge. This saves several months.

IMPOSING STRICT DEADLINES

In 1995 the "arbitrazh courts" became responsible for dealing with commercial disputes in the Russian Federation. In 2002, to make proceedings faster, the Russian Federation revised its commercial procedural code. Its most significant innovation was to introduce strict mandatory time limits: 2 months for a full hearing, 1 month for accelerated procedures.

Most Central Asian countries copied the Russian procedural rules, including the strict deadlines. Judges are held accountable for respecting the deadlines, with those who do best standing better chances for promotion. Not surprisingly, of the 10 economies with the fastest average times to enforce a contract, half are in Eastern Europe and Central Asia.

NOTES

1. Wojkowska (2006).
2. Safavian and Sharma (2007).
3. Dabla-Norris, Gradstein and Inchauste (2008).
4. World Bank Enterprise Surveys http://www.enterprisesurveys.org).

Closing a business

FIGURE 11.1

Higher recovery rates associated with more access to credit

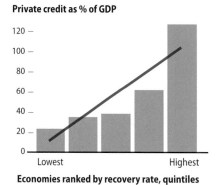

Private credit as % of GDP

Economies ranked by recovery rate, quintiles

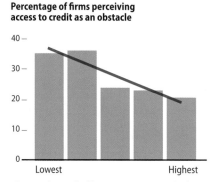

Percentage of firms perceiving access to credit as an obstacle

Economies ranked by recovery rate, quintiles

Note: Relationships are significant at the 1% level and remain significant when controlling for income per capita.
Source: Doing Business database; World Bank, World Development Indicators database; World Bank Enterprise Surveys.

Carlos, the owner of a large Colombian manufacturing firm, got bad news: his main customer had just entered bankruptcy. Carlos feared that it might take years to recover the company's loan—and that his business could suffer harm.

But there is good news too. Colombia's new insolvency law came into effect at the end of 2007, streamlining bankruptcy procedures. Before, a debtor could object to every claim from any creditor, greatly delaying the court process. Now all objections must be resolved in one court hearing. The new law also tightens procedural time limits. And it gives creditors more power to influence the proceedings, such as allowing them to remove and replace the liquidator.

Efficient bankruptcy regulations improve access to credit. Where insol-

TABLE 11.1

Where is it easy to close a business—and where not?

Easiest	Recovery rate	Most difficult	Recovery rate
Japan	92.5	Liberia	8.3
Singapore	91.3	Suriname	8.1
Norway	89.0	Mauritania	6.7
Canada	88.7	Venezuela	6.0
Finland	87.3	Congo, Dem. Rep.	5.4
Ireland	86.6	Philippines	4.4
Denmark	86.5	Micronesia	3.5
Belgium	86.3	Haiti	2.7
United Kingdom	84.2	Zimbabwe	0.0
Netherlands	82.7	Central African Republic	0.0

Note: Rankings are based on the recovery rate: how many cents on the dollar claimants (creditors, tax authorities and employees) recover from the insolvent firm. See Data notes for details.
Source: Doing Business database.

vency laws are most effective, creditors—confident that they will be able to collect on loans—are more likely to lend.[1]

The benefits of efficient bankruptcy regulations are particularly evident when comparing rich economies. Recent studies in Europe find that actual returns to creditors are 92% of the value of the loan in the United Kingdom, 80% in the Netherlands, 67% in Germany and 56% in France.[2] Why the big spread? In part because it takes only a year to finish the insolvency process in London, 13 months in Amsterdam and 15 months in Berlin, but almost 2 years in Paris, according to Doing Business data.

Good bankruptcy laws do 3 main things. They seek to rehabilitate viable businesses and liquidate unviable ones. They aim to maximize the value received by creditors, shareholders, employees and other stakeholders by requiring that businesses be turned around, sold as going concerns or liquidated—whichever generates the greatest total value. And they establish a system for clearly ranking creditors. Countries with laws meeting these 3 objectives achieve a higher recovery rate than countries without such laws.

Doing Business studies the time, cost and outcomes of bankruptcy proceedings involving domestic entities. Speed, low cost and continuation of viable business operations characterize the top-performing economies. In these economies businesses are more likely to be sold or reor-

ganized as a going concern rather than liquidated through piecemeal sales. And most allow creditors significant input into the appointment of administrators and require special qualifications for trustees (figure 11.3).

In Canada, Ireland, Japan, Norway and Singapore foreclosure, reorganization or liquidation is completed within a year (table 11.1). Canada and Ireland have specialized bankruptcy courts and statutory time limits. They also limit procedural appeals. Denmark introduced a "floating charge" in 2006 to allow secured creditors to take security over an entire business. This increases the likelihood that a viable business will be sold as a going concern. In Colombia, Kuwait, Norway and Singapore it costs only about 1% of the bankrupt estate's value to resolve insolvency (table 11.2).

FIGURE 11.2

Rankings on closing a business are based on 1 subindicator

Function of time, cost and other factors such as lending rate and the likelihood of the company continuing to operate

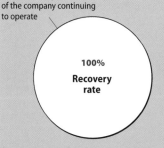

100%
Recovery
rate

Note: Time and cost do not count separately for the ranking. See Data notes for details.

FIGURE 11.3
Higher recovery rates in economies with specialized courts and trustees
Recovery rate (cents on the dollar)

Source: Doing Business database.

WHO REFORMED IN 2007/08?

Poland was the top reformer in closing a business in 2007/08 (table 11.3). Its Law on Trustee Licensing took effect on October 10, 2007. The new law tightened professional requirements for administrators to ensure they have the skills and education needed to oversee bankruptcy proceedings. Obtaining a trustee's license now requires passing an exam in economics, law, finance and management. The reform also limits trustees' pay to 3% of the bankrupt estate's value, down from 5%.

Three economies in Latin America and the Caribbean rank close behind Poland as top reformers. Colombia, the runner-up reformer, introduced 2 new insolvency proceedings: a reorganization procedure to restructure insolvent companies and a mandatory liquidation procedure. Its new insolvency law tightens time limits for negotiating reorganization agreements. Before, the term allowed was 6 months, with a possible extension of 8 months. The new law limits the term to 4 months, and the extension to 2.

Mexico amended its bankruptcy law. Now debtors and creditors may enter into a reorganization agreement at any stage of the insolvency procedure. St. Vincent and the Grenadines enacted a bankruptcy law in 2007. The law is the country's first set of rules regulating the bankruptcy of private enterprises since its independence.

Four Eastern European economies joined Poland in streamlining bankruptcy procedures. Latvia passed a new insolvency law in November 2007. Now financially distressed companies can choose to continue operating by pursuing reorganization. Like Poland, Latvia also tightened the qualification standards for bankruptcy administrators. So did Bosnia and Herzegovina. The Czech Republic's Insolvency Act took effect on January 1, 2008. The law introduces reorganization as the preferred method for resolving insolvency, mandates stricter deadlines, establishes an electronic insolvency register and sets new qualification standards for trustees.

Bulgaria passed 2 laws: the Civil Procedure Code and the Law for the Commercial Registry. The first specifies that appeals will now take place at 2 levels: first before the court of appeals and then before the supreme court. Bulgaria's supreme court will be the final arbiter, with the discretion to decide whether or not to hear a case. Before, court decisions could be appealed only before the supreme court—which usually sent cases back to the district court—resulting in long delays. Another first for Bulgaria: major decisions and rulings of the bankruptcy court are posted on the commercial registry's website.

In East Asia and Pacific, Hong Kong (China) and Cambodia were the only reformers. Hong Kong (China) issued the Bankruptcy Amendment Rules for 2007,

strengthening trustees' role and powers. Cambodia adopted the 2007 Bankruptcy Law, its first regulating the bankruptcy of private enterprises. The law introduces a reorganization procedure to restructure insolvent companies.

Five OECD high-income economies joined the list of reformers in 2007/08. Finland streamlined court-supervised reorganization. Now a simple majority of creditors can approve simplified reorganization plans; before, unanimous consent was required. Finland revised its Restructuring of Enterprises Act, accelerating hearings and making the entire process more flexible. Germany amended its insolvency code to make it easier to maintain a debtor's business as a going concern. The new law allows the insolvency court to suspend enforcement actions against assets essential to continuing the business.

Portugal cut the formality of publishing insolvency notices in newspapers. It also introduced a fast-track procedure

TABLE 11.2
Where is bankruptcy the most efficient—and where the least?

Time (years)			
Fastest		**Slowest**	
Ireland	0.4	Ecuador	5.3
Japan	0.6	Indonesia	5.5
Canada	0.8	Haiti	5.7
Singapore	0.8	Philippines	5.7
Belgium	0.9	Belarus	5.8
Finland	0.9	Angola	6.2
Norway	0.9	Czech Republic	6.5
Australia	1.0	Maldives	6.7
Belize	1.0	Mauritania	8.0
Iceland	1.0	India	10.0

Cost (% of estate)			
Least		**Most**	
Colombia	1.0	Micronesia	38.0
Kuwait	1.0	Philippines	38.0
Norway	1.0	Samoa	38.0
Singapore	1.0	Solomon Islands	38.0
Bahamas, The	3.5	Vanuatu	38.0
Belgium	3.5	Venezuela	38.0
Brunei	3.5	Sierra Leone	42.0
Canada	3.5	Ukraine	42.0
Finland	3.5	Liberia	42.5
Georgia	3.5	Central African Republic	76.0

Source: Doing Business database.

TABLE 11.3

Establishing or promoting reorganization procedures—a popular reform feature in 2007/08

Established or promoted reorganization procedure	Colombia, Czech Republic, Finland, Germany, Greece, Latvia, Mexico, New Zealand
Developed the trustee profession	Bosnia and Herzegovina, Czech Republic, Hong Kong (China), Latvia, Poland
Introduced or tightened time limits and streamlined procedural appeals	Bulgaria, Colombia, Portugal, Saudi Arabia
Established a first bankruptcy law	Cambodia, St. Vincent and the Grenadines
Granted priority to secured creditors	Czech Republic

Source: Doing Business database.

for debtors with less than €5,000 in assets and new procedures to accelerate payments to insolvency administrators. In addition, Portugal limited procedural appeals by unifying its appeals process and raising the value threshold for claims heard in the courts of first and second instance. In the future, appeals of appeals court decisions that confirm first-instance decisions will be possible only in limited circumstances. This is expected to cut the number of appeals before the supreme court.

New Zealand introduced a reorganization procedure similar to the one in Australia. The aim is to provide an alternative to liquidation and receivership and maximize a company's chances of continuing as a going concern. Greece thoroughly revised its bankruptcy system to maximize creditors' recovery of debt. A new law aims to reorganize financially distressed companies, preserve the business assets, treat creditors equally and prevent piecemeal sale. This law is expected to lead to a boom in restructurings and, together with a better early detection system, allow more companies to continue as going concerns.

Saudi Arabia was the only reformer in the Middle East and North Africa. Its Ministry of Commerce introduced strict deadlines for bankruptcy procedures. Auctions of debtors' assets are expected to take place quicker than before.

Bolivia made going through bankruptcy more complex, by suspending applications for voluntary restructuring. The only option now is a bankruptcy procedure that typically takes years.

WHAT ARE THE REFORM TRENDS?

Reform continues even in the jurisdictions with the best performance. *Doing Business* has recorded 58 reforms making it easier to close a business in the past 5 years. Most focused on expanding creditors' rights and speeding bankruptcy proceedings in the court.

Economies in Eastern Europe and Central Asia have had the most reforms making it easier to close a business in the past 5 years, especially in speeding bankruptcy proceedings (figure 11.4). High-income OECD economies follow close behind, focusing more on empow-

ering creditors.

Elsewhere in the world reform has been moving more slowly. The 10 reforms in Latin America and the Caribbean, Sub-Saharan Africa and South Asia have ranged from introducing stricter deadlines to establishing specialized bankruptcy courts. In 2006 Burundi enacted its first bankruptcy law, setting clear time limits for procedures. In the Middle East and North Africa only Tunisia and Saudi Arabia have reformed.

EXPANDING CREDITORS' RIGHTS

Expanding creditors' rights has been the most popular reform feature over the past 5 years (figure 11.5). Seventeen economies have empowered creditors: China, the Czech Republic, Denmark, Finland, France, Hungary, Indonesia, Italy, Korea, Poland, Portugal, Puerto Rico, Romania, Serbia, Slovakia, the United States and Vietnam. Giving creditors more say in the process speeds the resolution of bankruptcy and is likely to result in the continuation of the business. Allowing creditors a greater role in decision making increases the recovery rate.

Reforms expanding the powers of

FIGURE 11.4

Most reforms in Eastern Europe & Central Asia and rich economies

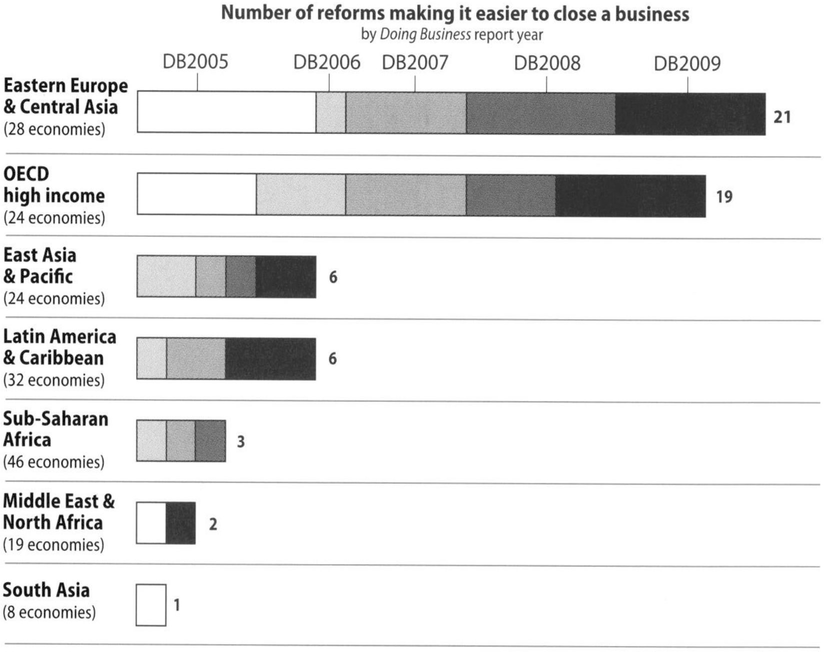

Number of reforms making it easier to close a business
by *Doing Business* report year

Note: A reform is counted as 1 reform per reforming economy per year.
Source: Doing Business database.

FIGURE 11.5

**Top 5 reform features in
closing a business**

Reforms including feature since DB2005 (%)

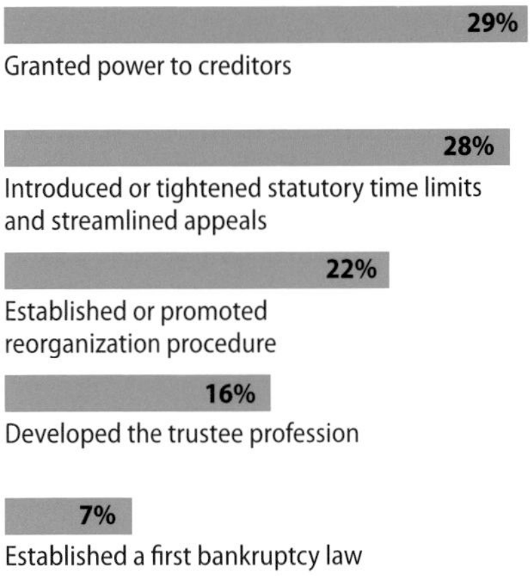

Granted power to creditors	29%
Introduced or tightened statutory time limits and streamlined appeals	28%
Established or promoted reorganization procedure	22%
Developed the trustee profession	16%
Established a first bankruptcy law	7%

Note: A reform may include several reform features.
Source: Doing Business database.

creditors have been most concentrated among OECD high-income economies. Finland gave creditors the right to set up a creditors' committee to advise the administrator. France and Korea now allow the creditors' committee to vote on the reorganization plan. Denmark encouraged creditors to report to the court any trustee actions that appear to delay the process. The court can then replace the trustee if it decides—based on the creditors' reports—that the trustee is incompetent.

Several economies, including Finland and France, granted higher priority to creditors in bankruptcy claims. France gave a "supersecured" position to creditors that lend money to distressed companies, giving them priority over previous secured creditors. That makes it easier for such companies to obtain new loans and continue operating.

OECD high-income economies have also promoted reorganization. Finland, France, Italy and Korea made reorganization more accessible to troubled companies. Italy now allows distressed companies to seek an agreement with creditors before entering formal bankruptcy and with no prerequisites. That permits the companies to continue operating.[3]

Besides OECD high-income economies, several in East Asia and Pacific also empowered creditors. Indonesia expanded the powers of creditors' committees so they can file and vote on reorganization plans. China adopted a new bankruptcy law in 2007, its first since 1949, significantly strengthening creditors' rights. Secured creditors now rank first in payment priority.[4] Vietnam also gave higher priority to secured creditors, and removed priority for tax claims, when it changed its 1993 bankruptcy law in 2004.

SPEEDING BANKRUPTCY PROCEEDINGS

The second most popular reform feature in closing a business has been introducing or tightening deadlines in court procedures and streamlining appeals. Sixteen economies have undertaken such reforms: Armenia, Bulgaria, Colombia, Estonia, Georgia, Lithuania, Portugal, Puerto Rico, Romania, Saudi Arabia, Serbia, Slovakia, Spain, Tunisia, the United Kingdom and the United States. Imposing time limits facilitates fast resolution of bankruptcy, avoiding deterioration in a company's value over time.

This type of reform has been most popular in Eastern Europe and Central Asia, where no fewer than 8 economies have reformed in this direction in the past 5 years. Romania, Bulgaria and Estonia restricted procedural appeals. In 2004 Romania reduced the time allowed for each appeal from 30 days to 10, shortening the total duration of the bankruptcy procedure from 55 months to 40. Bulgaria restricted opportunities for procedural appeals. Before the reform, the initial decision could be appealed to 2 higher levels of courts. Now only 1 appeal is possible. Estonia allows debt recovery to continue even when there is an appeal, avoiding disruption of the process.

Armenia, Bulgaria, Estonia, Georgia, Lithuania, Serbia and Slovakia introduced or tightened procedural time limits. Armenia passed a new law incorporating time limits into the reorganization procedure. Serbia set strict time limits: claimants have 5 days to raise objections to the resolution, appeals must be made within 8 days after the rul-ing, and the court has 30 days to issue a decision on an appeal. Slovakia tightened time limits, speeding bankruptcy by at least 9 months in 2006.

GETTING THE FOCUS RIGHT

When it comes to reforming bankruptcy regulations, it is often assumed that reorganization is always the best course of action. But in low-income economies reorganization does not always lead to the highest return for creditors.

Mandatory reorganization procedures in some African economies often make matters worse. Take for example Benin, the Republic of Congo and Côte d'Ivoire. All have mandatory reorganization provisions, but their judicial systems lack the capacity to handle these types of cases. Among the main problems: frequent adjournments and courts that fail to hand down timely decisions.

In such systems, reorganization usually ends in liquidation. The time spent in reorganization only delays the process and increases the cost. Reforms that focus on debt enforcement or foreclosure are more likely to show results in those countries. And reforms that ensure properly resourced and well-functioning courts can help a larger number of viable businesses to reorganize successfully.

Overall, economies around the world are reforming toward more efficient bankruptcy systems. In the years since *Doing Business* started collecting data on the topic, the average time to complete bankruptcy proceedings has declined by 4%.

NOTES

1. Djankov and others (2006).
2. Davydenko and Franks (2008) and de Jong and Couwenberg (2007).
3. Beye and Nasr (2008).
4. Only wage claims made before the new law came into effect have priority over secured creditors.

References

Aghion, Philippe, Robin Burgess, Stephen Redding and Fabrizio Zilibotti. Forthcoming. "The Unequal Effects of Liberalization: Evidence from Dismantling the License Raj in India." *American Economic Review.*

Ahmad, Manzoor. 2008. "Reforming Trade Facilitation: Experience of Pakistan." Presentation to Trade Logistics Advisory Program, World Bank, Washington, DC. Pakistan Mission to World Trade Organization, Geneva.

Alesina, Alberto, Silvia Ardagna, Giuseppe Nicoletti and Fabio Schiantarelli. 2005. "Regulation and Investment." *Journal of the European Economic Association* 3 (4): 791–825.

Almeida, Rita, and Pedro Carneiro. Forthcoming. "Enforcement of Labor Regulation and Firm Size." *Journal of Comparative Economics.*

Amin, Mohammad. Forthcoming. "Labor Regulation and Employment in India's Retail Stores." *Journal of Comparative Economics.*

Antunes, Antonio, and Tiago Cavalcanti. 2007. "Start Up Costs, Limited Enforcement, and the Hidden Economy." *European Economic Review* 51 (1): 203–24.

Ardagna, Silvia, and Annamaria Lusardi. 2008. *Explaining International Differences in Entrepreneurship: The Roles of Individual Characteristics and Regulatory Constraints.* NBER Working Paper 14012. Cambridge, MA: National Bureau of Economic Research.

Barseghyan, Levon. 2008. "Entry Costs and Cross-Country Differences in Productivity and Output." *Journal of Economic Growth* 13 (2): 145–67.

Bayerisches Staatsministerium des Innern. 2002. *Erfahrungsbericht BayBO 1998.* Munich.

Benmelech, Effi, and Nittai Bergman. 2008. "Vintage Capital and Creditor Protection." Working Paper, Department of Economics, Harvard University, Cambridge, MA.

Besley, Timothy, and Robin Burgess. 2004. "Can Labor Regulation Hinder Economic Performance? Evidence from India." *Quarterly Journal of Economics* 119(1): 91–134.

Beye, Mema, and Joanna Nasr. 2008. "Repaying Creditors without Imprisoning Debtors." In World Bank, *Celebrating Reform 2008.* Washington, DC: World Bank Group and U.S. Agency for International Development.

Botero, Juan C., Simeon Djankov, Rafael La Porta, Florencio López-de-Silanes and Andrei Shleifer. 2004. "The Regulation of Labor." *Quarterly Journal of Economics* 119 (4): 1339–82.

Brown, Martin, and Christian Zehnder. 2007. "Credit Registries, Relationship Banking, and Loan Repayment." *Journal of Money, Credit and Banking* 39 (8): 1883–918.

Brown, Martin, Tullio Jappelli and Marco Pagano. 2008. "Information Sharing and Credit: Firm-Level Evidence from Transition Countries." Finance Working Paper 201, European Corporate Governance Institute, Brussels.

Bruhn, Miriam. 2008. "License to Sell: The Effect of Business Registration Reform on Entrepreneurial Activity in Mexico." Policy Research Working Paper 4538, World Bank, Washington, DC.

Bureau, Jean-Christophe, Raja Chakir and Jacques Gallezot. 2007. "The Utilization of EU and US Trade Preferences for Developing Countries in the Agri-Food Sector." Working Paper, Trinity College, Dublin.

Chang, Roberto, Linda Kaltani and Norman Loayza. Forthcoming. "Openness Can Be Good for Growth: The Role of Policy Complementarities." *Journal of Development Economics.*

Chari, Amalavoyal. 2008. "License Reform in India: Theory and Evidence." Department of Economics, Yale University, New Haven, CT.

Ciccone, Antonio, and Elias Papaioannou. 2007. "Red Tape and Delayed Entry." *Journal of the European Economic Association* 5 (2–3): 444–58.

Claessens, Stijn, and Enrico Perotti. 2007. "Finance and Inequality: Channels and Evidence." *Journal of Comparative Economics* 35 (4): 748–73.

Clasen, Jochen, and Elke Viebrock. 2008. "Voluntary Unemployment Insurance and Trade Union Membership: Investigating the Connections in Denmark and Sweden." *Journal of Social Policy* 37 (3): 433–51.

Coma-Cunill, Roger, and Marie Delion. 2008. "Honduras: Slashing the Time to Register a Property from 18 Months to 15 Days." In World Bank, *Celebrating Reform 2008.* Washington, DC: World Bank Group and U.S. Agency for International Development.

Cruz-Osorio, Jose, and Gabriela Enrigue. 2008. "Compare, Compete, and Cooperate: How Mexican States Improve Regulation with the Help of Subnational Doing Business." Subnational Doing Business Case Studies Series, World Bank Group, Washington, DC.

Cuñat, Alejandro, and Marc Melitz. 2007. *Volatility, Labor Market Flexibility, and the Pattern of Comparative Advantage.* NBER Working Paper 13062. Cambridge, MA: National Bureau of Economic Research.

Dabla-Norris, Era, Mark Gradstein and Gabriela Inchauste. 2008. "What Causes Firms to Hide Output? The Determinants of Informality." *Journal of Development Economics* 85 (1): 1–27.

Dahya, Jay, Orlin Dimitrov and John McConnell. 2008. "Dominant Shareholders, Corporate Boards, and Corporate Value: A Cross-Country Analysis." *Journal of Financial Economics* 87 (1): 73–100.

Davydenko, Sergei, and Julian Franks. 2008. "Do Bankruptcy Codes Matter? A Study of Defaults in France, Germany and the UK." *Journal of Finance* 63 (2): 565–608.

de Jong, Abe, and Oscar Couwenberg. 2007. "Costs and Recovery Rates in the Dutch Liquidation-Based Bankruptcy System." Working paper, Faculty of Law, University of Groningen.

de Soto, Hernando. 2000. *The Mystery of Capital: Why Capital Triumphs in the West and Fails Everywhere Else.* New York: Basic Books.

Djankov, Simeon, and Rita Ramalho. 2008. "The Regulation of Labor in Developing Countries." Working paper, Global Indicators and Analysis Department, World Bank, Washington, DC.

Djankov, Simeon, Caroline Freund and Cong Pham. Forthcoming. "Trading on Time." *Review of Economics and Statistics.*

Djankov, Simeon, Caralee McLiesh and Andrei Shleifer. 2007. "Private Credit in 129 Countries." *Journal of Financial Economics* 84 (2): 299–329.

Djankov, Simeon, Oliver Hart, Caralee McLiesh and Andrei Shleifer. 2006. *Debt Enforcement around the World.* NBER Working Paper 12807. Cambridge, MA: National Bureau of Economic Research.

Djankov, Simeon, Rafael La Porta, Florencio López-de-Silanes and Andrei Shleifer. 2002. "The Regulation of Entry." *Quarterly Journal of Economics* 117 (1): 1–37.

———. 2003. "Courts." *Quarterly Journal of Economics* 118 (2): 453–517.

———. 2008. "The Law and Economics of Self-Dealing." *Journal of Financial Economics* 88 (3): 430–65.

Djankov, Simeon, Darshini Manraj, Caralee McLiesh and Rita Ramalho. 2005. "Doing Business Indicators: Why Aggregate, and How to Do It." World Bank, Washington, DC. http://www.doingbusiness.org/documents/how_to_aggregate.pdf.

Djankov, Simeon, Tim Ganser, Caralee McLiesh, Rita Ramalho and Andrei Shleifer. 2008. *The Effect of Corporate Taxes on Investment and Entrepreneurship.* NBER Working Paper 13756. Cambridge, MA: National Bureau of Economic Research.

Doidge, Craig, Andrew Karolyi and René M. Stulz. 2007. "Why Do Countries Matter So Much for Corporate Governance?" *Journal of Financial Economics* 86 (1): 1–39.

Ellis, Amanda, Claire Manuel and Mark Blackden. 2006. *Gender and Economic Growth in Uganda: Unleashing the Power of Women.* Directions in Development series. Washington, DC: World Bank.

Eurobarometer. 2006. *Europeans and Mobility: First Results of an EU-Wide Survey.* http://ec.europa.eu/employment_social/workersmobility_2006/uploaded_files/documents/FIRST%20RESULTS_Web%20version_06.02.06.pdf.

Feldmann, Horst. 2008. "Business Regulation and Labor Market Performance around the World." *Journal of Regulatory Economics* 33 (2): 201–35.

Fisman, Raymond, and Virginia Sarria-Allende. 2004. *Regulation of Entry and the Distortion of Industrial Organization.* NBER Working Paper 10929. Cambridge, MA: National Bureau of Economic Research.

Freund, Caroline, and Bineswaree Bolaky. Forthcoming. "Trade, Regulation and Income." *Journal of Development Economics.*

Geginat, Carolin, and Jana Malinska. 2008. "Czech Republic: Creating a New Profession from Scratch." In World Bank, *Celebrating Reform 2008.* Washington, DC: World Bank Group and U.S. Agency for International Development.

Hacibeyoglu, Cemile. 2008. "Ghana: When Enough Is Enough." In World Bank, *Celebrating Reform 2008.* Washington, DC: World Bank Group and U.S. Agency for International Development.

Haidar, Jamal Ibrahim. 2008. "Egypt: How to Raise Revenues by Lowering Fees." In World Bank, *Celebrating Reform 2008.* Washington, DC: World Bank Group and U.S. Agency for International Development.

Helpman, Elhanan, and Oleg Itskhoki. 2007. *Labor Market Rigidities, Trade, and Unemployment.* NBER Working Paper 13365. Cambridge, MA: National Bureau of Economic Research.

Helpman, Elhanan, Marc Melitz and Yona Rubinstein. 2008. "Estimating Trade Flows: Trading Partners and Trading Volumes." *Quarterly Journal of Economics* 123 (2): 441–87.

Hertveldt, Sabine. 2008. "Rwanda: Pragmatism Leads the Way in Setting Up Specialized Commercial Court." In World Bank, *Celebrating Reform 2008.* Washington, DC: World Bank Group and U.S. Agency for International Development.

Ivanova, Anna, Michael Keen and Alexander Klemm. 2005. "The Russian Flat Tax Reform." IMF Working Paper 5/16, International Monetary Fund, Washington, DC.

Johns, Melissa, and Jean Michel Lobet. 2007. "Protecting Investors from Self-Dealing." In World Bank, *Celebrating Reform 2007.* Washington, DC: World Bank Group and U.S. Agency for International Development.

Kaplan, David. Forthcoming. "Job Creation and Labor Reform in Latin America." *Journal of Comparative Economics.*

Kaplan, David, Eduardo Piedra and Enrique Seira. 2008. "Entry Regulation and Business Start-Ups: Evidence from Mexico." Working Paper, Enterprise Analysis Unit, World Bank, Washington, DC.

Klapper, Leora, Luc Laeven and Raghuram Rajan. 2006. "Entry Regulation as a Barrier to Entrepreneurship." *Journal of Financial Economics* 82 (3): 591–629.

Klapper, Leora, Raphael Amit, Mauro F. Guillén and Juan Manuel Quesada Delgado. 2008. "Entrepreneurship and Firm Formation across Countries." Policy Research Working Paper 4313, World Bank, Washington, DC.

Lobet, Jean Michel. 2008. "Vietnam: Protecting Minority Shareholders to Boost Investment." In World Bank, *Celebrating Reform 2008.* Washington, DC: World Bank Group and U.S. Agency for International Development.

Marechal, Valerie, and Rachel (Raha) Shahid-Saless. 2008. "Peru: Bringing More Credit to the Private Sector." In World Bank, *Celebrating Reform 2008.* Washington, DC: World Bank Group and U.S. Agency for International Development.

Masatlioglu, Yusufcan, and Jamele Rigolini. 2008. "Informality Traps." Department of Economics, University of Michigan, Ann Arbor.

McKinsey & Company. 2002. *McKinsey Global Investor Opinion Survey on Corporate Governance.* http://www.mckinsey.com/clientservice/organizationleadership/service/corpgovernance/pdf/globalinvestoropinionsurvey2002.pdf.

Miceli, Thomas, and Joseph Kieyah. 2003. "The Economics of Land Title Reform." *Journal of Comparative Economics* 31 (2): 246–56.

Monteiro, Joana, and Juliano Assunção. 2008. "Outgoing the Shadows: Estimating the Impact of Bureaucratic Simplification and Tax Cuts on Informality and Investment." Department of Economics, Pontifícia Universidade Católica, Rio de Janeiro.

Narayan, Deepa, Robert Chambers, Meera Kaul Shah and Patti Petesh. 2000. *Voices of the Poor: Crying Out for Change.* Washington, DC: World Bank.

Nordas, Hildegunn, Enrico Pinali and Massimo Geloso-Grosso. 2006. "Logistics and Time as a Trade Barrier." OECD Trade Policy Working Paper 35, Organisation for Economic Co-operation and Development, Paris.

Perotti, Enrico, and Paolo Volpin. 2004. "Lobbying on Entry." CEPR Discussion Paper 4519, Centre for Economic Policy Research, London.

PricewaterhouseCoopers. 2005. "The Economic Impact of Accelerating Permit Processes on Local Development and Government Revenues." Report prepared for American Institute of Architects, Washington, DC.

Ramos, Camille. 2008. "One-Stop Shopping in Portugal." In World Bank, *Celebrating Reform 2008.* Washington, DC: World Bank Group and U.S. Agency for International Development.

Sadikov, Azim. 2007. "Border and Behind-the-Border Trade Barriers and Country Exports." IMF Working Paper 7/292, International Monetary Fund, Washington, DC.

Safavian, Mehnaz, and Siddharth Sharma. 2007. "When Do Creditor Rights Work?" *Journal of Comparative Economics* 35 (3): 484–508.

Schneider, Friedrich. 2005. "The Informal Sector in 145 Countries." Department of Economics, University of Linz.

Sitta, Samuel. 2005. "Integrity Environment and Investment Promotion: The Case of Tanzania." Paper presented at the Organisation for Economic Co-operation and Development, New Partnership for

Africa's Development and Transparency International conference Alliance for Integrity—Government & Business Roles in Enhancing African Standards of Living, Addis Ababa, March 7–8. Tanzania Investment Center, Dar es Salaam.

van Stel, André, David Storey and Roy Thurik. 2007. "The Effect of Business Regulations on Nascent and Young Business Entrepreneurship." *Small Business Economics* 28 (2): 171–86.

Wangda, Pema. Forthcoming. *Reforming the Labor Administration in Bhutan*. IFC Smart Lesson Series. Washington, DC: World Bank Group.

WEF (World Economic Forum). 2007. *The Global Competitiveness Report 2007–2008*. New York: Palgrave Macmillan.

Wojkowska, Ewa. 2006. "Doing Justice: How Informal Justice Systems Can Contribute." Oslo Governance Centre, United Nations Development Programme, Oslo.

World Bank. 2003. *Doing Business in 2004: Understanding Regulation*. Washington, DC: World Bank Group.

———. 2004. *Doing Business in 2005: Removing Obstacles to Growth*. Washington, DC: World Bank Group.

———. 2005. *Doing Business in 2006: Creating Jobs*. Washington, DC: World Bank Group.

———. 2006a. *Doing Business in Mexico 2007: Comparing Regulation in the 31 States and Mexico City*. Washington, DC: World Bank Group.

———. 2006b. *Doing Business 2007: How to Reform*. Washington, DC: World Bank Group.

———. 2006c. "Vietnam: Report on the Observance of Standards and Codes (ROSC)." World Bank Group, Washington, DC.

———. 2007a. *Celebrating Reform 2007*. Washington, DC: World Bank Group and U.S. Agency for International Development.

———. 2007b. *Doing Business 2008: Comparing Regulation in 178 Economies*. Washington, DC: World Bank Group.

———. 2007c. *Reforming Collateral Laws and Registries: International Best Practices and the Case of China*. Washington, DC: World Bank Group. http://www.ifc.org/ifcext/fias.nsf/Content/FIAS_Resources_Country_Reports.

———. 2008a. *Doing Business: Women in Africa*. Washington, DC: World Bank Group.

———. 2008b. *World Development Indicators 2008*. Washington, DC: World Bank Group.

World Bank Independent Evaluation Group. 2008. *Doing Business: An Independent Evaluation—Taking the Measure of the World Bank–IFC Doing Business Indicators*. Washington, DC: World Bank Group.

WTO (World Trade Organization). 2005. "Customs Border Cooperation between Norway, Sweden and Finland." Communication from Norway. Document TN/TF/W/48. Negotiating Group on Trade Facilitation, WTO, Geneva.

Yakovlev, Evgeny, and Ekaterina Zhuravskaya. 2008. "Deregulation of Business." New Economic School, Moscow. http://ssrn.com/abstract=965838.

Data notes

The indicators presented and analyzed in *Doing Business* measure business regulation and the protection of property rights—and their effect on businesses, especially small and medium-size domestic firms. First, the indicators document the degree of regulation, such as the number of procedures to start a business or to register and transfer commercial property. Second, they gauge regulatory outcomes, such as the time and cost to enforce a contract, go through bankruptcy or trade across borders. Third, they measure the extent of legal protections of property, for example, the protections of investors against looting by company directors or the range of assets that can be used as collateral according to secured transactions laws. Fourth, they measure the flexibility of employment regulation. Finally, a set of indicators documents the tax burden on businesses. For details on how the rankings on these indicators are constructed, see Ease of doing business, page 79.

The data for all sets of indicators in *Doing Business 2009* are for June 2008.[1] Three new economies—The Bahamas, Bahrain and Qatar—were added to the sample, now comprising 181 economies.

METHODOLOGY

The *Doing Business* data are collected in a standardized way. To start, the *Doing Business* team, with academic advisers, designs a survey. The survey uses a simple business case to ensure comparability across economies and over time—with assumptions about the legal form of the business, its size, its location and the nature of its operations. Surveys are administered through more than 6,700 local experts, including lawyers, business consultants, accountants, freight forwarders, government officials and other professionals routinely administering or advising on legal and regulatory requirements (table 12.1). These experts have several (typically 4) rounds of interaction with the *Doing Business* team, involving conference calls, written correspondence and visits by the team. For *Doing Business 2009* team members visited 73 economies to verify data and recruit respondents. The data from surveys are subjected to numerous tests for robustness, which lead to revisions or expansions of the information collected.

The *Doing Business* methodology offers several advantages. It is transparent, using factual information about what laws and regulations say and allowing multiple interactions with local respondents to clarify potential misinterpretations of questions. Having representative samples of respondents is not an issue, as the texts of the relevant laws and regulations are collected and answers checked for accuracy. The methodology is inexpensive and easily replicable, so data can be collected in a large sample of economies. Because standard assumptions are used in the data collection, comparisons and benchmarks are valid across economies. Finally, the data not only highlight the extent of specific regulatory obstacles to doing business but also identify their source and point to what might be reformed.

LIMITS TO WHAT IS MEASURED

The *Doing Business* methodology has 5 limitations that should be considered when interpreting the data. First, the collected data refer to businesses in the economy's largest business city and may not be representative of regulation in other parts of the economy. To address this limitation, subnational *Doing Business* indicators were created for 6 economies in 2007/08: China, Colombia, Egypt, Morocco, Nigeria and the Philippines.[2] Six other subnational studies are under way, in Central Asia, Southeast Europe, Indonesia, the Russian Federation, Southeast Asia and Ukraine. And some existing studies are updated annually, such as those in India, Mexico and Pakistan. These subnational studies point to significant differences in the speed of reform and the ease of doing business across cities in the same economy.

Second, the data often focus on a specific business form—generally a limited liability company (or its legal equivalent) of a specified size—and may not be representative of the regulation on other businesses, for example, sole proprietorships. Third, transactions described in a standardized case scenario refer to a specific set of issues and may not represent the full set of issues a business encounters. Fourth, the measures of time involve an element of judgment by the expert respondents. When sources indicate different estimates, the time indicators reported in *Doing Business* represent the median values of several responses given under the assumptions of the standardized case.

Finally, the methodology assumes that a business has full information on what is required and does not waste time when completing procedures. In practice, completing a procedure may take longer if the business lacks information or is unable to follow up promptly.

TABLE 12.1

How many experts does *Doing Business* consult?

Indicator set	Number of contributors
Starting a business	1,166
Dealing with construction permits	739
Employing workers	810
Registering property	907
Getting credit	1,033
Protecting investors	653
Paying taxes	862
Trading across borders	817
Enforcing contracts	767
Closing a business	727

Alternatively, the business may choose to disregard some burdensome procedures. For both reasons the time delays reported in *Doing Business 2009* could differ from the perceptions of entrepreneurs reported in the World Bank Enterprise Surveys or other perception surveys.

CHANGES IN WHAT IS MEASURED

The methodology for one of the *Doing Business* topics—getting credit—improved this year. Three main changes were made, affecting only the strength of legal rights index. First, a standardized case scenario with specific assumptions was introduced to bring this indicator into line with other *Doing Business* indicators. Second, the indicator now focuses not on tangible movable collateral, such as equipment, but on revolving movable collateral, such as accounts receivable and inventory. Third, the indicator no longer considers whether management remains in place during a reorganization procedure, better accommodating economies that adopt reorganization procedures similar to Chapter 11 reorganization or *redressement* procedures in civil law systems.

DATA CHALLENGES AND REVISIONS

Most laws and regulations underlying the *Doing Business* data are available on the *Doing Business* website at http://www .doingbusiness.org. All the sample surveys and the details underlying the indicators are also published on the website. Questions on the methodology and challenges to data can be submitted through the website's "Ask a Question" function at http://www.doingbusiness.org.

Doing Business publishes 8,900 indicators each year. To create these indicators, the team measures more than 52,000 data points, each of which is made available on the *Doing Business* website. Data time series for each indicator and economy are available on the website, beginning with the first year the indicator or economy was included in the report. To provide a comparable time series for research, the data set is back-calculated to adjust for changes in methodology and any revisions in data due to corrections. The website also makes available all original data sets used for background papers. The correction rate between *Doing Business 2008* and *Doing Business 2009* was 6%.

STARTING A BUSINESS

Doing Business records all procedures that are officially required for an entrepreneur to start up and formally operate an industrial or commercial business. These include obtaining all necessary licenses and permits and completing any required notifications, verifications or inscriptions for the company and employees with relevant authorities (table 12.2).

After a study of laws, regulations and publicly available information on business entry, a detailed list of procedures is developed, along with the time and cost of complying with each procedure under normal circumstances and the paid-in minimum capital requirements. Subsequently, local incorporation lawyers and government officials complete and verify the data.

Information is also collected on the sequence in which procedures are to be completed and whether procedures may be carried out simultaneously. It is assumed that any required information is readily available and that all agencies involved in the start-up process function without corruption. If answers by local experts differ, inquiries continue until the data are reconciled.

To make the data comparable across economies, several assumptions about the business and the procedures are used.

ASSUMPTIONS ABOUT THE BUSINESS

The business:
- Is a limited liability company. If there is more than one type of limited liability company in the economy, the limited liability form most popular among domestic firms is chosen. Information on the most popular form is obtained from incorporation lawyers or the statistical office.
- Operates in the economy's largest business city.
- Is 100% domestically owned and has 5 owners, none of whom is a legal entity.
- Has start-up capital of 10 times income per capita at the end of 2007, paid in cash.

Economy characteristics

GROSS NATIONAL INCOME (GNI) PER CAPITA

Doing Business 2009 reports 2007 income per capita as published in the World Bank's *World Development Indicators 2008*. Income is calculated using the Atlas method (current US$). For cost indicators expressed as a percentage of income per capita, 2007 GNI in local currency units is used as the denominator. GNI data were not available from the World Bank for The Bahamas, Bahrain, Puerto Rico, Qatar and the United Arab Emirates. In these cases GDP or GNP per capita data and growth rates from the International Monetary Fund's World Economic Outlook database, the Economist Intelligence Unit 2008 country profiles

and the U.S. State Department 2008 country profiles were used.

REGION AND INCOME GROUP

Doing Business uses the World Bank regional and income group classifications, available at http://www .worldbank.org/data/countryclass. Throughout the report the term *rich economies* refers to the high-income group, *middle-income economies* to the upper-middle-income group and *poor economies* to the lower-middle-income and low-income groups.

POPULATION

Doing Business 2009 reports midyear 2007 population statistics as published in *World Development Indicators 2008*.

TABLE 12.2
What does starting a business measure?

Procedures to legally start and operate a company *(number)*
· Preregistration (for example, name verification or reservation, notarization)
· Registration in the economy's largest business city
· Postregistration (for example, social security registration, company seal)

Time required to complete each procedure *(calendar days)*
· Does not include time spent gathering information
· Each procedure starts on a separate day
· Procedure completed once final document is received
· No prior contact with officials

Cost required to complete each procedure *(% of income per capita)*
· Official costs only, no bribes
· No professional fees unless services required by law

Paid-in minimum capital *(% of income per capita)*
· Deposited in a bank or with a notary before registration begins

Source: Doing Business database.

- Performs general industrial or commercial activities, such as the production or sale to the public of products or services. The business does not perform foreign trade activities and does not handle products subject to a special tax regime, for example, liquor or tobacco. It is not using heavily polluting production processes.
- Leases the commercial plant and offices and is not a proprietor of real estate.
- Does not qualify for investment incentives or any special benefits.
- Has at least 10 and up to 50 employees 1 month after the commencement of operations, all of them nationals.
- Has a turnover of at least 100 times income per capita.
- Has a company deed 10 pages long.

PROCEDURES

A procedure is defined as any interaction of the company founders with external parties (for example, government agencies, lawyers, auditors or notaries). Interactions between company founders or company officers and employees are not counted as procedures. Procedures that must be completed in the same building but in different offices are counted as separate procedures. If founders have to visit the same office several times for different sequential procedures, each is counted separately. The founders are assumed to complete all procedures themselves, without middlemen, facilitators, accountants or lawyers, unless the use of such a third party is mandated by law. If the services of professionals are required, procedures conducted by such professionals on behalf of the company are counted separately. Each electronic procedure is counted separately. If 2 procedures can be completed through the same website but require separate filings, they are counted as 2 procedures.

Both pre- and postincorporation procedures that are officially required for an entrepreneur to formally operate a business are recorded.

Procedures required for official correspondence or transactions with public agencies are also included. For example, if a company seal or stamp is required on official documents, such as tax declarations, obtaining the seal or stamp is counted. Similarly, if a company must open a bank account before registering for sales tax or value added tax, this transaction is included as a procedure. Shortcuts are counted only if they fulfill 4 criteria: they are legal, they are available to the general public, they are used by the majority of companies, and avoiding them causes substantial delays.

Only procedures required of all businesses are covered. Industry-specific procedures are excluded. For example, procedures to comply with environmental regulations are included only when they apply to all businesses conducting general commercial or industrial activities. Procedures that the company undergoes to connect to electricity, water, gas and waste disposal services are not included.

TIME

Time is recorded in calendar days. The measure captures the median duration that incorporation lawyers indicate is necessary to complete a procedure with minimum follow-up with government agencies and no extra payments. It is assumed that the minimum time required for each procedure is 1 day. Although procedures may take place simultaneously, they cannot start on the same day (that is, simultaneous procedures start on consecutive days). A procedure is considered completed once the company has received the final document, such as the company registration certificate or tax number. If a procedure can be accelerated for an additional cost, the fastest procedure is chosen. It is assumed that the entrepreneur does not waste time and commits to completing each remaining procedure without delay. The time that the entrepreneur spends on gathering information is ignored. It is assumed that the entrepreneur is aware of all entry regulations and their sequence from the beginning but has had no prior contact with any of the officials.

COST

Cost is recorded as a percentage of the economy's income per capita. It includes all official fees and fees for legal or professional services if such services are required by law. Fees for purchasing and legalizing company books are included if these transactions are required by law. The company law, the commercial code and specific regulations and fee schedules are used as sources for calculating costs. In the absence of fee schedules, a government officer's estimate is taken as an official source. In the absence of a government officer's estimate, estimates of incorporation lawyers are used. If several incorporation lawyers provide different estimates, the median reported value is applied. In all cases the cost excludes bribes.

PAID-IN MINIMUM CAPITAL

The paid-in minimum capital requirement reflects the amount that the entrepreneur needs to deposit in a bank or with a notary before registration and up to 3 months following incorporation and is recorded as a percentage of the economy's income per capita. The amount is typically specified in the commercial code or the company law. Many economies have a minimum capital requirement but allow businesses to pay only a part of it before registration, with the rest to be paid after the first year of operation. In Germany in June 2008, the minimum capital requirement for limited liability companies was €25,000, of which at least €12,500 was payable before registration. The paid-in minimum capital recorded for Germany is therefore €12,500, or 42.2% of income per capita. In Serbia the minimum capital requirement was €500, of which only half needed to be paid before registration. The paid-in minimum capital recorded for Serbia is therefore €250, or 7% of income per capita.

The data details on starting a business can be found for each economy at http://www.doingbusiness.org. This methodology was developed in Djankov and others (2002) and is adopted here with minor changes.

DEALING WITH CONSTRUCTION PERMITS

Doing Business records all procedures required for a business in the construction industry to build a standardized warehouse. These procedures include submitting all relevant project-specific documents (for example, building plans and site maps) to the authorities; obtaining all necessary clearances, licenses, permits and certificates; completing all

TABLE 12.3

What does dealing with construction permits measure?

Procedures to legally build a warehouse (number)

- Submitting all relevant documents and obtaining all necessary clearances, licenses, permits and certificates
- Completing all required notifications and receiving all necessary inspections
- Obtaining utility connections for electricity, water, sewerage and a land telephone line
- Registering the warehouse after its completion (if required for use as collateral or for transfer of warehouse)

Time required to complete each procedure (calendar days)

- Does not include time spent gathering information
- Each procedure starts on a separate day
- Procedure completed once final document is received
- No prior contact with officials

Cost required to complete each procedure (% of income per capita)

- Official costs only, no bribes

Source: Doing Business database.

required notifications; and receiving all necessary inspections. *Doing Business* also records procedures for obtaining connections for electricity, water, sewerage and a fixed land line. Procedures necessary to register the property so that it can be used as collateral or transferred to another entity are also counted (table 12.3). The survey divides the process of building a warehouse into distinct procedures and calculates the time and cost of completing each procedure in practice under normal circumstances.

Information is collected from experts in construction licensing, including architects, construction lawyers, construction firms, utility service providers and public officials who deal with building regulations, including approvals and inspections. To make the data comparable across economies, several assumptions about the business, the warehouse project and the utility connections are used.

ASSUMPTIONS ABOUT THE CONSTRUCTION COMPANY

The business (BuildCo):
- Is a limited liability company.
- Operates in the economy's largest business city.
- Is 100% domestically and privately owned.
- Has 5 owners, none of whom is a legal entity.
- Is fully licensed and insured to carry out construction projects, such as building warehouses.

- Has 60 builders and other employees, all of them nationals with the technical expertise and professional experience necessary to obtain construction permits and approvals.
- Has at least 1 employee who is a licensed architect and registered with the local association of architects.
- Has paid all taxes and taken out all necessary insurance applicable to its general business activity (for example, accidental insurance for construction workers and third-person liability insurance).
- Owns the land on which the warehouse is built.

ASSUMPTIONS ABOUT THE WAREHOUSE

The warehouse:
- Will be used for general storage activities, such as storage of books or stationery. The warehouse will not be used for any goods requiring special conditions, such as food, chemicals or pharmaceuticals.
- Has 2 stories, both above ground, with a total surface of approximately 1,300.6 square meters (14,000 square feet). Each floor is 3 meters (9 feet, 10 inches) high.
- Has road access and is located in the periurban area of the economy's largest business city (that is, on the fringes of the city but still within its official limits).

- Is not located in a special economic or industrial zone. The zoning requirements for warehouses are met by building in an area where similar warehouses can be found.
- Is located on a land plot of 929 square meters (10,000 square feet) that is 100% owned by BuildCo and is accurately registered in the cadastre and land registry.
- Is a new construction (there was no previous construction on the land).
- Has complete architectural and technical plans prepared by a licensed architect.
- Will include all technical equipment required to make the warehouse fully operational.
- Will take 30 weeks to construct (excluding all delays due to administrative and regulatory requirements).

ASSUMPTIONS ABOUT THE UTILITY CONNECTIONS

The electricity connection:
- Is 10 meters (32 feet, 10 inches) from the main electricity network.
- Is a medium-tension, 3-phase, 4-wire Y, 140-kVA connection. Three-phase service is available in the construction area.
- Will be delivered by an overhead service, unless overhead service is not available in the periurban area.
- Consists of a simple hookup unless installation of a private substation (transformer) or extension of network is required.
- Requires the installation of only one electricity meter.

BuildCo is assumed to have a licensed electrician on its team to complete the internal wiring for the warehouse.

The water and sewerage connection:
- Is 10 meters (32 feet, 10 inches) from the existing water source and sewer tap.
- Does not require water for fire protection reasons; a fire extinguishing system (dry system) will be used instead. If a wet fire protection system is required by law, it is assumed that the water demand specified below also covers the water needed for fire protection.
- Has an average water use of 662 liters (175 gallons) a day and an average wastewater flow of 568 liters (150 gallons) a day.
- Has a peak water use of 1,325 liters (350 gallons) a day and a peak wastewater flow of 1,136 liters (300 gallons) a day.
- Will have a constant level of water demand and wastewater flow throughout the year.

The telephone connection:
- Is 10 meters (32 feet, 10 inches) from the main telephone network.
- Is a fixed land line.

PROCEDURES

A procedure is any interaction of the company's employees or managers with external parties, including government agencies, notaries, the land registry, the cadastre, utility companies, public and private inspectors and technical experts apart from in-house architects and engineers. Interactions between company employees, such as development of the warehouse plans and inspections conducted by employees, are not counted as procedures. Procedures that the company undergoes to connect to electricity, water, sewerage and telephone services are included. All procedures that are legally or in practice required for building a warehouse are counted, even if they may be avoided in exceptional cases.

TIME

Time is recorded in calendar days. The measure captures the median duration that local experts indicate is necessary to complete a procedure in practice. It is assumed that the minimum time required for each procedure is 1 day. Although procedures may take place simultaneously, they cannot start on the same day (that is, simultaneous procedures start on consecutive days). If a procedure can be accelerated legally for an additional cost, the fastest procedure is chosen. It is assumed that BuildCo does not waste time and commits to completing each remaining procedure without delay. The time that BuildCo spends on gathering information is ignored. It is assumed that BuildCo is aware of all building requirements and their sequence from the beginning.

COST

Cost is recorded as a percentage of the economy's income per capita. Only official costs are recorded. All the fees associated with completing the procedures to legally build a warehouse are recorded, including those associated with obtaining land use approvals and preconstruction design clearances; receiving inspections before, during and after construction; getting utility connections; and registering the warehouse property. Nonrecurring taxes required for the completion of the warehouse project also are recorded. The building code, information from local experts and specific regulations and fee schedules are used as sources for costs. If several local partners provide different estimates, the median reported value is used.

The data details on dealing with construction permits can be found for each economy at http://www.doing business.org.

EMPLOYING WORKERS

Doing Business measures the regulation of employment, specifically as it affects the hiring and firing of workers and the rigidity of working hours.

In 2007 improvements were made to align the methodology for the employing workers indicators with the International Labour Organization (ILO) conventions. Only 4 of the 188 ILO conventions cover areas measured by *Doing Business*: employee termination, weekend work, holiday with pay and night work. The methodology was adapted to ensure full consistency with these 4 conventions. It is possible for an economy to receive the highest score on the ease of employing workers and comply with all relevant ILO conventions (specifically, the 4 related to *Doing Business*)—and no economy can achieve a better score by failing to comply with these conventions.

The ILO conventions covering areas related to the employing workers indicators do not include the ILO core labor standards—8 conventions covering the right to collective bargaining, the elimination of forced labor, the abolition of child labor and equitable treatment in employment practices. *Doing Business* supports the ILO core labor standards and this year includes information on their ratification. *Doing Business* does not measure or rank ratification or compliance with ILO conventions.

The data on employing workers are based on a detailed survey of employment regulations that is completed by local lawyers and public officials. Employment laws and regulations as well as secondary sources are reviewed to ensure accuracy. To make the data comparable across economies, several assumptions about the worker and the business are used.

ASSUMPTIONS ABOUT THE WORKER

The worker:

- Is a 42-year-old, nonexecutive, full-time, male employee.
- Has worked at the same company for 20 years.
- Earns a salary plus benefits equal to the economy's average wage during the entire period of his employment.
- Is a lawful citizen who belongs to the same race and religion as the majority of the economy's population.
- Resides in the economy's largest business city.
- Is not a member of a labor union, unless membership is mandatory.

ASSUMPTIONS ABOUT THE BUSINESS

The business:

- Is a limited liability company.
- Operates in the economy's largest business city.
- Is 100% domestically owned.
- Operates in the manufacturing sector.
- Has 201 employees.

- Is subject to collective bargaining agreements in economies where such agreements cover more than half the manufacturing sector and apply even to firms not party to them.
- Abides by every law and regulation but does not grant workers more benefits than mandated by law, regulation or (if applicable) collective bargaining agreement.

RIGIDITY OF EMPLOYMENT INDEX

The rigidity of employment index is the average of 3 subindices: a difficulty of hiring index, a rigidity of hours index and a difficulty of firing index (table 12.4). All the subindices have several components. And all take values between 0 and 100, with higher values indicating more rigid regulation.

The difficulty of hiring index measures (i) whether fixed-term contracts are prohibited for permanent tasks; (ii) the maximum cumulative duration of fixed-term contracts; and (iii) the ratio of the minimum wage for a trainee or first-time employee to the average value added per worker.[4] An economy is assigned a score of 1 if fixed-term contracts are prohibited for permanent tasks and a score of 0 if they can be used for any task. A score of 1 is assigned if the maximum cumulative duration of

fixed-term contracts is less than 3 years; 0.5 if it is 3 years or more but less than 5 years; and 0 if fixed-term contracts can last 5 years or more. Finally, a score of 1 is assigned if the ratio of the minimum wage to the average value added per worker is 0.75 or more; 0.67 for a ratio of 0.50 or more but less than 0.75; 0.33 for a ratio of 0.25 or more but less than 0.50; and 0 for a ratio of less than 0.25. In the Central African Republic, for example, fixed-term contracts are prohibited for permanent tasks (a score of 1), and they can be used for a maximum of 4 years (a score of 0.5). The ratio of the mandated minimum wage to the value added per worker is 0.62 (a score of 0.67). Averaging the 3 values and scaling the index to 100 gives the Central African Republic a score of 72.

The rigidity of hours index has 5 components: (i) whether night work is unrestricted; (ii) whether weekend work is unrestricted; (iii) whether the workweek can consist of 5.5 days; (iv) whether the workweek can extend to 50 hours or more (including overtime) for 2 months a year to respond to a seasonal increase in production; and (v) whether paid annual vacation is 21 working days or fewer. For each of these questions, if the answer is no, the economy is assigned a score of 1; otherwise a score of 0 is as-

TABLE 12.4
What does employing workers measure?

Difficulty of hiring index (0–100)

- Applicability and maximum duration of fixed-term contracts
- Minimum wage for trainee or first-time employee

Rigidity of hours index (0–100)

- Restrictions on night work and weekend work
- Allowed maximum length of the workweek in days and hours, including overtime
- Paid annual vacation days

Difficulty of firing index (0–100)

- Notification and approval requirements for termination of a redundant worker or group of redundant workers
- Obligation to reassign or retrain and priority rules for redundancy and reemployment

Rigidity of employment index (0–100)

- Simple average of the difficulty of hiring, rigidity of hours and difficulty of firing indices

Firing cost (weeks of salary)

- Notice requirements, severance payments and penalties due when terminating a redundant worker, expressed in weeks of salary

Source: Doing Business database.

signed. For example, the Czech Republic imposes restrictions on night work (a score of 1) and weekend work (a score of 1), allows 6-day workweeks (a score of 0), permits 50-hour workweeks for 2 months (a score of 0) and requires paid vacation of 20 working days (a score of 0). Averaging the scores and scaling the result to 100 gives a final index of 40 for the Czech Republic.

The difficulty of firing index has 8 components: (i) whether redundancy is disallowed as a basis for terminating workers; (ii) whether the employer needs to notify a third party (such as a government agency) to terminate 1 redundant worker; (iii) whether the employer needs to notify a third party to terminate a group of 25 redundant workers; (iv) whether the employer needs approval from a third party to terminate 1 redundant worker; (v) whether the employer needs approval from a third party to terminate a group of 25 redundant workers; (vi) whether the law requires the employer to reassign or retrain a worker before making the worker redundant; (vii) whether priority rules apply for redundancies; and (viii) whether priority rules apply for reemployment. For the first question an answer of yes for workers of any income level gives a score of 10 and means that the rest of the questions do not apply. An answer of yes to question (iv) gives a score of 2. For every other question, if the answer is yes, a score of 1 is assigned; otherwise a score of 0 is given. Questions (i) and (iv), as the most restrictive regulations, have greater weight in the construction of the index.

In Tunisia, for example, redundancy is allowed as grounds for termination (a score of 0). An employer has to both notify a third party (a score of 1) and obtain its approval (a score of 2) to terminate a single redundant worker, and has to both notify a third party (a score of 1) and obtain its approval (a score of 1) to terminate a group of 25 redundant workers. The law mandates retraining or alternative placement before termination (a score of 1). There are priority rules for termination (a score of 1) and reemployment (a score of 1). Adding the scores and scaling to 100 gives a final index of 80.

FIRING COST

The firing cost indicator measures the cost of advance notice requirements, severance payments and penalties due when terminating a redundant worker, expressed in weeks of salary. If the firing cost adds up to 8 or fewer weeks of salary, a score of 0 is assigned for the purposes of calculating the aggregate ease of doing business ranking. If the cost adds up to more than 8 weeks of salary, the score is the number of weeks. One month is recorded as 4 and 1/3 weeks. In Mauritius, for example, an employer is required to give 3 months' notice before a redundancy termination, and the severance pay for a worker with 20 years of service equals 5 months of wages. No penalty is levied. Altogether, the employer pays the equivalent of 35 weeks of salary to dismiss the worker.

The data details on employing workers can be found for each economy at http://www.doingbusiness.org. This methodology was developed in Botero and others (2004) and is adopted here with minor changes.

REGISTERING PROPERTY

Doing Business records the full sequence of procedures necessary for a business (buyer) to purchase a property from another business (seller) and to transfer the property title to the buyer's name so that the buyer can use the property for expanding its business, use the property as collateral in taking new loans or, if necessary, sell the property to another business (table 12.5). The process starts with obtaining the necessary documents, such as a copy of the seller's title if necessary, and conducting due diligence if required. The transaction is considered complete when the buyer can use the property as collateral for a bank loan.

Every procedure required by law or necessary in practice is included, whether it is the responsibility of the seller or the buyer or must be completed by a third party on their behalf. Local property lawyers, notaries and property registries provide information on procedures as well as the time and cost to complete each of them.

To make the data comparable across economies, several assumptions about the parties to the transaction, the property and the procedures are used.

ASSUMPTIONS ABOUT THE PARTIES

The parties (buyer and seller):
- Are limited liability companies.
- Are located in the periurban area of the economy's largest business city.
- Are 100% domestically and privately owned.
- Have 50 employees each, all of whom are nationals.
- Perform general commercial activities.

ASSUMPTIONS ABOUT THE PROPERTY

The property:
- Has a value of 50 times income per capita. The sale price equals the value.
- Is fully owned by the seller.
- Has no mortgages attached and has been under the same ownership for the past 10 years.
- Is registered in the land registry or cadastre, or both, and is free of title disputes.
- Is located in a periurban commercial zone, and no rezoning is required.
- Consists of land and a building. The land area is 557.4 square meters (6,000 square feet). A 2-story warehouse of 929 square meters (10,000 square feet) is located on the land. The warehouse is 10 years old, is in good condition and complies with all safety standards, building codes and other legal requirements. The property of land and building will be transferred in its entirety.
- Will not be subject to renovations or additional building following the purchase.

- Has no trees, natural water sources, natural reserves or historical monuments of any kind.
- Will not be used for special purposes, and no special permits, such as for residential use, industrial plants, waste storage or certain types of agricultural activities, are required.
- Has no occupants (legal or illegal), and no other party holds a legal interest in it.

PROCEDURES

A procedure is defined as any interaction of the buyer or the seller or their agents (if an agent is legally or in practice required) with external parties, including government agencies, inspectors, notaries and lawyers. Interactions between company officers and employees are not considered. All procedures that are legally or in practice required for registering property are recorded, even if they may be avoided in exceptional cases. It is assumed that the buyer follows the fastest legal option available and used by the majority of property owners. Although the buyer may use lawyers or other professionals where necessary in the registration process, it is assumed that it does not employ an outside facilitator in the registration process unless legally or in practice required to do so.

TIME

Time is recorded in calendar days. The measure captures the median duration that property lawyers, notaries or registry officials indicate is necessary to complete a procedure. It is assumed that the minimum time required for each procedure is 1 day. Although procedures may take place simultaneously, they cannot start on the same day. It is assumed that the buyer does not waste time and commits to completing each remaining procedure without delay. If a procedure can be accelerated for an additional cost, the fastest legal procedure available and used by the majority of property owners is chosen. If procedures can be undertaken simultaneously, it is assumed that they are. It is assumed that the parties

TABLE 12.5
What does registering property measure?

Procedures to legally transfer title on immovable property (number)

- Preregistration (for example, checking for liens, notarizing sales agreement, paying property transfer taxes)
- Registration in the economy's largest business city
- Postregistration (for example, filing title with municipality)

Time required to complete each procedure (calendar days)

- Does not include time spent gathering information
- Each procedure starts on a separate day
- Procedure completed once final document is received
- No prior contact with officials

Cost required to complete each procedure (% of property value)

- Official costs only, no bribes
- No value added or capital gains taxes included

Source: *Doing Business* database.

involved are aware of all regulations and their sequence from the beginning. Time spent on gathering information is not considered.

COST

Cost is recorded as a percentage of the property value, assumed to be equivalent to 50 times income per capita. Only official costs required by law are recorded, including fees, transfer taxes, stamp duties and any other payment to the property registry, notaries, public agencies or lawyers. Other taxes, such as capital gains tax or value added tax, are excluded from the cost measure. Both costs borne by the buyer and those borne by the seller are included. If cost estimates differ among sources, the median reported value is used.

The data details on registering property can be found for each economy at http://www.doingbusiness.org.

GETTING CREDIT

Doing Business constructs measures of the legal rights of borrowers and lenders and the sharing of credit information. The first set of indicators describes how well collateral and bankruptcy laws facilitate lending. The second set measures the coverage, scope, quality and accessibility of credit information available through public and private credit registries (table 12.6).

The data on the legal rights of borrowers and lenders are gathered through a survey of financial lawyers and verified through analysis of laws and regulations as well as public sources of information on collateral and bankruptcy laws. The data on credit information sharing are built in 2 stages. First, banking supervision authorities and public information sources are surveyed to confirm the presence of public credit registries and private credit information bureaus. Second, when applicable, a detailed survey on the public or private credit registry's structure, law and associated rules is administered to the credit registry. Survey responses are verified through several rounds of follow-up communication with respondents as well as by contacting third parties and consulting public sources. The survey data are confirmed through teleconference calls or on-site visits in all economies.

STRENGTH OF LEGAL RIGHTS INDEX

The strength of legal rights index measures the degree to which collateral and bankruptcy laws protect the rights of borrowers and lenders and thus facilitate lending. Two case scenarios are used to determine the scope of the secured transactions system, involving a secured borrower, the company ABC, and a secured lender, BizBank.

Several assumptions about the secured borrower and lender are used:

- ABC is a domestic, limited liability company.
- ABC has its headquarters and only base of operations in the economy's largest business city.
- To fund its business expansion plans, ABC obtains a loan from BizBank for an amount up to 10 times income per capita in local currency.
- Both ABC and BizBank are 100% domestically owned.

The case scenarios also involve assumptions. In case A, as collateral for the loan, ABC grants BizBank a nonpossessory security interest in one category of revolving movable assets, for example, its accounts receivable or its inventory. ABC wants to keep both possession and ownership of the collateral. In economies in which the law does not allow nonpossessory security interests in movable property, ABC and BizBank use a fiduciary transfer-of-title arrangement (or a similar substitute for nonpossessory security interests).

In case B, ABC grants BizBank a business charge, enterprise charge, floating charge or any charge or combination of charges that gives BizBank a security interest over ABC's combined assets (or as much of ABC's assets as possible). ABC keeps ownership and possession of the assets.

The strength of legal rights index includes 8 aspects related to legal rights in collateral law and 2 aspects in bankruptcy law. A score of 1 is assigned for each of the following features of the laws:

- Any business may use movable assets as collateral while keeping possession of the assets, and any financial institution may accept such assets as collateral.
- The law allows a business to grant a nonpossessory security right in a single category of revolving movable assets (such as accounts receivable or inventory), without requiring a specific description of the secured assets.
- The law allows a business to grant a nonpossessory security right in substantially all of its assets, without requiring a specific description of the secured assets.
- A security right may extend to future or after-acquired assets and may extend automatically to the products, proceeds or replacements of the original assets.
- General description of debts and obligations is permitted in collateral agreements and in registration documents, so that all types of obligations and debts can be secured by stating a maximum rather than a specific amount between the parties.
- A collateral registry is in operation that is unified geographically and by asset type and that is indexed by the name of the grantor of a security right.
- Secured creditors are paid first (for example, before general tax claims and employee claims) when a debtor defaults outside an insolvency procedure.

- Secured creditors are paid first (for example, before general tax claims and employee claims) when a business is liquidated.
- Secured creditors are not subject to an automatic stay or moratorium on enforcement procedures when a debtor enters a court-supervised reorganization procedure.
- The law allows parties to agree in a collateral agreement that the lender may enforce its security right out of court.

The index ranges from 0 to 10, with higher scores indicating that collateral and bankruptcy laws are better designed to expand access to credit.

DEPTH OF CREDIT INFORMATION INDEX

The depth of credit information index measures rules affecting the scope, accessibility and quality of credit information available through either public or private credit registries. A score of 1 is assigned for each of the following 6 features of the public registry or the private credit bureau (or both):

- Both positive credit information (for example, loan amounts and pattern of on-time repayments) and negative information (for example, late payments, number and amount of defaults and bankruptcies) are distributed.
- Data on both firms and individuals are distributed.
- Data from retailers, trade creditors or utility companies as well as financial institutions are distributed.
- More than 2 years of historical data are distributed. Registries that erase data on defaults as soon as they are repaid obtain a score of 0 for this indicator.
- Data on loans below 1% of income per capita are distributed. A registry must have a minimum coverage of 1% of the adult population to score a 1 for this indicator.
- Regulations guarantee borrowers the right to access their data in the largest registry in the economy.

TABLE 12.6

What does getting credit measure?

Strength of legal rights index (0–10)
· Protection of rights of borrowers and lenders through collateral and bankruptcy laws
· Security interest is a nonpossessory one in movable assets

Depth of credit information index (0–6)
· Scope and accessibility of credit information distributed by public and private credit registries
· Quality of data distributed by public and private credit registries

Public credit registry coverage (% of adults)
· Number of individuals and firms listed in a public credit registry as percentage of adult population

Private credit bureau coverage (% of adults)
· Number of individuals and firms listed in a private credit bureau as percentage of adult population

Source: Doing Business database.

The index ranges from 0 to 6, with higher values indicating the availability of more credit information, from either a public registry or a private bureau, to facilitate lending decisions. If the registry is not operational or has coverage of less than 0.1% of the adult population, the score on the depth of credit information index is 0.

In Turkey, for example, both a public and a private registry operate. Both distribute positive and negative information (a score of 1). The private bureau distributes data only on individuals, but the public registry covers firms as well as individuals (a score of 1). The public and private registries share data among financial institutions only; no data are collected from retailers or utilities (a score of 0). The private bureau distributes more than 2 years of historical data (a score of 1). The public registry collects data on loans of $3,493 (44% of income per capita) or more, but the private bureau collects information on loans of any value (a score of 1). Borrowers have the right to access their data in both the private and the public registry (a score of 1). Summing across the indicators gives Turkey a total score of 5.

PUBLIC CREDIT REGISTRY COVERAGE

The public credit registry coverage indicator reports the number of individuals and firms listed in a public credit registry with information on repayment history, unpaid debts or credit outstanding from the past 5 years. The number is expressed as a percentage of the adult population (the population aged 15 and above according to the World Bank's *World Development Indicators 2008*). A public credit registry is defined as a database managed by the public sector, usually by the central bank or the superintendent of banks, that collects information on the creditworthiness of borrowers (persons or businesses) in the financial system and makes it available to financial institutions. If no public registry operates, the coverage value is 0.

PRIVATE CREDIT BUREAU COVERAGE

The private credit bureau coverage indicator reports the number of individuals and firms listed by a private credit bureau with information on repayment history, unpaid debts or credit outstanding from the past 5 years. The number is expressed as a percentage of the adult population (the population aged 15 and above according to the World Bank's *World Development Indicators 2008*). A private credit bureau is defined as a private firm or nonprofit organization that maintains a database on the creditworthiness of borrowers (persons or businesses) in the financial system and facilitates the exchange of credit information among banks and financial institutions. Credit investigative bureaus and credit reporting firms that do not directly facilitate information exchange among banks and other financial institutions are not considered. If no private bureau operates, the coverage value is 0.

The data details on getting credit can be found for each economy at http://www .doingbusiness.org. This methodology was developed in Djankov, McLiesh and Shleifer (2007) and is adopted here with minor changes.

PROTECTING INVESTORS

Doing Business measures the strength of minority shareholder protections against directors' misuse of corporate assets for personal gain. The indicators distinguish 3 dimensions of investor protection: transparency of related-party transactions (extent of disclosure index), liability for self-dealing (extent of director liability index) and shareholders' ability to sue officers and directors for misconduct (ease of shareholder suits index) (table 12.7). The data come from a survey of corporate lawyers and are based on securities regulations, company laws and court rules of evidence.

To make the data comparable across economies, several assumptions about the business and the transaction are used.

ASSUMPTIONS ABOUT THE BUSINESS

The business (buyer):
- Is a publicly traded corporation listed on the economy's most important stock exchange. If the number of publicly traded companies listed on that exchange is less than 10, or if there is no stock exchange in the economy, it is assumed that buyer is a large private company with multiple shareholders.
- Has a board of directors and a chief executive officer (CEO) who may legally act on behalf of buyer where permitted, even if this is not specifically required by law.
- Is a food manufacturer.
- Has its own distribution network.

ASSUMPTIONS ABOUT THE TRANSACTION

- Mr. James is buyer's controlling shareholder and a member of buyer's board of directors. He owns 60% of buyer and elected 2 directors to buyer's 5-member board.
- Mr. James also owns 90% of seller, a company that operates a chain of retail hardware stores. Seller recently closed a large number of its stores.
- Mr. James proposes to buyer that it purchase seller's unused fleet of trucks to expand buyer's distribution of its food products. Buyer agrees. The price is equal to 10% of buyer's assets and is higher than the market value.
- The proposed transaction is part of the company's ordinary course of business and is not outside the authority of the company.
- Buyer enters into the transaction. All required approvals are obtained, and all required disclosures made (that is, the transaction is not fraudulent).
- The transaction is unfair to buyer. Shareholders sue Mr. James and the other parties that approved the transaction.

TABLE 12.7
What does protecting investors measure?

Extent of disclosure index *(0–10)*
- Who can approve related-party transactions
- Disclosure requirements in case of related-party transactions

Extent of director liability index *(0–10)*
- Ability of the shareholders to hold the interested party and the approving body liable in case of related-party transactions
- Available legal remedies (damages, repayment of profits, fines and imprisonment)
- Ability of shareholders to sue directly or derivatively

Ease of shareholder suits index *(0–10)*
- Documents and information available during trial
- Direct access to internal documents of the company and use of a government inspector without filing a suit in court

Strength of investor protection index *(0–10)*
- Simple average of the extent of disclosure, extent of director liability and ease of shareholder suits indices

Source: Doing Business database.

EXTENT OF DISCLOSURE INDEX

The extent of disclosure index has 5 components:
- What corporate body can provide legally sufficient approval for the transaction. A score of 0 is assigned if it is the CEO or the managing director alone; 1 if the board of directors or shareholders must vote and Mr. James is permitted to vote; 2 if the board of directors must vote and Mr. James is not permitted to vote; 3 if shareholders must vote and Mr. James is not permitted to vote.
- Whether immediate disclosure of the transaction to the public, the regulator or the shareholders is required. A score of 0 is assigned if no disclosure is required; 1 if disclosure on the terms of the transaction but not Mr. James's conflict of interest is required; 2 if disclosure on both the terms and Mr. James's conflict of interest is required.
- Whether disclosure in the annual report is required. A score of 0 is assigned if no disclosure on the transaction is required; 1 if disclosure on the terms of the transaction but not Mr. James's conflict of interest is required; 2 if disclosure on both the terms and Mr. James's conflict of interest is required.
- Whether disclosure by Mr. James to the board of directors is required. A score of 0 is assigned if no disclosure is required; 1 if a general disclosure of the existence of a conflict of interest is required without any specifics; 2 if full disclosure of all material facts relating to Mr. James's interest in the buyer-seller transaction is required.
- Whether it is required that an external body, for example, an external auditor, review the transaction before it takes place. A score of 0 is assigned if no; 1 if yes.

The index ranges from 0 to 10, with higher values indicating greater disclosure. In Poland, for example, the board of directors must approve the transaction and Mr. James is not allowed to vote (a score of 2). Buyer is required to disclose immediately all information affecting the stock price, including the conflict of interest (a score of 2). In its annual report buyer must also disclose the terms of the transaction and Mr. James's ownership in buyer and seller (a score of 2). Before the transaction Mr. James must disclose his conflict of interest to the other directors, but he is not required to provide specific information about it (a score of 1). Poland does not require an external body to review the transaction (a score of 0). Adding these numbers gives Poland a score of 7 on the extent of disclosure index.

EXTENT OF DIRECTOR LIABILITY INDEX

The extent of director liability index has 7 components:
- Whether a shareholder plaintiff is able to hold Mr. James liable for damage the buyer-seller transaction causes to the company. A score of 0 is assigned if Mr. James cannot be held liable or can be held liable only for fraud or bad faith; 1 if Mr. James can be held liable only if he influenced the approval of the transaction or was negligent; 2 if Mr. James can be held liable when the transaction is unfair or prejudicial to the other shareholders.
- Whether a shareholder plaintiff is able to hold the approving body (the CEO or board of directors) liable for damage the transaction causes to the company. A score of 0 is assigned if the approving body cannot be held liable or can be held liable only for fraud or bad faith; 1 if the approving body can be held liable for negligence; 2 if the approving body can be held liable when the transaction is unfair or prejudicial to the other shareholders.
- Whether a court can void the transaction upon a successful claim by a shareholder plaintiff. A score of 0 is assigned if rescission is unavailable or is available only in case of fraud or bad faith; 1 if rescission is available when the transaction is oppressive or prejudicial to the other shareholders; 2 if rescission is available when the transaction is unfair or entails a conflict of interest.
- Whether Mr. James pays damages for the harm caused to the company upon a successful claim by the shareholder plaintiff. A score of 0 is assigned if no; 1 if yes.
- Whether Mr. James repays profits made from the transaction upon a successful claim by the shareholder plaintiff. A score of 0 is assigned if no; 1 if yes.

- Whether fines and imprisonment can be applied against Mr. James. A score of 0 is assigned if no; 1 if yes.
- Whether shareholder plaintiffs are able to sue directly or derivatively for damage the transaction causes to the company. A score of 0 is assigned if suits are unavailable or are available only for shareholders holding more than 10% of the company's share capital; 1 if direct or derivative suits are available for shareholders holding 10% or less of share capital.

The index ranges from 0 to 10, with higher values indicating greater liability of directors. To hold Mr. James liable in Panama, for example, a plaintiff must prove that Mr. James influenced the approving body or acted negligently (a score of 1). To hold the other directors liable, a plaintiff must prove that they acted negligently (a score of 1). The unfair transaction cannot be voided (a score of 0). If Mr. James is found liable, he must pay damages (a score of 1) but he is not required to disgorge his profits (a score of 0). Mr. James cannot be fined or imprisoned (a score of 0). Direct suits are available for shareholders holding 10% or less of share capital (a score of 1). Adding these numbers gives Panama a score of 4 on the extent of director liability index.

EASE OF SHAREHOLDER SUITS INDEX

The ease of shareholder suits index has 6 components:

- What range of documents is available to the shareholder plaintiff from the defendant and witnesses during trial. A score of 1 is assigned for each of the following types of documents available: information that the defendant has indicated he intends to rely on for his defense; information that directly proves specific facts in the plaintiff's claim; any information relevant to the subject matter of the claim; and any information that may lead to the discovery of relevant information.
- Whether the plaintiff can directly examine the defendant and witnesses during trial. A score of 0 is assigned

if no; 1 if yes, with prior approval of the questions by the judge; 2 if yes, without prior approval.
- Whether the plaintiff can obtain categories of relevant documents from the defendant without identifying each document specifically. A score of 0 is assigned if no; 1 if yes.
- Whether shareholders owning 10% or less of the company's share capital can request that a government inspector investigate the buyer-seller transaction without filing suit in court. A score of 0 is assigned if no; 1 if yes.
- Whether shareholders owning 10% or less of the company's share capital have the right to inspect the transaction documents before filing suit. A score of 0 is assigned if no; 1 if yes.
- Whether the standard of proof for civil suits is lower than that for a criminal case. A score of 0 is assigned if no; 1 if yes.

The index ranges from 0 to 10, with higher values indicating greater powers of shareholders to challenge the transaction. In Greece, for example, the plaintiff can access documents that the defendant intends to rely on for his defense and that directly prove facts in the plaintiff's claim (a score of 2). The plaintiff can examine the defendant and witnesses during trial, though only with prior approval of the questions by the court (a score of 1). The plaintiff must specifically identify the documents being sought (for example, the buyer-seller purchase agreement of July 15, 2006) and cannot just request categories (for example, all documents related to the transaction) (a score of 0). A shareholder holding 5% of buyer's shares can request that a government inspector review suspected mismanagement by Mr. James and the CEO without filing suit in court (a score of 1). Any shareholder can inspect the transaction documents before deciding whether to sue (a score of 1). The standard of proof for civil suits is the same as that for a criminal case (a score of 0). Adding these numbers gives Greece a score of 5 on the ease of shareholder suits index.

STRENGTH OF INVESTOR PROTECTION INDEX

The strength of investor protection index is the average of the extent of disclosure index, the extent of director liability index and the ease of shareholder suits index. The index ranges from 0 to 10, with higher values indicating more investor protection.

The data details on protecting investors can be found for each economy at http://www.doingbusiness.org. This methodology was developed in Djankov, La Porta, López-de-Silanes and Shleifer (2008).

PAYING TAXES

Doing Business records the taxes and mandatory contributions that a medium-size company must pay in a given year, as well as measures of the administrative burden of paying taxes and contributions. Taxes and contributions measured include the profit or corporate income tax, social contributions and labor taxes paid by the employer, property taxes, property transfer taxes, dividend tax, capital gains tax, financial transactions tax, waste collection taxes and vehicle and road taxes.

Doing Business measures all taxes and contributions that are government mandated (at any level—federal, state or local), apply to the standardized business and have an impact in its income statements. In doing so, *Doing Business* goes beyond the traditional definition of a tax: as defined for the purposes of government national accounts, taxes include only compulsory, unrequited payments to general government (table 12.8). *Doing Business* departs from this definition because it measures imposed charges that affect business accounts, not government accounts. The main differences relate to labor contributions and value added tax. The *Doing Business* measure includes government-mandated contributions paid by the employer to a requited private pension fund or workers' insurance fund. The indicator includes, for example, Australia's

TABLE 12.8
What does paying taxes measure?

Tax payments for a manufacturing company in 2007 (number per year)
- Total number of taxes and contributions paid, including consumption taxes (value added tax, sales tax or goods and service tax)
- Method and frequency of payment

Time required to comply with 3 major taxes (hours per year)
- Hours to prepare, file and pay profit taxes, consumption taxes and labor taxes and contributions
- Collecting information to compute tax payable
- Completing tax return forms, filing with proper agencies
- Arranging payment or withholding
- Preparing separate tax accounting books, if required

Total tax rate (% of profit)
- Profit or corporate income tax
- Social contributions and labor taxes paid by the employer
- Property and property transfer taxes
- Dividend, capital gains and financial transactions taxes
- Waste collection, vehicle, road and other taxes

Source: Doing Business database.

compulsory superannuation guarantee and workers' compensation insurance. It excludes value added taxes from the total tax rate because they do not affect the accounting profits of the business—that is, they are not reflected in the income statement.

Doing Business has prepared a case scenario to measure the taxes and contributions paid by a standardized business and the complexity of an economy's tax compliance system. This case scenario uses a set of financial statements and assumptions about transactions made over the year. Tax experts in each economy compute the taxes and contributions due in their jurisdiction based on the standardized case facts. Information is also compiled on the frequency of filing, tax audits and other costs of compliance. The project was developed and implemented in cooperation with PricewaterhouseCoopers.

To make the data comparable across economies, several assumptions about the business and the taxes and contributions are used.

ASSUMPTIONS ABOUT THE BUSINESS
The business:
- Is a limited liability, taxable company. If there is more than one type of limited liability company in the economy, the limited liability form

most popular among domestic firms is chosen. The most popular form is reported by incorporation lawyers or the statistical office.
- Started operations on January 1, 2006. At that time the company purchased all the assets shown in its balance sheet and hired all its workers.
- Operates in the economy's largest business city.
- Is 100% domestically owned and has 5 owners, all of whom are natural persons.
- Has a start-up capital of 102 times income per capita at the end of 2006.
- Performs general industrial or commercial activities. Specifically, it produces ceramic flowerpots and sells them at retail. It does not participate in foreign trade (no import or export) and does not handle products subject to a special tax regime, for example, liquor or tobacco.
- At the beginning of 2007, owns 2 plots of land, 1 building, machinery, office equipment, computers and 1 truck and leases 1 truck.
- Does not qualify for investment incentives or any benefits apart from those related to the age or size of the company.
- Has 60 employees—4 managers, 8 assistants and 48 workers. All are

nationals, and 1 manager is also an owner.
- Has a turnover of 1,050 times income per capita.
- Makes a loss in the first year of operation.
- Has a gross margin (pretax) of 20% (that is, sales are 120% of the cost of goods sold).
- Distributes 50% of its net profits as dividends to the owners at the end of the second year.
- Sells one of its plots of land at a profit during the second year.
- Has annual fuel costs for its trucks equal to twice income per capita.
- Is subject to a series of detailed assumptions on expenses and transactions to further standardize the case. All financial statement variables are proportional to 2005 income per capita. For example, the owner who is also a manager spends 10% of income per capita on traveling for the company (20% of this owner's expenses are purely private, 20% are for entertaining customers and 60% for business travel).

ASSUMPTIONS ABOUT THE TAXES AND CONTRIBUTIONS
- All the taxes and contributions paid in the second year of operation (fiscal 2007) are recorded. A tax or contribution is considered distinct if it has a different name or is collected by a different agency. Taxes and contributions with the same name and agency, but charged at different rates depending on the business, are counted as the same tax or contribution.
- The number of times the company pays taxes and contributions in a year is the number of different taxes or contributions multiplied by the frequency of payment (or withholding) for each one. The frequency of payment includes advance payments (or withholding) as well as regular payments (or withholding).

TAX PAYMENTS

The tax payments indicator reflects the total number of taxes and contributions paid, the method of payment, the frequency of payment and the number of agencies involved for this standardized case during the second year of operation. It includes consumption taxes paid by the company, such as sales tax or value added tax. These taxes are traditionally collected from the consumer on behalf of the tax agencies. Although they do not affect the income statements of the company, they add to the administrative burden of complying with the tax system and so are included in the tax payments measure.

The number of payments takes into account electronic filing. Where full electronic filing and payment is allowed and it is used by the majority of medium-size businesses, the tax is counted as paid once a year even if payments are more frequent. For taxes paid through third parties, such as tax on interest withheld at source by a financial institution or fuel tax paid by the fuel distributor, only one payment is included even if payments are more frequent. These are taxes withheld or paid at source where no filing is required of the company.

Where 2 or more taxes or contributions are filed for and paid jointly using the same form, each of these joint payments is counted once. For example, if mandatory health insurance contributions and mandatory pension contributions are filed for and paid together, only one of these contributions would be included in the number of payments.

TIME

Time is recorded in hours per year. The indicator measures the time taken to prepare, file and pay 3 major types of taxes and contributions: the corporate income tax, value added or sales tax and labor taxes, including payroll taxes and social contributions. Preparation time includes the time to collect all information necessary to compute the tax payable. If separate accounting books must be kept for tax purposes—or separate calculations made—the time associated with these processes is included. This extra time is included only if the regular accounting work is not enough to fulfill the tax accounting requirements. Filing time includes the time to complete all necessary tax return forms and make all necessary calculations. Payment time considers the hours needed to make the payment online or at the tax authorities. Where taxes and contributions are paid in person, the time includes delays while waiting.

TOTAL TAX RATE

The total tax rate measures the amount of taxes and mandatory contributions borne by the business in the second year of operation, expressed as a share of commercial profit. *Doing Business 2009* reports the total tax rate for fiscal 2007. The total amount of taxes borne is the sum of all the different taxes and contributions payable after accounting for allowable deductions and exemptions. The taxes withheld (such as personal income tax) or collected by the company and remitted to the tax authorities (such as value added tax, sales tax or goods and service tax) but not borne by the company are excluded. The taxes included can be divided into 5 categories: profit or corporate income tax, social contributions and labor taxes paid by the employer (in respect of which all mandatory contributions are included, even if paid to a private entity such as a requited pension fund), property taxes, turnover taxes and other small taxes (such as municipal fees and vehicle and fuel taxes).

The total tax rate is designed to provide a comprehensive measure of the cost of all the taxes a business bears. It differs from the statutory tax rate, which merely provides the factor to be applied to the tax base. In computing the total tax rate, the actual tax payable is divided by commercial profit. Data for Sweden illustrate this (table 12.9).

Commercial profit is essentially net profit before all taxes borne. It differs from the conventional profit before tax, reported in financial statements. In computing profit before tax, many of the taxes borne by a firm are deductible. In computing commercial profit, these taxes are not deductible. Commercial profit therefore presents a clear picture of the actual profit of a business before any of the taxes it bears in the course of the fiscal year.

Commercial profit is computed as sales minus cost of goods sold, minus gross salaries, minus administrative expenses, minus other expenses, minus provisions, plus capital gains (from the property sale) minus interest expense, plus interest income and minus com-

TABLE 12.9

Computing the total tax rate for Sweden

Type of tax (tax base)	Statutory rate (r)	Statutory tax base (b)	Actual tax payable (a) a = r×b	Commercial profit[1] (c)	Total tax rate (t) t = a/c
		SKr	SKr	SKr	
Corporate income tax (taxable income)	28%	10,352,253	2,898,631	17,619,223	16.50%
Real estate tax (land and buildings)	0.38%	26,103,545	97,888	17,619,223	0.60%
Payroll tax (taxable wages)	32.28%	19,880,222	6,417,336	17,619,223	36.40%
Fuel tax (fuel price)	SKr 3.665 per liter	53,505 liters	196,095	17,619,223	1.10%
TOTAL			**9,609,950**		**54.50%**

1. Profit before all taxes borne.
Source: Doing Business database.

mercial depreciation. To compute the commercial depreciation, a straight-line depreciation method is applied, with the following rates: 0% for the land, 5% for the building, 10% for the machinery, 33% for the computers, 20% for the office equipment, 20% for the truck and 10% for business development expenses. Commercial profit amounts to 59.4 times income per capita.

This methodology is consistent with the Total Tax Contribution framework developed by PricewaterhouseCoopers. This framework measures taxes that are borne by companies and affect their income statements, as does *Doing Business*. But while PricewaterhouseCoopers bases its calculation on data from the largest companies in the economy, *Doing Business* focuses on a standardized medium-size company.

The data details on paying taxes can be found for each economy at http://www .doingbusiness.org. This methodology was developed in Djankov, Ganser, McLiesh, Ramalho and Shleifer (2008).

TRADING ACROSS BORDERS

Doing Business compiles procedural requirements for exporting and importing a standardized cargo of goods by ocean transport (table 12.10). Every official procedure for exporting and importing the goods is recorded—from the contractual agreement between the 2 parties to the delivery of goods—along with the time and cost necessary for completion. All documents needed by the trader for clearance of the goods across the border are also recorded. For exporting goods, procedures range from packing the goods at the factory to their departure from the port of exit. For importing goods, procedures range from the vessel's arrival at the port of entry to the cargo's delivery at the factory warehouse. The time and cost for ocean transport are not included. Payment is made by letter of credit, and the time, cost and documents required for the issuance of a letter of credit are taken into account.

Local freight forwarders, shipping lines, customs brokers, port officials and banks provide information on required documents and cost as well as the time to complete each procedure. To make the data comparable across economies, several assumptions about the business and the traded goods are used.

ASSUMPTIONS ABOUT THE BUSINESS

The business:
- Has 60 employees.
- Is located in the economy's largest business city.
- Is a private, limited liability company. It does not operate in an export processing zone or an industrial estate with special export or import privileges.
- Is domestically owned with no foreign ownership.
- Exports more than 10% of its sales.

ASSUMPTIONS ABOUT THE TRADED GOODS

The traded product travels in a dry-cargo, 20-foot, full container load. It weighs 10 tons and is valued at $20,000. The product:
- Is not hazardous nor does it include military items.
- Does not require refrigeration or any other special environment.
- Does not require any special phytosanitary or environmental safety standards other than accepted international standards.

DOCUMENTS

All documents required per shipment to export and import the goods are recorded. It is assumed that the contract has already been agreed upon and signed by both parties. Documents required for clearance by government ministries, customs authorities, port and container terminal authorities, health and technical control agencies and banks are taken into account. Since payment is by letter of credit, all documents required by banks for the issuance or securing of a letter of credit are also taken into account. Documents that are renewed at least annually

TABLE 12.10
What does trading across borders measure?

Documents required to export and import (number)
- Bank documents
- Customs clearance documents
- Port and terminal handling documents
- Transport documents

Time required to export and import (days)
- Obtaining all the documents
- Inland transport
- Customs clearance and inspections
- Port and terminal handling
- Does not include ocean transport time

Cost required to export and import (US$ per container)
- Obtaining all the documents
- Inland transport
- Customs clearance and inspections
- Port and terminal handling
- Official costs only, no bribes or tariffs

Source: Doing Business database.

and that do not require renewal per shipment (for example, an annual tax clearance certificate) are not included.

TIME

The time for exporting and importing is recorded in calendar days. The time calculation for a procedure starts from the moment it is initiated and runs until it is completed. If a procedure can be accelerated for an additional cost and is available to all trading companies, the fastest legal procedure is chosen. Fast-track procedures applying to firms located in an export processing zone are not taken into account because they are not available to all trading companies. Ocean transport time is not included. It is assumed that neither the exporter nor the importer wastes time and that each commits to completing each remaining procedure without delay. Procedures that can be completed in parallel are measured as simultaneous. The waiting time between procedures—for example, during unloading of the cargo—is included in the measure.

COST

Cost measures the fees levied on a 20-foot container in U.S. dollars. All the fees associated with completing the procedures to export or import the goods are included. These include costs for documents, administrative fees for customs clearance and technical control, terminal handling charges and inland transport. The cost measure does not include customs tariffs and duties or costs related to ocean transport. Only official costs are recorded.

The data details on trading across borders can be found for each economy at http:// www.doingbusiness.org. This methodology was developed in Djankov, Freund and Pham (forthcoming) and is adopted here with minor changes.

ENFORCING CONTRACTS

Indicators on enforcing contracts measure the efficiency of the judicial system in resolving a commercial dispute (table 12.11). The data are built by following the step-by-step evolution of a commercial sale dispute before local courts. The data are collected through study of the codes of civil procedure and other court regulations as well as surveys completed by local litigation lawyers (and, in a quarter of the economies, by judges as well). The name of the relevant court in each economy—the court in the largest business city with jurisdiction over commercial cases worth 200% of income per capita—is published at http://www .doingbusiness.org.

ASSUMPTIONS ABOUT THE CASE

- The value of the claim equals 200% of the economy's income per capita.
- The dispute concerns a lawful transaction between 2 businesses (Seller and Buyer), located in the economy's largest business city. Seller sells goods worth 200% of the economy's income per capita to Buyer. After Seller delivers the goods to Buyer, Buyer refuses to pay for the goods on the grounds that the delivered goods were not of adequate quality.

- Seller sues Buyer to recover the amount under the sales agreement (that is, 200% of the economy's income per capita). Buyer opposes Seller's claim, saying that the quality of the goods is not adequate. The claim is disputed on the merits.
- A court in the economy's largest business city with jurisdiction over commercial cases worth 200% of income per capita decides the dispute.
- Seller attaches Buyer's goods prior to obtaining a judgment because Seller fears that Buyer may become insolvent during the lawsuit.
- Expert opinions are given on the quality of the delivered goods. If it is standard practice in the economy for parties to call witnesses or expert witnesses to give an opinion on the quality of the goods, the parties each call one witness or expert witness. If it is standard practice for the judge to appoint an independent expert to give an expert opinion on the quality of the goods, the judge does so. In this case the judge does not allow opposing expert testimony.
- The judgment is 100% in favor of Seller: the judge decides that the goods are of adequate quality and that Buyer must pay the agreed price (200% of income per capita).
- Buyer does not appeal the judgment. The judgment becomes final.
- Seller takes all required steps for prompt enforcement of the judgment. The money is successfully collected through a public sale of Buyer's movable assets (for example, office equipment).

PROCEDURES

The list of procedural steps compiled for each economy traces the chronology of a commercial dispute before the relevant court. A procedure is defined as any interaction between the parties, or between them and the judge or court officer. This includes steps to file the case, steps for trial and judgment and steps necessary to enforce the judgment.

The survey allows respondents to

record procedures that exist in civil law but not common law jurisdictions, and vice versa. For example, in civil law countries the judge can appoint an independent expert, while in common law countries each party submits a list of expert witnesses to the court. To indicate the overall efficiency of court procedures, 1 procedure is now subtracted for economies that have specialized commercial courts and 1 procedure for economies that allow electronic filing of court cases. Procedural steps that take place simultaneously with or are included in other procedural steps are not counted in the total number of procedures.

TIME

Time is recorded in calendar days, counted from the moment Seller files the lawsuit in court until payment. This includes both the days when actions take place and the waiting periods between. The average duration of different stages of dispute resolution is recorded: the completion of filing and service of process and of pretrial attachment (time to file the case), the issuance of judgment (time for the trial and obtaining the judgment) and the moment of payment (time for enforcement of judgment).

TABLE 12.11

What does enforcing contracts measure?

Procedures to enforce a contract (number)
· Any interaction between the parties in a commercial dispute, or between them and the judge or court officer
· Steps to file the case
· Steps for trial and judgment
· Steps to enforce the judgment

Time required to complete each procedure (calendar days)
· Measured in calendar days
· Time to file the case
· Time for trial and obtaining judgment
· Time to enforce the judgment

Cost required to complete each procedure (% of claim)
· No bribes
· Average attorney fees
· Court costs, including expert fees
· Enforcement costs

Source: Doing Business database.

COST

Cost is recorded as a percentage of the claim, assumed to be equivalent to 200% of income per capita. No bribes are recorded. Three types of costs are recorded: court costs, enforcement costs and average attorney fees. Court costs include all costs Seller must advance to the court or to the expert regardless of the final cost to Seller. Expert fees, if required by law or necessary in practice, are included in court costs. Enforcement costs are all costs Seller must advance to enforce the judgment through a public sale of Buyer's movable assets, regardless of the final cost to Seller. Average attorney fees are the fees Seller must advance to a local attorney to represent Seller in the standardized case.

The data details on enforcing contracts can be found for each economy at http://www.doingbusiness.org. This methodology was developed in Djankov and others (2003) and is adopted here with minor changes.

CLOSING A BUSINESS

Doing Business studies the time, cost and outcomes of bankruptcy proceedings involving domestic entities (table 12.12). The data are derived from survey responses by local insolvency practitioners and verified through a study of laws and regulations as well as public information on bankruptcy systems.

To make the data comparable across economies, several assumptions about the business and the case are used.

ASSUMPTIONS ABOUT THE BUSINESS

The business:
- Is a limited liability company.
- Operates in the economy's largest business city.
- Is 100% domestically owned, with the founder, who is also the chairman of the supervisory board, owning 51% (no other shareholder holds more than 5% of shares).
- Has downtown real estate, where it runs a hotel, as its major asset.

- Has a professional general manager.
- Has had average annual revenue of 1,000 times income per capita over the past 3 years.
- Has 201 employees and 50 suppliers, each of which is owed money for the last delivery.
- Borrowed from a domestic bank 5 years ago (the loan has 10 years to full repayment) and bought real estate (the hotel building), using it as security for the bank loan.
- Has observed the payment schedule and all other conditions of the loan up to now.
- Has a floating charge or mortgage, with the value of its principal being exactly equal to the market value of the hotel.

ASSUMPTIONS ABOUT THE CASE

The business is experiencing liquidity problems. The company's loss in 2007 reduced its net worth to a negative figure. There is no cash to pay the bank interest or principal in full, due tomorrow. The business therefore defaults on its loan. Management believes that losses will be incurred in 2008 and 2009 as well.

The bank holds a floating charge against the hotel in economies where floating charges are possible. If the law does not permit a floating charge but contracts commonly use some other provision to that effect, this provision is specified in the lending contract.

The business has too many creditors to negotiate an informal out-of-court workout. It has the following options: a judicial procedure aimed at the rehabilitation or reorganization of the business to permit its continued operation; a judicial procedure aimed at the liquidation or winding-up of the company; or a debt enforcement or foreclosure procedure aimed at selling the hotel either piecemeal or as a going concern, enforced either in court (or through a government authority like a debt collection agency) or out of court (for example, by appointing a receiver).

If an economy has had fewer than 5 cases a year over the past 5 years involving a judicial reorganization, judicial liq-

uidation or debt enforcement procedure, the economy receives a "no practice" mark. This means that creditors are unlikely to recover their debt through the legal process (in or out of court).

TIME

Time for creditors to recover their debt is recorded in calendar years. Information is collected on the sequence of procedures and on whether any procedures can be carried out simultaneously. Potential delay tactics by the parties, such as the filing of dilatory appeals or requests for extension, are taken into consideration.

COST

The cost of the proceedings is recorded as a percentage of the estate's value. The cost is calculated on the basis of survey responses by insolvency practitioners and includes court fees as well as fees of insolvency practitioners, independent assessors, lawyers and accountants. Respondents provide cost estimates from among the following options: a specific percentage or less than 2%, 2–5%, 5–8%, 8–11%, 11–18%, 18–25%, 25–33%, 33–50%, 50–75% and more than 75% of the value of the business estate.

TABLE 12.12
What does closing a business measure?

Time required to recover debt (years)
- Measured in calendar years
- Appeals and requests for extension are included

Cost required to recover debt (% of estate)
- Measured as percentage of estate value
- Court fees
- Lawyers' fees
- Independent assessors' fees
- Accountants' fees

Recovery rate for creditors (cents on the dollar)
- Measures the cents on the dollar recovered by creditors
- Present value of debt recovered
- Official costs of the insolvency proceedings are deducted
- Depreciation of assets is taken into account
- Outcome for the business affects the maximum value that can be recovered

Source: Doing Business database.

RECOVERY RATE

The recovery rate is recorded as cents on the dollar recouped by creditors through the bankruptcy, insolvency or debt enforcement proceedings. The calculation takes into account whether the business emerges from the proceedings as a going concern as well as costs and the loss in value due to the time spent closing down. If the business keeps operating, no value is lost on the initial claim, set at 100 cents on the dollar. If it does not, the initial 100 cents on the dollar are reduced to 70 cents on the dollar. Then the official costs of the insolvency procedure are deducted (1 cent for each percentage of the initial value). Finally, the value lost as a result of the time the money remains tied up in insolvency proceedings is taken into account, including the loss of value due to depreciation of the hotel furniture. Consistent with international accounting practice, the depreciation rate for furniture is taken to be 20%. The furniture is assumed to account for a quarter of the total value of assets. The recovery rate is the present value of the remaining proceeds, based on end-2007 lending rates from the International Monetary Fund's *International Financial Statistics*, supplemented with data from central banks. The recovery rate for economies with "no practice" is zero.

This methodology was developed in Djankov and others (2006).

NOTES

1. The data for paying taxes refer to January–December 2007.

2. These are available at http://www.subnational.doingbusiness.org.

3. The average value added per worker is the ratio of an economy's GNI per capita to the working-age population as a percentage of the total population.

Ease of doing business

The ease of doing business index ranks economies from 1 to 181. For each economy the index is calculated as the ranking on the simple average of its percentile rankings on each of the 10 topics covered in *Doing Business 2009*. The ranking on each topic is the simple average of the percentile rankings on its component indicators (table 13.1).

If an economy has no laws or regulations covering a specific area—for example, bankruptcy—it receives a "no practice" mark. Similarly, an economy receives a "no practice" or "not possible" mark if regulation exists but is never used in practice or if a competing regulation prohibits such practice. Either way, a "no practice" or "not possible" mark puts the economy at the bottom of the ranking on the relevant indicator.

Here is one example of how the ranking is constructed. In Iceland it takes 5 procedures, 5 days and 2.6% of annual income per capita in fees to open a business. The minimum capital required amounts to 13.6% of income per capita. On these 4 indicators Iceland ranks in the 9th, 3rd, 13th and 58th percentiles. So on average Iceland ranks in the 21st percentile on the ease of starting a business. It ranks in the 48th percentile on protecting investors, 26th percentile on trading across borders, 8th percentile on enforcing contracts, 8th percentile on closing a business and so on. Higher rankings indicate simpler regulation and stronger protection of property rights. The simple average of Iceland's percentile rankings on all topics is 23%. When all economies are ordered by their average percentile rank, Iceland is in 11th place.

More complex aggregation methods—such as principal components and unobserved components—yield a nearly identical ranking.[1] The choice of aggregation method has little influence on the rankings because the 10 sets of indicators in *Doing Business* provide sufficiently broad coverage across topics. So *Doing Business* uses the simplest method.

The ease of doing business index is limited in scope. It does not account for an economy's proximity to large markets, the quality of its infrastructure services (other than services related to trading across borders or construction permits), the security of property from theft and looting, macroeconomic conditions or the strength of underlying institutions. There remains a large unfinished agenda for research into what regulation constitutes binding constraints, what package of reforms is most effective and how these issues are shaped by the context of an economy. The *Doing Business* indicators provide a new empirical data set that may improve understanding of these issues.

Doing Business also uses a simple method to calculate the top reformers. First, it selects the economies that implemented reforms making it easier to do business in 3 or more of the 10 *Doing Business* topics. One reform is counted per topic. For example, if an economy merged several procedures by creating a unified property registry and separately reduced the property transfer tax, this counts as 1 reform for the purposes of attaining the 3 reforms required to be a candidate for top reformer. This year 33 economies met this criterion: Albania, Azerbaijan, Belarus, Bosnia and Herzegovina, Botswana, Bulgaria, Burkina Faso, China, Colombia, the Czech Republic, the Dominican Republic, Egypt, Georgia, Greece, the Kyrgyz Republic, Liberia, the former Yugoslav Republic of Macedonia, Madagascar, Mauritius, Morocco, Mozambique, New Zealand, Portugal, Rwanda, Saudi Arabia, Senegal, Sierra Leone, Slovenia, Thailand, Tunisia, Ukraine, Uruguay and Zambia (table 13.2).

Second, *Doing Business* ranks these economies on the increase in their ranking on the ease of doing business from the previous year. For example, Albania, Burkina Faso and Rwanda each reformed in 4 aspects of business regulation. Albania's aggregate ranking on the ease of doing business improved from 135 to 86, Burkina Faso's from 164 to 148 and Rwanda's from 148 to 139. These changes represent an improve-

TABLE 13.1
Which indicators make up the ranking?

Starting a business	*Protecting investors*
Procedures, time, cost and paid-in minimum capital to open a new business	Strength of investor protection index: extent of disclosure index, extent of director liability index and ease of shareholder suits index
Dealing with construction permits	*Paying taxes*
Procedures, time and cost to obtain construction permits, inspections and utility connections	Number of tax payments, time to prepare and file tax returns and to pay taxes, total taxes as a share of profit before all taxes borne
Employing workers	*Trading across borders*
Difficulty of hiring index, rigidity of hours index, difficulty of firing index, firing cost	Documents, time and cost to export and import
Registering property	*Enforcing contracts*
Procedures, time and cost to transfer commercial real estate	Procedures, time and cost to resolve a commercial dispute
Getting credit	*Closing a business*
Strength of legal rights index, depth of credit information index	Recovery rate in bankruptcy

ment in the ranking by 49 places, 16 places and 9 places, respectively. Albania therefore ranks ahead of Burkina Faso in the list of top 10 reformers. Rwanda does not make the list.

In summary, top reformers are economies that have implemented 3 or more reforms making it easier to do business and, as a result, improved their position in the ease of doing business more than other economies. The change in ranking is calculated by comparing this year's ranking with last year's back-calculated ranking. To ensure consistency over time, data sets for previous years are adjusted to reflect any changes in methodology, additions of new economies and revisions in data.

NOTE

1. See Djankov and others (2005).

TABLE 13.2

Economy	Reforms in 2007/08									
	Starting a business	Dealing with construction permits	Employing workers	Registering property	Getting credit	Protecting investors	Paying taxes	Trading across borders	Enforcing contracts	Closing a business
Afghanistan										
Albania	✔				✔	✔	✔			
Algeria										
Angola	✔	✔								
Antigua and Barbuda							✔			
Argentina			✔							
Armenia		✔							✔	
Australia										
Austria									✔	
Azerbaijan	✔		✔	✔	✔	✔	✔		✔	
Bahamas, The										
Bahrain										
Bangladesh	✔			✔						
Belarus	✔	✔		✔	✔		✔	✔		
Belgium									✔	
Belize										
Benin		✗						✔		
Bhutan									✔	
Bolivia										✗
Bosnia and Herzegovina		✔		✔			✔			✔
Botswana	✔					✔	✗	✔		
Brazil								✔		
Brunei										
Bulgaria	✔	✗					✔		✔	✔
Burkina Faso		✔	✔	✔			✔			
Burundi										✔
Cambodia					✔					
Cameroon					✔					
Canada	✔						✔			
Cape Verde			✗							
Central African Republic					✔					
Chad					✔					
Chile										
China			✗		✔		✔		✔	
Colombia	✔	✔					✔	✔		✔
Comoros										
Congo, Dem. Rep.										
Congo, Rep.				✔	✔					
Costa Rica	✔									
Côte d'Ivoire							✔			
Croatia		✔						✔		
Czech Republic	✔		✔				✔			✔
Denmark							✔			
Djibouti								✔		
Dominica										
Dominican Republic	✔			✔			✔	✔		
Ecuador								✔		
Egypt	✔	✔		✔	✔	✔		✔		
El Salvador	✔							✔		

✔ Reforms making it easier to do business   ✗ Reforms making it more difficult to do business

Economy	Starting a business	Dealing with construction permits	Employing workers	Registering property	Getting credit	Protecting investors	Paying taxes	Trading across borders	Enforcing contracts	Closing a business
					Reforms in 2007/08					
Equatorial Guinea					✔			✗		
Eritrea								✔		
Estonia										
Ethiopia										
Fiji		✗	✗							
Finland					✔					✔
France							✔	✔		
Gabon					✔			✗		
Gambia, The			✗							
Georgia	✔			✔	✔		✔			
Germany							✔			✔
Ghana	✔									
Greece	✔					✔	✔			✔
Grenada										
Guatemala					✔					
Guinea										
Guinea-Bissau										
Guyana										
Haiti								✔		
Honduras							✔	✔		
Hong Kong, China		✔								✔
Hungary	✔			✔						
Iceland										
India								✔		
Indonesia	✗				✔					
Iran										
Iraq										
Ireland										
Israel										
Italy	✔		✗				✔			
Jamaica		✔		✔						
Japan										
Jordan	✔									
Kazakhstan			✗	✔	✔					
Kenya	✔							✔		
Kiribati										
Korea			✗					✔		
Kuwait										
Kyrgyz Republic	✔	✔				✔				
Lao PDR	—									
Latvia				✔						✔
Lebanon	✔									
Lesotho	✔									
Liberia	✔	✔			✔			✔		
Lithuania				✔						
Luxembourg										
Macedonia, former Yugoslav Republic of	✔			✔	✔		✔	✔	✔	
Madagascar	✔			✔			✔	✔		
Malawi										

✔ Reforms making it easier to do business   ✗ Reforms making it more difficult to do business

Economy	Reforms in 2007/08									
	Starting a business	Dealing with construction permits	Employing workers	Registering property	Getting credit	Protecting investors	Paying taxes	Trading across borders	Enforcing contracts	Closing a business
Malaysia	✔						✔			
Maldives										
Mali								✔		
Marshall Islands										
Mauritania	✔	✔								
Mauritius	✔			✔	✔					
Mexico							✔			✔
Micronesia										
Moldova	✔				✔					
Mongolia							✔	✔		
Montenegro		✗			✔					
Morocco					✔		✔	✔		
Mozambique			✔				✔		✔	
Namibia	✔									
Nepal										
Netherlands										
New Zealand	✔						✔			✔
Nicaragua										
Niger										
Nigeria								✔		
Norway										
Oman	✔									
Pakistan										
Palau								✔		
Panama	✔									
Papua New Guinea										
Paraguay										
Peru										
Philippines								✔		
Poland										✔
Portugal		✔							✔	✔
Puerto Rico										
Qatar										
Romania									✔	
Russian Federation										
Rwanda		✔		✔				✔	✔	
Samoa							✔			
São Tomé and Principe										
Saudi Arabia	✔			✔		✔				✔
Senegal	✔			✔				✔		
Serbia		✗		✔						
Seychelles										
Sierra Leone	✔	✔		✔				✔		
Singapore	✔	✔								
Slovakia	✔									
Slovenia	✔		✔				✔			
Solomon Islands										
South Africa	✔						✔			
Spain										
Sri Lanka					✔					

✔ Reforms making it easier to do business   ✗ Reforms making it more difficult to do business

Economy	Starting a business	Dealing with construction permits	Employing workers	Registering property	Getting credit	Protecting investors	Paying taxes	Trading across borders	Enforcing contracts	Closing a business
Reforms in 2007/08										
St. Kitts and Nevis										
St. Lucia										
St. Vincent and the Grenadines							✔			✔
Sudan										
Suriname										
Swaziland										
Sweden			✗							
Switzerland	✗									
Syria	✔							✔		
Taiwan, China					✔					
Tajikistan		✗				✔				
Tanzania										
Thailand				✔		✔	✔	✔		
Timor-Leste										
Togo										
Tonga	✔	✔								
Trinidad and Tobago										
Tunisia	✔				✔	✔	✔	✗		
Turkey						✔				
Uganda										
Ukraine		✗			✔		✔	✔		
United Arab Emirates					✔					
United Kingdom			✗							
United States										
Uruguay	✔						✔	✔		
Uzbekistan					✔					
Vanuatu					✔					
Venezuela							✗			
Vietnam					✔					
West Bank and Gaza	✔	✗			✔					
Yemen	✔									
Zambia	✔			✔			✔			
Zimbabwe		✗								

✔ Reforms making it easier to do business   ✗ Reforms making it more difficult to do business

Country
tables

AFGHANISTAN

		South Asia		GNI per capita (US$)	370
Ease of doing business (rank)	162	Low income		Population (m)	24.8

Starting a business (rank)	22	**Registering property** (rank)	174	**Trading across borders** (rank)	179
Procedures (number)	4	Procedures (number)	9	Documents to export (number)	12
Time (days)	9	Time (days)	250	Time to export (days)	74
Cost (% of income per capita)	59.5	Cost (% of property value)	7.0	Cost to export (US$ per container)	3,000
Minimum capital (% of income per capita)	0.0			Documents to import (number)	11
		Getting credit (rank)	178	Time to import (days)	77
Dealing with construction permits (rank)	140	Strength of legal rights index (0-10)	1	Cost to import (US$ per container)	2,600
Procedures (number)	13	Depth of credit information index (0-6)	0		
Time (days)	340	Public registry coverage (% of adults)	0.0	**Enforcing contracts** (rank)	160
Cost (% of income per capita)	14,918.9	Private bureau coverage (% of adults)	0.0	Procedures (number)	47
				Time (days)	1,642
Employing workers (rank)	30	**Protecting investors** (rank)	181	Cost (% of claim)	25.0
Difficulty of hiring index (0-100)	0	Extent of disclosure index (0-10)	0		
Rigidity of hours index (0-100)	40	Extent of director liability index (0-10)	0	**Closing a business** (rank)	181
Difficulty of firing index (0-100)	40	Ease of shareholder suits index (0-10)	2	Time (years)	NO PRACTICE
Rigidity of employment index (0-100)	27	Strength of investor protection index (0-10)	0.7	Cost (% of estate)	NO PRACTICE
Firing cost (weeks of salary)	0			Recovery rate (cents on the dollar)	0.0
		Paying taxes (rank)	49		
		Payments (number per year)	8		
		Time (hours per year)	275		
		Total tax rate (% of profit)	36.4		

ALBANIA

		Eastern Europe & Central Asia		GNI per capita (US$)	3,290
Ease of doing business (rank)	86	Lower middle income		Population (m)	3.2

Starting a business (rank)	67	**Registering property** (rank)	62	**Trading across borders** (rank)	77
Procedures (number)	6	Procedures (number)	6	Documents to export (number)	7
Time (days)	8	Time (days)	42	Time to export (days)	21
Cost (% of income per capita)	25.8	Cost (% of property value)	3.4	Cost to export (US$ per container)	770
Minimum capital (% of income per capita)	32.3			Documents to import (number)	9
		Getting credit (rank)	12	Time to import (days)	22
Dealing with construction permits (rank)	170	Strength of legal rights index (0-10)	9	Cost to import (US$ per container)	775
Procedures (number)	24	Depth of credit information index (0-6)	4		
Time (days)	331	Public registry coverage (% of adults)	8.3	**Enforcing contracts** (rank)	89
Cost (% of income per capita)	435.0	Private bureau coverage (% of adults)	0.0	Procedures (number)	39
				Time (days)	390
Employing workers (rank)	108	**Protecting investors** (rank)	14	Cost (% of claim)	38.7
Difficulty of hiring index (0-100)	44	Extent of disclosure index (0-10)	8		
Rigidity of hours index (0-100)	40	Extent of director liability index (0-10)	9	**Closing a business** (rank)	181
Difficulty of firing index (0-100)	20	Ease of shareholder suits index (0-10)	5	Time (years)	NO PRACTICE
Rigidity of employment index (0-100)	35	Strength of investor protection index (0-10)	7.3	Cost (% of estate)	NO PRACTICE
Firing cost (weeks of salary)	56			Recovery rate (cents on the dollar)	0.0
		Paying taxes (rank)	143		
		Payments (number per year)	44		
		Time (hours per year)	244		
		Total tax rate (% of profit)	50.5		

ALGERIA

		Middle East & North Africa		GNI per capita (US$)	3,620
Ease of doing business (rank)	132	Lower middle income		Population (m)	33.9

Starting a business (rank)	141	**Registering property** (rank)	162	**Trading across borders** (rank)	118
Procedures (number)	14	Procedures (number)	14	Documents to export (number)	8
Time (days)	24	Time (days)	51	Time to export (days)	17
Cost (% of income per capita)	10.8	Cost (% of property value)	7.5	Cost to export (US$ per container)	1,248
Minimum capital (% of income per capita)	36.6			Documents to import (number)	9
		Getting credit (rank)	131	Time to import (days)	23
Dealing with construction permits (rank)	112	Strength of legal rights index (0-10)	3	Cost to import (US$ per container)	1,428
Procedures (number)	22	Depth of credit information index (0-6)	2		
Time (days)	240	Public registry coverage (% of adults)	0.2	**Enforcing contracts** (rank)	126
Cost (% of income per capita)	46.8	Private bureau coverage (% of adults)	0.0	Procedures (number)	47
				Time (days)	630
Employing workers (rank)	118	**Protecting investors** (rank)	70	Cost (% of claim)	21.9
Difficulty of hiring index (0-100)	44	Extent of disclosure index (0-10)	6		
Rigidity of hours index (0-100)	60	Extent of director liability index (0-10)	6	**Closing a business** (rank)	49
Difficulty of firing index (0-100)	40	Ease of shareholder suits index (0-10)	4	Time (years)	2.5
Rigidity of employment index (0-100)	48	Strength of investor protection index (0-10)	5.3	Cost (% of estate)	7
Firing cost (weeks of salary)	17			Recovery rate (cents on the dollar)	41.7
		Paying taxes (rank)	166		
		Payments (number per year)	34		
		Time (hours per year)	451		
		Total tax rate (% of profit)	74.2		

ANGOLA

		Sub-Saharan Africa		GNI per capita (US$)	2,560
Ease of doing business (rank)	168	Lower middle income		Population (m)	17.0

Starting a business (rank)	156	**Registering property** (rank)	173	**Trading across borders** (rank)	172
Procedures (number)	8	Procedures (number)	7	Documents to export (number)	12
Time (days)	68	Time (days)	334	Time to export (days)	68
Cost (% of income per capita)	196.8	Cost (% of property value)	11.6	Cost to export (US$ per container)	2,250
Minimum capital (% of income per capita)	39.1			Documents to import (number)	9
		Getting credit (rank)	84	Time to import (days)	62
Dealing with construction permits (rank)	125	Strength of legal rights index (0-10)	4	Cost to import (US$ per container)	3,325
Procedures (number)	12	Depth of credit information index (0-6)	4		
Time (days)	328	Public registry coverage (% of adults)	2.7	**Enforcing contracts** (rank)	179
Cost (% of income per capita)	831.1	Private bureau coverage (% of adults)	0.0	Procedures (number)	46
				Time (days)	1,011
Employing workers (rank)	174	**Protecting investors** (rank)	53	Cost (% of claim)	44.4
Difficulty of hiring index (0-100)	67	Extent of disclosure index (0-10)	5		
Rigidity of hours index (0-100)	60	Extent of director liability index (0-10)	6	**Closing a business** (rank)	142
Difficulty of firing index (0-100)	70	Ease of shareholder suits index (0-10)	6	Time (years)	6.2
Rigidity of employment index (0-100)	66	Strength of investor protection index (0-10)	5.7	Cost (% of estate)	22
Firing cost (weeks of salary)	58			Recovery rate (cents on the dollar)	10.0
		Paying taxes (rank)	130		
		Payments (number per year)	31		
		Time (hours per year)	272		
		Total tax rate (% of profit)	53.2		

ANTIGUA AND BARBUDA

		Latin America & Caribbean		GNI per capita (US$)	11,520
Ease of doing business (rank)	42	High income		Population (m)	0.1

Starting a business (rank)	45	**Registering property** (rank)	97	**Trading across borders** (rank)	46
Procedures (number)	8	Procedures (number)	6	Documents to export (number)	5
Time (days)	21	Time (days)	26	Time to export (days)	15
Cost (% of income per capita)	11.6	Cost (% of property value)	10.9	Cost to export (US$ per container)	1,133
Minimum capital (% of income per capita)	0.0			Documents to import (number)	6
		Getting credit (rank)	109	Time to import (days)	15
Dealing with construction permits (rank)	22	Strength of legal rights index (0-10)	7	Cost to import (US$ per container)	1,133
Procedures (number)	13	Depth of credit information index (0-6)	0		
Time (days)	156	Public registry coverage (% of adults)	0.0	**Enforcing contracts** (rank)	73
Cost (% of income per capita)	25.8	Private bureau coverage (% of adults)	0.0	Procedures (number)	45
				Time (days)	351
Employing workers (rank)	46	**Protecting investors** (rank)	24	Cost (% of claim)	22.7
Difficulty of hiring index (0-100)	11	Extent of disclosure index (0-10)	4		
Rigidity of hours index (0-100)	0	Extent of director liability index (0-10)	8	**Closing a business** (rank)	61
Difficulty of firing index (0-100)	20	Ease of shareholder suits index (0-10)	7	Time (years)	3.0
Rigidity of employment index (0-100)	10	Strength of investor protection index (0-10)	6.3	Cost (% of estate)	7
Firing cost (weeks of salary)	52			Recovery rate (cents on the dollar)	35.5
		Paying taxes (rank)	136		
		Payments (number per year)	56		
		Time (hours per year)	207		
		Total tax rate (% of profit)	46.8		

ARGENTINA

		Latin America & Caribbean		GNI per capita (US$)	6,050
Ease of doing business (rank)	113	Upper middle income		Population (m)	39.5

Starting a business (rank)	135	**Registering property** (rank)	95	**Trading across borders** (rank)	106
Procedures (number)	15	Procedures (number)	5	Documents to export (number)	9
Time (days)	32	Time (days)	51	Time to export (days)	13
Cost (% of income per capita)	9.0	Cost (% of property value)	7.5	Cost to export (US$ per container)	1,480
Minimum capital (% of income per capita)	3.7			Documents to import (number)	7
		Getting credit (rank)	59	Time to import (days)	18
Dealing with construction permits (rank)	167	Strength of legal rights index (0-10)	4	Cost to import (US$ per container)	1,810
Procedures (number)	28	Depth of credit information index (0-6)	6		
Time (days)	338	Public registry coverage (% of adults)	31.2	**Enforcing contracts** (rank)	45
Cost (% of income per capita)	183.3	Private bureau coverage (% of adults)	100.0	Procedures (number)	36
				Time (days)	590
Employing workers (rank)	130	**Protecting investors** (rank)	104	Cost (% of claim)	16.5
Difficulty of hiring index (0-100)	44	Extent of disclosure index (0-10)	6		
Rigidity of hours index (0-100)	60	Extent of director liability index (0-10)	2	**Closing a business** (rank)	83
Difficulty of firing index (0-100)	0	Ease of shareholder suits index (0-10)	6	Time (years)	2.8
Rigidity of employment index (0-100)	35	Strength of investor protection index (0-10)	4.7	Cost (% of estate)	12
Firing cost (weeks of salary)	95			Recovery rate (cents on the dollar)	29.8
		Paying taxes (rank)	134		
		Payments (number per year)	9		
		Time (hours per year)	453		
		Total tax rate (% of profit)	108.1		

ARMENIA

Ease of doing business (rank)	44	Eastern Europe & Central Asia		GNI per capita (US$)	2,640
		Lower middle income		Population (m)	3.0

Starting a business (rank)	66	**Registering property** (rank)	5	**Trading across borders** (rank)	143
Procedures (number)	9	Procedures (number)	3	Documents to export (number)	7
Time (days)	18	Time (days)	4	Time to export (days)	30
Cost (% of income per capita)	3.6	Cost (% of property value)	0.3	Cost to export (US$ per container)	1,746
Minimum capital (% of income per capita)	2.3			Documents to import (number)	9
		Getting credit (rank)	28	Time to import (days)	24
Dealing with construction permits (rank)	42	Strength of legal rights index (0-10)	7	Cost to import (US$ per container)	1,981
Procedures (number)	19	Depth of credit information index (0-6)	5		
Time (days)	116	Public registry coverage (% of adults)	2.6	**Enforcing contracts** (rank)	61
Cost (% of income per capita)	28.0	Private bureau coverage (% of adults)	24.4	Procedures (number)	49
				Time (days)	285
Employing workers (rank)	54	**Protecting investors** (rank)	88	Cost (% of claim)	19.0
Difficulty of hiring index (0-100)	33	Extent of disclosure index (0-10)	5		
Rigidity of hours index (0-100)	40	Extent of director liability index (0-10)	2	**Closing a business** (rank)	47
Difficulty of firing index (0-100)	20	Ease of shareholder suits index (0-10)	8	Time (years)	1.9
Rigidity of employment index (0-100)	31	Strength of investor protection index (0-10)	5.0	Cost (% of estate)	4
Firing cost (weeks of salary)	13			Recovery rate (cents on the dollar)	41.8
		Paying taxes (rank)	150		
		Payments (number per year)	50		
		Time (hours per year)	958		
		Total tax rate (% of profit)	36.6		

AUSTRALIA

Ease of doing business (rank)	9	OECD: High Income		GNI per capita (US$)	35,960
		High income		Population (m)	21.0

Starting a business (rank)	3	**Registering property** (rank)	33	**Trading across borders** (rank)	45
Procedures (number)	2	Procedures (number)	5	Documents to export (number)	6
Time (days)	2	Time (days)	5	Time to export (days)	9
Cost (% of income per capita)	0.8	Cost (% of property value)	4.9	Cost to export (US$ per container)	1,200
Minimum capital (% of income per capita)	0.0			Documents to import (number)	6
		Getting credit (rank)	5	Time to import (days)	12
Dealing with construction permits (rank)	57	Strength of legal rights index (0-10)	9	Cost to import (US$ per container)	1,239
Procedures (number)	16	Depth of credit information index (0-6)	5		
Time (days)	221	Public registry coverage (% of adults)	0.0	**Enforcing contracts** (rank)	20
Cost (% of income per capita)	13.2	Private bureau coverage (% of adults)	100.0	Procedures (number)	28
				Time (days)	395
Employing workers (rank)	8	**Protecting investors** (rank)	53	Cost (% of claim)	20.7
Difficulty of hiring index (0-100)	0	Extent of disclosure index (0-10)	8		
Rigidity of hours index (0-100)	0	Extent of director liability index (0-10)	2	**Closing a business** (rank)	14
Difficulty of firing index (0-100)	10	Ease of shareholder suits index (0-10)	7	Time (years)	1.0
Rigidity of employment index (0-100)	3	Strength of investor protection index (0-10)	5.7	Cost (% of estate)	8
Firing cost (weeks of salary)	4			Recovery rate (cents on the dollar)	78.8
		Paying taxes (rank)	48		
		Payments (number per year)	12		
		Time (hours per year)	107		
		Total tax rate (% of profit)	50.3		

AUSTRIA

Ease of doing business (rank)	27	OECD: High Income		GNI per capita (US$)	42,700
		High income		Population (m)	8.3

Starting a business (rank)	104	**Registering property** (rank)	36	**Trading across borders** (rank)	19
Procedures (number)	8	Procedures (number)	3	Documents to export (number)	4
Time (days)	28	Time (days)	32	Time to export (days)	7
Cost (% of income per capita)	5.1	Cost (% of property value)	4.5	Cost to export (US$ per container)	1,125
Minimum capital (% of income per capita)	52.8			Documents to import (number)	5
		Getting credit (rank)	12	Time to import (days)	8
Dealing with construction permits (rank)	46	Strength of legal rights index (0-10)	7	Cost to import (US$ per container)	1,125
Procedures (number)	13	Depth of credit information index (0-6)	6		
Time (days)	194	Public registry coverage (% of adults)	1.3	**Enforcing contracts** (rank)	13
Cost (% of income per capita)	70.4	Private bureau coverage (% of adults)	40.9	Procedures (number)	25
				Time (days)	397
Employing workers (rank)	50	**Protecting investors** (rank)	126	Cost (% of claim)	18.0
Difficulty of hiring index (0-100)	0	Extent of disclosure index (0-10)	3		
Rigidity of hours index (0-100)	60	Extent of director liability index (0-10)	5	**Closing a business** (rank)	20
Difficulty of firing index (0-100)	40	Ease of shareholder suits index (0-10)	4	Time (years)	1.1
Rigidity of employment index (0-100)	33	Strength of investor protection index (0-10)	4.0	Cost (% of estate)	18
Firing cost (weeks of salary)	2			Recovery rate (cents on the dollar)	71.5
		Paying taxes (rank)	93		
		Payments (number per year)	22		
		Time (hours per year)	170		
		Total tax rate (% of profit)	54.5		

AZERBAIJAN

		Eastern Europe & Central Asia		GNI per capita (US$)	2,550
Ease of doing business (rank)	33	Lower middle income		Population (m)	8.6

Starting a business (rank)	13	**Registering property** (rank)	9	**Trading across borders** (rank)	174
Procedures (number)	6	Procedures (number)	4	Documents to export (number)	9
Time (days)	16	Time (days)	11	Time to export (days)	48
Cost (% of income per capita)	3.2	Cost (% of property value)	0.3	Cost to export (US$ per container)	3,075
Minimum capital (% of income per capita)	0.0			Documents to import (number)	14
		Getting credit (rank)	12	Time to import (days)	56
Dealing with construction permits (rank)	155	Strength of legal rights index (0-10)	8	Cost to import (US$ per container)	3,420
Procedures (number)	31	Depth of credit information index (0-6)	5		
Time (days)	207	Public registry coverage (% of adults)	3.1	**Enforcing contracts** (rank)	26
Cost (% of income per capita)	522.6	Private bureau coverage (% of adults)	0.0	Procedures (number)	39
				Time (days)	237
Employing workers (rank)	15	**Protecting investors** (rank)	18	Cost (% of claim)	18.5
Difficulty of hiring index (0-100)	0	Extent of disclosure index (0-10)	7		
Rigidity of hours index (0-100)	0	Extent of director liability index (0-10)	5	**Closing a business** (rank)	81
Difficulty of firing index (0-100)	10	Ease of shareholder suits index (0-10)	8	Time (years)	2.7
Rigidity of employment index (0-100)	3	Strength of investor protection index (0-10)	6.7	Cost (% of estate)	8
Firing cost (weeks of salary)	22			Recovery rate (cents on the dollar)	30.1
		Paying taxes (rank)	102		
		Payments (number per year)	23		
		Time (hours per year)	376		
		Total tax rate (% of profit)	41.1		

BAHAMAS, THE

		Latin America & Caribbean		GNI per capita (US$)	19,781
Ease of doing business (rank)	55	High income		Population (m)	0.3

Starting a business (rank)	45	**Registering property** (rank)	143	**Trading across borders** (rank)	51
Procedures (number)	7	Procedures (number)	7	Documents to export (number)	6
Time (days)	31	Time (days)	48	Time to export (days)	16
Cost (% of income per capita)	9.8	Cost (% of property value)	12.5	Cost to export (US$ per container)	930
Minimum capital (% of income per capita)	0.0			Documents to import (number)	6
		Getting credit (rank)	68	Time to import (days)	13
Dealing with construction permits (rank)	92	Strength of legal rights index (0-10)	9	Cost to import (US$ per container)	1,380
Procedures (number)	18	Depth of credit information index (0-6)	0		
Time (days)	197	Public registry coverage (% of adults)	0.0	**Enforcing contracts** (rank)	120
Cost (% of income per capita)	241.6	Private bureau coverage (% of adults)	0.0	Procedures (number)	49
				Time (days)	427
Employing workers (rank)	44	**Protecting investors** (rank)	104	Cost (% of claim)	28.9
Difficulty of hiring index (0-100)	11	Extent of disclosure index (0-10)	2		
Rigidity of hours index (0-100)	0	Extent of director liability index (0-10)	5	**Closing a business** (rank)	29
Difficulty of firing index (0-100)	40	Ease of shareholder suits index (0-10)	7	Time (years)	5.0
Rigidity of employment index (0-100)	17	Strength of investor protection index (0-10)	4.7	Cost (% of estate)	4
Firing cost (weeks of salary)	26			Recovery rate (cents on the dollar)	54.7
		Paying taxes (rank)	39		
		Payments (number per year)	17		
		Time (hours per year)	58		
		Total tax rate (% of profit)	47.0		

BAHRAIN

		Middle East & North Africa		GNI per capita (US$)	25,731
Ease of doing business (rank)	18	High income		Population (m)	0.8

Starting a business (rank)	49	**Registering property** (rank)	18	**Trading across borders** (rank)	21
Procedures (number)	7	Procedures (number)	2	Documents to export (number)	5
Time (days)	9	Time (days)	31	Time to export (days)	14
Cost (% of income per capita)	0.6	Cost (% of property value)	0.9	Cost to export (US$ per container)	805
Minimum capital (% of income per capita)	210.1			Documents to import (number)	6
		Getting credit (rank)	84	Time to import (days)	15
Dealing with construction permits (rank)	14	Strength of legal rights index (0-10)	4	Cost to import (US$ per container)	845
Procedures (number)	13	Depth of credit information index (0-6)	4		
Time (days)	56	Public registry coverage (% of adults)	0.0	**Enforcing contracts** (rank)	113
Cost (% of income per capita)	57.2	Private bureau coverage (% of adults)	35.8	Procedures (number)	48
				Time (days)	635
Employing workers (rank)	26	**Protecting investors** (rank)	53	Cost (% of claim)	14.7
Difficulty of hiring index (0-100)	0	Extent of disclosure index (0-10)	8		
Rigidity of hours index (0-100)	20	Extent of director liability index (0-10)	4	**Closing a business** (rank)	25
Difficulty of firing index (0-100)	50	Ease of shareholder suits index (0-10)	5	Time (years)	2.5
Rigidity of employment index (0-100)	23	Strength of investor protection index (0-10)	5.7	Cost (% of estate)	10
Firing cost (weeks of salary)	4			Recovery rate (cents on the dollar)	63.2
		Paying taxes (rank)	15		
		Payments (number per year)	25		
		Time (hours per year)	36		
		Total tax rate (% of profit)	15.0		

BANGLADESH

		South Asia		GNI per capita (US$)	470
Ease of doing business (rank)	110	Low income		Population (m)	158.6

Starting a business (rank)	90	**Registering property** (rank)	175	**Trading across borders** (rank)	105
Procedures (number)	7	Procedures (number)	8	Documents to export (number)	6
Time (days)	73	Time (days)	245	Time to export (days)	28
Cost (% of income per capita)	25.7	Cost (% of property value)	10.4	Cost to export (US$ per container)	970
Minimum capital (% of income per capita)	0.0			Documents to import (number)	8
		Getting credit (rank)	59	Time to import (days)	32
Dealing with construction permits (rank)	114	Strength of legal rights index (0-10)	8	Cost to import (US$ per container)	1,375
Procedures (number)	14	Depth of credit information index (0-6)	2		
Time (days)	231	Public registry coverage (% of adults)	0.9	**Enforcing contracts** (rank)	178
Cost (% of income per capita)	739.8	Private bureau coverage (% of adults)	0.0	Procedures (number)	41
				Time (days)	1,442
Employing workers (rank)	132	**Protecting investors** (rank)	18	Cost (% of claim)	63.3
Difficulty of hiring index (0-100)	44	Extent of disclosure index (0-10)	6		
Rigidity of hours index (0-100)	20	Extent of director liability index (0-10)	7	**Closing a business** (rank)	106
Difficulty of firing index (0-100)	40	Ease of shareholder suits index (0-10)	7	Time (years)	4.0
Rigidity of employment index (0-100)	35	Strength of investor protection index (0-10)	6.7	Cost (% of estate)	8
Firing cost (weeks of salary)	104			Recovery rate (cents on the dollar)	23.2
		Paying taxes (rank)	90		
		Payments (number per year)	21		
		Time (hours per year)	302		
		Total tax rate (% of profit)	39.5		

BELARUS

		Eastern Europe & Central Asia		GNI per capita (US$)	4,220
Ease of doing business (rank)	85	Upper middle income		Population (m)	9.7

Starting a business (rank)	97	**Registering property** (rank)	14	**Trading across borders** (rank)	134
Procedures (number)	8	Procedures (number)	4	Documents to export (number)	8
Time (days)	31	Time (days)	21	Time to export (days)	20
Cost (% of income per capita)	7.8	Cost (% of property value)	0.0	Cost to export (US$ per container)	1,772
Minimum capital (% of income per capita)	12.4			Documents to import (number)	8
		Getting credit (rank)	109	Time to import (days)	26
Dealing with construction permits (rank)	65	Strength of legal rights index (0-10)	2	Cost to import (US$ per container)	1,720
Procedures (number)	17	Depth of credit information index (0-6)	5		
Time (days)	210	Public registry coverage (% of adults)	2.4	**Enforcing contracts** (rank)	14
Cost (% of income per capita)	39.2	Private bureau coverage (% of adults)	0.0	Procedures (number)	28
				Time (days)	225
Employing workers (rank)	49	**Protecting investors** (rank)	104	Cost (% of claim)	23.4
Difficulty of hiring index (0-100)	0	Extent of disclosure index (0-10)	5		
Rigidity of hours index (0-100)	40	Extent of director liability index (0-10)	1	**Closing a business** (rank)	71
Difficulty of firing index (0-100)	40	Ease of shareholder suits index (0-10)	8	Time (years)	5.8
Rigidity of employment index (0-100)	27	Strength of investor protection index (0-10)	4.7	Cost (% of estate)	22
Firing cost (weeks of salary)	22			Recovery rate (cents on the dollar)	33.4
		Paying taxes (rank)	181		
		Payments (number per year)	112		
		Time (hours per year)	1,188		
		Total tax rate (% of profit)	117.5		

BELGIUM

		OECD: High Income		GNI per capita (US$)	40,710
Ease of doing business (rank)	19	High income		Population (m)	10.6

Starting a business (rank)	20	**Registering property** (rank)	168	**Trading across borders** (rank)	43
Procedures (number)	3	Procedures (number)	7	Documents to export (number)	4
Time (days)	4	Time (days)	132	Time to export (days)	8
Cost (% of income per capita)	5.2	Cost (% of property value)	12.7	Cost to export (US$ per container)	1,619
Minimum capital (% of income per capita)	19.9			Documents to import (number)	5
		Getting credit (rank)	43	Time to import (days)	9
Dealing with construction permits (rank)	44	Strength of legal rights index (0-10)	7	Cost to import (US$ per container)	1,600
Procedures (number)	14	Depth of credit information index (0-6)	4		
Time (days)	169	Public registry coverage (% of adults)	57.7	**Enforcing contracts** (rank)	22
Cost (% of income per capita)	65.2	Private bureau coverage (% of adults)	0.0	Procedures (number)	25
				Time (days)	505
Employing workers (rank)	37	**Protecting investors** (rank)	15	Cost (% of claim)	16.6
Difficulty of hiring index (0-100)	11	Extent of disclosure index (0-10)	8		
Rigidity of hours index (0-100)	40	Extent of director liability index (0-10)	6	**Closing a business** (rank)	8
Difficulty of firing index (0-100)	10	Ease of shareholder suits index (0-10)	7	Time (years)	0.9
Rigidity of employment index (0-100)	20	Strength of investor protection index (0-10)	7.0	Cost (% of estate)	4
Firing cost (weeks of salary)	16			Recovery rate (cents on the dollar)	86.3
		Paying taxes (rank)	64		
		Payments (number per year)	11		
		Time (hours per year)	156		
		Total tax rate (% of profit)	58.1		

BELIZE

Ease of doing business (rank)	78	Latin America & Caribbean Upper middle income		GNI per capita (US$)	3,800
				Population (m)	0.3

Starting a business (rank)	139	**Registering property** (rank)	121	**Trading across borders** (rank)	114
Procedures (number)	9	Procedures (number)	8	Documents to export (number)	7
Time (days)	44	Time (days)	60	Time to export (days)	21
Cost (% of income per capita)	51.1	Cost (% of property value)	4.7	Cost to export (US$ per container)	1,810
Minimum capital (% of income per capita)	0.0			Documents to import (number)	6
		Getting credit (rank)	84	Time to import (days)	21
Dealing with construction permits (rank)	2	Strength of legal rights index (0-10)	8	Cost to import (US$ per container)	2,145
Procedures (number)	11	Depth of credit information index (0-6)	0		
Time (days)	66	Public registry coverage (% of adults)	0.0	**Enforcing contracts** (rank)	168
Cost (% of income per capita)	17.8	Private bureau coverage (% of adults)	0.0	Procedures (number)	51
				Time (days)	892
Employing workers (rank)	25	**Protecting investors** (rank)	113	Cost (% of claim)	27.5
Difficulty of hiring index (0-100)	22	Extent of disclosure index (0-10)	3		
Rigidity of hours index (0-100)	20	Extent of director liability index (0-10)	4	**Closing a business** (rank)	24
Difficulty of firing index (0-100)	0	Ease of shareholder suits index (0-10)	6	Time (years)	1.0
Rigidity of employment index (0-100)	14	Strength of investor protection index (0-10)	4.3	Cost (% of estate)	23
Firing cost (weeks of salary)	24			Recovery rate (cents on the dollar)	63.4
		Paying taxes (rank)	53		
		Payments (number per year)	40		
		Time (hours per year)	147		
		Total tax rate (% of profit)	28.2		

BENIN

Ease of doing business (rank)	169	Sub-Saharan Africa Low income		GNI per capita (US$)	570
				Population (m)	9.0

Starting a business (rank)	149	**Registering property** (rank)	119	**Trading across borders** (rank)	129
Procedures (number)	7	Procedures (number)	4	Documents to export (number)	7
Time (days)	31	Time (days)	120	Time to export (days)	32
Cost (% of income per capita)	196.0	Cost (% of property value)	11.9	Cost to export (US$ per container)	1,237
Minimum capital (% of income per capita)	347.0			Documents to import (number)	7
		Getting credit (rank)	145	Time to import (days)	40
Dealing with construction permits (rank)	130	Strength of legal rights index (0-10)	3	Cost to import (US$ per container)	1,393
Procedures (number)	15	Depth of credit information index (0-6)	1		
Time (days)	410	Public registry coverage (% of adults)	10.5	**Enforcing contracts** (rank)	175
Cost (% of income per capita)	303.6	Private bureau coverage (% of adults)	0.0	Procedures (number)	42
				Time (days)	825
Employing workers (rank)	116	**Protecting investors** (rank)	150	Cost (% of claim)	64.7
Difficulty of hiring index (0-100)	39	Extent of disclosure index (0-10)	6		
Rigidity of hours index (0-100)	40	Extent of director liability index (0-10)	1	**Closing a business** (rank)	130
Difficulty of firing index (0-100)	40	Ease of shareholder suits index (0-10)	3	Time (years)	4.0
Rigidity of employment index (0-100)	40	Strength of investor protection index (0-10)	3.3	Cost (% of estate)	22
Firing cost (weeks of salary)	36			Recovery rate (cents on the dollar)	16.7
		Paying taxes (rank)	165		
		Payments (number per year)	55		
		Time (hours per year)	270		
		Total tax rate (% of profit)	73.2		

BHUTAN

Ease of doing business (rank)	124	South Asia Lower middle income		GNI per capita (US$)	1,770
				Population (m)	0.7

Starting a business (rank)	63	**Registering property** (rank)	38	**Trading across borders** (rank)	151
Procedures (number)	8	Procedures (number)	5	Documents to export (number)	8
Time (days)	46	Time (days)	64	Time to export (days)	38
Cost (% of income per capita)	8.5	Cost (% of property value)	0.0	Cost to export (US$ per container)	1,210
Minimum capital (% of income per capita)	0.0			Documents to import (number)	11
		Getting credit (rank)	172	Time to import (days)	38
Dealing with construction permits (rank)	116	Strength of legal rights index (0-10)	2	Cost to import (US$ per container)	2,140
Procedures (number)	25	Depth of credit information index (0-6)	0		
Time (days)	183	Public registry coverage (% of adults)	0.0	**Enforcing contracts** (rank)	37
Cost (% of income per capita)	158.4	Private bureau coverage (% of adults)	0.0	Procedures (number)	47
				Time (days)	225
Employing workers (rank)	13	**Protecting investors** (rank)	126	Cost (% of claim)	0.1
Difficulty of hiring index (0-100)	0	Extent of disclosure index (0-10)	5		
Rigidity of hours index (0-100)	0	Extent of director liability index (0-10)	3	**Closing a business** (rank)	181
Difficulty of firing index (0-100)	20	Ease of shareholder suits index (0-10)	4	Time (years)	NO PRACTICE
Rigidity of employment index (0-100)	7	Strength of investor protection index (0-10)	4.0	Cost (% of estate)	NO PRACTICE
Firing cost (weeks of salary)	10			Recovery rate (cents on the dollar)	0.0
		Paying taxes (rank)	82		
		Payments (number per year)	19		
		Time (hours per year)	274		
		Total tax rate (% of profit)	39.8		

BOLIVIA

Ease of doing business (rank)	150	Latin America & Caribbean		GNI per capita (US$)		1,260
		Lower middle income		Population (m)		9.5
Starting a business (rank)	165	**Registering property** (rank)	129	**Trading across borders** (rank)		117
Procedures (number)	15	Procedures (number)	7	Documents to export (number)		8
Time (days)	50	Time (days)	92	Time to export (days)		19
Cost (% of income per capita)	112.4	Cost (% of property value)	4.9	Cost to export (US$ per container)		1,425
Minimum capital (% of income per capita)	2.8			Documents to import (number)		7
		Getting credit (rank)	109	Time to import (days)		23
Dealing with construction permits (rank)	98	Strength of legal rights index (0-10)	1	Cost to import (US$ per container)		1,747
Procedures (number)	17	Depth of credit information index (0-6)	6			
Time (days)	249	Public registry coverage (% of adults)	11.9	**Enforcing contracts** (rank)		133
Cost (% of income per capita)	121.6	Private bureau coverage (% of adults)	29.7	Procedures (number)		40
				Time (days)		591
Employing workers (rank)	180	**Protecting investors** (rank)	126	Cost (% of claim)		33.2
Difficulty of hiring index (0-100)	78	Extent of disclosure index (0-10)	1			
Rigidity of hours index (0-100)	60	Extent of director liability index (0-10)	5	**Closing a business** (rank)		59
Difficulty of firing index (0-100)	100	Ease of shareholder suits index (0-10)	6	Time (years)		1.8
Rigidity of employment index (0-100)	79	Strength of investor protection index (0-10)	4.0	Cost (% of estate)		15
Firing cost (weeks of salary)	NOT POSSIBLE			Recovery rate (cents on the dollar)		37.3
		Paying taxes (rank)	176			
		Payments (number per year)	41			
		Time (hours per year)	1,080			
		Total tax rate (% of profit)	78.1			

BOSNIA AND HERZEGOVINA

Ease of doing business (rank)	119	Eastern Europe & Central Asia		GNI per capita (US$)		3,580
		Lower middle income		Population (m)		3.9
Starting a business (rank)	161	**Registering property** (rank)	144	**Trading across borders** (rank)		55
Procedures (number)	12	Procedures (number)	7	Documents to export (number)		6
Time (days)	60	Time (days)	128	Time to export (days)		16
Cost (% of income per capita)	30.8	Cost (% of property value)	5.2	Cost to export (US$ per container)		1,070
Minimum capital (% of income per capita)	36.3			Documents to import (number)		7
		Getting credit (rank)	59	Time to import (days)		16
Dealing with construction permits (rank)	137	Strength of legal rights index (0-10)	5	Cost to import (US$ per container)		1,035
Procedures (number)	16	Depth of credit information index (0-6)	5			
Time (days)	296	Public registry coverage (% of adults)	0.0	**Enforcing contracts** (rank)		123
Cost (% of income per capita)	666.9	Private bureau coverage (% of adults)	69.2	Procedures (number)		38
				Time (days)		595
Employing workers (rank)	117	**Protecting investors** (rank)	88	Cost (% of claim)		38.4
Difficulty of hiring index (0-100)	67	Extent of disclosure index (0-10)	3			
Rigidity of hours index (0-100)	40	Extent of director liability index (0-10)	6	**Closing a business** (rank)		60
Difficulty of firing index (0-100)	30	Ease of shareholder suits index (0-10)	6	Time (years)		3.3
Rigidity of employment index (0-100)	46	Strength of investor protection index (0-10)	5.0	Cost (% of estate)		9
Firing cost (weeks of salary)	31			Recovery rate (cents on the dollar)		35.9
		Paying taxes (rank)	154			
		Payments (number per year)	51			
		Time (hours per year)	428			
		Total tax rate (% of profit)	44.1			

BOTSWANA

Ease of doing business (rank)	38	Sub-Saharan Africa		GNI per capita (US$)		5,840
		Upper middle income		Population (m)		1.9
Starting a business (rank)	80	**Registering property** (rank)	29	**Trading across borders** (rank)		149
Procedures (number)	10	Procedures (number)	4	Documents to export (number)		6
Time (days)	78	Time (days)	11	Time to export (days)		31
Cost (% of income per capita)	2.3	Cost (% of property value)	5.0	Cost to export (US$ per container)		2,508
Minimum capital (% of income per capita)	0.0			Documents to import (number)		9
		Getting credit (rank)	43	Time to import (days)		42
Dealing with construction permits (rank)	119	Strength of legal rights index (0-10)	7	Cost to import (US$ per container)		3,064
Procedures (number)	24	Depth of credit information index (0-6)	4			
Time (days)	167	Public registry coverage (% of adults)	0.0	**Enforcing contracts** (rank)		92
Cost (% of income per capita)	311.9	Private bureau coverage (% of adults)	52.9	Procedures (number)		29
				Time (days)		987
Employing workers (rank)	73	**Protecting investors** (rank)	38	Cost (% of claim)		28.1
Difficulty of hiring index (0-100)	0	Extent of disclosure index (0-10)	7			
Rigidity of hours index (0-100)	20	Extent of director liability index (0-10)	8	**Closing a business** (rank)		26
Difficulty of firing index (0-100)	40	Ease of shareholder suits index (0-10)	3	Time (years)		1.7
Rigidity of employment index (0-100)	20	Strength of investor protection index (0-10)	6.0	Cost (% of estate)		15
Firing cost (weeks of salary)	90			Recovery rate (cents on the dollar)		60.3
		Paying taxes (rank)	17			
		Payments (number per year)	19			
		Time (hours per year)	140			
		Total tax rate (% of profit)	17.1			

BRAZIL

Ease of doing business (rank)	125	Latin America & Caribbean		GNI per capita (US$)	5,910
		Upper middle income		Population (m)	191.6

Starting a business (rank)	127	**Registering property** (rank)	111	**Trading across borders** (rank)	92
Procedures (number)	18	Procedures (number)	14	Documents to export (number)	8
Time (days)	152	Time (days)	42	Time to export (days)	14
Cost (% of income per capita)	8.2	Cost (% of property value)	2.7	Cost to export (US$ per container)	1,240
Minimum capital (% of income per capita)	0.0			Documents to import (number)	7
		Getting credit (rank)	84	Time to import (days)	19
Dealing with construction permits (rank)	108	Strength of legal rights index (0-10)	3	Cost to import (US$ per container)	1,275
Procedures (number)	18	Depth of credit information index (0-6)	5		
Time (days)	411	Public registry coverage (% of adults)	20.2	**Enforcing contracts** (rank)	100
Cost (% of income per capita)	46.7	Private bureau coverage (% of adults)	62.2	Procedures (number)	45
				Time (days)	616
Employing workers (rank)	121	**Protecting investors** (rank)	70	Cost (% of claim)	16.5
Difficulty of hiring index (0-100)	78	Extent of disclosure index (0-10)	6		
Rigidity of hours index (0-100)	60	Extent of director liability index (0-10)	7	**Closing a business** (rank)	127
Difficulty of firing index (0-100)	0	Ease of shareholder suits index (0-10)	3	Time (years)	4.0
Rigidity of employment index (0-100)	46	Strength of investor protection index (0-10)	5.3	Cost (% of estate)	12
Firing cost (weeks of salary)	37			Recovery rate (cents on the dollar)	17.1
		Paying taxes (rank)	145		
		Payments (number per year)	11		
		Time (hours per year)	2,600		
		Total tax rate (% of profit)	69.4		

BRUNEI

Ease of doing business (rank)	88	East Asia & Pacific		GNI per capita (US$)	36,216
		High income		Population (m)	0.4

Starting a business (rank)	130	**Registering property** (rank)	177	**Trading across borders** (rank)	42
Procedures (number)	18	Procedures (number)	NO PRACTICE	Documents to export (number)	6
Time (days)	116	Time (days)	NO PRACTICE	Time to export (days)	28
Cost (% of income per capita)	9.2	Cost (% of property value)	NO PRACTICE	Cost to export (US$ per container)	630
Minimum capital (% of income per capita)	0.0			Documents to import (number)	6
		Getting credit (rank)	109	Time to import (days)	19
Dealing with construction permits (rank)	72	Strength of legal rights index (0-10)	7	Cost to import (US$ per container)	708
Procedures (number)	32	Depth of credit information index (0-6)	0		
Time (days)	167	Public registry coverage (% of adults)	0.0	**Enforcing contracts** (rank)	157
Cost (% of income per capita)	5.3	Private bureau coverage (% of adults)	0.0	Procedures (number)	58
				Time (days)	540
Employing workers (rank)	5	**Protecting investors** (rank)	113	Cost (% of claim)	36.6
Difficulty of hiring index (0-100)	0	Extent of disclosure index (0-10)	3		
Rigidity of hours index (0-100)	20	Extent of director liability index (0-10)	2	**Closing a business** (rank)	35
Difficulty of firing index (0-100)	0	Ease of shareholder suits index (0-10)	8	Time (years)	2.5
Rigidity of employment index (0-100)	7	Strength of investor protection index (0-10)	4.3	Cost (% of estate)	4
Firing cost (weeks of salary)	4			Recovery rate (cents on the dollar)	47.2
		Paying taxes (rank)	35		
		Payments (number per year)	15		
		Time (hours per year)	144		
		Total tax rate (% of profit)	37.4		

BULGARIA

Ease of doing business (rank)	45	Eastern Europe & Central Asia		GNI per capita (US$)	4,590
		Upper middle income		Population (m)	7.6

Starting a business (rank)	81	**Registering property** (rank)	59	**Trading across borders** (rank)	102
Procedures (number)	4	Procedures (number)	8	Documents to export (number)	5
Time (days)	49	Time (days)	19	Time to export (days)	23
Cost (% of income per capita)	2.0	Cost (% of property value)	2.3	Cost to export (US$ per container)	1,626
Minimum capital (% of income per capita)	47.8			Documents to import (number)	7
		Getting credit (rank)	5	Time to import (days)	21
Dealing with construction permits (rank)	117	Strength of legal rights index (0-10)	8	Cost to import (US$ per container)	1,776
Procedures (number)	24	Depth of credit information index (0-6)	6		
Time (days)	139	Public registry coverage (% of adults)	30.7	**Enforcing contracts** (rank)	86
Cost (% of income per capita)	493.6	Private bureau coverage (% of adults)	5.0	Procedures (number)	39
				Time (days)	564
Employing workers (rank)	60	**Protecting investors** (rank)	38	Cost (% of claim)	23.8
Difficulty of hiring index (0-100)	17	Extent of disclosure index (0-10)	10		
Rigidity of hours index (0-100)	60	Extent of director liability index (0-10)	1	**Closing a business** (rank)	75
Difficulty of firing index (0-100)	10	Ease of shareholder suits index (0-10)	7	Time (years)	3.3
Rigidity of employment index (0-100)	29	Strength of investor protection index (0-10)	6.0	Cost (% of estate)	9
Firing cost (weeks of salary)	9			Recovery rate (cents on the dollar)	32.1
		Paying taxes (rank)	94		
		Payments (number per year)	17		
		Time (hours per year)	616		
		Total tax rate (% of profit)	34.9		

BURKINA FASO

		Sub-Saharan Africa		GNI per capita (US$)	430
Ease of doing business (rank)	148	Low income		Population (m)	14.8

Starting a business (rank)	113	**Registering property** (rank)	148	**Trading across borders** (rank)	173
Procedures (number)	5	Procedures (number)	6	Documents to export (number)	11
Time (days)	16	Time (days)	136	Time to export (days)	45
Cost (% of income per capita)	62.3	Cost (% of property value)	10.2	Cost to export (US$ per container)	2,132
Minimum capital (% of income per capita)	458.8			Documents to import (number)	11
		Getting credit (rank)	145	Time to import (days)	54
Dealing with construction permits (rank)	106	Strength of legal rights index (0-10)	3	Cost to import (US$ per container)	3,630
Procedures (number)	15	Depth of credit information index (0-6)	1		
Time (days)	214	Public registry coverage (% of adults)	1.9	**Enforcing contracts** (rank)	110
Cost (% of income per capita)	577.9	Private bureau coverage (% of adults)	0.0	Procedures (number)	37
				Time (days)	446
Employing workers (rank)	57	**Protecting investors** (rank)	142	Cost (% of claim)	107.4
Difficulty of hiring index (0-100)	33	Extent of disclosure index (0-10)	6		
Rigidity of hours index (0-100)	20	Extent of director liability index (0-10)	1	**Closing a business** (rank)	110
Difficulty of firing index (0-100)	10	Ease of shareholder suits index (0-10)	4	Time (years)	4.0
Rigidity of employment index (0-100)	21	Strength of investor protection index (0-10)	3.7	Cost (% of estate)	9
Firing cost (weeks of salary)	34			Recovery rate (cents on the dollar)	21.7
		Paying taxes (rank)	132		
		Payments (number per year)	45		
		Time (hours per year)	270		
		Total tax rate (% of profit)	44.6		

BURUNDI

		Sub-Saharan Africa		GNI per capita (US$)	110
Ease of doing business (rank)	177	Low income		Population (m)	8.5

Starting a business (rank)	138	**Registering property** (rank)	125	**Trading across borders** (rank)	170
Procedures (number)	11	Procedures (number)	5	Documents to export (number)	9
Time (days)	43	Time (days)	94	Time to export (days)	47
Cost (% of income per capita)	215.0	Cost (% of property value)	10.7	Cost to export (US$ per container)	2,147
Minimum capital (% of income per capita)	0.0			Documents to import (number)	10
		Getting credit (rank)	163	Time to import (days)	71
Dealing with construction permits (rank)	173	Strength of legal rights index (0-10)	2	Cost to import (US$ per container)	3,705
Procedures (number)	20	Depth of credit information index (0-6)	1		
Time (days)	384	Public registry coverage (% of adults)	0.3	**Enforcing contracts** (rank)	170
Cost (% of income per capita)	8,515.8	Private bureau coverage (% of adults)	0.0	Procedures (number)	44
				Time (days)	832
Employing workers (rank)	70	**Protecting investors** (rank)	150	Cost (% of claim)	38.6
Difficulty of hiring index (0-100)	0	Extent of disclosure index (0-10)	4		
Rigidity of hours index (0-100)	60	Extent of director liability index (0-10)	1	**Closing a business** (rank)	181
Difficulty of firing index (0-100)	30	Ease of shareholder suits index (0-10)	5	Time (years)	NO PRACTICE
Rigidity of employment index (0-100)	30	Strength of investor protection index (0-10)	3.3	Cost (% of estate)	NO PRACTICE
Firing cost (weeks of salary)	26			Recovery rate (cents on the dollar)	0.0
		Paying taxes (rank)	114		
		Payments (number per year)	32		
		Time (hours per year)	140		
		Total tax rate (% of profit)	278.7		

CAMBODIA

		East Asia & Pacific		GNI per capita (US$)	540
Ease of doing business (rank)	135	Low income		Population (m)	14.4

Starting a business (rank)	169	**Registering property** (rank)	108	**Trading across borders** (rank)	122
Procedures (number)	9	Procedures (number)	7	Documents to export (number)	11
Time (days)	85	Time (days)	56	Time to export (days)	22
Cost (% of income per capita)	151.7	Cost (% of property value)	4.4	Cost to export (US$ per container)	732
Minimum capital (% of income per capita)	43.9			Documents to import (number)	11
		Getting credit (rank)	68	Time to import (days)	30
Dealing with construction permits (rank)	147	Strength of legal rights index (0-10)	9	Cost to import (US$ per container)	872
Procedures (number)	23	Depth of credit information index (0-6)	0		
Time (days)	709	Public registry coverage (% of adults)	0.0	**Enforcing contracts** (rank)	136
Cost (% of income per capita)	64.3	Private bureau coverage (% of adults)	0.0	Procedures (number)	44
				Time (days)	401
Employing workers (rank)	134	**Protecting investors** (rank)	70	Cost (% of claim)	102.7
Difficulty of hiring index (0-100)	44	Extent of disclosure index (0-10)	5		
Rigidity of hours index (0-100)	60	Extent of director liability index (0-10)	9	**Closing a business** (rank)	181
Difficulty of firing index (0-100)	30	Ease of shareholder suits index (0-10)	2	Time (years)	NO PRACTICE
Rigidity of employment index (0-100)	45	Strength of investor protection index (0-10)	5.3	Cost (% of estate)	NO PRACTICE
Firing cost (weeks of salary)	39			Recovery rate (cents on the dollar)	0.0
		Paying taxes (rank)	24		
		Payments (number per year)	27		
		Time (hours per year)	137		
		Total tax rate (% of profit)	22.6		

CAMEROON

		Sub-Saharan Africa		GNI per capita (US$)	1,050
Ease of doing business (rank)	164	Lower middle income		Population (m)	18.5

Starting a business (rank)	171	**Registering property** (rank)	138	**Trading across borders** (rank)	137
Procedures (number)	13	Procedures (number)	5	Documents to export (number)	9
Time (days)	37	Time (days)	93	Time to export (days)	27
Cost (% of income per capita)	137.1	Cost (% of property value)	17.8	Cost to export (US$ per container)	995
Minimum capital (% of income per capita)	188.0			Documents to import (number)	8
		Getting credit (rank)	131	Time to import (days)	33
Dealing with construction permits (rank)	154	Strength of legal rights index (0-10)	3	Cost to import (US$ per container)	1,672
Procedures (number)	15	Depth of credit information index (0-6)	2		
Time (days)	426	Public registry coverage (% of adults)	4.9	**Enforcing contracts** (rank)	172
Cost (% of income per capita)	1,277.2	Private bureau coverage (% of adults)	0.0	Procedures (number)	43
				Time (days)	800
Employing workers (rank)	124	**Protecting investors** (rank)	113	Cost (% of claim)	46.6
Difficulty of hiring index (0-100)	28	Extent of disclosure index (0-10)	6		
Rigidity of hours index (0-100)	40	Extent of director liability index (0-10)	1	**Closing a business** (rank)	95
Difficulty of firing index (0-100)	70	Ease of shareholder suits index (0-10)	6	Time (years)	3.2
Rigidity of employment index (0-100)	46	Strength of investor protection index (0-10)	4.3	Cost (% of estate)	15
Firing cost (weeks of salary)	33			Recovery rate (cents on the dollar)	25.5
		Paying taxes (rank)	171		
		Payments (number per year)	41		
		Time (hours per year)	1,400		
		Total tax rate (% of profit)	51.4		

CANADA

		OECD: High Income		GNI per capita (US$)	39,420
Ease of doing business (rank)	8	High income		Population (m)	33.0

Starting a business (rank)	2	**Registering property** (rank)	32	**Trading across borders** (rank)	44
Procedures (number)	1	Procedures (number)	6	Documents to export (number)	3
Time (days)	5	Time (days)	17	Time to export (days)	7
Cost (% of income per capita)	0.5	Cost (% of property value)	1.8	Cost to export (US$ per container)	1,660
Minimum capital (% of income per capita)	0.0			Documents to import (number)	4
		Getting credit (rank)	28	Time to import (days)	11
Dealing with construction permits (rank)	29	Strength of legal rights index (0-10)	6	Cost to import (US$ per container)	1,785
Procedures (number)	14	Depth of credit information index (0-6)	6		
Time (days)	75	Public registry coverage (% of adults)	0.0	**Enforcing contracts** (rank)	58
Cost (% of income per capita)	103.7	Private bureau coverage (% of adults)	100.0	Procedures (number)	36
				Time (days)	570
Employing workers (rank)	18	**Protecting investors** (rank)	5	Cost (% of claim)	22.3
Difficulty of hiring index (0-100)	11	Extent of disclosure index (0-10)	8		
Rigidity of hours index (0-100)	0	Extent of director liability index (0-10)	9	**Closing a business** (rank)	4
Difficulty of firing index (0-100)	0	Ease of shareholder suits index (0-10)	8	Time (years)	0.8
Rigidity of employment index (0-100)	4	Strength of investor protection index (0-10)	8.3	Cost (% of estate)	4
Firing cost (weeks of salary)	28			Recovery rate (cents on the dollar)	88.7
		Paying taxes (rank)	28		
		Payments (number per year)	9		
		Time (hours per year)	119		
		Total tax rate (% of profit)	45.4		

CAPE VERDE

		Sub-Saharan Africa		GNI per capita (US$)	2,430
Ease of doing business (rank)	143	Lower middle income		Population (m)	0.5

Starting a business (rank)	163	**Registering property** (rank)	124	**Trading across borders** (rank)	56
Procedures (number)	12	Procedures (number)	6	Documents to export (number)	5
Time (days)	52	Time (days)	73	Time to export (days)	19
Cost (% of income per capita)	35.7	Cost (% of property value)	7.7	Cost to export (US$ per container)	1,325
Minimum capital (% of income per capita)	47.5			Documents to import (number)	5
		Getting credit (rank)	123	Time to import (days)	18
Dealing with construction permits (rank)	79	Strength of legal rights index (0-10)	3	Cost to import (US$ per container)	1,129
Procedures (number)	18	Depth of credit information index (0-6)	3		
Time (days)	120	Public registry coverage (% of adults)	21.8	**Enforcing contracts** (rank)	40
Cost (% of income per capita)	639.1	Private bureau coverage (% of adults)	0.0	Procedures (number)	37
				Time (days)	425
Employing workers (rank)	169	**Protecting investors** (rank)	126	Cost (% of claim)	21.8
Difficulty of hiring index (0-100)	33	Extent of disclosure index (0-10)	1		
Rigidity of hours index (0-100)	60	Extent of director liability index (0-10)	5	**Closing a business** (rank)	181
Difficulty of firing index (0-100)	70	Ease of shareholder suits index (0-10)	6	Time (years)	NO PRACTICE
Rigidity of employment index (0-100)	54	Strength of investor protection index (0-10)	4.0	Cost (% of estate)	NO PRACTICE
Firing cost (weeks of salary)	93			Recovery rate (cents on the dollar)	0.0
		Paying taxes (rank)	115		
		Payments (number per year)	57		
		Time (hours per year)	100		
		Total tax rate (% of profit)	54.0		

CENTRAL AFRICAN REPUBLIC

Sub-Saharan Africa			GNI per capita (US$)		380
Ease of doing business (rank)	180	Low income		Population (m)	4.3

Starting a business (rank)	152	**Registering property** (rank)	133	**Trading across borders** (rank)	175
Procedures (number)	10	Procedures (number)	5	Documents to export (number)	8
Time (days)	14	Time (days)	75	Time to export (days)	57
Cost (% of income per capita)	232.3	Cost (% of property value)	18.6	Cost to export (US$ per container)	5,121
Minimum capital (% of income per capita)	513.9			Documents to import (number)	18
		Getting credit (rank)	131	Time to import (days)	66
Dealing with construction permits (rank)	138	Strength of legal rights index (0-10)	3	Cost to import (US$ per container)	5,074
Procedures (number)	21	Depth of credit information index (0-6)	2		
Time (days)	239	Public registry coverage (% of adults)	1.2	**Enforcing contracts** (rank)	169
Cost (% of income per capita)	278.9	Private bureau coverage (% of adults)	0.0	Procedures (number)	43
				Time (days)	660
Employing workers (rank)	151	**Protecting investors** (rank)	126	Cost (% of claim)	82.0
Difficulty of hiring index (0-100)	72	Extent of disclosure index (0-10)	6		
Rigidity of hours index (0-100)	60	Extent of director liability index (0-10)	1	**Closing a business** (rank)	181
Difficulty of firing index (0-100)	50	Ease of shareholder suits index (0-10)	5	Time (years)	4.8
Rigidity of employment index (0-100)	61	Strength of investor protection index (0-10)	4.0	Cost (% of estate)	76
Firing cost (weeks of salary)	22			Recovery rate (cents on the dollar)	0.0
		Paying taxes (rank)	178		
		Payments (number per year)	54		
		Time (hours per year)	504		
		Total tax rate (% of profit)	203.8		

CHAD

Sub-Saharan Africa			GNI per capita (US$)		540
Ease of doing business (rank)	175	Low income		Population (m)	10.8

Starting a business (rank)	180	**Registering property** (rank)	132	**Trading across borders** (rank)	159
Procedures (number)	19	Procedures (number)	6	Documents to export (number)	6
Time (days)	75	Time (days)	44	Time to export (days)	78
Cost (% of income per capita)	175.0	Cost (% of property value)	22.7	Cost to export (US$ per container)	5,367
Minimum capital (% of income per capita)	365.1			Documents to import (number)	9
		Getting credit (rank)	145	Time to import (days)	102
Dealing with construction permits (rank)	70	Strength of legal rights index (0-10)	3	Cost to import (US$ per container)	6,020
Procedures (number)	9	Depth of credit information index (0-6)	1		
Time (days)	181	Public registry coverage (% of adults)	0.6	**Enforcing contracts** (rank)	166
Cost (% of income per capita)	974.7	Private bureau coverage (% of adults)	0.0	Procedures (number)	41
				Time (days)	743
Employing workers (rank)	139	**Protecting investors** (rank)	126	Cost (% of claim)	77.4
Difficulty of hiring index (0-100)	39	Extent of disclosure index (0-10)	6		
Rigidity of hours index (0-100)	60	Extent of director liability index (0-10)	1	**Closing a business** (rank)	181
Difficulty of firing index (0-100)	40	Ease of shareholder suits index (0-10)	5	Time (years)	NO PRACTICE
Rigidity of employment index (0-100)	46	Strength of investor protection index (0-10)	4.0	Cost (% of estate)	NO PRACTICE
Firing cost (weeks of salary)	36			Recovery rate (cents on the dollar)	0.0
		Paying taxes (rank)	130		
		Payments (number per year)	54		
		Time (hours per year)	122		
		Total tax rate (% of profit)	60.5		

CHILE

Latin America & Caribbean			GNI per capita (US$)		8,350
Ease of doing business (rank)	40	Upper middle income		Population (m)	16.6

Starting a business (rank)	55	**Registering property** (rank)	39	**Trading across borders** (rank)	53
Procedures (number)	9	Procedures (number)	6	Documents to export (number)	6
Time (days)	27	Time (days)	31	Time to export (days)	21
Cost (% of income per capita)	7.5	Cost (% of property value)	1.3	Cost to export (US$ per container)	745
Minimum capital (% of income per capita)	0.0			Documents to import (number)	7
		Getting credit (rank)	68	Time to import (days)	21
Dealing with construction permits (rank)	62	Strength of legal rights index (0-10)	4	Cost to import (US$ per container)	795
Procedures (number)	18	Depth of credit information index (0-6)	5		
Time (days)	155	Public registry coverage (% of adults)	28.1	**Enforcing contracts** (rank)	65
Cost (% of income per capita)	101.3	Private bureau coverage (% of adults)	34.5	Procedures (number)	36
				Time (days)	480
Employing workers (rank)	74	**Protecting investors** (rank)	38	Cost (% of claim)	28.6
Difficulty of hiring index (0-100)	33	Extent of disclosure index (0-10)	7		
Rigidity of hours index (0-100)	20	Extent of director liability index (0-10)	6	**Closing a business** (rank)	112
Difficulty of firing index (0-100)	20	Ease of shareholder suits index (0-10)	5	Time (years)	4.5
Rigidity of employment index (0-100)	24	Strength of investor protection index (0-10)	6.0	Cost (% of estate)	15
Firing cost (weeks of salary)	52			Recovery rate (cents on the dollar)	21.3
		Paying taxes (rank)	41		
		Payments (number per year)	10		
		Time (hours per year)	316		
		Total tax rate (% of profit)	25.9		

CHINA

Ease of doing business (rank)	83	East Asia & Pacific Lower middle income		GNI per capita (US$) Population (m)	2,360 1,320.0

Starting a business (rank)	151	**Registering property** (rank)	30	**Trading across borders** (rank)	48
Procedures (number)	14	Procedures (number)	4	Documents to export (number)	7
Time (days)	40	Time (days)	29	Time to export (days)	21
Cost (% of income per capita)	8.4	Cost (% of property value)	3.2	Cost to export (US$ per container)	460
Minimum capital (% of income per capita)	158.1			Documents to import (number)	6
		Getting credit (rank)	59	Time to import (days)	24
Dealing with construction permits (rank)	176	Strength of legal rights index (0-10)	6	Cost to import (US$ per container)	545
Procedures (number)	37	Depth of credit information index (0-6)	4		
Time (days)	336	Public registry coverage (% of adults)	58.8	**Enforcing contracts** (rank)	18
Cost (% of income per capita)	698.4	Private bureau coverage (% of adults)	0.0	Procedures (number)	34
				Time (days)	406
Employing workers (rank)	111	**Protecting investors** (rank)	88	Cost (% of claim)	11.1
Difficulty of hiring index (0-100)	11	Extent of disclosure index (0-10)	10		
Rigidity of hours index (0-100)	20	Extent of director liability index (0-10)	1	**Closing a business** (rank)	62
Difficulty of firing index (0-100)	50	Ease of shareholder suits index (0-10)	4	Time (years)	1.7
Rigidity of employment index (0-100)	27	Strength of investor protection index (0-10)	5.0	Cost (% of estate)	22
Firing cost (weeks of salary)	91			Recovery rate (cents on the dollar)	35.3
		Paying taxes (rank)	132		
		Payments (number per year)	9		
		Time (hours per year)	504		
		Total tax rate (% of profit)	79.9		

COLOMBIA

Ease of doing business (rank)	53	Latin America & Caribbean Lower middle income		GNI per capita (US$) Population (m)	3,250 46.1

Starting a business (rank)	79	**Registering property** (rank)	78	**Trading across borders** (rank)	96
Procedures (number)	9	Procedures (number)	9	Documents to export (number)	6
Time (days)	36	Time (days)	23	Time to export (days)	14
Cost (% of income per capita)	14.1	Cost (% of property value)	2.4	Cost to export (US$ per container)	1,690
Minimum capital (% of income per capita)	0.0			Documents to import (number)	8
		Getting credit (rank)	59	Time to import (days)	15
Dealing with construction permits (rank)	54	Strength of legal rights index (0-10)	5	Cost to import (US$ per container)	1,640
Procedures (number)	13	Depth of credit information index (0-6)	5		
Time (days)	114	Public registry coverage (% of adults)	0.0	**Enforcing contracts** (rank)	149
Cost (% of income per capita)	661.6	Private bureau coverage (% of adults)	42.5	Procedures (number)	34
				Time (days)	1,346
Employing workers (rank)	80	**Protecting investors** (rank)	24	Cost (% of claim)	52.6
Difficulty of hiring index (0-100)	11	Extent of disclosure index (0-10)	8		
Rigidity of hours index (0-100)	40	Extent of director liability index (0-10)	2	**Closing a business** (rank)	30
Difficulty of firing index (0-100)	20	Ease of shareholder suits index (0-10)	9	Time (years)	3.0
Rigidity of employment index (0-100)	24	Strength of investor protection index (0-10)	6.3	Cost (% of estate)	1
Firing cost (weeks of salary)	59			Recovery rate (cents on the dollar)	52.8
		Paying taxes (rank)	141		
		Payments (number per year)	31		
		Time (hours per year)	256		
		Total tax rate (% of profit)	78.4		

COMOROS

Ease of doing business (rank)	155	Sub-Saharan Africa Low income		GNI per capita (US$) Population (m)	680 0.6

Starting a business (rank)	160	**Registering property** (rank)	93	**Trading across borders** (rank)	129
Procedures (number)	11	Procedures (number)	5	Documents to export (number)	10
Time (days)	23	Time (days)	24	Time to export (days)	30
Cost (% of income per capita)	188.6	Cost (% of property value)	20.8	Cost to export (US$ per container)	1,073
Minimum capital (% of income per capita)	280.8			Documents to import (number)	10
		Getting credit (rank)	163	Time to import (days)	21
Dealing with construction permits (rank)	64	Strength of legal rights index (0-10)	3	Cost to import (US$ per container)	1,057
Procedures (number)	18	Depth of credit information index (0-6)	0		
Time (days)	164	Public registry coverage (% of adults)	0.0	**Enforcing contracts** (rank)	150
Cost (% of income per capita)	77.9	Private bureau coverage (% of adults)	0.0	Procedures (number)	43
				Time (days)	506
Employing workers (rank)	162	**Protecting investors** (rank)	126	Cost (% of claim)	89.4
Difficulty of hiring index (0-100)	39	Extent of disclosure index (0-10)	6		
Rigidity of hours index (0-100)	60	Extent of director liability index (0-10)	1	**Closing a business** (rank)	181
Difficulty of firing index (0-100)	40	Ease of shareholder suits index (0-10)	5	Time (years)	NO PRACTICE
Rigidity of employment index (0-100)	46	Strength of investor protection index (0-10)	4.0	Cost (% of estate)	NO PRACTICE
Firing cost (weeks of salary)	100			Recovery rate (cents on the dollar)	0.0
		Paying taxes (rank)	55		
		Payments (number per year)	20		
		Time (hours per year)	100		
		Total tax rate (% of profit)	48.8		

CONGO, DEM. REP.

		Sub-Saharan Africa		GNI per capita (US$)	140
Ease of doing business (rank)	181	Low income		Population (m)	62.4
Starting a business (rank)	154	**Registering property** (rank)	152	**Trading across borders** (rank)	160
Procedures (number)	13	Procedures (number)	8	Documents to export (number)	8
Time (days)	155	Time (days)	57	Time to export (days)	46
Cost (% of income per capita)	435.4	Cost (% of property value)	9.2	Cost to export (US$ per container)	2,607
Minimum capital (% of income per capita)	0.0			Documents to import (number)	9
		Getting credit (rank)	163	Time to import (days)	66
Dealing with construction permits (rank)	141	Strength of legal rights index (0-10)	3	Cost to import (US$ per container)	2,483
Procedures (number)	14	Depth of credit information index (0-6)	0		
Time (days)	322	Public registry coverage (% of adults)	0.0	**Enforcing contracts** (rank)	173
Cost (% of income per capita)	1,725.8	Private bureau coverage (% of adults)	0.0	Procedures (number)	43
				Time (days)	645
Employing workers (rank)	175	**Protecting investors** (rank)	150	Cost (% of claim)	151.8
Difficulty of hiring index (0-100)	72	Extent of disclosure index (0-10)	3		
Rigidity of hours index (0-100)	80	Extent of director liability index (0-10)	3	**Closing a business** (rank)	150
Difficulty of firing index (0-100)	70	Ease of shareholder suits index (0-10)	4	Time (years)	5.2
Rigidity of employment index (0-100)	74	Strength of investor protection index (0-10)	3.3	Cost (% of estate)	29
Firing cost (weeks of salary)	31			Recovery rate (cents on the dollar)	5.4
		Paying taxes (rank)	153		
		Payments (number per year)	32		
		Time (hours per year)	308		
		Total tax rate (% of profit)	229.8		

CONGO, REP.

		Sub-Saharan Africa		GNI per capita (US$)	1,540
Ease of doing business (rank)	178	Lower middle income		Population (m)	3.8
Starting a business (rank)	157	**Registering property** (rank)	171	**Trading across borders** (rank)	176
Procedures (number)	10	Procedures (number)	7	Documents to export (number)	11
Time (days)	37	Time (days)	116	Time to export (days)	50
Cost (% of income per capita)	106.4	Cost (% of property value)	16.5	Cost to export (US$ per container)	2,490
Minimum capital (% of income per capita)	131.2			Documents to import (number)	12
		Getting credit (rank)	131	Time to import (days)	62
Dealing with construction permits (rank)	68	Strength of legal rights index (0-10)	3	Cost to import (US$ per container)	2,959
Procedures (number)	14	Depth of credit information index (0-6)	2		
Time (days)	169	Public registry coverage (% of adults)	6.9	**Enforcing contracts** (rank)	155
Cost (% of income per capita)	345.6	Private bureau coverage (% of adults)	0.0	Procedures (number)	44
				Time (days)	560
Employing workers (rank)	170	**Protecting investors** (rank)	150	Cost (% of claim)	53.2
Difficulty of hiring index (0-100)	78	Extent of disclosure index (0-10)	6		
Rigidity of hours index (0-100)	60	Extent of director liability index (0-10)	1	**Closing a business** (rank)	117
Difficulty of firing index (0-100)	70	Ease of shareholder suits index (0-10)	3	Time (years)	3.0
Rigidity of employment index (0-100)	69	Strength of investor protection index (0-10)	3.3	Cost (% of estate)	24
Firing cost (weeks of salary)	33			Recovery rate (cents on the dollar)	20.4
		Paying taxes (rank)	179		
		Payments (number per year)	61		
		Time (hours per year)	606		
		Total tax rate (% of profit)	65.5		

COSTA RICA

		Latin America & Caribbean		GNI per capita (US$)	5,560
Ease of doing business (rank)	117	Upper middle income		Population (m)	4.5
Starting a business (rank)	123	**Registering property** (rank)	45	**Trading across borders** (rank)	94
Procedures (number)	12	Procedures (number)	6	Documents to export (number)	7
Time (days)	60	Time (days)	21	Time to export (days)	18
Cost (% of income per capita)	20.5	Cost (% of property value)	3.4	Cost to export (US$ per container)	1,050
Minimum capital (% of income per capita)	0.0			Documents to import (number)	8
		Getting credit (rank)	59	Time to import (days)	25
Dealing with construction permits (rank)	123	Strength of legal rights index (0-10)	5	Cost to import (US$ per container)	1,050
Procedures (number)	23	Depth of credit information index (0-6)	5		
Time (days)	191	Public registry coverage (% of adults)	5.9	**Enforcing contracts** (rank)	132
Cost (% of income per capita)	211.7	Private bureau coverage (% of adults)	51.6	Procedures (number)	40
				Time (days)	877
Employing workers (rank)	77	**Protecting investors** (rank)	164	Cost (% of claim)	24.3
Difficulty of hiring index (0-100)	44	Extent of disclosure index (0-10)	2		
Rigidity of hours index (0-100)	40	Extent of director liability index (0-10)	5	**Closing a business** (rank)	98
Difficulty of firing index (0-100)	0	Ease of shareholder suits index (0-10)	2	Time (years)	3.5
Rigidity of employment index (0-100)	28	Strength of investor protection index (0-10)	3.0	Cost (% of estate)	15
Firing cost (weeks of salary)	35			Recovery rate (cents on the dollar)	25.4
		Paying taxes (rank)	152		
		Payments (number per year)	43		
		Time (hours per year)	282		
		Total tax rate (% of profit)	55.7		

CÔTE D'IVOIRE

		Sub-Saharan Africa		GNI per capita (US$)	910
Ease of doing business (rank)	161	Low income		Population (m)	19.3

Starting a business (rank)	167	**Registering property** (rank)	139	**Trading across borders** (rank)	155
Procedures (number)	10	Procedures (number)	6	Documents to export (number)	10
Time (days)	40	Time (days)	62	Time to export (days)	23
Cost (% of income per capita)	135.1	Cost (% of property value)	13.9	Cost to export (US$ per container)	1,904
Minimum capital (% of income per capita)	215.9			Documents to import (number)	9
		Getting credit (rank)	145	Time to import (days)	43
Dealing with construction permits (rank)	160	Strength of legal rights index (0-10)	3	Cost to import (US$ per container)	2,437
Procedures (number)	21	Depth of credit information index (0-6)	1		
Time (days)	628	Public registry coverage (% of adults)	2.9	**Enforcing contracts** (rank)	124
Cost (% of income per capita)	243.3	Private bureau coverage (% of adults)	0.0	Procedures (number)	33
				Time (days)	770
Employing workers (rank)	112	**Protecting investors** (rank)	150	Cost (% of claim)	41.7
Difficulty of hiring index (0-100)	33	Extent of disclosure index (0-10)	6		
Rigidity of hours index (0-100)	60	Extent of director liability index (0-10)	1	**Closing a business** (rank)	68
Difficulty of firing index (0-100)	20	Ease of shareholder suits index (0-10)	3	Time (years)	2.2
Rigidity of employment index (0-100)	38	Strength of investor protection index (0-10)	3.3	Cost (% of estate)	18
Firing cost (weeks of salary)	49			Recovery rate (cents on the dollar)	34.0
		Paying taxes (rank)	148		
		Payments (number per year)	66		
		Time (hours per year)	270		
		Total tax rate (% of profit)	45.4		

CROATIA

		Eastern Europe & Central Asia		GNI per capita (US$)	10,460
Ease of doing business (rank)	106	Upper middle income		Population (m)	4.4

Starting a business (rank)	117	**Registering property** (rank)	109	**Trading across borders** (rank)	97
Procedures (number)	8	Procedures (number)	5	Documents to export (number)	7
Time (days)	40	Time (days)	174	Time to export (days)	20
Cost (% of income per capita)	11.5	Cost (% of property value)	5.0	Cost to export (US$ per container)	1,281
Minimum capital (% of income per capita)	16.6			Documents to import (number)	8
		Getting credit (rank)	68	Time to import (days)	16
Dealing with construction permits (rank)	163	Strength of legal rights index (0-10)	6	Cost to import (US$ per container)	1,141
Procedures (number)	19	Depth of credit information index (0-6)	3		
Time (days)	410	Public registry coverage (% of adults)	0.0	**Enforcing contracts** (rank)	44
Cost (% of income per capita)	655.2	Private bureau coverage (% of adults)	71.8	Procedures (number)	38
				Time (days)	561
Employing workers (rank)	146	**Protecting investors** (rank)	126	Cost (% of claim)	13.8
Difficulty of hiring index (0-100)	61	Extent of disclosure index (0-10)	1		
Rigidity of hours index (0-100)	40	Extent of director liability index (0-10)	5	**Closing a business** (rank)	79
Difficulty of firing index (0-100)	50	Ease of shareholder suits index (0-10)	6	Time (years)	3.1
Rigidity of employment index (0-100)	50	Strength of investor protection index (0-10)	4.0	Cost (% of estate)	15
Firing cost (weeks of salary)	39			Recovery rate (cents on the dollar)	30.5
		Paying taxes (rank)	33		
		Payments (number per year)	17		
		Time (hours per year)	196		
		Total tax rate (% of profit)	32.5		

CZECH REPUBLIC

		OECD: High Income		GNI per capita (US$)	14,450
Ease of doing business (rank)	75	High income		Population (m)	10.3

Starting a business (rank)	86	**Registering property** (rank)	65	**Trading across borders** (rank)	49
Procedures (number)	8	Procedures (number)	4	Documents to export (number)	4
Time (days)	15	Time (days)	123	Time to export (days)	17
Cost (% of income per capita)	9.6	Cost (% of property value)	3.0	Cost to export (US$ per container)	985
Minimum capital (% of income per capita)	31.8			Documents to import (number)	7
		Getting credit (rank)	43	Time to import (days)	20
Dealing with construction permits (rank)	86	Strength of legal rights index (0-10)	6	Cost to import (US$ per container)	1,087
Procedures (number)	36	Depth of credit information index (0-6)	5		
Time (days)	180	Public registry coverage (% of adults)	4.6	**Enforcing contracts** (rank)	95
Cost (% of income per capita)	16.9	Private bureau coverage (% of adults)	65.2	Procedures (number)	27
				Time (days)	820
Employing workers (rank)	59	**Protecting investors** (rank)	88	Cost (% of claim)	33.0
Difficulty of hiring index (0-100)	33	Extent of disclosure index (0-10)	2		
Rigidity of hours index (0-100)	40	Extent of director liability index (0-10)	5	**Closing a business** (rank)	113
Difficulty of firing index (0-100)	10	Ease of shareholder suits index (0-10)	8	Time (years)	6.5
Rigidity of employment index (0-100)	28	Strength of investor protection index (0-10)	5.0	Cost (% of estate)	15
Firing cost (weeks of salary)	22			Recovery rate (cents on the dollar)	20.9
		Paying taxes (rank)	118		
		Payments (number per year)	12		
		Time (hours per year)	930		
		Total tax rate (% of profit)	48.6		

DENMARK

		OECD: High Income		GNI per capita (US$)	54,910
Ease of doing business (rank)	5	High income		Population (m)	5.5

Starting a business (rank)	16	**Registering property** (rank)	43	**Trading across borders** (rank)	3
Procedures (number)	4	Procedures (number)	6	Documents to export (number)	4
Time (days)	6	Time (days)	42	Time to export (days)	5
Cost (% of income per capita)	0.0	Cost (% of property value)	0.6	Cost to export (US$ per container)	681
Minimum capital (% of income per capita)	40.1			Documents to import (number)	3
		Getting credit (rank)	12	Time to import (days)	5
Dealing with construction permits (rank)	7	Strength of legal rights index (0-10)	9	Cost to import (US$ per container)	681
Procedures (number)	6	Depth of credit information index (0-6)	4		
Time (days)	69	Public registry coverage (% of adults)	0.0	**Enforcing contracts** (rank)	29
Cost (% of income per capita)	60.9	Private bureau coverage (% of adults)	5.0	Procedures (number)	34
				Time (days)	380
Employing workers (rank)	10	**Protecting investors** (rank)	24	Cost (% of claim)	23.3
Difficulty of hiring index (0-100)	0	Extent of disclosure index (0-10)	7		
Rigidity of hours index (0-100)	20	Extent of director liability index (0-10)	5	**Closing a business** (rank)	7
Difficulty of firing index (0-100)	10	Ease of shareholder suits index (0-10)	7	Time (years)	1.1
Rigidity of employment index (0-100)	10	Strength of investor protection index (0-10)	6.3	Cost (% of estate)	4
Firing cost (weeks of salary)	0			Recovery rate (cents on the dollar)	86.5
		Paying taxes (rank)	13		
		Payments (number per year)	9		
		Time (hours per year)	135		
		Total tax rate (% of profit)	29.9		

DJIBOUTI

		Middle East & North Africa		GNI per capita (US$)	1,090
Ease of doing business (rank)	153	Lower middle income		Population (m)	0.8

Starting a business (rank)	173	**Registering property** (rank)	134	**Trading across borders** (rank)	35
Procedures (number)	11	Procedures (number)	7	Documents to export (number)	5
Time (days)	37	Time (days)	40	Time to export (days)	19
Cost (% of income per capita)	200.2	Cost (% of property value)	13.2	Cost to export (US$ per container)	1,058
Minimum capital (% of income per capita)	514.0			Documents to import (number)	5
		Getting credit (rank)	172	Time to import (days)	16
Dealing with construction permits (rank)	99	Strength of legal rights index (0-10)	1	Cost to import (US$ per container)	978
Procedures (number)	14	Depth of credit information index (0-6)	1		
Time (days)	195	Public registry coverage (% of adults)	0.2	**Enforcing contracts** (rank)	159
Cost (% of income per capita)	982.8	Private bureau coverage (% of adults)	0.0	Procedures (number)	40
				Time (days)	1,225
Employing workers (rank)	137	**Protecting investors** (rank)	177	Cost (% of claim)	34.0
Difficulty of hiring index (0-100)	67	Extent of disclosure index (0-10)	5		
Rigidity of hours index (0-100)	40	Extent of director liability index (0-10)	2	**Closing a business** (rank)	132
Difficulty of firing index (0-100)	30	Ease of shareholder suits index (0-10)	0	Time (years)	5.0
Rigidity of employment index (0-100)	46	Strength of investor protection index (0-10)	2.3	Cost (% of estate)	18
Firing cost (weeks of salary)	56			Recovery rate (cents on the dollar)	15.9
		Paying taxes (rank)	61		
		Payments (number per year)	35		
		Time (hours per year)	114		
		Total tax rate (% of profit)	38.7		

DOMINICA

		Latin America & Caribbean		GNI per capita (US$)	4,250
Ease of doing business (rank)	74	Upper middle income		Population (m)	0.1

Starting a business (rank)	21	**Registering property** (rank)	103	**Trading across borders** (rank)	82
Procedures (number)	5	Procedures (number)	5	Documents to export (number)	7
Time (days)	14	Time (days)	42	Time to export (days)	13
Cost (% of income per capita)	25.5	Cost (% of property value)	13.7	Cost to export (US$ per container)	1,297
Minimum capital (% of income per capita)	0.0			Documents to import (number)	8
		Getting credit (rank)	68	Time to import (days)	15
Dealing with construction permits (rank)	24	Strength of legal rights index (0-10)	9	Cost to import (US$ per container)	1,310
Procedures (number)	13	Depth of credit information index (0-6)	0		
Time (days)	182	Public registry coverage (% of adults)	0.0	**Enforcing contracts** (rank)	164
Cost (% of income per capita)	12.8	Private bureau coverage (% of adults)	0.0	Procedures (number)	47
				Time (days)	681
Employing workers (rank)	61	**Protecting investors** (rank)	24	Cost (% of claim)	36.0
Difficulty of hiring index (0-100)	11	Extent of disclosure index (0-10)	4		
Rigidity of hours index (0-100)	20	Extent of director liability index (0-10)	8	**Closing a business** (rank)	181
Difficulty of firing index (0-100)	20	Ease of shareholder suits index (0-10)	7	Time (years)	NO PRACTICE
Rigidity of employment index (0-100)	17	Strength of investor protection index (0-10)	6.3	Cost (% of estate)	NO PRACTICE
Firing cost (weeks of salary)	58			Recovery rate (cents on the dollar)	0.0
		Paying taxes (rank)	63		
		Payments (number per year)	38		
		Time (hours per year)	120		
		Total tax rate (% of profit)	37.0		

DOMINICAN REPUBLIC

		Latin America & Caribbean		GNI per capita (US$)	3,550
Ease of doing business (rank)	97	Lower middle income		Population (m)	9.8

Starting a business (rank)	84	**Registering property** (rank)	106	**Trading across borders** (rank)	32
Procedures (number)	8	Procedures (number)	7	Documents to export (number)	6
Time (days)	19	Time (days)	60	Time to export (days)	9
Cost (% of income per capita)	19.4	Cost (% of property value)	3.8	Cost to export (US$ per container)	916
Minimum capital (% of income per capita)	0.0			Documents to import (number)	7
		Getting credit (rank)	68	Time to import (days)	10
Dealing with construction permits (rank)	77	Strength of legal rights index (0-10)	3	Cost to import (US$ per container)	1,150
Procedures (number)	17	Depth of credit information index (0-6)	6		
Time (days)	214	Public registry coverage (% of adults)	33.9	**Enforcing contracts** (rank)	83
Cost (% of income per capita)	93.2	Private bureau coverage (% of adults)	35.0	Procedures (number)	34
				Time (days)	460
Employing workers (rank)	97	**Protecting investors** (rank)	126	Cost (% of claim)	40.9
Difficulty of hiring index (0-100)	44	Extent of disclosure index (0-10)	5		
Rigidity of hours index (0-100)	40	Extent of director liability index (0-10)	0	**Closing a business** (rank)	144
Difficulty of firing index (0-100)	0	Ease of shareholder suits index (0-10)	7	Time (years)	3.5
Rigidity of employment index (0-100)	28	Strength of investor protection index (0-10)	4.0	Cost (% of estate)	38
Firing cost (weeks of salary)	88			Recovery rate (cents on the dollar)	8.9
		Paying taxes (rank)	72		
		Payments (number per year)	9		
		Time (hours per year)	480		
		Total tax rate (% of profit)	35.7		

ECUADOR

		Latin America & Caribbean		GNI per capita (US$)	3,080
Ease of doing business (rank)	136	Lower middle income		Population (m)	13.3

Starting a business (rank)	158	**Registering property** (rank)	64	**Trading across borders** (rank)	124
Procedures (number)	14	Procedures (number)	9	Documents to export (number)	9
Time (days)	65	Time (days)	16	Time to export (days)	20
Cost (% of income per capita)	38.5	Cost (% of property value)	2.2	Cost to export (US$ per container)	1,345
Minimum capital (% of income per capita)	12.7			Documents to import (number)	7
		Getting credit (rank)	84	Time to import (days)	29
Dealing with construction permits (rank)	85	Strength of legal rights index (0-10)	3	Cost to import (US$ per container)	1,332
Procedures (number)	19	Depth of credit information index (0-6)	5		
Time (days)	155	Public registry coverage (% of adults)	37.7	**Enforcing contracts** (rank)	101
Cost (% of income per capita)	272.7	Private bureau coverage (% of adults)	46.8	Procedures (number)	39
				Time (days)	588
Employing workers (rank)	171	**Protecting investors** (rank)	126	Cost (% of claim)	27.2
Difficulty of hiring index (0-100)	44	Extent of disclosure index (0-10)	1		
Rigidity of hours index (0-100)	60	Extent of director liability index (0-10)	5	**Closing a business** (rank)	131
Difficulty of firing index (0-100)	50	Ease of shareholder suits index (0-10)	6	Time (years)	5.3
Rigidity of employment index (0-100)	51	Strength of investor protection index (0-10)	4.0	Cost (% of estate)	18
Firing cost (weeks of salary)	135			Recovery rate (cents on the dollar)	16.1
		Paying taxes (rank)	69		
		Payments (number per year)	8		
		Time (hours per year)	600		
		Total tax rate (% of profit)	34.9		

EGYPT

		Middle East & North Africa		GNI per capita (US$)	1,580
Ease of doing business (rank)	114	Lower middle income		Population (m)	75.5

Starting a business (rank)	41	**Registering property** (rank)	85	**Trading across borders** (rank)	24
Procedures (number)	6	Procedures (number)	7	Documents to export (number)	6
Time (days)	7	Time (days)	72	Time to export (days)	14
Cost (% of income per capita)	18.3	Cost (% of property value)	0.9	Cost to export (US$ per container)	737
Minimum capital (% of income per capita)	2.0			Documents to import (number)	6
		Getting credit (rank)	84	Time to import (days)	15
Dealing with construction permits (rank)	165	Strength of legal rights index (0-10)	3	Cost to import (US$ per container)	823
Procedures (number)	28	Depth of credit information index (0-6)	5		
Time (days)	249	Public registry coverage (% of adults)	2.2	**Enforcing contracts** (rank)	151
Cost (% of income per capita)	376.7	Private bureau coverage (% of adults)	4.7	Procedures (number)	42
				Time (days)	1,010
Employing workers (rank)	107	**Protecting investors** (rank)	70	Cost (% of claim)	26.2
Difficulty of hiring index (0-100)	0	Extent of disclosure index (0-10)	8		
Rigidity of hours index (0-100)	20	Extent of director liability index (0-10)	3	**Closing a business** (rank)	128
Difficulty of firing index (0-100)	60	Ease of shareholder suits index (0-10)	5	Time (years)	4.2
Rigidity of employment index (0-100)	27	Strength of investor protection index (0-10)	5.3	Cost (% of estate)	22
Firing cost (weeks of salary)	132			Recovery rate (cents on the dollar)	16.8
		Paying taxes (rank)	144		
		Payments (number per year)	29		
		Time (hours per year)	711		
		Total tax rate (% of profit)	46.1		

EL SALVADOR

		Latin America & Caribbean		GNI per capita (US$)		2,850
Ease of doing business (rank)	72	Lower middle income		Population (m)		6.9

Starting a business (rank)	103	**Registering property** (rank)	42	**Trading across borders** (rank)	57
Procedures (number)	8	Procedures (number)	5	Documents to export (number)	8
Time (days)	17	Time (days)	31	Time to export (days)	14
Cost (% of income per capita)	49.6	Cost (% of property value)	3.7	Cost to export (US$ per container)	880
Minimum capital (% of income per capita)	3.5			Documents to import (number)	9
		Getting credit (rank)	43	Time to import (days)	10
Dealing with construction permits (rank)	121	Strength of legal rights index (0-10)	5	Cost to import (US$ per container)	820
Procedures (number)	34	Depth of credit information index (0-6)	6		
Time (days)	155	Public registry coverage (% of adults)	18.4	**Enforcing contracts** (rank)	53
Cost (% of income per capita)	176.3	Private bureau coverage (% of adults)	83.0	Procedures (number)	30
				Time (days)	786
Employing workers (rank)	87	**Protecting investors** (rank)	113	Cost (% of claim)	19.2
Difficulty of hiring index (0-100)	33	Extent of disclosure index (0-10)	5		
Rigidity of hours index (0-100)	40	Extent of director liability index (0-10)	2	**Closing a business** (rank)	78
Difficulty of firing index (0-100)	0	Ease of shareholder suits index (0-10)	6	Time (years)	4.0
Rigidity of employment index (0-100)	24	Strength of investor protection index (0-10)	4.3	Cost (% of estate)	9
Firing cost (weeks of salary)	86			Recovery rate (cents on the dollar)	30.8
		Paying taxes (rank)	124		
		Payments (number per year)	53		
		Time (hours per year)	320		
		Total tax rate (% of profit)	34.9		

EQUATORIAL GUINEA

		Sub-Saharan Africa		GNI per capita (US$)		12,860
Ease of doing business (rank)	167	High income		Population (m)		0.5

Starting a business (rank)	174	**Registering property** (rank)	69	**Trading across borders** (rank)	133
Procedures (number)	20	Procedures (number)	6	Documents to export (number)	7
Time (days)	136	Time (days)	23	Time to export (days)	30
Cost (% of income per capita)	101.7	Cost (% of property value)	6.2	Cost to export (US$ per container)	1,411
Minimum capital (% of income per capita)	15.4			Documents to import (number)	7
		Getting credit (rank)	131	Time to import (days)	49
Dealing with construction permits (rank)	87	Strength of legal rights index (0-10)	3	Cost to import (US$ per container)	1,411
Procedures (number)	18	Depth of credit information index (0-6)	2		
Time (days)	201	Public registry coverage (% of adults)	2.7	**Enforcing contracts** (rank)	69
Cost (% of income per capita)	159.4	Private bureau coverage (% of adults)	0.0	Procedures (number)	40
				Time (days)	553
Employing workers (rank)	178	**Protecting investors** (rank)	142	Cost (% of claim)	18.5
Difficulty of hiring index (0-100)	67	Extent of disclosure index (0-10)	6		
Rigidity of hours index (0-100)	60	Extent of director liability index (0-10)	1	**Closing a business** (rank)	181
Difficulty of firing index (0-100)	70	Ease of shareholder suits index (0-10)	4	Time (years)	NO PRACTICE
Rigidity of employment index (0-100)	66	Strength of investor protection index (0-10)	3.7	Cost (% of estate)	NO PRACTICE
Firing cost (weeks of salary)	133			Recovery rate (cents on the dollar)	0.0
		Paying taxes (rank)	161		
		Payments (number per year)	46		
		Time (hours per year)	296		
		Total tax rate (% of profit)	59.5		

ERITREA

		Sub-Saharan Africa		GNI per capita (US$)		230
Ease of doing business (rank)	173	Low income		Population (m)		4.8

Starting a business (rank)	178	**Registering property** (rank)	165	**Trading across borders** (rank)	163
Procedures (number)	13	Procedures (number)	12	Documents to export (number)	9
Time (days)	84	Time (days)	101	Time to export (days)	50
Cost (% of income per capita)	102.2	Cost (% of property value)	5.2	Cost to export (US$ per container)	1,431
Minimum capital (% of income per capita)	396.7			Documents to import (number)	13
		Getting credit (rank)	172	Time to import (days)	60
Dealing with construction permits (rank)	181	Strength of legal rights index (0-10)	2	Cost to import (US$ per container)	1,581
Procedures (number)	NO PRACTICE	Depth of credit information index (0-6)	0		
Time (days)	NO PRACTICE	Public registry coverage (% of adults)	0.0	**Enforcing contracts** (rank)	51
Cost (% of income per capita)	NO PRACTICE	Private bureau coverage (% of adults)	0.0	Procedures (number)	39
				Time (days)	405
Employing workers (rank)	65	**Protecting investors** (rank)	104	Cost (% of claim)	22.6
Difficulty of hiring index (0-100)	0	Extent of disclosure index (0-10)	4		
Rigidity of hours index (0-100)	40	Extent of director liability index (0-10)	5	**Closing a business** (rank)	181
Difficulty of firing index (0-100)	20	Ease of shareholder suits index (0-10)	5	Time (years)	NO PRACTICE
Rigidity of employment index (0-100)	20	Strength of investor protection index (0-10)	4.7	Cost (% of estate)	NO PRACTICE
Firing cost (weeks of salary)	69			Recovery rate (cents on the dollar)	0.0
		Paying taxes (rank)	105		
		Payments (number per year)	18		
		Time (hours per year)	216		
		Total tax rate (% of profit)	84.5		

ESTONIA

		Eastern Europe & Central Asia		GNI per capita (US$)	13,200
Ease of doing business (rank)	22	High income		Population (m)	1.3

Starting a business (rank)	23	**Registering property** (rank)	24	**Trading across borders** (rank)	5
Procedures (number)	5	Procedures (number)	3	Documents to export (number)	3
Time (days)	7	Time (days)	51	Time to export (days)	5
Cost (% of income per capita)	1.7	Cost (% of property value)	0.4	Cost to export (US$ per container)	730
Minimum capital (% of income per capita)	23.7			Documents to import (number)	4
		Getting credit (rank)	43	Time to import (days)	5
Dealing with construction permits (rank)	19	Strength of legal rights index (0-10)	6	Cost to import (US$ per container)	740
Procedures (number)	14	Depth of credit information index (0-6)	5		
Time (days)	118	Public registry coverage (% of adults)	0.0	**Enforcing contracts** (rank)	30
Cost (% of income per capita)	27.5	Private bureau coverage (% of adults)	20.6	Procedures (number)	36
				Time (days)	425
Employing workers (rank)	163	**Protecting investors** (rank)	53	Cost (% of claim)	18.9
Difficulty of hiring index (0-100)	33	Extent of disclosure index (0-10)	8		
Rigidity of hours index (0-100)	80	Extent of director liability index (0-10)	3	**Closing a business** (rank)	58
Difficulty of firing index (0-100)	60	Ease of shareholder suits index (0-10)	6	Time (years)	3.0
Rigidity of employment index (0-100)	58	Strength of investor protection index (0-10)	5.7	Cost (% of estate)	9
Firing cost (weeks of salary)	35			Recovery rate (cents on the dollar)	37.5
		Paying taxes (rank)	34		
		Payments (number per year)	10		
		Time (hours per year)	81		
		Total tax rate (% of profit)	48.6		

ETHIOPIA

		Sub-Saharan Africa		GNI per capita (US$)	220
Ease of doing business (rank)	116	Low income		Population (m)	79.1

Starting a business (rank)	118	**Registering property** (rank)	154	**Trading across borders** (rank)	152
Procedures (number)	7	Procedures (number)	13	Documents to export (number)	8
Time (days)	16	Time (days)	43	Time to export (days)	46
Cost (% of income per capita)	29.8	Cost (% of property value)	7.1	Cost to export (US$ per container)	2,087
Minimum capital (% of income per capita)	693.6			Documents to import (number)	8
		Getting credit (rank)	123	Time to import (days)	42
Dealing with construction permits (rank)	59	Strength of legal rights index (0-10)	4	Cost to import (US$ per container)	2,893
Procedures (number)	12	Depth of credit information index (0-6)	2		
Time (days)	128	Public registry coverage (% of adults)	0.1	**Enforcing contracts** (rank)	78
Cost (% of income per capita)	790.7	Private bureau coverage (% of adults)	0.0	Procedures (number)	39
				Time (days)	690
Employing workers (rank)	95	**Protecting investors** (rank)	113	Cost (% of claim)	15.2
Difficulty of hiring index (0-100)	33	Extent of disclosure index (0-10)	4		
Rigidity of hours index (0-100)	40	Extent of director liability index (0-10)	4	**Closing a business** (rank)	74
Difficulty of firing index (0-100)	30	Ease of shareholder suits index (0-10)	5	Time (years)	3.0
Rigidity of employment index (0-100)	34	Strength of investor protection index (0-10)	4.3	Cost (% of estate)	15
Firing cost (weeks of salary)	40			Recovery rate (cents on the dollar)	32.2
		Paying taxes (rank)	37		
		Payments (number per year)	20		
		Time (hours per year)	198		
		Total tax rate (% of profit)	31.1		

FIJI

		East Asia & Pacific		GNI per capita (US$)	3,800
Ease of doing business (rank)	39	Upper middle income		Population (m)	0.8

Starting a business (rank)	87	**Registering property** (rank)	40	**Trading across borders** (rank)	108
Procedures (number)	8	Procedures (number)	3	Documents to export (number)	13
Time (days)	46	Time (days)	68	Time to export (days)	24
Cost (% of income per capita)	25.2	Cost (% of property value)	2.0	Cost to export (US$ per container)	654
Minimum capital (% of income per capita)	0.0			Documents to import (number)	13
		Getting credit (rank)	12	Time to import (days)	24
Dealing with construction permits (rank)	55	Strength of legal rights index (0-10)	9	Cost to import (US$ per container)	630
Procedures (number)	19	Depth of credit information index (0-6)	4		
Time (days)	135	Public registry coverage (% of adults)	0.0	**Enforcing contracts** (rank)	64
Cost (% of income per capita)	51.2	Private bureau coverage (% of adults)	42.3	Procedures (number)	34
				Time (days)	397
Employing workers (rank)	32	**Protecting investors** (rank)	38	Cost (% of claim)	38.9
Difficulty of hiring index (0-100)	11	Extent of disclosure index (0-10)	3		
Rigidity of hours index (0-100)	20	Extent of director liability index (0-10)	8	**Closing a business** (rank)	119
Difficulty of firing index (0-100)	20	Ease of shareholder suits index (0-10)	7	Time (years)	1.8
Rigidity of employment index (0-100)	17	Strength of investor protection index (0-10)	6.0	Cost (% of estate)	38
Firing cost (weeks of salary)	22			Recovery rate (cents on the dollar)	20.1
		Paying taxes (rank)	71		
		Payments (number per year)	33		
		Time (hours per year)	140		
		Total tax rate (% of profit)	41.5		

FINLAND

		OECD: High Income		GNI per capita (US$)		44,400
Ease of doing business (rank)	14	High income		Population (m)		5.3

Starting a business (rank)	18	**Registering property** (rank)	21	**Trading across borders** (rank)	4
Procedures (number)	3	Procedures (number)	3	Documents to export (number)	4
Time (days)	14	Time (days)	14	Time to export (days)	8
Cost (% of income per capita)	1.0	Cost (% of property value)	4.0	Cost to export (US$ per container)	495
Minimum capital (% of income per capita)	7.4			Documents to import (number)	5
		Getting credit (rank)	28	Time to import (days)	8
		Strength of legal rights index (0-10)	7	Cost to import (US$ per container)	575
Dealing with construction permits (rank)	43	Depth of credit information index (0-6)	5		
Procedures (number)	18	Public registry coverage (% of adults)	0.0	**Enforcing contracts** (rank)	5
Time (days)	38	Private bureau coverage (% of adults)	14.8	Procedures (number)	32
Cost (% of income per capita)	118.3			Time (days)	235
		Protecting investors (rank)	53	Cost (% of claim)	10.4
Employing workers (rank)	129	Extent of disclosure index (0-10)	6		
Difficulty of hiring index (0-100)	44	Extent of director liability index (0-10)	4	**Closing a business** (rank)	5
Rigidity of hours index (0-100)	60	Ease of shareholder suits index (0-10)	7	Time (years)	0.9
Difficulty of firing index (0-100)	40	Strength of investor protection index (0-10)	5.7	Cost (% of estate)	4
Rigidity of employment index (0-100)	48			Recovery rate (cents on the dollar)	87.3
Firing cost (weeks of salary)	26	**Paying taxes** (rank)	97		
		Payments (number per year)	20		
		Time (hours per year)	269		
		Total tax rate (% of profit)	47.8		

FRANCE

		OECD: High Income		GNI per capita (US$)		38,500
Ease of doing business (rank)	31	High income		Population (m)		61.7

Starting a business (rank)	14	**Registering property** (rank)	166	**Trading across borders** (rank)	22
Procedures (number)	5	Procedures (number)	9	Documents to export (number)	2
Time (days)	7	Time (days)	113	Time to export (days)	9
Cost (% of income per capita)	1.0	Cost (% of property value)	6.3	Cost to export (US$ per container)	1,078
Minimum capital (% of income per capita)	0.0			Documents to import (number)	2
		Getting credit (rank)	43	Time to import (days)	11
		Strength of legal rights index (0-10)	7	Cost to import (US$ per container)	1,248
Dealing with construction permits (rank)	18	Depth of credit information index (0-6)	4		
Procedures (number)	13	Public registry coverage (% of adults)	28.3	**Enforcing contracts** (rank)	10
Time (days)	137	Private bureau coverage (% of adults)	0.0	Procedures (number)	30
Cost (% of income per capita)	23.8			Time (days)	331
		Protecting investors (rank)	70	Cost (% of claim)	17.4
Employing workers (rank)	148	Extent of disclosure index (0-10)	10		
Difficulty of hiring index (0-100)	67	Extent of director liability index (0-10)	1	**Closing a business** (rank)	40
Rigidity of hours index (0-100)	60	Ease of shareholder suits index (0-10)	5	Time (years)	1.9
Difficulty of firing index (0-100)	40	Strength of investor protection index (0-10)	5.3	Cost (% of estate)	9
Rigidity of employment index (0-100)	56			Recovery rate (cents on the dollar)	44.7
Firing cost (weeks of salary)	32	**Paying taxes** (rank)	66		
		Payments (number per year)	11		
		Time (hours per year)	132		
		Total tax rate (% of profit)	65.4		

GABON

		Sub-Saharan Africa		GNI per capita (US$)		6,670
Ease of doing business (rank)	151	Upper middle income		Population (m)		1.3

Starting a business (rank)	148	**Registering property** (rank)	158	**Trading across borders** (rank)	128
Procedures (number)	9	Procedures (number)	8	Documents to export (number)	7
Time (days)	58	Time (days)	60	Time to export (days)	20
Cost (% of income per capita)	20.3	Cost (% of property value)	10.5	Cost to export (US$ per container)	1,945
Minimum capital (% of income per capita)	30.2			Documents to import (number)	8
		Getting credit (rank)	131	Time to import (days)	22
		Strength of legal rights index (0-10)	3	Cost to import (US$ per container)	1,955
Dealing with construction permits (rank)	60	Depth of credit information index (0-6)	2		
Procedures (number)	16	Public registry coverage (% of adults)	20.7	**Enforcing contracts** (rank)	147
Time (days)	210	Private bureau coverage (% of adults)	0.0	Procedures (number)	38
Cost (% of income per capita)	39.4			Time (days)	1,070
		Protecting investors (rank)	150	Cost (% of claim)	34.3
Employing workers (rank)	154	Extent of disclosure index (0-10)	6		
Difficulty of hiring index (0-100)	17	Extent of director liability index (0-10)	1	**Closing a business** (rank)	134
Rigidity of hours index (0-100)	60	Ease of shareholder suits index (0-10)	3	Time (years)	5.0
Difficulty of firing index (0-100)	80	Strength of investor protection index (0-10)	3.3	Cost (% of estate)	15
Rigidity of employment index (0-100)	52			Recovery rate (cents on the dollar)	15.2
Firing cost (weeks of salary)	43	**Paying taxes** (rank)	101		
		Payments (number per year)	26		
		Time (hours per year)	272		
		Total tax rate (% of profit)	44.7		

GAMBIA, THE

		Sub-Saharan Africa		GNI per capita (US$)	320
Ease of doing business (rank)	130	Low income		Population (m)	1.7
Starting a business (rank)	101	**Registering property** (rank)	111	**Trading across borders** (rank)	73
Procedures (number)	8	Procedures (number)	5	Documents to export (number)	6
Time (days)	27	Time (days)	371	Time to export (days)	24
Cost (% of income per capita)	254.9	Cost (% of property value)	4.6	Cost to export (US$ per container)	831
Minimum capital (% of income per capita)	0.0			Documents to import (number)	8
		Getting credit (rank)	131	Time to import (days)	23
Dealing with construction permits (rank)	74	Strength of legal rights index (0-10)	5	Cost to import (US$ per container)	922
Procedures (number)	17	Depth of credit information index (0-6)	0		
Time (days)	146	Public registry coverage (% of adults)	0.0	**Enforcing contracts** (rank)	63
Cost (% of income per capita)	394.0	Private bureau coverage (% of adults)	0.0	Procedures (number)	32
				Time (days)	434
Employing workers (rank)	55	**Protecting investors** (rank)	170	Cost (% of claim)	37.9
Difficulty of hiring index (0-100)	0	Extent of disclosure index (0-10)	2		
Rigidity of hours index (0-100)	40	Extent of director liability index (0-10)	1	**Closing a business** (rank)	120
Difficulty of firing index (0-100)	40	Ease of shareholder suits index (0-10)	5	Time (years)	3.0
Rigidity of employment index (0-100)	27	Strength of investor protection index (0-10)	2.7	Cost (% of estate)	15
Firing cost (weeks of salary)	26			Recovery rate (cents on the dollar)	19.5
		Paying taxes (rank)	175		
		Payments (number per year)	50		
		Time (hours per year)	376		
		Total tax rate (% of profit)	292.4		

GEORGIA

		Eastern Europe & Central Asia		GNI per capita (US$)	2,120
Ease of doing business (rank)	15	Lower middle income		Population (m)	4.4
Starting a business (rank)	4	**Registering property** (rank)	2	**Trading across borders** (rank)	81
Procedures (number)	3	Procedures (number)	2	Documents to export (number)	8
Time (days)	3	Time (days)	3	Time to export (days)	12
Cost (% of income per capita)	4.0	Cost (% of property value)	0.0	Cost to export (US$ per container)	1,380
Minimum capital (% of income per capita)	0.0			Documents to import (number)	7
		Getting credit (rank)	28	Time to import (days)	14
Dealing with construction permits (rank)	10	Strength of legal rights index (0-10)	6	Cost to import (US$ per container)	1,340
Procedures (number)	12	Depth of credit information index (0-6)	6		
Time (days)	113	Public registry coverage (% of adults)	0.0	**Enforcing contracts** (rank)	43
Cost (% of income per capita)	20.3	Private bureau coverage (% of adults)	4.5	Procedures (number)	36
				Time (days)	285
Employing workers (rank)	5	**Protecting investors** (rank)	38	Cost (% of claim)	29.9
Difficulty of hiring index (0-100)	0	Extent of disclosure index (0-10)	8		
Rigidity of hours index (0-100)	20	Extent of director liability index (0-10)	6	**Closing a business** (rank)	92
Difficulty of firing index (0-100)	0	Ease of shareholder suits index (0-10)	4	Time (years)	3.3
Rigidity of employment index (0-100)	7	Strength of investor protection index (0-10)	6.0	Cost (% of estate)	4
Firing cost (weeks of salary)	4			Recovery rate (cents on the dollar)	27.9
		Paying taxes (rank)	110		
		Payments (number per year)	30		
		Time (hours per year)	387		
		Total tax rate (% of profit)	38.6		

GERMANY

		OECD: High Income		GNI per capita (US$)	38,860
Ease of doing business (rank)	25	High income		Population (m)	82.3
Starting a business (rank)	102	**Registering property** (rank)	52	**Trading across borders** (rank)	11
Procedures (number)	9	Procedures (number)	4	Documents to export (number)	4
Time (days)	18	Time (days)	40	Time to export (days)	7
Cost (% of income per capita)	5.6	Cost (% of property value)	5.2	Cost to export (US$ per container)	822
Minimum capital (% of income per capita)	42.2			Documents to import (number)	5
		Getting credit (rank)	12	Time to import (days)	7
Dealing with construction permits (rank)	15	Strength of legal rights index (0-10)	7	Cost to import (US$ per container)	887
Procedures (number)	12	Depth of credit information index (0-6)	6		
Time (days)	100	Public registry coverage (% of adults)	0.7	**Enforcing contracts** (rank)	9
Cost (% of income per capita)	62.2	Private bureau coverage (% of adults)	98.4	Procedures (number)	30
				Time (days)	394
Employing workers (rank)	142	**Protecting investors** (rank)	88	Cost (% of claim)	14.4
Difficulty of hiring index (0-100)	33	Extent of disclosure index (0-10)	5		
Rigidity of hours index (0-100)	60	Extent of director liability index (0-10)	5	**Closing a business** (rank)	33
Difficulty of firing index (0-100)	40	Ease of shareholder suits index (0-10)	5	Time (years)	1.2
Rigidity of employment index (0-100)	44	Strength of investor protection index (0-10)	5.0	Cost (% of estate)	8
Firing cost (weeks of salary)	69			Recovery rate (cents on the dollar)	52.2
		Paying taxes (rank)	80		
		Payments (number per year)	16		
		Time (hours per year)	196		
		Total tax rate (% of profit)	50.5		

GHANA

Ease of doing business (rank)	87	Sub-Saharan Africa / Low income		GNI per capita (US$)		590
				Population (m)		23.5

Starting a business (rank)	137	**Registering property** (rank)	31	**Trading across borders** (rank)	76
Procedures (number)	9	Procedures (number)	5	Documents to export (number)	6
Time (days)	34	Time (days)	34	Time to export (days)	19
Cost (% of income per capita)	32.7	Cost (% of property value)	1.2	Cost to export (US$ per container)	1,003
Minimum capital (% of income per capita)	16.6			Documents to import (number)	7
		Getting credit (rank)	109	Time to import (days)	29
Dealing with construction permits (rank)	142	Strength of legal rights index (0-10)	7	Cost to import (US$ per container)	1,130
Procedures (number)	18	Depth of credit information index (0-6)	0		
Time (days)	220	Public registry coverage (% of adults)	0.0	**Enforcing contracts** (rank)	50
Cost (% of income per capita)	1,282.6	Private bureau coverage (% of adults)	0.0	Procedures (number)	36
				Time (days)	487
Employing workers (rank)	145	**Protecting investors** (rank)	38	Cost (% of claim)	23.0
Difficulty of hiring index (0-100)	22	Extent of disclosure index (0-10)	7		
Rigidity of hours index (0-100)	40	Extent of director liability index (0-10)	5	**Closing a business** (rank)	104
Difficulty of firing index (0-100)	50	Ease of shareholder suits index (0-10)	6	Time (years)	1.9
Rigidity of employment index (0-100)	37	Strength of investor protection index (0-10)	6.0	Cost (% of estate)	22
Firing cost (weeks of salary)	178			Recovery rate (cents on the dollar)	24.0
		Paying taxes (rank)	65		
		Payments (number per year)	33		
		Time (hours per year)	224		
		Total tax rate (% of profit)	32.7		

GREECE

Ease of doing business (rank)	96	OECD: High Income / High income		GNI per capita (US$)		29,630
				Population (m)		11.2

Starting a business (rank)	133	**Registering property** (rank)	101	**Trading across borders** (rank)	70
Procedures (number)	15	Procedures (number)	11	Documents to export (number)	5
Time (days)	19	Time (days)	22	Time to export (days)	20
Cost (% of income per capita)	10.2	Cost (% of property value)	3.8	Cost to export (US$ per container)	1,153
Minimum capital (% of income per capita)	19.6			Documents to import (number)	6
		Getting credit (rank)	109	Time to import (days)	25
Dealing with construction permits (rank)	45	Strength of legal rights index (0-10)	3	Cost to import (US$ per container)	1,265
Procedures (number)	15	Depth of credit information index (0-6)	4		
Time (days)	169	Public registry coverage (% of adults)	0.0	**Enforcing contracts** (rank)	85
Cost (% of income per capita)	46.4	Private bureau coverage (% of adults)	39.0	Procedures (number)	39
				Time (days)	819
Employing workers (rank)	133	**Protecting investors** (rank)	150	Cost (% of claim)	14.4
Difficulty of hiring index (0-100)	33	Extent of disclosure index (0-10)	1		
Rigidity of hours index (0-100)	80	Extent of director liability index (0-10)	4	**Closing a business** (rank)	41
Difficulty of firing index (0-100)	40	Ease of shareholder suits index (0-10)	5	Time (years)	2.0
Rigidity of employment index (0-100)	51	Strength of investor protection index (0-10)	3.3	Cost (% of estate)	9
Firing cost (weeks of salary)	24			Recovery rate (cents on the dollar)	44.2
		Paying taxes (rank)	62		
		Payments (number per year)	10		
		Time (hours per year)	224		
		Total tax rate (% of profit)	47.4		

GRENADA

Ease of doing business (rank)	84	Latin America & Caribbean / Upper middle income		GNI per capita (US$)		4,670
				Population (m)		0.1

Starting a business (rank)	40	**Registering property** (rank)	156	**Trading across borders** (rank)	63
Procedures (number)	6	Procedures (number)	8	Documents to export (number)	6
Time (days)	20	Time (days)	77	Time to export (days)	16
Cost (% of income per capita)	30.2	Cost (% of property value)	7.4	Cost to export (US$ per container)	1,131
Minimum capital (% of income per capita)	0.0			Documents to import (number)	5
		Getting credit (rank)	68	Time to import (days)	20
Dealing with construction permits (rank)	16	Strength of legal rights index (0-10)	9	Cost to import (US$ per container)	1,478
Procedures (number)	10	Depth of credit information index (0-6)	0		
Time (days)	149	Public registry coverage (% of adults)	0.0	**Enforcing contracts** (rank)	163
Cost (% of income per capita)	31.1	Private bureau coverage (% of adults)	0.0	Procedures (number)	47
				Time (days)	723
Employing workers (rank)	51	**Protecting investors** (rank)	24	Cost (% of claim)	32.6
Difficulty of hiring index (0-100)	44	Extent of disclosure index (0-10)	4		
Rigidity of hours index (0-100)	20	Extent of director liability index (0-10)	8	**Closing a business** (rank)	181
Difficulty of firing index (0-100)	0	Ease of shareholder suits index (0-10)	7	Time (years)	NO PRACTICE
Rigidity of employment index (0-100)	21	Strength of investor protection index (0-10)	6.3	Cost (% of estate)	NO PRACTICE
Firing cost (weeks of salary)	29			Recovery rate (cents on the dollar)	0.0
		Paying taxes (rank)	74		
		Payments (number per year)	30		
		Time (hours per year)	140		
		Total tax rate (% of profit)	45.3		

GUATEMALA

Ease of doing business (rank)	112	Latin America & Caribbean		GNI per capita (US$)	2,440
		Lower middle income		Population (m)	13.3

Starting a business (rank)	147	**Registering property** (rank)	27	**Trading across borders** (rank)	123
Procedures (number)	11	Procedures (number)	5	Documents to export (number)	10
Time (days)	26	Time (days)	30	Time to export (days)	19
Cost (% of income per capita)	50.6	Cost (% of property value)	1.1	Cost to export (US$ per container)	1,182
Minimum capital (% of income per capita)	26.3			Documents to import (number)	10
		Getting credit (rank)	28	Time to import (days)	18
Dealing with construction permits (rank)	164	Strength of legal rights index (0-10)	7	Cost to import (US$ per container)	1,302
Procedures (number)	22	Depth of credit information index (0-6)	5		
Time (days)	215	Public registry coverage (% of adults)	16.1	**Enforcing contracts** (rank)	106
Cost (% of income per capita)	1,204.1	Private bureau coverage (% of adults)	19.7	Procedures (number)	31
				Time (days)	1,459
Employing workers (rank)	106	**Protecting investors** (rank)	126	Cost (% of claim)	26.5
Difficulty of hiring index (0-100)	44	Extent of disclosure index (0-10)	3		
Rigidity of hours index (0-100)	40	Extent of director liability index (0-10)	3	**Closing a business** (rank)	90
Difficulty of firing index (0-100)	0	Ease of shareholder suits index (0-10)	6	Time (years)	3.0
Rigidity of employment index (0-100)	28	Strength of investor protection index (0-10)	4.0	Cost (% of estate)	15
Firing cost (weeks of salary)	101			Recovery rate (cents on the dollar)	28.2
		Paying taxes (rank)	120		
		Payments (number per year)	39		
		Time (hours per year)	344		
		Total tax rate (% of profit)	36.5		

GUINEA

Ease of doing business (rank)	171	Sub-Saharan Africa		GNI per capita (US$)	400
		Low income		Population (m)	9.4

Starting a business (rank)	177	**Registering property** (rank)	157	**Trading across borders** (rank)	110
Procedures (number)	13	Procedures (number)	6	Documents to export (number)	7
Time (days)	41	Time (days)	104	Time to export (days)	33
Cost (% of income per capita)	135.7	Cost (% of property value)	13.9	Cost to export (US$ per container)	720
Minimum capital (% of income per capita)	476.9			Documents to import (number)	9
		Getting credit (rank)	163	Time to import (days)	32
Dealing with construction permits (rank)	162	Strength of legal rights index (0-10)	3	Cost to import (US$ per container)	1,191
Procedures (number)	32	Depth of credit information index (0-6)	0		
Time (days)	255	Public registry coverage (% of adults)	0.0	**Enforcing contracts** (rank)	131
Cost (% of income per capita)	243.0	Private bureau coverage (% of adults)	0.0	Procedures (number)	50
				Time (days)	276
Employing workers (rank)	114	**Protecting investors** (rank)	170	Cost (% of claim)	45.0
Difficulty of hiring index (0-100)	33	Extent of disclosure index (0-10)	6		
Rigidity of hours index (0-100)	60	Extent of director liability index (0-10)	1	**Closing a business** (rank)	109
Difficulty of firing index (0-100)	40	Ease of shareholder suits index (0-10)	1	Time (years)	3.8
Rigidity of employment index (0-100)	44	Strength of investor protection index (0-10)	2.7	Cost (% of estate)	8
Firing cost (weeks of salary)	26			Recovery rate (cents on the dollar)	22.0
		Paying taxes (rank)	168		
		Payments (number per year)	56		
		Time (hours per year)	416		
		Total tax rate (% of profit)	49.9		

GUINEA-BISSAU

Ease of doing business (rank)	179	Sub-Saharan Africa		GNI per capita (US$)	200
		Low income		Population (m)	1.7

Starting a business (rank)	181	**Registering property** (rank)	170	**Trading across borders** (rank)	111
Procedures (number)	17	Procedures (number)	9	Documents to export (number)	6
Time (days)	233	Time (days)	211	Time to export (days)	25
Cost (% of income per capita)	257.7	Cost (% of property value)	5.4	Cost to export (US$ per container)	1,545
Minimum capital (% of income per capita)	1,015.0			Documents to import (number)	6
		Getting credit (rank)	145	Time to import (days)	24
Dealing with construction permits (rank)	109	Strength of legal rights index (0-10)	3	Cost to import (US$ per container)	2,349
Procedures (number)	15	Depth of credit information index (0-6)	1		
Time (days)	167	Public registry coverage (% of adults)	1.0	**Enforcing contracts** (rank)	139
Cost (% of income per capita)	2,628.9	Private bureau coverage (% of adults)	0.0	Procedures (number)	41
				Time (days)	1,140
Employing workers (rank)	176	**Protecting investors** (rank)	126	Cost (% of claim)	25.0
Difficulty of hiring index (0-100)	67	Extent of disclosure index (0-10)	6		
Rigidity of hours index (0-100)	60	Extent of director liability index (0-10)	1	**Closing a business** (rank)	181
Difficulty of firing index (0-100)	70	Ease of shareholder suits index (0-10)	5	Time (years)	NO PRACTICE
Rigidity of employment index (0-100)	66	Strength of investor protection index (0-10)	4.0	Cost (% of estate)	NO PRACTICE
Firing cost (weeks of salary)	87			Recovery rate (cents on the dollar)	0.0
		Paying taxes (rank)	117		
		Payments (number per year)	46		
		Time (hours per year)	208		
		Total tax rate (% of profit)	45.9		

GUYANA

		Latin America & Caribbean		GNI per capita (US$)	1,300
Ease of doing business (rank)	105	Lower middle income		Population (m)	0.7

Starting a business (rank)	100	**Registering property** (rank)	63	**Trading across borders** (rank)	113
Procedures (number)	8	Procedures (number)	6	Documents to export (number)	7
Time (days)	40	Time (days)	34	Time to export (days)	30
Cost (% of income per capita)	68.4	Cost (% of property value)	4.5	Cost to export (US$ per container)	1,050
Minimum capital (% of income per capita)	0.0			Documents to import (number)	8
		Getting credit (rank)	145	Time to import (days)	35
Dealing with construction permits (rank)	37	Strength of legal rights index (0-10)	4	Cost to import (US$ per container)	1,056
Procedures (number)	11	Depth of credit information index (0-6)	0		
Time (days)	133	Public registry coverage (% of adults)	0.0	**Enforcing contracts** (rank)	73
Cost (% of income per capita)	255.8	Private bureau coverage (% of adults)	0.0	Procedures (number)	36
				Time (days)	581
Employing workers (rank)	72	**Protecting investors** (rank)	70	Cost (% of claim)	25.2
Difficulty of hiring index (0-100)	22	Extent of disclosure index (0-10)	5		
Rigidity of hours index (0-100)	20	Extent of director liability index (0-10)	5	**Closing a business** (rank)	126
Difficulty of firing index (0-100)	20	Ease of shareholder suits index (0-10)	6	Time (years)	3.0
Rigidity of employment index (0-100)	21	Strength of investor protection index (0-10)	5.3	Cost (% of estate)	29
Firing cost (weeks of salary)	56			Recovery rate (cents on the dollar)	17.6
		Paying taxes (rank)	108		
		Payments (number per year)	34		
		Time (hours per year)	288		
		Total tax rate (% of profit)	39.4		

HAITI

		Latin America & Caribbean		GNI per capita (US$)	560
Ease of doing business (rank)	154	Low income		Population (m)	9.6

Starting a business (rank)	176	**Registering property** (rank)	128	**Trading across borders** (rank)	146
Procedures (number)	13	Procedures (number)	5	Documents to export (number)	8
Time (days)	195	Time (days)	405	Time to export (days)	43
Cost (% of income per capita)	159.6	Cost (% of property value)	6.4	Cost to export (US$ per container)	1,020
Minimum capital (% of income per capita)	26.6			Documents to import (number)	10
		Getting credit (rank)	145	Time to import (days)	37
Dealing with construction permits (rank)	126	Strength of legal rights index (0-10)	2	Cost to import (US$ per container)	1,560
Procedures (number)	11	Depth of credit information index (0-6)	2		
Time (days)	1,179	Public registry coverage (% of adults)	0.7	**Enforcing contracts** (rank)	92
Cost (% of income per capita)	675.2	Private bureau coverage (% of adults)	0.0	Procedures (number)	35
				Time (days)	508
Employing workers (rank)	35	**Protecting investors** (rank)	164	Cost (% of claim)	42.6
Difficulty of hiring index (0-100)	22	Extent of disclosure index (0-10)	2		
Rigidity of hours index (0-100)	40	Extent of director liability index (0-10)	3	**Closing a business** (rank)	153
Difficulty of firing index (0-100)	0	Ease of shareholder suits index (0-10)	4	Time (years)	5.7
Rigidity of employment index (0-100)	21	Strength of investor protection index (0-10)	3.0	Cost (% of estate)	30
Firing cost (weeks of salary)	17			Recovery rate (cents on the dollar)	2.7
		Paying taxes (rank)	91		
		Payments (number per year)	42		
		Time (hours per year)	160		
		Total tax rate (% of profit)	40.1		

HONDURAS

		Latin America & Caribbean		GNI per capita (US$)	1,600
Ease of doing business (rank)	133	Lower middle income		Population (m)	7.1

Starting a business (rank)	146	**Registering property** (rank)	90	**Trading across borders** (rank)	107
Procedures (number)	13	Procedures (number)	7	Documents to export (number)	7
Time (days)	20	Time (days)	23	Time to export (days)	20
Cost (% of income per capita)	52.6	Cost (% of property value)	5.6	Cost to export (US$ per container)	1,163
Minimum capital (% of income per capita)	20.0			Documents to import (number)	10
		Getting credit (rank)	28	Time to import (days)	23
Dealing with construction permits (rank)	71	Strength of legal rights index (0-10)	6	Cost to import (US$ per container)	1,190
Procedures (number)	17	Depth of credit information index (0-6)	6		
Time (days)	125	Public registry coverage (% of adults)	11.3	**Enforcing contracts** (rank)	176
Cost (% of income per capita)	464.6	Private bureau coverage (% of adults)	60.5	Procedures (number)	45
				Time (days)	900
Employing workers (rank)	156	**Protecting investors** (rank)	150	Cost (% of claim)	35.2
Difficulty of hiring index (0-100)	89	Extent of disclosure index (0-10)	1		
Rigidity of hours index (0-100)	20	Extent of director liability index (0-10)	5	**Closing a business** (rank)	115
Difficulty of firing index (0-100)	50	Ease of shareholder suits index (0-10)	4	Time (years)	3.8
Rigidity of employment index (0-100)	53	Strength of investor protection index (0-10)	3.3	Cost (% of estate)	15
Firing cost (weeks of salary)	74			Recovery rate (cents on the dollar)	20.8
		Paying taxes (rank)	137		
		Payments (number per year)	47		
		Time (hours per year)	224		
		Total tax rate (% of profit)	49.3		

HONG KONG, CHINA

		East Asia & Pacific		GNI per capita (US$)	31,610
Ease of doing business (rank)	4	High income		Population (m)	6.9

Starting a business (rank)	15	**Registering property** (rank)	74	**Trading across borders** (rank)	2
Procedures (number)	5	Procedures (number)	5	Documents to export (number)	4
Time (days)	11	Time (days)	54	Time to export (days)	6
Cost (% of income per capita)	2.0	Cost (% of property value)	5.0	Cost to export (US$ per container)	625
Minimum capital (% of income per capita)	0.0			Documents to import (number)	4
		Getting credit (rank)	2	Time to import (days)	5
Dealing with construction permits (rank)	20	Strength of legal rights index (0-10)	10	Cost to import (US$ per container)	633
Procedures (number)	15	Depth of credit information index (0-6)	5		
Time (days)	119	Public registry coverage (% of adults)	0.0	**Enforcing contracts** (rank)	1
Cost (% of income per capita)	18.7	Private bureau coverage (% of adults)	69.9	Procedures (number)	24
				Time (days)	211
Employing workers (rank)	20	**Protecting investors** (rank)	3	Cost (% of claim)	14.5
Difficulty of hiring index (0-100)	0	Extent of disclosure index (0-10)	10		
Rigidity of hours index (0-100)	0	Extent of director liability index (0-10)	8	**Closing a business** (rank)	13
Difficulty of firing index (0-100)	0	Ease of shareholder suits index (0-10)	9	Time (years)	1.1
Rigidity of employment index (0-100)	0	Strength of investor protection index (0-10)	9.0	Cost (% of estate)	9
Firing cost (weeks of salary)	62			Recovery rate (cents on the dollar)	79.8
		Paying taxes (rank)	3		
		Payments (number per year)	4		
		Time (hours per year)	80		
		Total tax rate (% of profit)	24.2		

HUNGARY

		OECD: High Income		GNI per capita (US$)	11,570
Ease of doing business (rank)	41	High income		Population (m)	10.1

Starting a business (rank)	27	**Registering property** (rank)	57	**Trading across borders** (rank)	68
Procedures (number)	4	Procedures (number)	4	Documents to export (number)	5
Time (days)	5	Time (days)	17	Time to export (days)	18
Cost (% of income per capita)	8.4	Cost (% of property value)	11.0	Cost to export (US$ per container)	1,300
Minimum capital (% of income per capita)	10.8			Documents to import (number)	7
		Getting credit (rank)	28	Time to import (days)	17
Dealing with construction permits (rank)	89	Strength of legal rights index (0-10)	7	Cost to import (US$ per container)	1,290
Procedures (number)	31	Depth of credit information index (0-6)	5		
Time (days)	204	Public registry coverage (% of adults)	0.0	**Enforcing contracts** (rank)	12
Cost (% of income per capita)	10.3	Private bureau coverage (% of adults)	10.0	Procedures (number)	33
				Time (days)	335
Employing workers (rank)	84	**Protecting investors** (rank)	113	Cost (% of claim)	13.0
Difficulty of hiring index (0-100)	0	Extent of disclosure index (0-10)	2		
Rigidity of hours index (0-100)	80	Extent of director liability index (0-10)	4	**Closing a business** (rank)	55
Difficulty of firing index (0-100)	10	Ease of shareholder suits index (0-10)	7	Time (years)	2.0
Rigidity of employment index (0-100)	30	Strength of investor protection index (0-10)	4.3	Cost (% of estate)	15
Firing cost (weeks of salary)	35			Recovery rate (cents on the dollar)	38.4
		Paying taxes (rank)	111		
		Payments (number per year)	14		
		Time (hours per year)	330		
		Total tax rate (% of profit)	57.5		

ICELAND

		OECD: High Income		GNI per capita (US$)	54,100
Ease of doing business (rank)	11	High income		Population (m)	0.3

Starting a business (rank)	17	**Registering property** (rank)	15	**Trading across borders** (rank)	34
Procedures (number)	5	Procedures (number)	3	Documents to export (number)	5
Time (days)	5	Time (days)	4	Time to export (days)	15
Cost (% of income per capita)	2.6	Cost (% of property value)	2.4	Cost to export (US$ per container)	1,109
Minimum capital (% of income per capita)	13.6			Documents to import (number)	5
		Getting credit (rank)	28	Time to import (days)	14
Dealing with construction permits (rank)	28	Strength of legal rights index (0-10)	7	Cost to import (US$ per container)	1,183
Procedures (number)	18	Depth of credit information index (0-6)	5		
Time (days)	75	Public registry coverage (% of adults)	0.0	**Enforcing contracts** (rank)	3
Cost (% of income per capita)	19.2	Private bureau coverage (% of adults)	100.0	Procedures (number)	26
				Time (days)	393
Employing workers (rank)	62	**Protecting investors** (rank)	70	Cost (% of claim)	6.2
Difficulty of hiring index (0-100)	44	Extent of disclosure index (0-10)	5		
Rigidity of hours index (0-100)	40	Extent of director liability index (0-10)	5	**Closing a business** (rank)	16
Difficulty of firing index (0-100)	10	Ease of shareholder suits index (0-10)	6	Time (years)	1.0
Rigidity of employment index (0-100)	31	Strength of investor protection index (0-10)	5.3	Cost (% of estate)	4
Firing cost (weeks of salary)	13			Recovery rate (cents on the dollar)	76.6
		Paying taxes (rank)	32		
		Payments (number per year)	31		
		Time (hours per year)	140		
		Total tax rate (% of profit)	26.8		

INDIA

South Asia			GNI per capita (US$)			950
Ease of doing business (rank)	122	Lower middle income		Population (m)		1,123.3

Starting a business (rank)	121	**Registering property** (rank)	105
Procedures (number)	13	Procedures (number)	6
Time (days)	30	Time (days)	45
Cost (% of income per capita)	70.1	Cost (% of property value)	7.5
Minimum capital (% of income per capita)	0.0		
		Getting credit (rank)	28
Dealing with construction permits (rank)	136	Strength of legal rights index (0-10)	8
Procedures (number)	20	Depth of credit information index (0-6)	4
Time (days)	224	Public registry coverage (% of adults)	0.0
Cost (% of income per capita)	414.7	Private bureau coverage (% of adults)	10.5
Employing workers (rank)	89	**Protecting investors** (rank)	38
Difficulty of hiring index (0-100)	0	Extent of disclosure index (0-10)	7
Rigidity of hours index (0-100)	20	Extent of director liability index (0-10)	4
Difficulty of firing index (0-100)	70	Ease of shareholder suits index (0-10)	7
Rigidity of employment index (0-100)	30	Strength of investor protection index (0-10)	6.0
Firing cost (weeks of salary)	56		
		Paying taxes (rank)	169
		Payments (number per year)	60
		Time (hours per year)	271
		Total tax rate (% of profit)	71.5

Trading across borders (rank)	90
Documents to export (number)	8
Time to export (days)	17
Cost to export (US$ per container)	945
Documents to import (number)	9
Time to import (days)	20
Cost to import (US$ per container)	960
Enforcing contracts (rank)	180
Procedures (number)	46
Time (days)	1,420
Cost (% of claim)	39.6
Closing a business (rank)	140
Time (years)	10.0
Cost (% of estate)	9
Recovery rate (cents on the dollar)	10.4

INDONESIA

East Asia & Pacific			GNI per capita (US$)			1,650
Ease of doing business (rank)	129	Lower middle income		Population (m)		225.6

Starting a business (rank)	171	**Registering property** (rank)	107
Procedures (number)	11	Procedures (number)	6
Time (days)	76	Time (days)	39
Cost (% of income per capita)	77.9	Cost (% of property value)	10.7
Minimum capital (% of income per capita)	74.2		
		Getting credit (rank)	109
Dealing with construction permits (rank)	80	Strength of legal rights index (0-10)	3
Procedures (number)	18	Depth of credit information index (0-6)	4
Time (days)	176	Public registry coverage (% of adults)	26.1
Cost (% of income per capita)	221.1	Private bureau coverage (% of adults)	0.0
Employing workers (rank)	157	**Protecting investors** (rank)	53
Difficulty of hiring index (0-100)	61	Extent of disclosure index (0-10)	9
Rigidity of hours index (0-100)	0	Extent of director liability index (0-10)	5
Difficulty of firing index (0-100)	60	Ease of shareholder suits index (0-10)	3
Rigidity of employment index (0-100)	40	Strength of investor protection index (0-10)	5.7
Firing cost (weeks of salary)	108		
		Paying taxes (rank)	116
		Payments (number per year)	51
		Time (hours per year)	266
		Total tax rate (% of profit)	37.3

Trading across borders (rank)	37
Documents to export (number)	5
Time to export (days)	21
Cost to export (US$ per container)	704
Documents to import (number)	6
Time to import (days)	27
Cost to import (US$ per container)	660
Enforcing contracts (rank)	140
Procedures (number)	39
Time (days)	570
Cost (% of claim)	122.7
Closing a business (rank)	139
Time (years)	5.5
Cost (% of estate)	18
Recovery rate (cents on the dollar)	13.7

IRAN

Middle East & North Africa			GNI per capita (US$)			3,470
Ease of doing business (rank)	142	Lower middle income		Population (m)		71.0

Starting a business (rank)	96	**Registering property** (rank)	147
Procedures (number)	8	Procedures (number)	9
Time (days)	47	Time (days)	36
Cost (% of income per capita)	4.6	Cost (% of property value)	10.6
Minimum capital (% of income per capita)	1.0		
		Getting credit (rank)	84
Dealing with construction permits (rank)	165	Strength of legal rights index (0-10)	5
Procedures (number)	19	Depth of credit information index (0-6)	3
Time (days)	670	Public registry coverage (% of adults)	21.7
Cost (% of income per capita)	514.2	Private bureau coverage (% of adults)	0.0
Employing workers (rank)	147	**Protecting investors** (rank)	164
Difficulty of hiring index (0-100)	11	Extent of disclosure index (0-10)	5
Rigidity of hours index (0-100)	60	Extent of director liability index (0-10)	4
Difficulty of firing index (0-100)	50	Ease of shareholder suits index (0-10)	0
Rigidity of employment index (0-100)	40	Strength of investor protection index (0-10)	3.0
Firing cost (weeks of salary)	91		
		Paying taxes (rank)	104
		Payments (number per year)	22
		Time (hours per year)	344
		Total tax rate (% of profit)	44.2

Trading across borders (rank)	142
Documents to export (number)	8
Time to export (days)	26
Cost to export (US$ per container)	1,011
Documents to import (number)	10
Time to import (days)	42
Cost to import (US$ per container)	1,656
Enforcing contracts (rank)	56
Procedures (number)	39
Time (days)	520
Cost (% of claim)	17.0
Closing a business (rank)	107
Time (years)	4.5
Cost (% of estate)	9
Recovery rate (cents on the dollar)	23.1

IRAQ

Ease of doing business (rank)	152	Middle East & North Africa		GNI per capita (US$)	1,224
		Lower middle income		Population (m)	28.5

Starting a business (rank)	175	**Registering property** (rank)	43	**Trading across borders** (rank)	178
Procedures (number)	11	Procedures (number)	5	Documents to export (number)	10
Time (days)	77	Time (days)	8	Time to export (days)	102
Cost (% of income per capita)	150.7	Cost (% of property value)	6.5	Cost to export (US$ per container)	3,900
Minimum capital (% of income per capita)	59.1			Documents to import (number)	10
		Getting credit (rank)	163	Time to import (days)	101
Dealing with construction permits (rank)	111	Strength of legal rights index (0-10)	3	Cost to import (US$ per container)	3,900
Procedures (number)	14	Depth of credit information index (0-6)	0		
Time (days)	215	Public registry coverage (% of adults)	0.0	**Enforcing contracts** (rank)	148
Cost (% of income per capita)	915.0	Private bureau coverage (% of adults)	0.0	Procedures (number)	51
				Time (days)	520
Employing workers (rank)	67	**Protecting investors** (rank)	113	Cost (% of claim)	32.5
Difficulty of hiring index (0-100)	33	Extent of disclosure index (0-10)	4		
Rigidity of hours index (0-100)	60	Extent of director liability index (0-10)	5	**Closing a business** (rank)	181
Difficulty of firing index (0-100)	20	Ease of shareholder suits index (0-10)	4	Time (years)	NO PRACTICE
Rigidity of employment index (0-100)	38	Strength of investor protection index (0-10)	4.3	Cost (% of estate)	NO PRACTICE
Firing cost (weeks of salary)	0			Recovery rate (cents on the dollar)	0.0
		Paying taxes (rank)	43		
		Payments (number per year)	13		
		Time (hours per year)	312		
		Total tax rate (% of profit)	24.7		

IRELAND

Ease of doing business (rank)	7	OECD: High Income		GNI per capita (US$)	48,140
		High income		Population (m)	4.4

Starting a business (rank)	5	**Registering property** (rank)	82	**Trading across borders** (rank)	18
Procedures (number)	4	Procedures (number)	5	Documents to export (number)	4
Time (days)	13	Time (days)	38	Time to export (days)	7
Cost (% of income per capita)	0.3	Cost (% of property value)	9.6	Cost to export (US$ per container)	1,109
Minimum capital (% of income per capita)	0.0			Documents to import (number)	4
		Getting credit (rank)	12	Time to import (days)	12
Dealing with construction permits (rank)	30	Strength of legal rights index (0-10)	8	Cost to import (US$ per container)	1,121
Procedures (number)	11	Depth of credit information index (0-6)	5		
Time (days)	185	Public registry coverage (% of adults)	0.0	**Enforcing contracts** (rank)	39
Cost (% of income per capita)	44.4	Private bureau coverage (% of adults)	100.0	Procedures (number)	20
				Time (days)	515
Employing workers (rank)	38	**Protecting investors** (rank)	5	Cost (% of claim)	26.9
Difficulty of hiring index (0-100)	11	Extent of disclosure index (0-10)	10		
Rigidity of hours index (0-100)	20	Extent of director liability index (0-10)	6	**Closing a business** (rank)	6
Difficulty of firing index (0-100)	20	Ease of shareholder suits index (0-10)	9	Time (years)	0.4
Rigidity of employment index (0-100)	17	Strength of investor protection index (0-10)	8.3	Cost (% of estate)	9
Firing cost (weeks of salary)	24			Recovery rate (cents on the dollar)	86.6
		Paying taxes (rank)	6		
		Payments (number per year)	9		
		Time (hours per year)	76		
		Total tax rate (% of profit)	28.8		

ISRAEL

Ease of doing business (rank)	30	Middle East & North Africa		GNI per capita (US$)	21,900
		High income		Population (m)	7.2

Starting a business (rank)	24	**Registering property** (rank)	160	**Trading across borders** (rank)	9
Procedures (number)	5	Procedures (number)	7	Documents to export (number)	5
Time (days)	34	Time (days)	144	Time to export (days)	12
Cost (% of income per capita)	4.4	Cost (% of property value)	7.5	Cost to export (US$ per container)	665
Minimum capital (% of income per capita)	0.0			Documents to import (number)	4
		Getting credit (rank)	5	Time to import (days)	12
Dealing with construction permits (rank)	120	Strength of legal rights index (0-10)	9	Cost to import (US$ per container)	605
Procedures (number)	20	Depth of credit information index (0-6)	5		
Time (days)	235	Public registry coverage (% of adults)	0.0	**Enforcing contracts** (rank)	102
Cost (% of income per capita)	112.8	Private bureau coverage (% of adults)	91.0	Procedures (number)	35
				Time (days)	890
Employing workers (rank)	92	**Protecting investors** (rank)	5	Cost (% of claim)	25.3
Difficulty of hiring index (0-100)	11	Extent of disclosure index (0-10)	7		
Rigidity of hours index (0-100)	60	Extent of director liability index (0-10)	9	**Closing a business** (rank)	39
Difficulty of firing index (0-100)	0	Ease of shareholder suits index (0-10)	9	Time (years)	4.0
Rigidity of employment index (0-100)	24	Strength of investor protection index (0-10)	8.3	Cost (% of estate)	23
Firing cost (weeks of salary)	91			Recovery rate (cents on the dollar)	44.9
		Paying taxes (rank)	77		
		Payments (number per year)	33		
		Time (hours per year)	230		
		Total tax rate (% of profit)	33.9		

ITALY

		OECD: High Income		GNI per capita (US$)		33,540
Ease of doing business (rank)	65	High income		Population (m)		59.4

Starting a business (rank)	53	**Registering property** (rank)	58	**Trading across borders** (rank)	60
Procedures (number)	6	Procedures (number)	8	Documents to export (number)	5
Time (days)	10	Time (days)	27	Time to export (days)	20
Cost (% of income per capita)	18.5	Cost (% of property value)	0.6	Cost to export (US$ per container)	1,305
Minimum capital (% of income per capita)	9.7			Documents to import (number)	5
		Getting credit (rank)	84	Time to import (days)	18
Dealing with construction permits (rank)	83	Strength of legal rights index (0-10)	3	Cost to import (US$ per container)	1,305
Procedures (number)	14	Depth of credit information index (0-6)	5		
Time (days)	257	Public registry coverage (% of adults)	11.8	**Enforcing contracts** (rank)	156
Cost (% of income per capita)	136.4	Private bureau coverage (% of adults)	74.9	Procedures (number)	41
				Time (days)	1,210
Employing workers (rank)	75	**Protecting investors** (rank)	53	Cost (% of claim)	29.9
Difficulty of hiring index (0-100)	33	Extent of disclosure index (0-10)	7		
Rigidity of hours index (0-100)	40	Extent of director liability index (0-10)	4	**Closing a business** (rank)	27
Difficulty of firing index (0-100)	40	Ease of shareholder suits index (0-10)	6	Time (years)	1.8
Rigidity of employment index (0-100)	38	Strength of investor protection index (0-10)	5.7	Cost (% of estate)	22
Firing cost (weeks of salary)	11			Recovery rate (cents on the dollar)	56.6
		Paying taxes (rank)	128		
		Payments (number per year)	15		
		Time (hours per year)	334		
		Total tax rate (% of profit)	73.3		

JAMAICA

		Latin America & Caribbean		GNI per capita (US$)		3,710
Ease of doing business (rank)	63	Upper middle income		Population (m)		2.7

Starting a business (rank)	11	**Registering property** (rank)	109	**Trading across borders** (rank)	100
Procedures (number)	6	Procedures (number)	5	Documents to export (number)	6
Time (days)	8	Time (days)	54	Time to export (days)	21
Cost (% of income per capita)	7.9	Cost (% of property value)	11.0	Cost to export (US$ per container)	1,750
Minimum capital (% of income per capita)	0.0			Documents to import (number)	6
		Getting credit (rank)	84	Time to import (days)	22
Dealing with construction permits (rank)	49	Strength of legal rights index (0-10)	8	Cost to import (US$ per container)	1,420
Procedures (number)	10	Depth of credit information index (0-6)	0		
Time (days)	156	Public registry coverage (% of adults)	0.0	**Enforcing contracts** (rank)	127
Cost (% of income per capita)	396.3	Private bureau coverage (% of adults)	0.0	Procedures (number)	35
				Time (days)	655
Employing workers (rank)	32	**Protecting investors** (rank)	70	Cost (% of claim)	45.6
Difficulty of hiring index (0-100)	11	Extent of disclosure index (0-10)	4		
Rigidity of hours index (0-100)	0	Extent of director liability index (0-10)	8	**Closing a business** (rank)	22
Difficulty of firing index (0-100)	0	Ease of shareholder suits index (0-10)	4	Time (years)	1.1
Rigidity of employment index (0-100)	4	Strength of investor protection index (0-10)	5.3	Cost (% of estate)	18
Firing cost (weeks of salary)	62			Recovery rate (cents on the dollar)	64.5
		Paying taxes (rank)	173		
		Payments (number per year)	72		
		Time (hours per year)	414		
		Total tax rate (% of profit)	51.3		

JAPAN

		OECD: High Income		GNI per capita (US$)		37,670
Ease of doing business (rank)	12	High income		Population (m)		127.8

Starting a business (rank)	64	**Registering property** (rank)	51	**Trading across borders** (rank)	17
Procedures (number)	8	Procedures (number)	6	Documents to export (number)	4
Time (days)	23	Time (days)	14	Time to export (days)	10
Cost (% of income per capita)	7.5	Cost (% of property value)	5.0	Cost to export (US$ per container)	989
Minimum capital (% of income per capita)	0.0			Documents to import (number)	5
		Getting credit (rank)	12	Time to import (days)	11
Dealing with construction permits (rank)	39	Strength of legal rights index (0-10)	7	Cost to import (US$ per container)	1,047
Procedures (number)	15	Depth of credit information index (0-6)	6		
Time (days)	187	Public registry coverage (% of adults)	0.0	**Enforcing contracts** (rank)	21
Cost (% of income per capita)	19.1	Private bureau coverage (% of adults)	76.2	Procedures (number)	30
				Time (days)	316
Employing workers (rank)	17	**Protecting investors** (rank)	15	Cost (% of claim)	22.7
Difficulty of hiring index (0-100)	0	Extent of disclosure index (0-10)	7		
Rigidity of hours index (0-100)	20	Extent of director liability index (0-10)	6	**Closing a business** (rank)	1
Difficulty of firing index (0-100)	30	Ease of shareholder suits index (0-10)	8	Time (years)	0.6
Rigidity of employment index (0-100)	17	Strength of investor protection index (0-10)	7.0	Cost (% of estate)	4
Firing cost (weeks of salary)	4			Recovery rate (cents on the dollar)	92.5
		Paying taxes (rank)	112		
		Payments (number per year)	13		
		Time (hours per year)	355		
		Total tax rate (% of profit)	55.4		

JORDAN

Ease of doing business (rank)	101	Middle East & North Africa		GNI per capita (US$)	2,850
		Lower middle income		Population (m)	5.7

Starting a business (rank)	131	**Registering property** (rank)	115	**Trading across borders** (rank)	74
Procedures (number)	10	Procedures (number)	8	Documents to export (number)	7
Time (days)	14	Time (days)	22	Time to export (days)	19
Cost (% of income per capita)	60.4	Cost (% of property value)	10.0	Cost to export (US$ per container)	730
Minimum capital (% of income per capita)	24.2			Documents to import (number)	7
		Getting credit (rank)	123	Time to import (days)	22
Dealing with construction permits (rank)	74	Strength of legal rights index (0-10)	4	Cost to import (US$ per container)	1,290
Procedures (number)	18	Depth of credit information index (0-6)	2		
Time (days)	122	Public registry coverage (% of adults)	1.0	**Enforcing contracts** (rank)	128
Cost (% of income per capita)	443.7	Private bureau coverage (% of adults)	0.0	Procedures (number)	39
				Time (days)	689
Employing workers (rank)	52	**Protecting investors** (rank)	113	Cost (% of claim)	31.2
Difficulty of hiring index (0-100)	11	Extent of disclosure index (0-10)	5		
Rigidity of hours index (0-100)	20	Extent of director liability index (0-10)	4	**Closing a business** (rank)	93
Difficulty of firing index (0-100)	60	Ease of shareholder suits index (0-10)	4	Time (years)	4.3
Rigidity of employment index (0-100)	30	Strength of investor protection index (0-10)	4.3	Cost (% of estate)	9
Firing cost (weeks of salary)	4			Recovery rate (cents on the dollar)	27.3
		Paying taxes (rank)	22		
		Payments (number per year)	26		
		Time (hours per year)	101		
		Total tax rate (% of profit)	31.1		

KAZAKHSTAN

Ease of doing business (rank)	70	Eastern Europe & Central Asia		GNI per capita (US$)	5,060
		Upper middle income		Population (m)	15.5

Starting a business (rank)	78	**Registering property** (rank)	25	**Trading across borders** (rank)	180
Procedures (number)	8	Procedures (number)	5	Documents to export (number)	11
Time (days)	21	Time (days)	40	Time to export (days)	89
Cost (% of income per capita)	5.2	Cost (% of property value)	0.1	Cost to export (US$ per container)	3,005
Minimum capital (% of income per capita)	15.9			Documents to import (number)	13
		Getting credit (rank)	43	Time to import (days)	76
Dealing with construction permits (rank)	175	Strength of legal rights index (0-10)	5	Cost to import (US$ per container)	3,055
Procedures (number)	38	Depth of credit information index (0-6)	6		
Time (days)	231	Public registry coverage (% of adults)	0.0	**Enforcing contracts** (rank)	28
Cost (% of income per capita)	1,431.8	Private bureau coverage (% of adults)	25.6	Procedures (number)	38
				Time (days)	230
Employing workers (rank)	29	**Protecting investors** (rank)	53	Cost (% of claim)	22.0
Difficulty of hiring index (0-100)	0	Extent of disclosure index (0-10)	7		
Rigidity of hours index (0-100)	40	Extent of director liability index (0-10)	1	**Closing a business** (rank)	100
Difficulty of firing index (0-100)	30	Ease of shareholder suits index (0-10)	9	Time (years)	3.3
Rigidity of employment index (0-100)	23	Strength of investor protection index (0-10)	5.7	Cost (% of estate)	18
Firing cost (weeks of salary)	9			Recovery rate (cents on the dollar)	25.3
		Paying taxes (rank)	49		
		Payments (number per year)	9		
		Time (hours per year)	271		
		Total tax rate (% of profit)	36.4		

KENYA

Ease of doing business (rank)	82	Sub-Saharan Africa		GNI per capita (US$)	680
		Low income		Population (m)	37.5

Starting a business (rank)	109	**Registering property** (rank)	119	**Trading across borders** (rank)	148
Procedures (number)	12	Procedures (number)	8	Documents to export (number)	9
Time (days)	30	Time (days)	64	Time to export (days)	29
Cost (% of income per capita)	39.7	Cost (% of property value)	4.1	Cost to export (US$ per container)	2,055
Minimum capital (% of income per capita)	0.0			Documents to import (number)	8
		Getting credit (rank)	5	Time to import (days)	26
Dealing with construction permits (rank)	9	Strength of legal rights index (0-10)	10	Cost to import (US$ per container)	2,190
Procedures (number)	10	Depth of credit information index (0-6)	4		
Time (days)	100	Public registry coverage (% of adults)	0.0	**Enforcing contracts** (rank)	107
Cost (% of income per capita)	46.3	Private bureau coverage (% of adults)	2.1	Procedures (number)	44
				Time (days)	465
Employing workers (rank)	68	**Protecting investors** (rank)	88	Cost (% of claim)	26.7
Difficulty of hiring index (0-100)	22	Extent of disclosure index (0-10)	3		
Rigidity of hours index (0-100)	0	Extent of director liability index (0-10)	2	**Closing a business** (rank)	76
Difficulty of firing index (0-100)	30	Ease of shareholder suits index (0-10)	10	Time (years)	4.5
Rigidity of employment index (0-100)	17	Strength of investor protection index (0-10)	5.0	Cost (% of estate)	22
Firing cost (weeks of salary)	47			Recovery rate (cents on the dollar)	31.6
		Paying taxes (rank)	158		
		Payments (number per year)	41		
		Time (hours per year)	417		
		Total tax rate (% of profit)	50.9		

KIRIBATI

		East Asia & Pacific		GNI per capita (US$)	1,170
Ease of doing business (rank)	79	Lower middle income		Population (m)	0.1

Starting a business (rank)	111	**Registering property** (rank)	68	**Trading across borders** (rank)	69
Procedures (number)	6	Procedures (number)	5	Documents to export (number)	6
Time (days)	21	Time (days)	513	Time to export (days)	21
Cost (% of income per capita)	64.6	Cost (% of property value)	0.1	Cost to export (US$ per container)	1,070
Minimum capital (% of income per capita)	34.9			Documents to import (number)	7
		Getting credit (rank)	131	Time to import (days)	21
Dealing with construction permits (rank)	76	Strength of legal rights index (0-10)	5	Cost to import (US$ per container)	1,070
Procedures (number)	14	Depth of credit information index (0-6)	0		
Time (days)	160	Public registry coverage (% of adults)	0.0	**Enforcing contracts** (rank)	75
Cost (% of income per capita)	717.5	Private bureau coverage (% of adults)	0.0	Procedures (number)	32
				Time (days)	660
Employing workers (rank)	21	**Protecting investors** (rank)	38	Cost (% of claim)	25.8
Difficulty of hiring index (0-100)	0	Extent of disclosure index (0-10)	6		
Rigidity of hours index (0-100)	0	Extent of director liability index (0-10)	5	**Closing a business** (rank)	181
Difficulty of firing index (0-100)	50	Ease of shareholder suits index (0-10)	7	Time (years)	NO PRACTICE
Rigidity of employment index (0-100)	17	Strength of investor protection index (0-10)	6.0	Cost (% of estate)	NO PRACTICE
Firing cost (weeks of salary)	4			Recovery rate (cents on the dollar)	0.0
		Paying taxes (rank)	10		
		Payments (number per year)	7		
		Time (hours per year)	120		
		Total tax rate (% of profit)	31.8		

KOREA

		OECD: High Income		GNI per capita (US$)	19,690
Ease of doing business (rank)	23	High income		Population (m)	48.5

Starting a business (rank)	126	**Registering property** (rank)	67	**Trading across borders** (rank)	12
Procedures (number)	10	Procedures (number)	7	Documents to export (number)	4
Time (days)	17	Time (days)	11	Time to export (days)	8
Cost (% of income per capita)	16.9	Cost (% of property value)	5.1	Cost to export (US$ per container)	767
Minimum capital (% of income per capita)	53.8			Documents to import (number)	6
		Getting credit (rank)	12	Time to import (days)	8
Dealing with construction permits (rank)	23	Strength of legal rights index (0-10)	7	Cost to import (US$ per container)	747
Procedures (number)	13	Depth of credit information index (0-6)	6		
Time (days)	34	Public registry coverage (% of adults)	0.0	**Enforcing contracts** (rank)	8
Cost (% of income per capita)	154.6	Private bureau coverage (% of adults)	90.4	Procedures (number)	35
				Time (days)	230
Employing workers (rank)	152	**Protecting investors** (rank)	70	Cost (% of claim)	10.3
Difficulty of hiring index (0-100)	44	Extent of disclosure index (0-10)	7		
Rigidity of hours index (0-100)	60	Extent of director liability index (0-10)	2	**Closing a business** (rank)	12
Difficulty of firing index (0-100)	30	Ease of shareholder suits index (0-10)	7	Time (years)	1.5
Rigidity of employment index (0-100)	45	Strength of investor protection index (0-10)	5.3	Cost (% of estate)	4
Firing cost (weeks of salary)	91			Recovery rate (cents on the dollar)	80.5
		Paying taxes (rank)	43		
		Payments (number per year)	14		
		Time (hours per year)	250		
		Total tax rate (% of profit)	33.7		

KUWAIT

		Middle East & North Africa		GNI per capita (US$)	31,640
Ease of doing business (rank)	52	High income		Population (m)	2.7

Starting a business (rank)	134	**Registering property** (rank)	83	**Trading across borders** (rank)	104
Procedures (number)	13	Procedures (number)	8	Documents to export (number)	8
Time (days)	35	Time (days)	55	Time to export (days)	20
Cost (% of income per capita)	1.3	Cost (% of property value)	0.5	Cost to export (US$ per container)	995
Minimum capital (% of income per capita)	81.7			Documents to import (number)	10
		Getting credit (rank)	84	Time to import (days)	20
Dealing with construction permits (rank)	82	Strength of legal rights index (0-10)	4	Cost to import (US$ per container)	1,152
Procedures (number)	25	Depth of credit information index (0-6)	4		
Time (days)	104	Public registry coverage (% of adults)	0.0	**Enforcing contracts** (rank)	94
Cost (% of income per capita)	171.4	Private bureau coverage (% of adults)	31.2	Procedures (number)	50
				Time (days)	566
Employing workers (rank)	43	**Protecting investors** (rank)	24	Cost (% of claim)	13.3
Difficulty of hiring index (0-100)	0	Extent of disclosure index (0-10)	7		
Rigidity of hours index (0-100)	40	Extent of director liability index (0-10)	7	**Closing a business** (rank)	66
Difficulty of firing index (0-100)	0	Ease of shareholder suits index (0-10)	5	Time (years)	4.2
Rigidity of employment index (0-100)	13	Strength of investor protection index (0-10)	6.3	Cost (% of estate)	1
Firing cost (weeks of salary)	78			Recovery rate (cents on the dollar)	34.5
		Paying taxes (rank)	9		
		Payments (number per year)	14		
		Time (hours per year)	118		
		Total tax rate (% of profit)	14.4		

KYRGYZ REPUBLIC

		Eastern Europe & Central Asia		GNI per capita (US$)	590
Ease of doing business (rank)	68	Low income		Population (m)	5.2

Starting a business (rank)	31	**Registering property** (rank)	52	**Trading across borders** (rank)	181
Procedures (number)	4	Procedures (number)	7	Documents to export (number)	13
Time (days)	15	Time (days)	8	Time to export (days)	64
Cost (% of income per capita)	7.4	Cost (% of property value)	3.9	Cost to export (US$ per container)	3,000
Minimum capital (% of income per capita)	0.4			Documents to import (number)	13
		Getting credit (rank)	28	Time to import (days)	75
Dealing with construction permits (rank)	58	Strength of legal rights index (0-10)	7	Cost to import (US$ per container)	3,250
Procedures (number)	13	Depth of credit information index (0-6)	5		
Time (days)	159	Public registry coverage (% of adults)	0.0	**Enforcing contracts** (rank)	52
Cost (% of income per capita)	405.7	Private bureau coverage (% of adults)	3.7	Procedures (number)	39
				Time (days)	177
Employing workers (rank)	81	**Protecting investors** (rank)	11	Cost (% of claim)	29.0
Difficulty of hiring index (0-100)	33	Extent of disclosure index (0-10)	9		
Rigidity of hours index (0-100)	40	Extent of director liability index (0-10)	5	**Closing a business** (rank)	137
Difficulty of firing index (0-100)	40	Ease of shareholder suits index (0-10)	9	Time (years)	4.0
Rigidity of employment index (0-100)	38	Strength of investor protection index (0-10)	7.7	Cost (% of estate)	15
Firing cost (weeks of salary)	17			Recovery rate (cents on the dollar)	14.2
		Paying taxes (rank)	155		
		Payments (number per year)	75		
		Time (hours per year)	202		
		Total tax rate (% of profit)	61.4		

LAO PDR

		East Asia & Pacific		GNI per capita (US$)	580
Ease of doing business (rank)	165	Low income		Population (m)	5.9

Starting a business (rank)	92	**Registering property** (rank)	159	**Trading across borders** (rank)	165
Procedures (number)	8	Procedures (number)	9	Documents to export (number)	9
Time (days)	103	Time (days)	135	Time to export (days)	50
Cost (% of income per capita)	14.1	Cost (% of property value)	4.1	Cost to export (US$ per container)	1,860
Minimum capital (% of income per capita)	0.0			Documents to import (number)	10
		Getting credit (rank)	145	Time to import (days)	50
Dealing with construction permits (rank)	110	Strength of legal rights index (0-10)	4	Cost to import (US$ per container)	2,040
Procedures (number)	24	Depth of credit information index (0-6)	0		
Time (days)	172	Public registry coverage (% of adults)	0.0	**Enforcing contracts** (rank)	111
Cost (% of income per capita)	172.1	Private bureau coverage (% of adults)	0.0	Procedures (number)	42
				Time (days)	443
Employing workers (rank)	85	**Protecting investors** (rank)	180	Cost (% of claim)	31.6
Difficulty of hiring index (0-100)	11	Extent of disclosure index (0-10)	0		
Rigidity of hours index (0-100)	40	Extent of director liability index (0-10)	3	**Closing a business** (rank)	181
Difficulty of firing index (0-100)	50	Ease of shareholder suits index (0-10)	2	Time (years)	NO PRACTICE
Rigidity of employment index (0-100)	34	Strength of investor protection index (0-10)	1.7	Cost (% of estate)	NO PRACTICE
Firing cost (weeks of salary)	19			Recovery rate (cents on the dollar)	0.0
		Paying taxes (rank)	113		
		Payments (number per year)	34		
		Time (hours per year)	560		
		Total tax rate (% of profit)	33.7		

LATVIA

		Eastern Europe & Central Asia		GNI per capita (US$)	9,930
Ease of doing business (rank)	29	Upper middle income		Population (m)	2.3

Starting a business (rank)	35	**Registering property** (rank)	77	**Trading across borders** (rank)	25
Procedures (number)	5	Procedures (number)	7	Documents to export (number)	6
Time (days)	16	Time (days)	50	Time to export (days)	13
Cost (% of income per capita)	2.3	Cost (% of property value)	2.0	Cost to export (US$ per container)	900
Minimum capital (% of income per capita)	16.9			Documents to import (number)	6
		Getting credit (rank)	12	Time to import (days)	12
Dealing with construction permits (rank)	78	Strength of legal rights index (0-10)	9	Cost to import (US$ per container)	850
Procedures (number)	25	Depth of credit information index (0-6)	4		
Time (days)	187	Public registry coverage (% of adults)	3.7	**Enforcing contracts** (rank)	4
Cost (% of income per capita)	20.6	Private bureau coverage (% of adults)	0.0	Procedures (number)	27
				Time (days)	279
Employing workers (rank)	103	**Protecting investors** (rank)	53	Cost (% of claim)	16.0
Difficulty of hiring index (0-100)	50	Extent of disclosure index (0-10)	5		
Rigidity of hours index (0-100)	40	Extent of director liability index (0-10)	4	**Closing a business** (rank)	86
Difficulty of firing index (0-100)	40	Ease of shareholder suits index (0-10)	8	Time (years)	3.0
Rigidity of employment index (0-100)	43	Strength of investor protection index (0-10)	5.7	Cost (% of estate)	13
Firing cost (weeks of salary)	17			Recovery rate (cents on the dollar)	29.0
		Paying taxes (rank)	36		
		Payments (number per year)	7		
		Time (hours per year)	279		
		Total tax rate (% of profit)	33.0		

LEBANON

Ease of doing business (rank)	99	Middle East & North Africa		GNI per capita (US$)	5,770
		Upper middle income		Population (m)	4.1

Starting a business (rank)	98	**Registering property** (rank)	102	**Trading across borders** (rank)	83
Procedures (number)	5	Procedures (number)	8	Documents to export (number)	5
Time (days)	11	Time (days)	25	Time to export (days)	27
Cost (% of income per capita)	87.5	Cost (% of property value)	5.9	Cost to export (US$ per container)	872
Minimum capital (% of income per capita)	57.0			Documents to import (number)	7
		Getting credit (rank)	84	Time to import (days)	38
Dealing with construction permits (rank)	121	Strength of legal rights index (0-10)	3	Cost to import (US$ per container)	1,073
Procedures (number)	20	Depth of credit information index (0-6)	5		
Time (days)	211	Public registry coverage (% of adults)	6.8	**Enforcing contracts** (rank)	118
Cost (% of income per capita)	217.8	Private bureau coverage (% of adults)	0.0	Procedures (number)	37
				Time (days)	721
Employing workers (rank)	58	**Protecting investors** (rank)	88	Cost (% of claim)	30.8
Difficulty of hiring index (0-100)	44	Extent of disclosure index (0-10)	9		
Rigidity of hours index (0-100)	0	Extent of director liability index (0-10)	1	**Closing a business** (rank)	121
Difficulty of firing index (0-100)	30	Ease of shareholder suits index (0-10)	5	Time (years)	4.0
Rigidity of employment index (0-100)	25	Strength of investor protection index (0-10)	5.0	Cost (% of estate)	22
Firing cost (weeks of salary)	17			Recovery rate (cents on the dollar)	19.0
		Paying taxes (rank)	45		
		Payments (number per year)	19		
		Time (hours per year)	180		
		Total tax rate (% of profit)	36.0		

LESOTHO

Ease of doing business (rank)	123	Sub-Saharan Africa		GNI per capita (US$)	1,000
		Lower middle income		Population (m)	2.0

Starting a business (rank)	125	**Registering property** (rank)	135	**Trading across borders** (rank)	141
Procedures (number)	7	Procedures (number)	6	Documents to export (number)	6
Time (days)	40	Time (days)	101	Time to export (days)	44
Cost (% of income per capita)	37.8	Cost (% of property value)	8.2	Cost to export (US$ per container)	1,549
Minimum capital (% of income per capita)	14.5			Documents to import (number)	8
		Getting credit (rank)	84	Time to import (days)	49
Dealing with construction permits (rank)	150	Strength of legal rights index (0-10)	8	Cost to import (US$ per container)	1,715
Procedures (number)	15	Depth of credit information index (0-6)	0		
Time (days)	601	Public registry coverage (% of adults)	0.0	**Enforcing contracts** (rank)	104
Cost (% of income per capita)	817.1	Private bureau coverage (% of adults)	0.0	Procedures (number)	41
				Time (days)	695
Employing workers (rank)	63	**Protecting investors** (rank)	142	Cost (% of claim)	19.5
Difficulty of hiring index (0-100)	22	Extent of disclosure index (0-10)	2		
Rigidity of hours index (0-100)	40	Extent of director liability index (0-10)	1	**Closing a business** (rank)	69
Difficulty of firing index (0-100)	0	Ease of shareholder suits index (0-10)	8	Time (years)	2.6
Rigidity of employment index (0-100)	21	Strength of investor protection index (0-10)	3.7	Cost (% of estate)	8
Firing cost (weeks of salary)	44			Recovery rate (cents on the dollar)	33.9
		Paying taxes (rank)	54		
		Payments (number per year)	21		
		Time (hours per year)	324		
		Total tax rate (% of profit)	18.0		

LIBERIA

Ease of doing business (rank)	157	Sub-Saharan Africa		GNI per capita (US$)	150
		Low income		Population (m)	3.8

Starting a business (rank)	88	**Registering property** (rank)	172	**Trading across borders** (rank)	115
Procedures (number)	8	Procedures (number)	13	Documents to export (number)	10
Time (days)	27	Time (days)	50	Time to export (days)	20
Cost (% of income per capita)	100.2	Cost (% of property value)	14.7	Cost to export (US$ per container)	1,232
Minimum capital (% of income per capita)	0.0			Documents to import (number)	9
		Getting credit (rank)	131	Time to import (days)	17
Dealing with construction permits (rank)	177	Strength of legal rights index (0-10)	4	Cost to import (US$ per container)	1,212
Procedures (number)	25	Depth of credit information index (0-6)	1		
Time (days)	321	Public registry coverage (% of adults)	0.3	**Enforcing contracts** (rank)	165
Cost (% of income per capita)	60,988.7	Private bureau coverage (% of adults)	0.0	Procedures (number)	41
				Time (days)	1,280
Employing workers (rank)	105	**Protecting investors** (rank)	142	Cost (% of claim)	35.0
Difficulty of hiring index (0-100)	33	Extent of disclosure index (0-10)	4		
Rigidity of hours index (0-100)	20	Extent of director liability index (0-10)	1	**Closing a business** (rank)	146
Difficulty of firing index (0-100)	40	Ease of shareholder suits index (0-10)	6	Time (years)	3.0
Rigidity of employment index (0-100)	31	Strength of investor protection index (0-10)	3.7	Cost (% of estate)	43
Firing cost (weeks of salary)	84			Recovery rate (cents on the dollar)	8.3
		Paying taxes (rank)	59		
		Payments (number per year)	32		
		Time (hours per year)	158		
		Total tax rate (% of profit)	35.8		

LITHUANIA

Ease of doing business (rank)	28	Eastern Europe & Central Asia		GNI per capita (US$)	9,920
		Upper middle income		Population (m)	3.4

Starting a business (rank)	74	Registering property (rank)	4	Trading across borders (rank)	26
Procedures (number)	7	Procedures (number)	2	Documents to export (number)	6
Time (days)	26	Time (days)	3	Time to export (days)	10
Cost (% of income per capita)	2.7	Cost (% of property value)	0.5	Cost to export (US$ per container)	870
Minimum capital (% of income per capita)	35.9			Documents to import (number)	6
		Getting credit (rank)	43	Time to import (days)	13
Dealing with construction permits (rank)	63	Strength of legal rights index (0-10)	5	Cost to import (US$ per container)	980
Procedures (number)	17	Depth of credit information index (0-6)	6		
Time (days)	162	Public registry coverage (% of adults)	8.9	Enforcing contracts (rank)	16
Cost (% of income per capita)	109.9	Private bureau coverage (% of adults)	7.2	Procedures (number)	30
				Time (days)	210
Employing workers (rank)	131	Protecting investors (rank)	88	Cost (% of claim)	23.6
Difficulty of hiring index (0-100)	33	Extent of disclosure index (0-10)	5		
Rigidity of hours index (0-100)	80	Extent of director liability index (0-10)	4	Closing a business (rank)	34
Difficulty of firing index (0-100)	30	Ease of shareholder suits index (0-10)	6	Time (years)	1.7
Rigidity of employment index (0-100)	48	Strength of investor protection index (0-10)	5.0	Cost (% of estate)	7
Firing cost (weeks of salary)	30			Recovery rate (cents on the dollar)	48.0
		Paying taxes (rank)	57		
		Payments (number per year)	15		
		Time (hours per year)	166		
		Total tax rate (% of profit)	46.4		

LUXEMBOURG

Ease of doing business (rank)	50	OECD: High Income		GNI per capita (US$)	75,880
		High income		Population (m)	0.5

Starting a business (rank)	69	Registering property (rank)	118	Trading across borders (rank)	31
Procedures (number)	6	Procedures (number)	8	Documents to export (number)	5
Time (days)	26	Time (days)	29	Time to export (days)	6
Cost (% of income per capita)	6.5	Cost (% of property value)	10.3	Cost to export (US$ per container)	1,420
Minimum capital (% of income per capita)	21.3			Documents to import (number)	4
		Getting credit (rank)	109	Time to import (days)	6
Dealing with construction permits (rank)	40	Strength of legal rights index (0-10)	7	Cost to import (US$ per container)	1,420
Procedures (number)	13	Depth of credit information index (0-6)	0		
Time (days)	217	Public registry coverage (% of adults)	0.0	Enforcing contracts (rank)	2
Cost (% of income per capita)	20.0	Private bureau coverage (% of adults)	0.0	Procedures (number)	26
				Time (days)	321
Employing workers (rank)	167	Protecting investors (rank)	113	Cost (% of claim)	8.8
Difficulty of hiring index (0-100)	67	Extent of disclosure index (0-10)	6		
Rigidity of hours index (0-100)	80	Extent of director liability index (0-10)	4	Closing a business (rank)	48
Difficulty of firing index (0-100)	40	Ease of shareholder suits index (0-10)	3	Time (years)	2.0
Rigidity of employment index (0-100)	62	Strength of investor protection index (0-10)	4.3	Cost (% of estate)	15
Firing cost (weeks of salary)	39			Recovery rate (cents on the dollar)	41.7
		Paying taxes (rank)	14		
		Payments (number per year)	22		
		Time (hours per year)	59		
		Total tax rate (% of profit)	21.0		

MACEDONIA, FORMER YUGOSLAV REPUBLIC OF

Ease of doing business (rank)	71	Eastern Europe & Central Asia		GNI per capita (US$)	3,460
		Lower middle income		Population (m)	2.0

Starting a business (rank)	12	Registering property (rank)	88	Trading across borders (rank)	64
Procedures (number)	7	Procedures (number)	6	Documents to export (number)	6
Time (days)	9	Time (days)	66	Time to export (days)	17
Cost (% of income per capita)	3.8	Cost (% of property value)	3.4	Cost to export (US$ per container)	1,315
Minimum capital (% of income per capita)	0.0			Documents to import (number)	6
		Getting credit (rank)	43	Time to import (days)	15
Dealing with construction permits (rank)	152	Strength of legal rights index (0-10)	7	Cost to import (US$ per container)	1,325
Procedures (number)	21	Depth of credit information index (0-6)	4		
Time (days)	198	Public registry coverage (% of adults)	6.5	Enforcing contracts (rank)	70
Cost (% of income per capita)	1,862.8	Private bureau coverage (% of adults)	0.0	Procedures (number)	38
				Time (days)	385
Employing workers (rank)	125	Protecting investors (rank)	88	Cost (% of claim)	33.1
Difficulty of hiring index (0-100)	50	Extent of disclosure index (0-10)	5		
Rigidity of hours index (0-100)	60	Extent of director liability index (0-10)	6	Closing a business (rank)	129
Difficulty of firing index (0-100)	30	Ease of shareholder suits index (0-10)	4	Time (years)	3.7
Rigidity of employment index (0-100)	47	Strength of investor protection index (0-10)	5.0	Cost (% of estate)	28
Firing cost (weeks of salary)	26			Recovery rate (cents on the dollar)	16.7
		Paying taxes (rank)	27		
		Payments (number per year)	40		
		Time (hours per year)	75		
		Total tax rate (% of profit)	18.4		

MADAGASCAR

Ease of doing business (rank)	144	Sub-Saharan Africa Low income		GNI per capita (US$) Population (m)	320 19.7	

Starting a business (rank)	58	**Registering property** (rank)	145	**Trading across borders** (rank)	109
Procedures (number)	5	Procedures (number)	7	Documents to export (number)	4
Time (days)	7	Time (days)	74	Time to export (days)	23
Cost (% of income per capita)	11.0	Cost (% of property value)	7.5	Cost to export (US$ per container)	1,279
Minimum capital (% of income per capita)	289.8			Documents to import (number)	9
		Getting credit (rank)	172	Time to import (days)	27
Dealing with construction permits (rank)	102	Strength of legal rights index (0-10)	2	Cost to import (US$ per container)	1,660
Procedures (number)	16	Depth of credit information index (0-6)	0		
Time (days)	178	Public registry coverage (% of adults)	0.1	**Enforcing contracts** (rank)	153
Cost (% of income per capita)	764.8	Private bureau coverage (% of adults)	0.0	Procedures (number)	38
				Time (days)	871
Employing workers (rank)	153	**Protecting investors** (rank)	53	Cost (% of claim)	42.4
Difficulty of hiring index (0-100)	89	Extent of disclosure index (0-10)	5		
Rigidity of hours index (0-100)	60	Extent of director liability index (0-10)	6	**Closing a business** (rank)	181
Difficulty of firing index (0-100)	40	Ease of shareholder suits index (0-10)	6	Time (years)	NO PRACTICE
Rigidity of employment index (0-100)	63	Strength of investor protection index (0-10)	5.7	Cost (% of estate)	NO PRACTICE
Firing cost (weeks of salary)	30			Recovery rate (cents on the dollar)	0.0
		Paying taxes (rank)	92		
		Payments (number per year)	25		
		Time (hours per year)	238		
		Total tax rate (% of profit)	42.8		

MALAWI

Ease of doing business (rank)	134	Sub-Saharan Africa Low income		GNI per capita (US$) Population (m)	250 13.9	

Starting a business (rank)	122	**Registering property** (rank)	96	**Trading across borders** (rank)	167
Procedures (number)	10	Procedures (number)	6	Documents to export (number)	12
Time (days)	39	Time (days)	88	Time to export (days)	45
Cost (% of income per capita)	125.9	Cost (% of property value)	3.3	Cost to export (US$ per container)	1,671
Minimum capital (% of income per capita)	0.0			Documents to import (number)	10
		Getting credit (rank)	84	Time to import (days)	54
Dealing with construction permits (rank)	156	Strength of legal rights index (0-10)	8	Cost to import (US$ per container)	2,550
Procedures (number)	21	Depth of credit information index (0-6)	0		
Time (days)	213	Public registry coverage (% of adults)	0.0	**Enforcing contracts** (rank)	138
Cost (% of income per capita)	1,289.2	Private bureau coverage (% of adults)	0.0	Procedures (number)	42
				Time (days)	432
Employing workers (rank)	96	**Protecting investors** (rank)	70	Cost (% of claim)	142.4
Difficulty of hiring index (0-100)	56	Extent of disclosure index (0-10)	4		
Rigidity of hours index (0-100)	0	Extent of director liability index (0-10)	7	**Closing a business** (rank)	135
Difficulty of firing index (0-100)	20	Ease of shareholder suits index (0-10)	5	Time (years)	2.6
Rigidity of employment index (0-100)	25	Strength of investor protection index (0-10)	5.3	Cost (% of estate)	30
Firing cost (weeks of salary)	84			Recovery rate (cents on the dollar)	15.1
		Paying taxes (rank)	58		
		Payments (number per year)	19		
		Time (hours per year)	292		
		Total tax rate (% of profit)	31.4		

MALAYSIA

Ease of doing business (rank)	20	East Asia & Pacific Upper middle income		GNI per capita (US$) Population (m)	6,540 26.5	

Starting a business (rank)	75	**Registering property** (rank)	81	**Trading across borders** (rank)	29
Procedures (number)	9	Procedures (number)	5	Documents to export (number)	7
Time (days)	13	Time (days)	144	Time to export (days)	18
Cost (% of income per capita)	14.7	Cost (% of property value)	2.5	Cost to export (US$ per container)	450
Minimum capital (% of income per capita)	0.0			Documents to import (number)	7
		Getting credit (rank)	1	Time to import (days)	14
Dealing with construction permits (rank)	104	Strength of legal rights index (0-10)	10	Cost to import (US$ per container)	450
Procedures (number)	25	Depth of credit information index (0-6)	6		
Time (days)	261	Public registry coverage (% of adults)	52.9	**Enforcing contracts** (rank)	59
Cost (% of income per capita)	7.9	Private bureau coverage (% of adults)	..	Procedures (number)	30
				Time (days)	600
Employing workers (rank)	48	**Protecting investors** (rank)	4	Cost (% of claim)	27.5
Difficulty of hiring index (0-100)	0	Extent of disclosure index (0-10)	10		
Rigidity of hours index (0-100)	0	Extent of director liability index (0-10)	9	**Closing a business** (rank)	54
Difficulty of firing index (0-100)	30	Ease of shareholder suits index (0-10)	7	Time (years)	2.3
Rigidity of employment index (0-100)	10	Strength of investor protection index (0-10)	8.7	Cost (% of estate)	15
Firing cost (weeks of salary)	75			Recovery rate (cents on the dollar)	38.6
		Paying taxes (rank)	21		
		Payments (number per year)	12		
		Time (hours per year)	145		
		Total tax rate (% of profit)	34.5		

MALDIVES

Ease of doing business (rank)	69	South Asia		GNI per capita (US$)	3,200
		Lower middle income		Population (m)	0.3
Starting a business (rank)	38	**Registering property** (rank)	177	**Trading across borders** (rank)	121
Procedures (number)	5	Procedures (number)	NO PRACTICE	Documents to export (number)	8
Time (days)	9	Time (days)	NO PRACTICE	Time to export (days)	21
Cost (% of income per capita)	11.5	Cost (% of property value)	NO PRACTICE	Cost to export (US$ per container)	1,348
Minimum capital (% of income per capita)	4.8			Documents to import (number)	9
		Getting credit (rank)	145	Time to import (days)	20
Dealing with construction permits (rank)	8	Strength of legal rights index (0-10)	4	Cost to import (US$ per container)	1,348
Procedures (number)	9	Depth of credit information index (0-6)	0		
Time (days)	118	Public registry coverage (% of adults)	0.0	**Enforcing contracts** (rank)	90
Cost (% of income per capita)	26.3	Private bureau coverage (% of adults)	0.0	Procedures (number)	41
				Time (days)	665
Employing workers (rank)	4	**Protecting investors** (rank)	70	Cost (% of claim)	16.5
Difficulty of hiring index (0-100)	0	Extent of disclosure index (0-10)	0		
Rigidity of hours index (0-100)	0	Extent of director liability index (0-10)	8	**Closing a business** (rank)	123
Difficulty of firing index (0-100)	0	Ease of shareholder suits index (0-10)	8	Time (years)	6.7
Rigidity of employment index (0-100)	0	Strength of investor protection index (0-10)	5.3	Cost (% of estate)	4
Firing cost (weeks of salary)	9			Recovery rate (cents on the dollar)	18.2
		Paying taxes (rank)	1		
		Payments (number per year)	1		
		Time (hours per year)	0		
		Total tax rate (% of profit)	9.1		

MALI

Ease of doing business (rank)	166	Sub-Saharan Africa		GNI per capita (US$)	500
		Low income		Population (m)	12.3
Starting a business (rank)	162	**Registering property** (rank)	94	**Trading across borders** (rank)	166
Procedures (number)	11	Procedures (number)	5	Documents to export (number)	9
Time (days)	26	Time (days)	29	Time to export (days)	38
Cost (% of income per capita)	121.5	Cost (% of property value)	20.3	Cost to export (US$ per container)	2,012
Minimum capital (% of income per capita)	390.4			Documents to import (number)	11
		Getting credit (rank)	145	Time to import (days)	42
Dealing with construction permits (rank)	106	Strength of legal rights index (0-10)	3	Cost to import (US$ per container)	2,902
Procedures (number)	14	Depth of credit information index (0-6)	1		
Time (days)	208	Public registry coverage (% of adults)	4.1	**Enforcing contracts** (rank)	158
Cost (% of income per capita)	1,186.4	Private bureau coverage (% of adults)	0.0	Procedures (number)	39
				Time (days)	860
Employing workers (rank)	94	**Protecting investors** (rank)	150	Cost (% of claim)	52.0
Difficulty of hiring index (0-100)	33	Extent of disclosure index (0-10)	6		
Rigidity of hours index (0-100)	40	Extent of director liability index (0-10)	1	**Closing a business** (rank)	114
Difficulty of firing index (0-100)	40	Ease of shareholder suits index (0-10)	3	Time (years)	3.6
Rigidity of employment index (0-100)	38	Strength of investor protection index (0-10)	3.3	Cost (% of estate)	18
Firing cost (weeks of salary)	31			Recovery rate (cents on the dollar)	20.9
		Paying taxes (rank)	156		
		Payments (number per year)	58		
		Time (hours per year)	270		
		Total tax rate (% of profit)	51.4		

MARSHALL ISLANDS

Ease of doing business (rank)	93	East Asia & Pacific		GNI per capita (US$)	3,070
		Lower middle income		Population (m)	0.1
Starting a business (rank)	25	**Registering property** (rank)	177	**Trading across borders** (rank)	54
Procedures (number)	5	Procedures (number)	NO PRACTICE	Documents to export (number)	5
Time (days)	17	Time (days)	NO PRACTICE	Time to export (days)	21
Cost (% of income per capita)	17.3	Cost (% of property value)	NO PRACTICE	Cost to export (US$ per container)	875
Minimum capital (% of income per capita)	0.0			Documents to import (number)	5
		Getting credit (rank)	145	Time to import (days)	33
Dealing with construction permits (rank)	5	Strength of legal rights index (0-10)	4	Cost to import (US$ per container)	875
Procedures (number)	10	Depth of credit information index (0-6)	0		
Time (days)	55	Public registry coverage (% of adults)	0.0	**Enforcing contracts** (rank)	60
Cost (% of income per capita)	35.9	Private bureau coverage (% of adults)	0.0	Procedures (number)	36
				Time (days)	476
Employing workers (rank)	1	**Protecting investors** (rank)	150	Cost (% of claim)	27.4
Difficulty of hiring index (0-100)	0	Extent of disclosure index (0-10)	2		
Rigidity of hours index (0-100)	0	Extent of director liability index (0-10)	0	**Closing a business** (rank)	125
Difficulty of firing index (0-100)	0	Ease of shareholder suits index (0-10)	8	Time (years)	2.0
Rigidity of employment index (0-100)	0	Strength of investor protection index (0-10)	3.3	Cost (% of estate)	38
Firing cost (weeks of salary)	0			Recovery rate (cents on the dollar)	17.9
		Paying taxes (rank)	88		
		Payments (number per year)	21		
		Time (hours per year)	128		
		Total tax rate (% of profit)	64.9		

MAURITANIA

Sub-Saharan Africa			GNI per capita (US$)		840
Ease of doing business (rank)	160	Low income		Population (m)	3.1

Starting a business (rank)	143	**Registering property** (rank)	61	**Trading across borders** (rank)	158
Procedures (number)	9	Procedures (number)	4	Documents to export (number)	11
Time (days)	19	Time (days)	49	Time to export (days)	35
Cost (% of income per capita)	33.9	Cost (% of property value)	5.2	Cost to export (US$ per container)	1,520
Minimum capital (% of income per capita)	422.6			Documents to import (number)	11
		Getting credit (rank)	145	Time to import (days)	42
Dealing with construction permits (rank)	142	Strength of legal rights index (0-10)	3	Cost to import (US$ per container)	1,523
Procedures (number)	25	Depth of credit information index (0-6)	1		
Time (days)	201	Public registry coverage (% of adults)	0.2	**Enforcing contracts** (rank)	84
Cost (% of income per capita)	475.0	Private bureau coverage (% of adults)	0.0	Procedures (number)	46
				Time (days)	370
Employing workers (rank)	123	**Protecting investors** (rank)	142	Cost (% of claim)	23.2
Difficulty of hiring index (0-100)	56	Extent of disclosure index (0-10)	5		
Rigidity of hours index (0-100)	40	Extent of director liability index (0-10)	3	**Closing a business** (rank)	148
Difficulty of firing index (0-100)	40	Ease of shareholder suits index (0-10)	3	Time (years)	8.0
Rigidity of employment index (0-100)	45	Strength of investor protection index (0-10)	3.7	Cost (% of estate)	9
Firing cost (weeks of salary)	31			Recovery rate (cents on the dollar)	6.7
		Paying taxes (rank)	174		
		Payments (number per year)	38		
		Time (hours per year)	696		
		Total tax rate (% of profit)	98.7		

MAURITIUS

Sub-Saharan Africa			GNI per capita (US$)		5,450
Ease of doing business (rank)	24	Upper middle income		Population (m)	1.3

Starting a business (rank)	7	**Registering property** (rank)	127	**Trading across borders** (rank)	20
Procedures (number)	5	Procedures (number)	4	Documents to export (number)	5
Time (days)	6	Time (days)	210	Time to export (days)	17
Cost (% of income per capita)	5.0	Cost (% of property value)	10.8	Cost to export (US$ per container)	725
Minimum capital (% of income per capita)	0.0			Documents to import (number)	6
		Getting credit (rank)	84	Time to import (days)	16
Dealing with construction permits (rank)	36	Strength of legal rights index (0-10)	5	Cost to import (US$ per container)	677
Procedures (number)	18	Depth of credit information index (0-6)	3		
Time (days)	107	Public registry coverage (% of adults)	20.6	**Enforcing contracts** (rank)	76
Cost (% of income per capita)	41.0	Private bureau coverage (% of adults)	0.0	Procedures (number)	37
				Time (days)	750
Employing workers (rank)	64	**Protecting investors** (rank)	11	Cost (% of claim)	17.4
Difficulty of hiring index (0-100)	0	Extent of disclosure index (0-10)	6		
Rigidity of hours index (0-100)	20	Extent of director liability index (0-10)	8	**Closing a business** (rank)	70
Difficulty of firing index (0-100)	50	Ease of shareholder suits index (0-10)	9	Time (years)	1.7
Rigidity of employment index (0-100)	23	Strength of investor protection index (0-10)	7.7	Cost (% of estate)	15
Firing cost (weeks of salary)	35			Recovery rate (cents on the dollar)	33.6
		Paying taxes (rank)	11		
		Payments (number per year)	7		
		Time (hours per year)	161		
		Total tax rate (% of profit)	22.2		

MEXICO

Latin America & Caribbean			GNI per capita (US$)		8,340
Ease of doing business (rank)	56	Upper middle income		Population (m)	105.3

Starting a business (rank)	115	**Registering property** (rank)	88	**Trading across borders** (rank)	87
Procedures (number)	9	Procedures (number)	5	Documents to export (number)	5
Time (days)	28	Time (days)	74	Time to export (days)	17
Cost (% of income per capita)	12.5	Cost (% of property value)	4.8	Cost to export (US$ per container)	1,472
Minimum capital (% of income per capita)	11.0			Documents to import (number)	5
		Getting credit (rank)	59	Time to import (days)	23
Dealing with construction permits (rank)	33	Strength of legal rights index (0-10)	4	Cost to import (US$ per container)	2,700
Procedures (number)	12	Depth of credit information index (0-6)	6		
Time (days)	138	Public registry coverage (% of adults)	0.0	**Enforcing contracts** (rank)	79
Cost (% of income per capita)	131.0	Private bureau coverage (% of adults)	70.8	Procedures (number)	38
				Time (days)	415
Employing workers (rank)	141	**Protecting investors** (rank)	38	Cost (% of claim)	32.0
Difficulty of hiring index (0-100)	33	Extent of disclosure index (0-10)	8		
Rigidity of hours index (0-100)	40	Extent of director liability index (0-10)	5	**Closing a business** (rank)	23
Difficulty of firing index (0-100)	70	Ease of shareholder suits index (0-10)	5	Time (years)	1.8
Rigidity of employment index (0-100)	48	Strength of investor protection index (0-10)	6.0	Cost (% of estate)	18
Firing cost (weeks of salary)	52			Recovery rate (cents on the dollar)	64.2
		Paying taxes (rank)	149		
		Payments (number per year)	27		
		Time (hours per year)	549		
		Total tax rate (% of profit)	51.5		

MICRONESIA

Ease of doing business (rank)	126	East Asia & Pacific		GNI per capita (US$)		2,470
		Lower middle income		Population (m)		0.1

Starting a business (rank)	60	**Registering property** (rank)	177	**Trading across borders** (rank)	95
Procedures (number)	7	Procedures (number)	NO PRACTICE	Documents to export (number)	3
Time (days)	16	Time (days)	NO PRACTICE	Time to export (days)	30
Cost (% of income per capita)	137.5	Cost (% of property value)	NO PRACTICE	Cost to export (US$ per container)	1,255
Minimum capital (% of income per capita)	0.0			Documents to import (number)	6
		Getting credit (rank)	109	Time to import (days)	30
Dealing with construction permits (rank)	11	Strength of legal rights index (0-10)	7	Cost to import (US$ per container)	1,255
Procedures (number)	14	Depth of credit information index (0-6)	0		
Time (days)	73	Public registry coverage (% of adults)	0.0	**Enforcing contracts** (rank)	143
Cost (% of income per capita)	19.0	Private bureau coverage (% of adults)	0.0	Procedures (number)	34
				Time (days)	965
Employing workers (rank)	12	**Protecting investors** (rank)	170	Cost (% of claim)	66.0
Difficulty of hiring index (0-100)	22	Extent of disclosure index (0-10)	0		
Rigidity of hours index (0-100)	0	Extent of director liability index (0-10)	0	**Closing a business** (rank)	152
Difficulty of firing index (0-100)	0	Ease of shareholder suits index (0-10)	8	Time (years)	5.3
Rigidity of employment index (0-100)	7	Strength of investor protection index (0-10)	2.7	Cost (% of estate)	38
Firing cost (weeks of salary)	0			Recovery rate (cents on the dollar)	3.5
		Paying taxes (rank)	81		
		Payments (number per year)	21		
		Time (hours per year)	128		
		Total tax rate (% of profit)	58.7		

MOLDOVA

Ease of doing business (rank)	103	Eastern Europe & Central Asia		GNI per capita (US$)		1,260
		Lower middle income		Population (m)		3.8

Starting a business (rank)	89	**Registering property** (rank)	50	**Trading across borders** (rank)	135
Procedures (number)	9	Procedures (number)	6	Documents to export (number)	6
Time (days)	15	Time (days)	48	Time to export (days)	32
Cost (% of income per capita)	8.9	Cost (% of property value)	0.8	Cost to export (US$ per container)	1,775
Minimum capital (% of income per capita)	13.4			Documents to import (number)	7
		Getting credit (rank)	84	Time to import (days)	35
Dealing with construction permits (rank)	158	Strength of legal rights index (0-10)	8	Cost to import (US$ per container)	1,895
Procedures (number)	30	Depth of credit information index (0-6)	0		
Time (days)	292	Public registry coverage (% of adults)	0.0	**Enforcing contracts** (rank)	17
Cost (% of income per capita)	142.2	Private bureau coverage (% of adults)	0.0	Procedures (number)	31
				Time (days)	365
Employing workers (rank)	119	**Protecting investors** (rank)	104	Cost (% of claim)	16.6
Difficulty of hiring index (0-100)	44	Extent of disclosure index (0-10)	7		
Rigidity of hours index (0-100)	40	Extent of director liability index (0-10)	1	**Closing a business** (rank)	88
Difficulty of firing index (0-100)	40	Ease of shareholder suits index (0-10)	6	Time (years)	2.8
Rigidity of employment index (0-100)	41	Strength of investor protection index (0-10)	4.7	Cost (% of estate)	9
Firing cost (weeks of salary)	37			Recovery rate (cents on the dollar)	28.6
		Paying taxes (rank)	123		
		Payments (number per year)	53		
		Time (hours per year)	234		
		Total tax rate (% of profit)	42.1		

MONGOLIA

Ease of doing business (rank)	58	East Asia & Pacific		GNI per capita (US$)		1,290
		Lower middle income		Population (m)		2.6

Starting a business (rank)	59	**Registering property** (rank)	20	**Trading across borders** (rank)	156
Procedures (number)	7	Procedures (number)	5	Documents to export (number)	8
Time (days)	13	Time (days)	11	Time to export (days)	49
Cost (% of income per capita)	4.0	Cost (% of property value)	2.1	Cost to export (US$ per container)	2,131
Minimum capital (% of income per capita)	58.5			Documents to import (number)	8
		Getting credit (rank)	68	Time to import (days)	49
Dealing with construction permits (rank)	103	Strength of legal rights index (0-10)	6	Cost to import (US$ per container)	2,274
Procedures (number)	21	Depth of credit information index (0-6)	3		
Time (days)	215	Public registry coverage (% of adults)	22.7	**Enforcing contracts** (rank)	38
Cost (% of income per capita)	81.3	Private bureau coverage (% of adults)	0.0	Procedures (number)	32
				Time (days)	314
Employing workers (rank)	71	**Protecting investors** (rank)	24	Cost (% of claim)	30.6
Difficulty of hiring index (0-100)	22	Extent of disclosure index (0-10)	5		
Rigidity of hours index (0-100)	80	Extent of director liability index (0-10)	8	**Closing a business** (rank)	108
Difficulty of firing index (0-100)	0	Ease of shareholder suits index (0-10)	6	Time (years)	4.0
Rigidity of employment index (0-100)	34	Strength of investor protection index (0-10)	6.3	Cost (% of estate)	8
Firing cost (weeks of salary)	9			Recovery rate (cents on the dollar)	22.1
		Paying taxes (rank)	79		
		Payments (number per year)	42		
		Time (hours per year)	204		
		Total tax rate (% of profit)	30.3		

MONTENEGRO

Ease of doing business (rank)	90	Eastern Europe & Central Asia		GNI per capita (US$)	5,180		
		Upper middle income		Population (m)	0.6		

Starting a business (rank)	105	**Registering property** (rank)	123	**Trading across borders** (rank)	125
Procedures (number)	15	Procedures (number)	8	Documents to export (number)	9
Time (days)	21	Time (days)	86	Time to export (days)	18
Cost (% of income per capita)	4.4	Cost (% of property value)	3.3	Cost to export (US$ per container)	1,710
Minimum capital (% of income per capita)	0.0			Documents to import (number)	7
		Getting credit (rank)	43	Time to import (days)	19
Dealing with construction permits (rank)	167	Strength of legal rights index (0-10)	9	Cost to import (US$ per container)	1,910
Procedures (number)	20	Depth of credit information index (0-6)	2		
Time (days)	248	Public registry coverage (% of adults)	26.3	**Enforcing contracts** (rank)	130
Cost (% of income per capita)	1,323.2	Private bureau coverage (% of adults)	0.0	Procedures (number)	49
				Time (days)	545
Employing workers (rank)	104	**Protecting investors** (rank)	24	Cost (% of claim)	25.7
Difficulty of hiring index (0-100)	33	Extent of disclosure index (0-10)	5		
Rigidity of hours index (0-100)	40	Extent of director liability index (0-10)	8	**Closing a business** (rank)	42
Difficulty of firing index (0-100)	40	Ease of shareholder suits index (0-10)	6	Time (years)	2.0
Rigidity of employment index (0-100)	38	Strength of investor protection index (0-10)	6.3	Cost (% of estate)	8
Firing cost (weeks of salary)	39			Recovery rate (cents on the dollar)	43.7
		Paying taxes (rank)	139		
		Payments (number per year)	89		
		Time (hours per year)	372		
		Total tax rate (% of profit)	31.8		

MOROCCO

Ease of doing business (rank)	128	Middle East & North Africa		GNI per capita (US$)	2,250		
		Lower middle income		Population (m)	30.9		

Starting a business (rank)	62	**Registering property** (rank)	117	**Trading across borders** (rank)	64
Procedures (number)	6	Procedures (number)	8	Documents to export (number)	7
Time (days)	12	Time (days)	47	Time to export (days)	14
Cost (% of income per capita)	10.2	Cost (% of property value)	4.9	Cost to export (US$ per container)	700
Minimum capital (% of income per capita)	52.3			Documents to import (number)	10
		Getting credit (rank)	131	Time to import (days)	18
Dealing with construction permits (rank)	90	Strength of legal rights index (0-10)	3	Cost to import (US$ per container)	1,000
Procedures (number)	19	Depth of credit information index (0-6)	2		
Time (days)	163	Public registry coverage (% of adults)	2.4	**Enforcing contracts** (rank)	112
Cost (% of income per capita)	292.5	Private bureau coverage (% of adults)	0.0	Procedures (number)	40
				Time (days)	615
Employing workers (rank)	168	**Protecting investors** (rank)	164	Cost (% of claim)	25.2
Difficulty of hiring index (0-100)	100	Extent of disclosure index (0-10)	6		
Rigidity of hours index (0-100)	40	Extent of director liability index (0-10)	2	**Closing a business** (rank)	64
Difficulty of firing index (0-100)	50	Ease of shareholder suits index (0-10)	1	Time (years)	1.8
Rigidity of employment index (0-100)	63	Strength of investor protection index (0-10)	3.0	Cost (% of estate)	18
Firing cost (weeks of salary)	85			Recovery rate (cents on the dollar)	35.1
		Paying taxes (rank)	119		
		Payments (number per year)	28		
		Time (hours per year)	358		
		Total tax rate (% of profit)	44.6		

MOZAMBIQUE

Ease of doing business (rank)	141	Sub-Saharan Africa		GNI per capita (US$)	320		
		Low income		Population (m)	21.4		

Starting a business (rank)	144	**Registering property** (rank)	149	**Trading across borders** (rank)	140
Procedures (number)	10	Procedures (number)	8	Documents to export (number)	8
Time (days)	26	Time (days)	42	Time to export (days)	26
Cost (% of income per capita)	22.9	Cost (% of property value)	12.9	Cost to export (US$ per container)	1,200
Minimum capital (% of income per capita)	122.5			Documents to import (number)	10
		Getting credit (rank)	123	Time to import (days)	32
Dealing with construction permits (rank)	153	Strength of legal rights index (0-10)	2	Cost to import (US$ per container)	1,475
Procedures (number)	17	Depth of credit information index (0-6)	4		
Time (days)	381	Public registry coverage (% of adults)	1.9	**Enforcing contracts** (rank)	124
Cost (% of income per capita)	747.8	Private bureau coverage (% of adults)	0.0	Procedures (number)	30
				Time (days)	730
Employing workers (rank)	161	**Protecting investors** (rank)	38	Cost (% of claim)	142.5
Difficulty of hiring index (0-100)	67	Extent of disclosure index (0-10)	5		
Rigidity of hours index (0-100)	60	Extent of director liability index (0-10)	4	**Closing a business** (rank)	133
Difficulty of firing index (0-100)	20	Ease of shareholder suits index (0-10)	9	Time (years)	5.0
Rigidity of employment index (0-100)	49	Strength of investor protection index (0-10)	6.0	Cost (% of estate)	9
Firing cost (weeks of salary)	134			Recovery rate (cents on the dollar)	15.2
		Paying taxes (rank)	88		
		Payments (number per year)	37		
		Time (hours per year)	230		
		Total tax rate (% of profit)	34.3		

NAMIBIA

Ease of doing business (rank)	51	Sub-Saharan Africa		GNI per capita (US$)		3,360
		Lower middle income		Population (m)		2.1

Starting a business (rank)	112	**Registering property** (rank)	129	**Trading across borders** (rank)	150
Procedures (number)	10	Procedures (number)	9	Documents to export (number)	11
Time (days)	66	Time (days)	23	Time to export (days)	29
Cost (% of income per capita)	22.1	Cost (% of property value)	9.9	Cost to export (US$ per container)	1,686
Minimum capital (% of income per capita)	0.0			Documents to import (number)	9
		Getting credit (rank)	12	Time to import (days)	24
Dealing with construction permits (rank)	38	Strength of legal rights index (0-10)	8	Cost to import (US$ per container)	1,813
Procedures (number)	12	Depth of credit information index (0-6)	5		
Time (days)	139	Public registry coverage (% of adults)	0.0	**Enforcing contracts** (rank)	36
Cost (% of income per capita)	181.8	Private bureau coverage (% of adults)	59.6	Procedures (number)	33
				Time (days)	270
Employing workers (rank)	34	**Protecting investors** (rank)	70	Cost (% of claim)	29.9
Difficulty of hiring index (0-100)	0	Extent of disclosure index (0-10)	5		
Rigidity of hours index (0-100)	40	Extent of director liability index (0-10)	5	**Closing a business** (rank)	52
Difficulty of firing index (0-100)	20	Ease of shareholder suits index (0-10)	6	Time (years)	1.5
Rigidity of employment index (0-100)	20	Strength of investor protection index (0-10)	5.3	Cost (% of estate)	15
Firing cost (weeks of salary)	24			Recovery rate (cents on the dollar)	39.5
		Paying taxes (rank)	96		
		Payments (number per year)	37		
		Time (hours per year)	375		
		Total tax rate (% of profit)	25.3		

NEPAL

Ease of doing business (rank)	121	South Asia		GNI per capita (US$)		340
		Low income		Population (m)		28.1

Starting a business (rank)	73	**Registering property** (rank)	28	**Trading across borders** (rank)	157
Procedures (number)	7	Procedures (number)	3	Documents to export (number)	9
Time (days)	31	Time (days)	5	Time to export (days)	41
Cost (% of income per capita)	60.2	Cost (% of property value)	6.3	Cost to export (US$ per container)	1,764
Minimum capital (% of income per capita)	0.0			Documents to import (number)	10
		Getting credit (rank)	109	Time to import (days)	35
Dealing with construction permits (rank)	129	Strength of legal rights index (0-10)	5	Cost to import (US$ per container)	1,900
Procedures (number)	15	Depth of credit information index (0-6)	2		
Time (days)	424	Public registry coverage (% of adults)	0.0	**Enforcing contracts** (rank)	121
Cost (% of income per capita)	248.4	Private bureau coverage (% of adults)	0.2	Procedures (number)	39
				Time (days)	735
Employing workers (rank)	150	**Protecting investors** (rank)	70	Cost (% of claim)	26.8
Difficulty of hiring index (0-100)	56	Extent of disclosure index (0-10)	6		
Rigidity of hours index (0-100)	0	Extent of director liability index (0-10)	1	**Closing a business** (rank)	103
Difficulty of firing index (0-100)	70	Ease of shareholder suits index (0-10)	9	Time (years)	5.0
Rigidity of employment index (0-100)	42	Strength of investor protection index (0-10)	5.3	Cost (% of estate)	9
Firing cost (weeks of salary)	90			Recovery rate (cents on the dollar)	24.5
		Paying taxes (rank)	107		
		Payments (number per year)	34		
		Time (hours per year)	408		
		Total tax rate (% of profit)	34.1		

NETHERLANDS

Ease of doing business (rank)	26	OECD: High Income		GNI per capita (US$)		45,820
		High income		Population (m)		16.4

Starting a business (rank)	51	**Registering property** (rank)	23	**Trading across borders** (rank)	13
Procedures (number)	6	Procedures (number)	2	Documents to export (number)	4
Time (days)	10	Time (days)	5	Time to export (days)	6
Cost (% of income per capita)	5.9	Cost (% of property value)	6.1	Cost to export (US$ per container)	895
Minimum capital (% of income per capita)	51.7			Documents to import (number)	5
		Getting credit (rank)	43	Time to import (days)	6
Dealing with construction permits (rank)	94	Strength of legal rights index (0-10)	6	Cost to import (US$ per container)	1,020
Procedures (number)	18	Depth of credit information index (0-6)	5		
Time (days)	230	Public registry coverage (% of adults)	0.0	**Enforcing contracts** (rank)	34
Cost (% of income per capita)	112.1	Private bureau coverage (% of adults)	81.0	Procedures (number)	25
				Time (days)	514
Employing workers (rank)	98	**Protecting investors** (rank)	104	Cost (% of claim)	24.4
Difficulty of hiring index (0-100)	17	Extent of disclosure index (0-10)	4		
Rigidity of hours index (0-100)	40	Extent of director liability index (0-10)	4	**Closing a business** (rank)	10
Difficulty of firing index (0-100)	70	Ease of shareholder suits index (0-10)	6	Time (years)	1.1
Rigidity of employment index (0-100)	42	Strength of investor protection index (0-10)	4.7	Cost (% of estate)	4
Firing cost (weeks of salary)	17			Recovery rate (cents on the dollar)	82.7
		Paying taxes (rank)	30		
		Payments (number per year)	9		
		Time (hours per year)	180		
		Total tax rate (% of profit)	39.1		

NEW ZEALAND

		OECD: High Income		GNI per capita (US$)		28,780
Ease of doing business (rank)	2	High income		Population (m)		4.2

Starting a business (rank)	1
Procedures (number)	1
Time (days)	1
Cost (% of income per capita)	0.4
Minimum capital (% of income per capita)	0.0
Dealing with construction permits (rank)	2
Procedures (number)	7
Time (days)	65
Cost (% of income per capita)	25.8
Employing workers (rank)	14
Difficulty of hiring index (0-100)	11
Rigidity of hours index (0-100)	0
Difficulty of firing index (0-100)	10
Rigidity of employment index (0-100)	7
Firing cost (weeks of salary)	0

Registering property (rank)	3
Procedures (number)	2
Time (days)	2
Cost (% of property value)	0.1
Getting credit (rank)	5
Strength of legal rights index (0-10)	9
Depth of credit information index (0-6)	5
Public registry coverage (% of adults)	0.0
Private bureau coverage (% of adults)	100.0
Protecting investors (rank)	1
Extent of disclosure index (0-10)	10
Extent of director liability index (0-10)	9
Ease of shareholder suits index (0-10)	10
Strength of investor protection index (0-10)	9.7
Paying taxes (rank)	12
Payments (number per year)	8
Time (hours per year)	70
Total tax rate (% of profit)	35.6

Trading across borders (rank)	23
Documents to export (number)	7
Time to export (days)	10
Cost to export (US$ per container)	868
Documents to import (number)	5
Time to import (days)	9
Cost to import (US$ per container)	850
Enforcing contracts (rank)	11
Procedures (number)	30
Time (days)	216
Cost (% of claim)	22.0
Closing a business (rank)	17
Time (years)	1.3
Cost (% of estate)	4
Recovery rate (cents on the dollar)	76.2

NICARAGUA

		Latin America & Caribbean		GNI per capita (US$)		980
Ease of doing business (rank)	107	Lower middle income		Population (m)		5.6

Starting a business (rank)	85
Procedures (number)	6
Time (days)	39
Cost (% of income per capita)	121.0
Minimum capital (% of income per capita)	0.0
Dealing with construction permits (rank)	134
Procedures (number)	17
Time (days)	219
Cost (% of income per capita)	866.0
Employing workers (rank)	66
Difficulty of hiring index (0-100)	22
Rigidity of hours index (0-100)	60
Difficulty of firing index (0-100)	0
Rigidity of employment index (0-100)	27
Firing cost (weeks of salary)	24

Registering property (rank)	136
Procedures (number)	8
Time (days)	124
Cost (% of property value)	3.5
Getting credit (rank)	84
Strength of legal rights index (0-10)	3
Depth of credit information index (0-6)	5
Public registry coverage (% of adults)	13.4
Private bureau coverage (% of adults)	100.0
Protecting investors (rank)	88
Extent of disclosure index (0-10)	4
Extent of director liability index (0-10)	5
Ease of shareholder suits index (0-10)	6
Strength of investor protection index (0-10)	5.0
Paying taxes (rank)	162
Payments (number per year)	64
Time (hours per year)	240
Total tax rate (% of profit)	63.2

Trading across borders (rank)	99
Documents to export (number)	5
Time to export (days)	29
Cost to export (US$ per container)	1,300
Documents to import (number)	5
Time to import (days)	29
Cost to import (US$ per container)	1,420
Enforcing contracts (rank)	66
Procedures (number)	35
Time (days)	540
Cost (% of claim)	26.8
Closing a business (rank)	67
Time (years)	2.2
Cost (% of estate)	15
Recovery rate (cents on the dollar)	34.3

NIGER

		Sub-Saharan Africa		GNI per capita (US$)		280
Ease of doing business (rank)	172	Low income		Population (m)		14.2

Starting a business (rank)	159
Procedures (number)	11
Time (days)	19
Cost (% of income per capita)	170.1
Minimum capital (% of income per capita)	702.1
Dealing with construction permits (rank)	157
Procedures (number)	17
Time (days)	265
Cost (% of income per capita)	2,694.0
Employing workers (rank)	166
Difficulty of hiring index (0-100)	100
Rigidity of hours index (0-100)	60
Difficulty of firing index (0-100)	50
Rigidity of employment index (0-100)	70
Firing cost (weeks of salary)	35

Registering property (rank)	75
Procedures (number)	4
Time (days)	35
Cost (% of property value)	11.1
Getting credit (rank)	145
Strength of legal rights index (0-10)	3
Depth of credit information index (0-6)	1
Public registry coverage (% of adults)	0.9
Private bureau coverage (% of adults)	0.0
Protecting investors (rank)	150
Extent of disclosure index (0-10)	6
Extent of director liability index (0-10)	1
Ease of shareholder suits index (0-10)	3
Strength of investor protection index (0-10)	3.3
Paying taxes (rank)	120
Payments (number per year)	42
Time (hours per year)	270
Total tax rate (% of profit)	42.3

Trading across borders (rank)	169
Documents to export (number)	8
Time to export (days)	59
Cost to export (US$ per container)	3,545
Documents to import (number)	10
Time to import (days)	64
Cost to import (US$ per container)	3,545
Enforcing contracts (rank)	134
Procedures (number)	39
Time (days)	545
Cost (% of claim)	59.6
Closing a business (rank)	138
Time (years)	5.0
Cost (% of estate)	18
Recovery rate (cents on the dollar)	14.0

NIGERIA

		Sub-Saharan Africa		GNI per capita (US$)	930
Ease of doing business (rank)	118	Low income		Population (m)	148.0

Starting a business (rank)	91	**Registering property** (rank)	176	**Trading across borders** (rank)	144
Procedures (number)	8	Procedures (number)	14	Documents to export (number)	10
Time (days)	31	Time (days)	82	Time to export (days)	25
Cost (% of income per capita)	90.1	Cost (% of property value)	21.9	Cost to export (US$ per container)	1,179
Minimum capital (% of income per capita)	0.0			Documents to import (number)	9
		Getting credit (rank)	84	Time to import (days)	42
Dealing with construction permits (rank)	151	Strength of legal rights index (0-10)	8	Cost to import (US$ per container)	1,306
Procedures (number)	18	Depth of credit information index (0-6)	0		
Time (days)	350	Public registry coverage (% of adults)	0.1	**Enforcing contracts** (rank)	90
Cost (% of income per capita)	655.4	Private bureau coverage (% of adults)	0.0	Procedures (number)	39
				Time (days)	457
Employing workers (rank)	27	**Protecting investors** (rank)	53	Cost (% of claim)	32.0
Difficulty of hiring index (0-100)	0	Extent of disclosure index (0-10)	5		
Rigidity of hours index (0-100)	0	Extent of director liability index (0-10)	7	**Closing a business** (rank)	91
Difficulty of firing index (0-100)	20	Ease of shareholder suits index (0-10)	5	Time (years)	2.0
Rigidity of employment index (0-100)	7	Strength of investor protection index (0-10)	5.7	Cost (% of estate)	22
Firing cost (weeks of salary)	50			Recovery rate (cents on the dollar)	28.0
		Paying taxes (rank)	120		
		Payments (number per year)	35		
		Time (hours per year)	938		
		Total tax rate (% of profit)	32.2		

NORWAY

		OECD: High Income		GNI per capita (US$)	76,450
Ease of doing business (rank)	10	High income		Population (m)	4.7

Starting a business (rank)	33	**Registering property** (rank)	8	**Trading across borders** (rank)	7
Procedures (number)	6	Procedures (number)	1	Documents to export (number)	4
Time (days)	10	Time (days)	3	Time to export (days)	7
Cost (% of income per capita)	2.1	Cost (% of property value)	2.5	Cost to export (US$ per container)	780
Minimum capital (% of income per capita)	21.0			Documents to import (number)	4
		Getting credit (rank)	43	Time to import (days)	7
Dealing with construction permits (rank)	66	Strength of legal rights index (0-10)	7	Cost to import (US$ per container)	709
Procedures (number)	14	Depth of credit information index (0-6)	4		
Time (days)	252	Public registry coverage (% of adults)	0.0	**Enforcing contracts** (rank)	7
Cost (% of income per capita)	46.6	Private bureau coverage (% of adults)	100.0	Procedures (number)	33
				Time (days)	310
Employing workers (rank)	99	**Protecting investors** (rank)	18	Cost (% of claim)	9.9
Difficulty of hiring index (0-100)	61	Extent of disclosure index (0-10)	7		
Rigidity of hours index (0-100)	40	Extent of director liability index (0-10)	6	**Closing a business** (rank)	3
Difficulty of firing index (0-100)	40	Ease of shareholder suits index (0-10)	7	Time (years)	0.9
Rigidity of employment index (0-100)	47	Strength of investor protection index (0-10)	6.7	Cost (% of estate)	1
Firing cost (weeks of salary)	13			Recovery rate (cents on the dollar)	89.0
		Paying taxes (rank)	18		
		Payments (number per year)	4		
		Time (hours per year)	87		
		Total tax rate (% of profit)	41.6		

OMAN

		Middle East & North Africa		GNI per capita (US$)	11,120
Ease of doing business (rank)	57	High income		Population (m)	2.6

Starting a business (rank)	76	**Registering property** (rank)	19	**Trading across borders** (rank)	119
Procedures (number)	7	Procedures (number)	2	Documents to export (number)	10
Time (days)	14	Time (days)	16	Time to export (days)	22
Cost (% of income per capita)	3.6	Cost (% of property value)	3.0	Cost to export (US$ per container)	821
Minimum capital (% of income per capita)	461.2			Documents to import (number)	10
		Getting credit (rank)	123	Time to import (days)	26
Dealing with construction permits (rank)	133	Strength of legal rights index (0-10)	4	Cost to import (US$ per container)	1,037
Procedures (number)	16	Depth of credit information index (0-6)	2		
Time (days)	242	Public registry coverage (% of adults)	23.4	**Enforcing contracts** (rank)	105
Cost (% of income per capita)	721.4	Private bureau coverage (% of adults)	0.0	Procedures (number)	51
				Time (days)	598
Employing workers (rank)	24	**Protecting investors** (rank)	88	Cost (% of claim)	13.5
Difficulty of hiring index (0-100)	33	Extent of disclosure index (0-10)	8		
Rigidity of hours index (0-100)	40	Extent of director liability index (0-10)	5	**Closing a business** (rank)	63
Difficulty of firing index (0-100)	0	Ease of shareholder suits index (0-10)	2	Time (years)	4.0
Rigidity of employment index (0-100)	24	Strength of investor protection index (0-10)	5.0	Cost (% of estate)	4
Firing cost (weeks of salary)	4			Recovery rate (cents on the dollar)	35.1
		Paying taxes (rank)	8		
		Payments (number per year)	14		
		Time (hours per year)	62		
		Total tax rate (% of profit)	21.6		

PAKISTAN

		South Asia		GNI per capita (US$)	870
Ease of doing business (rank)	77	Low income		Population (m)	162.4

Starting a business (rank)	77	**Registering property** (rank)	97	**Trading across borders** (rank)	71
Procedures (number)	11	Procedures (number)	6	Documents to export (number)	9
Time (days)	24	Time (days)	50	Time to export (days)	24
Cost (% of income per capita)	12.6	Cost (% of property value)	5.3	Cost to export (US$ per container)	611
Minimum capital (% of income per capita)	0.0			Documents to import (number)	8
		Getting credit (rank)	59	Time to import (days)	18
Dealing with construction permits (rank)	93	Strength of legal rights index (0-10)	6	Cost to import (US$ per container)	680
Procedures (number)	12	Depth of credit information index (0-6)	4		
Time (days)	223	Public registry coverage (% of adults)	4.9	**Enforcing contracts** (rank)	154
Cost (% of income per capita)	734.0	Private bureau coverage (% of adults)	1.5	Procedures (number)	47
				Time (days)	976
Employing workers (rank)	136	**Protecting investors** (rank)	24	Cost (% of claim)	23.8
Difficulty of hiring index (0-100)	78	Extent of disclosure index (0-10)	6		
Rigidity of hours index (0-100)	20	Extent of director liability index (0-10)	6	**Closing a business** (rank)	53
Difficulty of firing index (0-100)	30	Ease of shareholder suits index (0-10)	7	Time (years)	2.8
Rigidity of employment index (0-100)	43	Strength of investor protection index (0-10)	6.3	Cost (% of estate)	4
Firing cost (weeks of salary)	90			Recovery rate (cents on the dollar)	39.2
		Paying taxes (rank)	124		
		Payments (number per year)	47		
		Time (hours per year)	560		
		Total tax rate (% of profit)	28.9		

PALAU

		East Asia & Pacific		GNI per capita (US$)	8,210
Ease of doing business (rank)	91	Upper middle income		Population (m)	0.0

Starting a business (rank)	83	**Registering property** (rank)	17	**Trading across borders** (rank)	120
Procedures (number)	8	Procedures (number)	5	Documents to export (number)	6
Time (days)	28	Time (days)	14	Time to export (days)	29
Cost (% of income per capita)	4.6	Cost (% of property value)	0.4	Cost to export (US$ per container)	1,170
Minimum capital (% of income per capita)	12.2			Documents to import (number)	10
		Getting credit (rank)	181	Time to import (days)	33
Dealing with construction permits (rank)	52	Strength of legal rights index (0-10)	0	Cost to import (US$ per container)	1,132
Procedures (number)	25	Depth of credit information index (0-6)	0		
Time (days)	118	Public registry coverage (% of adults)	0.0	**Enforcing contracts** (rank)	141
Cost (% of income per capita)	5.9	Private bureau coverage (% of adults)	0.0	Procedures (number)	38
				Time (days)	885
Employing workers (rank)	9	**Protecting investors** (rank)	170	Cost (% of claim)	35.3
Difficulty of hiring index (0-100)	11	Extent of disclosure index (0-10)	0		
Rigidity of hours index (0-100)	0	Extent of director liability index (0-10)	0	**Closing a business** (rank)	56
Difficulty of firing index (0-100)	0	Ease of shareholder suits index (0-10)	8	Time (years)	1.0
Rigidity of employment index (0-100)	4	Strength of investor protection index (0-10)	2.7	Cost (% of estate)	23
Firing cost (weeks of salary)	0			Recovery rate (cents on the dollar)	38.2
		Paying taxes (rank)	86		
		Payments (number per year)	19		
		Time (hours per year)	128		
		Total tax rate (% of profit)	73.0		

PANAMA

		Latin America & Caribbean		GNI per capita (US$)	5,510
Ease of doing business (rank)	81	Upper middle income		Population (m)	3.3

Starting a business (rank)	32	**Registering property** (rank)	75	**Trading across borders** (rank)	8
Procedures (number)	7	Procedures (number)	7	Documents to export (number)	3
Time (days)	13	Time (days)	44	Time to export (days)	9
Cost (% of income per capita)	19.6	Cost (% of property value)	2.4	Cost to export (US$ per container)	729
Minimum capital (% of income per capita)	0.0			Documents to import (number)	4
		Getting credit (rank)	28	Time to import (days)	9
Dealing with construction permits (rank)	73	Strength of legal rights index (0-10)	6	Cost to import (US$ per container)	879
Procedures (number)	21	Depth of credit information index (0-6)	6		
Time (days)	131	Public registry coverage (% of adults)	0.0	**Enforcing contracts** (rank)	116
Cost (% of income per capita)	123.3	Private bureau coverage (% of adults)	43.7	Procedures (number)	31
				Time (days)	686
Employing workers (rank)	172	**Protecting investors** (rank)	104	Cost (% of claim)	50.0
Difficulty of hiring index (0-100)	78	Extent of disclosure index (0-10)	1		
Rigidity of hours index (0-100)	60	Extent of director liability index (0-10)	4	**Closing a business** (rank)	72
Difficulty of firing index (0-100)	60	Ease of shareholder suits index (0-10)	9	Time (years)	2.5
Rigidity of employment index (0-100)	66	Strength of investor protection index (0-10)	4.7	Cost (% of estate)	18
Firing cost (weeks of salary)	44			Recovery rate (cents on the dollar)	32.4
		Paying taxes (rank)	172		
		Payments (number per year)	59		
		Time (hours per year)	482		
		Total tax rate (% of profit)	50.6		

PAPUA NEW GUINEA

		East Asia & Pacific		GNI per capita (US$)	850
Ease of doing business (rank)	95	Low income		Population (m)	6.3

Starting a business (rank)	92	**Registering property** (rank)	73	**Trading across borders** (rank)	89
Procedures (number)	8	Procedures (number)	4	Documents to export (number)	7
Time (days)	56	Time (days)	72	Time to export (days)	26
Cost (% of income per capita)	23.6	Cost (% of property value)	5.1	Cost to export (US$ per container)	664
Minimum capital (% of income per capita)	0.0			Documents to import (number)	9
		Getting credit (rank)	131	Time to import (days)	29
Dealing with construction permits (rank)	124	Strength of legal rights index (0-10)	5	Cost to import (US$ per container)	722
Procedures (number)	24	Depth of credit information index (0-6)	0		
Time (days)	217	Public registry coverage (% of adults)	0.0	**Enforcing contracts** (rank)	162
Cost (% of income per capita)	95.1	Private bureau coverage (% of adults)	0.0	Procedures (number)	43
				Time (days)	591
Employing workers (rank)	31	**Protecting investors** (rank)	38	Cost (% of claim)	110.3
Difficulty of hiring index (0-100)	11	Extent of disclosure index (0-10)	5		
Rigidity of hours index (0-100)	20	Extent of director liability index (0-10)	5	**Closing a business** (rank)	102
Difficulty of firing index (0-100)	0	Ease of shareholder suits index (0-10)	8	Time (years)	3.0
Rigidity of employment index (0-100)	10	Strength of investor protection index (0-10)	6.0	Cost (% of estate)	23
Firing cost (weeks of salary)	39			Recovery rate (cents on the dollar)	24.7
		Paying taxes (rank)	87		
		Payments (number per year)	33		
		Time (hours per year)	194		
		Total tax rate (% of profit)	41.7		

PARAGUAY

		Latin America & Caribbean		GNI per capita (US$)	1,670
Ease of doing business (rank)	115	Lower middle income		Population (m)	6.1

Starting a business (rank)	82	**Registering property** (rank)	70	**Trading across borders** (rank)	138
Procedures (number)	7	Procedures (number)	6	Documents to export (number)	9
Time (days)	35	Time (days)	46	Time to export (days)	35
Cost (% of income per capita)	67.9	Cost (% of property value)	3.5	Cost to export (US$ per container)	915
Minimum capital (% of income per capita)	0.0			Documents to import (number)	10
		Getting credit (rank)	68	Time to import (days)	33
Dealing with construction permits (rank)	96	Strength of legal rights index (0-10)	3	Cost to import (US$ per container)	1,200
Procedures (number)	13	Depth of credit information index (0-6)	6		
Time (days)	291	Public registry coverage (% of adults)	9.7	**Enforcing contracts** (rank)	103
Cost (% of income per capita)	342.2	Private bureau coverage (% of adults)	48.6	Procedures (number)	38
				Time (days)	591
Employing workers (rank)	177	**Protecting investors** (rank)	53	Cost (% of claim)	30.0
Difficulty of hiring index (0-100)	56	Extent of disclosure index (0-10)	6		
Rigidity of hours index (0-100)	60	Extent of director liability index (0-10)	5	**Closing a business** (rank)	116
Difficulty of firing index (0-100)	60	Ease of shareholder suits index (0-10)	6	Time (years)	3.9
Rigidity of employment index (0-100)	59	Strength of investor protection index (0-10)	5.7	Cost (% of estate)	9
Firing cost (weeks of salary)	113			Recovery rate (cents on the dollar)	20.7
		Paying taxes (rank)	102		
		Payments (number per year)	35		
		Time (hours per year)	328		
		Total tax rate (% of profit)	35.0		

PERU

		Latin America & Caribbean		GNI per capita (US$)	3,450
Ease of doing business (rank)	62	Lower middle income		Population (m)	27.9

Starting a business (rank)	116	**Registering property** (rank)	41	**Trading across borders** (rank)	93
Procedures (number)	10	Procedures (number)	5	Documents to export (number)	7
Time (days)	65	Time (days)	33	Time to export (days)	24
Cost (% of income per capita)	25.7	Cost (% of property value)	3.3	Cost to export (US$ per container)	875
Minimum capital (% of income per capita)	0.0			Documents to import (number)	8
		Getting credit (rank)	12	Time to import (days)	25
Dealing with construction permits (rank)	115	Strength of legal rights index (0-10)	7	Cost to import (US$ per container)	895
Procedures (number)	21	Depth of credit information index (0-6)	6		
Time (days)	210	Public registry coverage (% of adults)	23.7	**Enforcing contracts** (rank)	119
Cost (% of income per capita)	139.7	Private bureau coverage (% of adults)	33.2	Procedures (number)	41
				Time (days)	468
Employing workers (rank)	149	**Protecting investors** (rank)	18	Cost (% of claim)	35.7
Difficulty of hiring index (0-100)	44	Extent of disclosure index (0-10)	8		
Rigidity of hours index (0-100)	40	Extent of director liability index (0-10)	5	**Closing a business** (rank)	96
Difficulty of firing index (0-100)	60	Ease of shareholder suits index (0-10)	7	Time (years)	3.1
Rigidity of employment index (0-100)	48	Strength of investor protection index (0-10)	6.7	Cost (% of estate)	7
Firing cost (weeks of salary)	52			Recovery rate (cents on the dollar)	25.4
		Paying taxes (rank)	85		
		Payments (number per year)	9		
		Time (hours per year)	424		
		Total tax rate (% of profit)	41.2		

PHILIPPINES

		East Asia & Pacific		GNI per capita (US$)		1,620
Ease of doing business (rank)	140	Lower middle income		Population (m)		87.9

Starting a business (rank)	155
Procedures (number)	15
Time (days)	52
Cost (% of income per capita)	29.8
Minimum capital (% of income per capita)	6.0

Dealing with construction permits (rank)	105
Procedures (number)	24
Time (days)	203
Cost (% of income per capita)	90.1

Employing workers (rank)	126
Difficulty of hiring index (0-100)	56
Rigidity of hours index (0-100)	20
Difficulty of firing index (0-100)	30
Rigidity of employment index (0-100)	35
Firing cost (weeks of salary)	91

Registering property (rank)	97
Procedures (number)	8
Time (days)	33
Cost (% of property value)	4.3

Getting credit (rank)	123
Strength of legal rights index (0-10)	3
Depth of credit information index (0-6)	3
Public registry coverage (% of adults)	0.0
Private bureau coverage (% of adults)	5.4

Protecting investors (rank)	126
Extent of disclosure index (0-10)	2
Extent of director liability index (0-10)	2
Ease of shareholder suits index (0-10)	8
Strength of investor protection index (0-10)	4.0

Paying taxes (rank)	129
Payments (number per year)	47
Time (hours per year)	195
Total tax rate (% of profit)	50.8

Trading across borders (rank)	58
Documents to export (number)	8
Time to export (days)	16
Cost to export (US$ per container)	816
Documents to import (number)	8
Time to import (days)	16
Cost to import (US$ per container)	819

Enforcing contracts (rank)	114
Procedures (number)	37
Time (days)	842
Cost (% of claim)	26.0

Closing a business (rank)	151
Time (years)	5.7
Cost (% of estate)	38
Recovery rate (cents on the dollar)	4.4

POLAND

		Eastern Europe & Central Asia		GNI per capita (US$)		9,840
Ease of doing business (rank)	76	Upper middle income		Population (m)		38.1

Starting a business (rank)	145
Procedures (number)	10
Time (days)	31
Cost (% of income per capita)	18.8
Minimum capital (% of income per capita)	168.8

Dealing with construction permits (rank)	158
Procedures (number)	30
Time (days)	308
Cost (% of income per capita)	137.0

Employing workers (rank)	82
Difficulty of hiring index (0-100)	11
Rigidity of hours index (0-100)	60
Difficulty of firing index (0-100)	40
Rigidity of employment index (0-100)	37
Firing cost (weeks of salary)	13

Registering property (rank)	84
Procedures (number)	6
Time (days)	197
Cost (% of property value)	0.5

Getting credit (rank)	28
Strength of legal rights index (0-10)	8
Depth of credit information index (0-6)	4
Public registry coverage (% of adults)	0.0
Private bureau coverage (% of adults)	50.0

Protecting investors (rank)	38
Extent of disclosure index (0-10)	7
Extent of director liability index (0-10)	2
Ease of shareholder suits index (0-10)	9
Strength of investor protection index (0-10)	6.0

Paying taxes (rank)	142
Payments (number per year)	40
Time (hours per year)	418
Total tax rate (% of profit)	40.2

Trading across borders (rank)	41
Documents to export (number)	5
Time to export (days)	17
Cost to export (US$ per container)	884
Documents to import (number)	5
Time to import (days)	27
Cost to import (US$ per container)	884

Enforcing contracts (rank)	68
Procedures (number)	38
Time (days)	830
Cost (% of claim)	12.0

Closing a business (rank)	82
Time (years)	3.0
Cost (% of estate)	20
Recovery rate (cents on the dollar)	29.8

PORTUGAL

		OECD: High Income		GNI per capita (US$)		18,950
Ease of doing business (rank)	48	High income		Population (m)		10.6

Starting a business (rank)	34
Procedures (number)	6
Time (days)	6
Cost (% of income per capita)	2.9
Minimum capital (% of income per capita)	34.3

Dealing with construction permits (rank)	128
Procedures (number)	21
Time (days)	328
Cost (% of income per capita)	53.5

Employing workers (rank)	164
Difficulty of hiring index (0-100)	33
Rigidity of hours index (0-100)	60
Difficulty of firing index (0-100)	50
Rigidity of employment index (0-100)	48
Firing cost (weeks of salary)	95

Registering property (rank)	79
Procedures (number)	5
Time (days)	42
Cost (% of property value)	7.4

Getting credit (rank)	109
Strength of legal rights index (0-10)	3
Depth of credit information index (0-6)	4
Public registry coverage (% of adults)	76.4
Private bureau coverage (% of adults)	11.3

Protecting investors (rank)	38
Extent of disclosure index (0-10)	6
Extent of director liability index (0-10)	5
Ease of shareholder suits index (0-10)	7
Strength of investor protection index (0-10)	6.0

Paying taxes (rank)	73
Payments (number per year)	8
Time (hours per year)	328
Total tax rate (% of profit)	43.6

Trading across borders (rank)	33
Documents to export (number)	6
Time to export (days)	16
Cost to export (US$ per container)	685
Documents to import (number)	7
Time to import (days)	16
Cost to import (US$ per container)	999

Enforcing contracts (rank)	34
Procedures (number)	34
Time (days)	577
Cost (% of claim)	14.2

Closing a business (rank)	21
Time (years)	2.0
Cost (% of estate)	9
Recovery rate (cents on the dollar)	69.4

PUERTO RICO

		Latin America & Caribbean		GNI per capita (US$)	14,371
Ease of doing business (rank)	35	High income		Population (m)	3.9

Starting a business (rank)	9	**Registering property** (rank)	122	**Trading across borders** (rank)	101
Procedures (number)	7	Procedures (number)	8	Documents to export (number)	7
Time (days)	7	Time (days)	194	Time to export (days)	15
Cost (% of income per capita)	0.8	Cost (% of property value)	1.5	Cost to export (US$ per container)	1,250
Minimum capital (% of income per capita)	0.0			Documents to import (number)	10
		Getting credit (rank)	12	Time to import (days)	16
		Strength of legal rights index (0-10)	8	Cost to import (US$ per container)	1,250
Dealing with construction permits (rank)	144	Depth of credit information index (0-6)	5		
Procedures (number)	22	Public registry coverage (% of adults)	0.0	**Enforcing contracts** (rank)	97
Time (days)	209	Private bureau coverage (% of adults)	61.4	Procedures (number)	39
Cost (% of income per capita)	550.8			Time (days)	620
		Protecting investors (rank)	15	Cost (% of claim)	24.3
Employing workers (rank)	39	Extent of disclosure index (0-10)	7		
Difficulty of hiring index (0-100)	56	Extent of director liability index (0-10)	6	**Closing a business** (rank)	28
Rigidity of hours index (0-100)	0	Ease of shareholder suits index (0-10)	8	Time (years)	3.8
Difficulty of firing index (0-100)	20	Strength of investor protection index (0-10)	7.0	Cost (% of estate)	8
Rigidity of employment index (0-100)	25			Recovery rate (cents on the dollar)	55.2
Firing cost (weeks of salary)	0				
		Paying taxes (rank)	98		
		Payments (number per year)	16		
		Time (hours per year)	218		
		Total tax rate (% of profit)	64.7		

QATAR

		Middle East & North Africa		GNI per capita (US$)	72,849
Ease of doing business (rank)	37	High income		Population (m)	0.8

Starting a business (rank)	57	**Registering property** (rank)	54	**Trading across borders** (rank)	36
Procedures (number)	6	Procedures (number)	10	Documents to export (number)	5
Time (days)	6	Time (days)	16	Time to export (days)	21
Cost (% of income per capita)	9.1	Cost (% of property value)	0.3	Cost to export (US$ per container)	735
Minimum capital (% of income per capita)	75.4			Documents to import (number)	7
		Getting credit (rank)	131	Time to import (days)	20
		Strength of legal rights index (0-10)	3	Cost to import (US$ per container)	657
Dealing with construction permits (rank)	27	Depth of credit information index (0-6)	2		
Procedures (number)	19	Public registry coverage (% of adults)	..	**Enforcing contracts** (rank)	98
Time (days)	76	Private bureau coverage (% of adults)	0.0	Procedures (number)	43
Cost (% of income per capita)	0.8			Time (days)	570
		Protecting investors (rank)	88	Cost (% of claim)	21.6
Employing workers (rank)	88	Extent of disclosure index (0-10)	5		
Difficulty of hiring index (0-100)	0	Extent of director liability index (0-10)	6	**Closing a business** (rank)	31
Rigidity of hours index (0-100)	60	Ease of shareholder suits index (0-10)	4	Time (years)	2.8
Difficulty of firing index (0-100)	20	Strength of investor protection index (0-10)	5.0	Cost (% of estate)	22
Rigidity of employment index (0-100)	27			Recovery rate (cents on the dollar)	52.7
Firing cost (weeks of salary)	69				
		Paying taxes (rank)	2		
		Payments (number per year)	1		
		Time (hours per year)	36		
		Total tax rate (% of profit)	11.3		

ROMANIA

		Eastern Europe & Central Asia		GNI per capita (US$)	6,150
Ease of doing business (rank)	47	Upper middle income		Population (m)	21.5

Starting a business (rank)	26	**Registering property** (rank)	114	**Trading across borders** (rank)	40
Procedures (number)	6	Procedures (number)	8	Documents to export (number)	5
Time (days)	10	Time (days)	83	Time to export (days)	12
Cost (% of income per capita)	3.6	Cost (% of property value)	2.4	Cost to export (US$ per container)	1,275
Minimum capital (% of income per capita)	1.1			Documents to import (number)	6
		Getting credit (rank)	12	Time to import (days)	13
		Strength of legal rights index (0-10)	8	Cost to import (US$ per container)	1,175
Dealing with construction permits (rank)	88	Depth of credit information index (0-6)	5		
Procedures (number)	17	Public registry coverage (% of adults)	4.5	**Enforcing contracts** (rank)	31
Time (days)	243	Private bureau coverage (% of adults)	24.7	Procedures (number)	31
Cost (% of income per capita)	91.2			Time (days)	512
		Protecting investors (rank)	38	Cost (% of claim)	19.9
Employing workers (rank)	143	Extent of disclosure index (0-10)	9		
Difficulty of hiring index (0-100)	67	Extent of director liability index (0-10)	5	**Closing a business** (rank)	85
Rigidity of hours index (0-100)	80	Ease of shareholder suits index (0-10)	4	Time (years)	3.3
Difficulty of firing index (0-100)	40	Strength of investor protection index (0-10)	6.0	Cost (% of estate)	9
Rigidity of employment index (0-100)	62			Recovery rate (cents on the dollar)	29.5
Firing cost (weeks of salary)	8				
		Paying taxes (rank)	146		
		Payments (number per year)	113		
		Time (hours per year)	202		
		Total tax rate (% of profit)	48.0		

RUSSIAN FEDERATION

		Eastern Europe & Central Asia		GNI per capita (US$)	7,560
Ease of doing business (rank)	120	Upper middle income		Population (m)	141.6

Starting a business (rank)	65	**Registering property** (rank)	49	**Trading across borders** (rank)	161
Procedures (number)	8	Procedures (number)	6	Documents to export (number)	8
Time (days)	29	Time (days)	52	Time to export (days)	36
Cost (% of income per capita)	2.6	Cost (% of property value)	0.2	Cost to export (US$ per container)	2,150
Minimum capital (% of income per capita)	2.2			Documents to import (number)	13
		Getting credit (rank)	109	Time to import (days)	36
Dealing with construction permits (rank)	180	Strength of legal rights index (0-10)	3	Cost to import (US$ per container)	2,150
Procedures (number)	54	Depth of credit information index (0-6)	4		
Time (days)	704	Public registry coverage (% of adults)	0.0	**Enforcing contracts** (rank)	18
Cost (% of income per capita)	2,612.7	Private bureau coverage (% of adults)	10.0	Procedures (number)	37
				Time (days)	281
Employing workers (rank)	101	**Protecting investors** (rank)	88	Cost (% of claim)	13.4
Difficulty of hiring index (0-100)	33	Extent of disclosure index (0-10)	6		
Rigidity of hours index (0-100)	60	Extent of director liability index (0-10)	2	**Closing a business** (rank)	89
Difficulty of firing index (0-100)	40	Ease of shareholder suits index (0-10)	7	Time (years)	3.8
Rigidity of employment index (0-100)	44	Strength of investor protection index (0-10)	5.0	Cost (% of estate)	9
Firing cost (weeks of salary)	17			Recovery rate (cents on the dollar)	28.2
		Paying taxes (rank)	134		
		Payments (number per year)	22		
		Time (hours per year)	448		
		Total tax rate (% of profit)	48.7		

RWANDA

		Sub-Saharan Africa		GNI per capita (US$)	320
Ease of doing business (rank)	139	Low income		Population (m)	9.7

Starting a business (rank)	60	**Registering property** (rank)	60	**Trading across borders** (rank)	168
Procedures (number)	8	Procedures (number)	4	Documents to export (number)	9
Time (days)	14	Time (days)	315	Time to export (days)	42
Cost (% of income per capita)	108.9	Cost (% of property value)	0.6	Cost to export (US$ per container)	3,275
Minimum capital (% of income per capita)	0.0			Documents to import (number)	10
		Getting credit (rank)	145	Time to import (days)	42
Dealing with construction permits (rank)	90	Strength of legal rights index (0-10)	2	Cost to import (US$ per container)	5,070
Procedures (number)	14	Depth of credit information index (0-6)	2		
Time (days)	210	Public registry coverage (% of adults)	0.3	**Enforcing contracts** (rank)	48
Cost (% of income per capita)	607.1	Private bureau coverage (% of adults)	0.0	Procedures (number)	24
				Time (days)	310
Employing workers (rank)	93	**Protecting investors** (rank)	170	Cost (% of claim)	78.7
Difficulty of hiring index (0-100)	44	Extent of disclosure index (0-10)	2		
Rigidity of hours index (0-100)	40	Extent of director liability index (0-10)	5	**Closing a business** (rank)	181
Difficulty of firing index (0-100)	30	Ease of shareholder suits index (0-10)	1	Time (years)	NO PRACTICE
Rigidity of employment index (0-100)	38	Strength of investor protection index (0-10)	2.7	Cost (% of estate)	NO PRACTICE
Firing cost (weeks of salary)	26			Recovery rate (cents on the dollar)	0.0
		Paying taxes (rank)	56		
		Payments (number per year)	34		
		Time (hours per year)	160		
		Total tax rate (% of profit)	33.7		

SAMOA

		East Asia & Pacific		GNI per capita (US$)	2,430
Ease of doing business (rank)	64	Lower middle income		Population (m)	0.2

Starting a business (rank)	132	**Registering property** (rank)	72	**Trading across borders** (rank)	86
Procedures (number)	9	Procedures (number)	5	Documents to export (number)	7
Time (days)	35	Time (days)	147	Time to export (days)	27
Cost (% of income per capita)	39.8	Cost (% of property value)	1.7	Cost to export (US$ per container)	820
Minimum capital (% of income per capita)	0.0			Documents to import (number)	7
		Getting credit (rank)	123	Time to import (days)	31
Dealing with construction permits (rank)	47	Strength of legal rights index (0-10)	6	Cost to import (US$ per container)	848
Procedures (number)	18	Depth of credit information index (0-6)	0		
Time (days)	88	Public registry coverage (% of adults)	0.0	**Enforcing contracts** (rank)	79
Cost (% of income per capita)	90.9	Private bureau coverage (% of adults)	0.0	Procedures (number)	44
				Time (days)	455
Employing workers (rank)	16	**Protecting investors** (rank)	24	Cost (% of claim)	19.7
Difficulty of hiring index (0-100)	11	Extent of disclosure index (0-10)	5		
Rigidity of hours index (0-100)	20	Extent of director liability index (0-10)	6	**Closing a business** (rank)	136
Difficulty of firing index (0-100)	0	Ease of shareholder suits index (0-10)	8	Time (years)	2.5
Rigidity of employment index (0-100)	10	Strength of investor protection index (0-10)	6.3	Cost (% of estate)	38
Firing cost (weeks of salary)	9			Recovery rate (cents on the dollar)	14.3
		Paying taxes (rank)	60		
		Payments (number per year)	37		
		Time (hours per year)	224		
		Total tax rate (% of profit)	18.9		

SÃO TOMÉ AND PRINCIPE

		Sub-Saharan Africa		GNI per capita (US$)		870
Ease of doing business (rank)	176	Low income		Population (m)		0.2

Starting a business (rank)	136	**Registering property** (rank)	151	**Trading across borders** (rank)	88
Procedures (number)	10	Procedures (number)	7	Documents to export (number)	8
Time (days)	144	Time (days)	62	Time to export (days)	27
Cost (% of income per capita)	88.9	Cost (% of property value)	10.9	Cost to export (US$ per container)	690
Minimum capital (% of income per capita)	0.0			Documents to import (number)	8
		Getting credit (rank)	163	Time to import (days)	29
Dealing with construction permits (rank)	113	Strength of legal rights index (0-10)	3	Cost to import (US$ per container)	577
Procedures (number)	13	Depth of credit information index (0-6)	0		
Time (days)	255	Public registry coverage (% of adults)	0.0	**Enforcing contracts** (rank)	171
Cost (% of income per capita)	740.5	Private bureau coverage (% of adults)	0.0	Procedures (number)	43
				Time (days)	1,185
Employing workers (rank)	179	**Protecting investors** (rank)	150	Cost (% of claim)	34.8
Difficulty of hiring index (0-100)	50	Extent of disclosure index (0-10)	3		
Rigidity of hours index (0-100)	80	Extent of director liability index (0-10)	1	**Closing a business** (rank)	181
Difficulty of firing index (0-100)	60	Ease of shareholder suits index (0-10)	6	Time (years)	NO PRACTICE
Rigidity of employment index (0-100)	63	Strength of investor protection index (0-10)	3.3	Cost (% of estate)	NO PRACTICE
Firing cost (weeks of salary)	91			Recovery rate (cents on the dollar)	0.0
		Paying taxes (rank)	151		
		Payments (number per year)	42		
		Time (hours per year)	424		
		Total tax rate (% of profit)	47.2		

SAUDI ARABIA

		Middle East & North Africa		GNI per capita (US$)		15,440
Ease of doing business (rank)	16	High income		Population (m)		24.2

Starting a business (rank)	28	**Registering property** (rank)	1	**Trading across borders** (rank)	16
Procedures (number)	7	Procedures (number)	2	Documents to export (number)	5
Time (days)	12	Time (days)	2	Time to export (days)	17
Cost (% of income per capita)	14.9	Cost (% of property value)	0.0	Cost to export (US$ per container)	681
Minimum capital (% of income per capita)	0.0			Documents to import (number)	5
		Getting credit (rank)	59	Time to import (days)	18
Dealing with construction permits (rank)	50	Strength of legal rights index (0-10)	4	Cost to import (US$ per container)	678
Procedures (number)	18	Depth of credit information index (0-6)	6		
Time (days)	125	Public registry coverage (% of adults)	0.0	**Enforcing contracts** (rank)	137
Cost (% of income per capita)	74.7	Private bureau coverage (% of adults)	14.1	Procedures (number)	44
				Time (days)	635
Employing workers (rank)	45	**Protecting investors** (rank)	24	Cost (% of claim)	27.5
Difficulty of hiring index (0-100)	0	Extent of disclosure index (0-10)	8		
Rigidity of hours index (0-100)	40	Extent of director liability index (0-10)	8	**Closing a business** (rank)	57
Difficulty of firing index (0-100)	0	Ease of shareholder suits index (0-10)	3	Time (years)	1.5
Rigidity of employment index (0-100)	13	Strength of investor protection index (0-10)	6.3	Cost (% of estate)	22
Firing cost (weeks of salary)	80			Recovery rate (cents on the dollar)	37.5
		Paying taxes (rank)	7		
		Payments (number per year)	14		
		Time (hours per year)	79		
		Total tax rate (% of profit)	14.5		

SENEGAL

		Sub-Saharan Africa		GNI per capita (US$)		820
Ease of doing business (rank)	149	Low income		Population (m)		12.4

Starting a business (rank)	95	**Registering property** (rank)	161	**Trading across borders** (rank)	60
Procedures (number)	4	Procedures (number)	6	Documents to export (number)	6
Time (days)	8	Time (days)	124	Time to export (days)	14
Cost (% of income per capita)	72.7	Cost (% of property value)	20.6	Cost to export (US$ per container)	1,078
Minimum capital (% of income per capita)	236.2			Documents to import (number)	5
		Getting credit (rank)	145	Time to import (days)	18
Dealing with construction permits (rank)	118	Strength of legal rights index (0-10)	3	Cost to import (US$ per container)	1,920
Procedures (number)	16	Depth of credit information index (0-6)	1		
Time (days)	220	Public registry coverage (% of adults)	4.4	**Enforcing contracts** (rank)	146
Cost (% of income per capita)	528.7	Private bureau coverage (% of adults)	0.0	Procedures (number)	44
				Time (days)	780
Employing workers (rank)	165	**Protecting investors** (rank)	164	Cost (% of claim)	26.5
Difficulty of hiring index (0-100)	72	Extent of disclosure index (0-10)	6		
Rigidity of hours index (0-100)	60	Extent of director liability index (0-10)	1	**Closing a business** (rank)	77
Difficulty of firing index (0-100)	50	Ease of shareholder suits index (0-10)	2	Time (years)	3.0
Rigidity of employment index (0-100)	61	Strength of investor protection index (0-10)	3.0	Cost (% of estate)	7
Firing cost (weeks of salary)	38			Recovery rate (cents on the dollar)	31.6
		Paying taxes (rank)	170		
		Payments (number per year)	59		
		Time (hours per year)	666		
		Total tax rate (% of profit)	46.0		

SERBIA

		Eastern Europe & Central Asia		GNI per capita (US$)	4,730
Ease of doing business (rank)	94	Upper middle income		Population (m)	7.4

Starting a business (rank)	106	**Registering property** (rank)	97	**Trading across borders** (rank)	62
Procedures (number)	11	Procedures (number)	6	Documents to export (number)	6
Time (days)	23	Time (days)	111	Time to export (days)	12
Cost (% of income per capita)	7.6	Cost (% of property value)	2.9	Cost to export (US$ per container)	1,398
Minimum capital (% of income per capita)	6.9			Documents to import (number)	6
		Getting credit (rank)	28	Time to import (days)	14
Dealing with construction permits (rank)	171	Strength of legal rights index (0-10)	7	Cost to import (US$ per container)	1,559
Procedures (number)	20	Depth of credit information index (0-6)	5		
Time (days)	279	Public registry coverage (% of adults)	0.0	**Enforcing contracts** (rank)	96
Cost (% of income per capita)	2,177.7	Private bureau coverage (% of adults)	91.9	Procedures (number)	36
				Time (days)	635
Employing workers (rank)	91	**Protecting investors** (rank)	70	Cost (% of claim)	28.9
Difficulty of hiring index (0-100)	67	Extent of disclosure index (0-10)	7		
Rigidity of hours index (0-100)	20	Extent of director liability index (0-10)	6	**Closing a business** (rank)	99
Difficulty of firing index (0-100)	30	Ease of shareholder suits index (0-10)	3	Time (years)	2.7
Rigidity of employment index (0-100)	39	Strength of investor protection index (0-10)	5.3	Cost (% of estate)	23
Firing cost (weeks of salary)	25			Recovery rate (cents on the dollar)	25.4
		Paying taxes (rank)	126		
		Payments (number per year)	66		
		Time (hours per year)	279		
		Total tax rate (% of profit)	34.0		

SEYCHELLES

		Sub-Saharan Africa		GNI per capita (US$)	8,960
Ease of doing business (rank)	104	Upper middle income		Population (m)	0.1

Starting a business (rank)	68	**Registering property** (rank)	55	**Trading across borders** (rank)	90
Procedures (number)	9	Procedures (number)	4	Documents to export (number)	6
Time (days)	38	Time (days)	33	Time to export (days)	17
Cost (% of income per capita)	8.3	Cost (% of property value)	7.0	Cost to export (US$ per container)	1,839
Minimum capital (% of income per capita)	0.0			Documents to import (number)	5
		Getting credit (rank)	163	Time to import (days)	19
Dealing with construction permits (rank)	56	Strength of legal rights index (0-10)	3	Cost to import (US$ per container)	1,839
Procedures (number)	19	Depth of credit information index (0-6)	0		
Time (days)	144	Public registry coverage (% of adults)	0.0	**Enforcing contracts** (rank)	62
Cost (% of income per capita)	47.0	Private bureau coverage (% of adults)	0.0	Procedures (number)	38
				Time (days)	720
Employing workers (rank)	120	**Protecting investors** (rank)	53	Cost (% of claim)	14.3
Difficulty of hiring index (0-100)	44	Extent of disclosure index (0-10)	4		
Rigidity of hours index (0-100)	20	Extent of director liability index (0-10)	8	**Closing a business** (rank)	181
Difficulty of firing index (0-100)	50	Ease of shareholder suits index (0-10)	5	Time (years)	NO PRACTICE
Rigidity of employment index (0-100)	38	Strength of investor protection index (0-10)	5.7	Cost (% of estate)	NO PRACTICE
Firing cost (weeks of salary)	39			Recovery rate (cents on the dollar)	0.0
		Paying taxes (rank)	40		
		Payments (number per year)	16		
		Time (hours per year)	76		
		Total tax rate (% of profit)	46.6		

SIERRA LEONE

		Sub-Saharan Africa		GNI per capita (US$)	260
Ease of doing business (rank)	156	Low income		Population (m)	5.8

Starting a business (rank)	53	**Registering property** (rank)	163	**Trading across borders** (rank)	132
Procedures (number)	7	Procedures (number)	7	Documents to export (number)	7
Time (days)	17	Time (days)	86	Time to export (days)	29
Cost (% of income per capita)	56.2	Cost (% of property value)	12.9	Cost to export (US$ per container)	1,450
Minimum capital (% of income per capita)	0.0			Documents to import (number)	7
		Getting credit (rank)	145	Time to import (days)	34
Dealing with construction permits (rank)	169	Strength of legal rights index (0-10)	4	Cost to import (US$ per container)	1,535
Procedures (number)	25	Depth of credit information index (0-6)	0		
Time (days)	283	Public registry coverage (% of adults)	0.0	**Enforcing contracts** (rank)	141
Cost (% of income per capita)	452.2	Private bureau coverage (% of adults)	0.0	Procedures (number)	40
				Time (days)	515
Employing workers (rank)	173	**Protecting investors** (rank)	53	Cost (% of claim)	149.5
Difficulty of hiring index (0-100)	44	Extent of disclosure index (0-10)	3		
Rigidity of hours index (0-100)	60	Extent of director liability index (0-10)	6	**Closing a business** (rank)	145
Difficulty of firing index (0-100)	50	Ease of shareholder suits index (0-10)	8	Time (years)	2.6
Rigidity of employment index (0-100)	51	Strength of investor protection index (0-10)	5.7	Cost (% of estate)	42
Firing cost (weeks of salary)	189			Recovery rate (cents on the dollar)	8.5
		Paying taxes (rank)	160		
		Payments (number per year)	28		
		Time (hours per year)	399		
		Total tax rate (% of profit)	233.5		

SINGAPORE

Ease of doing business (rank)	1	East Asia & Pacific		GNI per capita (US$)	32,470	
		High income		Population (m)	4.6	

Starting a business (rank)	10	**Registering property** (rank)	16	**Trading across borders** (rank)	1
Procedures (number)	4	Procedures (number)	3	Documents to export (number)	4
Time (days)	4	Time (days)	9	Time to export (days)	5
Cost (% of income per capita)	0.7	Cost (% of property value)	2.8	Cost to export (US$ per container)	456
Minimum capital (% of income per capita)	0.0			Documents to import (number)	4
		Getting credit (rank)	5	Time to import (days)	3
Dealing with construction permits (rank)	2	Strength of legal rights index (0-10)	10	Cost to import (US$ per container)	439
Procedures (number)	11	Depth of credit information index (0-6)	4		
Time (days)	38	Public registry coverage (% of adults)	0.0	**Enforcing contracts** (rank)	14
Cost (% of income per capita)	21.2	Private bureau coverage (% of adults)	48.3	Procedures (number)	21
				Time (days)	150
Employing workers (rank)	1	**Protecting investors** (rank)	2	Cost (% of claim)	25.8
Difficulty of hiring index (0-100)	0	Extent of disclosure index (0-10)	10		
Rigidity of hours index (0-100)	0	Extent of director liability index (0-10)	9	**Closing a business** (rank)	2
Difficulty of firing index (0-100)	0	Ease of shareholder suits index (0-10)	9	Time (years)	0.8
Rigidity of employment index (0-100)	0	Strength of investor protection index (0-10)	9.3	Cost (% of estate)	1
Firing cost (weeks of salary)	4			Recovery rate (cents on the dollar)	91.3
		Paying taxes (rank)	5		
		Payments (number per year)	5		
		Time (hours per year)	84		
		Total tax rate (% of profit)	27.9		

SLOVAKIA

Ease of doing business (rank)	36	OECD: High Income		GNI per capita (US$)	11,730
		High income		Population (m)	5.4

Starting a business (rank)	48	**Registering property** (rank)	7	**Trading across borders** (rank)	116
Procedures (number)	6	Procedures (number)	3	Documents to export (number)	6
Time (days)	16	Time (days)	17	Time to export (days)	25
Cost (% of income per capita)	3.3	Cost (% of property value)	0.1	Cost to export (US$ per container)	1,445
Minimum capital (% of income per capita)	30.4			Documents to import (number)	8
		Getting credit (rank)	12	Time to import (days)	25
Dealing with construction permits (rank)	53	Strength of legal rights index (0-10)	9	Cost to import (US$ per container)	1,445
Procedures (number)	13	Depth of credit information index (0-6)	4		
Time (days)	287	Public registry coverage (% of adults)	1.4	**Enforcing contracts** (rank)	47
Cost (% of income per capita)	13.1	Private bureau coverage (% of adults)	39.9	Procedures (number)	30
				Time (days)	565
Employing workers (rank)	83	**Protecting investors** (rank)	104	Cost (% of claim)	25.7
Difficulty of hiring index (0-100)	17	Extent of disclosure index (0-10)	3		
Rigidity of hours index (0-100)	60	Extent of director liability index (0-10)	4	**Closing a business** (rank)	37
Difficulty of firing index (0-100)	30	Ease of shareholder suits index (0-10)	7	Time (years)	4.0
Rigidity of employment index (0-100)	36	Strength of investor protection index (0-10)	4.7	Cost (% of estate)	18
Firing cost (weeks of salary)	13			Recovery rate (cents on the dollar)	45.9
		Paying taxes (rank)	126		
		Payments (number per year)	31		
		Time (hours per year)	325		
		Total tax rate (% of profit)	47.4		

SLOVENIA

Ease of doing business (rank)	54	Eastern Europe & Central Asia		GNI per capita (US$)	20,960
		High income		Population (m)	2.0

Starting a business (rank)	41	**Registering property** (rank)	104	**Trading across borders** (rank)	78
Procedures (number)	5	Procedures (number)	6	Documents to export (number)	6
Time (days)	19	Time (days)	391	Time to export (days)	20
Cost (% of income per capita)	0.1	Cost (% of property value)	2.0	Cost to export (US$ per container)	1,075
Minimum capital (% of income per capita)	46.8			Documents to import (number)	8
		Getting credit (rank)	84	Time to import (days)	21
Dealing with construction permits (rank)	69	Strength of legal rights index (0-10)	6	Cost to import (US$ per container)	1,130
Procedures (number)	15	Depth of credit information index (0-6)	2		
Time (days)	208	Public registry coverage (% of adults)	2.7	**Enforcing contracts** (rank)	79
Cost (% of income per capita)	112.2	Private bureau coverage (% of adults)	0.0	Procedures (number)	32
				Time (days)	1,350
Employing workers (rank)	158	**Protecting investors** (rank)	18	Cost (% of claim)	18.6
Difficulty of hiring index (0-100)	78	Extent of disclosure index (0-10)	3		
Rigidity of hours index (0-100)	60	Extent of director liability index (0-10)	9	**Closing a business** (rank)	38
Difficulty of firing index (0-100)	40	Ease of shareholder suits index (0-10)	8	Time (years)	2.0
Rigidity of employment index (0-100)	59	Strength of investor protection index (0-10)	6.7	Cost (% of estate)	8
Firing cost (weeks of salary)	37			Recovery rate (cents on the dollar)	45.5
		Paying taxes (rank)	78		
		Payments (number per year)	22		
		Time (hours per year)	260		
		Total tax rate (% of profit)	36.7		

SOLOMON ISLANDS

Ease of doing business (rank)	89	East Asia & Pacific		GNI per capita (US$)	730	
		Low income		Population (m)	0.5	

Starting a business (rank)	99	**Registering property** (rank)	169	**Trading across borders** (rank)	75
Procedures (number)	7	Procedures (number)	10	Documents to export (number)	7
Time (days)	57	Time (days)	297	Time to export (days)	24
Cost (% of income per capita)	53.6	Cost (% of property value)	4.8	Cost to export (US$ per container)	1,011
Minimum capital (% of income per capita)	0.0			Documents to import (number)	4
		Getting credit (rank)	145	Time to import (days)	21
Dealing with construction permits (rank)	35	Strength of legal rights index (0-10)	4	Cost to import (US$ per container)	1,194
Procedures (number)	12	Depth of credit information index (0-6)	0		
Time (days)	62	Public registry coverage (% of adults)	0.0	**Enforcing contracts** (rank)	108
Cost (% of income per capita)	471.1	Private bureau coverage (% of adults)	0.0	Procedures (number)	37
				Time (days)	455
Employing workers (rank)	42	**Protecting investors** (rank)	53	Cost (% of claim)	78.9
Difficulty of hiring index (0-100)	11	Extent of disclosure index (0-10)	3		
Rigidity of hours index (0-100)	0	Extent of director liability index (0-10)	7	**Closing a business** (rank)	105
Difficulty of firing index (0-100)	20	Ease of shareholder suits index (0-10)	7	Time (years)	1.0
Rigidity of employment index (0-100)	10	Strength of investor protection index (0-10)	5.7	Cost (% of estate)	38
Firing cost (weeks of salary)	44			Recovery rate (cents on the dollar)	23.6
		Paying taxes (rank)	47		
		Payments (number per year)	33		
		Time (hours per year)	80		
		Total tax rate (% of profit)	36.3		

SOUTH AFRICA

Ease of doing business (rank)	32	Sub-Saharan Africa		GNI per capita (US$)	5,760
		Upper middle income		Population (m)	47.6

Starting a business (rank)	47	**Registering property** (rank)	87	**Trading across borders** (rank)	147
Procedures (number)	6	Procedures (number)	6	Documents to export (number)	8
Time (days)	22	Time (days)	24	Time to export (days)	30
Cost (% of income per capita)	6.0	Cost (% of property value)	8.8	Cost to export (US$ per container)	1,445
Minimum capital (% of income per capita)	0.0			Documents to import (number)	9
		Getting credit (rank)	2	Time to import (days)	35
Dealing with construction permits (rank)	48	Strength of legal rights index (0-10)	9	Cost to import (US$ per container)	1,721
Procedures (number)	17	Depth of credit information index (0-6)	6		
Time (days)	174	Public registry coverage (% of adults)	0.0	**Enforcing contracts** (rank)	82
Cost (% of income per capita)	27.5	Private bureau coverage (% of adults)	64.8	Procedures (number)	30
				Time (days)	600
Employing workers (rank)	102	**Protecting investors** (rank)	9	Cost (% of claim)	33.2
Difficulty of hiring index (0-100)	56	Extent of disclosure index (0-10)	8		
Rigidity of hours index (0-100)	40	Extent of director liability index (0-10)	8	**Closing a business** (rank)	73
Difficulty of firing index (0-100)	30	Ease of shareholder suits index (0-10)	8	Time (years)	2.0
Rigidity of employment index (0-100)	42	Strength of investor protection index (0-10)	8.0	Cost (% of estate)	18
Firing cost (weeks of salary)	24			Recovery rate (cents on the dollar)	32.2
		Paying taxes (rank)	23		
		Payments (number per year)	9		
		Time (hours per year)	200		
		Total tax rate (% of profit)	34.2		

SPAIN

Ease of doing business (rank)	49	OECD: High Income		GNI per capita (US$)	29,450
		High income		Population (m)	44.9

Starting a business (rank)	140	**Registering property** (rank)	46	**Trading across borders** (rank)	52
Procedures (number)	10	Procedures (number)	4	Documents to export (number)	6
Time (days)	47	Time (days)	18	Time to export (days)	9
Cost (% of income per capita)	14.9	Cost (% of property value)	7.2	Cost to export (US$ per container)	1,121
Minimum capital (% of income per capita)	13.1			Documents to import (number)	8
		Getting credit (rank)	43	Time to import (days)	10
Dealing with construction permits (rank)	51	Strength of legal rights index (0-10)	6	Cost to import (US$ per container)	1,121
Procedures (number)	11	Depth of credit information index (0-6)	5		
Time (days)	233	Public registry coverage (% of adults)	45.8	**Enforcing contracts** (rank)	54
Cost (% of income per capita)	62.3	Private bureau coverage (% of adults)	8.1	Procedures (number)	39
				Time (days)	515
Employing workers (rank)	160	**Protecting investors** (rank)	88	Cost (% of claim)	17.2
Difficulty of hiring index (0-100)	78	Extent of disclosure index (0-10)	5		
Rigidity of hours index (0-100)	60	Extent of director liability index (0-10)	6	**Closing a business** (rank)	19
Difficulty of firing index (0-100)	30	Ease of shareholder suits index (0-10)	4	Time (years)	1.0
Rigidity of employment index (0-100)	56	Strength of investor protection index (0-10)	5.0	Cost (% of estate)	15
Firing cost (weeks of salary)	56			Recovery rate (cents on the dollar)	73.2
		Paying taxes (rank)	84		
		Payments (number per year)	8		
		Time (hours per year)	234		
		Total tax rate (% of profit)	60.2		

SRI LANKA

		South Asia		GNI per capita (US$)	1,540
Ease of doing business (rank)	102	Lower middle income		Population (m)	19.9

Starting a business (rank)	29	**Registering property** (rank)	141	**Trading across borders** (rank)	66
Procedures (number)	4	Procedures (number)	8	Documents to export (number)	8
Time (days)	38	Time (days)	83	Time to export (days)	21
Cost (% of income per capita)	7.1	Cost (% of property value)	5.1	Cost to export (US$ per container)	865
Minimum capital (% of income per capita)	0.0			Documents to import (number)	6
		Getting credit (rank)	68	Time to import (days)	20
Dealing with construction permits (rank)	161	Strength of legal rights index (0-10)	4	Cost to import (US$ per container)	895
Procedures (number)	21	Depth of credit information index (0-6)	5		
Time (days)	214	Public registry coverage (% of adults)	0.0	**Enforcing contracts** (rank)	135
Cost (% of income per capita)	1,486.5	Private bureau coverage (% of adults)	8.7	Procedures (number)	40
				Time (days)	1,318
Employing workers (rank)	110	**Protecting investors** (rank)	70	Cost (% of claim)	22.8
Difficulty of hiring index (0-100)	0	Extent of disclosure index (0-10)	4		
Rigidity of hours index (0-100)	20	Extent of director liability index (0-10)	5	**Closing a business** (rank)	43
Difficulty of firing index (0-100)	60	Ease of shareholder suits index (0-10)	7	Time (years)	1.7
Rigidity of employment index (0-100)	27	Strength of investor protection index (0-10)	5.3	Cost (% of estate)	5
Firing cost (weeks of salary)	169			Recovery rate (cents on the dollar)	43.4
		Paying taxes (rank)	164		
		Payments (number per year)	62		
		Time (hours per year)	256		
		Total tax rate (% of profit)	63.7		

ST. KITTS AND NEVIS

		Latin America & Caribbean		GNI per capita (US$)	9,630
Ease of doing business (rank)	67	Upper middle income		Population (m)	0.0

Starting a business (rank)	72	**Registering property** (rank)	146	**Trading across borders** (rank)	27
Procedures (number)	8	Procedures (number)	6	Documents to export (number)	6
Time (days)	45	Time (days)	81	Time to export (days)	12
Cost (% of income per capita)	12.5	Cost (% of property value)	13.3	Cost to export (US$ per container)	850
Minimum capital (% of income per capita)	0.0			Documents to import (number)	6
		Getting credit (rank)	84	Time to import (days)	14
Dealing with construction permits (rank)	6	Strength of legal rights index (0-10)	8	Cost to import (US$ per container)	938
Procedures (number)	14	Depth of credit information index (0-6)	0		
Time (days)	67	Public registry coverage (% of adults)	0.0	**Enforcing contracts** (rank)	114
Cost (% of income per capita)	5.1	Private bureau coverage (% of adults)	0.0	Procedures (number)	47
				Time (days)	578
Employing workers (rank)	22	**Protecting investors** (rank)	24	Cost (% of claim)	20.5
Difficulty of hiring index (0-100)	11	Extent of disclosure index (0-10)	4		
Rigidity of hours index (0-100)	20	Extent of director liability index (0-10)	8	**Closing a business** (rank)	181
Difficulty of firing index (0-100)	20	Ease of shareholder suits index (0-10)	7	Time (years)	NO PRACTICE
Rigidity of employment index (0-100)	17	Strength of investor protection index (0-10)	6.3	Cost (% of estate)	NO PRACTICE
Firing cost (weeks of salary)	13			Recovery rate (cents on the dollar)	0.0
		Paying taxes (rank)	95		
		Payments (number per year)	24		
		Time (hours per year)	172		
		Total tax rate (% of profit)	52.7		

ST. LUCIA

		Latin America & Caribbean		GNI per capita (US$)	5,530
Ease of doing business (rank)	34	Upper middle income		Population (m)	0.2

Starting a business (rank)	36	**Registering property** (rank)	66	**Trading across borders** (rank)	80
Procedures (number)	6	Procedures (number)	6	Documents to export (number)	5
Time (days)	20	Time (days)	16	Time to export (days)	15
Cost (% of income per capita)	22.6	Cost (% of property value)	7.4	Cost to export (US$ per container)	1,425
Minimum capital (% of income per capita)	0.0			Documents to import (number)	8
		Getting credit (rank)	84	Time to import (days)	18
Dealing with construction permits (rank)	13	Strength of legal rights index (0-10)	8	Cost to import (US$ per container)	1,470
Procedures (number)	9	Depth of credit information index (0-6)	0		
Time (days)	139	Public registry coverage (% of adults)	0.0	**Enforcing contracts** (rank)	161
Cost (% of income per capita)	30.3	Private bureau coverage (% of adults)	0.0	Procedures (number)	47
				Time (days)	635
Employing workers (rank)	23	**Protecting investors** (rank)	24	Cost (% of claim)	37.3
Difficulty of hiring index (0-100)	0	Extent of disclosure index (0-10)	4		
Rigidity of hours index (0-100)	20	Extent of director liability index (0-10)	8	**Closing a business** (rank)	45
Difficulty of firing index (0-100)	0	Ease of shareholder suits index (0-10)	7	Time (years)	2.0
Rigidity of employment index (0-100)	7	Strength of investor protection index (0-10)	6.3	Cost (% of estate)	9
Firing cost (weeks of salary)	56			Recovery rate (cents on the dollar)	42.9
		Paying taxes (rank)	29		
		Payments (number per year)	32		
		Time (hours per year)	61		
		Total tax rate (% of profit)	34.0		

ST. VINCENT AND THE GRENADINES

Latin America & Caribbean		GNI per capita (US$)	4,210
Ease of doing business (rank)	66	Upper middle income	Population (m)	0.1

Starting a business (rank)	39	**Registering property** (rank)	129	**Trading across borders** (rank)	72
Procedures (number)	8	Procedures (number)	7	Documents to export (number)	6
Time (days)	12	Time (days)	38	Time to export (days)	12
Cost (% of income per capita)	26.8	Cost (% of property value)	11.9	Cost to export (US$ per container)	1,770
Minimum capital (% of income per capita)	0.0			Documents to import (number)	6
		Getting credit (rank)	84	Time to import (days)	13
Dealing with construction permits (rank)	1	Strength of legal rights index (0-10)	8	Cost to import (US$ per container)	1,769
Procedures (number)	11	Depth of credit information index (0-6)	0		
Time (days)	74	Public registry coverage (% of adults)	0.0	**Enforcing contracts** (rank)	109
Cost (% of income per capita)	8.4	Private bureau coverage (% of adults)	0.0	Procedures (number)	45
				Time (days)	394
Employing workers (rank)	41	**Protecting investors** (rank)	24	Cost (% of claim)	30.3
Difficulty of hiring index (0-100)	0	Extent of disclosure index (0-10)	4		
Rigidity of hours index (0-100)	20	Extent of director liability index (0-10)	8	**Closing a business** (rank)	181
Difficulty of firing index (0-100)	20	Ease of shareholder suits index (0-10)	7	Time (years)	NO PRACTICE
Rigidity of employment index (0-100)	13	Strength of investor protection index (0-10)	6.3	Cost (% of estate)	NO PRACTICE
Firing cost (weeks of salary)	54			Recovery rate (cents on the dollar)	0.0
		Paying taxes (rank)	76		
		Payments (number per year)	36		
		Time (hours per year)	117		
		Total tax rate (% of profit)	42.6		

SUDAN

Sub-Saharan Africa		GNI per capita (US$)	960
Ease of doing business (rank)	147	Lower middle income	Population (m)	38.6

Starting a business (rank)	107	**Registering property** (rank)	35	**Trading across borders** (rank)	139
Procedures (number)	10	Procedures (number)	6	Documents to export (number)	6
Time (days)	39	Time (days)	9	Time to export (days)	35
Cost (% of income per capita)	50.8	Cost (% of property value)	3.1	Cost to export (US$ per container)	2,050
Minimum capital (% of income per capita)	0.0			Documents to import (number)	6
		Getting credit (rank)	131	Time to import (days)	49
Dealing with construction permits (rank)	135	Strength of legal rights index (0-10)	5	Cost to import (US$ per container)	2,900
Procedures (number)	19	Depth of credit information index (0-6)	0		
Time (days)	271	Public registry coverage (% of adults)	0.0	**Enforcing contracts** (rank)	143
Cost (% of income per capita)	240.3	Private bureau coverage (% of adults)	0.0	Procedures (number)	53
				Time (days)	810
Employing workers (rank)	144	**Protecting investors** (rank)	150	Cost (% of claim)	19.8
Difficulty of hiring index (0-100)	39	Extent of disclosure index (0-10)	0		
Rigidity of hours index (0-100)	20	Extent of director liability index (0-10)	6	**Closing a business** (rank)	181
Difficulty of firing index (0-100)	50	Ease of shareholder suits index (0-10)	4	Time (years)	NO PRACTICE
Rigidity of employment index (0-100)	36	Strength of investor protection index (0-10)	3.3	Cost (% of estate)	NO PRACTICE
Firing cost (weeks of salary)	118			Recovery rate (cents on the dollar)	0.0
		Paying taxes (rank)	67		
		Payments (number per year)	42		
		Time (hours per year)	180		
		Total tax rate (% of profit)	31.6		

SURINAME

Latin America & Caribbean		GNI per capita (US$)	4,730
Ease of doing business (rank)	146	Upper middle income	Population (m)	0.5

Starting a business (rank)	170	**Registering property** (rank)	136	**Trading across borders** (rank)	98
Procedures (number)	13	Procedures (number)	4	Documents to export (number)	8
Time (days)	694	Time (days)	193	Time to export (days)	25
Cost (% of income per capita)	125.2	Cost (% of property value)	13.9	Cost to export (US$ per container)	975
Minimum capital (% of income per capita)	0.8			Documents to import (number)	7
		Getting credit (rank)	131	Time to import (days)	25
Dealing with construction permits (rank)	95	Strength of legal rights index (0-10)	5	Cost to import (US$ per container)	885
Procedures (number)	14	Depth of credit information index (0-6)	0		
Time (days)	431	Public registry coverage (% of adults)	0.0	**Enforcing contracts** (rank)	177
Cost (% of income per capita)	105.7	Private bureau coverage (% of adults)	0.0	Procedures (number)	44
				Time (days)	1,715
Employing workers (rank)	53	**Protecting investors** (rank)	178	Cost (% of claim)	37.1
Difficulty of hiring index (0-100)	0	Extent of disclosure index (0-10)	1		
Rigidity of hours index (0-100)	20	Extent of director liability index (0-10)	0	**Closing a business** (rank)	147
Difficulty of firing index (0-100)	50	Ease of shareholder suits index (0-10)	5	Time (years)	5.0
Rigidity of employment index (0-100)	23	Strength of investor protection index (0-10)	2.0	Cost (% of estate)	30
Firing cost (weeks of salary)	26			Recovery rate (cents on the dollar)	8.1
		Paying taxes (rank)	26		
		Payments (number per year)	17		
		Time (hours per year)	199		
		Total tax rate (% of profit)	27.9		

SWAZILAND

		Sub-Saharan Africa		GNI per capita (US$)		2,580
Ease of doing business (rank)	108	Lower middle income		Population (m)		1.1
Starting a business (rank)	153	**Registering property** (rank)	153	**Trading across borders** (rank)		154
Procedures (number)	13	Procedures (number)	11	Documents to export (number)		9
Time (days)	61	Time (days)	46	Time to export (days)		21
Cost (% of income per capita)	35.1	Cost (% of property value)	7.1	Cost to export (US$ per container)		2,184
Minimum capital (% of income per capita)	0.6			Documents to import (number)		11
		Getting credit (rank)	43	Time to import (days)		33
Dealing with construction permits (rank)	21	Strength of legal rights index (0-10)	6	Cost to import (US$ per container)		2,249
Procedures (number)	13	Depth of credit information index (0-6)	5			
Time (days)	93	Public registry coverage (% of adults)	0.0	**Enforcing contracts** (rank)		129
Cost (% of income per capita)	94.9	Private bureau coverage (% of adults)	43.5	Procedures (number)		40
				Time (days)		972
Employing workers (rank)	40	**Protecting investors** (rank)	178	Cost (% of claim)		23.1
Difficulty of hiring index (0-100)	0	Extent of disclosure index (0-10)	0			
Rigidity of hours index (0-100)	20	Extent of director liability index (0-10)	1	**Closing a business** (rank)		65
Difficulty of firing index (0-100)	20	Ease of shareholder suits index (0-10)	5	Time (years)		2.0
Rigidity of employment index (0-100)	13	Strength of investor protection index (0-10)	2.0	Cost (% of estate)		15
Firing cost (weeks of salary)	53			Recovery rate (cents on the dollar)		34.9
		Paying taxes (rank)	52			
		Payments (number per year)	33			
		Time (hours per year)	104			
		Total tax rate (% of profit)	36.6			

SWEDEN

		OECD: High Income		GNI per capita (US$)		46,060
Ease of doing business (rank)	17	High income		Population (m)		9.1
Starting a business (rank)	30	**Registering property** (rank)	10	**Trading across borders** (rank)		6
Procedures (number)	3	Procedures (number)	1	Documents to export (number)		4
Time (days)	15	Time (days)	2	Time to export (days)		8
Cost (% of income per capita)	0.6	Cost (% of property value)	3.0	Cost to export (US$ per container)		697
Minimum capital (% of income per capita)	30.3			Documents to import (number)		3
		Getting credit (rank)	68	Time to import (days)		6
Dealing with construction permits (rank)	17	Strength of legal rights index (0-10)	5	Cost to import (US$ per container)		735
Procedures (number)	8	Depth of credit information index (0-6)	4			
Time (days)	116	Public registry coverage (% of adults)	0.0	**Enforcing contracts** (rank)		55
Cost (% of income per capita)	103.5	Private bureau coverage (% of adults)	100.0	Procedures (number)		30
				Time (days)		508
Employing workers (rank)	114	**Protecting investors** (rank)	53	Cost (% of claim)		31.3
Difficulty of hiring index (0-100)	33	Extent of disclosure index (0-10)	6			
Rigidity of hours index (0-100)	60	Extent of director liability index (0-10)	4	**Closing a business** (rank)		18
Difficulty of firing index (0-100)	40	Ease of shareholder suits index (0-10)	7	Time (years)		2.0
Rigidity of employment index (0-100)	44	Strength of investor protection index (0-10)	5.7	Cost (% of estate)		9
Firing cost (weeks of salary)	26			Recovery rate (cents on the dollar)		75.1
		Paying taxes (rank)	42			
		Payments (number per year)	2			
		Time (hours per year)	122			
		Total tax rate (% of profit)	54.5			

SWITZERLAND

		OECD: High Income		GNI per capita (US$)		59,880
Ease of doing business (rank)	21	High income		Population (m)		7.6
Starting a business (rank)	52	**Registering property** (rank)	13	**Trading across borders** (rank)		39
Procedures (number)	6	Procedures (number)	4	Documents to export (number)		4
Time (days)	20	Time (days)	16	Time to export (days)		8
Cost (% of income per capita)	2.1	Cost (% of property value)	0.4	Cost to export (US$ per container)		1,537
Minimum capital (% of income per capita)	27.6			Documents to import (number)		5
		Getting credit (rank)	12	Time to import (days)		9
Dealing with construction permits (rank)	32	Strength of legal rights index (0-10)	8	Cost to import (US$ per container)		1,505
Procedures (number)	14	Depth of credit information index (0-6)	5			
Time (days)	154	Public registry coverage (% of adults)	0.0	**Enforcing contracts** (rank)		32
Cost (% of income per capita)	52.1	Private bureau coverage (% of adults)	22.5	Procedures (number)		32
				Time (days)		417
Employing workers (rank)	19	**Protecting investors** (rank)	164	Cost (% of claim)		24.0
Difficulty of hiring index (0-100)	0	Extent of disclosure index (0-10)	0			
Rigidity of hours index (0-100)	40	Extent of director liability index (0-10)	5	**Closing a business** (rank)		36
Difficulty of firing index (0-100)	10	Ease of shareholder suits index (0-10)	4	Time (years)		3.0
Rigidity of employment index (0-100)	17	Strength of investor protection index (0-10)	3.0	Cost (% of estate)		4
Firing cost (weeks of salary)	13			Recovery rate (cents on the dollar)		46.8
		Paying taxes (rank)	19			
		Payments (number per year)	24			
		Time (hours per year)	63			
		Total tax rate (% of profit)	28.9			

SYRIA

		Middle East & North Africa			GNI per capita (US$)	1,760
Ease of doing business (rank)	137	Lower middle income			Population (m)	19.9

Starting a business (rank)	124	**Registering property** (rank)	71	**Trading across borders** (rank)	111
Procedures (number)	8	Procedures (number)	4	Documents to export (number)	8
Time (days)	17	Time (days)	19	Time to export (days)	15
Cost (% of income per capita)	18.2	Cost (% of property value)	28.0	Cost to export (US$ per container)	1,190
Minimum capital (% of income per capita)	4,353.8			Documents to import (number)	9
		Getting credit (rank)	178	Time to import (days)	21
Dealing with construction permits (rank)	132	Strength of legal rights index (0-10)	1	Cost to import (US$ per container)	1,625
Procedures (number)	26	Depth of credit information index (0-6)	0		
Time (days)	128	Public registry coverage (% of adults)	0.0	**Enforcing contracts** (rank)	174
Cost (% of income per capita)	697.0	Private bureau coverage (% of adults)	0.0	Procedures (number)	55
				Time (days)	872
Employing workers (rank)	122	**Protecting investors** (rank)	113	Cost (% of claim)	29.3
Difficulty of hiring index (0-100)	11	Extent of disclosure index (0-10)	6		
Rigidity of hours index (0-100)	40	Extent of director liability index (0-10)	5	**Closing a business** (rank)	84
Difficulty of firing index (0-100)	50	Ease of shareholder suits index (0-10)	2	Time (years)	4.1
Rigidity of employment index (0-100)	34	Strength of investor protection index (0-10)	4.3	Cost (% of estate)	9
Firing cost (weeks of salary)	80			Recovery rate (cents on the dollar)	29.5
		Paying taxes (rank)	99		
		Payments (number per year)	20		
		Time (hours per year)	336		
		Total tax rate (% of profit)	43.5		

TAIWAN, CHINA

		East Asia & Pacific			GNI per capita (US$)	17,930
Ease of doing business (rank)	61	High income			Population (m)	22.9

Starting a business (rank)	119	**Registering property** (rank)	26	**Trading across borders** (rank)	30
Procedures (number)	8	Procedures (number)	3	Documents to export (number)	7
Time (days)	42	Time (days)	5	Time to export (days)	13
Cost (% of income per capita)	4.1	Cost (% of property value)	6.2	Cost to export (US$ per container)	757
Minimum capital (% of income per capita)	177.4			Documents to import (number)	7
		Getting credit (rank)	68	Time to import (days)	12
Dealing with construction permits (rank)	127	Strength of legal rights index (0-10)	4	Cost to import (US$ per container)	769
Procedures (number)	29	Depth of credit information index (0-6)	5		
Time (days)	193	Public registry coverage (% of adults)	0.0	**Enforcing contracts** (rank)	88
Cost (% of income per capita)	123.6	Private bureau coverage (% of adults)	62.7	Procedures (number)	47
				Time (days)	510
Employing workers (rank)	159	**Protecting investors** (rank)	70	Cost (% of claim)	17.7
Difficulty of hiring index (0-100)	78	Extent of disclosure index (0-10)	7		
Rigidity of hours index (0-100)	40	Extent of director liability index (0-10)	4	**Closing a business** (rank)	11
Difficulty of firing index (0-100)	40	Ease of shareholder suits index (0-10)	5	Time (years)	1.9
Rigidity of employment index (0-100)	53	Strength of investor protection index (0-10)	5.3	Cost (% of estate)	4
Firing cost (weeks of salary)	91			Recovery rate (cents on the dollar)	80.9
		Paying taxes (rank)	100		
		Payments (number per year)	23		
		Time (hours per year)	340		
		Total tax rate (% of profit)	40.4		

TAJIKISTAN

		Eastern Europe & Central Asia			GNI per capita (US$)	460
Ease of doing business (rank)	159	Low income			Population (m)	6.7

Starting a business (rank)	168	**Registering property** (rank)	46	**Trading across borders** (rank)	177
Procedures (number)	13	Procedures (number)	6	Documents to export (number)	10
Time (days)	49	Time (days)	37	Time to export (days)	82
Cost (% of income per capita)	27.6	Cost (% of property value)	1.8	Cost to export (US$ per container)	3,150
Minimum capital (% of income per capita)	216.8			Documents to import (number)	10
		Getting credit (rank)	172	Time to import (days)	83
Dealing with construction permits (rank)	178	Strength of legal rights index (0-10)	2	Cost to import (US$ per container)	4,550
Procedures (number)	32	Depth of credit information index (0-6)	0		
Time (days)	351	Public registry coverage (% of adults)	0.0	**Enforcing contracts** (rank)	23
Cost (% of income per capita)	1,420.7	Private bureau coverage (% of adults)	0.0	Procedures (number)	34
				Time (days)	295
Employing workers (rank)	128	**Protecting investors** (rank)	150	Cost (% of claim)	20.5
Difficulty of hiring index (0-100)	33	Extent of disclosure index (0-10)	4		
Rigidity of hours index (0-100)	80	Extent of director liability index (0-10)	1	**Closing a business** (rank)	97
Difficulty of firing index (0-100)	40	Ease of shareholder suits index (0-10)	5	Time (years)	3.0
Rigidity of employment index (0-100)	51	Strength of investor protection index (0-10)	3.3	Cost (% of estate)	9
Firing cost (weeks of salary)	22			Recovery rate (cents on the dollar)	25.4
		Paying taxes (rank)	159		
		Payments (number per year)	54		
		Time (hours per year)	224		
		Total tax rate (% of profit)	85.5		

TANZANIA

		Sub-Saharan Africa		GNI per capita (US$)	400
Ease of doing business (rank)	127	Low income		Population (m)	40.4

Starting a business (rank)	109	**Registering property** (rank)	142	**Trading across borders** (rank)	103
Procedures (number)	12	Procedures (number)	9	Documents to export (number)	5
Time (days)	29	Time (days)	73	Time to export (days)	24
Cost (% of income per capita)	41.5	Cost (% of property value)	4.4	Cost to export (US$ per container)	1,262
Minimum capital (% of income per capita)	0.0			Documents to import (number)	7
		Getting credit (rank)	84	Time to import (days)	31
Dealing with construction permits (rank)	172	Strength of legal rights index (0-10)	8	Cost to import (US$ per container)	1,475
Procedures (number)	21	Depth of credit information index (0-6)	0		
Time (days)	308	Public registry coverage (% of adults)	0.0	**Enforcing contracts** (rank)	33
Cost (% of income per capita)	2,087.0	Private bureau coverage (% of adults)	0.0	Procedures (number)	38
				Time (days)	462
Employing workers (rank)	140	**Protecting investors** (rank)	88	Cost (% of claim)	14.3
Difficulty of hiring index (0-100)	100	Extent of disclosure index (0-10)	3		
Rigidity of hours index (0-100)	40	Extent of director liability index (0-10)	4	**Closing a business** (rank)	111
Difficulty of firing index (0-100)	50	Ease of shareholder suits index (0-10)	8	Time (years)	3.0
Rigidity of employment index (0-100)	63	Strength of investor protection index (0-10)	5.0	Cost (% of estate)	22
Firing cost (weeks of salary)	18			Recovery rate (cents on the dollar)	21.3
		Paying taxes (rank)	109		
		Payments (number per year)	48		
		Time (hours per year)	172		
		Total tax rate (% of profit)	45.1		

THAILAND

		East Asia & Pacific		GNI per capita (US$)	3,400
Ease of doing business (rank)	13	Lower middle income		Population (m)	63.8

Starting a business (rank)	44	**Registering property** (rank)	5	**Trading across borders** (rank)	10
Procedures (number)	8	Procedures (number)	2	Documents to export (number)	4
Time (days)	33	Time (days)	2	Time to export (days)	14
Cost (% of income per capita)	4.9	Cost (% of property value)	1.1	Cost to export (US$ per container)	625
Minimum capital (% of income per capita)	0.0			Documents to import (number)	3
		Getting credit (rank)	68	Time to import (days)	13
Dealing with construction permits (rank)	12	Strength of legal rights index (0-10)	4	Cost to import (US$ per container)	795
Procedures (number)	11	Depth of credit information index (0-6)	5		
Time (days)	156	Public registry coverage (% of adults)	0.0	**Enforcing contracts** (rank)	25
Cost (% of income per capita)	9.4	Private bureau coverage (% of adults)	31.8	Procedures (number)	35
				Time (days)	479
Employing workers (rank)	56	**Protecting investors** (rank)	11	Cost (% of claim)	14.3
Difficulty of hiring index (0-100)	33	Extent of disclosure index (0-10)	10		
Rigidity of hours index (0-100)	20	Extent of director liability index (0-10)	7	**Closing a business** (rank)	46
Difficulty of firing index (0-100)	0	Ease of shareholder suits index (0-10)	6	Time (years)	2.7
Rigidity of employment index (0-100)	18	Strength of investor protection index (0-10)	7.7	Cost (% of estate)	36
Firing cost (weeks of salary)	54			Recovery rate (cents on the dollar)	42.4
		Paying taxes (rank)	82		
		Payments (number per year)	23		
		Time (hours per year)	264		
		Total tax rate (% of profit)	37.8		

TIMOR-LESTE

		East Asia & Pacific		GNI per capita (US$)	1,510
Ease of doing business (rank)	170	Lower middle income		Population (m)	1.1

Starting a business (rank)	150	**Registering property** (rank)	177	**Trading across borders** (rank)	79
Procedures (number)	10	Procedures (number)	NO PRACTICE	Documents to export (number)	6
Time (days)	83	Time (days)	NO PRACTICE	Time to export (days)	25
Cost (% of income per capita)	6.6	Cost (% of property value)	NO PRACTICE	Cost to export (US$ per container)	1,010
Minimum capital (% of income per capita)	331.1			Documents to import (number)	7
		Getting credit (rank)	178	Time to import (days)	26
Dealing with construction permits (rank)	100	Strength of legal rights index (0-10)	1	Cost to import (US$ per container)	1,015
Procedures (number)	22	Depth of credit information index (0-6)	0		
Time (days)	208	Public registry coverage (% of adults)	0.0	**Enforcing contracts** (rank)	181
Cost (% of income per capita)	62.9	Private bureau coverage (% of adults)	0.0	Procedures (number)	51
				Time (days)	1,800
Employing workers (rank)	78	**Protecting investors** (rank)	126	Cost (% of claim)	163.2
Difficulty of hiring index (0-100)	33	Extent of disclosure index (0-10)	3		
Rigidity of hours index (0-100)	20	Extent of director liability index (0-10)	4	**Closing a business** (rank)	181
Difficulty of firing index (0-100)	50	Ease of shareholder suits index (0-10)	5	Time (years)	NO PRACTICE
Rigidity of employment index (0-100)	34	Strength of investor protection index (0-10)	4.0	Cost (% of estate)	NO PRACTICE
Firing cost (weeks of salary)	17			Recovery rate (cents on the dollar)	0.0
		Paying taxes (rank)	75		
		Payments (number per year)	15		
		Time (hours per year)	640		
		Total tax rate (% of profit)	28.3		

TOGO

Sub-Saharan Africa		GNI per capita (US$)	360
Ease of doing business (rank) 163	Low income	Population (m)	6.6

Starting a business (rank)	179	**Registering property** (rank)	155	**Trading across borders** (rank)	84
Procedures (number)	13	Procedures (number)	5	Documents to export (number)	6
Time (days)	53	Time (days)	295	Time to export (days)	24
Cost (% of income per capita)	251.3	Cost (% of property value)	13.4	Cost to export (US$ per container)	940
Minimum capital (% of income per capita)	559.9			Documents to import (number)	8
		Getting credit (rank)	145	Time to import (days)	29
Dealing with construction permits (rank)	145	Strength of legal rights index (0-10)	3	Cost to import (US$ per container)	963
Procedures (number)	15	Depth of credit information index (0-6)	1		
Time (days)	277	Public registry coverage (% of adults)	2.6	**Enforcing contracts** (rank)	151
Cost (% of income per capita)	1,400.1	Private bureau coverage (% of adults)	0.0	Procedures (number)	41
				Time (days)	588
Employing workers (rank)	155	**Protecting investors** (rank)	142	Cost (% of claim)	47.5
Difficulty of hiring index (0-100)	72	Extent of disclosure index (0-10)	6		
Rigidity of hours index (0-100)	60	Extent of director liability index (0-10)	1	**Closing a business** (rank)	94
Difficulty of firing index (0-100)	40	Ease of shareholder suits index (0-10)	4	Time (years)	3.0
Rigidity of employment index (0-100)	57	Strength of investor protection index (0-10)	3.7	Cost (% of estate)	15
Firing cost (weeks of salary)	36			Recovery rate (cents on the dollar)	26.6
		Paying taxes (rank)	147		
		Payments (number per year)	53		
		Time (hours per year)	270		
		Total tax rate (% of profit)	48.2		

TONGA

East Asia & Pacific		GNI per capita (US$)	2,320
Ease of doing business (rank) 43	Lower middle income	Population (m)	0.1

Starting a business (rank)	19	**Registering property** (rank)	113	**Trading across borders** (rank)	50
Procedures (number)	4	Procedures (number)	4	Documents to export (number)	7
Time (days)	25	Time (days)	108	Time to export (days)	19
Cost (% of income per capita)	9.6	Cost (% of property value)	10.2	Cost to export (US$ per container)	650
Minimum capital (% of income per capita)	0.0			Documents to import (number)	6
		Getting credit (rank)	109	Time to import (days)	25
Dealing with construction permits (rank)	31	Strength of legal rights index (0-10)	7	Cost to import (US$ per container)	725
Procedures (number)	11	Depth of credit information index (0-6)	0		
Time (days)	76	Public registry coverage (% of adults)	0.0	**Enforcing contracts** (rank)	57
Cost (% of income per capita)	371.6	Private bureau coverage (% of adults)	0.0	Procedures (number)	37
				Time (days)	350
Employing workers (rank)	5	**Protecting investors** (rank)	104	Cost (% of claim)	30.5
Difficulty of hiring index (0-100)	0	Extent of disclosure index (0-10)	3		
Rigidity of hours index (0-100)	20	Extent of director liability index (0-10)	3	**Closing a business** (rank)	101
Difficulty of firing index (0-100)	0	Ease of shareholder suits index (0-10)	8	Time (years)	2.7
Rigidity of employment index (0-100)	7	Strength of investor protection index (0-10)	4.7	Cost (% of estate)	22
Firing cost (weeks of salary)	0			Recovery rate (cents on the dollar)	25.2
		Paying taxes (rank)	31		
		Payments (number per year)	23		
		Time (hours per year)	164		
		Total tax rate (% of profit)	27.5		

TRINIDAD AND TOBAGO

Latin America & Caribbean		GNI per capita (US$)	14,100
Ease of doing business (rank) 80	High income	Population (m)	1.3

Starting a business (rank)	56	**Registering property** (rank)	164	**Trading across borders** (rank)	47
Procedures (number)	9	Procedures (number)	8	Documents to export (number)	5
Time (days)	43	Time (days)	162	Time to export (days)	14
Cost (% of income per capita)	0.9	Cost (% of property value)	7.0	Cost to export (US$ per container)	866
Minimum capital (% of income per capita)	0.0			Documents to import (number)	6
		Getting credit (rank)	28	Time to import (days)	26
Dealing with construction permits (rank)	84	Strength of legal rights index (0-10)	8	Cost to import (US$ per container)	1,100
Procedures (number)	20	Depth of credit information index (0-6)	4		
Time (days)	261	Public registry coverage (% of adults)	0.0	**Enforcing contracts** (rank)	167
Cost (% of income per capita)	5.5	Private bureau coverage (% of adults)	37.6	Procedures (number)	42
				Time (days)	1,340
Employing workers (rank)	36	**Protecting investors** (rank)	18	Cost (% of claim)	33.5
Difficulty of hiring index (0-100)	0	Extent of disclosure index (0-10)	4		
Rigidity of hours index (0-100)	0	Extent of director liability index (0-10)	9	**Closing a business** (rank)	181
Difficulty of firing index (0-100)	20	Ease of shareholder suits index (0-10)	7	Time (years)	NO PRACTICE
Rigidity of employment index (0-100)	7	Strength of investor protection index (0-10)	6.7	Cost (% of estate)	NO PRACTICE
Firing cost (weeks of salary)	67			Recovery rate (cents on the dollar)	0.0
		Paying taxes (rank)	51		
		Payments (number per year)	40		
		Time (hours per year)	114		
		Total tax rate (% of profit)	33.1		

TUNISIA

		Middle East & North Africa		GNI per capita (US$)		3,200
Ease of doing business (rank)	73	Lower middle income		Population (m)		10.2

Starting a business (rank)	37	**Registering property** (rank)	55	**Trading across borders** (rank)	38
Procedures (number)	10	Procedures (number)	4	Documents to export (number)	5
Time (days)	11	Time (days)	39	Time to export (days)	17
Cost (% of income per capita)	7.9	Cost (% of property value)	6.1	Cost to export (US$ per container)	733
Minimum capital (% of income per capita)	0.0			Documents to import (number)	7
		Getting credit (rank)	84	Time to import (days)	23
Dealing with construction permits (rank)	101	Strength of legal rights index (0-10)	3	Cost to import (US$ per container)	858
Procedures (number)	20	Depth of credit information index (0-6)	5		
Time (days)	84	Public registry coverage (% of adults)	14.9	**Enforcing contracts** (rank)	72
Cost (% of income per capita)	1,017.8	Private bureau coverage (% of adults)	0.0	Procedures (number)	39
				Time (days)	565
Employing workers (rank)	113	**Protecting investors** (rank)	142	Cost (% of claim)	21.8
Difficulty of hiring index (0-100)	28	Extent of disclosure index (0-10)	0		
Rigidity of hours index (0-100)	40	Extent of director liability index (0-10)	5	**Closing a business** (rank)	32
Difficulty of firing index (0-100)	80	Ease of shareholder suits index (0-10)	6	Time (years)	1.3
Rigidity of employment index (0-100)	49	Strength of investor protection index (0-10)	3.7	Cost (% of estate)	7
Firing cost (weeks of salary)	17			Recovery rate (cents on the dollar)	52.3
		Paying taxes (rank)	106		
		Payments (number per year)	22		
		Time (hours per year)	228		
		Total tax rate (% of profit)	59.1		

TURKEY

		Eastern Europe & Central Asia		GNI per capita (US$)		8,020
Ease of doing business (rank)	59	Upper middle income		Population (m)		73.9

Starting a business (rank)	43	**Registering property** (rank)	34	**Trading across borders** (rank)	59
Procedures (number)	6	Procedures (number)	6	Documents to export (number)	7
Time (days)	6	Time (days)	6	Time to export (days)	14
Cost (% of income per capita)	14.9	Cost (% of property value)	3.0	Cost to export (US$ per container)	940
Minimum capital (% of income per capita)	10.9			Documents to import (number)	8
		Getting credit (rank)	68	Time to import (days)	15
Dealing with construction permits (rank)	131	Strength of legal rights index (0-10)	4	Cost to import (US$ per container)	1,063
Procedures (number)	25	Depth of credit information index (0-6)	5		
Time (days)	188	Public registry coverage (% of adults)	12.7	**Enforcing contracts** (rank)	27
Cost (% of income per capita)	249.3	Private bureau coverage (% of adults)	26.3	Procedures (number)	35
				Time (days)	420
Employing workers (rank)	138	**Protecting investors** (rank)	53	Cost (% of claim)	18.8
Difficulty of hiring index (0-100)	44	Extent of disclosure index (0-10)	9		
Rigidity of hours index (0-100)	40	Extent of director liability index (0-10)	4	**Closing a business** (rank)	118
Difficulty of firing index (0-100)	30	Ease of shareholder suits index (0-10)	4	Time (years)	3.3
Rigidity of employment index (0-100)	38	Strength of investor protection index (0-10)	5.7	Cost (% of estate)	15
Firing cost (weeks of salary)	95			Recovery rate (cents on the dollar)	20.2
		Paying taxes (rank)	68		
		Payments (number per year)	15		
		Time (hours per year)	223		
		Total tax rate (% of profit)	45.5		

UGANDA

		Sub-Saharan Africa		GNI per capita (US$)		340
Ease of doing business (rank)	111	Low income		Population (m)		30.9

Starting a business (rank)	129	**Registering property** (rank)	167	**Trading across borders** (rank)	145
Procedures (number)	18	Procedures (number)	13	Documents to export (number)	6
Time (days)	25	Time (days)	227	Time to export (days)	39
Cost (% of income per capita)	100.7	Cost (% of property value)	4.1	Cost to export (US$ per container)	3,090
Minimum capital (% of income per capita)	0.0			Documents to import (number)	7
		Getting credit (rank)	109	Time to import (days)	37
Dealing with construction permits (rank)	81	Strength of legal rights index (0-10)	7	Cost to import (US$ per container)	3,290
Procedures (number)	16	Depth of credit information index (0-6)	0		
Time (days)	143	Public registry coverage (% of adults)	0.0	**Enforcing contracts** (rank)	117
Cost (% of income per capita)	703.5	Private bureau coverage (% of adults)	0.0	Procedures (number)	38
				Time (days)	535
Employing workers (rank)	11	**Protecting investors** (rank)	126	Cost (% of claim)	44.9
Difficulty of hiring index (0-100)	0	Extent of disclosure index (0-10)	2		
Rigidity of hours index (0-100)	0	Extent of director liability index (0-10)	5	**Closing a business** (rank)	51
Difficulty of firing index (0-100)	10	Ease of shareholder suits index (0-10)	5	Time (years)	2.2
Rigidity of employment index (0-100)	3	Strength of investor protection index (0-10)	4.0	Cost (% of estate)	30
Firing cost (weeks of salary)	13			Recovery rate (cents on the dollar)	41.1
		Paying taxes (rank)	70		
		Payments (number per year)	32		
		Time (hours per year)	222		
		Total tax rate (% of profit)	34.5		

UKRAINE

		Eastern Europe & Central Asia		GNI per capita (US$)		2,550
Ease of doing business (rank)	145	Lower middle income		Population (m)		46.4

Starting a business (rank)	128	**Registering property** (rank)	140	**Trading across borders** (rank)	131
Procedures (number)	10	Procedures (number)	10	Documents to export (number)	6
Time (days)	27	Time (days)	93	Time to export (days)	31
Cost (% of income per capita)	5.5	Cost (% of property value)	2.9	Cost to export (US$ per container)	1,230
Minimum capital (% of income per capita)	174.2			Documents to import (number)	10
		Getting credit (rank)	28	Time to import (days)	36
Dealing with construction permits (rank)	179	Strength of legal rights index (0-10)	9	Cost to import (US$ per container)	1,250
Procedures (number)	30	Depth of credit information index (0-6)	3		
Time (days)	471	Public registry coverage (% of adults)	0.0	**Enforcing contracts** (rank)	49
Cost (% of income per capita)	1,901.7	Private bureau coverage (% of adults)	3.0	Procedures (number)	30
				Time (days)	354
Employing workers (rank)	100	**Protecting investors** (rank)	142	Cost (% of claim)	41.5
Difficulty of hiring index (0-100)	44	Extent of disclosure index (0-10)	1		
Rigidity of hours index (0-100)	60	Extent of director liability index (0-10)	3	**Closing a business** (rank)	143
Difficulty of firing index (0-100)	30	Ease of shareholder suits index (0-10)	7	Time (years)	2.9
Rigidity of employment index (0-100)	45	Strength of investor protection index (0-10)	3.7	Cost (% of estate)	42
Firing cost (weeks of salary)	13			Recovery rate (cents on the dollar)	9.1
		Paying taxes (rank)	180		
		Payments (number per year)	99		
		Time (hours per year)	848		
		Total tax rate (% of profit)	58.4		

UNITED ARAB EMIRATES

		Middle East & North Africa		GNI per capita (US$)	26,210
Ease of doing business (rank)	46	High income		Population (m)	4.4

Starting a business (rank)	113	**Registering property** (rank)	11	**Trading across borders** (rank)	14
Procedures (number)	8	Procedures (number)	3	Documents to export (number)	5
Time (days)	17	Time (days)	6	Time to export (days)	10
Cost (% of income per capita)	13.4	Cost (% of property value)	2.0	Cost to export (US$ per container)	618
Minimum capital (% of income per capita)	311.9			Documents to import (number)	7
		Getting credit (rank)	68	Time to import (days)	10
Dealing with construction permits (rank)	41	Strength of legal rights index (0-10)	4	Cost to import (US$ per container)	587
Procedures (number)	21	Depth of credit information index (0-6)	5		
Time (days)	125	Public registry coverage (% of adults)	6.5	**Enforcing contracts** (rank)	145
Cost (% of income per capita)	1.5	Private bureau coverage (% of adults)	7.7	Procedures (number)	50
				Time (days)	607
Employing workers (rank)	47	**Protecting investors** (rank)	113	Cost (% of claim)	26.2
Difficulty of hiring index (0-100)	0	Extent of disclosure index (0-10)	4		
Rigidity of hours index (0-100)	40	Extent of director liability index (0-10)	7	**Closing a business** (rank)	141
Difficulty of firing index (0-100)	0	Ease of shareholder suits index (0-10)	2	Time (years)	5.1
Rigidity of employment index (0-100)	13	Strength of investor protection index (0-10)	4.3	Cost (% of estate)	30
Firing cost (weeks of salary)	84			Recovery rate (cents on the dollar)	10.2
		Paying taxes (rank)	4		
		Payments (number per year)	14		
		Time (hours per year)	12		
		Total tax rate (% of profit)	14.4		

UNITED KINGDOM

		OECD: High Income		GNI per capita (US$)	42,740
Ease of doing business (rank)	6	High income		Population (m)	61.0

Starting a business (rank)	8	**Registering property** (rank)	22	**Trading across borders** (rank)	28
Procedures (number)	6	Procedures (number)	2	Documents to export (number)	4
Time (days)	13	Time (days)	21	Time to export (days)	13
Cost (% of income per capita)	0.8	Cost (% of property value)	4.1	Cost to export (US$ per container)	1,030
Minimum capital (% of income per capita)	0.0			Documents to import (number)	4
		Getting credit (rank)	2	Time to import (days)	13
Dealing with construction permits (rank)	61	Strength of legal rights index (0-10)	9	Cost to import (US$ per container)	1,350
Procedures (number)	19	Depth of credit information index (0-6)	6		
Time (days)	144	Public registry coverage (% of adults)	0.0	**Enforcing contracts** (rank)	24
Cost (% of income per capita)	64.2	Private bureau coverage (% of adults)	100.0	Procedures (number)	30
				Time (days)	404
Employing workers (rank)	28	**Protecting investors** (rank)	9	Cost (% of claim)	23.4
Difficulty of hiring index (0-100)	11	Extent of disclosure index (0-10)	10		
Rigidity of hours index (0-100)	20	Extent of director liability index (0-10)	7	**Closing a business** (rank)	9
Difficulty of firing index (0-100)	10	Ease of shareholder suits index (0-10)	7	Time (years)	1.0
Rigidity of employment index (0-100)	14	Strength of investor protection index (0-10)	8.0	Cost (% of estate)	6
Firing cost (weeks of salary)	22			Recovery rate (cents on the dollar)	84.2
		Paying taxes (rank)	16		
		Payments (number per year)	8		
		Time (hours per year)	105		
		Total tax rate (% of profit)	35.3		

UNITED STATES

		OECD: High Income		GNI per capita (US$)	46,040
Ease of doing business (rank)	3	High income		Population (m)	301.6

Starting a business (rank)	6	**Registering property** (rank)	12	**Trading across borders** (rank)	15
Procedures (number)	6	Procedures (number)	4	Documents to export (number)	4
Time (days)	6	Time (days)	12	Time to export (days)	6
Cost (% of income per capita)	0.7	Cost (% of property value)	0.5	Cost to export (US$ per container)	990
Minimum capital (% of income per capita)	0.0			Documents to import (number)	5
		Getting credit (rank)	5	Time to import (days)	5
Dealing with construction permits (rank)	26	Strength of legal rights index (0-10)	8	Cost to import (US$ per container)	1,245
Procedures (number)	19	Depth of credit information index (0-6)	6		
Time (days)	40	Public registry coverage (% of adults)	0.0	**Enforcing contracts** (rank)	6
Cost (% of income per capita)	13.1	Private bureau coverage (% of adults)	100.0	Procedures (number)	32
				Time (days)	300
Employing workers (rank)	1	**Protecting investors** (rank)	5	Cost (% of claim)	9.4
Difficulty of hiring index (0-100)	0	Extent of disclosure index (0-10)	7		
Rigidity of hours index (0-100)	0	Extent of director liability index (0-10)	9	**Closing a business** (rank)	15
Difficulty of firing index (0-100)	0	Ease of shareholder suits index (0-10)	9	Time (years)	1.5
Rigidity of employment index (0-100)	0	Strength of investor protection index (0-10)	8.3	Cost (% of estate)	7
Firing cost (weeks of salary)	0			Recovery rate (cents on the dollar)	76.7
		Paying taxes (rank)	46		
		Payments (number per year)	10		
		Time (hours per year)	187		
		Total tax rate (% of profit)	42.3		

URUGUAY

		Latin America & Caribbean		GNI per capita (US$)	6,380
Ease of doing business (rank)	109	Upper middle income		Population (m)	3.3

Starting a business (rank)	120	**Registering property** (rank)	149	**Trading across borders** (rank)	127
Procedures (number)	11	Procedures (number)	8	Documents to export (number)	10
Time (days)	44	Time (days)	66	Time to export (days)	19
Cost (% of income per capita)	43.5	Cost (% of property value)	7.1	Cost to export (US$ per container)	1,100
Minimum capital (% of income per capita)	0.0			Documents to import (number)	10
		Getting credit (rank)	43	Time to import (days)	22
Dealing with construction permits (rank)	139	Strength of legal rights index (0-10)	5	Cost to import (US$ per container)	1,330
Procedures (number)	30	Depth of credit information index (0-6)	6		
Time (days)	234	Public registry coverage (% of adults)	15.4	**Enforcing contracts** (rank)	99
Cost (% of income per capita)	108.0	Private bureau coverage (% of adults)	98.0	Procedures (number)	40
				Time (days)	720
Employing workers (rank)	79	**Protecting investors** (rank)	88	Cost (% of claim)	19.0
Difficulty of hiring index (0-100)	33	Extent of disclosure index (0-10)	3		
Rigidity of hours index (0-100)	60	Extent of director liability index (0-10)	4	**Closing a business** (rank)	44
Difficulty of firing index (0-100)	0	Ease of shareholder suits index (0-10)	8	Time (years)	2.1
Rigidity of employment index (0-100)	31	Strength of investor protection index (0-10)	5.0	Cost (% of estate)	7
Firing cost (weeks of salary)	31			Recovery rate (cents on the dollar)	43.0
		Paying taxes (rank)	167		
		Payments (number per year)	53		
		Time (hours per year)	336		
		Total tax rate (% of profit)	58.5		

UZBEKISTAN

		Eastern Europe & Central Asia		GNI per capita (US$)	730
Ease of doing business (rank)	138	Low income		Population (m)	26.9

Starting a business (rank)	70	**Registering property** (rank)	125	**Trading across borders** (rank)	171
Procedures (number)	7	Procedures (number)	12	Documents to export (number)	7
Time (days)	15	Time (days)	78	Time to export (days)	80
Cost (% of income per capita)	10.3	Cost (% of property value)	1.5	Cost to export (US$ per container)	3,100
Minimum capital (% of income per capita)	17.7			Documents to import (number)	11
		Getting credit (rank)	123	Time to import (days)	104
Dealing with construction permits (rank)	148	Strength of legal rights index (0-10)	3	Cost to import (US$ per container)	4,600
Procedures (number)	26	Depth of credit information index (0-6)	3		
Time (days)	260	Public registry coverage (% of adults)	2.3	**Enforcing contracts** (rank)	46
Cost (% of income per capita)	123.4	Private bureau coverage (% of adults)	2.2	Procedures (number)	42
				Time (days)	195
Employing workers (rank)	76	**Protecting investors** (rank)	113	Cost (% of claim)	22.2
Difficulty of hiring index (0-100)	33	Extent of disclosure index (0-10)	4		
Rigidity of hours index (0-100)	40	Extent of director liability index (0-10)	6	**Closing a business** (rank)	122
Difficulty of firing index (0-100)	30	Ease of shareholder suits index (0-10)	3	Time (years)	4.0
Rigidity of employment index (0-100)	34	Strength of investor protection index (0-10)	4.3	Cost (% of estate)	10
Firing cost (weeks of salary)	22			Recovery rate (cents on the dollar)	18.7
		Paying taxes (rank)	162		
		Payments (number per year)	106		
		Time (hours per year)	196		
		Total tax rate (% of profit)	90.6		

VANUATU

Ease of doing business (rank)	60	East Asia & Pacific Lower middle income		GNI per capita (US$) Population (m)	1,840 0.2	

Starting a business (rank)	94
Procedures (number)	8
Time (days)	39
Cost (% of income per capita)	54.8
Minimum capital (% of income per capita)	0.0

Dealing with construction permits (rank)	24
Procedures (number)	7
Time (days)	51
Cost (% of income per capita)	356.7

Employing workers (rank)	86
Difficulty of hiring index (0-100)	22
Rigidity of hours index (0-100)	40
Difficulty of firing index (0-100)	10
Rigidity of employment index (0-100)	24
Firing cost (weeks of salary)	56

Registering property (rank)	115
Procedures (number)	2
Time (days)	188
Cost (% of property value)	11.0

Getting credit (rank)	84
Strength of legal rights index (0-10)	8
Depth of credit information index (0-6)	0
Public registry coverage (% of adults)	0.0
Private bureau coverage (% of adults)	0.0

Protecting investors (rank)	70
Extent of disclosure index (0-10)	5
Extent of director liability index (0-10)	6
Ease of shareholder suits index (0-10)	5
Strength of investor protection index (0-10)	5.3

Paying taxes (rank)	20
Payments (number per year)	31
Time (hours per year)	120
Total tax rate (% of profit)	8.4

Trading across borders (rank)	136
Documents to export (number)	7
Time to export (days)	26
Cost to export (US$ per container)	1,497
Documents to import (number)	9
Time to import (days)	30
Cost to import (US$ per container)	1,392

Enforcing contracts (rank)	67
Procedures (number)	30
Time (days)	430
Cost (% of claim)	74.7

Closing a business (rank)	50
Time (years)	2.6
Cost (% of estate)	38
Recovery rate (cents on the dollar)	41.2

VENEZUELA

Ease of doing business (rank)	174	Latin America & Caribbean Upper middle income		GNI per capita (US$) Population (m)	7,320 27.5	

Starting a business (rank)	142
Procedures (number)	16
Time (days)	141
Cost (% of income per capita)	26.8
Minimum capital (% of income per capita)	0.0

Dealing with construction permits (rank)	96
Procedures (number)	11
Time (days)	395
Cost (% of income per capita)	344.7

Employing workers (rank)	180
Difficulty of hiring index (0-100)	78
Rigidity of hours index (0-100)	60
Difficulty of firing index (0-100)	100
Rigidity of employment index (0-100)	79
Firing cost (weeks of salary)	NOT POSSIBLE

Registering property (rank)	92
Procedures (number)	8
Time (days)	47
Cost (% of property value)	2.2

Getting credit (rank)	163
Strength of legal rights index (0-10)	3
Depth of credit information index (0-6)	0
Public registry coverage (% of adults)	0.0
Private bureau coverage (% of adults)	0.0

Protecting investors (rank)	170
Extent of disclosure index (0-10)	3
Extent of director liability index (0-10)	3
Ease of shareholder suits index (0-10)	2
Strength of investor protection index (0-10)	2.7

Paying taxes (rank)	177
Payments (number per year)	70
Time (hours per year)	864
Total tax rate (% of profit)	56.6

Trading across borders (rank)	164
Documents to export (number)	8
Time to export (days)	49
Cost to export (US$ per container)	2,590
Documents to import (number)	9
Time to import (days)	71
Cost to import (US$ per container)	2,868

Enforcing contracts (rank)	71
Procedures (number)	29
Time (days)	510
Cost (% of claim)	43.7

Closing a business (rank)	149
Time (years)	4.0
Cost (% of estate)	38
Recovery rate (cents on the dollar)	6.0

VIETNAM

Ease of doing business (rank)	92	East Asia & Pacific Low income		GNI per capita (US$) Population (m)	790 85.1	

Starting a business (rank)	108
Procedures (number)	11
Time (days)	50
Cost (% of income per capita)	16.8
Minimum capital (% of income per capita)	0.0

Dealing with construction permits (rank)	67
Procedures (number)	13
Time (days)	194
Cost (% of income per capita)	313.3

Employing workers (rank)	90
Difficulty of hiring index (0-100)	11
Rigidity of hours index (0-100)	20
Difficulty of firing index (0-100)	40
Rigidity of employment index (0-100)	24
Firing cost (weeks of salary)	87

Registering property (rank)	37
Procedures (number)	4
Time (days)	57
Cost (% of property value)	1.2

Getting credit (rank)	43
Strength of legal rights index (0-10)	7
Depth of credit information index (0-6)	4
Public registry coverage (% of adults)	13.4
Private bureau coverage (% of adults)	0.0

Protecting investors (rank)	170
Extent of disclosure index (0-10)	6
Extent of director liability index (0-10)	0
Ease of shareholder suits index (0-10)	2
Strength of investor protection index (0-10)	2.7

Paying taxes (rank)	140
Payments (number per year)	32
Time (hours per year)	1,050
Total tax rate (% of profit)	40.1

Trading across borders (rank)	67
Documents to export (number)	6
Time to export (days)	24
Cost to export (US$ per container)	734
Documents to import (number)	8
Time to import (days)	23
Cost to import (US$ per container)	901

Enforcing contracts (rank)	42
Procedures (number)	34
Time (days)	295
Cost (% of claim)	31.0

Closing a business (rank)	124
Time (years)	5.0
Cost (% of estate)	15
Recovery rate (cents on the dollar)	18.0

WEST BANK AND GAZA

		Middle East & North Africa		GNI per capita (US$)	1,230
Ease of doing business (rank)	131	Lower middle income		Population (m)	3.9

Starting a business (rank)	166	**Registering property** (rank)	80	**Trading across borders** (rank)	85
Procedures (number)	11	Procedures (number)	7	Documents to export (number)	6
Time (days)	49	Time (days)	63	Time to export (days)	25
Cost (% of income per capita)	69.1	Cost (% of property value)	0.9	Cost to export (US$ per container)	835
Minimum capital (% of income per capita)	56.1			Documents to import (number)	6
		Getting credit (rank)	163	Time to import (days)	40
Dealing with construction permits (rank)	149	Strength of legal rights index (0-10)	0	Cost to import (US$ per container)	1,225
Procedures (number)	21	Depth of credit information index (0-6)	3		
Time (days)	199	Public registry coverage (% of adults)	7.8	**Enforcing contracts** (rank)	122
Cost (% of income per capita)	1,399.9	Private bureau coverage (% of adults)	0.0	Procedures (number)	44
				Time (days)	700
Employing workers (rank)	109	**Protecting investors** (rank)	38	Cost (% of claim)	21.2
Difficulty of hiring index (0-100)	33	Extent of disclosure index (0-10)	6		
Rigidity of hours index (0-100)	40	Extent of director liability index (0-10)	5	**Closing a business** (rank)	181
Difficulty of firing index (0-100)	20	Ease of shareholder suits index (0-10)	7	Time (years)	NO PRACTICE
Rigidity of employment index (0-100)	31	Strength of investor protection index (0-10)	6.0	Cost (% of estate)	NO PRACTICE
Firing cost (weeks of salary)	91			Recovery rate (cents on the dollar)	0.0
		Paying taxes (rank)	25		
		Payments (number per year)	27		
		Time (hours per year)	154		
		Total tax rate (% of profit)	16.8		

YEMEN

		Middle East & North Africa		GNI per capita (US$)	870
Ease of doing business (rank)	98	Low income		Population (m)	22.4

Starting a business (rank)	50	**Registering property** (rank)	48	**Trading across borders** (rank)	126
Procedures (number)	7	Procedures (number)	6	Documents to export (number)	6
Time (days)	13	Time (days)	19	Time to export (days)	31
Cost (% of income per capita)	93.0	Cost (% of property value)	3.8	Cost to export (US$ per container)	1,129
Minimum capital (% of income per capita)	0.0			Documents to import (number)	9
		Getting credit (rank)	172	Time to import (days)	28
Dealing with construction permits (rank)	33	Strength of legal rights index (0-10)	2	Cost to import (US$ per container)	1,475
Procedures (number)	13	Depth of credit information index (0-6)	0		
Time (days)	107	Public registry coverage (% of adults)	0.1	**Enforcing contracts** (rank)	41
Cost (% of income per capita)	189.7	Private bureau coverage (% of adults)	0.0	Procedures (number)	37
				Time (days)	520
Employing workers (rank)	69	**Protecting investors** (rank)	126	Cost (% of claim)	16.5
Difficulty of hiring index (0-100)	0	Extent of disclosure index (0-10)	6		
Rigidity of hours index (0-100)	60	Extent of director liability index (0-10)	4	**Closing a business** (rank)	87
Difficulty of firing index (0-100)	40	Ease of shareholder suits index (0-10)	2	Time (years)	3.0
Rigidity of employment index (0-100)	33	Strength of investor protection index (0-10)	4.0	Cost (% of estate)	8
Firing cost (weeks of salary)	17			Recovery rate (cents on the dollar)	28.6
		Paying taxes (rank)	138		
		Payments (number per year)	44		
		Time (hours per year)	248		
		Total tax rate (% of profit)	47.8		

ZAMBIA

		Sub-Saharan Africa		GNI per capita (US$)	800
Ease of doing business (rank)	100	Low income		Population (m)	11.9

Starting a business (rank)	71	**Registering property** (rank)	91	**Trading across borders** (rank)	153
Procedures (number)	6	Procedures (number)	6	Documents to export (number)	6
Time (days)	18	Time (days)	39	Time to export (days)	53
Cost (% of income per capita)	28.6	Cost (% of property value)	6.6	Cost to export (US$ per container)	2,664
Minimum capital (% of income per capita)	1.5			Documents to import (number)	9
		Getting credit (rank)	68	Time to import (days)	64
Dealing with construction permits (rank)	146	Strength of legal rights index (0-10)	9	Cost to import (US$ per container)	3,335
Procedures (number)	17	Depth of credit information index (0-6)	0		
Time (days)	254	Public registry coverage (% of adults)	0.0	**Enforcing contracts** (rank)	87
Cost (% of income per capita)	1,023.1	Private bureau coverage (% of adults)	0.1	Procedures (number)	35
				Time (days)	471
Employing workers (rank)	135	**Protecting investors** (rank)	70	Cost (% of claim)	38.7
Difficulty of hiring index (0-100)	22	Extent of disclosure index (0-10)	3		
Rigidity of hours index (0-100)	60	Extent of director liability index (0-10)	6	**Closing a business** (rank)	80
Difficulty of firing index (0-100)	20	Ease of shareholder suits index (0-10)	7	Time (years)	2.7
Rigidity of employment index (0-100)	34	Strength of investor protection index (0-10)	5.3	Cost (% of estate)	9
Firing cost (weeks of salary)	178			Recovery rate (cents on the dollar)	30.2
		Paying taxes (rank)	38		
		Payments (number per year)	37		
		Time (hours per year)	132		
		Total tax rate (% of profit)	16.1		

ZIMBABWE

Ease of doing business (rank)	158	Sub-Saharan Africa		GNI per capita (US$)		325
		Low income		Population (m)		13.4

Starting a business (rank)	164	**Registering property** (rank)	85	**Trading across borders** (rank)	162
Procedures (number)	10	Procedures (number)	4	Documents to export (number)	7
Time (days)	96	Time (days)	30	Time to export (days)	53
Cost (% of income per capita)	432.7	Cost (% of property value)	25.0	Cost to export (US$ per container)	2,678
Minimum capital (% of income per capita)	3.4			Documents to import (number)	9
		Getting credit (rank)	84	Time to import (days)	73
Dealing with construction permits (rank)	174	Strength of legal rights index (0-10)	8	Cost to import (US$ per container)	3,999
Procedures (number)	19	Depth of credit information index (0-6)	0		
Time (days)	1,426	Public registry coverage (% of adults)	0.0	**Enforcing contracts** (rank)	77
Cost (% of income per capita)	16,368.8	Private bureau coverage (% of adults)	0.0	Procedures (number)	38
				Time (days)	410
Employing workers (rank)	127	**Protecting investors** (rank)	113	Cost (% of claim)	32.0
Difficulty of hiring index (0-100)	0	Extent of disclosure index (0-10)	8		
Rigidity of hours index (0-100)	40	Extent of director liability index (0-10)	1	**Closing a business** (rank)	154
Difficulty of firing index (0-100)	60	Ease of shareholder suits index (0-10)	4	Time (years)	3.3
Rigidity of employment index (0-100)	33	Strength of investor protection index (0-10)	4.3	Cost (% of estate)	22
Firing cost (weeks of salary)	446			Recovery rate (cents on the dollar)	0.1
		Paying taxes (rank)	157		
		Payments (number per year)	52		
		Time (hours per year)	256		
		Total tax rate (% of profit)	63.7		

Ratification status of the ILO core labor standards

✓ Convention ratified
□ Convention not ratified
D Ratification denounced

Economy	Freedom of association and collective bargaining		Elimination of forced and compulsory labour		Elimination of discrimination in respect of employment and occupation		Abolition of child labour	
	Convention 87	Convention 98	Convention 29	Convention 105	Convention 100	Convention 111	Convention 138	Convention 182
Afghanistan	□	□	□	✓	✓	✓	□	□
Albania	✓	✓	✓	✓	✓	✓	✓	✓
Algeria	✓	✓	✓	✓	✓	✓	✓	✓
Angola	✓	✓	✓	✓	✓	✓	✓	✓
Antigua and Barbuda	✓	✓	✓	✓	✓	✓	✓	✓
Argentina	✓	✓	✓	✓	✓	✓	✓	✓
Armenia	✓	✓	✓	✓	✓	✓	✓	✓
Australia	✓	✓	✓	✓	✓	✓	□	✓
Austria	✓	✓	✓	✓	✓	✓	✓	✓
Azerbaijan	✓	✓	✓	✓	✓	✓	✓	✓
Bahamas, The	✓	✓	✓	✓	✓	✓	✓	✓
Bahrain	□	□	✓	✓	□	✓	□	✓
Bangladesh	✓	✓	✓	✓	✓	✓	□	✓
Belarus	✓	✓	✓	✓	✓	✓	✓	✓
Belgium	✓	✓	✓	✓	✓	✓	✓	✓
Belize	✓	✓	✓	✓	✓	✓	✓	✓
Benin	✓	✓	✓	✓	✓	✓	✓	✓
Bhutan	□	□	□	□	□	□	□	□
Bolivia	✓	✓	✓	✓	✓	✓	✓	✓
Bosnia and Herzegovina	✓	✓	✓	✓	✓	✓	✓	✓
Botswana	✓	✓	✓	✓	✓	✓	✓	✓
Brazil	□	✓	✓	✓	✓	✓	✓	✓
Brunei	□	□	□	□	□	□	□	✓
Bulgaria	✓	✓	✓	✓	✓	✓	✓	✓
Burkina Faso	✓	✓	✓	✓	✓	✓	✓	✓
Burundi	✓	✓	✓	✓	✓	✓	✓	✓
Cambodia	✓	✓	✓	✓	✓	✓	✓	✓
Cameroon	✓	✓	✓	✓	✓	✓	✓	✓
Canada	✓	□	□	✓	✓	✓	□	✓
Cape Verde	✓	✓	✓	✓	✓	✓	□	✓
Central African Republic	✓	✓	✓	✓	✓	✓	✓	✓
Chad	✓	✓	✓	✓	✓	✓	✓	✓
Chile	✓	✓	✓	✓	✓	✓	✓	✓
China	□	□	□	□	✓	✓	✓	✓
Colombia	✓	✓	✓	✓	✓	✓	✓	✓
Comoros	✓	✓	✓	✓	✓	✓	✓	✓
Congo, Dem. Rep.	✓	✓	✓	✓	✓	✓	✓	✓
Congo, Rep.	✓	✓	✓	✓	✓	✓	✓	✓
Costa Rica	✓	✓	✓	✓	✓	✓	✓	✓
Côte d'Ivoire	✓	✓	✓	✓	✓	✓	✓	✓
Croatia	✓	✓	✓	✓	✓	✓	✓	✓
Czech Republic	✓	✓	✓	✓	✓	✓	✓	✓
Denmark	✓	✓	✓	✓	✓	✓	✓	✓
Djibouti	✓	✓	✓	✓	✓	✓	✓	✓
Dominica	✓	✓	✓	✓	✓	✓	✓	✓
Dominican Republic	✓	✓	✓	✓	✓	✓	✓	✓
Ecuador	✓	✓	✓	✓	✓	✓	✓	✓
Egypt	✓	✓	✓	✓	✓	✓	✓	✓
El Salvador	✓	✓	✓	✓	✓	✓	✓	✓

Ratification status of the ILO core labor standards

✓ Convention ratified
□ Convention not ratified
D Ratification denounced

Economy	Freedom of association and collective bargaining		Elimination of forced and compulsory labour		Elimination of discrimination in respect of employment and occupation		Abolition of child labour	
	Convention 87	Convention 98	Convention 29	Convention 105	Convention 100	Convention 111	Convention 138	Convention 182
Equatorial Guinea	✓	✓	✓	✓	✓	✓	✓	✓
Eritrea	✓	✓	✓	✓	✓	✓	✓	□
Estonia	✓	✓	✓	✓	✓	✓	✓	✓
Ethiopia	✓	✓	✓	✓	✓	✓	✓	✓
Fiji	✓	✓	✓	✓	✓	✓	✓	✓
Finland	✓	✓	✓	✓	✓	✓	✓	✓
France	✓	✓	✓	✓	✓	✓	✓	✓
Gabon	✓	✓	✓	✓	✓	✓	□	✓
Gambia, The	✓	✓	✓	✓	✓	✓	✓	✓
Georgia	✓	✓	✓	✓	✓	✓	✓	✓
Germany	✓	✓	✓	✓	✓	✓	✓	✓
Ghana	✓	✓	✓	✓	✓	✓	□	✓
Greece	✓	✓	✓	✓	✓	✓	✓	✓
Grenada	✓	✓	✓	✓	✓	✓	✓	✓
Guatemala	✓	✓	✓	✓	✓	✓	✓	✓
Guinea	✓	✓	✓	✓	✓	✓	✓	✓
Guinea-Bissau	□	✓	✓	✓	✓	✓	□	□
Guyana	✓	✓	✓	✓	✓	✓	✓	✓
Haiti	✓	✓	✓	✓	✓	✓	□	✓
Honduras	✓	✓	✓	✓	✓	✓	✓	✓
Hong Kong, China[a]	—	—	—	—	—	—	—	—
Hungary	✓	✓	✓	✓	✓	✓	✓	✓
Iceland	✓	✓	✓	✓	✓	✓	✓	✓
India	□	□	✓	✓	✓	✓	□	□
Indonesia	✓	✓	✓	✓	✓	✓	✓	✓
Iran	□	□	✓	✓	✓	✓	□	✓
Iraq	□	✓	✓	✓	✓	✓	✓	✓
Ireland	✓	✓	✓	✓	✓	✓	✓	✓
Israel	✓	✓	✓	✓	✓	✓	✓	✓
Italy	✓	✓	✓	✓	✓	✓	✓	✓
Jamaica	✓	✓	✓	✓	✓	✓	✓	✓
Japan	✓	✓	✓	□	✓	□	✓	✓
Jordan	□	✓	✓	✓	✓	✓	✓	✓
Kazakhstan	✓	✓	✓	✓	✓	✓	✓	✓
Kenya	□	✓	✓	✓	✓	✓	✓	✓
Kiribati	✓	✓	✓	✓	□	□	□	□
Korea	□	□	□	□	✓	✓	✓	✓
Kuwait	✓	✓	✓	✓	□	✓	✓	✓
Kyrgyz Republic	✓	✓	✓	✓	✓	✓	✓	✓
Lao PDR	□	□	✓	□	✓	✓	✓	✓
Latvia	✓	✓	✓	✓	✓	✓	✓	✓
Lebanon	□	✓	✓	✓	✓	✓	✓	✓
Lesotho	✓	✓	✓	✓	✓	✓	✓	✓
Liberia	✓	✓	✓	✓	□	✓	□	✓
Lithuania	✓	✓	✓	✓	✓	✓	✓	✓
Luxembourg	✓	✓	✓	✓	✓	✓	✓	✓
Macedonia, former Yugoslav Republic of	✓	✓	✓	✓	✓	✓	✓	✓
Madagascar	✓	✓	✓	✓	✓	✓	✓	✓
Malawi	✓	✓	✓	✓	✓	✓	✓	✓

Ratification status of the ILO core labor standards

✓ Convention ratified
□ Convention not ratified
D Ratification denounced

Economy	Freedom of association and collective bargaining		Elimination of forced and compulsory labour		Elimination of discrimination in respect of employment and occupation		Abolition of child labour	
	Convention 87	Convention 98	Convention 29	Convention 105	Convention 100	Convention 111	Convention 138	Convention 182
Malaysia	□	✓	✓	D	✓	□	✓	✓
Maldives	□	□	□	□	□	□	□	□
Mali	✓	✓	✓	✓	✓	✓	✓	✓
Marshall Islands	□	□	□	□	□	□	□	□
Mauritania	✓	✓	✓	✓	✓	✓	✓	✓
Mauritius	✓	✓	✓	✓	✓	✓	✓	✓
Mexico	✓	□	✓	✓	✓	✓	□	✓
Micronesia	□	□	□	□	□	□	□	□
Moldova	✓	✓	✓	✓	✓	✓	✓	✓
Mongolia	✓	✓	✓	✓	✓	✓	✓	✓
Montenegro	✓	✓	✓	✓	✓	✓	✓	✓
Morocco	□	✓	✓	✓	✓	✓	✓	✓
Mozambique	✓	✓	✓	✓	✓	✓	✓	✓
Namibia	✓	✓	✓	✓	□	✓	✓	✓
Nepal	□	✓	✓	✓	✓	✓	✓	✓
Netherlands	✓	✓	✓	✓	✓	✓	✓	✓
New Zealand	□	✓	✓	✓	✓	✓	□	✓
Nicaragua	✓	✓	✓	✓	✓	✓	✓	✓
Niger	✓	✓	✓	✓	✓	✓	✓	✓
Nigeria	✓	✓	✓	✓	✓	✓	✓	✓
Norway	✓	✓	✓	✓	✓	✓	✓	✓
Oman	□	□	✓	✓	□	□	✓	✓
Pakistan	✓	✓	✓	✓	✓	✓	✓	✓
Palau	□	□	□	□	□	□	□	□
Panama	✓	✓	✓	✓	✓	✓	✓	✓
Papua New Guinea	✓	✓	✓	✓	✓	✓	✓	✓
Paraguay	✓	✓	✓	✓	✓	✓	✓	✓
Peru	✓	✓	✓	✓	✓	✓	✓	✓
Philippines	✓	✓	✓	✓	✓	✓	✓	✓
Poland	✓	✓	✓	✓	✓	✓	✓	✓
Portugal	✓	✓	✓	✓	✓	✓	✓	✓
Puerto Rico[a]	—	—	—	—	—	—	—	—
Qatar	□	□	✓	✓	□	✓	✓	✓
Romania	✓	✓	✓	✓	✓	✓	✓	✓
Russian Federation	✓	✓	✓	✓	✓	✓	✓	✓
Rwanda	✓	✓	✓	✓	✓	✓	✓	✓
Samoa	✓	✓	✓	✓	✓	✓	□	✓
São Tomé and Principe	✓	✓	✓	✓	✓	✓	✓	✓
Saudi Arabia	□	□	✓	✓	✓	✓	□	✓
Senegal	✓	✓	✓	✓	✓	✓	✓	✓
Serbia	✓	✓	✓	✓	✓	✓	✓	✓
Seychelles	✓	✓	✓	✓	✓	✓	✓	✓
Sierra Leone	✓	✓	✓	✓	✓	✓	□	□
Singapore	□	✓	✓	D	✓	□	✓	✓
Slovakia	✓	✓	✓	✓	✓	✓	✓	✓
Slovenia	✓	✓	✓	✓	✓	✓	✓	✓
Solomon Islands	□	□	✓	□	□	□	□	□
South Africa	✓	✓	✓	✓	✓	✓	✓	✓
Spain	✓	✓	✓	✓	✓	✓	✓	✓
Sri Lanka	✓	✓	✓	✓	✓	✓	✓	✓

Ratification status of the ILO core labor standards

✔ Convention ratified
☐ Convention not ratified
D Ratification denounced

Economy	Freedom of association and collective bargaining		Elimination of forced and compulsory labour		Elimination of discrimination in respect of employment and occupation		Abolition of child labour	
	Convention 87	Convention 98	Convention 29	Convention 105	Convention 100	Convention 111	Convention 138	Convention 182
St. Kitts and Nevis	✓	✓	✓	✓	✓	✓	✓	✓
St. Lucia	✓	✓	✓	✓	✓	✓	☐	✓
St. Vincent and the Grenadines	✓	✓	✓	✓	✓	✓	✓	✓
Sudan	☐	✓	✓	✓	✓	✓	✓	✓
Suriname	✓	✓	✓	✓	☐	☐	☐	✓
Swaziland	✓	✓	✓	✓	✓	✓	✓	✓
Sweden	✓	✓	✓	✓	✓	✓	✓	✓
Switzerland	✓	✓	✓	✓	✓	✓	✓	✓
Syria	✓	✓	✓	✓	✓	✓	✓	✓
Taiwan, China[a]	—	—	—	—	—	—	—	—
Tajikistan	✓	✓	✓	✓	✓	✓	✓	✓
Tanzania	✓	✓	✓	✓	✓	✓	✓	✓
Thailand	☐	☐	✓	✓	✓	☐	✓	✓
Timor-Leste	☐	☐	☐	☐	☐	☐	☐	☐
Togo	✓	✓	✓	✓	✓	✓	✓	✓
Tonga	☐	☐	☐	☐	☐	☐	☐	☐
Trinidad and Tobago	✓	✓	✓	✓	✓	✓	✓	✓
Tunisia	✓	✓	✓	✓	✓	✓	✓	✓
Turkey	✓	✓	✓	✓	✓	✓	✓	✓
Uganda	✓	✓	✓	✓	✓	✓	✓	✓
Ukraine	✓	✓	✓	✓	✓	✓	✓	✓
United Arab Emirates	☐	☐	✓	✓	✓	✓	✓	✓
United Kingdom	✓	✓	✓	✓	✓	✓	✓	✓
United States	☐	☐	☐	✓	☐	☐	☐	✓
Uruguay	✓	✓	✓	✓	✓	✓	✓	✓
Uzbekistan	☐	✓	✓	✓	✓	✓	☐	✓
Vanuatu	✓	✓	✓	✓	✓	✓	☐	✓
Venezuela	✓	✓	✓	✓	✓	✓	✓	✓
Vietnam	☐	☐	✓	☐	✓	✓	✓	✓
West Bank and Gaza	☐	☐	☐	☐	☐	☐	☐	☐
Yemen	✓	✓	✓	✓	✓	✓	✓	✓
Zambia	✓	✓	✓	✓	✓	✓	✓	✓
Zimbabwe	✓	✓	✓	✓	✓	✓	✓	✓

Note: The table shows the ratification status of the 8 ILO conventions regarding core labor standards for the 181 economies included in *Doing Business 2009* as of July 28, 2008. The ratification of these conventions is not included in the *Doing Business* employing workers indicators. Nor does *Doing Business* measure compliance with the core labor standards. *Doing Business* will conduct further analysis on compliance with these standards in the coming years. One issue to be further explored concerns the relationship between national law and the ILO conventions. In some cases, for example, national law may go beyond what is required in some of the ILO conventions and may not allow ratification for this reason. And in some cases where the ILO conventions have been ratified, national law may be in contradiction with some of the ILO conventions and may specifically give priority to the national over the international provisions.

a. Hong Kong (China), Puerto Rico and Taiwan (China) are not independent members of the ILO.

Source: ILO, ILOLEX database (http://www.ilo.org/ilolex/).

Acknowledgments

Doing Business 2009 was prepared by a team led by Sylvia Solf, Simeon Djankov (through March 2008) and Penelope Brook (from April 2008) under the general direction of Michael Klein. The team comprised Teymour Abdel Aziz, Svetlana Bagaudinova, Karim O. Belayachi, Mema Beye, Frederic Bustelo, César Chaparro Yedro, Maya Choueiri, Roger Coma-Cunill, Santiago Croci Downes, Marie Delion, Allen Dennis, Jacqueline den Otter, Alejandro Espinosa-Wang, Monica Fonseca Fernandez, Kjartan Fjeldsted, Elena Gasol Ramos, Carolin Geginat, Cemile Hacibeyoglu, Jamal Haidar, Sabine Hertveldt, Palarp Jumpasut, Dahlia Khalifa, Jean Michel Lobet, Oliver Lorenz, Valerie Marechal, Andres Martinez, Alexandra Mincu, Sushmitha Narsiah, Joanna Nasr, Dana Omran, Caroline Otonglo, Nadia Ram, Rita Ramalho, Camille Ramos, Ivana Rossi, Yara Salem, Pilar Salgado-Otónel, Umar Shavurov, Larisa Smirnova, Jayashree Srinivasan, Susanne Szymanski, Tea Trumbic, Caroline van Coppenolle, Bryan Welsh, Justin Yap and Lior Ziv. Jan Bezem, Sonali Bishop, Tara Sabre Collier, Sarah Iqbal, Alice Ouedraogo, Babacar Sedikh Faye and Jennifer Yip assisted in the months prior to publication.

Oliver Hart and Andrei Shleifer provided academic advice on the project. The paying taxes project was conducted in collaboration with Pricewaterhouse-Coopers, led by Robert Morris.

Alison Strong copyedited the manuscript. Gerry Quinn designed the report and the graphs. Kim Bieler assisted in the typesetting. Alexandra Quinn provided desktopping services. The online service of the *Doing Business* database is managed by Ramin Aliyev, Felipe Iturralde Escudero and Graeme Littler under the direction of Suzanne Smith.

We are grateful for valuable comments provided by colleagues across the World Bank Group and for the guidance of World Bank Group Executive Directors.

The report was made possible by the generous contribution of more than 6,700 lawyers, accountants, judges, businesspeople and public officials in 181 economies. Global and regional contributors are firms that have completed multiple surveys in their various offices around the world.

Quotations in this report are from *Doing Business* local partners unless otherwise indicated. The names of those wishing to be acknowledged individually are listed on the following pages. Contact details are posted on the *Doing Business* website at http://www.doingbusiness.org.

Contact details for local partners are available on the Doing Business website at http://www.doingbusiness.org

GLOBAL CONTRIBUTORS

ALLEN & OVERY LLP

APL LTD

BAKER & MCKENZIE

CLEARY GOTTLIEB STEEN & HAMILTON LLP

HAWKAMAH – THE INSTITUTE FOR CORPORATE GOVERNANCE

IUS LABORIS, ALLIANCE OF LABOR, EMPLOYMENT, BENEFITS AND PENSIONS LAW FIRMS

LAWYERS WITHOUT BORDERS

LEX MUNDI, ASSOCIATION OF INDEPENDENT LAW FIRMS

PRICEWATERHOUSECOOPERS

PRICEWATERHOUSECOOPERS LEGAL SERVICES

SDV INTERNATIONAL LOGISTICS

THE ADORA GROUP LTD (FREIGHTNET)

TOBOC INC.

REGIONAL CONTRIBUTORS

ABU-GHAZALEH LEGAL

EAST AFRICA LAW SOCIETY

FEDERACIÓN INTERAMERICANA DE LA INDUSTRIA DE LA CONSTRUCCIÓN

GARCIA & BODAN

GLOBALINK TRANSPORTATION & LOGISTICS WORLDWIDE LLP

IKRP ROKAS & PARTNERS

M&M LOGISTICS

TRANSUNION INTERNATIONAL

UNIVERSITY OF SOUTH PACIFIC

AFGHANISTAN

Najibullah Amiri
AFGHANISTAN BANKS ASSOCIATION

BEARINGPOINT

Bahauddin Baha
SUPREME COURT

A. Farid Barakzai
TNT INTERNATIONAL EXPRESS

Amanda Galton
ORRICK, HERRINGTON & SUTCLIFFE

Shahzad Haider
AFGHANISTAN INTERNATIONAL BANK

Muslimul Haq
AFGHANISTAN BANKS ASSOCIATION

Abdul Wassay Haqiqi
HAQIQI LEGAL SERVICES

Saduddin Haziq
AFGHANISTAN INTERNATIONAL BANK

Rashid Ibrahim
A.F. FERGUSON & CO.

Yasin Khosti
SOCIETY OF AFGHAN ARCHITECTS AND ENGINEERS

Gaurav Lekh Raj Kukreja
AFGHAN CONTAINER TRANSPORT COMPANY

Zahoor Malla
GLOBALINK LOGISTICS GROUP

T. Ud-Din A. Mirza
A.F. FERGUSON & CO.

Kevin O'Brien
USAID/BEARING POINT

Habibullah Peerzada
ACCL INTERNATIONAL

Abdul Rahman Watanwal
MBC CONSTRUCTION

ALBANIA

Erjola Aliaj
IKRP ROKAS & PARTNERS

Artur Asllani
TONUCCI & PARTNERS

Ledia Beçi
HOXHA, MEMI & HOXHA

Ilir Bejleri
SON GROUP, ENGINEERING AND CONSTRUCTION

Jona Bica
KALO & ASSOCIATES

Rene Bijvoet
PRICEWATERHOUSECOOPERS

Alban Caushi
KALO & ASSOCIATES

Dorian Collaku
BANK OF ALBANIA

Ilir Daci
KALO & ASSOCIATES

Besnik Duraj
HOXHA, MEMI & HOXHA

Sokol Elmazaj
BOGA & ASSOCIATES

Valbona Gjonçari
BOGA & ASSOCIATES

Jola Gjuzi
KALO & ASSOCIATES

Vilma Gjyshi
KALO & ASSOCIATES

Anteo Gremi
ZIG CONSULTING FIRM

Emel Haxhillari
KALO & ASSOCIATES

Shpati Hoxha
HOXHA, MEMI & HOXHA

Erald Ibro
ZIG CONSULTING FIRM

Olsi Ibro
ZIG CONSULTING FIRM

Ilir Johollari
HOXHA, MEMI & HOXHA

Perparim Kalo
KALO & ASSOCIATES

Renata Leka
BOGA & ASSOCIATES

Georgios K. Lemonis
IKRP ROKAS & PARTNERS

Elton Lula
KALO & ASSOCIATES

Andi Memi
HOXHA, MEMI & HOXHA

Loreta Peci
PRICEWATERHOUSECOOPERS

Ermira Pervizi
IKRP ROKAS & PARTNERS

Laura Qorlaze
PRICEWATERHOUSECOOPERS

Miranda Ramajj
BANK OF ALBANIA

Ardjana Shehi
KALO & ASSOCIATES

SHPRESA D

Elda Shuraja
HOXHA, MEMI & HOXHA

SKY NET ALBANIA

Gerhard Velaj
BOGA & ASSOCIATES

Silva Velaj
BOGA & ASSOCIATES

Agim Vërshevci
ALIMENTI NATURALI & PB

Elda Zaimi
ZIG CONSULTING FIRM

ALGERIA

Branka Achari-Djokic
BANQUE D'ALGÉRIE

Salima Aloui
LAW FIRM GOUSSANEM & ALOUI

Hadda Ammara
BOUCHAIB LAW FIRM

Khodja Bachir
SNC KHODJA & CO.

Hassan Djamel Belloula
CABINET BELLOULA

Tayeb Belloula
CABINET BELLOULA

Adnane Bouchaib
BOUCHAIB LAW FIRM

Fatma Zohra Bouchemla
ATTORNEY-AT-LAW

Jean-Pierre Comunale
SDV

Arezki Djadour
GIDE LOYRETTE NOUEL, MEMBER OF LEX MUNDI

Asmaa El Ouazzani
LANDWELL & ASSOCIÉS - PRICEWATERHOUSECOOPERS LEGAL SERVICES

Malik Elkettas
ELKETTAS INTERNATIONAL

Brahim Embouazza
MCDCONSULTING

Mohamed Lehbib Goubi
BANQUE D'ALGÉRIE

Khaled Goussanem
LAW FIRM GOUSSANEM & ALOUI

Samir Hamouda
CABINET D'AVOCATS SAMIR HAMOUDA

Samy Laghouati
GIDE LOYRETTE NOUEL, MEMBER OF LEX MUNDI

Nadia Larbaoui
BOUCHAIB LAW FIRM

Karine Lasne
LANDWELL & ASSOCIÉS - PRICEWATERHOUSECOOPERS LEGAL SERVICES

Michel Lecerf
LANDWELL & ASSOCIÉS - PRICEWATERHOUSECOOPERS LEGAL SERVICES

Adnane Merad
ETUDE DE ME KADDOUR MERAD

Narimane Naas
GIDE LOYRETTE NOUEL, MEMBER OF LEX MUNDI

Fériel Oulounis
CABINET D'AVOCATS SAMIR HAMOUDA

Maya Sator
CABINET SATOR

Mohamed Sator
CABINET SATOR

Marc Veuillot
ALLEANCE ADVISORY MAROC

Tarik Zahzah
GHELLAL & MEKERBA

Nabiha Zerigui
CABINET D'AVOCATS SAMIR HAMOUDA

ANGOLA

José Rodrigues Alentejo
CÂMARA DE COMÉRCIO E INDÚSTRIA DE ANGOLA

Fernando Barros
PRICEWATERHOUSECOOPERS

Alain Brachet
SDV AMI INTERNATIONAL LOGISTICS

Pedro Calixto
PRICEWATERHOUSECOOPERS

Olainde Camache
AVM ADVOGADOS

Maurice Campbell
CROWN AGENTS

Caetano Capitão
CENTRO DE APOIO EMPRESARIAL- CAE

Nahary Cardoso
FÁTIMA FREITAS ADVOGADOS

CONSERVATÓRIA DO REGISTRO PREDIAL DE LUANDA (⬛ª SECÇÃO)

Esperança Costa
ALEXANDRE PEGADO - ESCRITÓRIO DE ADVOGADOS

João Viegas de Abreu
CONSULANA

Miguel de Avillez Pereira
ABREU ADVOGADOS

Francisca de Oliveira
ASSOCIAÇÃO DE MULHERES EMPRESARIAS DA PROVÍNCIA DE LUANDA (ASSOMEL)

Fernando F. Bastos
FARIA DE BASTOS, SEBASTIÃO E LOPES - ADVOGADOS ASSOCIADOS

Ana Fernandes
PRICEWATERHOUSECOOPERS

Lourdes Caposso Fernandes
RCJE ADVOGADOS ASSOCIADOS

Conceição Manita Ferreira
RUI C. FERREIRA & GUILHERMINA PRATA

Luís Folhadela
KPMG

Fátima Freitas
FÁTIMA FREITAS ADVOGADOS

Brian Glazier
EDI ARCHITECTURE INC.

Adelaide Godinho
AG & LP

Raul Gomes
ATS LOGISTICS CO.

Blake Hinderyckx
CAE/CDC

Helder da Conceição José
INSTITUTO DE PLANEAMENTO E GESTÃO URBANA DO GOVERNO PROVINCIAL DE LUANDA

Victor Leonel
ORDEM DOS ARQUITECTOS

Guiomar Lopes
FARIA DE BASTOS, SEBASTIÃO E LOPES - ADVOGADOS ASSOCIADOS

Paulette Lopes
FARIA DE BASTOS, SEBASTIÃO E LOPES - ADVOGADOS ASSOCIADOS

Teresinha Lopes
FARIA DE BASTOS, SEBASTIÃO E LOPES - ADVOGADOS ASSOCIADOS

Chindalena Lourenco
FÁTIMA FREITAS ADVOGADOS

Manuel Malufuene
ORDEM DOS ARQUITECTOS

Ulanga Gaspar Martins
BANCO PRIVADO ATLÂNTICO

Josephine Matambo
KPMG

Filomeno Henrique C. Mendonça da Silva
MINISTERIO DOS TRANSPORTES

Manuel Nazareth Neto
PORTO DE LUANDA

Eduardo Paiva
PRICEWATERHOUSECOOPERS

Mário A. Palhares
BANCO DE NEGÓCIOS INTERNACIONAL

Alexandre Pegado
ALEXANDRE PEGADO - ESCRITÓRIO DE ADVOGADOS

Jorge Leão Peres
Banco Nacional

Douglas Pillinger
Panalpina

Luis Filipe Pizarro
AG & LP

Laurinda Prazeres
Faria de Bastos, Sebastião e Lopes - Advogados Associados

Elisa Rangel Nunes
ERN Advogados

Víctor Anjos Santos
AVM Advogados

Guilherme Santos Silva
Abreu Advogados

Isabel Serrão
KPMG

Maikel Steve
Luanda Incubadora de Empresas

Bento Tati
Guiché Único de Empresa

N'Gunu Tiny
RCJE Advogados Asociados

Isabel Tormenta
Guiché Único de Empresa

ANTIGUA AND BARBUDA

Mitzie Bockley
Registrar, Intellectual Property and Commerce Office, Ministry of Justice

Rhodette F.C. Brown
Phillips, Phillips & Archibald

Everett Christian
ABI Bank Ltd.

Neil Coates
PricewaterhouseCoopers

Brian D'Ornellas
OBM International, Antigua Ltd.

Vernon Edwards
Freight Forwarding & Deconsolidating

Phillip Jr. Isaacs
OBM International, Antigua Ltd.

Alfred McKelly James
James & Associates

Efrain Laureano
Caribbean Open Trade Support (USAID)

Gloria Martin
Francis Trading Agency Limited

Marscha Prince
PricewaterhouseCoopers

Septimus A. Rhudd
Rhudd & Associates

Stacy A. Richards-Anjo
Richards & Co.

Alice N. Roberts
Roberts & Co.

Clare K. Roberts
Roberts & Co.

Carl Samuel
Antigua Public Utility Authority

Cassandra Simmons

Arthur Thomas
Thomas, John & Co.

Charles Walwyn
PricewaterhouseCoopers

Marietta Warren
Interfreight Ltd.

Hesketh Williams
Ministry of Labor

Roslyn Yearwood
Integrity Commission Antigua & Barbuda

ARGENTINA

Dolores Aispuru
PricewaterhouseCoopers

Lisandro A. Allende
Brons & Salas Abogados

Ana Candelaria Alonso Negre
Alfaro Abogados

Vanesa Balda
Vitale, Manoff & Feilbogen

Gonzalo Carlos Ballester
J.P. O'Farrell Abogados

Ignacio Fernández Borzese
TWR Abogados

Agustina Caratti
PricewaterhouseCoopers

Mariano Ezequiel Carricart
Fornieles Abogados

Gustavo Casir
Quattrini, Laprida & Asociados

Pablo L. Cavallaro
Estudio Cavallaro Abogados

Albert Chamorro
Alfaro Abogados

Julian A. Collados
Accountant

Hernán Gonzalo Cuenca Martínez
PricewaterhouseCoopers Legal Services

Oscar Alberto del Río
Central Bank

Andrés Edelstein
PricewaterhouseCoopers

Joaquín Eppens
Murray, Díaz Cordero & Sirito de Zavalía

Diego Etchepare
PricewaterhouseCoopers

Fernando Fucci
Grant Thorton

Ignacio Funes de Rioja
Funes de Rioja & Asociados, member of Ius Laboris

Claudia Gizzi
GPM

María Laura González
PricewaterhouseCoopers

Pablo González del Solar
PricewaterhouseCoopers

Pablo Grillo Ciocchini
Brons & Salas Abogados

Fabián Hilal
Campos, Etcheverry & Asociados

Walter Keiniger
Marval, O'Farrell & Mairal, member of Lex Mundi

Santiago Laclau
Marval, O'Farrell & Mairal, member of Lex Mundi

Guillermo Lalanne
Estudio O'Farrell

Rodrigo Marchan
GPM

Agustín Marra
Alfaro Abogados

Pablo Mastromarino
Estudio Beccar Varela

José Oscar Mira
Central Bank

Jorge Miranda
Clippers S.A.

Enrique Monsegur
Clippers S.A.

Miguel P. Murray
Murray, Díaz Cordero & Sirito de Zavalía

Isabel Muscolo
Quattrini, Laprida & Asociados

Alfredo Miguel O'Farrell
Marval, O'Farrell & Mairal, member of Lex Mundi

Mariano Payaslian
GPM

María Ximena Pérez Dirrocco
Marval, O'Farrell & Mairal, member of Lex Mundi

Julio Alberto Pueyrredon
PricewaterhouseCoopers

Pablo Ramos
Comercial del Oeste

Sebastián Rodrigo
Alfaro Abogados

Ignacio Rodriguez
PricewaterhouseCoopers

Nicolás Rossi Bunge
Marval, O'Farrell & Mairal, member of Lex Mundi

Adolfo Rouillon
The World Bank

Patricia Ruhman Seggiaro
Marval, O'Farrell & Mairal, member of Lex Mundi

Sonia Salvatierra
Marval, O'Farrell & Mairal, member of Lex Mundi

Jorge Sanchez Diaz
Ecobamboo S.A.

Liliana Cecilia Segade
Quattrini, Laprida & Asociados

Miguel Teson
Estudio O'Farrell

Eduardo J. Viñales
Funes de Rioja & Asociados, member of Ius Laboris

Joaquín Emilio Zappa
J.P. O'Farrell Abogados

Octavio Miguel Zenarruza
Álvarez Prado & Asociados

Carlos Zima
PricewaterhouseCoopers

ARMENIA

Artak Arzoyan
ACRA Credit Bureau

Vardan Bezhanyan
Yerevan State University

Gevorg Chakmishyan
PricewaterhouseCoopers

Aikanush Edigaryan
Trans-Alliance

Courtney Fowler
PricewaterhouseCoopers

Gagik Galstyan
Horizon ⊠

Hayk Ghazazyan
KPMG

Mher Grigoryan
VTB Bank

Sargis H. Martirosyan
Trans-Alliance

Davit Harutyunyan
PricewaterhouseCoopers

Vahe Kakoyan
Investment Law Group LLC

Karine Khachatryan
BearingPoint

Rajiv Nagri
Globalink Logistics Group

Artur Nikoyan
Trans-Alliance

Mikayel Pashayan
The State Committee of the Real Property Cadastre

Alex Poghossian
Alpha Plus Consulting

Aram Poghosyan
Grant Thornton Amyot

David Sargsyan
Ameria cjsc

Gayane Shimshiryan
Central Bank

Hakob Tadevosyan
Grant Thornton Amyot

Matthew Tallarovic
PricewaterhouseCoopers

Armen Ter-Tachatyan
Ter-Tachatyan Legal and Business Consulting

Artur Tunyan
Judicial Reform Project

AUSTRALIA

Lucy Adamson
Clayton Utz, member of Lex Mundi

Matthew Allison
Veda Advantage

Lynda Brumm
PricewaterhouseCoopers

David Buda
RBHM Commercial Lawyers

Alicia Castillo
Alicia Castillo Wealthing Group

Caterina Cavallaro
Baker & McKenzie

Joe Collins
Clayton Utz, member of Lex Mundi

Marcus Connor
Chang, Pistilli & Simmons

Tim Cox
PricewaterhouseCoopers

Michael Daniel
PricewaterhouseCoopers

Anne Davis
Clayton Utz, member of Lex Mundi

Jenny Davis
EnergyAustralia

Raymond Fang
Gadens Lawyers

Brett Feltham
PricewaterhouseCoopers

Joan Fitzhenry
Baker & McKenzie

Mark Geniale
Office of State Revenue, NSW Treasury

Mark Grdovich
Blake Dawson

Owen Hayford
Clayton Utz, member of Lex Mundi

David Hing
PricewaterhouseCoopers

Ian Humphreys
Blake Dawson

Eric Ip
Onward Business Consultants PTY LTD

Doug Jones
Clayton Utz, member of Lex Mundi

Morgan Kelly
Ferrier Hodgson

Mark Kingston
Tradesafe Australia Pty. Ltd.

Ricky Lee
PricewaterhouseCoopers Legal Services

John Lobban
Blake Dawson

John Martin
Thomson Playford

Mitchell Mathas
Deacons

Nick Mavrakis
Clayton Utz, member of Lex Mundi

Christie McGregor
PricewaterhouseCoopers

Mark Pistilli
Chang, Pistilli & Simmons

Ann Previtera
PricewaterhouseCoopers

John Reid
Office of State Revenue, NSW Treasury

Bob Ronai
Import-Export Services Pty. Ltd.

Luke Sayers
PricewaterhouseCoopers

Damian Sturzaker
Gadens Lawyers

Mark Swan
PricewaterhouseCoopers Legal Services

Nick Thomas
Clayton Utz, member of Lex Mundi

Simon Truskett
Clayton Utz, member of Lex Mundi

David Twigg
EnergyAustralia

Megan Valsinger-Clark
Gadens Lawyers

Andrew Wheeler
PricewaterhouseCoopers

David Zwi
Thomson Playford

AUSTRIA

Thomas Bareder
OeNB

Georg Brandstetter
Brandstetter Pritz & Partner

Martin Eckel
E|N|W|C Natlacen Walderdorff Cancola Rechtsanwälte GmbH

Tibor Fabian
Binder Grösswang Rechtsanwälte

Julian Feichtinger
Cerha Hempel Spiegelfeld Hlawati

Andreas Hable
Binder Grösswang Rechtsanwälte

Rudolf Kaindl
Koehler, Kaindl, Duerr & Partner, Civil Law Notaries

Susanne Kappel
Kunz Schima Wallentin Rechtsanwälte KEG, member of Ius Laboris

Kraus & Co Warenhandelsgesellschaft mbH

Florian Kremslehner
Dorda Brugger Jordis

Rudolf Krickl
PricewaterhouseCoopers

Ulrike Langwallner
Schönherr Rechtsanwälte GmbH / Attorneys-at-Law

Gregor Maderbacher
Brauneis Klauser Prändl Rechtsanwälte GmbH

Peter Madl
Schönherr Rechtsanwälte GmbH / Attorneys-at-Law

Irene Mandl
Austrian Institute for SME Research

Wolfgang Messeritsch
National Bank

Marguerita Müller
Dorda Brugger Jordis

Alfred Nepf
Ministry of Finance

Michael Podesser
PricewaterhouseCoopers

Ulla Reisch
Urbanek Lind Schmied Reisch Rechtsanwälte OG

Friedrich Roedler
PricewaterhouseCoopers

Ruth Rosenkranz
Graf & Pitkowitz Rechtsanwälte GmbH

Heidi Scheichenbauer
Austrian Institute for SME Research

Georg Schima
Kunz Schima Wallentin Rechtsanwälte KEG, member of Ius Laboris

Stephan Schmalzl
WallnöferSchmalzl-Rechtsanwälte

Ernst Schmidt

Karin Schöpp
Binder Grösswang Rechtsanwälte

Benedikt Spiegelfeld
Cerha Hempel Spiegelfeld Hlawati

Birgit Vogt-Majarek
Kunz Schima Wallentin Rechtsanwälte KEG, member of Ius Laboris

Lothar A. Wachter
Wolf Theiss

Gerhard Wagner
KSV ████

Irene Welser
Cerha Hempel Spiegelfeld Hlawati

Gerold Zeiler
Schönherr Rechtsanwälte GmbH / Attorneys-at-Law

AZERBAIJAN

Shirzad Abdullayev
National Bank

Sabit Abdullayev
OMNI Law Firm

Eldar Adilzade
IFC

Anar Aliyev
IFC

Azer Amiraslan Aliyev
IFC

Aykhan Asadov
Baker & McKenzie - CIS, Ltd.

Ismail Askerov
MGB Law offices

Rufat Aslanli
National Bank

Sabit A. Bagirov
Entrepreneurship Development Foundation

Samira Bakhshiyeva
Deloitte & Touche LLC

Samir Balayev
Unibank

Rana Dramali
Roseville Premium Residence

Mehriban Efendiyeva
Michael Wilson & Partners Ltd.

Zaur Fati-Zadeh
Ministry of Taxes

Vusal Gafarov
Baker & McKenzie - CIS, Ltd.

Rashad Gafarov
Panalpina

Rufat Gasinov
Baku Cargo

Rizvan Gubiyev
PricewaterhouseCoopers

Abbas Guliyev
Baker & McKenzie - CIS, Ltd.

Arif Guliyev
PricewaterhouseCoopers

Rashad Gulmaliyev
The State Register Service of Real Estate

Sabina Gulmaliyeva
MGB Law Offices

Jeyhun Gurbanov
AGL Ltd.

Elchin Habibov
National Bank

Faiq Haci-Ismaylov
INCE MMC

Adil Hajaliyev
BM International LLC

Arzu Hajiyeva
Ernst & Young

Samir Hasanov
Gosselin

Zaur Huseynov
OJSC Bakielektrikshebeke

Emin Huseynov
National Bank

Faig Huseynov
Unibank

Jeyhun Huseynzada
PricewaterhouseCoopers

Zohrad Ismayilov
Association for Assistance to Free Economy

Dilyara Israfilova
BM International LLC

Fakhiyar Jabbarov
IFC

Gunduz Karimov
Baker & McKenzie - CIS, Ltd.

Nuran Karimov
Deloitte & Touche LLC

Sahib Mammadov
Citizens' Labour Rights Protection League

Kamil Mammadov
Mammadov & Partners Law Firm

Elchin Mammadov
MGB Law Offices

Vugar Mammadov
PricewaterhouseCoopers

Rena Mammadova
Deloitte & Touche LLC

Faiq S. Manafov
Unibank

Daniel Matthews
Baker & McKenzie

Farhad Mirzayev
BM International LLC

Ruslan Mukhtarov
BM International LLC

Samir Nuriyev
Ministry of Economic Development

Movlan Pashayev
PricewaterhouseCoopers

Tamer Pektas
Aral group

Givi Petriashvili
IFC

John Quinn
ACE Forwarding Caspian

Karim N. Ramazanov
Ministry of Economic Development

Gamar Rustamova
OMNI Law Firm

Nailya Safrova
Swiss Cooperation Office for the South Caucasus, Embassy of Switzerland

Suleyman Gasan ogly Suleymanov
Caspian Service International Construction Company

Kamil Valiyev
McGrigors Baku Limited

Murad Yahyayev
Unibank

Ismail Zargarli
OMNI Law Firm

Ulviyya Zeynalova
MGB Law Offices

BAHAMAS, THE

McKinney, Bancroft & Hughes

Tropical Shipping

Kevin A. Basden
Bahamas Electricity Corporation

Rodney W. Braynen
Design Häus

Registry of the Registrar General's Office

Craig G. Delancy
The Commonwealth of the Bahamas, Ministry of Works & Transport

Rochelle A. Deleveaux
Central Bank

Chaunece M. Ferguson
Mackay & Moxey Chambers

Amos J. Ferguson jr.
Ferguson Associates & Planners

Anthony S. Forbes
Bahamas Electricity Corporation

Wendy Forsythe
Import Export Brokers Ltd.

Higgs & Johnson

Graham, Thompson & Co.

Debi Hancock-Williams
Williams Law Chambers

Colin Higgs
Ministry of Works & Transport

Lennox Paton

Gordon Major
The Commonwealth of the Bahamas, Ministry of Works & Transport

Shane A. Miller
Registrar General's Department

Michael Moss
Valuation and Business License Unit of the Ministry of Finance

Wayne R. Munroe
Bahamas Bar Council

Donna D. Newton
Supreme Court

Kevin Seymour
PricewaterhouseCoopers

Everette B. Sweeting
Bahamas Electricity Corporation

Tex I. Turnquest
Department of Lands & Surveys

BAHRAIN

Khalid Abdulla
Tameer

Aysha Mohammed Abdulmalik
Elham Ali Hassan & Associates

Khaled Hassan Ajaji
Ministry of Justice & Islamic Affairs

Mohammed Abdullah Al Sisi Al Buainain
Al Boainain Legal Services

Nawaf Bin Ebrahim Al Kalifa
Electricity & Water Authority

Hamed Mohamed Al Khalifa
Ministry of Municipalities & Agriculture Urban Planning

Haider Hashim Al Noami
Ministry of Municipalities & Agriculture Affairs. Municipal One Stop Shop

Mohammed Al Noor
Al-Twaijri and Partners Law Firm

Mohammed Hasan Al Zaimoor
Ministry of Industry & Commerce

Samer Al-Ajjawi
Ernst & Young

Abdulmajeed Ali Alawadhi
Electricity & Water Authority

Fatima Alhasan
Qays H. Zu'bi

Ebtihal Al-Hashimi
Ministry of Municipalities & Agriculture Affairs. Municipal One Stop Shop

Shaji Alukkal
Panalpina

Bilal Ambikapathy
Norton Rose

Maaria Ashraf
Hatim S. Zu'bi & Partners

Mohammed R. Awadh
Bahrain Investors Center

Mohammed Mirza A. Hussain Bin Jaffer
Ministry of Municipalities & Agriculture Affairs. Municipal One Stop Shop

Hussain Saleh Dhaif
Mela Bahrain

Michael Durgavich
Al-Sarraf & Al-Ruwayeh

Yousif A. Humood
Ministry of Finance

Abdulwahid A. Janahi
The Benefit Company

Jawad Habib Jawad
BDO Jawad Habib

Sara Jawahery
Elham Ali Hassan & Associates

Ebrahim Karolia
PricewaterhouseCoopers

Elie Kassis
Agility Logistics

Mubeen Khadir
Ernst & Young

Mohammed Abdul Khaliq
Tameer

Abdul-Haq Mohammed
Trowers & Hamlins

Abdullah Mutawi
Trowers & Hamlins

Hassan Ali Radhi
Hassan Radhi & Associates

Hameed Yousif Rahma
Ministry of Industry & Commerce

Najma A. Redha Hasan
Ministry of Municipalities & Agriculture Affairs. Municipal One Stop Shop

Mohamed Salahuddin
Mohamed Salahuddin Consulting Engineering Bureau

Latifa Salahuddin
Qays H. Zu'bi

E. Hugh Stokes
Hatim S. Zu'bi & Partners

Judith Tosh
Norton Rose

Robin Watson
The Benefit Company

Adrian Woodcock
Norton Rose

Hatim S. Zu'bi
Hatim S. Zu'bi & Partners

BANGLADESH

Mohammad Abdul Wazed
Directorate of Land Records and Surveys

Md. Abdul Maleque Mian Abdullah
Credit Information Bureau, Bangladesh Bank

Zainul Abedin
A. Qasem & Co. / PricewaterhouseCoopers

Munir Uddin Ahamed
Integrated Transportation Services Ltd., Agent of Panalpina

Tanjib-ul Alam
Dr. Kamal Hossain & Associates

MD. Nurul Amin
Development Constructions Ltd.

Mehedy Amin
Development Constructions Ltd.

Saady Amin
Development Constructions Ltd.

Noorul Azhar
Government of Bangladesh

Probir Barua

Md. Halim Bepari
Halim Law Associate

Sharif Bhuiyan
Dr. Kamal Hossain & Associates

Jamilur Reza Choudhury

Aparup Chowdhury
Ministry of Law, Justice and Parliamentary Affairs

Badrud Doulah
Doulah & Doulah Advocates

Nasirud Doulah
Doulah & Doulah Advocates

Shamsud Doulah
Doulah & Doulah Advocates

Mohammad Firoz Mia
Ministry of Establishment

Moin Ghani
Dr. Kamal Hossain & Associates

K M A Halim
Upright Textile Supports

Raquibul Haque Miah
Advocate & Attorneys Law Firm

Mirza Quamrul Hasan
Adviser's Legal Alliance

Abdullah Hasan
Dr. Kamal Hossain & Associates

Md. Nazmul Hasan
Protex International

Kazi Rashed Hassan Ferdous
Proactive

Ikhtiar Hossain
Overseas Business

Abdul Hamid Howlader
Dhaka District Registry Office

Mohammad Zeeshan Hyder
Lee, Khan & Partners

Shariful Islam

Md Aminul Islam
City Apparel-Tex Co.

Samsul Islam
Executive Magistrate and Deputy Commissioner Office

Mohammed Aminul Islam
V-Sign Sweaters Ltd.

Sohel Kasem
A. Qasem & Co. / PricewaterhouseCoopers

Leatherex Footwear Ind. Ltd.

Qazi Mahtab-uz-Zaman

A.I.M Monsoor

S A Mortoza
Oishi Trade Associates

Sheikh Nurul

Eva Quasem
Amir & Amir Law Associates, member of Lex Mundi

A.F.M. Rahamatul Bari
Globe Link Associates Ltd

Md. Mahbubur Rahman
Amiq Computer & Electronics

Moinur Rahman
Aspect Ratio Creative Communication

Al Amin Rahman
Al Amin Rahman & Associates

M.A. Reza
Tailorⓧ

Ruma Leather Industries Ltd.

Deloar Siddique
M. Abu Bakar & Co.

Shahriar Syeed
V-Teac Fashion Pvt Ltd.

S S Tex Link

Babla Topy

BELARUS

Ivan Alievich
Vlasova Mikhel & Partners

Yuri M. Alymov
National Bank

Alexey Anischenko
Vlasova, Mikhel and Partners LLC

Svetlana Babintseva
DICSA Audit, Law & Consulting

Ron J. Barden
PricewaterhouseCoopers

Vladimir G. Biruk
Capital Ltd.

Bokemin Ltd.

Dmitry Bokhan
Businessconsult

Alexander Bondar
Businessconsult

Alexander Botian
Borovtsov & Salei Law Offices

Vitaly Braginiec
Braginiec & Partners

Aliaksandr Danilevich
Danilevich

Igor Dankov
PricewaterhouseCoopers

Vladimir Didenko
PricewaterhouseCoopers

Anton Dolgovechny
National Bank

Dmitry Dorofeev
National Bank

Marina Dymovich
Borovtsov & Salei Law Offices

Kuksenko Ivan Gennadievich
ARS Group

Gennadiy Glinskiy
DICSA International Group of Lawyers

Alexandr Ignatov
National Bank

Antonina Ivanova
DICSA International Group of Lawyers

Dmitry L. Kalechits
National Bank

Nina Knyazeva
Businessconsult

Irina Koikova
DICSA International Group of Lawyers

Mikhail E. Kostyukov
Attorney at Law

Dmitry Labetsky
Businessconsult

Oksana Loban
Ernst & Young

Sergei Logvinov
Krafttrans

Ekaterina Lukyanova
State Committee for Real Estate Registration

Konstantin Mikhel
Vlasova Mikhel & Partners

Alexei Nazarov
National Bank

Vladimir Nemov
DICSA Audit, Law & Consulting

Magdalena Patrzyk
PricewaterhouseCoopers

Victor Plenkin
National Bank

Vassili I. Salei
Borovtsov & Salei Law Offices

Sergei Senchuk
State Committee for Real Estate Registration

Vitaly P. Sevroukevitch
Belarussian Scientific Industrial Association

Alexander Shevko
National Bank

Lubov Slobodchikova
National Bank

Viktar Strachuk
Deloitte & Touche

Sergey Strelchik
Valex Consult

Natalia Talai
Vlasova Mikhel & Partners

Yuri M. Truhan
National Bank

Alexander Vasilevsky
Valex Consult

Anna Yakubenko
PricewaterhouseCoopers

Vyacheslav Zhuk
IFC

BELGIUM

Allen & Overy LLP

Cour de Cassation

Hubert André-Dumont
McGuire Woods LLP

Christiaan Barbier
Monard-D'Hulst

Thierry Bosly
White & Case

Gilles Carbonez
McGuire Woods LLP

Ortwin Carron
Monard-D'Hulst

Koen Cooreman

Steven De Schrijver
Van Bael & Bellis

Amaury Della Faille
PricewaterhouseCoopers

Frank Dierckx
PricewaterhouseCoopers

David Du Pont
Ashurst

Jürgen Egger
Monard-D'Hulst

Pierrette Fraisse
SPF Finances - AGDP

Kurt Grillet
Altius

Sandrine Hirsch
Simont Braun

Thomas Hürner
National Bank

Stephan Legein
Federal Public Service Finance

Luc Legon
PricewaterhouseCoopers

Alexis Lemmerling
Berquin Notaires

Axel Maeterlinck
Simont Braun

Philippe Massart
Sibelga

MedicCleanAir

Robert Meunier
Notary

Carl Meyntjens
Ashurst

Dominique Mougenot
Commercial Court Mons

Didier Muraille
National Bank

Peter Neefs
National Bank

Sabrina Otten
PricewaterhouseCoopers

Panalpina World Transport N.V.

Peter Rooryck
Monard-D'Hulst

Katrien Schillemans
PricewaterhouseCoopers

Frédéric Souchon
PricewaterhouseCoopers

Jan Van Celst
DLA Piper LLP

Mieke van den Bunder
PricewaterhouseCoopers Business Advisors

Ruben Van Impe
Van Impe Accountancy BVBA

Dirk Van Strijthem
PricewaterhouseCoopers

Suzy Vande Wiele
Loyens & Loeff

Bart Vanham
PricewaterhouseCoopers

Patrick Vercauteren
APL

Reinout Vleugels
Van Bael & Bellis

Christian Willems
Loyens & Loeff

BELIZE

Emil Arguelles
Arguelles & Company LLC

Rudy Castillo
The Belize Bank Ltd.

Gian C. Gandhi
International Financial Services Commission

Mirna Lara
Eurocaribe Belize Shipping Services

Russell Longsworth
Caribbean Shipping Agencies Ltd.

Fred Lumor
Fred Lumor & Co.

Reynaldo F. Magana
Frontier International Business Services Ltd.

Tania Moody
Barrow & Williams

Patricia Rodriguez
Belize Companies and Corporate Affairs Registry

Dan Roth
Sterling Freight Services

Janelle Tillett
Eurocaribe Belize Shipping Services

Saidi Vaccaro
Arguelles & Company LLC

Philip Zuniga
Barrister & Attorney-at-Law

BENIN

Jean-Claude Adandedjan
Continental Bank

Ganiou Adechy
Etude de Me Ganiou Adechy

Eurydice Adjovi
Continental Bank

Victoire Agbanrin-Elisha
Cabinet d'Avocat Agbanrin-Elisha

Saïdou Agbantou
Cabinet d'Avocats

Paul Agbonihoue
SBEE

Jean-Paul T. Hervé Ahoyo
Societe Beninoise D'Energie Electrique

Sybel Akueshson
FCA

Rafikou Alabi
Cabinet Me Alabi

Dieu-Donné Mamert Assogba
Cabinet Maître Adjai

Innocent Sourou Avognon
Ministère de la Justice et de la Legislation

Zachari Baba Body
Cabinet SPA Baba Body, Quenum et Sambaou

Charles Badou
Cabinet d'Avocat Charles Badou

Gabriel Bankole
Continental Bank

Agnès A. Campbell
Campbell & Associés

Eugene Capo-chichi
Ministère des Transports et des Travaux Publics

Michèle A. O. Carrena
Tribunal de Première Instance de Cotonou

Dae Stores Limited

Johannès Dagnon
Groupe Helios Afrique

Armand Dakehoun
Ministere des Mines, de l'Energie et de l'Eau

Dansou
Imoteph

Jonathan Darboux
BCEAO

Fatimatou Zahra Diop
BCEAO

Henri Fadonougbo
Tribunal de Premiere Instance

Francis Sètondji Fagnibo
Ministère des Finances et de l'Economie

Guy Médard Agbo Fayemi
Ordre National des Architectes et des Urbanistes

Jean Claude Gnamien
FIDAFRICA / PricewaterhouseCoopers

Hermann Gnango
FIDAFRICA / PricewaterhouseCoopers

Denis Hazoume
Continental Bank

Dominique Lales
Addax & Oryx Group

Evelyne M'Bassidgé
FIDAFRICA / PricewaterhouseCoopers

Adeline Messou
FIDAFRICA / PricewaterhouseCoopers

Severin-Maxime Quenum
Cabinet SPA Baba Body, Quenum et Sambaou

Dakehoun Armand S. Raoul
Ministère des Mines, de l'Energies et de l'Eau

Mohammed Rabiou Salouf
Chambre de Commerce et d'Industrie du Benin

Zakari Djibril Sambaou

Alice Codjia Sohouenou
Attorney-at-Law

Didier Sterlingot
SDV - SAGA

Dominique Taty
FIDAFRICA / PricewaterhouseCoopers

Chakirou Tidjani
Agence Béninoise de Promotion des Echanges Commerciaux

Abdoul' Azis Tidjani
Direction Générale des Impôts et des Domaines

Jean-Bosco Todjinou
Ordre National des Architectes et des Urbanistes

Roger Tohoundjo
Haute Cour de Justice

Fousséni Traoré
FIDAFRICA / PricewaterhouseCoopers

Konate Yacouba
France Transfo

Zitty Sarl

Donatien Adannou Zonon
Chambre de Commerce et d'Industrie du Benin

BHUTAN

Susan Collier
Orrick, Herrington & Sutcliffe LLP

Kincho Dorjee
Leko Packers

Ugyen Dorji
Thimphu City Corporation

Laxmi Prasad Giri
Bhutan National Bank Ltd

Tharchin Lhendup
Ministry of Finance

S.N. Muruli
Thimphu City Corporation

Sangay Penjore
Thimpu Municipal Co.

Sonam Tshering
Ministry of Finance

Sonam Wangchuk
Ministry of Finance

Tshering Wangchuk
Royal Court of Justice

Sonam P. Wangdi
Ministry of Economic Affairs

Tashi Wangmo
Ministry of Labour and Human Resources

BOLIVIA

Fernando Aguirre
Bufete Aguirre Soc. Civ.

Carolina Aguirre Urioste
Bufete Aguirre Soc. Civ.

Oswaldo Alvarez Wills
S&V Asociados S.R.L.

Daniela Aragones Cortez
Sanjines & Asociados Soc. Civ. Abogados

Jaime Araujo Camacho
Ferrere

Raúl A. Baldivia
Baldivia Unzaga & Asociados

Adrian Barrenechea Bazoberry
Criales, Urcullo & Antezana

Enrique Barrios
Guevara & Gutiérrez S.C.

Alexandra Blanco
Guevara & Gutiérrez S.C.

Francisco Bollini Roca
Ferrere

Walter B. Calla Cardenas
Colegio Departamental de Arquitectos de La Paz

Franklin Carrillo
PricewaterhouseCoopers

Jose A. Criales
Criales, Urcullo & Antezana

J. Christian Davila C.
SD Arquitectos

Karen Yovana Egüez Palma
Ferrere

Jeannine Forgues
Ferrere

Nicolas Franulic Casasnovas
Infocred - Servicio de Informacion Crediticia BIC s.a.

Jose E. Gamboa T.
Colegio Departamental de Arquitectos de La Paz

Michelle Giraldi Lacerda
PricewaterhouseCoopers

Renato Goitia Machicao
Hermes S.R.L.

Adriana Grizante de Almeida
PricewaterhouseCoopers

Ramiro Guevara
Guevara & Gutiérrez S.C.

Primitivo Gutiérrez
Guevara & Gutiérrez S.C.

Enrique F. Hurtado
Superintencia de Bancos y Entidades Financieras

Marcelo Hurtado-Sandoval
Salazar, Salazar

Carlos Alberto Iacia
PricewaterhouseCoopers

Jorge Luis Inchauste
Guevara & Gutiérrez S.C.

Paola Justiniano Arias
Sanjines & Asociados Soc. Civ. Abogados

Cesar Lora
PricewaterhouseCoopers

Reynaldo Marconi O.
Finrural

Gonzalo Mendieta Romero
Estudio de Abogados Mendieta Romero & Asociados

Luis Meneses M.
Alpasur

Jaime Merida Alvarez
Colegio Departamental de Arquitectos de La Paz

Ariel Morales Vasquez
C.R.& F. Rojas Abogados

Evany Oliveira
PricewaterhouseCoopers

Elidie P. Bifano
PricewaterhouseCoopers

Alejandro Peláez Kay
Indacochea & Asociados

Mariana Pereira Nava
Indacochea & Asociados

Oscar Antonio Plaza Ponte
Entidad De Servicios De Información Enserbic S.A.

Julio Quintanilla Quiroga
Quintanilla & Soria, Soc. Civ.

Carlos Ramirez Arroyo
C.R. & F. Rojas, member of Lex Mundi

Diego Rojas
C.R. & F. Rojas, member of Lex Mundi

Fernando Rojas
C.R. & F. Rojas, member of Lex Mundi

Mariela Rojas
Entidad De Servicios De Información Enserbic S.A.

Pilar Salasar
Bufete Aguirre Soc. Civ.

Sergio Salazar-Machicado
Salazar, Salazar

Fernando Salazar-Paredes
Salazar, Salazar

Sandra Salinas
C.R. & F. Rojas, member of Lex Mundi

Raoul Rodolpho Sanjines Elizagoyen
Sanjines & Asociados Soc. Civ. Abogados

Jennifer Shepard
SD Arquitectos

A. Mauricio Torrico Galindo
Quintanilla & Soria, Soc. Civ.

Roberto Viscafé Ureña
PricewaterhouseCoopers

Mauricio Zambrana Cuéllar
Infocred - Servicio de Informacion Crediticia BIC s.a.

BOSNIA AND HERZEGOVINA

Sabina Buco
PricewaterhouseCoopers

Emir Corhodzić
DLA Piper Weiss -Tessbach

Mark Davidson
PricewaterhouseCoopers

Višnja Dizdarević
Marić Law Office

Petros Doukas
IKRP Rokas & Partners

Ezmana Hadziavdić
Marić Law Office

Emin Hadzić
Marić Law Office

Senada Havić Hrenovica
LRC Credit Bureau

Ismeta Huremović
Land Registry Office of the Sarajevo Municipal Court

Nusmir Huskić
Marić Law Office

Haris Mesinović
IFC

Arela Jusufbašić
LAWYERS' OFFICE BOJANA TKALCIC-DJULIC, OLODAR PREBANIC & ADELA DRAGANOVIC

Muhidin Karšić
LAW OFFICE OF EMIR KOVAČEVIČ

Emmanuel Koenig
PRICEWATERHOUSECOOPERS

Vildana Mandalović
IKRP ROKAS & PARTNERS

Branko Marić
MARIĆ LAW OFFICE

Emir Pasanović
DLA PIPER WEISS -TESSBACH

Edisa Peštek
DLA PIPER WEISS -TESSBACH

Hasib Salkić
INTERŠPED

Mehmed Spaho
LAW OFFICE SPAHO

Anisa Strujić
MARIĆ LAW OFFICE

Bojana Tkalčić-Djulić
LAWYERS' OFFICE BOJANA TKALCIC-DJULIC, OLODAR PREBANIC & ADELA DRAGANOVIC

Mira Todorović-Symeonidi
IKRP ROKAS & PARTNERS

Selver Zaimović
LAW OFFICE SPAHO

BOTSWANA

Staffnurse Bangu T. Lesetedi-Keothepile
REGISTRAR OF COMPANIES, TRADE MARKS, PATENTS AND DESIGNS

John Carr-Hartley
ARMSTRONGS ATTORNEYS

Rizwan Desai
COLLINS NEWMAN & CO

Diba M. Diba
MINCHIN & KELLY ATTORNEYS

Guri Dobo
DOBSON AND COMPANY, CERTIFIED PUBLIC ACCOUNTANTS

Edward W. Fasholé-Luke II
LUKE & ASSOCIATES

Vincent Galeromeloe
TRANSUNION ITC

Laknath Jayawickrama
PRICEWATERHOUSECOOPERS

Bokani Machinya
COLLINS NEWMAN & CO

Dineo Makati-Mpho
COLLINS NEWMAN & CO

Mercia Bonzo Makgaleme
CHIBANDA, MAKGALEME & CO.

Finola McMahon
OSEI-OFEI SWABI & CO.

Diniar Minwalla
PRICEWATERHOUSECOOPERS

Claude A. Mojafi
MINISTRY OF LABOUR AND HOME AFFAIRS

Mmatshipi Motsepe
MANICA AFRICA PTY. LTD.

Jack Allan Mutua
TECTURA INTERNATIONAL BOTSWANA

Alfred B. Ngowi
UNIVERSITY OF BOTSWANA

Rajesh Narasimhan
GRANT THORNTON

Godfrey N. Nthomiwa
ADMINISTRATION OF JUSTICE

Kwadwo Osei-Ofei
OSEI-OFEI SWABI & CO.

Butler Phirie
PRICEWATERHOUSECOOPERS

Nikola Stojanovic
ABB (PTY) LTD

Juliana White
BOTSWANA STOCK EXCHANGE

Dave Williams
MINCHIN & KELLY

BRAZIL

Pedro Aguiar de Freitas
COMPANHIA VALE DO RIO DOCE

Antonio Aires
DEMAREST E ALMEIDA ADVOGADOS

Donizeet Andonio da Silva
DAS CONSULTORIA

Pedro Vitor Araujo da Costa
ESCRITORIO DE ADVOCACIA GOUVÊA VIEIRA

Flavia Bailone Marcilio Barbosa
VEIRANO ADVOGADOS

Priscyla Barbosa
VEIRANO ADVOGADOS

Renato Berger
TOZZINI FREIRE ADVOGADOS

Camila Biral
DEMAREST E ALMEIDA ADVOGADOS

Richard Blanchet
LOESER E PORTELA ADVOGADOS

Adriano Borges
DE VIVO WHITAKER E CASTRO ADVOGADOS

Daniel Bortolotto
CARGO LOGISTICS

Sergio Bronstein
VEIRANO ADVOGADOS

Júlio César Bueno
PINHEIRO NETO ADVOGADOS

Paulo Campana
FELSBERG, PEDRETTI, MANNRICH E AIDAR ADVOGADOS E CONSULTORES LEGAIS

Plinio Cesar Romanini
BANCO CENTRAL

Renato Chiodaro
DE VIVO WHITAKER E CASTRO ADVOGADOS

CENTRO UNIVERSITÁRIO CURITIBA

Fernanda Cirne Montorfano
ESCRITORIO DE ADVOCACIA GOUVÊA VIEIRA

Gilberto Deon Corrêa Junior
VEIRANO ADVOGADOS

Sidinei Corrêa Marques
BANCO CENTRAL

Adriana Daiuto
DEMAREST E ALMEIDA ADVOGADOS

Cleber Dal Rovere Peluzo
VISEU CUNHA ORICCHIO ADVOGADOS

Eduardo Depassier
LOESER E PORTELA ADVOGADOS

Roberta dos Reis Matheus
TRENCH ROSSI E WATANABE ADVOGADOS

José Ricardo dos Santos Luz Júnior
DUARTE GARCIA, CASELLI GUIMARÃES E TERRA ADVOGADOS

Roberta Feiten Silva
VEIRANO ADVOGADOS

Vanessa Felício
VEIRANO ADVOGADOS

Thomas Benes Felsberg
FELSBERG, PEDRETTI, MANNRICH E AIDAR ADVOGADOS E CONSULTORES LEGAIS

Danielle Ferreiro
PINHEIRO GUIMARÃES ADVOGADOS

Rafael Frota Indio do Brasil Ferraz
ESCRITORIO DE ADVOCACIA GOUVÊA VIEIRA

Rafael Gagliardi
DEMAREST E ALMEIDA ADVOGADOS

Flavia Bailone Marcilio Barbosa
Thiago Giantomassi
DEMAREST E ALMEIDA ADVOGADOS

Michelle Giraldi Lacerda
PRICEWATERHOUSECOOPERS

Adriana Grizante de Almeida
PRICEWATERHOUSECOOPERS

Enrique Hadad
LOESER E PORTELA ADVOGADOS

Mery Ellen Hidalgo
NEW DEAL

Carlos Alberto Iacia
PRICEWATERHOUSECOOPERS

Christopher Jarvinen
PINHEIRO NETO ADVOGADOS

Esther Jerussalmy
ARAÚJO E POLICASTRO ADVOGADOS

Fernando Loeser
LOESER E PORTELA ADVOGADOS

Marina Maccabelli
DEMAREST E ALMEIDA ADVOGADOS

André Marques
PINHEIRO NETO ADVOGADOS

Georges Louis Martens Filho
DE VIVO, WHITAKER, CASTRO E GONÇALVES ADVOGADOS

Thiago Martins
ARAÚJO E POLICASTRO ADVOGADOS

Jose Augusto Martins
BAKER & MCKENZIE

Laura Massetto Meyer
PINHEIRO GUIMARÃES ADVOGADOS

Rodrigo Matos
MBM TRADING

Eduardo Augusto Mattar
PINHEIRO GUIMARÃES ADVOGADOS

Anneliese Moritz
FELSBERG, PEDRETTI, MANNRICH E AIDAR ADVOGADOS E CONSULTORES LEGAIS

Walter Abrahão Nimir Junior
DE VIVO, WHITAKER, CASTRO E GONÇALVES ADVOGADOS

Evany Oliveira
PRICEWATERHOUSECOOPERS

Andrea Oricchio Kirsh
VISEU CUNHA ORICCHIO ADVOGADOS

Elidie P. Bifano
PRICEWATERHOUSECOOPERS

Maria Fernanada Pecora
VEIRANO ADVOGADOS

Fabio Luis Pereira Barboza
VISEU CUNHA ORICCHIO ADVOGADOS

Andréa Pitthan Françolin
DE VIVO, WHITAKER, CASTRO E GONÇALVES ADVOGADOS

Durval Portela
LOESER E PORTELA ADVOGADOS

PONTIFÍCIA UNIVERSIDADE CATÓLICA DO PARANÁ

Eliane Ribeiro Gago
DUARTE GARCIA, CASELLI GUIMARÃES E TERRA ADVOGADOS

Guilherme Rizzo Amaral
VEIRANO ADVOGADOS

João Rodrigues
VEIRANO ADVOGADOS

Carlos Santos
SANTOS CONSULTING

Camilla Sisti
ARAÚJO E POLICASTRO ADVOGADOS

Claudio Taveira
PINHEIRO NETO ADVOGADOS

Enrique Tello Hadad
LOESER E PORTELA ADVOGADOS

Marcos Tiraboschi
VEIRANO ADVOGADOS

Fábio Tokars
JUNTA COMERCIAL DO PARANA

Luiz Fernando Valente De Paiva
PINHEIRO NETO ADVOGADOS

José Wahle
VEIRANO ADVOGADOS

Eduardo Guimarães Wanderley
VEIRANO ADVOGADOS

Celso Xavier
DEMAREST E ALMEIDA ADVOGADOS

BRUNEI

ARKITEK IBRAHIM

Danny Chua
BRUNEI TRANSPORTING COMPANY

Michael Guan
LEE CORPORATEHOUSE ASSOCIATES

Nancy Lai
LEE CORPORATEHOUSE ASSOCIATES

Kin Chee Lee
LEE CORPORATEHOUSE ASSOCIATES

Yew Choh Lee
Y.C. LEE & LEE ADVOCATES & SOLICITORS

Teck Guan Lim
ERNST & YOUNG

Kelvin Lim
K. LIM & CO.

Guillaume Madru
SDV

Colin Ong
DR. COLIN ONG LEGAL SERVICES

BULGARIA

Svetlin Adrianov
PENKOV, MARKOV & PARTNERS

Nikolay Bandakov
KAMBOUROV & PARTNERS

Christo Batchvarov
PRICEWATERHOUSECOOPERS

Ilian Beslemeshki
GEORGIEV, TODOROV & CO.

Nikolai Bozhilov
UNIMASTERS LOGISTICS PLC.

Stella Bozova
STOEVA, KUYUMDJIEVA & VITLIEMOV

Emil Cholakov
LM LEGAL SERVICES LTD.

Marta Del Coto
LANDWELL, PRICEWATERHOUSECOOPERS LEGAL SERVICES

Borislav Dimitrov
LANDWELL, PRICEWATERHOUSECOOPERS LEGAL SERVICES

Kristina Dimitrova
LANDWELL, PRICEWATERHOUSECOOPERS LEGAL SERVICES

Elina Dimova
LIC - PENKOV, MARKOV & PARTNERS

Lora Docheva
PRICEWATERHOUSECOOPERS

Bogdan Drenski
GEORGIEV, TODOROV & CO.

ECONOMOU INTERNATIONAL SHIPPING AGENCY LIMITED, VARNA

Georgy Georgiev
LANDWELL, PRICEWATERHOUSECOOPERS LEGAL SERVICES

Marieta Getcheva
PRICEWATERHOUSECOOPERS

Ralitsa Gougleva
DJINGOV, GOUGINSKI, KYUTCHUKOV & VELICHKOV

Katerina Gramatikova
DOBREV, KINKIN & LYUTSKANOV

Iassen Hristev
DOBREV, KINKIN &
LYUTSKANOV

Ginka Iskrova
PRICEWATERHOUSECOOPERS

Angel Kalaidjiev
KALAIDJIEV, GEORGIEV &
MINCHEV

Yabor Kambourov
KAMBOUROV & PARTNERS

Hristina Kirilova
KAMBOUROV & PARTNERS

Lilia Kisseva
DJINGOV, GOUGINSKI,
KYUTCHUKOV & VELICHKOV

Donko Kolev
ASTA BRIDGE INTERNATIONAL

Ilya Komarevski
LANDWELL,
PRICEWATERHOUSECOOPERS
LEGAL SERVICES

Boika Komsulova
PRICEWATERHOUSECOOPERS

Dessislava Lukarova
ARSOV NATCHEV GANEVA

Ivan Markov
LIC - PENKOV, MARKOV &
PARTNERS

Gergana Monovska
DJINGOV, GOUGINSKI,
KYUTCHUKOV & VELICHKOV

Vladimir Natchev
ARSOV NATCHEV GANEVA

Yordan Naydenov
BORISLAV BOYANOV & CO.

Violeta Nikolova
ARSOV NATCHEV GANEVA

Darina Oresharova
EXPERIAN BULGARIA EAD

Alexander Pachamanov
GEORGIEV, TODOROV & CO.

Yordanka Panchovska
GEORGIEV, TODOROV & CO.

Miglena Peneva
GEORGIEV, TODOROV & CO.

Vladimir Penkov
PENKOV, MARKOV & PARTNERS

Galina Petkova
ARSOV NATCHEV GANEVA

Borislava Pokrass
STOEVA, KUYUMDJIEVA &
VITLIEMOV

Gerdana Popova
GEORGIEV, TODOROV & CO.

Nikolav Radev
DOBREV, KINKIN &
LYUTSKANOV

Nevena Radlova
STOEVA, KUYUMDJIEVA &
VITLIEMOV

Alexander Rangelov
PRICEWATERHOUSECOOPERS

Anna Saeva
BORISLAV BOYANOV & CO.

Stela Slavcheva
ASPOLLY CARRASS
INTERNATIONAL LTD.

Violeta Slavova
EXPERIAN BULGARIA EAD

Irina Stoeva
STOEVA, KUYUMDJIEVA &
VITLIEMOV

Roman Stoyanov
LIC - PENKOV, MARKOV &
PARTNERS

Margarita Stoyanova
KAMBOUROV & PARTNERS

Peter Takov
LANDWELL,
PRICEWATERHOUSECOOPERS
LEGAL SERVICES

Laura Thomas
LM LEGAL SERVICES LTD.

Svilen Todorov
TODOROV & DOYKOVA LAW
FIRM

Matea Tsenkova
DJINGOV, GOUGINSKI,
KYUTCHUKOV & VELICHKOV

Stefan Tzakov
KAMBOUROV & PARTNERS,
ATTORNEYS AT LAW

Maria Urmanova
LANDWELL,
PRICEWATERHOUSECOOPERS
LEGAL SERVICES

Miroslav Varnaliev
UNIMASTERS LOGISTICS PLC.

Pavel Vitliemov
STOEVA, KUYUMDJIEVA &
VITLIEMOV

Vera Yaneva
PENKOV, MARKOV & PARTNERS

BURKINA FASO

Campene A Theophile

Fortune Bicaba

Dieudonne Bonkoungou

Birika Jean Claude Bonzi

B. Thierry Compaoré
INGENIERIE-DESIGN-
ARCHITECTURE

Bernardin Dabire
CABINET BERNARDIN DABIRE

Laurent-Michel Dabire
CABINET BERNARDIN DABIRE

Jonathan Darboux
BCEAO

Denis Dawende
OFFICE NOTARIAL ME JEAN
CELESTIN ZOURE

Sylvie Dembelé

Daouda Diallo
FISC CONSULTING
INTERNATIONAL

Fatimatou Zahra Diop
BCEAO

Jean Claude Gnamien
FIDAFRICA /
PRICEWATERHOUSECOOPERS

Hermann Gnango
FIDAFRICA /
PRICEWATERHOUSECOOPERS

Sibi Desire Gouba
OFFICE NOTARIAL ME JEAN
CELESTIN ZOURE

Issaka Kargourou
MAISON DE L'ENTREPRISE DU
BURKINA FASO

Barthélemy Kere
CABINET D'AVOCATS
BARTHÉLEMY KERE

Gilbert Kibtonre
CEFAC

Messan Lawson

Colette Lefebvre
INSPECTION DU TRAVAIL

Ido Leocaldie
CABINET BERNARDIN DABIRE

Evelyne Mandessi Bell
CABINET OUEDRAOGO &
BONKOUNGOU

Evelyne M'Bassidgé
FIDAFRICA /
PRICEWATERHOUSECOOPERS

Adeline Messou
FIDAFRICA /
PRICEWATERHOUSECOOPERS

Oumarou Ouedraogo
AVOCAT À LA COUR

N. Henri Ouedraogo
MINISTERE DES FINANCES ET
DU BUDGET

François de Salle Ouedraogo
SOCIETE NATIONALE
D'ELECTRICITE DU BURKINA

Benewende S. Sankara
CABINET MAITRE SANKARA

Hermann Sanon
OFFICE NOTARIAL ME JEAN
CELESTIN ZOURE

Michel Sawadogo
UNIVERSITÉ DE
OUAGADOUGOU

Moussa Sogodogo
AVOCAT À LA COUR

Barterlé Mathieu Some
AVOCAT À LA COUR

Thombiano Sylvain
EPURE

Dominique Taty
FIDAFRICA /
PRICEWATERHOUSECOOPERS

Clément Toe
GÉNÉRAL D'ELECTRICITÉ ET
DIVERS

Fousséni Traoré
FIDAFRICA /
PRICEWATERHOUSECOOPERS

Bouba Yaguibou

Seydou Roger Yamba
CABINET MAITRE SANKARA

Gilles Corneille Yaméogo
BARREAU DU BURKINA FASO

Ousmane Prosper Zoungrana

Théophane Noël Zoure
OFFICE NOTARIAL ME JEAN
CELESTIN ZOURE

BURUNDI

Bireha Audace
BANQUES-MICROFINANCE-
GESTION IMMOBILIÈRE

Joseph Bahizi
BANQUE DE LA RÉPUBLIQUE
DU BURUNDI

Sylvestre Banzubaze
AVOCAT AU BARREAU DU
BURUNDI

Emmanuel Hakizimana
CAB. D'AVOCATS-CONSEILS

Dominik Kohlhagen
CHERCHEUR AU LABORATOIRE
D'ANTHROPOLOGIE JURIDIQUE
DE PARIS

Augustin Mabushi
A & JN MABUSHI CABINET
D'AVOCATS

Jean Marie Mudende
REPUBLIQUE DE BURUNDI
MINISTERE DE LA JUSTICE

Bonaventure Nicimpaye
INTERCONTACT SERVICES, S.A.

Bernard Ntahiraja
CABINET WILLY RUBEYA

Tharcisse Ntakiyica
BARREAU DU BURUNDI

Daniel Ntawurishira
SDV TRANSAMI - GROUPE
BOLLORÉ

François Nyamoya
AVOCAT À LA COUR

Déogratias Nzemba
AVOCAT À LA COUR

Laurent Nzeyimana
PRESIDENT DU CONSEIL
D'ARBITRAGE CEBAC

Phillipe Pasquali
SDV TRANSAMI - GROUPE
BOLLORÉ

Prosper Ringuyeneza
ARCHITECTURE ET
CONSTRUCTION (A.C.)

Willy Rubeya
CABINET WILLY RUBEYA

Benjamin Rufagari
DELOITTE & TOUCHE

Clémence Rwamo
MINISTÈRE DE LA JUSTICE

Fabien Segatwa
ETUDE ME SEGATWA

Gabriel Sinarinzi
CABINET ME GABRIEL
SINARINZI

Salvatore Sindayihebura
SDV TRANSAMI - GROUPE
BOLLORÉ

Audace Sunzu
REGIDESO-BURUNDI

CAMBODIA

Chan Koulika Bo
B.N.G.

Kate Bugeja
ARBITRATION COUNCIL
FOUNDATION

Keokolreak Buth
VANNA & ASSOCIATES LAW
FIRM

Huot Chea
THE WORLD BANK

Michael Cheah
SAGGARA CORPORATION

Phanin Cheam
MUNICIPALITY OF PHNOM
PENH BUREAU OF URBAN
AFFAIRS

Rithy Chey
B.N.G

Boyan Chhan
INDOCHINA RESEARCH

Ngov Chong
PRICEWATERHOUSECOOPERS

Brennan Coleman
DFDL MEKONG LAW GROUP

Sandra D'Amico
HR INC. (CAMBODIA) CO.,
LTD.

Louis-Martin Desautels
DFDL MEKONG LAW GROUP

Senaka Fernando
PRICEWATERHOUSECOOPERS

Rob Force
DFDL MEKONG LAW GROUP

Stephane Guimbert
THE WORLD BANK GROUP

Phea Ham
CHHUN VINITA LAW OFFICE

Svay Hay
ACLEDA BANK PLC.

Kent Helmers
INDOCHINA RESEARCH

Naryth H Hour
B.N.G.

Tim Holzer
DFDL MEKONG LAW GROUP

Santhea Houn
NARITA LOGISTICS &
SERVICES/PANALPINA

Dourng Kakada
ECONOMIC INSTITUTE OF
CAMBODIA

May Kano
ACLEDA BANK PLC.

Sakhan Khom
ARBITRATION COUNCIL
FOUNDATION

Chhung Kong
DFDL MEKONG LAW GROUP

Kheng Leang
NARITA LOGISTICS &
SERVICES/PANALPINA

Jean Loi
PRICEWATERHOUSECOOPERS

Janet H. Lueckenhausen
FUNCTIONAL ENGINEERING

Tayseng Ly
HBS LAW FIRM &
CONSULTANTS

Nimmith Men
ARBITRATION COUNCIL
FOUNDATION

Jacqueline Menyhart
B.N.G

Eric Metayer
NARITA LOGISTICS &
SERVICES/PANALPINA

Long Mom
RAF INTERNATIONAL
FORWARDING INC.

Kaing Monika
THE GARMENT
MANUFACTURERS
ASSOCIATION IN CAMBODIA

Laurent Notin
INDOCHINA RESEARCH

Ry Ouk
BOU NOU OUK & PARTNERS

Phan Phalla
SUPREME NATIONAL
ECONOMIC COUNSEL

Pisetha Pin
SAMNANG CRM COMPANY
LIMITED

Soleil Della Pong
HR INC. (CAMBODIA) CO.,
LTD.

Sour Por
GLOBAL LINK SERVICE PTE LTD.

Sovannorak Rath
NATIONAL BANK

Kuntheapini Saing
ARBITRATION COUNCIL FOUNDATION

Denora Sarin
SARIN & ASSOCIATES

Chanthy Sin
LINEX

Sorya Sin
SHA TRANSPORT EXPRESS CO. LTD.

Billie Jean Slott
SCIARONI & ASSOCIATES

Lor Sok
ARBITRATION COUNCIL FOUNDATION

Chamnan Som
CAMBODIAN FEDERATION OF EMPLOYERS AND BUSINESS ASSOCIATIONS

Sorphea Sou
ARBITRATION COUNCIL FOUNDATION

David Symansky
HR INC. (CAMBODIA) CO., LTD.

Michael Tan
RAF INTERNATIONAL FORWARDING INC.

Vann Tho
ACLEDA BANK PLC

Janvibol Tip
TIP & PARTNERS

Iv Visal
ELECTRICITE DU CAMBODGE

Sal Viseth
SAL CHANTHA

CAMEROON

Mobeh Andre
MAERSK S.A.

Gilbert Awah Bongam
ACHU AND FON-NDIKUM LAW FIRM

Richard Batchato
SERVICE DU CADASTRE

David Boyo
JING & PARTNERS

Anne Marie Dibounje Jocke
CABINET MAITRE ELISE LOTTIN

Paul Marie Djamen
BICEC

Laurent Dongmo
JING & PARTNERS

Ivonne Egbe
SERVICES DES DOMAINES

Evariste Elundou
MAERSK S.A.

Lucas Florent Essomba
CABINET ESSOMBA & ASSOCIÉS

Jean Pierre Eyoum Mandengue
ETUDE NOTARIALE EYOUM MANDENGUE

Atsishi Fon Ndikum
ACHU AND FON-NDIKUM LAW FIRM

Philippe Fouda Fouda
BEAC

Caroline Idrissou-Belingar
BEAC

Angoh Angoh Jacob
NICO HALLE & CO. LAW FIRM

Paul Jing
JING & PARTNERS

Henri Pierre Job
CABINET D'AVOCATS HENRI JOB

Serge Jokung
CABINET MAÎTRE MARIE ANDRÉE NGWE

Jean Aime Kounga
CABINET D'AVOCATS ABENG ROLAND

Kumfa Jude Kwenyui
JURIS CONSUL LAW FIRM

Ariane Marceau-Cotte
CABINET MAÎTRE MARIE ANDRÉE NGWE

Danielle Mbape
JING & PARTNERS

Alain Serges Mbebi
CABINET CADIRE

Augustin Yves Mbock Keked
CABINET CADIRE

Clarence Mireille Moni Nseke Epse Etame
CABINET MAITRE ELISE LOTTIN

Bérangère Monin
FIDAFRICA / PRICEWATERHOUSECOOPERS

Jean Jacques Moukory Eyango
CABINET MAITRE ELISE LOTTIN

Raoul Mouthe
NIMBA CONSEIL

Aimé Ndock Len
M & N LAW FIRM, CABINET D'AVOCATS

Marcelin Ndoum
ETUDE DE NOTAIRE Wo'o

Isidore Baudouin Ndzana
FIDAFRICA / PRICEWATERHOUSECOOPERS

Simon Pierre Nemba
CABINET MAÎTRE MARIE ANDRÉE NGWE

Julius Ngu Tabe Achu
ACHU AND FON-NDIKUM LAW FIRM

Marie-Andrée Ngwe
CABINET MAÎTRE MARIE ANDRÉE NGWE

Mbah Martin Njah
NICO HALLE & CO. LAW FIRM

Pierre Njigui
ABB CAMEROON

Patrice Guy Njoya
CABINET MAÎTRE MARIE ANDRÉE NGWE

Jacques Nyemb
CABINET NYEMB

Christian O'Jeanson
MAERSK S.A.

André-Marie Owono
CABINET NYEMB

Blaise Talla
CABINET JURIDIQUE MOUTHE & ASSOCIES SARL

Dominique Taty
FIDAFRICA / PRICEWATERHOUSECOOPERS

Charles Tchuente
CABINET NYEMB

Jude Yong Yeh
CABINET CADIRE

CANADA

David Bish
GOODMANS LLP

Jay A. Carfagnini
GOODMANS LLP

Allan Coleman
OSLER, HOSKIN & HARCOURT LLP

David Cooper
BORDEN LADNER GERVAIS LLP

Gilles Demers
GROUPE OPTIMUM

Jeremy Fraiberg
OSLER, HOSKIN & HARCOURT LLP

Anne Glover
BLAKE, CASSELS & GRAYDON, MEMBER OF LEX MUNDI

Yoine Goldstein
McMILLAN BINCH MENDELSOHN

Steven Golick

Pamela S. Hughes
BLAKE, CASSELS & GRAYDON, MEMBER OF LEX MUNDI

Andrew Kent
McMILLAN BINCH MENDELSOHN

Matthew Kindree
BAKER & McKENZIE LLP

Joshua Kochath
COMAGE CONTAINER LINES

Susan Leslie
FIRST CANADIAN TITLE

Charles Magerman
BAKER & McKENZIE LLP

Thomas O'Brien
PRICEWATERHOUSECOOPERS

Alfred Page
BORDEN LADNER GERVAIS LLP

John Pirie
BAKER & McKENZIE LLP

Sam Rappos

Bruce Reynolds
BORDEN LADNER GERVAIS LLP

Damian Rigolo
OSLER, HOSKIN & HARCOURT LLP

Paul Robinson
CORPORATIONS CANADA

Kelly Russell
PRICEWATERHOUSECOOPERS

Paul Schabas
BLAKE, CASSELS & GRAYDON, MEMBER OF LEX MUNDI

Irina Schnitzer
DAVIS LLP

Nicholas Scheib
McMILLAN BINCH MENDELSOHN

SDV

Sharon Vogel
BORDEN LADNER GERVAIS LLP

Kim Wood
PRICEWATERHOUSECOOPERS

CAPE VERDE

Hermínio Afonso
PRICEWATERHOUSECOOPERS

Janira Hopffer Almada
D. HOPFFER ALMADA E ASSOCIADOS

Nandixany Andrade
ARNALDO SILVA & ASSOCIADOS

Vera Andrade
CWV ADVOGADOS

Braz de Andrade
FIRMA BRAZ DE ANDRADE

Mary Braz de Andrade
FIRMA BRAZ DE ANDRADE

Susana Caetano
PRICEWATERHOUSECOOPERS

Vasco Carvalho Oliveira Ramos
ENGIC

Ilíldio Cruz
GABINETE DE ADVOCACIA CONSULTORIA E PROCURADORIA JURIDICA

Zacarias De Pina
ENGEOBRA

Victor Adolfo de Pinto Osório
ATTORNEY-AT-LAW

Jorge Lima Delgado Lopes
NÚCLEO OPERACIONAL DA SOCIEDADE DE INFORMAÇÃO

João Dono
JOÃO DONO ADVOGADOS

Ana Duarte
PRICEWATERHOUSECOOPERS

John Duggan
PRICEWATERHOUSECOOPERS

Djassi Fonseca
NOSI

Florentino Jorge Fonseca Jesus
MUNICIPALIDADE PRAIA

Paulo Godinho
PRICEWATERHOUSECOOPERS

Eduardo Nascimento Gomes
EMPRESA PÚBLICA DE ELECTRICIDADE E ÁGUA

Joana Gomes Rosa
ADVOGADA

Agnaldo Laice
MAERSK LINE

Jose Manuel Fausto Lima
ELECTRA PRAIA

Ana Denise Lima Barber
CWV ADVOGADOS

Antonio Lopes
PRICEWATERHOUSECOOPERS

Maria de Fatima Lopes Varela
BANCO CENTRAL DE CABO VERDE

Ricardo Martins
ELECTRA

Paulo Noel Martins
PRIME CONSULTING GROUP

João M.A. Mendes
AUDITEC - AUDITORES & CONSULTORES

Carlos Pereira Modesto
MODESTO - DESPACHANTE

Fernando Aguiar Monteiro
ADVOGADOS ASSOCIADOS

Ricardo Cláudio Monteiro Gonçlaves
PALÁCIO DE JUSTIÇA DO TRIBUNAL DA COMARCA DA PRAIA

Milton Paiva
D. HOPFFER ALMADA E ASSOCIADOS

Carlos Gregorio Lopes Pereira Goncalves
CONSERVATORIA DE REGISTOS PREDIAL COMERCIAL & AUTOMOVEIS

Eldetrudes Pires Neves
ARAÚJO, NEVES, SANTOS & MIRANDA, ADVOGADOS ASSOCIADOS

Armando J.F. Rodrigues
PRICEWATERHOUSECOOPERS

José Rui de Sena
AGÊNCIA DE DESPACHO ADUANEIRO FERREIRA E SENA LDA

Tito Lívio Santos Oliveira Ramos
ENGIC

Henrique Semedo Borges
ADVOGADO

Arnaldo Silva
ARNALDO SILVA & ASSOCIADOS

Maria Fernanda Silva Ramos
BCA - GABINETE JURIDICO

Mario Alberto Tavares
MUNICIPALITY

João Carlos Tavares Fidalgo
BANCO CENTRAL

Elsa Tavazes
CWV ADVOGADOS

Jorge Lima Teixeira
ARCHITECT

Tereza Teixeira B. Amado
AMADO & MEDINA ADVOGADAS

Leendert Verschoor
PRICEWATERHOUSECOOPERS

CENTRAL AFRICAN REPUBLIC

Richard Anokonayen
MINISTERIE DE LA FONCTION PUBLIQUE

Max Symphorien Babdiba
CLUB OHADA

Jean Christophe Bakossa
L'ORDRE CENTRAFICAIN DES ARCHITECTES

Emile Bizon
CABINET TIANGAYE - UNIVERSITÉ DE BANGUI

Michel Desprez
SDV CENTRAFRIQUE - GROUPE BOLLORÉ

Maurice Dibert- Dollet
MINISTÈRE DE LA JUSTICE

Bertin-Rufin Dimanche
MINISTÈRE DES FINANCES, DIRECTION GÉNÉRALE DES IMPÔTS ET DES DOMAINES

Christiane Doraz-Serefessenet
SECRÉTAIRE GÉNÉRALE DE LA CHAMBRE DES NOTAIRES

Marie-Edith Douzima-Lawson
Cabinet Douzima
&Ministère de la fonction
publique

Energie Centrafricaine
(ENERCA)

Philippe Fouda Fouda
BEAC

Dolly Gotilogue

Isidore Grothe
Ministère des Finances et
du Budget

Gabriel Houndoni
Club OHADA

Caroline Idrissou-Belingar
BEAC

Noel Kelembho
SDV - Groupe Bolloré

Bouna Loumandet Chrésia
Etude Notariale

Jean Paul Maradas Nado
Ministere de l'Urbanisme

Anasthasie Mbo-Gaudeuille
Chambre de Commerce
d'Industrie des mines et de
L'artisanat

Serge Médard Missamou
Club OHADA

Yves Namkomokoina
Magistrat, Commerce
Tribunal

Jean Baptiste Nouganga
Bureau Comptable Fiscal -
Cabinet Nouganga

Bako Sah
Architect

CHAD

Abdelkerim Ahmat
SDV

Oscar D'Estaing Deffosso
FIDAFRICA /
PricewaterhouseCoopers

Baba Dina
Stat N'Djaména

Mahamat Djibrine
STD

N'Doningar Djimasna
Faculté de Droit,
Université de N'Djamena

Philippe Fouda Fouda
BEAC

Caroline Idrissou-Belingar
BEAC

Narcisse Madjiyore Dongar

Issa Ngarmbassa
Etude Me Issa Ngar mbassa

Nissaouabé Passang
Etude Me Passang

Nicolas Ronzié
FIDAFRICA /
PricewaterhouseCoopers

Gilles Schwarz
SDV

Dominique Taty
FIDAFRICA /
PricewaterhouseCoopers

Nadine Tinen Tchangoum
FIDAFRICA /
PricewaterhouseCoopers

Sobdibé Zoua
Law Firm SCPP

CHILE

Angie Armer Rios
Alvarez Hinzpeter Jana

Sandra Benedetto
PricewaterhouseCoopers

Jorge Benitez Urrutia
Urrutia & Cía

Jimena Bronfman
Guerrero, Olivos, Novoa y
Errázuriz

Héctor Carrasco
Superintendencia de
Bancos e Instituciones
Financieras

Paola Casorzo
Philippi, Yrarrazaval,
Pulido & Brunner

Andrés Chirgwin
Alvarez Hinzpeter Jana

Camilo Cortés
Alessandri & Compañía

Sergio Cruz
Cruz & Cia. Abogados

José Ignacio Díaz
Yrarrázaval, Ruiz-
Tagle,Goldenberg,Lagos
& Silva

Cristián S. Eyzaguirre
Eyzaguirre & Cía.

Silvio Figari Napoli
Databusiness

Cristian Garcia-Huidobro
Boletin Comercial

Juan Pablo Gonzalez M.
Guerrero, Olivos, Novoa y
Errázuriz

Mauricio Hederra
Cruz & Cía Abogados

Javier Hurtado
Camara Chilena de la
Construccion

Fernando Jamarne
Alessandri & Compañía

Didier Lara
PricewaterhouseCoopers

León Larrain
Baker & McKenzie (Cruzat,
Ortúzar y Mackenna
Ltda.)

Enrique Munita
Philippi, Yrarrazaval,
Pulido & Brunner

Cristian Olavarria
Philippi, Yrarrazaval,
Pulido & Brunner

Gerardo Ovalle Mahns
Yrarrázaval, Ruiz-Tagle,
Goldenberg, Lagos &Silva

Luis Parada Hoyl
Bahamondez, Alvarez &
Zegers

Pablo Paredes
Albagli Zaliasnik
Abogados

Beatriz Recar
Baker & McKenzie (Cruzat,
Ortúzar y Mackenna
Ltda.)

Sebastián Riesco
Eyzaguirre & Cía.

Claudio Rivera
Carey y Cía Ltda.

Edmundo Rojas García
Conservador de Bienes
Raíces de Santiago

Alvaro Rosenblut
Albagli Zaliasnik
Abogados

Carlos Saavedra
Cruz & Cia. Abogados

Adriana Salias
Redlines Group

Martín Santa María O.
Guerrero, Olivos, Novoa y
Errázuriz

Carlos Saveedra
Cruz & Cía Abogados

Esteban Tomic
Cruz & Cia. Abogados

Jorge Valenzuela
Philippi, Yrarrazaval,
Pulido & Brunner

Sebastián Valdivieso
Yrarrázaval, Ruiz - Tagle,
Goldenberg, Lagos &Silva

Osvaldo Villagra
PricewaterhouseCoopers

Arturo Yrarrázaval
Covarrubias
Yrarrazaval, Ruiz - Tagle
Goldenburg, Lagos & Silva

Sebastián Yunge
Guerrero, Olivos, Novoa y
Errázuriz

Rony Zimerman M.
Alvarez Hinzpeter Jana

CHINA

Russell Brown
LehmanBrown

Robin Cai
BNP Service

Rico Chan
Baker & McKenzie

John Chan
Fuzhou Relax Co., Ltd.

Rex Chan
PricewaterhouseCoopers

Yixin Chen
Davis Polk & Wardwell

Caro Chen
Dniya Ornaments Co., Ltd.

Lisa Chen
Jiahua Co.

Jie Chen
Jun He Law Offices, member
of Lex Mundi

Barry Cheung
KPMG Huazhen

Bolivia Cheung
KPMG Huazhen

Taylor Chuang
Innovation Medical
Instrument Co., Ltd.

Yw Chung
Baker Botts LLP

Tony Diao
Shaughnessy Holdings Ltd.

Wayne Forfine
Forfine Marketing &
Service

Wei Gao
ZY & Partners

Leo Ge
Global Star Logistics Co.
Ltd.

Alex Gee
Shanghai Pegasus
Materials Co., Ltd.

Alexander Gong
Baker & McKenzie

Kejun Guo
DeHeng Law Offices

Felix Hu
Shanghai Meiyao Aviation
Co., Ltd.

Simon Huang
LehmanBrown

Haining XinGuangYuan
Lighting Co., Ltd.

Kone Jerry
Zhejiang Gangzida
Industry & Trade Co., Ltd.

Zhou Jianming
Ningbo Jingcheng Meter

John T. Kuzmik
Baker Botts LLP

John Kuznik
Baker Botts LLP

Jony Lee
Sanli Group

Berry Lin
SDV Ltd.

Zhiqiang Liu
King & Wood

Lucy Lu
King & Wood

George Luo
Pinsent Masons

Mikkaworks Organics

Nicky Ning
Luoyang Chundi Import &
Export Co., Ltd.

Nonnon Pan
Medplus Inc.

Catherine Rown

Han Shen
Davis Polk & Wardwell

Cathy Shi
Orrick, Herrington &
Sutcliffe LLP

Frank Shu
Paul Hasting

Jessie Tang
Global Star Logistics Co.
Ltd.

Youshan Tang
Ningbo Flight Rigging &
Tool Co., Ltd.

Emily Tang
Orrick, Herrington &
Sutcliffe LLP

Lu Terry
Shenyang Longyuan Group
Co., Ltd.

Wafangdian Yushi Energy
Co., Ltd.

Celia Wang
PricewaterhouseCoopers

Fenghe Wang
Dacheng Law Offices

William Wang
PricewaterhouseCoopers

Luke Wang
Shanghai Deso Industry
Co., Ltd

Waynex Industrial Co., Ltd.

Cassie Wong
PricewaterhouseCoopers

Kent Woo
Kingson Law Firm

Annie Xun

Qing Yang
Yang Fit Co., Ltd.

Bill Yao
Simple Technic Co., Ltd.

Susan Ye
KPMG Huazhen

Jerry Ye
Orrick

Jonathan You
Orrick, Herrington &
Sutcliffe LLP

Xianghau Yu
Shanghai Xu Xiao Qing Law
Office

Xianghua Yunge
Shanghai Xu Xiao Qing Law
Office

Libin Zhang
Baker Botts LLP

Yi Zhang
King & Wood PRC Lawyers

Johnson Zheng
Xiamen All Carbon
Corporation

COLOMBIA

Carlos Alcala
José Lloreda Camacho
& Co.

Mauricio Angulo
Computec - DataCrédito

Patricia Arrázola-Bustillo
Gómez-Pinzón Abogados

Luis Alfredo Barragán
Brigard & Urrutia, member
of Lex Mundi

Pablo Barraquer-Uprimny
Brigard & Urrutia, member
of Lex Mundi

Guillermo Hernando Bayona
Combariza
Notaria ☒ de Bogotá

Juliana Bazzani Botero
José Lloreda Camacho
& Co.

Juan Guillermo Becerra
PricewaterhouseCoopers

Claudia Benavides
Gómez-Pinzón Abogados

Nicolás Botero
Holguín, Neira & Pombo
Abogados

Carlos Rodríguez Calero
PricewaterhouseCoopers

Maria Paula Camacho
Cámara Colombiana de la
Construcción

Bibiana Camacho
Cavelier Abogados

Carolina Camacho
Posse Herrera & Ruiz

Darío Cárdenas
Cárdenas & Cárdenas

Natalia Caroprese
BAKER & MCKENZIE

Felipe Cuberos
PRIETO & CARRIZOSA S.A.

María Helena Díaz Méndez
PRICEWATERHOUSECOOPERS

Jose Duran
EXCELLENTIA STRATEGIC

Lucas Fajardo-Gutierrez
BRIGARD & URRUTIA, MEMBER OF LEX MUNDI

Gustavo Florez
SOCIEDAD PORTUARIA REGIONAL DE CARTAGENA

Carlos Fradique-Méndez
BRIGARD & URRUTIA, MEMBER OF LEX MUNDI

Ana Giraldo
PRIETO & CARRIZOSA S.A.

Santiago Gutiérrez
JOSÉ LLOREDA CAMACHO & CO.

Viviana Hernández Grajales
CÁMARA COLOMBIANA DE LA CONSTRUCCIÓN

Wilson Herrera Robles
PRICEWATERHOUSE COOPERS

Santiago Higuera
CÁMARA COLOMBIANA DE LA CONSTRUCCIÓN

Mario Hoyos
JOSÉ LLOREDA CAMACHO & CO.

Jorge Lara-Urbaneja
BAKER & MCKENZIE

Alessandra Laureiro
GÓMEZ-PINZÓN ABOGADOS

Cristina Lloreda
BRIGARD & URRUTIA, MEMBER OF LEX MUNDI

Santiago Lopez
PRICEWATERHOUSECOOPERS LEGAL SERVICES

Natalia López
POSSE HERRERA & RUIZ

Gabriela Mancero
CAVELIER ABOGADOS

Carlos Monroy
CONIKA CONSTRUCCIONES

Ana Maria Navarrete
POSSE HERRERA & RUIZ

Luis E. Nieto
NIETO & CHALELA

Ana Maria Olaya
POSSE HERRERA & RUIZ

Juan Carlos Paredes
BRIGARD & URRUTIA, MEMBER OF LEX MUNDI

Carlo Polo
COMPUTEC – DATACRÉDITO

Raul Quevedo
JOSÉ LLOREDA CAMACHO & CO.

Fernan Restrepo
BRIGARD & URRUTIA, MEMBER OF LEX MUNDI

Cristina Rueda Londono
BAKER & MCKENZIE

Juan Carlos Ruiz
JOSÉ LLOREDA CAMACHO & CO.

José Roberto Sáchica Méndez
BAKER & MCKENZIE

Paula Samper Salazar
GÓMEZ-PINZÓN ABOGADOS

Felipe Sandoval Villamil
GÓMEZ-PINZÓN ABOGADOS

José Luis Suárez
GÓMEZ-PINZÓN ABOGADOS

Raúl Alberto Suárez Arcila

Jose Alejandro Torres
POSSE HERRERA & RUIZ

Beatriz Uribe Botero
CÁMARA COLOMBIANA DE LA CONSTRUCCIÓN

Claudia Vargas
PRICEWATERHOUSECOOPERS

Diego Vega
PRICEWATERHOUSECOOPERS LEGAL SERVICES

Alberto Zuleta
GÓMEZ-PINZÓN ABOGADOS

COMOROS

Harimia Ahmed Ali
CABINET ME HARIMIA

Remy Grondin
VITOGAZ COMORES

Ahamada Mahamoudou
AVOCAT À LA COUR

Youssouf Yahaya
IMPOTS DE LA GRANDE COMORE

CONGO, DEM. REP.

Jean Adolphe Bitenu
ANAPI

Etienne Blocaille
FIDAFRICA / PRICEWATERHOUSECOOPERS

Alain Buhendwa
CABINET MWAKA & ASSOCIATES

Deo Bukayafwa
MBM CONSEIL

Jean Michel Cardino
SOCIÉTÉ MINIÈRE DE DÉVELOPPEMENT/RJ TRADERS

Victor Créspel Musafiri
CABINET D'AVOCAT JCC & A

Regis de Oliveira
AGETRAF S.A.R.L. - SDV

Yves Debiesme
AGETRAF S.A.R.L. - SDV

Hervé Diakiese
AVOCAT À LA COUR

Papy Djuma Bilali
CABINET MASAMBA

David Guarnieri
FIDAFRICA / PRICEWATERHOUSECOOPERS

Amisi Herady
ANAPI

Sandra Kabuya
CABINET MWAKA & ASSOCIATES

Robert Katambu
CABINET MWAKA & ASSOCIATES

Pierre Kazadi Tshibanda
CABINET MASAMBA

Arly Khuty

Francis Lugunda Lubamba
CABINET LUGUNDA LUBAMBA

Angèle Mabondo Ngoyi
CABINET MASAMBA

Nkusu Makengo
CABINET MASAMBA

Babala Mangala
GTS EXPRESS

Roger Masamba Makela
AVOCAT DOYEN DE FACULTÉ

Jean Paul Matanga
CABINET MWAKA & ASSOCIATES

Paulin Mbalanda
MBM CONSEIL

Didier Mopiti
MBM CONSEIL

Louman Mpoy
CABINET MPOY - LOUMAN & ASSOCIÉS

Jean Bosco Mwaka
CABINET MWAKA & ASSOCIATES

Victorine Bibiche Nsimba Kilembe
BARREAU DE KINSHASA/ MATETE

SOCIÉTÉ NATIONALE D'ELECTRICITÉ (SNEL)

Christie Madudu Sulubika
CABINET G.B. MOKA NGOLO & ASSOCIÉS

Dominique Taty
FIDAFRICA / PRICEWATERHOUSECOOPERS

Marius Tshiey-A-Tshiey
CABINET MBAKI ET ASSOCIÉS

Toto Wa Kinkela
CABINET TOTO

CONGO, REP.

Prosper Bizitou
FIDAFRICA / PRICEWATERHOUSECOOPERS

David Bourion
FIDAFRICA / PRICEWATERHOUSECOOPERS

Mohammad Daoudou
FIDAFRICA / PRICEWATERHOUSECOOPERS

Jean-Philippe Esseau
CABINET ESSEAU

Mathias Essereke
CABINET D'AVOCATS CLAUDE COELHO

Ludovic Désiré Essou
CABINET ESSOU

Philippe Fouda Fouda
BEAC

ETUDE DE MAITRES SÉRAPHIN MCAKOSSO-DOUTA ET NORBERT M'FOUTOU

Henriette Lucie Arlette Galiba
OFFICE NOTARIAL ME GALIBA

Caroline Idrissou-Belingar
BEAC

Sylvert Bérenger Kymbassa Boussi
ETUDE MAITRE BÉATRICE DIANZOLO, HUISSIER DE JUSTICE

François Lavanant
SDV

Emmanuel Le Bras
FIDAFRICA / PRICEWATERHOUSECOOPERS

Bruno Ossebi
CABINET ESSOU

Chimène Prisca Nina Pongui
ETUDE DE ME CHIMÈNE PRISCA NINA PONGUI

Roberto Prota
SDV

COSTA RICA

BUFETE FACIO & CAÑAS, MEMBER OF IUS LABORIS & LEX MUNDI

Alejandro Antillon
PACHECO COTO

Carlos Barrantes
PRICEWATERHOUSECOOPERS

Alejandro Bettoni Traube
DONINELLI & DONINELLI - ASESORES JURÍDICOS ASOCIADOS

Caroline Bono
PRICEWATERHOUSECOOPERS

Eduardo Calderón-Odio
BLP ABOGADOS

Gastón Certad
BATALLA & ASOCIADOS

Silvia Chacon
ALFREDO FOURNIER & ASOCIADOS

María Fernanda Chavarría B
CORDERO & CORDERO ABOGADOS

Daniel Chaves
CINDE

Ricardo Cordero B.
CORDERO & CORDERO ABOGADOS

Daniel De la Garza
JD CANO

Melania Dittel
ARIAS & MUÑOZ

Anamari Echeverría
PARQUE EMPRESARIAL FORUM

Alejandro Fernández de Castro
PRICEWATERHOUSECOOPERS

Octavio Fournier
ALFREDO FOURNIER & ASOCIADOS

Neftali Garro
BLP ABOGADOS

Andrés Gómez
PRICEWATERHOUSECOOPERS

Andrea González-Rojas
BLP ABOGADOS

Jorge Guzmán
LEX COUNSEL

María del Mar Herrera
BLP ABOGADOS

Randall Zamora Hidalgo
COSTA RICA ABC

Roberto Leiva
FACIO & CAÑAS, MEMBER OF LEX MUNDI

Vicente Lines
ARIAS & MUÑOZ

Andrés López
BLP ABOGADOS

Ivannia Méndez Rodríguez
OLLER ABOGADOS

Jorge Montenegro
SCGMT ARQUITECTURA Y DISEÑO

Eduardo Montoya Solano
SUPERINTENDENCIA GENERAL DE ENTIDADES FINANCIERAS

Cecilia Naranjo
LEX COUNSEL

Pedro Oller
OLLER ABOGADOS

Ramón Ortega
PRICEWATERHOUSECOOPERS

Marianne Pál - Hegedüs
AGUILAR CASTILLO LOVE

Andrea Paniagua
PRICEWATERHOUSECOOPERS

Felix Pecou Johnson
JAPDEVA CARIBBEAN PORT AUTHORITY

Laura Perez
CINDE

Julio Pinedo
PRICEWATERHOUSECOOPERS

Monica Romero
PRICEWATERHOUSECOOPERS

Miguel Ruiz Herrera
LEX COUNSEL

Andrea Saenz
AGUILAR CASTILLO LOVE

Mauricio Salas
BLP ABOGADOS

Jose Luis Salinas
SCGMT ARQUITECTURA Y DISEÑO

Walter Anderson Salomons
JAPDEVA CARIBBEAN PORT AUTHORITY

Ana Victoria Sandoval
JD CANO

Juan Tejada
PRICEWATERHOUSECOOPERS

Natalia Van der Laat
BLP ABOGADOS

Marianela Vargas
PRICEWATERHOUSECOOPERS

Sebastián Wong
JD CANO

Rodrigo Zapata
LEX COUNSEL

Jafet Zúñiga Salas
SUPERINTENDENCIA GENERAL DE ENTIDADES FINANCIERAS

CÔTE D'IVOIRE

ANY RAY & PARTNERS

César Asman
CABINET N'GOAN, ASMAN & ASSOCIÉS

Joachim Bile-Aka
BNETD

Jonathan Darboux
BCEAO

Fatimatou Zahra Diop
BCEAO

Dorothée K. Dreesen
ETUDE MAITRE DREESEN

Bertrand Fleury
SDV - SAGA CI

Jean Claude Gnamien
*FIDAFRICA /
PRICEWATERHOUSECOOPERS*

Hermann Gnango
*FIDAFRICA /
PRICEWATERHOUSECOOPERS*

Seyanne Groga
*CABINET JEAN-FRANÇOIS
CHAUVEAU*

Guillaume Koffi
*CONSEIL NATIONAL DE
L'ORDRE DES ARCHITECTES*

Herman Kouao

Evelyne M'Bassidgé
*FIDAFRICA /
PRICEWATERHOUSECOOPERS*

Adeline Messou
*FIDAFRICA /
PRICEWATERHOUSECOOPERS*

Georges N'Goan
*CABINET N'GOAN, ASMAN &
ASSOCIÉS*

Patricia N'guessan
*CABINET JEAN-FRANÇOIS
CHAUVEAU*

Jacques Otro
*CONSEIL NATIONAL DE
L'ORDRE DES ARCHITECTES*

Athanase Raux
*CABINET RAUX, AMIEN &
ASSOCIÉS*

Serge Roux
ETUDE MAITRE ROUX

Dominique Taty
*FIDAFRICA /
PRICEWATERHOUSECOOPERS*

Fousséni Traoré
*FIDAFRICA /
PRICEWATERHOUSECOOPERS*

Nadia Vanie
*CABINET N'GOAN, ASMAN &
ASSOCIÉS*

Abbé Yao
*SCPA DOGUÉ-ABBÉ YAO &
ASSOCIÉS*

CROATIA

Boris Andrejas
BABI⬛ & PARTNERS

Ivo Bijelić
PRICEWATERHOUSECOOPERS

Natko Bilić
STUDIO ⬛LHD

Andrej Bolfek
LEKO & PARTNERS

Marko Borsky
*DIVJAK, TOPIC &
BAHTIJAREVIC*

Marijana Božić
DTB

Belinda Čačić
ČA⬛⬛ & PARTNERS

Jasmina Crnalić
CMS ZAGREB

Stefanija Čukman
JURI⬛ LAW OFFICES

Martina Čulap
LEKO & PARTNERS

Gordana Delić
TRANSADRIA

Saša Divjak
*DIVJAK, TOPIC &
BAHTIJAREVIC*

Amela Dizdarević
SIHTAR ATTORNEYS AT LAW

Ivana Dominković
CMS ZAGREB

Ivan Dušić
VUKMIR LAW OFFICE

Hrvoje Filipović
LAW OFFICES NOGOLICA

Tamiko Rochelle Franklin
LEGAL CONSULTANT

Bojan Fras
ZURIC & PARTNERS

Ivan Gjurgjan
*POROBIJA & POROBIJA LAW
FIRM*

Kresimir Golubić

Lidija Hanžek
HROK

*HEP DISTRIBUTION SYSTEM
OPERATOR LTD.*

Anita Heršak Klobučarević
*POROBIJA & POROBIJA LAW
FIRM*

Jana Hitrec
ČA⬛⬛ & PARTNERS

Branimir Iveković
IVEKOVI⬛ & VIDAN

Irina Jelčić
*HANŽEKOVI⬛, RADAKOVI⬛ &
PARTNERS, MEMBER OF LEX
MUNDI*

Marijana Jelić
LAW OFFICE JELIC

Sanja Jurković
PRICEWATERHOUSECOOPERS

Mirna Kette
PRICEWATERHOUSECOOPERS

Margita Kiš-Kapetanović
*POROBIJA & POROBIJA LAW
FIRM*

Miroslav Leko
LEKO & PARTNERS

Krešimir Ljubić
LEKO & PARTNERS

Marko Lovirić
*DIVJAK, TOPIC &
BAHTIJAREVIC*

Miroljub Mačešić
*MA⬛E⬛I⬛ & PARTNERS,
ODVJETNICKO DRUSTVO*

Josip Marohnić
*DIVJAK, TOPIC &
BAHTIJAREVIC*

Tin Matić
TIN MATI⬛ LAW OFFICE

Andrej Matijevich
MATIJEVICH LAW OFFICE

Iain McGuire
PRICEWATERHOUSECOOPERS

Martina Mladina Kavurić
MAMI⬛ REBERSKI & PARTNERS

Ivana Mucić
CMS ZAGREB

Ljiljana Nogolica
GEOLEGES D. O. O.

Zvonko Nogolica
LAW OFFICES NOGOLICA

Marija Petrović
*DIVJAK, TOPIC &
BAHTIJAREVIC*

Sanja Porobija
*POROBIJA & POROBIJA LAW
FIRM*

Tihana Posavec
*DIVJAK, TOPIC &
BAHTIJAREVIC*

Marko Praljak
*DIVJAK, TOPIC &
BAHTIJAREVIC*

Ronald Pusić
PRICEWATERHOUSECOOPERS

Gordan Rotkvić
PRICEWATERHOUSECOOPERS

Djuro Sessa
COUNTY COURT IN ZAGREB

Ana Sihtar
SIHTAR ATTORNEYS AT LAW

Manuela Špoljarić
LEKO & PARTNERS

Mario Stefanić
TRANSADRIA

Goran Šverko
LAW OFFICES NOGOLICA

Luka Tadić-Čolić
BABI⬛ & PARTNERS

Zoran Tasić
CMS ZAGREB

Iva Tokić
*POROBIJA & POROBIJA LAW
FIRM*

Hrvoje Vidan
IVEKOVIC AND VIDAN

Arn Willems
CB RICHARD ELLIS D.O.O.

CZECH REPUBLIC

*ALLEN & OVERY, PRAHA
ADVOKÁTNÍ KANCELÁ⬛*

Tomas Babacek
*AMBRUZ & DARK
ADVOKÁTI, V.O.S.
PRICEWATERHOUSECOOPERS
LEGAL SERVICES*

Libor Basl
BAKER & MCKENZIE

Martin Bohuslav
*AMBRUZ & DARK
ADVOKÁTI, V.O.S.
PRICEWATERHOUSECOOPERS
LEGAL SERVICES*

Stephen B. Booth
PRICEWATERHOUSECOOPERS

Jiří Černý
PETERKA & PARTNERS

Matěj Daněk
*PROCHÁZKA RANDL KUBR,
MEMBER OF IUS LABORIS &
LEX MUNDI*

Svatava Dokoupilova
*CZECH OFFICE FOR
SURVEYING, MAPPING AND
CADASTRE*

Jitka Ernestova
PETERKA & PARTNERS

Kristýna Fišerová
PETERKA & PARTNERS

Jakub Hajek
*AMBRUZ & DARK
ADVOKÁTI, V.O.S.
PRICEWATERHOUSECOOPERS
LEGAL SERVICES*

Michal Hanko
BUBNIK, MYSLIL & PARTNERS

Jarmila Hanzalova
*PROCHÁZKA RANDL KUBR,
MEMBER OF IUS LABORIS &
LEX MUNDI*

Vlastimil Hokr
BDO PRIMA AUDIT S.R.O.

Vít Horáček
*GLATZOVÁ AND CO. LAW
OFFICES*

Hana Hrbacova
*AMBRUZ & DARK
ADVOKÁTI, V.O.S.
PRICEWATERHOUSECOOPERS
LEGAL SERVICES*

Iva Hromková
*GLATZOVÁ AND CO. LAW
OFFICES*

Ludvik Juřička
*AMBRUZ & DARK
ADVOKÁTI, V.O.S.
PRICEWATERHOUSECOOPERS
LEGAL SERVICES*

Robert Jurka
BDO PRIMA AUDIT S.R.O.

Jiri Klimicek
*SQUIRE, SANDERS & DEMPSEY,
V.O.S. ADVOKÁT KANCELÁ⬛*

Miroslav Kocman
ICCRUE S.R.O.

Adela Krbcová
PETERKA & PARTNERS

Petr Kucera
*CCB - CZECH BANKING
CREDIT BUREAU*

Lenka Mrazova
PRICEWATERHOUSECOOPERS

David Musil
PRICEWATERHOUSECOOPERS

Jarmila Musilova
NATIONAL BANK

Stanislav Myslil
*CERMAK HOREJS MYSLIL A
SPOL.*

Jörg Nürnberger
DLA PIPER

Athanassios Pantazopoulos
*IKRP ROKAS & PARTNERS AND
DR. A. PANTAZOPOULOS*

Marketa Penazova
*AMBRUZ & DARK
ADVOKÁTI, V.O.S.
PRICEWATERHOUSECOOPERS
LEGAL SERVICES*

Jan Petřík
*BRZOBOHATÝ BROŽ & HONSA,
V.O.S.*

Kristýna Pohlová
*GLATZOVÁ AND CO. LAW
OFFICES*

Pavla Přikrylová
PETERKA & PARTNERS

Jan Procházka
*AMBRUZ & DARK
ADVOKÁTI, V.O.S.
PRICEWATERHOUSECOOPERS
LEGAL SERVICES*

Nataša Randlová
*PROCHÁZKA RANDL KUBR,
MEMBER OF IUS LABORIS &
LEX MUNDI*

Tomas Richter
*CLIFFORD CHANCE LLP/
INSTITUTE OF ECONOMIC
STUDIES, FACULTY OF*

*SOCIAL SCIENCES, CHARLES
UNIVERSITY*

Zdenek Rosicky
*SQUIRE, SANDERS & DEMPSEY,
V.O.S. ADVOKÁT KANCELÁ⬛*

Leona Sevcikova
PANALPINA S.R.O.

Robert Sgariboldi
PANALPINA S.R.O.

Dana Sládečková
NATIONAL BANK

Marie Strachotová
PETERKA & PARTNERS

Miroslav Tichý
DLA PIPER

Růžena Trojánková
LINKLATERS

Klára Valentová
*AMBRUZ & DARK
ADVOKÁTI, V.O.S.
PRICEWATERHOUSECOOPERS
LEGAL SERVICES*

Luďk Vrána
LINKLATERS

Markéta Zachová
VEJMELKA & WÜNSCH, S.R.O.

Veronika Žaloudková
ICCRUE S.R.O.

DENMARK

Elsebeth Aaes-Jørgensen
*NORRBOM VINDING, MEMBER
OF IUS LABORIS*

Christine Lægteskov Aon
*KROMANN REUMERT, MEMBER
OF LEX MUNDI*

Peter Bang

Steffen Bang-Olsen
*KROMANN REUMERT, MEMBER
OF LEX MUNDI*

Thomas Bech Olsen
*PANALPINA WORLD
TRANSPORT LTD*

Christel Berning
PRICEWATERHOUSECOOPERS

Jonas Bøgelund
*GORRISSEN FEDERSPIEL
KIERKEGAARD*

Ole Borch
BECH-BRUUN LAW FIRM

Thomas Booker
*ACCURA
ADVOKATAKTIESELSKAB*

Christian Bredtoft Guldmann
*KROMANN REUMERT, MEMBER
OF LEX MUNDI*

Mogens Ebeling
JONAS BRUUN

Eivind Einersen
PHILIP & PARTNERE

Henrik Faust Pedersen
PRICEWATERHOUSECOOPERS

Lars Fogh
*ACCURA
ADVOKATAKTIESELSKAB*

Alice Folker
*GORRISSEN FEDERSPIEL
KIERKEGAARD*

Arne Gehring
PRICEWATERHOUSECOOPERS

Jens Hjortskov
PHILIP & PARTNERE

Heidi Hoelgaard
EXPERIAN NORTHERN EUROPE

Jens Steen Jensen
KROMANN REUMERT, MEMBER OF LEX MUNDI

Jeppe Jørgensen
BECH-BRUUN LAW FIRM

Ann Kell
PRICEWATERHOUSECOOPERS

Aage Krogh
MAGNUSSON

Christine Larsen

Susanne Schjølin Larsen
KROMANN REUMERT, MEMBER OF LEX MUNDI

Lars Lindencrone
BECH-BRUUN LAW FIRM

Andreas Nielsen
JONAS BRUUN

Tim Nielsen
KROMANN REUMERT, MEMBER OG LEX MUNDI

Betri Pihl Schultze
PRICEWATERHOUSECOOPERS

Soren Plomgaard
JONAS BRUUN

Louise Krarup Simonsen
KROMANN REUMERT, MEMBER OF LEX MUNDI

Niels Bang Sørensen
GORRISSEN FEDERSPIEL KIERKEGAARD

Jesper Trommer Volf
ACCURA ADVOKATAKTIESELSKAB

Knud Villemoes Hansen
NATIONAL SURVEY AND CADASTRE - DENMARK/KORT & MATRIKELSTYRELSEN

Anders Worsøe
MAGNUSSON

DJIBOUTI

Rahma Abdi Abdillahi
BANQUE CENTRALE

Wabat Daoud
AVOCAT À LA COUR

Bruno Détroyat

Ibrahim Hamadou Hassan

Ibrahim Mohamed Omar
CABINET CECA

Oubah Mohamed Omar
SOCIÉTÉ MARITIME L. SAVON & RIES

Aicha Youssouf
CABINET CECA

DOMINICA

Eddie Beaupierre
ELEMENT AGENCIES

Alix Boyd-Knights

Kathy Buffong
ATTORNEY GENERAL'S CHAMBERS

Gerald D. Burton
GERALD D. BURTON'S CHAMBERS

DEVELOPMENT AND PLANNING DIVISION

Gina Dyer
DYER & DYER

Marvlyn Estrado
KPB CHARTERED ACCOUNTANTS

Kerry George
C I S ENTERPRISES LTD.

F. Adler Hamlet
REALCO COMPANY LIMITED

Foued Issa
ISSA TRADING LTD.

Alick C. Lawrence
LAWRENCE ALICK C. CHAMBERS

Severin McKenzie
MCKENZIE ARCHITECTURAL & CONSTRUCTION SERVICES INC.

Richard Peterkin
PRICEWATERHOUSECOOPERS

Joan K.R. Prevost
PREVOST & ROBERTS

J. Gildon Richards
J. GILDON RICHARDS CHAMBERS

Mark Riddle
DOMLEC

Eugene G. Royer
EUGENE G. ROYER CHARTERED ARCHITECT

Linda Singletary
C I S ENTERPRISES LTD.

Jason Timothy
DOMLEC

Ossie Walsh
SUPREME COURT/ REGISTRY

Reginald Winston
SUPREME COURT/ REGISTRY

DOMINICAN REPUBLIC

Carla Alsina
BIAGGI & MESSINA

Hilda Patricia Polanco Morales
SÁNCHEZ RAFUL SICARD & POLANCO

Mario Ariza
HEADRICK RIZIK ALVAREZ & FERNÁNDEZ

Caroline Bono
PRICEWATERHOUSECOOPERS

Ana Isabel Caceres
TRONCOSO Y CACERES

Juan Manuel Caceres
TRONCOSO Y CACERES

Giselle Castillo
SUPERINTENDENCIA DE BANCOS

Leandro Corral
ESTRELLA & TUPETE

José Cruz Campillo
JIMÉNEZ CRUZ PEÑA

Sarah de León
HEADRICK, RIZIK, ALVAREZ & FERNANDEZ

Rosa Díaz
JIMÉNEZ CRUZ PEÑA

Rafael Dickson Morales
MG&A MEDINA GARNES & ASOCIADOS ABOGADOS

Edward Fernandez
BIAGGI & MESSINA

Alejandro Fernández de Castro
PRICEWATERHOUSECOOPERS

Mary Fernández Rodríguez
HEADRICK RIZIK ALVAREZ & FERNÁNDEZ

Gloria Gasso
HEADRICK RIZIK ALVAREZ & FERNÁNDEZ

Pablo Gonzalez Tapia
BIAGGI & MESSINA

Fabio Guzmán-Ariza
GUZMÁN ARIZA

Mónika Infante
SAXUM LEGAL

Philippe Lescuras
PANALPINA

Xavier Marra Martínez
DHIMES & MARRA

Fernando Marranzini
HEADRICK RIZIK ALVAREZ & FERNÁNDEZ

Carlos Marte
PANALPINA

Patricia Media Coste
HEADRICK RIZIK ALVAREZ & FERNÁNDEZ

Fabiola Medina
MG&A MEDINA GARNES & ASOCIADOS ABOGADOS

Ramón Ortega
PRICEWATERHOUSECOOPERS

Andrea Paniagua
PRICEWATERHOUSECOOPERS

Valeria Pérez Modena
JIMÉNEZ CRUZ PEÑA

Carolina Pichardo
BIAGGI & MESSINA

Edward Piña
BIAGGI & MESSINA

Rafael Piña
HEADRICK RIZIK ALVAREZ & FERNÁNDEZ

Julio Pinedo
PRICEWATERHOUSECOOPERS

Sabrina Angulo Pucheu
SÁNCHEZ RAFUL SICARD & POLANCO

Maria Portes
CASTILLO Y CASTILLO

Sóstenes Rodriguez Segura
RUSSIN, VECCHI AND HEREDIA BONETTI

Wilferdo Senior
CONSULTANT

Maricell Silvestre Rodriguez
JIMÉNEZ CRUZ PEÑA

Juan Tejada
PRICEWATERHOUSECOOPERS

Vilma Veras Terrero
JIMÉNEZ CRUZ PEÑA

TransUNION

Guiraldis Velásquez Ramos
DHIMES & MARRA

Vilma Verras Terrero
JIMÉNEZ CUZ PEÑA

Patricia Villar
PANALPINA

ECUADOR

Pablo Aguirre
PRICEWATERHOUSECOOPERS

Christof Baer
PRICEWATERHOUSECOOPERS

Hernán Batallas-Gómez
FALCONI PUIG ABOGADOS

Xavier Bravo Ruales
SUPERINTENDENCIA DE BANCOS Y SEGUROS

Diego Cabezas-Klaere
ORTEGA MOREIRA & ORTEGA TRUJILLO

Silvana Coka G.
GEOTRANSPORT S.A.

Fernando Coral
PANALPINA

Lucía Cordero Ledergerber
FALCONI PUIG ABOGADOS

Fernando Del Pozo Contreras
GALLEGOS, VALAREZO & NEIRA

Gonzalo Diez P.
GONZALO DIEZ

Miguel Falconi-Puig
FALCONI PUIG ABOGADOS

Jorge Eduardo Fernández Perdomo
ACREDITA BURÓ DE INFORMACIÓN CREDITICIA S.A

Juan Carlos Gallegos Happle
GALLEGOS, VALAREZO & NIERA

Leopoldo González R.
PAZ HOROWITZ

Francisco Grijalva M.
IUS & LAW

Iván A. Intriago
IUS & LAW

Maggio Irigoyen V.
API

Vanessa Izquierdo D.
BUSTAMANTE & BUSTAMANTE

Alvaro Jarrín
SUPERINTENDENCIA DE BANCOS Y SEGUROS

Juan Manuel Marchán
PÉREZ, BUSTAMANTE Y PONCE, MEMBER OF LEX MUNDI

Christian Morales
PANALPINA

Francisco Javier Naranjo Grijalva
PAZ HOROWITZ

Priscilla Ortega
ARÍZAGA & CO. ABOGADOS

Pablo Padilla Muirragui
ECUADOR CARGO SYSTEM

Jorge Paz Durini
PAZ HOROWITZ

Bruno Pineda-Cordero
PÉREZ, BUSTAMANTE Y PONCE, MEMBER OF LEX MUNDI

Xavier Amador Pino
ESTUDIO JURIDICO AMADOR

Daniel Pino Arroba
CORONEL Y PÉREZ

Jorge Pizarro Páez
BUSTAMANTE & BUSTAMANTE

Patricia Ponce Arteta
BUSTAMANTE & BUSTAMANTE

Sandra Reed
PÉREZ, BUSTAMANTE Y PONCE, MEMBER OF LEX MUNDI

Gustavo Romero
ROMERO ARTETA PONCE

Myriam Dolores Rosales Garcés
SUPERINTENDENCIA DE BANCOS Y SEGUROS

Veronica Sofia Ruales Díaz
BUSTAMANTE & BUSTAMANTE

Montserrate Sánchez
CORONEL Y PÉREZ

Pablo F. Sarzosa J.
API ECUADOR

SUPERINTENDENCIA DE COMPAÑIAS

César Vélez Calderón
COVELCAL

EGYPT

Abdel Aal Aly
AFIFI WORLD TRANSPORT

Naguib Abadir
NACITA CORPORATION

Walid Abbas
ADVANCED GROUP

Girgis Abd El-Shahid
SARWAT A. SHAHID LAW FIRM

Sara Abdel Gabbar
TROWERS & HAMLINS

Ahmed Abdel Warith
AAW CONSULTING ENGINEERS

Ramez Mounir Abdel-Nour
KARIM ADEL LAW OFFICE

Mohamed Abo -Shady
MODERN AGRICULTURAL EST.

Ahmed Abou Ali
HASSOUNA & ABOU ALI

Gamal Abou Ali
HASSOUNA & ABOU ALI

Nermine Abulata
MINISTRY OF TRADE & INDUSTRY

Ghada Adel
PRICEWATERHOUSECOOPERS

Hazem Ahmed
HASSOUNA & ABOU ALI

Mahmoud Ahmed Bassiem

Ashraf El Al Arabi
MINISTRY OF FINANCE

Abd El Wahab Aly Ibrahim
ABD EL WAHAB SONS

Tim Armsby
TROWERS & HAMLINS

Amr Mohamed Mahmoud Atta
KARIM ADEL LAW OFFICE

Adel Awadalla
S.S.I.B.

Ziad Bahaa El Dian
GENERAL AUTHORITY FOR INVESTMENT AND FREE ZONES

Louis Bishara
BTM

Ibrahim Hassan Dakr
KARIM ADEL LAW OFFICE

Hussein Mahmoud Gaafar El Gebaly
MINISTRY OF HOUSING, UTILITIES, AND URBAN DEVELOPMENT

Mohamed EL Gindy
WAAD TRADE & DEVELOPMENT CO.

Mohamed El Homosany
MINISTRY OF JUSTICE

Mohamed Refaat El Houshy
THE EGYPTIAN CREDIT BUREAU "I-SCORE"

Amr El Monayer
MINISTRY OF FINANCE

Hasan El Shafiey
NADOURY NAHAS LAW OFFICES

Karim Elhelaly
PRICEWATERHOUSECOOPERS

Ashraf Elibrachy
IBRACHY LAW FIRM

Mohamed El-Labboudy
NADOURY & NAHAS LAW OFFICES

Hassan Fahmy
MINISTRY OF INVESTMENT

Heba Foaad
PRICEWATERHOUSECOOPERS

Ashraf Gamal El-Din
EGYPTIAN INSTITUTE OF DIRECTORS

Yaser Gamaluddin Hamam
THE EGYPTIAN LAW FIRM

Ahmed Gawish
MINISTRY OF TRANSPORT

Hend Abdel Ghany
MENA ASSOCIATES, MEMBER OF AMERELLER RECHTSANWÄLTE

Karim Adel Kamel Ghobrial
KARIM ADEL LAW OFFICE

Zeinab Saieed Gohar
CENTRAL BANK

Rimon Hakim
SARWAT GROUP FOR EXPORT AND IMPORT

Emad Hassan
MINISTRY OF STATE FOR ADMINISTRATIVE DEVELOPMENT

Omneia Helmy
THE EGYPTIAN CENTER FOR ECONOMIC STUDIES

Lobna Mohamed Hilal
CENTRAL BANK

Mamdoh Farghli Kassem
THE EGYPTIAN LAW FIRM

Sherif Mansour
PRICEWATERHOUSECOOPERS

Nouran Mohamed
PRICEWATERHOUSECOOPERS

Mohamed Mohamed
PRIVATE PRACTICE

Mostafa Mostafa
AL KAMEL LAW OFFICE

Ashraf Nadoury
NADOURY & NAHAS LAW OFFICES

Mariama Sabet

Mohamed Serry
SERRY LAW OFFICE

Wael Shaker
ISLAND GROUP

Safwat Sobhy
PRICEWATERHOUSECOOPERS

SOUTH CAIRO ELECTRICITY DISTRIBUTION COMPANY

Cath Welch
PRICEWATERHOUSECOOPERS

Eman Zakaria
MINISTRY OF MANPOWER & MIGRATION

Mona Zobaa
MINISTRY OF INVESTMENT

EL SALVADOR

Carlos Roberto Alfaro
PRICEWATERHOUSECOOPERS

Ana Margoth Arévalo
SUPERINTENDENCIA DEL SISTEMA FINANCIERO

Francisco Armando Arias Rivera
ARIAS & MUÑOZ

Irene Arrieta de Díaz Nuila
ARRIETA BUSTAMANTE

Francisco José Barrientos
AGUILAR CASTILLO LOVE

Caroline Bono
PRICEWATERHOUSECOOPERS

Diana Castro
LEXINCORP

Ricardo Cevallos
CONSORTIUM CENTRO AMÉRICA ABOGADOS

Walter Chávez Velasco
GOLD SERVICE / MSI

David Claros
GARCÍA & BODÁN

Geraldo Cruz
GARCÍA & BODÁN

Karla de Martínez
ARRIETA BUSTAMANTE

Mayra de Morán
PRESIDENTIAL PROGRAM "EL SALVADOR EFICIENTE"

Maria Marta Delgado
ARIAS & MUÑOZ

Alejandro Fernández de Castro
PRICEWATERHOUSECOOPERS

Roberta Gallardo de Cromeyer
ARIAS & MUÑOZ

Ernesto Hempe
PRICEWATERHOUSECOOPERS

Carlos Henriquez
GOLD SERVICE / MSI

Juan Carlos Herrera
ARIAS & MUÑOZ

Thelma Dinora Lizama de Osorio
SUPERINTENDENCIA DEL SISTEMA FINANCIERO

Karla Martinez
ARRIETA BUSTAMANTE

Daniel Martinez
GARCÍA & BODÁN

Luis Medina
RUSCONI, VALDEZ, MEDINA & ASOCIADOS

Astrud María Meléndez
ASOCIACIÓN PROTECTORA DE CRÉDITOS DE EL SALVADOR (PROCREDITO)

José Walter Meléndez
CUSTOMS

Mauricio Melhado
GOLD SERVICE / MSI

Camilo Mena
GOLD SERVICE / MSI

Antonio R. Mendez Llort
ROMERO PINEDA & ASOCIADOS, MEMBER OF LEX MUNDI AND TERRA LEX

Miriam Eleana Mixco Reyna
GOLD SERVICE / MSI

Jocelyn Mónico
AGUILAR CASTILLO LOVE

Ramón Ortega
PRICEWATERHOUSECOOPERS

Andrea Paniagua
PRICEWATERHOUSECOOPERS

Carlos Pastrana

Julio Pinedo
PRICEWATERHOUSECOOPERS

Francisco Eduardo Portillo
CEPA

Ana Patricia Portillo Reyes
GUANDIQUE SEGOVIA QUINTANILLA

Flor de Maria Rodriguez
ARIAS & MUÑOZ

Kelly Romero
RUSCONI, VALDEZ, MEDINA & ASOCIADOS

Adonay Rosales
PRICEWATERHOUSECOOPERS

Oscar Samour
CONSORTIUM CENTRO AMÉRICA ABOGADOS

Juan Tejada
PRICEWATERHOUSECOOPERS

Manuel Telles Suvillaga
LEXINCORP

Mauricio Antonio Urrutia
SUPERINTENDENCIA DEL SISTEMA FINANCIERO

Julio Valdés
ARIAS & MUÑOZ

Juan Vásquez
GOLD SERVICE / MSI

EQUATORIAL GUINEA

Leoncio-Mitogo Edjang Avoro
ATTORNEY-AT-LAW

Philippe Fouda Fouda
BEAC

Caroline Idrissou-Belingar
BEAC

Sébastien Lechêne
FIDAFRICA / PRICEWATERHOUSECOOPERS

Franck Mamelin
PANALPINA TRANSPORTES MUNDIALES S.A.R.L.

Ponciano Mbomio Nvo
GABINETE JURIDICO

François Münzer
FIDAFRICA / PRICEWATERHOUSECOOPERS

Dominique Taty
FIDAFRICA / PRICEWATERHOUSECOOPERS

ERITREA

Rahel Abera
BERHANE GILA-MICHAEL LAW FIRM

Berhane Gila-Michael
BERHANE GILA-MICHAEL LAW FIRM

Senai W. Andemariam
UNIVERSITY OF ASMARA

Kebreab Habte Michael

Michael Joseph
ERNST & YOUNG

Tekeste Mesghenna
MTD ENTERPRISES PLC

ESTONIA

Anne Adamson
SORAINEN LAW OFFICES

Angela Agur
MAQS LAW FIRM

Mike Ahern
PRICEWATERHOUSECOOPERS

Katrin Altmets
SORAINEN LAW OFFICES

Jane Eespöld
SORAINEN LAW OFFICES

Silja Elunurm
GLIKMAN & PARTNERS

Diana Freivald
MINISTRY OF JUSTICE

Cameron Greaves
PRICEWATERHOUSECOOPERS

Pirkko-Liis Harkmaa
LEPIK & LUHAÄÄR LAWIN

Triinu Hiob
LEPIK & LUHAÄÄR LAWIN

Andres Juss
ESTONIAN LAND BOARD

Aidi Kallavus
KPMG AS

Gerli Kilusk
LEPIK & LUHAÄÄR LAWIN

Risto Koovit
CORVUS GRUPP TRANSPORT

Ermo Kosk
LEPIK & LUHAÄÄR LAWIN

Tanja Kriisa
PRICEWATERHOUSECOOPERS

Mikk Läänemets
LAW OFFICE TARK & CO.

Liina Lins
LEPIK & LUHAÄÄR LAWIN

Karin Madisson
SORAINEN LAW OFFICES

Olger Marjak
LAW OFFICE TARK & CO.

Marko Mehilane
LEPIK & LUHAÄÄR LAWIN

Veiko Meos
KREDIIDIINFO A.S.

Jaanus Mody
LUIGA MODY HÄÄL BORENIUS

Margus Mugu
LUIGA MODY HÄÄL BORENIUS

Kaspar Noor
MAQS LAW FIRM

Arne Ots
RAIDLA & PARTNERS

Kirsti Pent
LAW OFFICE TARK & CO.

Daniel Polawski
PAUL VARUL

Kristiina Puuste
KPMG AS

Ants Ratas
CF & S AS

Heidi Rätsep
CENTRE OF REGISTERS AND INFORMATION SYSTEM

Martin Simovart
LEPIK & LUHAÄÄR LAWIN

Monika Tamm
LEPIK & LUHAÄÄR LAWIN

Marjaa Teder
LUIGA MODY HÄÄL BORENIUS

Tanel Tikan
LEPIK & LUHAÄÄR LAWIN

Villi Töntson
PRICEWATERHOUSECOOPERS

Veikko Toomere
MAQS LAW FIRM

Karolina Ullman
MAQS LAW FIRM

Neve Uudelt
RAIDLA & PARTNERS

Toomas Vaher
RAIDLA & PARTNERS

Paul Varul
PAUL VARUL

Urmas Veinberg
MAQS LAW FIRM

Andres Vinkel
HANSA LAW OFFICES

Vesse Võhma

Joel Zernask
KPMG AS

ETHIOPIA

Nethanet Alemu

Daniel Alemu
ATTORNEY-AT-LAW

Ato Wondimeneh Asrat
NATIONAL BANK

Bekure Assefa
BEKURE ASSEFA LAW OFFICE

Yonas Kidane Demiyesus
DASHEN BANK S.C.

Shimelise Eshete
MIDROC CONSTRUCTION PLC

Teshome G.M. Bokan
TGMB LAW OFFICE

Nega Getahun
CITY ADMINISTRATION OF ADDIS ABABA

Berhane Ghebray
BERHANE GHEBRAY & ASSOCIATES

Yosef Kebede
DASHEN BANK S.C.

Emebet Ketema

Tadesse Kiros
TADESSE, GETACHEW & ABATE LAW OFFICE

Taddesse Lencho
ADDIS ABABA UNIVERSITY

Molla Mengistu
Addis Ababa University

Fikremarkos Merso
Addis Ababa University

Woldegabriel Naizghi
HST & Co.

Getahun Nana
National Bank

Mehari Redae
Addis Ababa University

Abiot Seleshi
National Bank

Seyoum Yonhannes Tesfy
Addis Ababa University

Mekbib Tsegaw
Attorney-at-Law

Aklilu Wolde Amanuel

Aklilu Woldemariam
Ethiopian Investment Agency

FIJI

David Aidney
Williams & Gosling Ltd.

Eddielin Almonte
PricewaterhouseCoopers

John Apted
Munro Leys Notaries Public

Nehla Basawaiya
Munro Leys Notaries Public

William Wylie Clarke
Howards Lawyers

Jamnadas Dilip
Jamnadas and Associates

Delores Elliott
Databureau, Baycorp Advantage

Isireli Fa
The Fiji Law Society / FA & Company Barristers & Solicitors

Anthea S. Fong
Crompton Solicitors

Freddy Fonmoa
Williams & Gosling Ltd.

Jerome Kado
PricewaterhouseCoopers

Sashi Lochan
Titles Office

Litiana Morris
Howards Lawyers

Richard Naidu
Munro Leys Notaries Public

Ramesh Prakash
Mishra Prakash & Associates

Ramesh Prasad Lal
Carpenters Shipping

Colin Radford
LHM, Larsen Holtom Maybin & company limited, Architec, Engineers & interior designers

Abhi Ram
Companies Registrar

Roneel Ram
FEA (Fiji Electricity Authority)

Ana Rasovo
Howards Lawyers

Jenny Seeto
PricewaterhouseCoopers

Varun Shandil
Munro Leys Notaries Public

Shelvin Singh
Parshotam & Co.

Narotam Solanki
PricewaterhouseCoopers

Moto Solvalu
Williams & Gosling Ltd.

Mark Swamy
LHM, Larsen Holtom Maybin & company limited, Architec, Engineers & interior designers

Jay Udit
High Court

Chirk Yam
PricewaterhouseCoopers

Eddie Yuen
Williams & Gosling Ltd.

FINLAND

Sakari Aalto
Roschier Attorneys Ltd., member of Ius Laboris & Lex Mundi

Ville Ahtola
Castrén & Snellman Attorneys Ltd.

Manne Airaksinen
Roschier Attorneys Ltd., member of Ius Laboris & Lex Mundi

Claudio Busi
Castrén & Snellman Attorneys Ltd.

Mikko Eerola
Waselius & Wist

Tiina Hakri
Roschier Attorneys Ltd., member of Ius Laboris & Lex Mundi

Johanna Haltia-Tapio
Hannes Snellman, Attorneys-at-Law Ltd.

Tuija Hartikainen
PricewaterhouseCoopers

Olav Hermanson
Roschier Attorneys Ltd., member of Ius Laboris & Lex Mundi

Jani Hovila
Hannes Snellman, Attorneys-at-Law Ltd.

Pekka Jaatinen
Castrén & Snellman Attorneys Ltd.

Juuso Jokela
Suomen Asiakastieto Oy - Finska

Milla Kokko-Lehtinen
PricewaterhouseCoopers

Elina Kumpulainen
PricewaterhouseCoopers Legal Services

Risto Löf
PricewaterhouseCoopers

Tuomas Lukkarinen
National Land Survey

Lasse Luukkainen
Castrén & Snellman Attorneys Ltd.

Jyrki Mustonen
Hedman Osborne Clarke

Eva Nordman-Rajaharju
Roschier Attorneys Ltd., member of Ius Laboris & Lex Mundi

Ilona Paakkala
PricewaterhouseCoopers

Mikko Peltoniemi
Waselius & Wist

Merja Raunio
PricewaterhouseCoopers

Mikko Reinikainen
PricewaterhouseCoopers

Tatu Simula
Roschier Attorneys Ltd., member of Ius Laboris & Lex Mundi

Sini Soini
Roschier Attorneys Ltd., member of Ius Laboris & Lex Mundi

Timo Tammelin
Mega Trend Nordica Oy

Sanna Väänänen
PricewaterhouseCoopers

Helena Viita
Roschier Attorneys Ltd., member of Ius Laboris & Lex Mundi

Gunnar Westerlund
Roschier Attorneys Ltd., member of Ius Laboris & Lex Mundi

Kai Wist
PricewaterhouseCoopers

FRANCE

Allen & Overy LLP

APL

Faiza Alleg
Vaughan Avocats

Christophe Asselineau
Simmons & Simmons

Bertrand Barrier
Gide Loyrette Nouel, member of Lex Mundi

Christopher Baker
Skadden, Arps, Slate, Meagher & Flom LLP/ Fauvet La Giraudière & Associés

Roger J. Benrubi
Cleary Gottlieb Steen & Hamilton LLP

Franck Buffand
Lamy Lexel

Arnaud Chastel

Frédérique Chifflot Bourgeois
Lawyer at the Bar of Paris

Francis Collins
Landwell & Associés - PricewaterhouseCoopers Legal Services

Luis Comas
PricewaterhouseCoopers Legal Services

Confédération Française du Commerce Interentreprises (CGI)

Christian Courivaud
SCP Courivaud - Morange - Volniac

Ann Creelman
Vatier & Associés

Isabelle Didier
Vaughan Avocats

Electricité de France

Stephanie Ernould

Benoit Fauvelet
Banque de France

Christine Fortune

Sylvie Ghesquiere
Banque de France

Raymond Gianno
Affina Legal

Florence Grillier
Cabinet TAJ

Sabrina Henocq
Delsol & Associés

Cécile Jaouën
Simmons & Simmons

Marc Jobert
Jobert & Associés

Renaud Jouffroy

Jennifer Juvénal
Landwell & Associés

Daniel Arthur Laprès
Cabinet d'Avocats

Benoît Le Bars
Landwell & Associés - PricewaterhouseCoopers Legal Services

Anne-Marie Moulin
Banque de France

Panalpina

Michele Pennings
Landwell & Associés - PricewaterhouseCoopers Legal Services

Laure Poindessault-Bernard

Jacques Pourciel
Paris Notaire

Emmanuel Raingeard

Bernard Reynis

Frédéric Roussel
Fontaine, Roussel & Associés

Hugues Roux
Banque de France

Rizwan A Siddique
XG - TECC

Isabelle Smith Monnerville
Vaughan Avocats

Caroline Stéphane
Delsol & Associés

Bruno Thomas
Landwell & Associés - PricewaterhouseCoopers Legal Services

Marcia Winitzer
Marcia J. Winitzer

Philippe Xavier-Bender
Gide Loyrette Nouel, member of Lex Mundi

Roger J. Benrubi
Cleary Gottlieb Steen & Hamilton LLP

GABON

Eyang Abessolo Nauby
Controleur des Impots

Charles Adenet
FIDAFRICA/ PricewaterhouseCoopers

Y.A. Adetona
Cabinet Fidexce

Marcellin Massila Akendengue
SEEG, Societe d'Energie et d'Eau du Gabon

Stephanie Angue Boussougou
Inspecteur Central des Impots

Gianni Ardizzone
Panalpina

Marie Carmel Ketty Ayimambenwe
Banque Internationale pour le Commerce et l'Industrie

Claude Barone

Henri Bernhardt
GETMA

Agnese Biye Ngou
Huissier de Justice

Jean Delahaye
Bollore

Léopold Effah
Etude Mekam'Ne & Effah Avocats Associés

Steeve Romuald Engandza Loussou
Ministere de l'Economie des Finances, du Budget et de la Privatisation

Philippe Fouda Fouda
BEAC

Anne Gey Bekale
Notary

Caroline Idrissou-Belingar
BEAC

Jacques Lebama
Ministere de la Justice, Garde des Sceaux

Athanase Ndoye Loury
Syndic Judiciaire

Orphée Yvan Mandji
Agence de Promotions des Investissements Privés

Itchola Mano
Avocat

Pélagie Massamba Mouckocko
FIDAFRICA / PricewaterhouseCoopers

Jean-Joel Mebaley
Destiny Executives Architects - Agence du Bord de Mer

J.R. Lassi Mikala
Avocat à la Cour

Abel Mouloungui
Notary

Aliette Mounguengui Magnogunou
Inspecteur Central des Impots

Jean Hilaire Moussavou
FUMU Technologie

Haymand Moutsinga
Avocat à la Cour

Steeve Romuald Mve
PUBLISH WHAT YOU PAY

Reteno N'Diaye Brice
*DIRECTION GENERAL DES
IMPOTS*

Joel Ndong
*SERVICE ETUDES D'URBANISME
AT THE DIRECTION GENERALE
D'URBANISME*

Ruben Mindonga Ndongo
CABINET ME ANGUILER

Thierry Ngomo
ARCHIPRO INTERNATIONAL

Lubin Ntoutoume
AVOCAT

Olivier P. N'Zahou
JURISTE

Ferdinand Obiang
*MINISTERE DE L'ECONOMIE
DES FINANCES, DU BUDGET ET
DE LA PRIVATISATION*

Josette Cadie Olendo
CABINET OLENDO

César Apollinaire Ondo Mve
*COUR D'APPEL JUDICIAIRE DE
LIBREVILLE*

Marie-Jose Ongo Mendou
FFA JURIDIQUE & FISCAL

Paulette Oyane-Ondo
ATTORNEY-AT-LAW

Carine Peron
UNION GABONAISE DE BANQUE

Laurent Pommera
*FIDAFRICA /
PRICEWATERHOUSECOOPERS*

Laurette Poulain
TRANSFORM

Christophe A. Relongoué
*FIDAFRICA /
PRICEWATERHOUSECOOPERS*

Gomes Rene Fidel
*AVOCAT AU BARREAU
NATIONAL DU GABON*

Justine Adondjo Reteno
AVOCAT

Francois Salangros
*GEE - GABONAISE D'ETUDES
ET D'EXPERTISES BATIMENT*

Laurent Boris Skitt
*AGENCE DE PROMOTIONS DES
INVESTISSEMENTS PRIVÉS*

Dominique Taty
*FIDAFRICA /
PRICEWATERHOUSECOOPERS*

Didier Thoreau

GAMBIA, THE

Kelvin Abdallah
PRICEWATERHOUSECOOPERS

Victoria Andrews
AMIE BENSOUDA & CO.

Gideon Ayi-Owoo
PRICEWATERHOUSECOOPERS

Momodou M. Bah
*KANIFING MUNICIPAL
COUNCIL*

Awa Bah
*DEPARTMENT OF STATE FOR
JUSTICE*

Alpha Amadou Barry
DELOITTE

Amie N.D. Bensouda
AMIE BENSOUDA & CO.

Lamin B.S. Camara
DANDIMAYO CAMBERS

Neneh-Cham Cham Chongan
BASANGSANG CHAMBERS

Emmanuel E. Chime
CHIME CHAMBERS

Sulayman B. Chune
TAF CONSTRUCTION

A.N.M Ousainu Darboe
BASANGSANG CHAMBERS

Ida Denise Drameh
IDA D. DRAMEH & ASSOCIATES

Dzidzedze Fiadjoe
PRICEWATERHOUSECOOPERS

Michel Gaye

Birgitta Hardmark
MAERSK LINE

Haruna Jaiteh
OFFICE OF THE CHIEF JUSTICE

Ousman B. Jallow
*GAMBIA PUBLIC
PROCUREMENT AUTHORITY*

Alhaji Jallow
*NATIONAL WATER &
ELECTRICITY COMPANY LTD.*

Abdoulie Jammel
*DEPARTMENT OF STATE
FOR TRADE INDUSTRY AND
EMPLOYMENT*

Amadou Janneh
*NATIONAL WATER &
ELECTRICITY COMPANY LTD.*

Lamin S. Jatta
DELOITTE

Zainab Jawara-Alami
GAMBIA REVENUE AUTHORITY

Sulayman M. Joof
S.M. JOOF AGENCY

Amie Joof Conteh
KUNNI BOY CHAMBERS

Nani Juwara
*NATIONAL WATER AND
ELECTRICITY COMPANY LTD.*

Ismaila Kah
*DEVELOPMENT CONTROL UNIT
- DEPARTMENT OF PHYSICAL
PLANNING AND HOUSING*

Yusupha Kah
*DEPARTMENT OF STATE
FOR TRADE INDUSTRY AND
EMPLOYMENT*

Amadou Kebbeh
*GAMBIA PUBLIC
PROCUREMENT AUTHORITY*

George Kwatia
PRICEWATERHOUSECOOPERS

Thomas Nielsen
GAMBIA SHIPPING AGENCIES

Omar Njie
LAW FIRM OMAR NJIE

Pa M. M. N'jie
TRUST BANK LTD

Mary Abdoulie Samba-
Christensen
LEGAL PRACTITIONER

Jainaba Bah Sambou
*DEPARTMENT OF STATE FOR
JUSTICE*

Ebrima Sambou
*OFFICE OF THE CHIEF JUSTICE,
JUDICIARY OF THE GAMBIA*

Joseph E. Sarre
*GAMBIA ARCHITECTURAL AND
PLANNING CONSULTANTS*

Mama Fatima Singhateh
GT BANK

Hawa Sisay-Sabally
HAWA SISAY-SABALLY

Raymond Sock

Lamin Trawally
MAERSK LINE

Darcy White
PRICEWATERHOUSECOOPERS

GEORGIA

David Abuladze
*PRESIDENT OF THE UNION OF
ARCHITECTS OF GEORGIA*

Irakli Adeishvili
*TBILISI CITY COURT, CHAMBER
OF CIVIL CASES*

Natalia Babakishvili
*MGALOBLISHVILI, KIPIANI,
DZIDZIGURI (MKD) LAW FIRM*

Niko Bakashvili
*AUDITORIAL FIRM BAKASHVILI
& CO.*

Giorgi Begiashvili
*BEGIASHVILI & CO. LIMITED
LAW OFFICES*

Revaz Beridze
*USAID BUSINESS CLIMATE
REFORM*

Sandro Bibilashvili
BGI LEGAL

Bondo Bolkvadze
*CHEMONICS USAID
CONTRACTOR*

Temur Bolotashvili
*USAID BUSINESS CLIMATE
REFORM PROJECT*

Suliko Chachava
CARGO LOGISTICS GROUP

Vazha Chopikashvili
*ASSOCIATION FOR PROTECTION
OF LANDOWNERS RIGHTS
(APLR)*

Katie Dolidze
ALLIANCE GROUP HOLDING

Tsotne Ebralidze
*ARCI ARCHITECTURE &
DEVELOPMENT*

Courtney Fowler
PRICEWATERHOUSECOOPERS

Mariam Gabunia
*MINISTRY OF ECONOMIC
DEVELOPMENT*

David Giorgadze
*ASSOCIATION FOR PROTECTION
OF LANDOWNERS RIGHTS
(APLR)*

Lasha Gogiberidze
BGI LEGAL

Alexander Gomiashvili
JSC CREDIT INFO GEORGIA

Mamuka Gordeziani
GTS TRANS LOGISTICS

Tamuna Gvaramia
BGI LEGAL

Irakli Gvilia
CREDIT INFO GEORGIA

Gia Jandieri
*NEW ECONOMIC SCHOOL -
GEORGIA*

David Kakabadze
*GEORGIAN LEGAL
PARTNERSHIP*

Grigol Kakauridze
*MINISTRY OF ECONOMIC
DEVELOPMENT*

Luisa Khitarishvili
BOOZ ALLEN HAMILTON

Tamaz Khizanishvili
TBILISI STOCK EXCHANGE

Ivan Khokhlov
*DLA PIPER GVINADZE &
PARTNERS LP*

Maka Khutsishvili
CAUCASTRANSEXPRESS

Victor Kipiani
*MGALOBLISHVILI, KIPIANI,
DZIDZIGURI (MKD) LAW FIRM*

Anastasia Kipiani
PRICEWATERHOUSECOOPERS

Sergi Kobakhidze
PRICEWATERHOUSECOOPERS

Aieti Kukava
ALLIANCE GROUP HOLDING

Vakhtang Lejhava

David Lelashvili
*CHEMONICS, USAID
CONTRACTOR*

Giorgi Liluashvili
BGI LEGAL

Jaba Mamulashvili
BEGIASHVILI & CO.

Ekaterine Meskhidze
*NATIONAL AGENCY OF PUBLIC
REGISTRY*

Roin Migriauli
*LAW OFFICE "MIGRIAULI &
PARTNERS"*

Maia Okruashvili
*GEORGIAN LEGAL
PARTNERSHIP*

Mamuka Papuashvili
ENERGO PRO GEORGIA

Givi Petriashvili
IFC

Joseph Salukvadze
TBILISI STATE UNIVERSITY

Manzoor Shah
GLOBALINK LOGISTICS GROUP

Vakhtang Shevardnadze
*MGALOBLISHVILI, KIPIANI,
DZIDZIGURI (MKD) LAW FIRM*

Irakli Songulia
*ASSOCIATION FOR PROTECTION
OF LANDOWNERS RIGHTS
(APLR)*

Rusa Sreseli
PRICEWATERHOUSECOOPERS

Anna Tabidze
*MGALOBLISHVILI, KIPIANI,
DZIDZIGURI (MKD) LAW FIRM*

Matthew Tallarovic
PRICEWATERHOUSECOOPERS

Giorgi Tatalishvili
ENERGO PRO

Giorgi Tavartkiladze
DELOITTE

Tamara Tevdoradze
BGI LEGAL

Maia Tevzadze
*USAID BUSINESS CLIMATE
REFORM PROJECT*

Vladimir Tsophurashvili
CAUCASBUSINESSAUDIT LTD

Aleksandre Tvildiani
ALLIANCE GROUP CAPITAL

Tato Urjumelashvili
*USAID BUSINESS CLIMATE
REFORM PROJECT*

GERMANY

Allen & Overy LLP

Florian Amereller
AMERELLER RECHTSANWÄLTE

Gabriele Apfelbacher
*CLEARY GOTTLIEB STEEN &
HAMILTON LLP*

Kai Bandilla
*PRICEWATERHOUSECOOPERS
LEGAL*

Sven Bäumler
*VATTENFALL EUROPE
DISTRIBUTION HAMBURG
GMBH*

Henning Berger
WHITE & CASE

Astrid Berle
SCHUFA HOLDING AG

Jennifer Bierly
AVOCADO RECHTSANWÄLTE

Thomas Buhl
*CLEARY GOTTLIEB STEEN &
HAMILTON LLP*

Thomas Büssow
PRICEWATERHOUSECOOPERS

Pia Dorfmueller
PRICEWATERHOUSECOOPERS

Andreas Eckhardt
*PRICEWATERHOUSECOOPERS
LEGAL*

Dieter Endres
PRICEWATERHOUSECOOPERS

Horst Engelhardt
*DR. ENGELHARDT
TREUHAND GMBH
WIRTSCHAFTSPRÜFUNGS-
GESELLSCHAFT*

Sigrun Erber-Faller
*NOTARE ERBER-FALLER UND
VORAN*

Hanno Fierdag
RECHTSANWALT DR. FIERDAG

Markus J. Goetzmann
C·B·H RECHTSANWÄLTE

Andrea Gruss
ASHURST

Robert Gutte
*CLEARY GOTTLIEB STEEN &
HAMILTON LLP*

Rüdiger Harms
*CLEARY GOTTLIEB STEEN &
HAMILTON LLP*

Manfred Heinrich
DEUTSCHE BUNDESBANK

Götz-Sebastian Hök
*DR. HÖK STIEGLMEIER &
PARTNER*

Andrea Hosenfeld
ASHURST

Kai Christian Jaenecke
*PRICEWATERHOUSECOOPERS
LEGAL SERVICES*

Andre Jahn
*DR. HÖK STIEGLMEIER &
PARTNER*

Jörg Kraffel
White & Case

Peter Limmer
Notare Dr. Limmer & Dr. Friederich

Frank Lohrmann
Cleary Gottlieb Steen & Hamilton LLP

Max Lurati
PricewaterhouseCoopers Legal

Cornelia Marquardt
Norton Rose

Susanne Mattern
PricewaterhouseCoopers

Werner Meier
Cleary Gottlieb Steen & Hamilton LLP

Dirk Meyer-Claassen
Senatsverwaltung für Stadtentwicklung Berlin

Werner M. Mues
C·B·H Rechtsanwälte

Eike Najork
C·B·H Rechtsanwälte

Bernd Oberbossel

Dirk Otto
Norton Rose

Daniel Panajotow
Cleary Gottlieb Steen & Hamilton LLP

Peter Polke
Cleary Gottlieb Steen & Hamilton LLP

Sebastian Prügel
White & Case

Christopher Schauenburg
Cleary Gottlieb Steen & Hamilton LLP

Friedrich Tobias Schoene
Hogan & Hartson LLP

Thomas Schulz
Nörr Stiefenhofer Lutz, member of Lex Mundi

Hanno Sperlich
Cleary Gottlieb Steen & Hamilton LLP

Dirk Stiller
PricewaterhouseCoopers Legal Services

Dieter Straub
CMS Hasche Sigle

Tobias Taetzner
PricewaterhouseCoopers

Holger Thomas
SJ Berwin LLP

Valentin Todorow
Hogan & Hartson LLP

Christoph Torwegge
PricewaterhouseCoopers Legal

Heiko Vogt
Panalpina Welttransport GmbH

Annekatrens Werthmann-Feldhues
PricewaterhouseCoopers Legal

Karl-Heinz Wewetzer
Senatsverwaltung für Stadtentwicklung Berlin

Wilhelm Zeddies
Surveying Authorities - AdV c/o LGN

GHANA

Kelvin Abdallah
PricewaterhouseCoopers

Seth Adom-Asomaning
Peasah-Boadu & Co.

Seth Agyapong-Mensah
Fugar & Co.

Nene Amegatcher
Sam Okudzeto & Associates

Wilfred Kwabena Anim-Odame
Land Valuation Board

Adwoa S. Asamoah Addo
Fugar & Co.

Gideon Ayi-Owoo
PricewaterhouseCoopers

Elsie A. Awadzi
Lawfields Consulting

Emefa Baeta
Laryea, Laryea & Co. P.C.

Ellen Bannerman
Bruce-Lyle Bannerman & Thompson

Reginald Bannerman
Bruce-Lyle Bannerman & Thompson

Gwendy Bannerman
Fugar & Co.

Juliet Boabang
Bentsi-Enchill & Letsa, member of Lex Mundi

Abed Buabur
Andah and Andah

Dzidzedze Fiadjoe
PricewaterhouseCoopers

William Edem Fugar
Fugar & Co.

John Robert Jenkins
Golden Jubilee Terminal

Rosa Kudoadzi
Bentsi-Enchill & Letsa, member of Lex Mundi

George Kwatia
PricewaterhouseCoopers

Kenneth D. Laryea
Laryea, Laryea & Co. P.C.

Woodsworth Odame Larbi
Ministry of Lands, Forestry & Mines

Sam Okudzeto
Sam Okudzeto & Associates

Jacob Saah
Saah & Co.

Benjamin Sackar
Bruce-Lyle Bannerman & Thompson

Darcy White
PricewaterhouseCoopers

GREECE

George Apostolakos
Apostolakos Architects

Ioanna Argyraki
Kyriakides Georgopoulos & Daniolos Issaias, member of SEE Legal

Andreas Bagias
Kelemenis & Co.

Panayotis Bernitsas
M & P Bernitsas Law Offices

Alkistis Christofilou
IKRP Rokas & Partners

Sotiris Constantinou
Grant Thornton

Theodora D. Karagiorgou
Law Office T.J. Koutalidis

Eleni Dikonimaki
Teiresias S.A. Interbanking Information Systems

Anastasia Dritsa
Kyriakides Georgopoulos & Daniolos Issaias, member of SEE Legal

Margarita Flerianou
Economou International Shipping Agencies

Maira Galani
IKRP Rokas & Partners

Antigoni Gkarla
PricewaterhouseCoopers

Yannis Kelemenis
Kelemenis & Co.

Nicholas Kontizas
Zepos & Yannopoulos, member of Lex Mundi

Roula Koumparouli
Kremalis Law Firm, member of Ius Laboris

Yannis Kourniotis
M & P Bernitsas Law Offices

Dimitrios Kremalis
Kremalis Law Firm, member of Ius Laboris

Tom Kyriakopoulos
Kelemenis & Co.

Olga Maria Kyritsi
Kremalis Law Firm, member of Ius Laboris

Vassiliki G. Lazarakou
Zepos & Yannopoulos, member of Lex Mundi

Ioanna Lazaridou - Elmaloglou
Kelemenis & Co.

Evangelia Martinovits
IKRP Rokas & Partners

John Mazarakos
Elias Paraskevas Attorneys ✕✕✕✕

Yiannis Mazarakos
Elias Paraskevas Attorneys ✕✕✕✕

Effie G. Mitsopoulou
Kyriakides Georgopoulos & Daniolos Issaias, member of SEE Legal

Athanassios Pantazopoulos
IKRP Rokas & Partners and Dr. A. Pantazopoulos

Antonios Papadimitropoulos
Roussos & Partners

Athanassia Papantoniou
Kelemenis & Co.

Dimitris E. Paraskevas
Elias Paraskevas Attorneys ✕✕✕✕

Konstantinos Pistiolis
Elias Paraskevas Attorneys ✕✕✕✕

Katerina Politi
Kyriakides Georgopoulos & Daniolos Issaias, member of SEE Legal

Mary Psylla
PricewaterhouseCoopers

Kleanthis Roussos
Roussos & Partners

Alexandros Sakipis
PricewaterhouseCoopers

Ioannis Samios
Kyriakides Georgopoulos & Daniolos Issaias, member of SEE Legal

Harris Skordakis
PricewaterhouseCoopers Business Solutions S.A.

Alexia Stratou
Kremalis Law Firm, member of Ius Laboris

Spyridon Tsallas
IKRP Rokas & Partners

Antonios Tsavdaridis
IKRP Rokas & Partners

Christina Vlachtsis

Mariantzela Vlagopoulou
Kremalis Law Firm, member of Ius Laboris

Vicky Xourafa
Kyriakides Georgopoulos & Daniolos Issaias Law Firm

Freddy Yatracou
PricewaterhouseCoopers

Anna Zaravinou

GRENADA

Robert Branch
Supreme Court

James Bristol
Henry, Henry & Bristol

Evelyn Cenac
Customs

Zarah Chase
Grenada Electricity Services Ltd.

Anslem DeBourg
Labour Department

Ruggles Ferguson
Ciboney Chambers

Leroy Flavigny
Customs

Cosmus George
Reasonable Services Ltd

Henry Joseph
Accountants & Business Services

Kurt LaBarrie
Creative Design

Dickon Mitchell
Grant Joseph & Co., member of Lex Mundi

Niel Noel
Henry Hudson - Phillips & Co.

David Sinclair
Sinclair Enterprises Limited

Casandra Slocombe
Grenada Electricity Services Ltd.

Trevor St. Bernard
Lewis & Renwick

Phinsley St. Louis
St. Louis Service

Supreme Court Registry

Roselyn Wilkinson
Wilkinson, Wilkinson & Wilkinson

Daniella Williams
Danny Williams & Co.

GUATEMALA

Rodolfo Alegria Toruno
Beltranena, de la Cerda y Chavez

Maria Andrea Rimola Monroy
Cámara Guatemalteca de la Construcción

Pedro Aragón
Aragón & Aragón

Norka Aragón
Mayora & Mayora, S.C.

Ruby María Asturias Castillo
ACZALAW

Alexander Aziendadt
Beltranena, de la Cerda y Chavez

María de los Angeles Barillas Buchhalter
Saravia & Muñoz

Amaury Barrera
DHV Consultants

Roberto Batres
Carrillo & Asociados

Guillermo Bonillo
Bonilla, Montano, Toriello & Barrios

Maria del Pilar Bonillo
Bonilla, Montano, Toriello & Barrios

Caroline Bono
PricewaterhouseCoopers

Mario Adolfo Búcaro Flores
Díaz-Durán & Asociados Central Law

Agustín Buezo
Arrow Cargo

Eva Cacacho González
Quiñones, Ibargüen & Luján

Rodrigo Callejas Aquino
Carrillo & Asociados

Juan Pablo Carrasco de Groote
Díaz-Durán & Asociados - Central Law

Alfonso Carrillo
Carrillo & Asociados

Francisco José Castillo Chacón
Aguilar Castillo Love

Juan Carlos Castillo Chacón
Aguilar Castillo Love

Vanessa Castro Mirón
Mayora & Mayora, S.C.

José Cerezo
PricewaterhouseCoopers Legal Services

Paola van der Beek de Andrino
Cámara Guatemalteca de la Construcción

Karla de Mata
CPS Logistics

Rolando De Paz Barrientos
TransUnion

Estuardo Enrique Echeverria Nova
Superintendencia de Bancos

FedEx

Alejandro Fernández de Castro
PricewaterhouseCoopers

Walter Figueroa
Cámara Guatemalteca de la Construcción

Rodolfo Fuentes
Protectora de Crèdito Comercial

Veronika Sofia Gonzalez Bran
Díaz-Durán & Asociados - Central Law

Miguel Angel Gualim
DHV Consultants

Bethsy Hernandez
DHV Consultants

Juan Jegerlehner
Saravia & Muñoz

Christian Lanuza
Díaz-Durán & Asociados Central Law

Guillermo Lopez-Davis
Bufete Lopez Cordero

Andrés Lowenthal
Mayora & Mayora, S.C.

María Isabel Luján Zilbermann
Quiñones, Ibargüen & Luján

Sasha Maldonado
Aguilar Castillo Love

Enrique Maldonado
Ministry of Economy

Marco Antonio Martinez
CPS Logistics

Estuardo Mata Palmieri
Quiñones, Ibargüen & Luján

Edgar Mendoza
PricewaterhouseCoopers

Hugo Menes
Ayora & Mayora, S.C.

Guillermo Montano
Transactel Inc.

Ramón Ortega
PricewaterhouseCoopers

Marco Antonio Palacios
Palacios & Asociados

Andrea Paniagua
PricewaterhouseCoopers

Luis Pellecer
Carrillo & Asociados

Luis Rene Pellecer Lopez
Carrillo & Asociados

Jose Enrique Pensabene
Palacios y Asociados

Rita Pérez
Aragón & Aragón

Manuel Pérez
Carrillo & Asociados

Francisco Pilona
DHV Consultants

Julio Pinedo
PricewaterhouseCoopers

Gloria. E. Polanco
Frutas Tropicales de Guatemala, S.A. (FRUTESA)

Andres Porras Castillo
TransUnion

Fernando Quezado Toruño Quezada
Bufete Quezada Toruño, S.A.

Marco Tulio Reyna
Cámara Guatemalteca de la Construcción

Alfredo Rodríguez Mahuad
Rodriguez, Castellanos, Solares & Aguilar, S.C. -Consortium legal

Jorge Rolando Barrios

Salvador A. Saravia Castillo
Saravia & Muñoz

Klamcy Solorzano
DHV Consultants

Juan Tejada
PricewaterhouseCoopers

José Augusto Toledo Cruz
Arias & Muñoz

Arelis Torres de Alfaro
Superintendencia de Bancos

Elmer Vargas
ACZALAW

Raquel Villeda
Mayora & Mayora, S.C.

Julio Yon
DISAGRO, Soluciones Logisticas

GUINEA

Thierno A T Bah
Cabinet IRDED

Aminata Bah Tall
Nimba Conseil

Alpha Bakar Barry
Cabinet Karamoko Alpha Barry

Thérèse Beticka
Nimba Conseil

Sékou Camara
Direction Nationale des Impôts

Elhadj Ibrahima Sory Cissé
Tribunal du Travail de Conakry

Aïssata Diakite
Nimba Conseil

Mamadou Aliou Chérif Diallo
Koutou

Safiatou Kalissa
FIDAFRICA / PricewaterhouseCoopers

Mohamed Lahlou
FIDAFRICA / PricewaterhouseCoopers

Soumah Mama Aïssata
Ministère du Commerce

Raoul Mouthe
Nimba Conseil

Guy Piam
Nimba Conseil

Raffi Raja
Cabinet Koùmy

Nanamoudou Sangare
AEAE

André Sangare
Cabinet UIBG

SOCOPAO - SDV

Yansane Soumah
Manquepas

Facinet Soumah
Tribunal Première Instance de Kaloum

Ibrahima Sory Sow
Banque Centrale

Momoya Sylla
Nimba Conseil

Dominique Taty
FIDAFRICA / PricewaterhouseCoopers

Alphonse Temedieu
Nimba Conseil

GUINEA⊠BISSAU

Duarte Adolfo
Banco da África Ocidental, S. A.

Adelaida Mesa D'Almeida
Sole practicioner

Jonathan Darboux
BCEAO

Fatimatou Zahra Diop
BCEAO

Octávio Lopes
Octávio Lopes Advogados - Miranda Alliance

Miguel Mango
Audi - Conta Lda

Armando Mango
Ordem dos Advogados da Guiné-Bissau

Jaló Pires
Ministerio da Justica

Augusto Regala
Regala

Ribeiro
Regala

João Daniel Vaz Jr.
TransVaz, Lda

GUYANA

Ashton Chase
Law Office of Ashton Chase Associates

Deeds Registry

Lucia Loretta Desir
D & J Shipping Services

Guyana Office for Investment

High Court

Rexford Jackson
Singh, Doodnauth Law Firm

Land Registry

Rakesh Latchana
Ram & McRae

Colin Murray
Coastal Construction Services

Christopher Ram
Ram & McRae

Josephine Whitehead
Cameron & Shepherd

HAITI

Lionel Allen
Architect

Gemma Anglade
Brown Legal Group

Joel Baussan
CARIMPEX

Samuel Bien Aime
Ministere du Commerce et de l'Industrie

Brierre Pierre
Cabinet de Lespinasse

Jean Baptiste Brown
Brown Legal Group

Steve Christian Brown
Brown Legal Group

Martin Camille Cangé
Electricité d'Haïti

Raoul Celestin
Les Entreprises Commerciales Joseph Nadal S.A.

Djacaman Charles
Cabinet Gassant

Philippe-Victor Chatelain
Chatelain Cargo Services

Diggan d'Adesky
D'Adesky Import Export S.A.

Christian De Lespinasse
Cabinet de Lespinasse

Berto Dorcé
Juris Excel

Rigaud Duplan

Jean Gerard Eveillard
Cabinet Eveillard

Camille Fievre
Juris Excel

Irma Frederic
Avocat

Enerlio Gassant
Cabinet Gassant

Saurel Gilet
Ministere du Commerce et de l'Industrie

Emile Giordani

Gilbert Giordani
Etude Brisson Cassagnol

Archimelec Guerrier
Cabinet Gassant

Sylvie Handal
Hudicourt-Woolley

Chantal Hudicourt-Ewald
Cabinet Hudicourt-Woolley

Marc Hebert Ignace
Banque de la République d'Haiti

Luciner Joseph
Mairie de Petionville

Kareen T. Laplanche
UN Habitat

Wilhelm E. Lemke, Jr
ENMARCOLDA (D'adesky)

Louis Gary Lissade
Cabinet Lissade

Roberson Louis
Cabinet Gassant

Freshnel Lucien
Cabinet Gassant

Kathia Magloire
Cabinet Gassant

Alexandrine Nelson
Chatelain Cargo Services

Joseph Paillant
Ordre des Comptables Professionels Agrees d'Haiti

Jean Frederic Sales
Cabinet Sales

Margarette Sanon
Banque de la Republique d'Haiti

Paul Emile Simon
Architect

Salim Succar
Cabinet Lissade

Jean Vandal
Vandal & Vandal

HONDURAS

Fernando Aguilera
FIDE

Juan José Alcerro Milla
Aguilar Castillo Love

Lidabel Almendárez de Vijil
COHEP (Consejo Hondureño de la Empresa Privada)

Caroline Bono
PricewaterhouseCoopers

Claudia Patricia Cartagena
Oficina de Transparencia del Congreso Nacional de Honduras

Héctor Danilo Cartagena Gamero
PricewaterhouseCoopers

Janeth Castañeda de Aquino
Grupo Cropa Panalpina

Joel Castillo
Agencia Aduanera y Marítima CARE

Carmen Chevez
Comision Nacional de Bancos y Seguros

Ramón Discua
Batres, Discus, Martinez Abogados

Francisco Guillermo Durón Lopez
Bufete Durón

Fernando Fernández
PricewaterhouseCoopers Legal Services

Alejandro Fernández de Castro
PricewaterhouseCoopers

Lillizeth Garay
CNBS

Dania Waldina Gomez
Deloitte S.A. de C.V.

Santiago Herrera
FIDE

Marcela López Carrillo
PricewaterhouseCoopers

Heidi Luna
García & Bodán

Dennis Matamoros Batson
Arias & Muñoz

Rafael Enrique Medina Elvir
Instituto de la Propiedad

Juan Carlos Mejía Cotto
Instituto de la Propiedad

Ramón E. Morales
PricewaterhouseCoopers

Orestila Muñoz
Empresa Nacional de Energía Eléctrica

Jazna Vanessa Oquelí
García & Bodán

Ramón Ortega
PricewaterhouseCoopers

Andrea Paniagua
PricewaterhouseCoopers

Jose Ramon Paz
J.R. Paz & Asociados

Julio Pinedo
PricewaterhouseCoopers

Mauricio Quiñónez
PricewaterhouseCoopers

Dino Rietti
Arquitecnic

Milton Rivera
PricewaterhouseCoopers Legal Services

José Rafael Rivera Ferrari
J.R. Paz & Asociados

Enrique Rodriguez Burchard
Aguilar Castillo Love

Fanny Rodríguez del Cid
Arias & Muñoz

Martha R Saenz
Zacarías & Asociados

Godofredo Siercke
García & Bodán

Edgardo H. Sosa
Empresa Nacional de Energía Eléctrica

Cristian Stefan Handal
Zacarías & Asociados

Juan Tejada
PricewaterhouseCoopers

Jorge Torres
COHEP (Consejo Hondureño de la Empresa Privada)

Armando Urtecho López
COHEP (Consejo Hondureño de la Empresa Privada)

Roberto Manuel Zacarías Urrutia
Zacarías & Asociados

HONG KONG, CHINA

Brian Barron
Baker & McKenzie

Nicholas Chan
Squire, Sanders & Dempsey LLP

Albert P.C. Chan
The Hong Kong Polytechnic University

Alex Chan
The Land Registry

Vashi Chandi
Excellence International

Deborah Cheng
Squire, Sanders & Dempsey L.L.P.

Winnie Cheung
The Land Registry

Patrick Fontaine
Linklaters

Alexander Gong
Baker & McKenzie

Andrew Halkyard

Keith Man Kei Ho
Wilkinson & Grist

Rod Houng-Lee
PricewaterhouseCoopers

Kwok Ho Lam
CLP Power Limited

Cindy Lam
The Land Registry

David Lawrence
Deacons

Damasus Mak
Interlite Company Limited

Andrea Pellicani
Overseas Asia

Randolph Perry
Orrick, Herrington & Sutcliffe LLP

Martinal Quan
Metopro Associates Ltd.

Sara Tong
Temple Chambers

Anita Tsang
PricewaterhouseCoopers

Lawrence Tsong Tsong
TransUnion

Tak Kei Wan
CLP Power Limited

Susanne Wong
Hong Kong Economic & Trade Office

Raymond Wong
PricewaterhouseCoopers

Alexander Yuen
TransUnion

HUNGARY

Morley Allen & Overy Iroda

Pethő Ádám
BISZ Central Credit Information Ltd

Mark Balastyai
Futureal Holding Co.

Péter Bárdos

Sándor Békési
Partos & Noblet Lovells

Judit Bókai
Dr Bókai Notary Office

Hedi Bozsonyik
Szecskay Attorneys-at-Law

Zsuzsanna Cseri
Bárd, Cseri & Partners Law Firm

István Sándor
Kelemen, Meszaros, Sandor & Partners

Dalma Dudás
Réti, Antall & Madl Landwell

Gabriella Erdos
PricewaterhouseCoopers

György Fehér
Bellák & Partners Law Office, member of Ius Laboris

Anna Gáspár
Build-Econ Ltd.

Karolina Gombos
IB Grant Thornton Consulting Kft.

IFS Ltd.

Norbert Izer
PricewaterhouseCoopers

Zsuzsa Kardos
Bellák & Partners Law Office, member of Ius Laboris

Zsuzsanna Károlyi
Bellák & Partners Law Office, member of Ius Laboris

Adrienn Keller
Bellák & Partners Law Office, member of Ius Laboris

Andrea Kocziha
PricewaterhouseCoopers

Russell Lambert
PricewaterhouseCoopers

Petra Lencs
Bárd, Cseri & Partners Law Firm

Dóra Máthé
PricewaterhouseCoopers

Richárd Medve
Réti, Antall & Madl Landwell Law Firm

Lívia Mihovics
Réti, Antall & Madl Landwell Law Firm

László Mohai

Judit Nagy
Bellák & Partners Law Office, member of Ius Laboris

Sándor Németh
Szecskay Attorneys-at-Law

Tamás Pásztor
Nagy és Trócsányi Law Office, member of Lex Mundi

Tibor Szabó
Réti, Antall & Madl Landwell Law Firm

András Szecskay
Szecskay Attorneys-at-Law

Ilona Szarka
IB Grant Thornton Consulting Kft.

Ágnes Szent-Ivány
Sándor Szegedi Szent-Ivány Komáromi Eversheds

Viktória Szilágyi
Nagy és Trócsányi Law Office, member of Lex Mundi

László Szűcs
Réti, Antall & Madl Landwell Law Firm

Tibor Torok
PricewaterhouseCoopers

Ádám Tóth
Dr. Tóth & Dr. Gáspár Közjegyzői Iroda

Gábor Varga
BISZ Central Credit Information Ltd

Agnes Wolford
Budapest VIII. district Municipality

Blanka Zombori
PricewaterhouseCoopers

ICELAND

Elin Arnadottir
PricewaterhouseCoopers.

Kristján Ásgeirsson
Arkitektastofan OG

Guðrún Bergsteinsdóttir
BBA Legal

Þórður Búason
Reykjavik Construction Agency

Ólafur Eyjólfsson
PricewaterhouseCoopers

Skuli Th. Fjeldsted
Fjeldsted, Blöndal & Fjeldsted

Erlendur Gíslason
Logos, member of Lex Mundi

Ingibjörg Guðbjartsdóttir
BBA Legal

Elísabet Guðbjörnsdóttir
PricewaterhouseCoopers Legal Services

Reynir Haraldsson
Jónar Transport

Margrét Hauksdóttir
The Land Registry

Kristín Helga
PricewaterhouseCoopers Legal Services

Jón Ingi Ingibergsson
PricewaterhouseCoopers.

Erlingur E. Jónasson
Istak

Hróbjartur Jónatansson
AM Praxis Law Offices

Ásta Kristjánsdóttir
PricewaterhouseCoopers Legal Services

Ragna Matthíasdóttir
Istak

Daði Ólafsson
BBA Legal

Kristján Pálsson
Jónar Transport

Eyvindur Sólnes
LVA

Heiðar Stefánsson
Logos, member of Lex Mundi

Gunnar Sturluson
Logos, member of Lex Mundi

Rúnar Svavar Svavarsson
Orkuveita Reykjavíkur, Distribution-Electrical System

Bergþór Þormóðsson
Istak

INDIA

Nagarajan A.
Karthik Diesel Sales & Service

Rajan A.
Sweka International

Dulal Acharyya
Parasnath Tech Garments Pvt., Ltd.

Amit Agarwal
PricewaterhouseCoopers

Rohini Aggarwal
PricewaterhouseCoopers

Jameel Ahmed
AlifBiz

Ajit Bhuta and Associates

Rajiv Anand
PricewaterhouseCoopers

Palanikumar Arumugam
Variety Fashions

Aum Aruchitects

Pavithra B.
Maharani Laxmi Ammani Centre for Social Science Research

Rohit Bajaj
Chawla & Co.

Vikas Bansal
PricewaterhouseCoopers

Daksha Bara
Maharani Laxmi Ammani Centre for Social Science Research

Aditya Bhardwaj
Singhania & Partners, Solicitors & Advocates

Prachi Bhardwaj
Trilegal

Nitesh Bhasin
Trilegal

Bhasin International

Leena Chacko
Amarchand & Mangaldas & Suresh A. Shroff & Co.

Aman Chanda
PricewaterhouseCoopers

Harshala Chandorkar
Credit Information Bureau Ltd.

Vipul Chaturvedi
Innovative Eco-Care Pvt. Ltd.

Jyoti Chaudhari
Legasis Services Pvt. Ltd.

Anamika Chaudhary
Infini Juridique

Harminder Chawla
Chawla & Co.

Manjula Chawla
MCA Legal

Nimish Choudhary
PricewaterhouseCoopers

Sachin Chugh
Singhi Chugh & Kumar, Chartered Accountants

Kamlesh Desai
Mangal Exports

Prashant Dharia
Anant Industries

Rahul Dhawan
Fox Mandal

Thambi Durai
T. Durai & Co.

Koshy G. George
Karthik Diesel Sales & Service

C.V. Ganesh
Karthik Diesel Sales & Service

Rahul Garg
PricewaterhouseCoopers

G.D. Smabhare and Co.

Mayur Ghadia
*BHAVNA ELECTRICAL
INDUSTRIES*

Rajesh Gopinath
REGENT TELECOM

Dinesh Gupta
HARI OM INTERNATIONAL

Anil Gupta
HITECH GROUP

Chander Gupta
MR TOBACCO PVT., LTD.

Vinay Gupta
VINAY K GUPTA & CO.

Mano Haran
ACE OVERSEAS

Akil Hirani
MAJMUDAR & CO.

*INDIA BUSINESS DATABASE.
COM*

Vipin Jain
*SHREE BHIKSHU MARBLE AND
GRANITES*

Ashok Jain
SURAJ OVERSEAS

Atul Jani
*GAYATRI POLYMERS &
GEOSYNTHETICS.*

Malini Jayakumar
SRIBALAJI COSMETICS

Dharmendra Johari
STONEX INC.

G. D. Joseph
JOSEPH & CO.

Swaminathan Kalyanaraman
*DAKSHIN KREATIONS PRIVATE
LIMITED*

Dinesh Kanabar
PRICEWATERHOUSECOOPERS

A.V. Kane
*THE BRIHAN MUMBAI
ELECTRIC SUPPLY &
TRANSPORT UNDERTAKING*

Vaishal Kapadia
SHIDIMO INTERAUX PVT. LTD.

Deepti Kapoor
FOX MANDAL

Sushmita Kapur
FOX MANDAL

Rajas Kasbekar
LITTLE & CO.

Arun Kedia
VAV LIFE SCIENCES P. LTD.

Rajesh Khandelwal
SUMAN ENTERPRISES

Avinash Kumar
CHAWLA & CO.

Suraj Kumar
CHAWLA & CO.

Sailesh Kumar
*DRAGON EXPRESS FREIGHT
PVT LTD.*

Debashis Kumar
GANAPATI UDYOG

Abhishek Kumar
*SINGHANIA & PARTNERS,
SOLICITORS & ADVOCATES*

Karsh Kumar
*SINGHI CHUGH & KUMAR,
CHARTERED ACCOUNTANTS*

Vinu Kurian
*BETA HEALTHCARE PRODUCTS
PRIVATE LTD.*

Poonam Lila
*LEO CIRCUIT BOARDS PVT.
LTD.*

Manjunath Madhav
RIECO

Manish Madhukar
INFINI JURIDIQUE

*MAHARANI LAXMI AMMANNI
CENTRE FOR SOCIAL SCIENCE
RESEARCH*

Som Mandal
FOX MANDAL

Vipender Mann
*KNM & PARTNERS, LAW
OFFICES*

Kapish Mehta

Dara Mehta
LITTLE & CO.

Gajendra Mehta
NIMBUS CORPORATION

Jitesh Mehta
SOURCE INDIA

R.K. Mishra
METRO ASSOCIATES

Sharad Mishra
NEO MULTIMEDIAN

Saurabh Misra
*PARAS KUHAD & ASSOCIATES,
ADVOCATES ("PKA")*

Deepti Mittal
VINAY K GUPTA & CO.

Ravi Modi
DEV ROADLINES PVT. LTD.

Vikash Mohta
P.A. INTERNATIONAL

R. Muralidharan
PRICEWATERHOUSECOOPERS

Satish Murti
*MURTI & MURTI
INTERNATIONAL LAW
PRACTICE*

Anshoo Nayar
FOX MANDAL

NINE INTERNATIONAL

Anand Nivas
*DRAGON EXPRESS FREIGHT
PVT. LTD.*

Rajesh Palavankar
*INDOGLOBAL HEALTH
SCIENCES PRIVATE LIMITED*

Janak Pandya
NISHITH DESAI ASSOCIATES

Sujit Parakh
PRICEWATERHOUSECOOPERS

N. B. Patel
R.K. PLAST & ENGINEERS

Sanjay Patil

Ashish Patole
ACCENT TRENDZ

Niti Paul
CHAWLA & CO.

Francisca Philip
*SINGHANIA & PARTNERS,
SOLICITORS & ADVOCATES*

Nitin Potdar
*J. SAGAR ASSOCIATES,
ADVOCATES & SOLICITORS*

M. Prabhakaran
CONSULTA JURIS

Anand Prasad
TRILEGAL

Ahuja Punita
*SINGHI CHUGH & KUMAR,
CHARTERED ACCOUNTANTS*

Atramuddin Qureshi
HANDMADE CREATIONS

RAHUL EXPORTS

Capt Raj
*BRAHMA SHIPPING &
LOGISTICS*

Karthik Raja
*KNITTED GARMENTS
EXPORTER*

Sundar Rajan
CASSANOVA TEXTILES

Mohan Rajasekharan
MCA LEGAL

Krishnamurthy
Ramachandran
LEGASIS SERVICES PVT. LTD.

Mohan Ramakrishnan
*SATHYA AUTO PRIVATE
LIMITED*

Rangaswamy Ramakrishnan
TOP METROLOGY PVT. LTD.

Ashok Ramgir
HARSH IMPEX

Dipak Rao
*SINGHANIA & PARTNERS,
SOLICITORS & ADVOCATES*

Jessica Maria Rodrigues
*KAVJESS EXPORT IMPORT
TRADING COMPANY*

Martin Clifford Rodrigues
MAX EXPORTS

*ROOPA TEXTILES AND
TRIMMINGS*

Sameer Sah
MAJMUDAR & CO.

Abhishek Saket
INFINI JURIDIQUE

Dushir Saksena
*ICFAI SCHOOL OF FINANCIAL
STUDIES*

Sudhir Saksena
*ICFAI SCHOOL OF FINANCIAL
STUDIES*

Richie Sancheti
NISHITH DESAI ASSOCIATES

Deepak Sanghavi
ARL GLOBAL

Radhika Sankaran
FOX MANDAL

V. Siva Sankaran
T.S. CLASSIQUE

Mohit Saraf
LUTHRA & LUTHRA

Neha Satav
LEGASIS SERVICES PVT. LTD.

Srinivasan Seenu
AIR TRAVELS

Ratnika Sehgal
CHAWLA & CO.

Ramani Seshadri

Dilip Shah

Parag Shah
FOX MANDAL

Prakash Shah
PARIJAT MARKETING SERVICES

Ramasamy Shankar

Purushotam Sharma
GAJRAJ MEHANDI UYDOG

Ranjan Sharma
NET LINK COMPUTER

Anand Sharma
R.K. INDUSTRIES

Shivanand Shenoy

Tushar Shinde
*PRECISE BIOPHARMA PVT.
LTD.*

Vikram Shroff
NISHITH DESAI ASSOCIATES

Rajnish Shukla
*SINGHI CHUGH & KUMAR,
CHARTERED ACCOUNTANTS*

Sukhpreet Singh
CHAWLA & CO.

Ravinder Singh
INTERNATIONAL TOOLS CO.

Amaresh Kumar Singh
LUTHRA & LUTHRA

Kaviraj Singh
TRUSTMAN & CO

Ravinder Singhania
*SINGHANIA & PARTNERS,
SOLICITORS & ADVOCATES*

Arvind Sinha
BUSINESS ADVISORS GROUP

Uppu Sivaiah
ESPRIT DE CORPS INDIA

Ramamurthy Srinivasan
TRANSDEALS INC.

Rudra Srivastava
CHAWLA & CO.

Joseph Starr
STARLINE SHIPPING

STRETCH FASHIONS

Madhu Sweta
*SINGHANIA & PARTNERS,
SOLICITORS & ADVOCATES*

Niranjan Talati
SHREEJI MARKETING

Mahesh Thaker
M J & COMPANY

Krupa Thakkar
RUSHIL DECOR LTD.

Hira Tikoo
UNITED INTERNATIONAL

Aparna Tripathy
INFINI JURIDIQUE

Suhas Tuljapurkar
LEGASIS SERVICES PVT. LTD.

Sunil Upadhyaya
NATIONAL FOODS

Ratandeep Uppal
B M METAL CRAFTS

Kannan Venkatasamy
PERIPHERALCONNEXIONS

Saji Vijayadas
*DRAGON EXPRESS FREIGHT
PVT. LTD.*

Jude Xavier
REPPIN INTERNATIONAL

ZEDD TRADE

INDONESIA

Yose M. Adams
BANK INDONESIA

Nafis Adwani
*ALI BUDIARDJO, NUGROHO,
REKSODIPUTRO, MEMBER OF
LEX MUNDI*

Almer Apon
*PT BUANA MAS CITRA
LESTARI*

Hamud M. Balfas
*ALI BUDIARDJO, NUGROHO,
REKSODIPUTRO, MEMBER OF
LEX MUNDI*

Rick Beckmann
*BRIGITTA I. RAHAYOE &
SYAMSUDDIN*

Fabian Buddy Pascoal
*HANAFIAH PONGGAWA &
PARTNERS*

Ira A. Eddymurthy
*SOEWITO SUHARDIMAN
EDDYMURTHY KARDONO*

Sani Eka Duta
BANK INDONESIA

Greg Elms
IFC

Bambang Eryudhawan
*INDONESIAN INSTITUTE OF
ARCHITECTS*

Ahmad Fadli
*BRIGITTA I. RAHAYOE &
SYAMSUDDIN*

Iqbal Hadromi
HADROMI & PARTNERS

Djoko Hastowo
PLN KANTOR PUSAT

Ray Headifen
*PT PRIMA WAHANA CARAKA /
PRICEWATERHOUSECOOPERS*

Reno Hirdarisvita
HADROMI & PARTNERS

Rahayu N. Hoed
MAKARIM & TAIRA S.

Brigitta Imam Rahayoe
*BRIGITTA I. RAHAYOE &
SYAMSUDDIN*

Darrell R. Johnson
*INDONESIAN LEGAL
CONSULTANTS*

Mohammad Kamal
FURNITURE FIKAMAR

Mirza Karim
KARIMSYAH LAW FIRM

Ketua Kehormatan
*IKATAN ARKSITEK INDONESIA
JAKARTA*

David Knight
*AGRI-DEVELOPMENTS
INTERNATIONAL SA (PTY)
LIMITED*

Herry N. Kurniawan
*ALI BUDIARDJO, NUGROHO,
REKSODIPUTRO, MEMBER OF
LEX MUNDI*

Rudy Kusmanto
MAKARIM & TAIRA S.

Winita E. Kusnandar
KUSNANDAR & CO.

Erma Kusumawati
BANK INDONESIA

Julien Lallemand
PT SDV LOGISTICS

Ferry P. Madian
*ALI BUDIARDJO, NUGROHO,
REKSODIPUTRO, MEMBER OF
LEX MUNDI*

Ahmad Malkan
PT TRIHARPINDO MANDIRI

Eric Mancini
PT SDV LOGISTICS

Gopinath Menon
PT PricewaterhouseCoopers FAS

Karen Mills
KarimSyah Law Firm

Norma Mutalib
Makarim & Taira S.

Feria Ningsih
Makarim & Taira S.

Hartono Parbudi
Attorney-at-Law

Gita Petrimalia
Hadromi & Partners

Sandra Pranoto
IFC

Arno F. Rizaldi
Kusnandar & Co

L. Peter Rosner
Bank Dunia I the World Bank

Adam Sack
IFC

Isyana W. Sadjarwo
Notaris & Pejabot Pembuot Akio Tanoh

Pieter Henrianto Salean
Makarim & Taira S.

Henry Sandee
Bank Dunia I the World Bank

Gatot Sanyoto
Kusnandar & Co

Nur Asyura Anggini Sari
Bank Indonesia

Nasri Sebayang
PT PLN (Persero) Indonesia State Electricity Corporation

Indra Setiawan
Ali Budiardjo, Nugroho, Reksodiputro, member of Lex Mundi

Hans C. Shrader
IFC

Kevin Omar Sidharta
Ali Budiardjo, Nugroho, Reksodiputro, member of Lex Mundi

Ricardo Simanjuntak
Ricardo Simanjuntak & Partners

A. Kemalsjah Siregar
Kemalsjah & Associates

Bambang Soelaksono
The SMERU Research Institute

Pak Subani, SH
Amir Syamsuddin & Partners

Bernadeta Sulistyarimi
IFC

Galinar R. Kartakusuma Summitmas
Makarim & Taira S.

Yukiko LU. Tambunan
Bank Indonesia

Ernst G. Tehuteru
Ali Budiardjo, Nugroho, Reksodiputro, member of Lex Mundi

Gatot Triprasetio
Widyawan & Partners

Fararatri Widyadari
IFC

Robertus Winarto
PT Prima Wahana Caraka / PricewaterhouseCoopers

Ferry Zulkarnaen
Widyawan & Partners

IRAN

Mohammad Adib
Adib Law Firm

Behrooz Akhlaghi
International Law Office of Dr. Behrooz Akhlaghi & Associates

Reza Askari
Foreign Legal Affairs Group

Akhlaghi Behrooz
International Law Office of Dr Behrooz Akhlaghi & Associates

Gholamhossein Davani
Dayarayan Auditing & Financial Services

Saeed Hashemian
Adib Law Firm

Mehdi Heidarzadeh
Alvand Sayan International Trading Co, Ltd.

Javad Javaheri

Parisa Mazaheri
Atieh Associates

Mozaffar Mohammadian
Teema Bar International Transport

Yahya Rayegani
Farjam Law Office

Behrooz Rezazadeh
PSDC Group

Jamal Seifi
Dr. Jamal Seifi & Associates

Mir Shahbiz Shafe
Dr. Jamal Seifi & Associates

Cyrus Shafizadeh
Tavakoli & Shahabi

Mostafa Shahabi
Tavakoli & Shahabi

IRAQ

Hadeel Salih Abboud Al-Janabi
Mena Associates, member of Amereller Rechtsanwälte

Hadeel Al Janabi
Mena Associates, member of Amereller Rechtsanwälte

Ahmad Al Jannabi
Mena Associates, member of Amereller Rechtsanwälte

Farquad Al-Salman
F.H. Al-Salman & Co.

Florian Amereller
Amereller Rechtsanwälte

Blund Faridoon Arif Najeb
Attorney-at-Law

Husam Addin Hatim

Stephan Jäger
Amereller Rechtsanwälte

Imad Makki
Al Qarya Group Co.

IRELAND

Arthur Cox, member of Lex Mundi

Margaret Austin
Eugene F. Collins Solicitors

Alan Browning
LK Shields Solicitors, member of Ius Laboris

Jonathan Cullen
LK Shields Solicitors, member of Ius Laboris

Richard Curran
LK Shields Solicitors, member of Ius Laboris

Gavin Doherty
Eugene F. Collins Solicitors

Ciara Garry
ESB Networks

Paul Glenfield
Matheson Ormsby Prentice

Micheál Grace
Mason Hayes & Curran

Colm Kelly
PricewaterhouseCoopers

Ian Lavelle
LK Shields Solicitors, member of Ius Laboris

Margaret Masterson
PricewaterhouseCoopers

Gavan Neary
PricewaterhouseCoopers

Shane Neville
LK Shields Solicitors, member of Ius Laboris

Malichi O'Callaghan
Duncan & Grehan Partners

Panalpina World Transport Ltd.

Judith Riordan
Mason Hayes & Curran

Brendan Sharkey
Reddy Charlton McKnight

Gavin Simons
Eugene F. Collins Solicitors

Michael Treacy
Property Registration Authority

Colm Walsh
Irish International Freight Association

Maeve Walsh
Reddy Charlton McKnight

ISRAEL

Ronen Bar-Even
Weiss- Porat & Co.

Paul Baris
Yigal Arnon & Co.

Ofer Bar-On
Shavit Bar-On Gal-On Tzin Nov Yagur, Law Offices

Koby Cohen
PricewaterhouseCoopers

Lior Crystal
PricewaterhouseCoopers

Clifford Davis
S. Horowitz & Co., member of Lex Mundi

Roee Hecht
Shavit Bar-On Gal-On Tzin Nov Yagur, Law Offices

Aaron Jaffe
Yigal Arnon & Co.

Zeev Katz
PricewaterhouseCoopers

Vered Kirshner
PricewaterhouseCoopers

Gideon Koren
Ben Zvi Koren & Co. Law Offices

Orna Kornreich-Cohen
Shavit Bar-On Gal-On Tzin Nov Yagur, Law Offices

Michael Lagon
The Israel Electric Corporation Ltd.- Dan district

Michelle Liberman
S. Horowitz & Co., member of Lex Mundi

David Rosen
Idility Consulting

Gerry Seligman
PricewaterhouseCoopers

Yifat Shkedi-Shatz
S. Horowitz & Co., member of Lex Mundi

Edward Shtaif
The Israel Electric Corporation Ltd.- Dan district

Daniel Singerman
Business Data Israel + Personal Check

Nir Zalmanov
B.A.S

ITALY

Allen & Overy LLP

APL

Marianna Abbatticchio
Ristuccia & Tufarelli

Fabrizio Acerbis
PricewaterhouseCoopers

Paola Albano
Cleary Gottlieb Steen & Hamilton LLP

Gaetano Arnò
TLS / PricewaterhouseCoopers Legal Services

Maria Pia Ascenzo
Bank of Italy

Romina Ballana
PricewaterhouseCoopers

Paola Barazzetta
TLS / PricewaterhouseCoopers Legal Services

Susanna Beltramo
Studio Legale Beltramo

Antonino Boeti
Penelope S.R.L.

Roberto Bonsignore
Cleary Gottlieb Steen & Hamilton LLP

Luigi Brunetti
SDV

Carlo Bruno
Ashurst

Manuela Caccialanza
Jones Day

Sergio Calderara
Nunziante Magrone

Stefano Cancarini
TLS / PricewaterhouseCoopers Legal Services

Alessandro Caridi
PricewaterhouseCoopers

Gennaro Cassiani
GC Architecture Buro

Giorgio Cherubini
Pirola Pennuto Zei Associati

Domenico Colella
Portolano Colella Cavallo Studio Legale

Fabrizio Colonna
Camozzi Bonissoni Varrenti & Associati

Mattia Colonnelli de Gasperis
Lombardi Molinari e Associati Studio Legale

Barbara Corsetti
Portolano Colella Cavallo Studio Legale

Filippo Corsini
Chiomenti Studio Legale

CRIF S.p.A.

Luis Cristalli
Opdel Snc Di Ilario Dell Agnolo & Co.

Salvatore Cuzzocrea
PricewaterhouseCoopers

Antonio de Martinis
Spasaro De Martinis Law Firm

Elena D'errico
Abbatescianni Studio Legale e Tributario

Claudio Di Falco
Cleary Gottlieb Steen & Hamilton LLP

Domenico Di Pietro
Chiomenti Studio Legale

Marco Ettorre
Camozzi Bonissoni Varrenti & Associati

Carlo Falcetto
Nunziante Magrone

Emanuele Ferrari
Studio Notarile Ferrari

Linda Frigo
Studio Legale Macchi di Cellere e Gangemi

Ivana Genestrone
TLS Associazione Professionale di Avvocati e Commercialisti

Francesca Gesualdi
Cleary Gottlieb Steen & Hamilton LLP

Lucio Ghia
Ghia Law Firm

Vincenzo Giannantonio
Ashurst

Maurizio Giuntoni
Ecoproget S.R.L.

Federico Guasti
STUDIO LEGALE GUASTI

Giovanni Izzo
ABBATESCIANNI STUDIO LEGALE E TRIBUTARIO

Arena Lanfranco
PRODITAL LEATHERS

Stefano Macchi di Cellere
JONES DAY

Barbara Magn
CAMOZZI BONISSONI VARRENTI & ASSOCIATI

Fabrizio Mariotti

Mario Miccoli
NOTAIO MICCOLI

Valeria Morossini

Francesca Napoletano
CHIOMENTI STUDIO LEGALE

Gianmatteo Nunziante
NUNZIANTE MAGRONE

Francesco Nuzzolo
PRICEWATERHOUSECOOPERS

Luciano Panzani
SUPREME COURT

Paolo Pasqualis
NOTARY

Giovanni Patti
ABBATESCIANNI STUDIO LEGALE E TRIBUTARIO

Paolo Pedrazzoli
STUDIO NOTAIO PEDRAZZOLI

Andrea Pellicani
OVERSEAS ASIA

Federica Peres
PORTOLANO COLELLA CAVALLO STUDIO LEGALE

Laura Prosperetti
CLEARY GOTTLIEB STEEN & HAMILTON LLP

Giuseppe Ramondelli
STUDIO LEGALE NOTARILE DI FABIO RAMONDELLI CANTAMAGLI

Giuseppe Antonio Recchia
DIPARTIMENTO SUI RAPPORTI DI LAVORO E SULLE RELAZIONI INDUSTRIALI - UNIVERSITY OF BARI

Tommaso Romolotti
CAMOZZI BONISSONI VARRENTI & ASSOCIATI

Giovanni B. Sandicchi
CLEARY GOTTLIEB STEEN & HAMILTON LLP

Lamberto Schiona
STUDIO LEGALE SCHIONA

Massimiliano Silvetti
NUNZIANTE MAGRONE

Piervincenzo Spasaro
SPASARO DE MARTINIS LAW FIRM

Giovanni Stefanin
TLS ASSOCIAZIONE PROFESSIONALE DI AVVOCATI E COMMERCIALISTI

Robert Sturgess
SDV

Maria Antonietta Tanico
TANICO LAW FIRM

Silvio Tersilla
LOVELLS

Tommaso Tomaiuolo
TLS ASSOCIAZIONE PROFESSIONALE DI AVVOCATI E COMMERCIALISTI

Luca Tufarelli
RISTUCCIA & TUFARELLI

Benedetta Vannini
CLEARY GOTTLIEB STEEN & HAMILTON LLP

Emanuela Vittelo
CLEARY GOTTLIEB STEEN & HAMILTON LLP

Angelo Zambelli
LABLAW STUDIO LEGALE - FAILLA, ROTONDI & ZAMBELLI

Filippo Zucchinelli
TLS / PRICEWATERHOUSECOOPERS LEGAL SERVICES

JAMAICA

Theresa Bowen
LEX CARIBBEAN

Arlene E. Burton
PRICEWATERHOUSECOOPERS

Eric Alexander Crawford
PRICEWATERHOUSECOOPERS

EAGLE AND WHALE LTD.

Nicole Foga
FOGA DALEY & CO.

Stephanie Gordon
LEX CARIBBEAN

Herbert Winston Grant
GRANT, STEWART, PHILLIPS & CO.

Michael Hall
PRICEWATERHOUSECOOPERS

Corrine N. Henry
MYERS, FLETCHER & GORDON, MEMBER OF LEX MUNDI

Alicia P. Hussey
MYERS, FLETCHER & GORDON, MEMBER OF LEX MUNDI

Emile G.R. Leiba
MYERS, FLETCHER & GORDON, MEMBER OF LEX MUNDI

Sandra Minott-Phillips
MYERS, FLETCHER & GORDON, MEMBER OF LEX MUNDI

Viveen Morrison
PRICEWATERHOUSECOOPERS

Hilary Reid
MYERS, FLETCHER & GORDON, MEMBER OF LEX MUNDI

Natalie Farrell Ross
MYERS, FLETCHER & GORDON, MEMBER OF LEX MUNDI

Lisa N. Russell
MYERS, FLETCHER & GORDON, MEMBER OF LEX MUNDI

Humprey Taylor
TAYLOR CONSTRUCTION LTD.

Lorraine Thomas
LTN LOGISTICS INTERNATIONAL CO. LTD

Maliaca Wong
MYERS, FLETCHER & GORDON, MEMBER OF LEX MUNDI

JAPAN

ALLEN & OVERY

APL

Miho Arimura
HATASAWA & WAKAI LAW FIRM

CREDIT INFORMATION CENTER CORP.

Mijo Fujita
ADACHI, HENDERSON, MIYATAKE & FUJITA

Yoshimasa Furuta
ANDERSON MORI & TOMOTSUNE

Shigeru Hasegawa
ZEIRISHI-HOJIN PRICEWATERHOUSECOOPERS

Tamotsu Hatasawa
HATASAWA & WAKAI LAW FIRM

Takashi Hirose
OH-EBASHI LPC & PARTNERS

Yuko Inui
ORRICK, HERRINGTON & SUTCLIFFE LLP

Muriuki Kaindio
TOKYO TRADING CO. LTD.

Yosuke Kanegae
OH-EBASHI LPC & PARTNERS

Hideki Thurgood Kano
ANDERSON MORI & TOMOTSUNE

Yutaro Kawabata
NISHIMURA & ASAHI

Susumi Kawaguchi
OBAYASHI CORPORATION

Kotaku Kimu
ZEIRISHI-HOJIN PRICEWATERHOUSECOOPERS

Kenichi Kojima
USHIJIMA & PARTNERS

Toshio Miyatake
ADACHI, HENDERSON, MIYATAKE & FUJITA

Michihiro Mori
NISHIMURA & ASAHI

Tohru Motobayashi
MORI HAMADA & MATSUMOTO

Takafumi Nihei
NISHIMURA & ASAHI

Miho Niunoya
ATSUMI & PARTNERS

Naoko Sato
ANDERSON MORI & TOMOTSUNE

Tetsuro Sato
BAKER & MCKENZIE

Eri Sugihara
NISHIMURA & ASAHI

Hidetaka Sumomogi
NISHIMURA & ASAHI

Hiroyuki Suzuki
ZEIRISHI-HOJIN PRICEWATERHOUSECOOPERS

Toshio Taikoji
KAJIMA CORPORATION

Junichi Tobimatsu
MORI HAMADA & MATSUMOTO

Jun Yamada
ANDERSON MORI & TOMOTSUNE

Michi Yamagami
ANDERSON MORI & TOMOTSUNE

Akio Yamamoto
KAJIMA CORPORATION

Kazuhiro Yanagida
NISHIMURA & ASAHI

Setsuko Yufu
ATSUMI & PARTNERS

JORDAN

Saleh Abdelati
ALI SHARIF ZU'BI, ADVOCATES & LEGAL CONSULTANTS, MEMBER OF LEX MUNDI

Chaled Abu-Gharbieh
ARCH EPE, ENTERPRISE BUSINESS SOLUTIONS

Anas Abunameh
LAW & ARBITRATION CENTRE

Ibrahim Abunameh
LAW & ARBITRATION CENTRE

Bassam Abu-Rumman
ALI SHARIF ZU'BI, ADVOCATES & LEGAL CONSULTANTS, MEMBER OF LEX MUNDI

Sabri Al Khassib
AMMAN CHAMBER OF COMMERCE

Tamara Al-Banna
KHALIFEH & PARTNERS

Eman M. Al-Dabbas
INTERNATIONAL BUSINESS LEGAL ASSOCIATES

Arafat Alfayoumi
CENTRAL BANK

Omar Aljazy
ALJAZY & CO.ADVOCATES & LEGAL CONSULTANTS

Francis Bawab
PRICEWATERHOUSECOOPERS

Stephen Carpenter
CUSTOMS ADMINISTRATION MODERNIZATION PROGRAM (CAMP)

Micheal T. Dabit
MICHAEL T. DABIT & ASSOCIATES

Anwar Elliyan
THE JORDANIAN ELECTRIC POWER CO. LTD. (JEPCO)

GREATER AMMAN MUNICIPALITY

David H. Harrell
CUSTOMS ADMINISTRATION MODERNIZATION PROGRAM (CAMP)

George Hazboun

Zeina Jaradat
PRICEWATERHOUSECOOPERS

Rasha Laswi
ZALLOUM & LASWI LAW FIRM

Husam Jamil Madanat
LAND AND SURVEY DIRECTORATE

Firas Malhas
INTERNATIONAL BUSINESS LEGAL ASSOCIATES

Munaf Malkawi
MUFIDA ART MOSAIC

Maher Melhem
ABU-GHAZALEH PROFESSIONAL CONSULTING (AGPC)

Amer Mofleh
INTERNATIONAL BUSINESS LEGAL ASSOCIATES

Khaldoun Nazer
KHALIFEH & PARTNERS

OMQ AL BIHAR EST.

Ahmad Quandour
KHALIFEH & PARTNERS

Osama Y. Sabbagh
THE JORDANIAN ELECTRIC POWER CO. LTD. (JEPCO)

Stephan Stephan
PRICEWATERHOUSECOOPERS

Azzam Zalloum
ZALLOUM & LASWI LAW FIRM

Iyad Zawaideh
ALI SHARIF ZU'BI, ADVOCATES & LEGAL CONSULTANTS, MEMBER OF LEX MUNDI

Kareem Zureikat
ALI SHARIF ZU'BI, ADVOCATES & LEGAL CONSULTANTS, MEMBER OF LEX MUNDI

KAZAKHSTAN

Bolat Abaidullayev
BUSINESS ENVIRONMENT IMPROVEMENT PROJECT/ PRAGMA CORPORATION

Ardak Aiyekeyeva
PRICEWATERHOUSECOOPERS

Anvar Akhmedov
FIRST CREDIT BUREAU

Aman Aliev
ASSISTANCE, LLC LAW FIRM

Askar Baigazin
PRICEWATERHOUSECOOPERS LEGAL SERVICES

Nurlan Baimurzayev
MINISTRY OF JUSTICE

Ildus Bariev
GLOBALINK LOGISTICS GROUP

Aliya Baysenova
ASSISTANCE, LLC LAW FIRM

Gulnur Bekmukhanbetova
MCGUIREWOODS KAZAKHSTAN LLP

Shamshidin Bizhkenov
ARISTAN PROJECT MANAGEMENT GROUP (APMG)

Sergey Chetverikov
PRICEWATERHOUSECOOPERS

Michael Dark
MICHAEL WILSON & PARTNERS LTD.

Almaz Dosserbekov
ARISTAN PROJECT MANAGEMENT GROUP (APMG)

Ardak Dyussembayeva
AEQUITAS LAW FIRM

Courtney Fowler
PRICEWATERHOUSECOOPERS

Oleg Gnoevykh
M&M LOGISTICS

Semion Issyk
AEQUITAS LAW FIRM

Vladimir Ivlev
FIRST CREDIT BUREAU

Thomas Johnson
DENTON WILDE SAPTE

Elena Kaeva
PRICEWATERHOUSECOOPERS

Dina Kali
PricewaterhouseCoopers Legal Services

Nursultan Kassenov
Aristan Project Management Group (APMG)

Pasha Karim
Globalink Logistics Group

Yekaterina Kim
Michael Wilson & Partners Ltd.

Alexander Kurganov
M&M Logistics

Abdulkhamid Muminov
PricewaterhouseCoopers

Assel Musina
Denton Wilde Sapte

Berik Nurgaziyev
Aristan Project Management Group (APMG)

Yuliya Penzova
Aequitas Law Firm

Saniya Perzadayeva
Macleod Dixon

Elvis Robert
M&M Logistics

Asem Shaidildinova
PricewaterhouseCoopers

Kanat Skakov
Salans

Zhaniya Ussen
Assistance, LLC Law Firm

Dubek Zhabykenov
BA Services International LLC

Danat Zhakenov
Zhakenov & Partners in association with Grundberg Mocatta Rakison

Valerie A. Zhakenov
Zhakenov & Partners in association with Grundberg Mocatta Rakison

Liza Zhumakhmetova
PricewaterhouseCoopers Legal Services

Ainur Zhumanbayeva
Michael Wilson & Partners Ltd.

KENYA

George Akoto
Akoto & Company Advocates

George Arego
Siginon Freight Ltd

Anil Madhavan Changwony
Siginon Freight Ltd

Oliver Fowler
Kaplan & Stratton

Fiona Fox
Chunga Associates

Peter Gachuhi
Kaplan & Stratton

Francis Gichuhi
Prism Designs Africa

Edmond Gichuru
Gichuru Kiplagat & Advocates

William Ikutha Maema
Iseme, Kamau & Maema Advocates

Karori Kamau
Iseme, Kamau & Maema Advocates

Patrick Karara
PricewaterhouseCoopers

Peter Kenani
Homeline Consolidation Services Ltd.

Morris Kimuli
B.M. Musau & Co. Advocates

Felix Kioko
B.M. Musau & Co. Advocates

Meshack T. Kipturgo
Siginon Freight Ltd

Owen Koimburi
SCI Koimburi Tucker & Co.

Alexandra Kontos
Walker Kontos Advocates

Gilbert Langat
Kenya Shippers Council

Nicholas Malonza
B.M. Musau & Co. Advocates

Victor Majani
Osoro and Co, Certified Public Accountants

Sam Mbugua
Philton

Rosemary Mburu
Institute of Trade Development

Metropol East Africa Ltd.

Osoro Moses Osano
Muriu Mungai& Co Advocates

Washington Muthamia
Alexandria Freight Forwarders Ltd.

Judy Mwangi
Chunga Associates

Wachira Ndege
Credit Reference Bureau Africa Ltd.

Stephen Okello
PricewaterhouseCoopers

Erastus K. Omolo
Erastus & Co. Certified Public Accountants

Elisha Ongoya
Asiema & Co Advocates

Tom Onyango
Ochieng, Onyango, Kibet & Ohaga

Cephas Osoro
Osoro and Co, Certified Public Accountants

Mohammed Ramadhan
Del Ray Cargo

Sonal Sejpal
Anjarwalla & Khanna Advocates

Rodgers Abwire Sekwe
Muriu Mungai & Co Advocates

Deepen Shah
Walker Kontos Advocates

Mahat Somane
Kaplan & Straton

John Syekei Nyandieka
Muriu Mungai & Co Advocates

Joseph Taracha
The Central Bank

Adrian Topoti
B.M. Musau & Co. Advocates

KIRIBATI

Kenneth Barden
Attorney-at-Law

William Wylie Clarke
Howards Lawyers

Lawrence Muller
Betio City Council

Tion Neemia
Shipping Agency of Kiribati

Ports Authority

Matereta Raiman
Ministry of Finance & Economic Development

KOREA

Yong Seok Ahn
Lee & Ko

Dong-Ook Byun
Customs Service

Min-Sook Chae
Korea Credit Bureau

Hyeong-Tae Cho
Samil PricewaterhouseCoopers

Han-Jun Chon
Samil PricewaterhouseCoopers

Eui Jong Chung
Bae, Kim & Lee LLC

Lionel Darrieutort
SDV

Marc Fally
SDV

Sang-goo Han
Yoon Yang Kim Shin & Yu

Sean C. Hayes
Ahnse Law Offices

Baek Huh
Hwang Mok Park P.C., member of Lex Mundi

C.W. Hyun
Kim & Chang

James I.S. Jeon
Sojong Partners

Young-Cheol Jeong
Yonsei University

Kim Jung In
Korea Credit Bureau

Gee-Hong Kim
Horizon Law Group

Jung-In Kim
Korea Credit Bureau

Yong-Deog Kim
Korea Credit Bureau

Kyu-Dong Kim
Samil PricewaterhouseCoopers

S.E. Stephan Kim
Sojong Partners

Wonhyung Kim
Yoon Yang Kim Shin & Yu

Korea Information Service

Jung Myung Lee
Hwang Mok Park P.C., member of Lex Mundi

Hye Jeong Lee
Ahnse Law Offices

Sung Whan Lee
Ahnse Law Offices

Kwon Lee
Kim & Chang

Kyu Wha Lee
Lee & Ko

Jada Soyun Lee
Orrick, Herrington & Sutcliffe LLP

Sun-Kyoo Lee
Samil PricewaterhouseCoopers

June Ha Lim
Hwang Mok Park P.C., member of Lex Mundi

Patrick J. Monaghan
Kim & Chang

Sung-Ho Moon
Horizon Law Group

Ho Joon Moon
Lee & Ko

Je-Sik Myoung
Korea Credit Bureau

Byung-Hun Nam
NamSun Industries co.

Panalpina IAF Ltd.

Sang Il Park
Hwang Mok Park P.C., member of Lex Mundi

J.T. Park
Kim & Chang

Jung-Taek Park
Kim & Chang

Jeong Seo
Kim & Chang

Dong-Suk Wang
Korea Credit Bureau

Kim Ji Woong
Korea Credit Bureau

Jee-Yeon Yu
Kim & Chang

KUWAIT

Ihab AbbasCalderon
Al-Fahad & Co, Deloitte & Touche

Labeed Abdal
The Law Firm of Labeed Abdal

Amal Abdallah
Al-Saleh & Partners

Mahmoud Abdulfattah
The Law Offices of Mishari Al-Ghazali

Lina A. Adlouni
The Law office of Al-Essa & Partners

Abdullah Al-Ayoub
Abdullah Kh. Al-Ayoub & Associates, member of Lex Mundi

Ammar Al-Fouzan
The Law Offices of Mishari Al-Ghazali

Mishari M. Al-Ghazali
The Law Offices of Mishari Al-Ghazali

Mohammed Al Noor
Al-Twaijri And Partners Law Firm

Reema Ali
Ali & Partners

Abdullah Bin Ali
Packaging and Plastic Industries Co. (KSC)

Tim Bullock
Al-Fahad & Co, Deloitte & Touche

Paul Day
Al Sarraf & Al Ruwayeh

Sam Habbas
Al Sarraf & Al Ruwayeh

Nazih Abdul Hameed
Al-Saleh & Partners

Sunil Jose
Abu-Ghazaleh Consulting and Intellectual Property

Mazen A. Khoursheed
Packaging and Plastic Industries Co. (KSC)

Jasmin Paurus Kohina
Abdullah Kh. Al-Ayoub & Associates, member of Lex Mundi

Chirine Krayem Moujaes
The Law Offices of Mishari Al-Ghazali

Dany Labaky
The Law Offices of Mishari Al-Ghazali

Shaik Haneef Moinuddin
Law Offices of Jamal Ahmed Abdullah

Mohamed Omar
Al Markaz Law Firm

Omar Hamad Yousuf Al-Essa
The Law office of Al-Essa & Partners

Ahmed Zakaria
Al Sarraf & Al Ruwayeh

KYRGYZ REPUBLIC

Ainura Abdyrakunova
Lorenz Law Firm

Gulnara Ahmatova
International Business Council

Nursulu Ahmetova
USAID Business Environment Improvement Project

Renat Akhmetov
PricewaterhouseCoopers

Sabyrbek Akimabev
USAID Business Environment Improvement Project

Niyazbek Aldashev
Lorenz Law Firm

Natalia Alenkina
Consultant Holding

Petrova Alevtina
Engineering Service Ltd

Dogadin Andrei
Union of Entrepreneurs of Kyrgyzstan

Talaybek Asylbekov
International Business Council

Denis Bagrov
Grata Law Firm

Zharkymbai Baiganchuk
CONSTRUCTION COMPANY
-KEP STROI LTD

Julia Bulatova
LAW FIRM "PARTNER"

Natalia Dolinskaya
INTERNATIONAL BUSINESS
COUNCIL

Akjoltoi Elebesova
CREDIT INFORMATION BUREAU
ISHENIM

Damir Esenaliev
THE WORLD BANK

Saltanat Ismailova
PRICEWATERHOUSECOOPERS

Nurbek Ismankulov
M&M LOGISTICS

Kalberdiev Junus
Kalmamtovich
THE GOSREGISTER OF THE
KYRGZ REPUBLIC

Abykeev Kadyr
AVANGARD STYLE LTD

Vitaliy Khabarov
LAW FIRM "PARTNER"

Tatyana Kim
CHAMBER OF TAX
CONSULTANTS

Galina Kucheryavaya
ORGANISATION GROUP OF
PROCREDIT HOLDING

Nurdin Kumushbekov
USAID BUSINESS
ENVIRONMENT IMPROVEMENT
PROJECT

Usen Kydyraliev
ENTREPRENEURS' UNION OF
KYRGYZSTAN

Erkin Madmarov
IBC

Barno Marazykova
LAW FIRM "PARTNER"

Tatyana Marchenko
LORENZ LAW FIRM

Olga Moreva
USAID BUSINESS
ENVIRONMENT IMPROVEMENT
PROJECT

Janybek Musaev

Almas Nakipov
PRICEWATERHOUSECOOPERS

Aidin Nazekov
USAID BUSINESS
ENVIRONMENT IMPROVEMENT
PROJECT

Sergey Oseledko

Erkin Sakiev

Kanat Seidaliev
GRATA LAW FIRM

Yulia Shapovalova
USAID BUSINESS
ENVIRONMENT IMPROVEMENT
PROJECT

Anastasia Shloeva
GLOBALINK LOGISTICS GROUP

Mirgul Smanalieva
LAW FIRM "PARTNER"

Kalybek Sultanov
AVANGARD STYLE LTD

Rakhat Suyumkulov
MENS LTD.

Azim Usmanov
GRATA LAW FIRM

Alexander Vachtel
SENTYABR STROI LTD

LAO PDR

Kelly Bird
ASIAN DEVELOPMENT BANK

Sithong Chanthasouk
DFDL MEKONG LAW GROUP

Lasonexay Chanthavong
DFDL MEKONG LAW GROUP

Sounthorn Chanthavong
DFDL MEKONG LAW GROUP

Aristotle David
DFDL MEKONG LAW GROUP

Chanthaly Douangvilay
PEOPLE'S COURT OF
VIENTIANE CAPITAL

Daodeuane Duangdara
PRICEWATERHOUSECOOPERS

Grant Follett
DFDL MEKONG LAW GROUP

Daniel Horngren
VASCO LTD.

Richard Irwin
PRICEWATERHOUSECOOPERS

Khamkhong Liemphrachan
MINISTRY OF JUSTICE

Ketsana Phommachanh
MINISTRY OF JUSTICE,
LAW RESEARCH AND
INTERNATIONAL COOPERATION
INSTITUTE

Thavorn Rujivanarom
PRICEWATERHOUSECOOPERS

Khongsy Saisouttha
JUDGEMENT ENFORCEMENT
OFFICE OF VIENTIANE
CAPITAL

Sivath Sengdouangchanh
CONSULTANT

Khamphone Sipaseuth
MINISTRY OF JUSTICE

Danyel Thomson
DFDL MEKONG LAW GROUP

Andrea Wilson
DFDL MEKONG LAW GROUP

LATVIA

Ilze Abika
SKUDRA & UDRIS LAW
OFFICES

Mike Ahern
PRICEWATERHOUSECOOPERS

Martins Aljens
LEJINS, TORGANS & PARTNERS,
MEMBER OF IUS LABORIS

Laura Ausekle
LATVIJAS BANKA

Elina Bedanova
LEJINS, TORGANS & PARTNERS,
MEMBER OF IUS LABORIS

Eva Berlaus-Gulbe
SORAINEN

Iveta Berzina
SKUDRA & UDRIS LAW
OFFICES

Ilze Bukaldere
LIEPA, SKOPINA/ BORENIUS

Andis Burkevics
SORAINEN LAW OFFICES

Andis Čonka
LATVIJAS BANKA

Zane Džule
LIEPA, SKOPIⓃA/BORENIUS

Zlata Elksnina-Zascirinska
PRICEWATERHOUSECOOPERS

Ivars Grunte
LOZE, GRUNTE & CERS

Andris Ignatenko
ESTMA SIA

Aija Klavinska
PRICEWATERHOUSECOOPERS

LAW OFFICES BLUEGER &
PLAUDE

Oleg Litskevich
MARITIME TRANSPORT &
AGENCIES

Janis Loze
SORAINEN

Zane Paeglite
SORAINEN

Baiba Plaude
BLUEGER &PLAUDE

Ivars Pommers
LAWFIRM OF GLIMSTEDT AND
PARTNERS

Inese Rendeniece
LOZE, GRUNTE & CERS

Sergejs Rudans
LIEPA, SKOPIⓃA/BORENIUS

Dace Silava-Tomsone
LEJINS, TORGANS & PARTNERS,
MEMBER OF IUS LABORIS

Mihails Špika
JSC DZINTARS

Sarmis Spilbergs
KLAVINS&SLAIDINS/LAWIN,
MEMBER OF LEX MUNDI

Zane Stalberga - Markvarte
MARKVARTE & PARTNERI LAW
OFFICE

Pāvels Tjuševs
EVERSHEDS BITⓃNS -
ATTORNEYS-AT-LAW

Maris Vainovskis
EVERSHEDS BITⓃNS -
ATTORNEYS-AT-LAW

Vilmars Vanags
RE & RE LTD.

Maija Volkova
LEJINS, TORGANS & PARTNERS,
MEMBER OF IUS LABORIS

Agate Ziverte
PRICEWATERHOUSECOOPERS

LEBANON

ASSOCIATION OF BANKS IN
LEBANON (ABL)

Nada Abdelsater-Abusamra
RAPHAËL & ASSOCIÉS

Wadih Abou Nasr
PRICEWATERHOUSECOOPERS

Soha Al Masri
ABU GHAZALEH- LEGAL

Manal Assir
UNDP

Jean Baroudi
BAROUDI & ASSOCIATES

Rita Bou Habib
AUDIT DEPARTMENT - VAT
DIRECTORATE

Najib Choucair
CENTRAL BANK

Bernard Choueiri
MINISTRY OF JUSTICE

Sanaa Daakour
THE LEVANT LAWYERS

Bassam Darwich
P & G LEVANT

Theodore De Mar Youssef
BADRI AND SALIM EL
MEOUCHI LAW FIRM, MEMBER
OF INTERLEGES

ELECTRICITÉ DU LIBAN

Chadia El Meouchi
BADRI AND SALIM EL
MEOUCHI LAW FIRM, MEMBER
OF INTERLEGES

Dania George
PRICEWATERHOUSECOOPERS

Samer Ghalayini
THE LEVANT LAWYERS

Fady Ghanem
BADRI AND SALIM EL
MEOUCHI LAW FIRM, MEMBER
OF INTERLEGES

Greta Habib
BADRI AND SALIM EL
MEOUCHI LAW FIRM, MEMBER
OF INTERLEGES

Louay Hajj Chehadeh
MINISTRY OF FINANCE

Abdallah Hayek
HAYEK GROUP

Wajih Hechaime
HECHAIME LAW FIRM

Fady Jamaleddine
THE LEVANT LAWYERS

Maria Jreissat
BADRI AND SALIM EL
MEOUCHI LAW FIRM, MEMBER
OF INTERLEGES

Georges Jureidini
COSERV SARL - PANALPINA
AGENTS

Georges Kadige
KADIGE & KADIGE LAW FIRM

Michel Kadige
KADIGE & KADIGE LAW FIRM

Wael Khaddage
MINISTRY OF FINANCE

Najib Khattar
KHATTAR ASSOCIATES

Albert Laham

Georges Maarawi
MINISTRY OF FINANCE

Eddy Maghariki
HYAM G. MALLAT LAW FIRM

Georges Mallat
HYAM G. MALLAT LAW FIRM

Nabil Mallat
HYAM G. MALLAT LAW FIRM

Rachad Medawar
OBEID & MEDAWAR LAW FIRM

Fadi Moghaizel
MOGHAIZEL LAW FIRM,
MEMBER OF LEX MUNDI

Mario Mohanna
PATRIMOINE CONSEIL SARL

Mirvat Mostafa
THE LEVANT LAWYERS

Rahaf Nabbouh
UNDP PROJECT OF THE
MINISTRY OF FINANCE

Toufic Nehme
LAW OFFICE OF ALBERT
LAHAM

Hermes Peter
INCOME TAX DEPARTMENT-
BEIRUT

Moussa Raphaël
RAPHAËL & ASSOCIÉS

Mazen Rasamny
BADRI AND SALIM EL
MEOUCHI LAW FIRM, MEMBER
OF INTERLEGES

Mireille Richa
TYAN & ZGHEIB LAW FIRM

Jihad Rizkallah
BADRI AND SALIM EL
MEOUCHI LAW FIRM, MEMBER
OF INTERLEGES

Elias A. Saadé
MOGHAIZEL LAW FIRM,
MEMBER OF LEX MUNDI

Joseph Safar
HAYEK GROUP

Christel Salem
BADRI AND SALIM EL
MEOUCHI LAW FIRM, MEMBER
OF INTERLEGES

Rached Sarkis
RACHED SARKIS OFFICE

Camille C. Sifri
PRICEWATERHOUSECOOPERS

Nady Tyan
TYAN & ZGHEIB LAW FIRM

Patricia Yammine
PRICEWATERHOUSECOOPERS

Ray Yazbeck
BADRI AND SALIM EL
MEOUCHI LAW FIRM, MEMBER
OF INTERLEGES

LESOTHO

Mark Badenhorst
PRICEWATERHOUSECOOPERS

Paul De Chalain
PRICEWATERHOUSECOOPERS

Thuso Green
PROCELL

Gerhard Gouws
NEDBANK LTD.

HARLEY & MORRIS

Mankhebe Makume
LESOTHO ELECTRICITY
COMPANY (PTY) LTD

João Martins
PRICEWATERHOUSECOOPERS

Mathias Matshe
SHEERAN & ASSOCIATES

Kuena Mophethe
K.MOPHETHE LAW CHAMBERS

Thabo Mpaka
MPAKA CHAMBERS

Theodore Ntlatlapa
DNT ARCHITECTS

Malaika Ribeiro
PRICEWATERHOUSECOOPERS

Peter Sands
SDV (PTY) LTD

Duduzile Seamatha
SHEERAN & ASSOCIATES

Tiisetso Sello-Mafatle
SELLO - MAFATLE CHAMBERS

Lindiwe Sephomolo
*ASSOCIATION OF LESOTHO
EMPLOYERS AND BUSINESS*

Phoka Thene
SELLO - MAFATLE CHAMBERS

LIBERIA

Kelvin Abdallah
PRICEWATERHOUSECOOPERS

Gideon Ayi-Owoo
PRICEWATERHOUSECOOPERS

Golda A. Bonah
SHERMAN & SHERMAN

G. Raymond Bright
*ACE PLANNING &
CONSULTING GROUP*

F. Augustus Caesar, Jr.
CAESAR ARCHITECTS, INC.

Roy Chalkley
UMARCO

*CITY CORPORATION OF
MONROVIA*

Henry Reed Cooper
COOPER & TOGBAH LAW FIRM

Frank Musah Dean
DEAN & ASSOCIATES

Peter Doe-Sumah
GBEHZON HOLDINGS INC.

Dzidzedze Fiadjoe
PRICEWATERHOUSECOOPERS

Christine Sonpon Freeman
COOPER & TOGBAH LAW FIRM

Cyril Jones
JONES & JONES

George Kwatia
PRICEWATERHOUSECOOPERS

Martha Lackay
*LIBERIA ELECTRICITY
CORPORATION*

Steven Neufville
MINISTRY OF PUBLIC WORKS

Togba Ngangana
MINISTRY OF PUBLIC WORKS

Sylvanus O' Connor
AEP CONSULTANTS INC.

Chan-Chan A. Paegar
SHERMAN & SHERMAN

Joseph N. Siaway
MAERSK LTD.

G. Lahaison Waritay
MINISTRY OF PUBLIC WORKS

Darcy White
PRICEWATERHOUSECOOPERS

Ben Wolo
*LIBERIA
TELECOMMUNICATIONS
CORPORATION*

Melvin Yates
*COMPASS INC., CLEARING AND
FORWARDING*

Harvy T. Yuan, Sr.
*LIBERIA ELECTRICITY
CORPORATION*

LITHUANIA

Kęstutis Adamonis
SORAINEN

Mike Ahern
PRICEWATERHOUSECOOPERS

Petras Baltusevicius
DSV TRANSPORT UAB

Kim Bartholdy
DSV TRANSPORT UAB

Kristina Bartuseviciene
PRICEWATERHOUSECOOPERS

Vilius Bernatonis
*SUTKIENE, PILKAUSKAS &
PARTNERS*

Renata Beržanskienė
SORAINEN LAW OFFICES

Vilma Brilinkeviciene
*SUTKIENE, PILKAUSKAS &
PARTNERS*

Dovilė Burgienė
*LAW FIRM LIDEIKA,
PETRAUSKAS, VALI🞖NAS IR
PARTNERIAI LAWIN, MEMBER
OF LEX MUNDI*

Sergej Butov
*LAW FIRM LIDEIKA,
PETRAUSKAS, VALI🞖NAS IR
PARTNERIAI LAWIN, MEMBER
OF LEX MUNDI*

Robertas Ciocys
*LAW FIRM LIDEIKA,
PETRAUSKAS, VALI🞖NAS IR
PARTNERIAI LAWIN, MEMBER
OF LEX MUNDI*

Radville Ciricaite
*FOIGT & PARTNERS / REGIJA
BORENIUS*

Giedre Domkute
*LAW FIRM AAA BALTIC
SERVICE COMPANY*

Ieva Dosinaite
*NORCOUS & PARTNERS,
MEMBER OF IUS LABORIS*

Mindaugas Dovidauskas
FORTUNE LAW GROUP

Vilma Dovidauskiene
*COMPETENT AMERINDE
CONSOLIDATED*

Stasys Drazdauskas
*FOIGT & PARTNERS / REGIJA
BORENIUS*

Rolandas Galvėnas
*LAW FIRM LIDEIKA,
PETRAUSKAS, VALI🞖NAS IR
PARTNERIAI LAWIN, MEMBER
OF LEX MUNDI*

Simas Gudynas
*LAW FIRM LIDEIKA,
PETRAUSKAS, VALI🞖NAS IR
PARTNERIAI, MEMBER OF LEX
MUND*

Agne Jakaite
*LAW FIRM LIDEIKA,
PETRAUSKAS, VALI🞖NAS IR
PARTNERIAI LAWIN, MEMBER
OF LEX MUNDI*

Agne Jonaitytė
SORAINEN LAW OFFICES

Viktorija Kapustinskaja
SORAINEN LAW OFFICES

Jurgita Karvelė
*FOIGT & PARTNERS / REGIJA
BORENIUS*

Jonas Kiauleikis
*FOIGT & PARTNERS / REGIJA
BORENIUS*

Mindaugas Kiškis
*LAW FIRM LIDEIKA,
PETRAUSKAS, VALI🞖NAS IR
PARTNERIAI LAWIN, MEMBER
OF LEX MUNDI*

Raminta Klumbyte

Egidijus Kundelis
PRICEWATERHOUSECOOPERS

Žilvinas Kvietkus
*NORCOUS & PARTNERS,
MEMBER OF IUS LABORIS*

Asta Macijauskiene
*LAW FIRM BERNOTAS &
DOMINAS GLIMSTEDT*

Gytis Malinauskas
SORAINEN LAW OFFICES

Linas Margevicius
*LEGAL BUREAU OF LINAS
MARGEVICIUS*

Kipras Mensevicius

Tomas Mieliauskas
LAW FIRM FORESTA

Bronislovas Mikuta

Ieva Navickaitė
*LAW FIRM ZABIELA
ZABIELAITE & PARTNERS*

Žygimantas Pacevičius
*FOIGT & PARTNERS / REGIJA
BORENIUS*

Rytis Paukste
*LAW FIRM LIDEIKA,
PETRAUSKAS, VALI🞖NAS IR
PARTNERIAI LAWIN, MEMBER
OF LEX MUNDI*

Algirdas Pekšys
SORAINEN

Jonas Pilkauskas
*SUTKIENE, PILKAUSKAS &
PARTNERS*

Thomas Saulenas
*FORESTA BUSINESS LAW
GROUP*

Rimantas Simaitis
*NORCOUS & PARTNERS,
MEMBER OF IUS LABORIS*

Julija Solovjova
PRICEWATERHOUSECOOPERS

Daiva Ušinskaitė
*LAW FIRM AAA BALTIC
SERVICE COMPANY*

Vilija Vaitkutė Pavan
*LAW FIRM LIDEIKA,
PETRAUSKAS, VALI🞖NAS IR
PARTNERIAI LAWIN, MEMBER
OF LEX MUNDI*

Agne Vilutiene
LAW FIRM FORESTA

Lina Vosyliene
KPMG

Darius Zabiela
*LAW FIRM ZABIELA,
ZABIELAITE & PARTNERS*

Indre Zakalskyte
ERNST & YOUNG

Jūratė Zarankienė
ERNST & YOUNG

Ernesta Zutautaite
LAW FIRM FORESTA

Audrius Žvybas
*BERNOTAS & DOMINAS
GLIMSTEDT*

LUXEMBOURG

ALLEN & OVERY LLP

Lara Aherne
*BONN SCHMITT STEICHEN,
MEMBER OF LEX MUNDI*

Rene Beltjens
PRICEWATERHOUSECOOPERS

Denis Cantele
OOSTVOGELS PFISTER FEYTEN

Guy Castegnaro
*CASTEGNARO CABINET
D'AVOCATS, MEMBER OF IUS
LABORIS*

Christel Dumont
OOSTVOGELS PFISTER FEYTEN

Thomas Ecker
*VILLE DE LUXEMBOURG -
SERVICE DE L'ÉLECTRICITÉ*

Gérard Eischen
*CHAMBER OF COMMERCE
OF THE GRAND-DUCHY OF
LUXEMBOURG*

Martine Gerber Lemaire
OOSTVOGELS PFISTER FEYTEN

Anabela Fernandes
PRICEWATERHOUSECOOPERS

Jean Luc Heiby
*SDV INTERNATIONAL
LOGISTICS*

Isabelle Lapietra
PRICEWATERHOUSECOOPERS

Roxanne Le Ligeour
LOYENS & LOEFF

Michaël Lockman
PRICEWATERHOUSECOOPERS

Tom Loesch
LINKLATERS

Nuria Martin
LOYENS & LOEFF

Séverine Moca
PRICEWATERHOUSECOOPERS

Peter Moons
LOYENS & LOEFF

Anne Murrath
PRICEWATERHOUSECOOPERS

Elisabeth Omes
*BONN SCHMITT STEICHEN,
MEMBER OF LEX MUNDI*

Laurent Paquet
PRICEWATERHOUSECOOPERS

Simon Paul
LOYENS & LOEFF

*PAUL WURTH S.A.
ENGINEERING & PROJECT
MANAGEMENT*

Françoise Pfeiffer
OOSTVOGELS PFISTER FEYTEN

Dominique Robinet
PRICEWATERHOUSECOOPERS

Serge Saussoy
PRICEWATERHOUSECOOPERS

Jean-Luc Schaus
LOYENS & LOEFF

Alex Schmitt
*BONN SCHMITT STEICHEN,
MEMBER OF LEX MUNDI*

Marleen Vandenput
PRICEWATERHOUSECOOPERS

Davide Visin
PRICEWATERHOUSECOOPERS

MACEDONIA, FORMER YUGOSLAV REPUBLIC OF

Violeta Angelova Gerovska
IKRP ROKAS & PARTNERS

Zlatko Antevski
LAWYERS ANTEVSKI

Benita Beleskova
IKRP ROKAS & PARTNERS

Goran Bonevski
PUBLIC REVENUE OFFICE

Biljana Čakmakova
*MENS LEGIS CAKMAKOVA
ADVOCATES*

Katerina Carceva
PRICEWATERHOUSECOOPERS

Zoran Cvetanoski
*STATE AUTHORITY FOR
GEODETIC WORKS*

Pavlinka Dameska
*MENS LEGIS CAKMAKOVA
ADVOCATES*

Aleksandar Dimić
POLENAK LAW FIRM

Aleksandra Donevska
LAWYERS ANTEVSKI

Vesna Gavriloska
*MENS LEGIS CAKMAKOVA
ADVOCATES*

Ana Hadzieva
POLENAK LAW FIRM

Solobodan Hristovski
POLENAK LAW FIRM

Biljana Ickovska
LAW OFFICE NIKOLOVSKI

Aleksandar Ickovski
LAW OFFICE NIKOLOVSKI

Nena Ivanovska
*JUDICIAL REFORM
IMPLEMENTATION PROJECT*

Katerina Jordanova
LAWYERS ANTEVSKI

Kristijan Karapančevski
KARAPANCEVSKI COMPANY

Dejan Knezović
*LAW OFFICE KNEZOVIC &
ASSOCIATES*

Emmanuel Koenig
PRICEWATERHOUSECOOPERS

Mirjana Markovska
MARKOVSKA & ANDREVSKI

Irena Mitkovska
LAWYERS ANTEVSKI

Goce Mojsoski
PRICEWATERHOUSECOOPERS

NATIONAL BANK

Goran Nikolovski
LAW OFFICE NIKOLOVSKI

Ljupcho Nikolovski
MARKOVSKA & ANDREVSKI

Vesna Paunkoska

Valentin Pepeljugoski
LAW OFFICE PEPELJUGOSKI

Sonja Peshevska
LAW OFFICE PEPELJUGOSKI

Kristijan Polenak
POLENAK LAW FIRM

Tatjana Popovski Buloski
POLENAK LAW OFFICE

Ljubica Ruben
MENS LEGIS LAW FIRM

Tatjana Siskovska
POLENAK LAW FIRM

Dejan Stojanoski
LAW OFFICE PEPELJUGOSKI

Dzuli Stojanova
*MENS LEGIS CAKMAKOVA
ADVOCATES*

Suzana Stojkoska
MARKOVSKA & ANDREVSKI

Biljana Tofiloska
LAWYERS ANTEVSKI

Slavica Trckova
LAW OFFICE TRCKOVA

Natasa Trifunoska
EMPIRIA INTERNATIONAL

Vladimir Vasilevski
BETASPED INTERNATIONAL FREIGHT FORWARDING

Eva Veljanovska
MENS LEGIS CAKMAKOVA ADVOCATES

Sanja Veljanovska
MENS LEGIS LAW FIRM

Metodija Velkov
POLENAK LAW FIRM

Darko Vuksanović

Milica Zafirova
MARKOVSKA & ANDREVSKI

MADAGASCAR

Lalao Andriamanga
ECONOMIC DEVELOPMENT BOARD OF MADAGASCAR

Eric Andriamihaja Robson
ECONOMIC DEVELOPMENT BOARD OF MADAGASCAR

Tsiry Andriamisamanana
MADAGASCAR CONSEIL INTERNATIONAL

Josoa Lucien Andrianelinjaka
BANQUE CENTRALE

Philippe Buffier
ESPACE INGÉNIERIE

Dseyre
MADAGASCAR CONSEIL INTERNATIONAL

Yves Duchateau
SDV

John Hargreaves
ECONOMIC DEVELOPMENT BOARD OF MADAGASCAR

Raphaël Jakoba
MADAGASCAR CONSEIL INTERNATIONAL

Pascaline R. Rasamoeliarisoa
CABINET DELTA AUDIT DELOITTE

Sahondra Rabenarivo
KEYSERLINGK - RABENARIVO ASSOCIÉS

Pierrette Rajaonarisoa
SDV

Aina Rakotondrazaka

Lanto Tiana Ralison
FIDAFRICA / PRICEWATERHOUSECOOPERS

André Randranto
ANCIEN BÂTONNIER

William Randrianarivelo
FIDAFRICA / PRICEWATERHOUSECOOPERS

Sahondra Rasoarisoa
DELTA AUDIT DELOITTE

Théodore Raveloarison
JARY - BUREAU D'ÉTUDES ARCHITECTURE INGENIERIE

Andriamisa Ravelomanana
FIDAFRICA / PRICEWATERHOUSECOOPERS

Jean Marcel Razafimahenina
CABINET DELTA AUDIT DELOITTE

Njiva Razanatsoa
BANQUE CENTRALE

Louis Sagot
CABINET D'AVOCAT LOUIS SAGOT

Dominique Taty
FIDAFRICA / PRICEWATERHOUSECOOPERS

MALAWI

Kevin M. Carpenter
PRICEWATERHOUSECOOPERS

Richard Chakana
PS CARGO CO.

Marshal Chilenga
TF & PARTNERS

Alan Chinula

Stuart Forster

Jim Ghobede
PRICEWATERHOUSECOOPERS

Roseline Gramani
SAVJANI & CO.

Aamir Rashid Jakhura
FARGO GROUP OF COMPANIES

Chimwemwe Kalua
GOLDEN & LAW

Anthony Kamanga, SC
MINISTRY OF JUSTICE

Dannie J. Kamwaza
KAMWAZA DESIGN PARTNERSHIP

Alfred Majamanda
MBENDERA & NKHONO ASSOCIATES

Modecai Msisha
NYIRENDA & MSISHA LAW OFFICES

Misheck Msiska
PRICEWATERHOUSECOOPERS

Isaac Nsamala

Krishna Savjani
SAVJANI & CO.

Duncan Singano
SAVJANI & CO.

Don Whayo
KNIGHT FRANK

MALAYSIA

Nadia Aim Ab. Wahab
AZMI & ASSOCIATES

Nor Azimah Abdul Aziz
COMPANIES COMMISSION OF MALAYSIA

Noor Azhar
S.G. EMAS SENDIRIAN BERHAD

Zain Azlan
ZAIN & CO.

BANK NEGARA MALAYSIA

Michel Barbesier
SDV SDN BHD

Tan Kee Beng
SDV SDN BHD

Hong Yun Chang
TAY & PARTNERS

Ying Cheng Chee
PRICEWATERHOUSECOOPERS

Boon Hong Chen
SKRINE & CO., MEMBER OF LEX MUNDI

Yuan Yuan Cheng
SKRINE & CO., MEMBER OF LEX MUNDI

Chee Hoong Chia
ZAIN & CO.

Sharon Chooi
PRICEWATERHOUSECOOPERS

Tze Keong Chung
CTOS SDN BHD

Nancy Gan
RASLAN - LOONG

Hazlan Hassan

Nordin Hassan
ARMEIRA TECHNOLOGIES SDN. BHD.

Sien Yian Hee
PRICEWATERHOUSECOOPERS

Kumar Kanagabai
SKRINE & CO., MEMBER OF LEX MUNDI

Geeta Kaur
SDV SDN BHD

Chuan Keat Khoo
PRICEWATERHOUSECOOPERS

Christopher Lee
WONG & PARTNERS

Theresa Lim
PRICEWATERHOUSECOOPERS

Koon Huan Lim
SKRINE & CO., MEMBER OF LEX MUNDI

Caesar Loong
RASLAN - LOONG

Len Toong Low
NORTH PORT

Khin Lian Low
ZAIN & CO.

Suhara Mohamad Sidik
AZMI & ASSOCIATES

Azmi Mohd Ali
AZMI & ASSOCIATES

Zuhaidi Mohd Shahari
AZMI & ASSOCIATES

Shahri Omar
NORTH PORT

Normaizan Rahim
AZMI & ASSOCIATES

Gayathiry Ramalingam
ZAIN & CO.

Chandran Ramasamy
PRICEWATERHOUSECOOPERS

Dinesh Ratnarajah
AZMAN, DAVIDSON & CO.

Hsian Siong
WONG & PARTNERS

Ee Ling Tan
TAY & PARTNERS

Heng Choon Wan
PRICEWATERHOUSECOOPERS

Peter Wee
PRICEWATERHOUSECOOPERS

Kim Hoe Yeo
NORTH PORT

Melina Yong
RASLAN - LOONG

MALDIVES

Mohamed Akhsan
ARCHENG PVT LTD.

Mohideen Bawa
HORIZON FISHERIES PVT. LIMITED

Jatindra Bhattray
PRICEWATERHOUSECOOPERS

Mohamed Hameed
ANTRAC PVT. LTD.

Nadiya Hassan

Dheena Hussain
SHAH, HUSSAIN & CO. BARRISTERS & ATTORNEYS

Yudhishtran Kanagasabai
PRICEWATERHOUSECOOPERS

Laila Manik
SHAH, HUSSAIN & CO. BARRISTERS & ATTORNEYS

Aishath Rizna
SHAH, HUSSAIN & CO. BARRISTERS & ATTORNEYS.

Aminath Rizna
SHAH, HUSSAIN & CO. BARRISTERS & ATTORNEYS

Aishath Samah
BANK OF MALDIVES PLC.

Shuaib M. Shah
SHAH, HUSSAIN & CO. BARRISTERS & ATTORNEYS

MALI

Traore Baba
TMS - TRANSIT MANUTENTION SERVICES SARL

Baya Berthé

Amadou Camara
SCP CAMARA TRAORÉ

Jonathan Darboux
BCEAO

Fatima Diarra
OFFICE NOTARIAL AHMADOU TOURE, NOTAIRE A BAMAKO

Mohamed Abdoulaye Diop
SDV

Fatimatou Zahra Diop
BCEAO

Jean Claude Gnamien
FIDAFRICA / PRICEWATERHOUSECOOPERS

Hermann Gnango
FIDAFRICA / PRICEWATERHOUSECOOPERS

Mamadou Ismaïla Konate
JURIFIS CONSULT MALI

Mamadou Maiga
L'UNION DES CAISSES MUTUELLES DEPAGNE ET DES CRÉDITS DU MALI

Evelyne M'Bassidgé
FIDAFRICA / PRICEWATERHOUSECOOPERS

Adeline Messou
FIDAFRICA / PRICEWATERHOUSECOOPERS

Malick Badara Sow
ATELIER D'ARCHITECTURE ET D'URBANISME

Salif Tall
ETUDE DE ME TOURE

Dominique Taty
FIDAFRICA / PRICEWATERHOUSECOOPERS

Ahmadou Toure
OFFICE NOTARIAL AHMADOU TOURE, NOTAIRE A BAMAKO

Madhou Traore
CENTRE NATIONAL DE PROMOTION DES INVESTISSEMENTS - CNPI

Fousséni Traoré
FIDAFRICA / PRICEWATERHOUSECOOPERS

MARSHALL ISLANDS

Kenneth Barden
ATTORNEY-AT-LAW

Jerry Kramer
PACIFIC INTERNATIONAL, INC.

Philip Welch
MICRONESIAN SHIPPING AGENCIES INC.

MAURITANIA

Tidiane Bal
BSD & ASSOCIÉS

Youssoupha Diallo
BSD & ASSOCIÉS

Maouloud Vall El Hady Seyid
ETUDE HADY MAOULOUDVALL

Hamoud Ismail
SMPN

Cheikani Jules
CABINET ME JULES

Mohamed Lam
BSD & ASSOCIÉS

Wedou Mohamed
MAURIHANDLING

Ahmed Salem Ould Bouhoubeyni
CABINET BOUHOUBEYNI

Ahmed Salem Ould Hacen
BANQUE CENTRALE

Mohamedou Ould Hacen
BUREAU TASMIM

Hamdi Ould Mahjoub
PRIVATE PRACTICE

Aliou Sall
ASSURIM CONSULTING

Cheikh Sall
ETUDE HADY MAOULOUDVALL

Dominique Taty
FIDAFRICA / PRICEWATERHOUSECOOPERS

Ould Yahya Yeslem
ETUDE MAÎTRE YESLEM O.YAHYA

MAURITIUS

Ryan Allas
PRICEWATERHOUSECOOPERS

BPML FREEPORT SERVICES LTD

Philip Bond
PRICEWATERHOUSECOOPERS

André Bonieux
PRICEWATERHOUSECOOPERS

Urmila Boolell
BANYMANDHUB BOOLELL CHAMBERS

Thierry Chellen
BENOIT CHAMBERS

Yandraduth Googoolye
BANK OF MAURITIUS

Thierry Koenig
DE COMARMOND & KOENIG

LEGIS & PARTNERS

Didier Lenette
PRICEWATERHOUSECOOPERS

Damien Mamet
*PRICEWATERHOUSECOOPERS
LEGAL SERVICES*

Jean Pierre Montocchio

Loganayagan Munian
ARTISCO INTERNATIONAL

Khalil Munseea
FARFAT ENTERPRISE LTD.

Camille Pouletty
DE COMARMOND & KOENIG

Iqbal Rajahbalee
BLC CHAMBERS

Andre Robert
ATTORNEY-AT-LAW

Deviantee Sobarun
*REGISTRAR-GENERAL'S
DEPARTMENT*

Vikash Takoor
BANK OF MAURITIUS

Parikshat Teeluck
MAERSK LTD.

Bobby Yerkiah
PRICEWATERHOUSECOOPERS

MEXICO

Gabriel I. Aguilar Bustamente
PRICEWATERHOUSECOOPERS

Silvia Aguiñiga
PRICEWATERHOUSECOOPERS

Isis Anaya
SEDECO

Alberto Balderas
*JÁUREGUI, NAVARRETE Y
NADER, S.C.*

Carlos Cano
PRICEWATERHOUSECOOPERS

María Casas López
BAKER & MCKENZIE

Nallieli Cid
PRICEWATERHOUSECOOPERS

Rodrigo Conesa
RITCH MUELLER, S.C.

Eduardo Corzo Ramos
*HOLLAND & KNIGHT-
GALLÁSTEGUI Y LOZANO, S.C.*

Raul de la Sierra Scauley
*BARRERA, SIQUEIROS Y TORRES
LANDA*

Oscar de La Vega
*BASHAM, RINGE Y CORREA,
MEMBER OF IUS LABORIS*

Dolores Enriquez
PRICEWATERHOUSECOOPERS

Mariano Enriquez-Mejia
BAKER & MCKENZIE

Salvador Esquivel Bernal
PRICEWATERHOUSECOOPERS

César Fernando Gomez
*BARRERA, SIQUEIROS Y TORRES
LANDA*

Julio Flores Luna
*GOODRICH, RIQUELME Y
ASOCIADOS, MEMBER OF LEX
MUNDI*

Carlos Frias
PRICEWATERHOUSECOOPERS

Manuel Galicia
GALICIA Y ROBLES, S.C.

Celina Cossette Garcia
*PRICEWATERHOUSECOOPERS
LEGAL SERVICES*

Hans Goebel
*JÁUREGUI, NAVARRETE Y
NADER, S.C.*

Dalia Goldsmit
PRICEWATERHOUSECOOPERS

Daniel Gómez Alba
CAAAREM

Teresa de Lourdes Gómez
Neri
*GOODRICH, RIQUELME Y
ASOCIADOS, MEMBER OF LEX
MUNDI*

Hugo Gonzalez
BAKER & MCKENZIE

Cesar Gonzalez
PRICEWATERHOUSECOOPERS

Eugenia González Rivas
*GOODRICH, RIQUELME Y
ASOCIADOS*

Alvaro Gonzalez-Schiaffino
PRICEWATERHOUSECOOPERS

Benito Guerrero
GLUCSA DEL PACIFICO

Yves Hayaux-du-Tilly
*JÁUREGUI, NAVARRETE Y
NADER, S.C.*

Rodrigo Hernández Terán
PRICEWATERHOUSECOOPERS

Alejandro Ledesma
PRICEWATERHOUSECOOPERS

Adriana Lopez
*PRICEWATERHOUSECOOPERS
LEGAL SERVICES*

Ana Paula López Padilla y
Lapuente
*BARRERA, SIQUEIROS Y TORRES
LANDA*

Gerardo Lozano Alarcón
*HOLLAND & KNIGHT-
GALLÁSTEGUI Y LOZANO, S.C.*

Lorenza Luengo Gomezmont
BAKER & MCKENZIE

Laura Macarty
PRICEWATERHOUSECOOPERS

Carlos Manuel Martinez
PRICEWATERHOUSECOOPERS

Edgar Francisco Martínez
Herrasti
*GOODRICH, RIQUELME Y
ASOCIADOS*

Bernardo Martínez Negrete
GALICIA Y ROBLES, S.C.

Fernando Medel
*NOTARY PUBLIC XXX OF THE
FEDERAL DISTRICT*

Carla Mendoza
BAKER & MCKENZIE

Carlos E. Montemayor
PRICEWATERHOUSECOOPERS

Alonso Martin Montes
*PRICEWATERHOUSECOOPERS
LEGAL SERVICES*

Rocío Montes
PRICEWATERHOUSECOOPERS

Michelle Muciño
PMC ASOCIADOS

Gabriela Nassau
RITCH MUELLER, S.C.

Marco Nava
PRICEWATERHOUSECOOPERS

Arturo Pedromo
GALICIA Y ROBLES, S.C.

Lázaro Peña
PRICEWATERHOUSECOOPERS

Juan Manuel Perez
*PRICEWATERHOUSECOOPERS
LEGAL SERVICES*

Nicolás Pérez
GALICIA Y ROBLES, S.C.

Gabriela Pérez Castro Ponce
de León
MIRANDA & ESTAVILLO, S.C.

Pablo Perezalonso Eguía
RITCH MUELLER, S. C.

Leonel Pereznieto
*JÁUREGUI, NAVARRETE Y
NADER, S.C.*

Guillermo Piecarchic
PMC ASOCIADOS

José Piecarchic
PMC ASOCIADOS

Claudia Ríos
PRICEWATERHOUSECOOPERS

Mario Alberto Rocha
PRICEWATERHOUSECOOPERS

Cecilia Rojas
GALICIA Y ROBLES, S.C.

Arturo Ruiz Massieu
PRICEWATERHOUSECOOPERS

Israel Saldaña
PRICEWATERHOUSECOOPERS

Jorge Sanchez
*GOODRICH, RIQUELME Y
ASOCIADOS*

Paola Sánchez Hernandez
*BARRERA, SIQUEIROS Y TORRES
LANDA*

Cristina Sánchez-Urtiz
MIRANDA & ESTAVILLO, S.C.

Fernando Santamaria-Linares
*PRICEWATERHOUSECOOPERS
LEGAL SERVICES*

Monica Schiaffino Pérez
*BASHAM, RINGE Y CORREA,
MEMBER OF IUS LABORIS*

Juan Francisco Torres Landa
Ruffo
*BARRERA, SIQUEIROS Y TORRES
LANDA*

Antonio Torres-Cabello
CAAAREM

Maribel Trigo Aja
*GOODRICH, RIQUELME Y
ASOCIADOS, MEMBER OF LEX
MUNDI*

Layla Vargas Muga
*GOODRICH, RIQUELME Y
ASOCIADOS, MEMBER OF LEX
MUNDI*

Carlos Vela
PRICEWATERHOUSECOOPERS

MICRONESIA

Eric Emeka Akamigbo
POHNPEI STATE GOVERNMENT

Kenneth Barden
ATTORNEY-AT-LAW

MOLDOVA

Dinu Armasu
*FOREIGN INVESTORS
ASSOCIATION*

Maxim Banaga
PRICEWATERHOUSECOOPERS

Eduard Boian
PRICEWATERHOUSECOOPERS

Vitaliy Nikolaevich Bulgac
INDEPENDENT CONSULTANT

Victor Burac
VICTOR BURAC LAW FIRM

Mihail Buruiana
BURUIANA & PARTNERS

Victor Burunsus
THE WORLD BANK

Andrei Caciurenco
ACI PARTNERS

Georghu Calugharu
*UNION OF EMPLOYERS IN
BUILDING AND CONSTRUCTION
MATERIALS INDUSTRY*

Andrian Candu
*PRICEWATERHOUSECOOPERS
LEGAL SERVICES*

Octavian Cazac
TURCAN & TURCAN

Svetlana Ceban
PRICEWATERHOUSECOOPERS

Vitalie Ciofu
GLADEI & PARTNERS

Bogdan Ciubotaru
TURCAN &TURCAN

Aureliu Anatol Colenco
COMMERCIAL COURT

Alla Cotos
PRICEWATERHOUSECOOPERS

Sergiu Dumitrasco
PRICEWATERHOUSECOOPERS

Serghei Filatov
ACI PARTNERS

Feodosia Furculita
CUSTOMS SERVICE

Roger Gladei
GLADEI & PARTNERS

Silvia Grosu
PRICEWATERHOUSECOOPERS

Roman Gutu

Oxana Guțu

Valeriu Lazar
BIS

Victor A. Levintsa
LEVINTSA & ASSOCIATES

Andrei Lopusneac
*UNION FENOSA
INTERNATIONAL*

Cristina Martin
ACI PARTNERS

Mihaela Mitroi
PRICEWATERHOUSECOOPERS

Marin Moraru
PRICEWATERHOUSECOOPERS

Gleb Morozov

Alexandru Munteanu
PRICEWATERHOUSECOOPERS

Igor Odobescu
ACI PARTNERS

Ruslan Pirnevu
*QUEHENBERGER-HELLMANN
SRL*

Maria Popescu
PRICEWATERHOUSECOOPERS

Nicolae Posturusu
CUSTOMS SERVICE

Silvia Radu
*UNION FENOSA
INTERNATIONAL*

Ion Railean
*UNION OF EMPLOYERS IN
BUILDING AND CONSTRUCTION
MATERIALS INDUSTRY*

Mihai Roscovan
*BUSINESS CONSULTING
INSTITUTE*

Pavel Sarghi
PRICEWATERHOUSECOOPERS

Antonina Sevcenco

Viorel Sirghi
BSMB LEGAL COUNSELLORS

Tatiana Stavinschi
PRICEWATERHOUSECOOPERS

Serghei Toncu
PRICEWATERHOUSECOOPERS

Nicolae Triboi
*NATIONAL ENERGY
REGULATORY AGENCY*

Alexander Turcan
TURCAN & TURCAN

Evgeniy Untilo
*UNION OF EMPLOYERS IN
BUILDING AND CONSTRUCTION
MATERIALS INDUSTRY*

Irina Verhovetchi
ACI PARTNERS

Daniela Zaharia
ACI PARTNERS

Marina Zanoga
TURCAN & TURCAN

MONGOLIA

Tomas Balco
PRICEWATERHOUSECOOPERS

Badarch Bayarmaa
LYNCH & MAHONEY

Batzaya Bodikhuu
*ANAND & BATZAYA
ADVOCATES*

David Buxbaum
ANDERSON & ANDERSON

Batbayar Byamba
GTS ADVOCATES

Enkh-Amgalan
Choidogdemid
GOBI CORPORATION

Khatanbat Dashdarjaa
ARLEX CONSULTING SERVICES

Delgermaa
GOBI CORPORATION

Courtney Fowler
PRICEWATERHOUSECOOPERS

Damdinsuren Khand
TSETS LAW FIRM

Odmaa Khurelbold
ANDERSON & ANDERSON

Daniel Mahoney
LYNCH & MAHONEY

Leylim Mizamkhan
PRICEWATERHOUSECOOPERS

Odonhuu Muuzee
TSETS LAW FIRM

Bayartsetseg N.
CHONO CORPORATION

Enkhriimaa N.
TUUSHIN COMPANY LTD.

Zorigt N.
TUUSHIN COMPANY LTD.

Sarantsatsral Ochirpurev
URKH COMPANY

Christian Packard
ANDERSON & ANDERSON

Uranbaatar S.
ARLEX CONSULTING SERVICES

Jocelyn Steiner
LYNCH & MAHONEY

Odbaatar Sukhbaatar
ANDERSON & ANDERSON

Tsogt Tsend
*ADMINISTRATIVE COURT OF
CAPITAL CITY*

Amangyeld Tuul
CREDIT REGISTRY

Arslaa Urjin
*ULAANBAATAR ELECTRICITY
DISTRIBUTION NETWORK
COMPANY*

Michelle Zorig
ARLEX CONSULTING SERVICES

MONTENEGRO

Rene Bijvoet
PRICEWATERHOUSECOOPERS

Bojana Bogojević
PRICEWATERHOUSECOOPERS

Vasilije Bošković
LAW FIRM BOŠKOVIⵣ

ČELEBIⵣ COMPANY

Mark Crowford
OPPORTUNITY BANK

Jelena Djokić
PRICEWATERHOUSECOOPERS

Jovana Ilić
PRICEWATERHOUSECOOPERS

Nada Jovanović
CENTRAL BANK

Ana Karanikić
*MONTENEGRIN EMPLOYERS
FEDERATION*

Radoš Kastratović
KASTRATOVIⵣ LAW OFFICE

Đorđe Krivokapić
KARANOVIⵣ & NIKOLIⵣ

Ana Krsmanović
*INSTITUTE FOR STRATEGIC
STUDIES AND PROGNOSES*

*MONTENEGRO BUSINESS
ALLIANCE*

Aleksandar Miljković
PRICEWATERHOUSECOOPERS

Veljko Pavičević
OPPORTUNITY BANK

Predrag Pavličić
MONTECCO INC

Zorica Peshić
LAW OFFICE VUJACIⵣ

Novica Pešić
LAW OFFICE VUJACIⵣ

Snežana Pešić
PRICEWATERHOUSECOOPERS

Dragana Radević
*CENTER FOR
ENTERPRENEURSHIP AND
ECONOMIC DEVELOPMENT*

Jelena Vujišić
LAW OFFICE VUJACIⵣ

Lana Vukmirović
PRELEVIC LAW FIRM

Veselin Vuković
CENTRAL BANK

MOROCCO

BANK AL-MAGHRIB

Aziz Abouelouafa
GLOBEX MARITIME CO.

Mly Hicham Alaoui
GLOBEX MARITIME CO.

Myriam Emmanuelle Bennani
*AMIN HAJJI & ASSOCIÉS
ASSOCIATION D'AVOCATS*

Rachid Benzakour
*CABINET D'AVOCATS
BENZAKOUR & LAHBABI*

Richard Cantin
*JURISTRUCTURES - PROJECT
MANAGEMENT & LEGAL
ADVISORY SERVICES LLP*

Mahat Chraibi
ALLEANCE ADVISORY MAROC

Driss Debbagh
KETTANI LAW FIRM

Youssef El Falah
*ABA RULE OF LAW
INITIATIVE-MOROCCO*

Hafid Elbaze
ALLEANCE ADVISORY MAROC

Mourad Faouzi
OULAMINE LAW GROUP

Nawal Jellouli
*MINISTÈRE DE L'ÉCONOMIE ET
DES FINANCES*

Azeddine Kabbaj
BARREAU DE CASABLANCA

Mehdi Kettani
ALI KETTANI LAW OFFICE

Nadia Kettani
KETTANI LAW FIRM

Rita Kettani
KETTANI LAW FIRM

Bouchaib Labkiri
GLOBEXLINE SARL

Wilfried Le Bihan
*CMS BUREAU FRANCIS
LEFEBVRE*

Michel Lecerf
ALLEANCE ADVISORY MAROC

Réda Oulamine
OULAMINE LAW GROUP

Hassan Rahmouni
HASSAN RAHMOUNI LAW FIRM

Nesrine Roudane
NERO BOUTIQUE LAW FIRM

Morgane Saint-Jalmes
KETTANI LAW FIRM

Houcine Sefrioui
PRESIDENT DE LA CAAF

Rachid Senhaji
*ORDRE DES ARCHITECTES DE
CASABLANCA*

Marc Veuillot
ALLEANCE ADVISORY MAROC

MOZAMBIQUE

Salimo Abdula
*CONFEDERATION OF BUSINESS
ASSOCIATIONS*

Mark Badenhorst
PRICEWATERHOUSECOOPERS

Carolina Balate
PRICEWATERHOUSECOOPERS

Armindo Braz Barradas
*MINISTRY OF INDUSTRY AND
COMMERCE*

Timothy W. Born
USAID

José Manuel Caldeira
*SAL & CALDEIRA -
ADVOGADOS E CONSULTORES,
LDA*

Eduardo Calú
*SAL & CALDEIRA -
ADVOGADOS E CONSULTORES,
LDA*

Alexandra Carvalho
Monjardino

Kátia Cassamo
MOZLEGAL LDA

Henrique Castro-Arnaro
*ARQUITECTOS E ASSOCIADOS,
LDA*

Paulo Centeio
*MGA ADVOGADOS &
CONSULTORES*

Pedro Chabela
*ELECTRICIDADE DE
MOÇAMBIQUE E.P.*

Pedro Ernesto Chambe
MOCARGO

Anastácia Chamusse
BANCO DE MOÇAMBIQUE

Dipak Chandulal
*MGA ADVOGADOS &
CONSULTORES*

Mucio Chebete
MOCARGO

Jonas Chitsumba
*ELECTRICIDADE DE
MOÇAMBIQUE E.P.*

Ahmad Chothia
*MANICA FREIGHT SERVICES
S.A.R.L*

Carol Christie Smit
MOZLEGAL LDA

Pedro Couto
*H. GAMITO, COUTO,
GONÇALVES PEREIRA
E CASTELO BRANCO &
ASSOCIADOS*

Simeai Cuamba
CUAMBA ADVOGADO

Paul De Chalain
PRICEWATERHOUSECOOPERS

Carlos de Sousa e Brito
*CARLOS DE SOUSA & BRITO &
ASSOCIADOS*

Fulgêncio Dimande
*MANICA FREIGHT SERVICES
S.A.R.L*

Maria João Dionísio
*PIMENTA, DIONÍSIO E
ASSOCIADOS*

Telmo Ferreira
*H. GAMITO, COUTO,
GONÇALVES PEREIRA
E CASTELO BRANCO &
ASSOCIADOS*

Jose Forjaz
JOSE FORJAZ ARQUITECTOS

Adrian Frey
MOZLEGAL LDA

Paulo Fumane
*CONFEDERATION OF BUSINESS
ASSOCIATIONS*

Martins Garrine
*MANICA FREIGHT SERVICES
S.A.R.L*

Jennifer Garvey

Nipul Kailashcumar Govan
*PIMENTA, DIONÍSIO E
ASSOCIADOS*

Jorge Graça
*MGA ADVOGADOS &
CONSULTORES*

Soraia Issufo
*SAL & CALDEIRA -
ADVOGADOS E CONSULTORES,
LDA*

Jorge Jorge Graça
*MGA ADVOGADOS &
CONSULTORES*

Neima Jossub
MOZLEGAL LDA

Friedrich Kaufmann
*MINISTÉRIO DA INDÚSTRIA E
COMÉRCIO*

Jim Lafleur
*CONFEDERATION OF
BUSINESS ASSOCIATIONS OF
MOZAMBIQUE*

Rufino Lucas
*TEC TÉNICOS CONSTRUTORES,
LDA*

Eugénio Luis
BANCO DE MOÇAMBIQUE

Ivan Carlos Macôo
*SAL & CALDEIRA -
ADVOGADOS E CONSULTORES,
LDA*

Jaime Magumbe
*SAL & CALDEIRA -
ADVOGADOS E CONSULTORES,
LDA*

Samuel Munzele Maimbo
THE WORLD BANK

Manuel Didier Malunga
*NATIONAL DIRECTORATE OF
REGISTRY AND NOTARIES*

João Martins
PRICEWATERHOUSECOOPERS

Camilo Mate
*MGA ADVOGADOS &
CONSULTORES*

Carlos Rafa Mate
ROYAL NORWEGIAN EMBASSY

Genaro Moura
*MANICA FREIGHT SERVICES
S.A.R.L*

Julio Mutisse
*SAL & CALDEIRA -
ADVOGADOS E CONSULTORES,
LDA*

Lara Narcy
*H. GAMITO, COUTO,
GONÇALVES PEREIRA
E CASTELO BRANCO &
ASSOCIADOS*

Auxílio Eugénio Nhabanga
*FERNANDA LOPES &
ASSOCIADOS ADVOGADOS*

Emilio R. Nhamissitane
ADVOGADO

Ilidio Alexandre Ombe
*ELECTRICIDADE DE
MOÇAMBIQUE E.P.*

Miguel Paiva
MOZLEGAL LDA

Paulo Pimenta
*PIMENTA, DIONÍSIO E
ASSOCIADOS*

António de Vasconcelos Porto
*VASCONCELOS PORTO &
ASSOCIADOS*

José Augusto Tomo Psico
BANCO DE MOÇAMBIQUE

Malaika Ribeiro
PRICEWATERHOUSECOOPERS

Luís Filipe Rodrigues
*SAL & CALDEIRA -
ADVOGADOS E CONSULTORES,
LDA*

Ana Filipa Russo de Sá
SILVA GARCIA

Firza Sadek
*PIMENTA, DIONÍSIO E
ASSOCIADOS*

Carlos Schwalbach
JOSE FORJAZ ARQUITECTOS

Muchimba Sikumba-Dils
MSD INVESTMENTS

Katia Tourais
*SAL & CALDEIRA -
ADVOGADOS E CONSULTORES,
LDA*

António Veloso
*PIMENTA, DIONÍSIO E
ASSOCIADOS*

NAMIBIA

Joos Agenbach
KOEP PARTNERS

Mark Badenhorst
PRICEWATERHOUSECOOPERS

Benita Blume
H.D. BOSSAU & CO.

Hanno D. Bossau
H.D. BOSSAU & CO.

Albé Botha
PRICEWATERHOUSECOOPERS

Lorna Celliers
BDO SPENCER STEWARD

Esi Chase
ADVOCATE

Andy Chase
*STAUCH+PARTNERS
ARCHITECTS*

Paul De Chalain
PRICEWATERHOUSECOOPERS

Eddie Dichtl
WOKER FREIGHT SERVICES

Ferdinand Diener
*CITY OF WINDHOEK POWER
DEPARTMENT*

Nellie du Toit
PRICEWATERHOUSECOOPERS

Hans-Bruno Gerdes
ENGLING, STRITTER &
PARTNERS

Ismarelda Hangue
DEEDS OFFICE

Sebby Kankondi
PORTS AUTHORITY

Herman Charl Kinghorn
KINGHORN ASSOCIATESF

Peter Frank Koep
P.F. KOEP & CO.

Frank Köpplinger
G.F. KÖPPLINGER LEGAL
PRACTITIONERS

Norbert Liebich
TRANSWORLD CARGO (PTY)
LTD.

John D. Mandy
STOCK EXCHANGE

Richard Traugott Diethelm
Mueller
KOEP PARTNERS

Brigitte Nependa
H.D. BOSSAU & CO.

Carina Oberholzer
PRICEWATERHOUSECOOPERS

Jesse Schickerling
THE LAW SOCIETY OF NAMIBIA

Ndapewa Shipopyeni

Retha Steinmann
THE LAW SOCIETY OF
NAMIBIA

Axel Stritter
ENGLING, STRITTER &
PARTNERS

Marius van Breda
TRANSUNION NAMIBIA

Lourens Willers
G.F. KÖPPLINGER LEGAL
PRACTITIONERS

Renate Williamson
P.F. KOEP & CO.

Paul A. E. Wolff
MANICA GROUP PTY. LTD.

NEPAL

Anil Chandra Adhikari
CREDIT INFORMATION BUREAU

Ajay Ghimire
APEX LAW CHAMBER

Jagat B. Khadka
SHANGRI-LA FREIGHT PVT.
LTD.

LD Mahat
CSC & CO. /
PRICEWATERHOUSECOOPERS

Ashok Man Kapali
SHANGRI-LA FREIGHT PVT.
LTD.

Purnachitra Pradhan
KARJA SUCHANA KENDRA
LTD(CIB)

Devendra Pradhan
PRADHAN & ASSOCIATES

Madan Krishna Sharma
CSC & CO. /
PRICEWATERHOUSECOOPERS

Sudheer Shrestha
KUSUM LAW FIRM

Ramji Shrestha
PRADHAN & ASSOCIATES

Ram Chandra Subedi
SUPREME COURT OF NEPAL,
APEX LAW CHAMBER

Anup Upreti
PIONEER LAW ASSOCIATES

NETHERLANDS

Richard Bakker
OCEAN - TRANS
INTERNATIONAL B.V.

BDO CAMPSOBERS
ACCOUNTANTS &
BELASTINGADVISEURS B.V.

Jan Bezem
PRICEWATERHOUSECOOPERS

Karin W.M. Bodewes
BAKER & MCKENZIE N.V.

Jacqueline van den Bosch
HOUTHOFF BURUMA N.V.

Roland Brandsma
PRICEWATERHOUSECOOPERS

Huub Brinkman
BAKER & MCKENZIE N.V.

Margriet de Boer
DE BRAUW BLACKSTONE
WESTBROEK N.V.

Rolef de Weijs
HOUTHOFF BURUMA N.V.

Friso Feitsma
PRICEWATERHOUSECOOPERS

Jeroen Holland
NAUTADUTILH ATTORNEYS

Fons Hoogeveen
PRICEWATERHOUSECOOPERS

Jan-Wilem de Jong
HOUTHOFF BURUMA N.V.

Alexander Kaarls
HOUTHOFF BURUMA N.V.

Martine Kos
HOUTHOFF BURUMA N.V.

Filip Krsteski
VAN DOORNE N.V.

Hans Mensonide
KENNEDY VAN DER LAAN

Martijn Molenaar
NAUTADUTILH ATTORNEYS

Charlotte Niggebrugge
HOUTHOFF BURUMA N.V.

Hugo Oppelaar
HOUTHOFF BURUMA N.V.

Ralf Pieters
PRICEWATERHOUSECOOPERS

Mark G. Rebergen
DE BRAUW BLACKSTONE
WESTBROEK N.V.

Hugo Reumkens
VAN DOORNE N.V.

Stefan Sagel
DE BRAUW BLACKSTONE
WESTBROEK N.V.

Jan Willem Schenk
BAKER & MCKENZIE N.V.

Robert Schrage
ROYAL NETHERLANDS
NOTARIAL ORGANIZATION

Piet Schroeder
BAKER & MCKENZIE N.V.

Hans Londonck Sluijk
HOUTHOFF BURUMA N.V.

SDV B.V.

Jellienke Stamhuis
DE BRAUW BLACKSTONE
WESTBROEK N.V.

Maarten Tinnemans
DE BRAUW BLACKSTONE
WESTBROEK N.V.

Jaap Jan Trommel
NAUTADUTILH ATTORNEYS

Helene van Bommel
PRICEWATERHOUSECOOPERS

Caspar van den Thillart
MINISTRY OF HOUSING,
SPATIAL PLANNING AND THE
ENVIRONMENT - GOVERNMENT
BUILDINGS AGENCY

Cees van den Udenhout

Paul van der Molen
CADASTRE, LAND REGISTRY
AND MAPPING AGENCY

Liane van der Vrugt
VÉDÉVÉ LEGAL B.V.

Sjaak van Leeuwen

Jan van Oorschot
NV CONTINUON

Frederic Verhoeven
HOUTHOFF BURUMA N.V.

Marcel Willems
KENNEDY VAN DER LAAN

Christiaan Zijderveld
HOUTHOFF BURUMA N.V.

Kim Zwartscholten
PRICEWATERHOUSECOOPERS

NEW ZEALAND

Douglas Alderslade
CHAPMAN TRIPP

Matthew Allison
VEDA ADVANTAGE

Jania Baigent
SIMPSON GRIERSON, MEMBER
OF LEX MUNDI

Kevin Best
PRICEWATERHOUSECOOPERS

Geoff Bevan
CHAPMAN TRIPP

Shelley Cave
SIMPSON GRIERSON, MEMBER
OF LEX MUNDI

John Cuthbertson
PRICEWATERHOUSECOOPERS

James Gibson
BELL GULLY

Richard Holden
SIMPSON GRIERSON, MEMBER
OF LEX MUNDI

Wanita Lala
PRICEWATERHOUSECOOPERS

Kate Lane
MINTER ELLISON RUDD WATTS

Thomas Leslie
BELL GULLY

Aaron Lloyd
MINTER ELLISON RUDD WATTS

Robert Muir
LAND INFORMATION NEW
ZEALAND

Ian Page
BRANZ

Mihai Pascariu
MINTER ELLISON RUDD WATTS

John Powell
RUSSELL MCVEAGH

Mark Russell
SIMPSON GRIERSON, MEMBER
OF LEX MUNDI

Neil Tier
GRANT THORNTON LTD.

SDV

Murray Tingey
BELL GULLY

Ross vander Schyff
MINISTRY OF ECONOMIC
DEVELOPMENT

Simon Vannini

Daniel Vizor
BELL GULLY

NICARAGUA

Diana Aguilar
ACZALAW

Guillermo Alemán Gómez
ACZALAW

Bernardo Arauz
BAUTRANS & LOGISTICS

Bertha Argüello de Rizo
F.A. ARIAS & MUÑOZ

David Urcuyo Báez
PRICEWATERHOUSECOOPERS

Minerva Adriana Bellorín
Rodríguez
ACZALAW

BENDAÑA & BENDAÑA

Caroline Bono
PRICEWATERHOUSECOOPERS

Thelma Carrion
AGUILAR CASTILLO LOVE

Humberto Carrión
CARRIÓN, SOMARRIBA &
ASOCIADOS

Gloria Maria de Alvarado
ALVARADO Y ASOCIADOS,
MEMBER OF LEX MUNDI

Francis Díaz
GARCÍA & BODÁN

Maricarmen Espinosa Segura
MOLINA & ASOCIADOS
CENTRAL LAW

Mervin Estrada
GARCÍA & BODÁN

Alejandro Fernández de
Castro
PRICEWATERHOUSECOOPERS

Terencio García Montenegro
GARCÍA & BODÁN

Gerardo Hernandez
CONSORTIUM - TABOADA &
ASOCIADOS

Ruth Huete
PRICEWATERHOUSECOOPERS

Mariela Jiménez
ACZALAW

Pablo Mogollon
TRANSUNION

Yalí Molina Palacios
MOLINA & ASOCIADOS
CENTRAL LAW

Alvaro Molina Vaca
MOLINA & ASOCIADOS
CENTRAL LAW

Roberto Montes
ARIAS & MUÑOZ

Soraya Montoya Herrera
MOLINA & ASOCIADOS
CENTRAL LAW

Amilcar Navarro
GARCÍA & BODÁN

Ramón Ortega
PRICEWATERHOUSECOOPERS

Silvio G. Otero Q.
GLOBALTRANS
INTERNACIONAL

Andrea Paniagua
PRICEWATERHOUSECOOPERS

Róger Pérez
ARIAS & MUÑOZ

Julio Pinedo
PRICEWATERHOUSECOOPERS

Carlos Taboada Rodríguez
CONSORTIUM - TABOADA &
ASOCIADOS

Carlos Jose Salinas Blandino
ALVARADO Y ASOCIADOS,
MEMBER OF LEX MUNDI

Felipe Sánchez
ACZALAW

Alfonso José Sandino Granera
CONSORTIUM - TABOADA &
ASOCIADOS

Julio E. Sequeira
EVENOR VALDIVIA P. &
ASOCIADOS

Arnulfo Somarriba
TRANSUNION

Rodrigo Taboada Rodríguez
CONSORTIUM - TABOADA &
ASOCIADOS

Juan Tejada
PRICEWATERHOUSECOOPERS

Carlos Tellez
GARCÍA & BODÁN

David Urcuyo
PRICEWATERHOUSECOOPERS

NIGER

Aliou Amadou
S.C.P.A. MANDELA

Karim Arzika
CONSERVATION FONCIÈRE

Mahamane Baba
SDV

Alain Blambert
SDV

Moussa Coulibaly
CABINET D'AVOCATS SOUNA-
COULIBALY

Jonathan Darboux
BCEAO

Aïssa Degbey
ECOBANK

Fatimatou Zahra Diop
BCEAO

Bernard Duffros
SOCIÉTÉ D'EXPLOITATION DES
EAUX DU NIGER

Jean Claude Gnamien
FIDAFRICA /
PRICEWATERHOUSECOOPERS

Hermann Gnango
FIDAFRICA /
PRICEWATERHOUSECOOPERS

Souley Hammi Illiassou
ETUDE D'AVOCATS - MARC LE
BIHAN & COLLABORATEURS

Diaouga Haoua
*ETUDE DE MAÎTRE DJIBO
AÏSSATOU*

Dodo Dan Gado Haoua
*ETUDE DE MAÎTRE DODO DAN
GADO HAOUA*

Issoufou Issa
*DIRECTION GÉNÉRALE DES
IMPÔTS*

Seybou Issifi
*COMMUNAUTÉ URBAINE DE
NIAMEY*

Bernar-Oliver Kouaovi
CABINET KOUAOVI

Fati Kountche-Adji
CABINET FATI KOUNTCHE

Fatouma Lanto
*ETUDE D'AVOCATS MARC LE
BIHAN ET COLLABORATEURS*

Marc Le Bihan
*ETUDE D'AVOCATS MARC LE
BIHAN & COLLABORATEURS*

Diallo Rayanatou Loutou
*CABINET LOUTOU -
ARCHITECTES*

Laouali Madougou
*ETUDE D'AVOCATS MARC LE
BIHAN & COLLABORATEURS*

Boubacar Nouhou Maiga
E.N.G.E.

Saadou Maiguizo
*BUREAU D'ETUDES
TECHNIQUES D'ASSISTANCE
ET DE SUIRVEILLANCE EN
CONSTRUCTION CIVILE*

Marie-Virginie Mamoudou
*CHAMBRE NATIONALE DES
NOTAIRES DU NIGER*

Aoula Mamoudou
*MINISTÈRE DE L'URBANISME,
DE L'HABITAT ET DU
CADASTRE*

Mamane Sani Manane
*BUREAU D'ETUDES BALA &
HIMO*

Evelyne M'Bassidgé
*FIDAFRICA /
PRICEWATERHOUSECOOPERS*

Adeline Messou
*FIDAFRICA /
PRICEWATERHOUSECOOPERS*

Yayé Mounkaïla
*CABINET D'AVOCATS
MOUNKAILA-NIANDOU*

Ibrahim Mounouni
*BUREAU D'ETUDES BALA &
HIMO*

Mayaki Oumarou
DESS NOTARIAL

Sahabi Oumarou
*THEMIS INTERNATIONAL
CONSULTANTS*

Achimi M. Riliwanou
*ETUDE DE MAÎTRE ACHIMI
RILIWANOU*

Abdou Yacouba Saïdou
CABINET ASPAU

Mano Salaou
*CABINET D'AVOCATS MANO
SALAOU*

Boubacar Salaou
*ETUDE DE MAÎTRE BOUBACAR
SALAOU*

Daouda Samna
S.C.P.A. MANDELA

Halilou Sani
NIGER

Abdou Moussa Sanoussi
E.N.G.E.

Dominique Taty
*FIDAFRICA /
PRICEWATERHOUSECOOPERS*

Idrissa Tchernaka
*ETUDE D'AVOCATS - MARC LE
BIHAN & COLLABORATEURS*

Fousséni Traoré
*FIDAFRICA /
PRICEWATERHOUSECOOPERS*

Hamadou Yacouba
*ETUDE DE MAÎTRE DJIBO
AÏSSATOU*

NIGERIA

Oluseyi Abiodun Akinwunmi
*AKINWUNMI & BUSARI, LEGAL
PRACTIONERS (A & B)*

Olaleye Adebiyi
WTS ADEBIYI & ASSOCIATES

Temitayo Adegoke
ALUKO & OYEBODE

Adeola Adeiye
UDO UDOMA & BELO-OSAGIE

Saheed A. Aderemi

Francis Adewale
*VISTA BRIDGE GLOBAL
RESOURCES LIMITED*

Adesegun Agbebiyi
ALUKO & OYEBODE

Gboalhan Agboluaje
*AELEX, LEGAL PRACTITIONERS
& ARBITRATORS*

Daniel Agbor
UDO UDOMA & BELO-OSAGIE

Kenneth Aitken
PRICEWATERHOUSECOOPERS

Uche Ajaegbu
*NIGERIA EMPLOYERS'
CONSULTATIVE ASSEMBLY*

Owolabi Animashaun
*SCOTECH UNIVERSAL
RESOURCES LIMITED*

Linda Arifayan
WTS ADEBIYI & ASSOCIATES

Barr. N.U. Chianakwalam
LEGAL STANDARD CONSULTING

Akinbo A. A. Cornerstone
*YOMM KINBOSS NIGERIA
LIMITED*

Kofo Dosekun
ALUKO & OYEBODE

Emmanuel Egwuagu
OBLA & CO.

Jude Bienose Ehiedu
*OLISA AGBAKOBA &
ASSOCIATES*

Nnenna Ejekam
NNENNA EJEKAM ASSOCIATES

Olusoji Elias
OLUSOJI ELIAS AND COMPANY

Anse Agu Ezetah
*CHIEF LAW AGU EZETAH
& CO.*

Yemi Idowu
PRICEWATERHOUSECOOPERS

Agent Benjamin Ihua-
Maduenyi
IHUA & IHUA

Femi David Ikotun
ZIONGATE CHAMERS

Okorie Kalu
*PUNUKA ATTORNEYS &
SOLICITORS*

Folajimi Mohammed
OLUSOJI ELIAS AND COMPANY

Ramat Muhammad
J.K. ADAMU & CO

Victor Nwakasi
*OLISA AGBAKOBA &
ASSOCIATES*

Godwin Obla
OBLA & CO.

Motunrayo Odumosu
PRICEWATERHOUSECOOPERS

Ozofu Ogiemudia
UDO UDOMA & BELO-OSAGIE

Mathias Okojie
*PUNUKA ATTORNEYS &
SOLICITORS*

Patrick Okonjo
OKONJO, ODIAWA & EBIE

Dozie Okwuosah
CENTRAL BANK

Titilola Olateju
OKONJO, ODIAWA & EBIE

Ayodeji Olomojobi
ALUKO & OYEBODE

Friday Omoregbee
*ADONO-SEE RESOURCES
NIGERIA LIMITED*

Fred Onuobia
*G. ELIAS & CO. SOLICITORS
AND ADVOCATES*

Tochukwu Onyiuke
*PUNUKA ATTORNEYS &
SOLICITORS*

Tunde Osasona
*WHITESTONE WORLDWIDE
LTD.*

Olufemi Ososanya
HLB Z.O. OSOSANYA & CO.

Gbenga Oyebode
ALUKO & OYEBODE

Olushola Salau
WTS ADEBIYI & ASSOCIATES

Mohammed Sani
*SMAH INTEGRATED SERVICES
LTD.*

Tunji Tiamiyu
*MULTIFREIGHTLOGISTICS
NIG LTD.*

Reginald Udom
ALUKO & OYEBODE

Uche Ugoi
*AKINWUNMI & BUSARI, LEGAL
PRACTIONERS (A & B)*

Aniekan Ukpanah
UDO UDOMA & BELO-OSAGIE

Maxwell Ukpebor
WTS ADEBIYI & ASSOCIATES

Adamu M. Usman
F.O. AKINRELE & CO.

Tokunbo Wahab
ALUKO & OYEBODE

NORWAY

Anders Aasland Kittelsen
*ADVOKATFIRMAET SCHJØDT
DA*

Bjørn Erik Andersen
DnB NOR

Jan L. Backer
WIKBORG, REIN & CO.

Stig Berge
*THOMMESSEN KREFTING
GREVE LUND AS, MEMBER OF
LEX MUNDI*

Carl Arthur Christiansen
RAEDER ADVOKATFIRMA

Magnar Danielsen
*NORWEGIAN MAPPING
AUTHORITY, CADASTRE AND
LAND REGISTRY*

Knut Ekern
PRICEWATERHOUSECOOPERS

Stein Fagerhaug
DALAN ADVOKATFIRMA DA

Marie Fjulsrud
*ADVOKATFIRMAET HJORT DA,
MEMBER OF IUS LABORIS*

Claus R. Flinder
SIMONSEN ADVOKATFIRMA DA

Amund Fougner
*ADVOKATFIRMAET HJORT DA,
MEMBER OF IUS LABORIS*

Geir Frøholm
*ADVOKATFIRMAET SCHJØDT
D.A.*

Mads Fuglesang
*ADVOKATFIRMAET SELMER
D.A.*

Ingenborg Gjølstad
*THOMMESSEN KREFTING
GREVE LUND AS, MEMBER OF
LEX MUNDI*

Pål Hasner
PRICEWATERHOUSECOOPERS

Renate Iren Heggelund
*ADVOKATFIRMAET SELMER
D.A.*

Odd Hylland
PRICEWATERHOUSECOOPERS

Tove Ihle-Hansen
PRICEWATERHOUSECOOPERS

JÓNAR TRANSPORT

Hanne Karlsen
RAEDER ADVOKATFIRMA

Niels R. Kiaer
RIME ADVOKATFIRMA DA

Bjørn H. Kise
*ADVOKATFIRMA VOGT &
WIIG A.S.*

Ole Fredrik Melleby
RAEDER ADVOKATFIRMA

Karl Erik Nedregotten
PRICEWATERHOUSECOOPERS

Thomas Nordgård
VOGT & WIIG AS

Ole Kristian Olsby
*HOMBLE OLSBY
advokatfirma AS*

Johan Ratvik
DLA PIPER NORWAY DA

Anne Ulset Sande
*KVALE & CO. ADVOKATFIRMA
ANS*

Vegard Sivertsen
*DELOITTE, MEMBER OF
DELOITTE TOUCHE TOHMATSU*

Ståle Skutle Arneson
*ADVOKATFIRMA VOGT &
WIIG A.S.*

Simen Smeby Lium
WIKBORG, REIN & CO.

Christel Spannow
PRICEWATERHOUSECOOPERS

Bernt Olav Steinland
*ADVOKATFIRMAET SELMER
D.A.*

Svein Sulland
*ADVOKATFIRMAET SELMER
D.A.*

Espen Trædal
PRICEWATERHOUSECOOPERS

OMAN

Abdulhakeem Zahran al-Abri
MINISTRY OF HOUSING

Hazem H. Abu-Ghazaleh
*ABU GHAZEL INTELLECTUAL
PROPERTY*

Syed Nasir Ahmed
DAMCO

Zubaida Fakir Mohamed Al
Balushi
CENTRAL BANK

Ahmed Al Barwani
DENTON WILDE SAPTE

Azzan Qasim Al Busaidi
*INTERNATIONAL RESEARCH
FOUNDATION*

Khamis Abdullah Al-Farsi
*MINISTRY OF COMMERCE AND
INDUSTRY*

Said bin Saad Al Shahry
SAID AL SHAHRY LAW OFFICE

Ali Nassir Seif Al-Bualy
*AL-BUALY ATTORNEYS AT LAW
& LEGAL CONSULTANTS*

Mohsin Ahmed Alawi
Al-Hadad
*MOHSIN AL-HADAD & AMUR
AL-KIYUMI & PARTNERS*

Khalid Khamis Al-Hashmi
MUSCAT MUNICIPALITY

Abdullah Alsaidi
*DR. ABDULLAH ALSAIDI LAW
office*

Saif Al-Saidi
*DR. SAIF AL-SAIDI ADVOCATES
AND LEGAL CONSULTANTS*

Mohammed Alshahri
*MOHAMMED ALSHAHRI &
ASSOCIATES*

MINISTRY OF HOUSING.

Hamad M. Al-Sharji
*HAMAD AL-SHARJI, PETER
MANSOUR & CO.*

Jihad Al-Taie
JIHAD AL-TAIE & ASSOCIATES

Majid Al Toki
TROWERS & HAMLINS

Sami Salim Al Asmi
*THE OMANI CENTER FOR
INVESTMENT PROMOTION
& EXPORT DEVELOPMENT
(OCIPED)*

Gaby Cobos
*CURTIS MALLET - PREVOST,
COLT & MOSLE LLP*

M.K. Das
BANK MUSCAT

Mehreen B. Elahi
*AL ALAWI, MANSOOR JAMAL
& CO.*

Abshaer M. Elgalal
Dr. Saif Al-Saidi Advocates and Legal Consultants

Alessandro Gugolz
Said Al Shahry Law Office

Dali Habboub
Denton Wilde Sapte

Sunil Joseph
Maersk Line

P.E. Lalachen MJ
Hassan Al Ansari Legal Consultancy

Mohamded Magdi
J. Nassir & Partners

Pushpa Malani
PricewaterhouseCoopers

Mansoor Jamal Malik
Al Alawi, Mansoor Jamal & Co.

Kapil Mehta
Maersk Line

Subha Mohan
Curtis Mallet - Prevost, Colt & Mosle LLP

Ala Hassan Moosa
Muscat Electricity Distribution Company

Jessica Morris
Denton Wilde Sapte

Bruce Palmer
Curtis Mallet - Prevost, Colt & Mosle LLP

Marian Paul
Al Alawi, Mansoor Jamal & Co.

Reji Paul
Dr. Abdullah Alsaidi Law Office

Madhu Sathyaseelan
Jihad Al-Taie & Associates

Peter Sayer
Said Al Shahry Law Office

Charles Schofield
Trowers & Hamlins

Paul Sheridan
Denton Wilde Sapte

Paul Suddaby
PricewaterhouseCoopers

Jeff Todd
PricewaterhouseCoopers

Thomas Willan
Denton Wilde Sapte

Norman Williams
Majan Engineering Consultants

Sarah Wright
Denton Wilde Sapte

PAKISTAN

Sh. Farooq Abdullah
Abraham & Sarwana

Ali Jafar Abidi
State Bank of Paksitan

Waheed Ahmad
Chaudhary Law Associates

Masood Ahmed
Abraham & Sarwana

Amjad Ali
Cotton Loop

Aroma Surgical Co.

Shariq Aziz
Online Shipping & Logistics

Major Javed Bashir
Greenfields International

Kashif Butt
Zeeshan Enterprises

Bunker Logistics

Ikram Fayaz
Qamar Abbas & Co.

Tahseen Ghani
Hussain Home Textile

Khalid Habibullah
Abraham & Sarwana

Javed Hassan
Sojitz Corporation

Waqar Hussain
Abraham & Sarwana

Hamid Hussain
Crown Movers Worldwide

Rashid Ibrahim
A.F. Ferguson & Co.

Ali Adnan Ibrahim
Georgetown University Law Center

Aman Ullah Iqbal
Crown Trading Company

Tariq Nasim Jan
Datacheck Pvt. Ltd.

Shaukat Ali Khan
Alhabib Textile Industries

Arif Khan
Qamar Abbas & Co.

Asim Khan Hameed
Ivon Trading Company Pvt. Ltd.

Muhammad Maki
Abraham & Sarwana

Mehmood Y. Mandviwalla
Mandviwalla & Zafar

Rashid Mehmood

Yasir Mehmood
Al Hafiz Enterprises

T. Ud-Din A. Mirza
A.F. Ferguson & Co.

Moazzam Mughal
Boxing Winner

Mohammad Qasim Qureshi
Azam Chaudhry Law Associates

Shaheer Asghar Qureshi
Sahil Freight Pakistan Private Limited

Faiza Rafique
Chaudhary Law Associates

Adnan Rafique
Parian International

Abdul Rahman
Qamar Abbas & Co.

Waqar Rana
Cornelius Lane & Mufti

Abid Rauf
ARC International

Mehdi Raza
Moosa Textile Mills (Pvt) Ltd

Sajjad Raza
Transocean Shipping Agencies

Abdul Razzaq
Qamar Abbas & Co.

Jawad A. Sarwana
Abraham & Sarwana

Mohammad Shafique
Online Shipping & Logistics

Ghulam Haider Shamsi
Haider Shamsi & Co., Chartered Accountants

Mohammed Shoukat
Aircon Logistic International

Zubair Umer
Textile Home

Ilyas Zafar
Zafar & Associates LLP.

PALAU

Kenneth Barden
Attorney-at-Law

Cristina Castro
Western Caroline Trading Co.

Lolita Gibbons-Decheny
Koror Planning and Zoning Office

David Shadel
The Law Office of Kirk and Shadel

PANAMA

Alejandro Alemán
Alfaro, Ferrer & Ramírez

Amanda C. Barraza de Wong
PricewaterhouseCoopers

Francisco A. Barrios G.
PricewaterhouseCoopers

Caroline Bono
PricewaterhouseCoopers

Jose A. Bozzo
Garrido & Garrido

Jose Ignacio Bravo
Cocolplan

Luis Chalhoub
Icaza, Gonzalez-Ruiz & Aleman

Shanina J. Contreras
Arosemena Noriega & Contreras, member of Ius Laboris and Lex Mundi

Julio Cesar Contreras III
Arosemena Noriega & Contreras, member of Ius Laboris and Lex Mundi

Guadalupe de Coparropa
CEVA Logistics

Ricardo Eskildsen Morales
Eskildsen & Eskildsen

Michael Fernandez
CAPAC (Cámara Panameña de la Construcción)

Alejandro Fernández de Castro
PricewaterhouseCoopers

Enna Ferrer
Alfaro, Ferrer & Ramírez

Einys K. Fuentes
Panamá Soluciones Logísticas Int. - PSLI

Jorge Garrido
Garrido & Garrido

Jorge R. González Byrne
Arias, Alemán & Mora

Ricardo Madrid
PricewaterhouseCoopers

Ana Lucia Márquez
Arosemena Noriega & Contreras, member of Ius Laboris and Lex Mundi

Ivette Elisa Martínez Saenz
Patton, Moreno & Asvat

Yadira I. Moreno
Aguilar Castillo Love

Erick Rogelio Muñoz
Sucre Arias & Reyes

José Miguel Navarrete
Arosemena Noriega & Contreras, member of Ius Laboris and Lex Mundi

Ramón Ortega
PricewaterhouseCoopers

Andrea Paniagua
PricewaterhouseCoopers

Sebastian Perez
Union Fenosa - EDEMET - EDECHI

Julio Pinedo
PricewaterhouseCoopers

Alfredo Ramírez Jr.
Alfaro, Ferrer & Ramírez

Manuel E. Rodriguez
Union Fenosa - EDEMET - EDECHI

Luz María Salamina
Asociación Panameña de Crédito

Juan Tejada
PricewaterhouseCoopers

Valentín Ureña III
Arosemena Noriega & Contreras, member of Ius Laboris and Lex Mundi

Patricia Urriola
Panalpina

Ramón Varela
Morgan & Morgan

PAPUA NEW GUINEA

Tyson Boboro
Allens Arthur Robinson

Vincent Bull
Allens Arthur Robinson

David Caradus
PricewaterhouseCoopers

Richard Flynn
Blake Dawson

Justin Haiara
Steeles Lawyers

Peter Joseph Heystraten
Sea Horse Pacific

Antonia Laki
PricewaterhouseCoopers

David Lavery
Blake Dawson

John Leahy
Peter Allan Lowing Lawyers

Simon Nutley
Peter Allan Lowing Lawyers

Steven O'Brien
O'Briens

Kapu Rageau
Rageau, Manua & Kikira Lawyers

Steamships Trading Company Ltd.

Thomas Taberia
Peter Allan Lowing Lawyers

PARAGUAY

Perla Alderete
Vouga & Olmedo Abogados

Hugo T. Berkemeyer
Berkemeyer, Attorneys & Counselors

Luis Alberto Breuer
Berkemeyer, Attorneys & Counselors

Esteban Burt
Peroni, Sosa, Tellechea, Burt & Narvaja, member of Lex Mundi

María Debattisti
Servimex SACI

Lorena Dolsa
Berkemeyer, Attorneys & Counselors

Blas Dos Santos
Ferrere Attorneys

Estefanía Elicetche
Peroni, Sosa, Tellechea, Burt & Narvaja, member of Lex Mundi

Jorge Figueredo
Vouga & Olmedo Abogados

Néstor Gamarra
Servimex SACI

Ilse Gonzalez
Ilse Gonzalez & Asoc

Larisa Guillén
PricewaterhouseCoopers

Jorge Jimenez Rey
Banco Central

Nestor Loizaga
Ferrere Attorneys

Carmela Martínez
PricewaterhouseCoopers

María Esmeralda Moreno
Moreno Ruffinelli & Asociados

Roberto Moreno Rodríguez Alcalá
Moreno Ruffinelli & Asociados

Hector Palazon
Ferrere Attorneys

Rocío Penayo
Moreno Ruffinelli & Asociados

Yolanda Pereira
Berkemeyer, Attorneys & Counselors

Armindo Riquelme
Fiorio, Cardozo & Alvarado

Belen Saldivar Romañach
Ferrere Attorneys

Angela Schaerer de Sosa
Escribana Pública

Ruben Taboada
PricewaterhouseCoopers

PERU

Walter Aguirre
PricewaterhouseCoopers

Marco Antonio Alarcón Piana
ESTUDIO ECHECOPAR

Humberto Allemant
PRICEWATERHOUSECOOPERS

Gisella Alvarado Caycho
ESTUDIO ECHECOPAR

Guilhermo Auler
FORSYTH & ARBE ABOGADOS

Raul Barrios
BARRIOS FUENTES GALLO ABOGADOS

German Barrios
BARRIOS FUENTES GALLO ABOGADOS

Vanessa Barzola
PRICEWATERHOUSECOOPERS LEGAL SERVICES

Marianell Bonomini
PRICEWATERHOUSECOOPERS LEGAL SERVICES

José Ignacio Castro
ESTUDIO RUBIO, LEGUÍA, NORMAND Y ASOCIADOS

Fernando Castro Kahn
MUÑIZ, RAMÍREZ, PERÉZ-TAIMAN & LUNA VICTORIA ATTORNEYS AT LAW

Javier de la Vega
PRICEWATERHOUSECOOPERS

Alfonso De Los Heros Pérez Albela
ESTUDIO ECHECOPAR

Mariana De Olazaval
ESTUDIO OLAECHEA, MEMBER OF LEX MUNDI

Paula Devescovi
BARRIOS FUENTES GALLO ABOGADOS

Juan Carlos Durand Grahammer
DURAND ABOGADOS

Arturo Ferrari
MUÑIZ, RAMÍREZ, PERÉZ-TAIMAN & LUNA VICTORIA ATTORNEYS AT LAW

Guillermo Ferrero
ESTUDIO FERRERO ABOGADOS

Luís Fuentes
BARRIOS FUENTES GALLO ABOGADOS

Juan García Montúfar
ESTUDIO RUBIO, LEGUÍA, NORMAND Y ASOCIADOS

Anabelí González
ESTUDIO FERRERO ABOGADOS

Cecilia Guzman-Barron
BARRIOS FUENTES GALLO ABOGADOS

Jose A. Honda
ESTUDIO OLAECHEA, MEMBER OF LEX MUNDI

Rafael Junco
CAMARA PERUANA DE LA CONSTRUCCION

Kuno Kafka Prado
ESTUDIO RUBIO, LEGUÍA, NORMAND Y ASOCIADOS

Adolfo Lopez
PRICEWATERHOUSECOOPERS

German Lora
PAYET, REY, CAUVI ABOGADOS

Raul Lozano-Merino
PEÑA, LOZANO, FAURA & ASOCIADOS

Milagros Maravi
ESTUDIO RUBIO, LEGUÍA, NORMAND Y ASOCIADOS

Jesús Matos
ESTUDIO OLAECHEA, MEMBER OF LEX MUNDI

Milagros Mendoza
ESTUDIO RUBIO, LEGUÍA, NORMAND Y ASOCIADOS

Anna Julia Mendoza
PAYET, REY, CAUVI ABOGADOS

Marlene Molero
ESTUDIO RUBIO, LEGUÍA, NORMAND Y ASOCIADOS

Miguel Mur
PRICEWATERHOUSECOOPERS

Franco Muschi
PAYET, REY, CAUVI ABOGADOS

Gabriel Musso
ESTUDIO RUBIO, LEGUÍA, NORMAND Y ASOCIADOS

Carmen Padrón
ESTUDIO RUBIO, LEGUÍA, NORMAND Y ASOCIADOS

Adolfo J. Pinillos
DURAND ABOGADOS

Lucianna Polar
ESTUDIO OLAECHEA, MEMBER OF LEX MUNDI

Carlos Javier Rabanal Sobrino
DURAND ABOGADOS

Fernando M. Ramos
BARRIOS FUENTES GALLO ABOGADOS

Sonia L. Rengifo
BARRIOS FUENTES GALLO ABOGADOS

Alonso Rey Bustamante
PAYET, REY, CAUVI ABOGADOS

Guillermo Acuña Roeder
ESTUDIO RUBIO, LEGUÍA, NORMAND Y ASOCIADOS

Augusto Ruiloba Morante
ESTUDIO ECHECOPAR

Emil Ruppert Yañez
ESTUDIO RUBIO, LEGUÍA, NORMAND Y ASOCIADOS

Carolina Sáenz
ESTUDIO RUBIO, LEGUÍA, NORMAND Y ASOCIADOS

Adolfo Sanabria Mercado
MUÑIZ, RAMÍREZ, PERÉZ-TAIMAN & LUNA VICTORIA ATTORNEYS AT LAW

Diego Sanchez
PRICEWATERHOUSECOOPERS

Martin Serkovic
ESTUDIO OLAECHEA, MEMBER OF LEX MUNDI

Hugo Silva
RODRIGO, ELÍAS, MEDRANO ABOGADOS

José Antonio Valdez
ESTUDIO OLAECHEA, MEMBER OF LEX MUNDI

Valery Vicente
FORSYTH & ARBE ABOGADOS

Manuel Villa-García
ESTUDIO OLAECHEA, MEMBER OF LEX MUNDI

Ursula Villanueva
ESTUDIO RUBIO, LEGUÍA, NORMAND Y ASOCIADOS

Monica Yoland Arteaga Chaparro
REGISTRO PREDIAL URBANO

PHILIPPINES

Emilio Amaranto
PUYAT JACINTO SANTOS LAW OFFICE

Myla Gloria Amboy
JIMENEZ GONZALES LIWANAG BELLO VALDEZ CALUYA & FERNANDEZ

Jazmin Banal
ROMULO, MABANTA, BUENAVENTURA, SAYOC & DE LOS ANGELES, MEMBER OF LEX MUNDI

Manuel Batallones
BAP CREDIT BUREAU

Alexander B. Cabrera
PRICEWATERHOUSECOOPERS / ISLA LIPANA & CO.

Rusvie Cadiz
RVFREIGHT AND SERVICES

Joseph Omar A. Castillo
PUYAT JACINTO SANTOS LAW OFFICE

Kenneth Chua
QUISUMBING TORRES, MEMBER FIRM OF BAKER AND McKENZIE

Emerico O. de Guzman
ANGARA ABELLO CONCEPCION REGALA & CRUZ LAW OFFICES (ACCRALAW)

Juana M. Dela Cruz
INTERNATIONAL CONSOLIDATOR PHILIPPINES, INC.

Rachelle Diaz
QUISUMBING TORRES, MEMBER FIRM OF BAKER AND McKENZIE

Ma. Lourdes Dino
JIMENEZ GONZALES LIWANAG BELLO VALDEZ CALUYA & FERNANDEZ

Rachel Follosco
FOLLOSCO MORALLOS & HERCE

Catherine Franco
QUISUMBING TORRES, MEMBER FIRM OF BAKER AND McKENZIE

Gilberto Gallos
ANGARA ABELLO CONCEPCION REGALA & CRUZ LAW OFFICES (ACCRALAW)

Geraldine S. Garcia
FOLLOSCO MORALLOS & HERCE

Gwen Grecia-de Vera
PJS LAW

Rafael Khan
SIGUION REYNA MONTECILLO & ONGSIAKO

Genevieve M. Limbo
PRICEWATERHOUSECOOPERS / ISLA LIPANA & CO.

Victoria Limkico
JIMENEZ GONZALES LIWANAG BELLO VALDEZ CALUYA & FERNANDEZ

Erich H. Lingad
INTERNATIONAL CONSOLIDATOR PHILIPPINES, INC.

Herminio Liwanag
JIMENEZ GONZALES LIWANAG BELLO VALDEZ CALUYA & FERNANDEZ

Lory Anne Manuel-McMullin
JIMENEZ GONZALES LIWANAG BELLO VALDEZ CALUYA & FERNANDEZ

Yolanda Mendoza-Eleazar
CASTILLO LAMAN TAN PANTALEON & SAN JOSE LAW OFFICES

Elmer R. Mitra, Jr
PRICEWATERHOUSECOOPERS / ISLA LIPANA & CO.

Jesusito G. Morallos
FOLLOSCO MORALLOS & HERCE

Freddie Naagas
OOCL LOGISTICS

Alan Ortiz
FOLLOSCO MORALLOS & HERCE

Nicanor N. Padilla
SIGUION REYNA MONTECILLO & ONGSIAKO

Emmanuel C. Paras
SYCIP SALAZAR HERNANDEZ & GATMAITAN

Zayber B. Protacio
PRICEWATERHOUSECOOPERS / ISLA LIPANA & CO.

Janice Kae Ramirez
QUASHA ANCHETA PENA & NOLASCO

Roderick Reyes
JIMENEZ GONZALES LIWANAG BELLO VALDEZ CALUYA & FERNANDEZ

Ricardo J. Romulo
ROMULO, MABANTA, BUENAVENTURA, SAYOC AND DE LOS ANGELES, MEMBER OF LEX MUNDI

Roy Enrico Santos
PUYAT JACINTO SANTOS LAW OFFICE

Sheryl Tanquilut
ROMULO, MABANTA, BUENAVENTURA, SAYOC & DE LOS ANGELES, MEMBER OF LEX MUNDI

Bianca Torres
PJS LAW

Ma. Melva Valdez
JIMENEZ GONZALES LIWANAG BELLO VALDEZ CALUYA & FERNANDEZ

Redentor C. Zapata
QUASHA ANCHETA PENA & NOLASCO

Gil Roberto Zerrudo
QUISUMBING TORRES, MEMBER FIRM OF BAKER AND McKENZIE

POLAND

ALLEN & OVERY A. PĘDZICH SP.K.

Grzegorz Banasiukj
GIDE LOYRETTE NOUEL POLSKA

Aleksander Borowicz
BIURO INFORMACJI KREDYTOWEJ S.A.

Tomasz Brudkowski
KOCHAŃSKI, BRUDKOWSKI & PARTNERS

Krzysztof Cichocki
SKS LEGAL

Krzysztof Ciepliński
GIDE LOYRETTE NOUEL POLSKA

Bożena Ciosek
WIERZBOWSKI EVERSHEDS, MEMBER OF EVERSHEDS INTERNATIONAL LTD.

Tomasz Duchniak
SKS LEGAL

Lech Giliciński
WHITE & CASE W. DANIŁOWICZ, W. JURCEWICZ I WSPÓLNICY SP. K.

Paweł Grześkowiak
GIDE LOYRETTE NOUEL POLSKA

Fidala Jaroslaw
TOKARCZUK, JĘDRZEJCZYK, WSPÓLNICY. KANCELARIA PRAWNA GIDE LOYRETTE NOUEL POLSKA

Piotr Kaim
PRICEWATERHOUSECOOPERS

Tomasz Kański
SOŁTYSIŃSKI KAWECKI & SZLĘZAK

Iwona Karasek
JAGIELLONIAN UNIVERSITY KRAKOW

Edyta Kolkowska

Ewa Lachowska - Brol
WIERZBOWSKI EVERSHEDS, MEMBER OF EVERSHEDS INTERNATIONAL LTD.

Dagmara Lipka-Chudzik
MAGNUSSON

Agata Mierzwa
WIERZBOWSKI EVERSHEDS, MEMBER OF EVERSHEDS INTERNATIONAL LTD.

Dariusz Okolski
OKOLSKI LAW OFFICE

Krzysztof Pawlak
SOŁTYSIŃSKI KAWECKI & SZLĘZAK

Weronika Pelc
WARDYŃSKI & PARTNERS, MEMBER OF LEX MUNDI

Anna Maria Pukszto
SALANS

Bartłomiej Raczkowski
BARTŁOMIEJ RACZKOWSKI KANCELARIA PRAWA PRACY

Piotr Sadownik
GIDE LOYRETTE NOUEL POLSKA

Katarzyna Sarek
BARTŁOMIEJ RACZKOWSKI KANCELARIA PRAWA PRACY

Zbigniew Skórczyński
CHADBOURNE & PARKE LLP

Dariusz Smiechowski
UNION OF POLISH ARCHITECTS

Iwona Smith
PRICEWATERHOUSECOOPERS

Ewelina Stobiecka
EISELSBERG NATLACEN WALDERDORFF CANCOLA RECHTSANWÄLTE GMBH

Dariusz Tokarczuk
*GIDE LOYRETTE NOUEL
POLSKA*

Wojciech Wądołowsk
MAGNUSSON

Radoslaw Waszkiewicz
*SOŁTYSIŃSKI KAWECKI &
SZLĘZAK*

Ewa Wiśniewska

Tomasz Zabost

PORTUGAL

Victor Abrantes
*VICTOR ABRANTES -
INTERNATIONAL SALES AGENT*

Filipa Arantes Pedroso
*MORAIS LEITÃO, GALVÃO
TELES, SOARES DA SILVA &
ASSOCIADOS, MEMBER OF LEX
MUNDI*

Miguel Azevedo
GARRIGUES

Manuel P. Barrocas
BARROCAS SARMENTO NEVES

José Pedro Briosa e Gala
BARROCAS SARMENTO NEVES

Rita Carvalho
PRICEWATERHOUSECOOPERS

Tiago Castanheira Marques
ABREU ADVOGADOS

Susana Cebola
*DIRECTORATE GENERAL OF
REGISTRY & NOTARY CIVIL
SERVICE*

Gabriel Cordeiro
*DIRECÇÃO MUNICIPAL DE
GESTÃO URBANÍSTICA*

João Cadete de Matos
BANCO DE PORTUGAL

Carlos de Sousa e Brito
*CARLOS DE SOUSA & BRITO &
ASSOCIADOS*

Cristina Dein
DEIN ADVOGADOS

John Duggan
PRICEWATERHOUSECOOPERS

Bruno Ferreira
GARRIGUES

Jorge Figueiredo
PRICEWATERHOUSECOOPERS

Inga Kilikeviciene

Martim Krupenski
BARROCAS SARMENTO NEVES

Maria Manuel Leitão Marques
*SECRETARY OF STATE
FOR ADMINISTRATIVE
MODERNISATION*

Diogo Léonidas Rocha
GARRIGUES

Jorge Pedro Lopes
*POLYTECHNIC INSTITUTE OF
BRAGANÇA*

Marta Elisa Machado
PRICEWATERHOUSECOOPERS

Ana Margarida Maia
*MIRANDA CORREIA
AMENDOEIRA & ASSOCIADOS*

Miguel Marques dos Santos
GARRIGUES

Filipa Marques Junior
*MORAIS LEITÃO, GALVÃO
TELES, SOARES DA SILVA &*

*ASSOCIADOS, MEMBER OF LEX
MUNDI*

Isabel Martínez de Salas
GARRIGUES

Susana Melo
*GRANT THORNTON
CONSULTORES, LDA*

Joaquim Luis Mendes
*GRANT THORNTON
CONSULTORES, LDA.*

João Moucheira
*DIRECTORATE GENERAL OF
REGISTRY & NOTARY CIVIL
SERVICE*

*MOUTEIRA GUERREIRO, ROSA
AMARAL & ASSOCIADOS -
SOCIEDADE DE ADVOGADOS
R.L.*

Rita Nogueira Neto
GARRIGUES

Felipe Oliviera
*CARLOS DE SOUSA & BRITO &
ASSOCIADOS*

Rui Peixoto Duarte
ABREU ADVOGADOS

Pedro Pereira Coutinho
GARRIGUES

Acácio Pita Negrão
*PLEN - SOCIEDADE DE
ADVOGADOS, RL*

Margarida Ramalho
*ASSOCIAÇÃO DE EMPRESAS
DE CONSTRUÇÃO E OBRAS
PÚBLICAS*

Paulo Ribeiro
QUINTA DO FIGUEIRAL

Filomena Rosa
*DIRECTORATE GENERAL OF
REGISTRY & NOTARY CIVIL
SERVICE*

David Salgado Areias
ABREU ADVOGADOS

Pedro Santos
ANDROMEDA

Pedro Santos
*GRANT THORNTON
CONSULTORES, LDA*

Raquel Santos
*MORAIS LEITÃO, GALVÃO
TELES, SOARES DA SILVA &
ASSOCIADOS, MEMBER OF LEX
MUNDI*

Manuel Silveira Botelho
*ANTÓNIO FRUTUOSO DE MELO
E ASSOCIADOS - SOCIEDADE DE
ADVOGADOS, R.L.*

Carmo Sousa Machado
ABREU ADVOGADOS

João Paulo Teixeira de Matos
GARRIGUES

PUERTO RICO

Viviana Aguilu
PRICEWATERHOUSECOOPERS

Israel Alicea
QUIÑONES & SÁNCHEZ, PSC

Ignacio Alvarez
*PIETRANTONI MÉNDEZ &
ALVAREZ LLP*

Alfredo Alvarez-Ibañez
O'NEILL & BORGES

Juan Aquino
O'NEILL & BORGES

Javier Arbona
QUIÑONES & SÁNCHEZ, PSC

James A. Arroyo
TRANSUNION

Hermann Bauer
O'NEILL & BORGES

Nikos Buxeda Ferrer
*ADSUAR MUÑIZ GOYCO SEDA
& PÉREZ-OCHOA, P.S.C*

Mildred Caban
*GOLDMAN ANTONETTI &
CÓRDOVA P.S.C*

Jorge Capo
O'NEILL & BORGES

Walter F. Chow
O'NEILL & BORGES

Myrtelena Díaz Pedora
*ADSUAR MUÑIZ GOYCO SEDA
& PÉREZ-OCHOA, P.S.C*

Alberto G. Estrella
*WILLIAM ESTRELLA LAW
OFFICES*

Carla Garcia
O'NEILL & BORGES

Carlos Hernandez
REICHARD & ESCALERA

Gerardo Hernandez
*WILLIAM ESTRELLA LAW
OFFICES*

Francisco Hernández-Ruiz
REICHARD & ESCALERA

Donald E. Hull
*PIETRANTONI MÉNDEZ &
ALVAREZ LLP*

Luis Marini
O'NEILL & BORGES

Rubén M. Medina-Lugo
*CANCIO, NADAL, RIVERA &
DÍAZ*

Oscar O Meléndez - Sauri
*COTO MALLEY & TAMARGO,
LLP*

Pedro A. Morell
*GOLDMAN ANTONETTI &
CÓRDOVA P.S.C*

Carlos Nieves
QUIÑONES & SÁNCHEZ, PSC

Joaquin M Nieves
SUN AIR EXPEDITE SERVICE

Jorge Peirats
*PIETRANTONI MÉNDEZ &
ALVAREZ LLP*

Edwin Quiñones
QUIÑONES & SÁNCHEZ, PSC

Victor Rodriguez
*MULTITRANSPORT & MARINE
CO.*

Victor Rodriguez
PRICEWATERHOUSECOOPERS

Jorge M. Ruiz Montilla
MCCONNELL VALDÉS LLC

Javier Sánchez

Ineabelle Santiago
REICHARD & ESCALERA

Yasmin Umpierre-Chaar
O'NEILL & BORGES

Carlos Valldejuly
O'NEILL & BORGES

Fernando Van Derdys
REICHARD & ESCALERA

Travis Wheatley
O'NEILL & BORGES

QATAR

Naveed Abdulla
GULF STAR GROUP

Shawki Abu Nada
*CENTRAL TENDERS
COMMITTEE*

Abdelmoniem Abutiffa
*QATAR INTERNATIONAL LAW
FIRM*

Ali Al Amari
CENTRAL BANK

Kholoud Al Faihani

Maitha Al Hajri

Mohammed Saleh Al Jilani
CENTRAL BANK

Hassan Abdulla Al Khouri

Abdullah Al Muslemani
LEGAL ADVISOR

Nada Mubarak Al Sulaiti
*AL SULAITI, ATTORNEYS,
LEGAL CONSULTANTS &
ARBITRATORS*

Mohammed A. Ali
*AL KHORRI ADVOCATE &
LEGAL CONSULTANTS*

Adnan Ali
PRICEWATERHOUSECOOPERS

Abdul Rahman Ali Almotawa
*CUSTOMS AND PORTS
GENERAL AUTHORITY*

A. Rahman Mohamed
Al-Jufairi
*A. RAHMAN MOHAMED
AL-JUFAIRI*

Juma Ali Rashed Al-Kaabi
*MINISTRY OF ECONOMY &
COMMERCE*

Rashid Bin Abdulla Al-Khalifa
*LAW OFFICE OF RASHID BIN
ABDULLA AI-KHALIFA*

Khalil Al-Mulla
*CUSTOMS AND PORTS
GENERAL AUTHORITY*

Muna Al-Mutawa
*ADVOCATE & LEGAL
CONSULTANT*

Mohammed H. Al-Naimi
*CENTRAL TENDERS
COMMITTEE*

Ahmad Al-Remehi
*REAL ESTATE REGISTRATION
DEPARTMENT*

Ahmed Mohammed
Al-Rmehy
MINISTRY OF JUSTICE

Walid A. Moneim Amen
LABOUR DEPARTMENT

Ian Clay
PRICEWATERHOUSECOOPERS

Dalal K. Farhat
ARAB ENGINEERING BUREAU

Steuart Anthony Greig
*BIN YOUSEF CARGO EXPRESS
W.L.L*

Robert A. Hager
PATTON BOGGS LLP

Tajeldin Idris Babiker
ABN LAW FIRM

Samar A. Ismail
KHATIB & ALAMI

Ibrahim Jaidah
ARAB ENGINEERING BUREAU

Abdul Jaleel
LEX CHAMBERS.

Milan Joshi
*BIN YOUSEF CARGO EXPRESS
W.L.L*

Upuli Kasthuriarachchi
PRICEWATERHOUSECOOPERS

Sajid Khan
PRICEWATERHOUSECOOPERS

Ali Kudah
*CUSTOMS AND PORTS
GENERAL AUTHORITY*

Ahmed Sayed Rekaby Mansy
*LAW OFFICE OF RASHID BIN
ABDULLA AI-KHALIFA*

Abdul Muttalib
GULF STAR GROUP

Najwan Nayef
*CLYDE & CO.LEGAL
CONSULTANTS*

Ali Said Othman
*CENTRAL TENDERS
COMMITTEE*

Mohammed SHK. Qasem
KHATIB & ALAML

Annette Seiffert
*CLYDE & CO. LEGAL
CONSULTANTS*

Sarah Simms
*CLYDE & CO. LEGAL
CONSULTANTS*

Laura Warren
*CLYDE & CO. LEGAL
CONSULTANTS*

Terence G.C. Witzmann
HSBC

ROMANIA

Adriana Almasan
*STOICA & ASOCIATII
ATTORNEYS-AT-LAW*

Alina Badea
MUŞAT & ASOCIAŢII

Emanuel Bancila
PRICEWATERHOUSECOOPERS

Irina Bănică
MUŞAT & ASOCIAŢII

Irina Barbu
D & B DAVID SI BAIAS S.C.A.

Cristian Bichi
NATIONAL BANK

Monica Biciusca
ANGHEL STABB & PARTNERS

Roxana Bolea
D & B DAVID SI BAIAS S.C.A.

Cosmin Bonea
SALANS

Cezara Chirica
D & B DAVID SI BAIAS S.C.A.

Anamaria Corbescu
SALANS

Dorín Coza
*BABIUC SULICA
PROTOPOPESCU VONICA*

Tiberiu Csaki
SALANS

Peter De Ruiter
PRICEWATERHOUSECOOPERS

Luminita Dima
*NESTOR NESTOR DICULESCU
KINGSTON PETERSEN, MEMBER*

OF IUS LABORIS, OF LEX MUNDI & OF SEE LEGAL

Alexandru Dobrescu
LINA & GUIA S.C.A

Ion Dragulin
NATIONAL BANK

Laura Adina Duca
NESTOR NESTOR DICULESCU KINGSTON PETERSEN, MEMBER OF IUS LABORIS, OF LEX MUNDI & OF SEE LEGAL

Cristina Ene
PRICEWATERHOUSECOOPERS

Serban Epure
BIROUL DE CREDIT

Adriana Gaspar
NESTOR NESTOR DICULESCU KINGSTON PETERSEN, MEMBER OF IUS LABORIS, OF LEX MUNDI & OF SEE LEGAL

Gina Gheorghe
TANASESCU, LEAUA, CADAR & ASOCIATII

Sergiu Gidei
D & B DAVID SI BAIAS S.C.A.

Alexandru Gosa
D & B DAVID SI BAIAS S.C.A.

Veronica Gruzsniczki
BABIUC SULICA PROTOPOPESCU VONICA

Mihai Guia
LINA & GUIA S.C.A

Nicolae Hariuc
ZAMFIRESCU RACOTI PREDOIU LAW PARTNERSHIP

HIDROPNEUMATICA

Roxana Ionescu
NESTOR NESTOR DICULESCU KINGSTON PETERSEN, MEMBER OF IUS LABORIS, OF LEX MUNDI & OF SEE LEGAL

Iulian Iosif
MUŞAT & ASOCIAŢII

Crenguta Leaua
TANASESCU, LEAUA, CADAR & ASOCIATII

Cristian Lina
LINA & GUIA S.C.A

Dumitru Viorel Manescu
NATIONAL UNION OF ROMANIAN NOTARIES

Alina Manescu
PRICEWATERHOUSECOOPERS

Oana Manuceanu
PRICEWATERHOUSECOOPERS

Gelu Titus Maravela
MUŞAT & ASOCIAŢII

Carmen Medar
D & B DAVID SI BAIAS S.C.A

Raluca Mocanu
PRICEWATERHOUSECOOPERS

Dominic Morega
MUŞAT & ASOCIAŢII

Adriana Neagoe
NATIONAL BANK

Manuela Marina Nestor
NESTOR NESTOR DICULESCU KINGSTON PETERSEN, MEMBER OF IUS LABORIS, OF LEX MUNDI & OF SEE LEGAL

Madalin Niculeasa
NESTOR NESTOR DICULESCU KINGSTON PETERSEN, MEMBER

OF IUS LABORIS, OF LEX MUNDI & OF SEE LEGAL

Lavinia Nucu
ANGHEL STABB & PARTNERS

Alina Oancea
PRICEWATERHOUSECOOPERS

Marius Pătrăşcanu
MUŞAT & ASOCIAŢII

Cristina Popescu
LINA & GUIA S.C.A

Alina Popescu
MUŞAT & ASOCIAŢII

Mariana Popescu
NATIONAL BANK

Diana Emanuela Precup
NESTOR NESTOR DICULESCU KINGSTON PETERSEN, MEMBER OF IUS LABORIS, OF LEX MUNDI & OF SEE LEGAL

Irina Preoteasa
PRICEWATERHOUSECOOPERS

Alina Proteasa
LINA & GUIA S.C.A

Adriana Puscas
BABIUC SULICA PROTOPOPESCU VONICA

Raluca Radu
SALANS

Laura Radu
STOICA & ASOCIATII ATTORNEYS-AT-LAW

Alina Rafaila
PRICEWATERHOUSECOOPERS

Angela Rosca
TAXHOUSE SRL

Alex Rosca
TAXHOUSE SRL

Ana-Maria Rusu
SALANS

Romana Schuster
PRICEWATERHOUSECOOPERS

Cristina Simion
PRICEWATERHOUSECOOPERS

Alexandru Slujitoru
D & B DAVID SI BAIAS S.C.A.

Alexandra Sova
SOVA & PARTNERS

Ileana Sovaila
MUŞAT & ASOCIAŢII

David Stabb
ANGHEL STABB & PARTNERS

Marta Stefan
ANGHEL STABB & PARTNERS

Cristiana Stoica
STOICA & ASOCIATII ATTORNEYS-AT-LAW

Sorin Corneliu Stratula
STRATULA TOMOSOIU MOCANU

Potyesz Tiberu
BITRANS LTD., MEMBER OF WORLD MEDIATRANS GROUP

Anca Vatasoiu
SALANS

Mihai Vintu
PRICEWATERHOUSECOOPERS

RUSSIAN FEDERATION

Marat Agabalyan
HERBERT SMITH CIS LLP

Darya Angelo
LAW FIRM ALRUD

Ekaterina Avilova
PRICEWATERHOUSECOOPERS LEGAL SERVICES

Fedor Bogatyrev
LAW FIRM ALRUD

Alexia Borisov
ANDREAS NEOCLEOUS & CO., LEGAL CONSULTANTS

Julia Borozdna
BAKER & MCKENZIE

Maria Bykovskaya
GIDE LOYRETTE NOUEL, MEMBER OF LEX MUNDI

ESPRO REAL ESTATE

Valery Getmanenko
BAKER & MCKENZIE

Maria Gorban
GIDE LOYRETTE NOUEL, MEMBER OF LEX MUNDI

Evgeniy Gouk
PRICEWATERHOUSECOOPERS CIS LAW OFFICES B.V.

Marlena Hurley
TransUnion CRIF DECISION SOLUTION

Irina Im
PRICEWATERHOUSECOOPERS

Sergej Juzovitski
RAMBOLL

Maxim Kandyba
PRICEWATERHOUSECOOPERS CIS LAW OFFICES B.V.

Ekaterina Kotova
PRICEWATERHOUSECOOPERS CIS LAW OFFICES B.V.

Dmitry Kurochkin
HERBERT SMITH CIS LLP

Sergei L. Lazarev
RUSSIN & VECCHI, LLC.

Maxim Likholetov
MAGNUSSON

Dmitry Lyakhov
RUSSIN & VECCHI, LLC.

Anastasia Malashkevich
PRICEWATERHOUSECOOPERS

Irina Martakova
PRICEWATERHOUSECOOPERS

Vladimir Melnikov
HERBERT SMITH CIS LLP

Lyudmila Merzlikina
ALRUD LAW FIRM

Yuri Monastyrsky
MONASTYRSKY, ZYUBA, STEPANOV & PARTNERS

OAO PIGMENT

Gennady Odarich
PRICEWATERHOUSECOOPERS LEGAL SERVICES

Tatiana Ponomareva

Igor Porokhin
MAGNUSSON

Maria Priezzheva
ORRICK HERRINGTON & SUTCLIFFE LLP

Roman Reshetyuk
PRICEWATERHOUSECOOPERS LEGAL SERVICES

Evgeny Reyzman
BAKER & MCKENZIE

Konstantin Salichev

Andrey Shpak
PRICEWATERHOUSECOOPERS

Olga Sirodoeva
ORRICK HERRINGTON & SUTCLIFFE LLP

Steven Snaith
PRICEWATERHOUSECOOPERS

Pavel Solovyev
MAGNUSSON

Irina Strizhakova
ANDREAS NEOCLEOUS & CO., LEGAL CONSULTANTS

Elena Subocheva
RUSSIN & VECCHI, LLC

Mikhail Usubyan
ORRICK, HERRINGTON & SUTCLIFFE LLP

Andrey Zhdanov
BAKER & MCKENZIE

RWANDA

BANQUE COMMERCIALE DU RWANDA

Emmanuel Abijuru
UNIVERSITÉ LIBRE DE KIGALI

Alberto Basomingera
CABINET D'AVOCATS MHAYIMANA

Pierre Célestin Bumbakare
RWANDA REVENUE AUTHORITY

José Habimana
UMWLIMU SACCO

Jean Havugimana
RWANDA REVENUE AUTHORITY

Suzanne Iyakaremye
SDV

Project Kaburege
CABINET D'AVOCAT KABUREGE

Annie Kairaba-Kyambadde
RWANDA INITIATIVE FOR SUSTAINABLE DEVELOPMENT / LANDNET

Marcellin Kamanzi

Robert Kamugisha
MINISTRY OF JUSTICE

Angélique Kantengwa
NATIONAL BANK

Theophile Kazaneza
KIGALI BAR ASSOCIATION

Rodolphe Kembukuswa
SDV

Narasimha Kollegal
WORLD FREIGHT S.A.R.L.

Isaïe Mhayimana
CABINET D'AVOCATS MHAYIMANA

Minette Mutoni
BARREAU DE KIGALI

Pothin Muvara

David Ngaracu
WORLD FREIGHT S.A.R.L.

Athanase Rutabingwa
KIGALI ALLIED ADVOCATES

Vincent Shyirambere
OFFICE OF THE REGISTRAR OF LAND TITLES

André Verbruggen

SAMOA

Tiffany Acton
QUANTUM CONTRAX LTD

Mike Betham
TRANSAM LTD.

Lawrie Burich
QUANTUM CONTRAX LTD

Murray Drake
DRAKE & CO.

Ruby Drake
DRAKE & CO.

George Latu
LATU EY & CLARKE LAWYERS

Arthur R. Penn
LESA MA PENN

John Ryan
TRANSAM LTD.

Shan Shiraz Ali Usman
TRADEPAC MARKETING LTD.

SÃO TOMÉ AND PRINCIPE

António de Barros A. Aguiar
SOCOGESTA

André Aureliano Aragão
ANDRÉ AURELIANO ARAGÃO JURISCONSULTA & ADVOGADO

Fernando Barros
PRICEWATERHOUSECOOPERS

Jorge Bonfim
DIRECÇÃO DO COMÉRCIO

Pedro Calixto
PRICEWATERHOUSECOOPERS

Edmar Carvalho
MIRANDA CORREIA AMENDOEIRA & ASOCIADOS

Abreu Conceição
SOARES DA COSTA

João Cristovão
BANCO INTERNACIONAL DE SÃO TOMÉ E PRÍNCIPE

Frederico da Glória
TRIBUNAL DE PRIMEIRA INSTÂNCIA DE SÃO TOMÉ

Pascoal Daio
PASCOAL DAIO - ADVOGADO & CONSULTORE

Abílio de Carvalho Dema
CABINET AFRICAIN DE GESTION INFORMATIQUE ET CONTABLE

Celiza Deus Lima
JPALMS ADVOGADOS

DIRECÇÃO DAS ALFÂNDEGAS

Agostinho Q.S.A. Fernandes
DIRECTORATE OF TAXES

Cesaltino Fernandes
SERVIÇOS GEOGRAFICOS E CADASTRAIS

Raul Gomes
ATS LOGISTICS Co.

METALURGICA SANTO AMARO

Jean-Paul Migan
ECOBANK

Faustino Manuel Neto
EMAE

Eduardo Paiva
PRICEWATERHOUSECOOPERS

Luisélio Pinto
United Investments

Guilherme Posser da Costa
De Juris - Advocacia e Consultoria, Lda.

Cosme Bonfim Afonso Rita
Câmara de Comércio, Agricultura e Serviços

Deodato Gomes Rodrigues
Enaport

Maria do Céu Silveira
Direcção de Obras Públicas e Urbanismo

Carlos Stock
Direcção dos Registros e Notariado

Sara Ranito Trigueiros
Banco Internacional de São Tomé e Príncipe

Rui Veríssimo
Soares Da Costa

SAUDI ARABIA

Emad Fareed Abdul Jawad
Globe Marine Services Co.

Abdulaziz Abdullatif
Al-Soaib Law Firm

Ali Abedi
The Allaince of Abbas F. Ghazzawi & Co. and Hammad, Al-Mehdar & Co.

Nasreldin Ahmed
The Law Firm of Salah Al-Hejailany

Omar Al Saab
Mohanned Bin saudi Al Rasheed Law Firm in Association with Baker Botts L.L.P

Nasser Alfaraj
Baker & McKenzie Ltd.

Mohammed Al-Ghamdi
Fulbright & Jaworski LLP

Hesham Al-Homoud
The Law Firm of Dr. Hesham Al-Homoud

Mohammed Al-Jaddan
The Law Firm of Yousef and Mohammed Al-Jaddan

Nabil Abdullah Al-Mubarak
Saudi Credit Bureau - SIMAH

Fayez Al-Nemer
Talal Bin Naif Al-Harbi Law Firm

Sami Al-Sarraj
Al Juraid & Company / PricewaterhouseCoopers

Mohammed Al-Soaib
Al-Soaib Law Firm

Ali Awais
Baker Botts LLP

Joseph Castelluccio
Fulbright & Jaworski LLP

Maher El Belbeisi
Abu-Ghazaleh Legal office

Adel El Said
Panalpina

Adel ElZein
Mohamed Ben Laden Law Firm

Imad El-Dine Ghazi
Law Office of Hassan Mahassni

Shadi Haroon
Baker Botts LLP

Jochen Hundt
Al-Soaib Law Firm

David K. Johnson
Al Juraid & Company / PricewaterhouseCoopers

Marcus Latta
The Law Firm of Salah Al-Hejailany

Muhammad Lotfi
Toban Law Firm

Hassan Mahassni
Law Office of Hassan Mahassni

Muntasir Osman
Law Office of Hassan Mahassni

K. Joseph Rajan
Globe Marine Services Co.

Mustafa Saleh
Turner International

Abdul Shakoor
Globe Marine Services Co.

Sameh M. Toban
Toban Law Firm

Natasha Zahid
Baker Botts LLP

Abdul Aziz Zaibag
Alzaibag Consultants

Soudki Zawaydeh
Al Juraid & Company / PricewaterhouseCoopers

Ebaish Zebar
The Law Firm of Salah Al-Hejailany

SENEGAL

Ibrahima Abdoulaye
Senelec

Khaled Abou El Houda
Cabinet Kanjo Koita

Cabinet Sarr & Associés, member of Lex Mundi

Magatte Dabo
Transfret Dakar

Jonathan Darboux
BCEAO

Fallou Diéye
APIX -Agence chargée de la Promotion de l'Investissement et des Grands Travaux

Issa Dione
Senelec

Patricia Lake Diop

Fodé Diop
Art Ingeierie Afrique

Fatimatou Zahra Diop
BCEAO

Amadou Drame
Cabinet d'Avocat

Cheikh Fall
Cabinet d'Avocat

Aïssatou Fall
FIDAFRICA / PricewaterhouseCoopers

Mame Adama Gueye
Mame Adama Gueye & Associes

Khaled A. Houda
Avocat à la Cour

Matthias Hubert
FIDAFRICA / PricewaterhouseCoopers

Oumy Kalsoum Gaye
Chambre de Commerce d'Industrie et d'Agriculture de Dakar

Seydina Kane
Senelec

Sidy Kanoute
Avocat à la Cour

Moussa Mbacke
Etude notariale Moussa Mbacke

Mamadou Mbaye
SCP Mame Adama Gueye & Associés

Ibrahima Mbodj
Avocat à la Cour

Pierre Michaux
FIDAFRICA / PricewaterhouseCoopers

Pape Oumar Ndiaye
Avocat à la Cour

Cheikh Tidiane Ndiaye
Secom

Moustapha Ndoye
Cabinet d'Avocats

Cheikh Oumar Sall

Mbacké Sene
Senelec

Daniel-Sedar Senghor
Notaire

Djibril Sy
SDV

Djibril Sy
Secom

Dominique Taty
FIDAFRICA / PricewaterhouseCoopers

Ibra Thiombane
SCP Mame Adama Gueye & Associés

Moustapha Thioune
Societe Generale de Banques au Senegal

Adama Traore
SCP Mame Adama Gueye & Associés

Baba Traore
Transfret

SERBIA

Rade Bačković
Association of Serbian Banks

Rene Bijvoet
PricewaterhouseCoopers

Bojana Bogojević
PricewaterhouseCoopers

Marija Bojović
PricewaterhouseCooper

Nataša Cvetićanin
Law Offices Janković, Popović & Mitić

Aleksandar Dimitrov
Prica & Partners Law Office

Jelena Djokić
PricewaterhouseCoopers

Uroš Djordjević
Zivkovic & Samardzic Law Office

Jelena Edelman
Prica & Partners Law Office

Olga Serb Gretić
Ninković Law Office

Oliver Haussmann
Moravčevic, Vojnović & Zdravković o.a.d. u saradnji sa Schönherr

Harrison Solicitors

Jovana Ilić
PricewaterhouseCoopers

Anna Jankov
PricewaterhouseCoopers

Nikola Janković
Law Offices Janković, Popović & Mitić

Martina Jović
PricewaterhouseCoopers

Mirko Kevac
PricewaterhouseCoopers

Dubravka Kosić
Law Office Kosic

Marija Kostić
Law Offices Janković, Popović & Mitić

Ivan Krsikapa
Ninković Law Office

Aleksandar Mančev
Prica & Partners Law Office

Aleksandar Miljković
PricewaterhouseCoopers

Dimitrije Nikolić
Cargo T. Weiss

Djurdje Ninković
Ninković Law Office

Darija Ognjenović
Prica & Partners Law Office

Igor Oljačić
Law Office Kosic

Vladimir Perić
Prica & Partners Law Office

Snežana Pešić
PricewaterhouseCoopers

Mihajlo Prica
Prica & Partners Law Office

Marko Repić
Law Office Kosic

Vladimir Savić
CPI Investement

Nenad Stanković
Joksovic, Stojanovic and Partners

Ana Stanković
Moravčevic, Vojnović & Zdravković o.a.d. u saradnji sa Schönherr

Petar Stojanović
Joksovic, Stojanovic and Partners

Jovana Stojanović
PricewaterhouseCoopers

Zoran Teodosijević
Law Offices Janković, Popović & Mitić

Jovana Tomašević
Živković & Samardžić Law Office

Clare Vernon
PricewaterhouseCoopers

Miloš Vulić
Prica & Partners Law Office

Relja Zdravković
Moravčevic, Vojnović & Zdravković o.a.d. u saradnji sa Schönherr

Branislav Živković
Zivkovic & Samardzic Law Office

Miloš Živković
Živković & Samardžić Law office

SEYCHELLES

Gerry Adam
Mahe Shipping Co. Ltd.

Jules G. Baker
Ports Authority

France Gonzalves Bonte

Andre D. Ciseau
Seychelles Ports Authority

Alex Ellenberger
Locus Architecture Pty. Ltd.

Daniel Houareau
Ports Authority

Joe Morin
Mahe Shipping Co. Ltd.

Bernard L. Pool
Pool & Patel

Roddy Ramanjooloo
Hoolooman Project Services

Unice Romain
Ports Authority

Serge Rouillon
Attorney-at-Law

SIERRA LEONE

Kelvin Abdallah
PricewaterhouseCoopers

Gideon Ayi-Owoo
PricewaterhouseCoopers

Mohamed Sahid Bangura
Macauley, Bangura & Co.

H.A. Bloomer
Ports Authority

A.Y Brewah
Brewah & Co.

Nicholas Colin Browne-Marke
Court of Appeals

Charles Campbell
Charles Campbell & Co.

John Carter
KPMG

Leslie Theophilus Clarkson
Ahmry Services

Neneh Dabo
Anti-Corruption Commission

Vidal Decker
KPMG

Mariama Dumbuya
Renner Thomas & Co., Adele Chambers

Dzidzedze Fiadjoe
PricewaterhouseCoopers

Cecil French
NATIONAL POWER AUTHORITY

Denis John Scott Garvie
NATIONAL POWER AUTHORITY

Eke Ahmed Halloway
HALLOWAY & PARTNERS

Millicent Hamilton-Hazeley
CLAS LEGAL

Michael A.O. Johnson
MINISTRY OF LANDS, COUNTRY PLANNING AND THE ENVIRONMENT

Mariama Kallay
GOVERNMENT OF SIERRA LEONE

Alex Konoima
MINISTRY OF LANDS, COUNTRY PLANNING AND THE ENVIRONMENT

George Kwatia
PRICEWATERHOUSECOOPERS

Centus Macauley Esq.
MACAULEY, BANGURA & CO.

Joseph Daniel Mahayei
MINISTRY OF ENERGY & POWER

Sullay A. Mannah
BANK OF SIERRA LEONE

Noah Mansaray
PORTS AUTHORITY

Corneleius Adeyemi Max-Williams I
SHIPPING AGENCIES LTD.

A.P. Moller-Maersk
MAERSK LTD.

Augustine Musa, Esq.
BREWAH & CO.

Oliver Onylander
ADELE CHAMBERS

Eduard Parkinson
NATIONAL POWER AUTHORITY

Prashatn Poduval
MAERSK LTD.

Roger Rogers
INTERNATIONAL CONSTRUCTION CO. LTD.

Susan Sisay
SISAY & ASSOCIATE

Lornard Taylor
MACAULEY, BANGURA & CO.

Alhaji Timbo
NATIONAL POWER AUTHORITY

Mohamed Ahmad Tunis
AHMRY SERVICES

Ayodele Wak-Williams
DEL-WAK AGENCIES

Darcy White
PRICEWATERHOUSECOOPERS

Claudius Williams-Tucker
KPMG

Amy Wright
ECOBANK SIERRA LEONE LTD.

Rowland Wright
WRIGHT & CO.

Alfred Yarteh
NATIONAL POWER AUTHORITY

SINGAPORE

Kala Anandarajah
RAJAH & TANN

Hui Jia Ang
PRICEWATERHOUSECOOPERS

Hooi Yen Chin
GATEWAY LAW CORPORATION

Paerin Choa
TSMP LAW CORPORATION

Kit Min Chye
TAN PENG CHIN LLC

Troy Doyle
CLIFFORD CHANCE WONG

Cyril Dumon
SDV INTERNATIONAL LOGISTICS

Paula Eastwood
PRICEWATERHOUSECOOPERS

Chi Duan Gooi
DONALDSON & BURKINSHAW

Muhammad Hattar
RODYK & DAVIDSON LLP

Ong Hway Cheng
RAJAH & TANN

Nanda Kumar
RAJAH & TANN

Lee Lay See
RAJAH & TANN

Airinn Loh
SCHENKER PTE. LTD.

MINISTRY OF TRADE AND INDUSTRY

Sheikh Babu Nooruddin
AL NOOR INTERNATIONAL PTE. LTD.

Beng Hong Ong
WONG TAN & MOLLY LIM LLC

QBB (PTE) LTD.

See Tiat Quek
PRICEWATERHOUSECOOPERS

Mark Rowley
CREDIT BUREAU PTE LTD.

Andrew Seah
SCHENKER PTE. LTD.

Priya Selvam
RAJAH & TANN

Lee Chuan Seng
BECA CARTER HOLDINGS & FERNER PTE LTD.

Nish Shetty
WONGPARTNERSHIP LLP

SHOOK LIN & BOK LLP (IN JOINT VENTURE WITH ALLEN & OVERY LLP)

May Yee Tan
WONG TAN & MOLLY LIM LLC

Winston Tay
CUSTOMS

Siu Ing Teng
SINGAPORE LAND AUTHORITY

Liew Yik Wee
WONGPARTNERSHIP LLP

Lim Wee Teck
RAJAH & TANN

Eddie Wong
CITY DEVELOPMENTS LTD.

Paul Wong
RODYK & DAVIDSON LLP

Valerie Wu
DONALDSON & BURKINSHAW

Stephanie Yuen Thio
TSMP LAW CORPORATION

SLOVAKIA

Zuzana Amrichova
PRICEWATERHOUSECOOPERS.

Martina Behuliaková
GEODESY, CARTOGRAPHY AND CADASTRE AUTHORITY OF THE SLOVAK REPUBLIC

Vladimir Beles
PRICEWATERHOUSECOOPERS

Radmila Benkova
PRICEWATERHOUSECOOPERS

Todd Bradshaw
PRICEWATERHOUSECOOPERS

Ján Budinský
SLOVAK CREDIT BUREAU, S.R.O.

Kristina Cermakova
PETERKA & PARTNERS

Elena Chorvátová
PETERKA & PARTNERS

Zuzana Dragúnová-Valerová
PRICEWATERHOUSECOOPERS

Viera Gregorova
PETERKA & PARTNERS

Simona Halakova
ČECHOVÁ & PARTNERS, MEMBER OF LEX MUNDI

Andrea Jezerska
ČECHOVÁ & PARTNERS, MEMBER OF LEX MUNDI

Tomas Jucha
PRICEWATERHOUSECOOPERS

Michaela Jurková
ČECHOVÁ & PARTNERS, MEMBER OF LEX MUNDI

Soňa Lehocká
ALIANCIAADVOKÁTOV AK, S.R.O.

Katarina Leitmannová
GEODESY, CARTOGRAPHY AND CADASTRE AUTHORITY

Marek Lovas
PRICEWATERHOUSECOOPERS

Michal Luknár
SQUIRE SANDERS S.R.O.

Přemysl Marek
PETERKA & PARTNERS

Tomáš Maretta
ČECHOVÁ & PARTNERS, MEMBER OF LEX MUNDI

Viktor Mišík
DEDÁK & PARTNERS

PANALPINA WELTTRANSPORT GMBH

Zora Puškáčová
ZUKALOVÁ COUNSELORS-AT-LAW

Peter Rozbora
ČECHOVÁ & PARTNERS, MEMBER OF LEX MUNDI

Gerta Sámelová-Flassiková
ALIANCIAADVOKÁTOV AK, S.R.O.

Peter Varga
PROCHÁZKA RANDL KUBR, MEMBER OF IUS LABORIS & LEX MUNDI

Clare Moger
PRICEWATERHOUSECOOPERS

Zuzana Wallova
NATIONAL BANK

Michal Zeman
ČECHOVÁ & PARTNERS, MEMBER OF LEX MUNDI

Dagmar Zukalová
ZUKALOVÁ COUNSELORS-AT-LAW

SLOVENIA

Ana Berce
ODVETNIKI ŠELIH & PARTNERJI

Crtomir Borec
PRICEWATERHOUSECOOPERS

Branko Boznik
EFT TRANSPORTAGENTUR GMBH

Nataša Božović
BANK OF SLOVENIA

Eva Budja
LAW OFFICE JADEK & PENSA D.O.O.

Nada Drobnic
DELOITTE D.O.O

Aleksander Ferk
PRICEWATERHOUSECOOPERS

Ana Filipov
SCHÖNHERR RECHTSANWÄLTE GMBH / ATTORNEYS-AT-LAW

Masa Grgurevic Alcin
THE SUPREME COURT

Barbara Guzina
DELOITTE D.O.O

Andrej Jarkovič
JANEŽ☒ & JARKOVI☒ ATTORNEYS-AT-LAW & PATENT ATTORNEYS

Aleksandra Jemc
LAW OFFICE JADEK & PENSA D.O.O.

Jernej Jeraj
SCHÖNHERR RECHTSANWÄLTE GMBH / ATTORNEYS-AT-LAW

Janos Kelemen
PRICEWATERHOUSECOOPERS

Danijel Kerševan
PANALPINA WELTTRANSPORT GMBH

Barbara Kozaric
DELOITTE D.O.O.

Bozena Lipej
SURVEYING & MAPPING AUTHORITY

Klemen Mir
PRICEWATERHOUSECOOPERS

Matjaz Nahtigal
ODVETNIKI ŠELIH & PARTNERJI

Sonja Omerza
PRICEWATERHOUSECOOPERS

Pavle Pensa
LAW OFFICE JADEK & PENSA D.O.O.

Tomaž Petrovič
SCHÖNHERR RECHTSANWÄLTE GMBH / ATTORNEYS-AT-LAW

Natasa Pipan Nahtigal
ODVETNIKI ŠELIH & PARTNERJI

Petra Plevnik
ATTORNEYS AT LAW MIRO SENICA IN ODVETNIKI

ELEKTRO LJUBLJANA D.D.

Anka Pogačnik
PRICEWATERHOUSECOOPERS

Tamara Šerdoner
PRICEWATERHOUSECOOPERS

Andreja Škofič-Klanjšček
DELOITTE D.O.O

Beta Štembal
PRICEWATERHOUSECOOPERS

Renata Šterbenc Štrus
LAW OFFICE JADEK & PENSA D.O.O.

Laura Thomson
PRICEWATERHOUSECOOPERS

Nives Uljan
PANALPINA WELTTRANSPORT GMBH

Matthias Wahl
SCHÖNHERR RECHTSANWÄLTE GMBH / ATTORNEYS-AT-LAW

Alenka Zaveršek
PRICEWATERHOUSECOOPERS

Brigita Žunič
DELOITTE D.O.O

Tina Žvanut Mioč
LAW OFFICE JADEK & PENSA D.O.O.

SOLOMON ISLANDS

Don Boykin
PACIFIC ARCHITECTS LTD

John Katahanas
SOL - LAW

Andrew Radclyff
BARRISTER & SOLICITOR

Roselle R. Rosales
PACIFIC ARCHITECTS, LTD.

Gregory Joseph Sojnocki
MORRIS & SOJNOCKI CHARTERED ACCOUNTANTS

Gerald Stenzil
TRADCO SHIPPING

SOUTH AFRICA

Theo Adendorff
KCSA

Ross Alcock
EDWARD NATHAN SONNENBERGS INC.

Mark Badenhorst
PRICEWATERHOUSECOOPERS

BAY LANGUAGE INSTITUTE

Kobus Blignaut
EDWARD NATHAN SONNENBERGS INC

Matthew Bonner
BAKER & McKENZIE LLP

Lloyd Chater
BOWMAN GILFILLAN, MEMBER OF LEX MUNDI

Paul Coetser
BRINK COHEN LE ROUX

Haydn Davies
WEBBER WENTZEL

Paul De Chalain
PRICEWATERHOUSECOOPERS

Gretchen De Smit
EDWARD NATHAN SONNENBERGS INC.

Tim Desmond
GARLICKE & BOUSFIELD INC

Rudolph Du Plessis
Bowman Gilfillan, member of Lex Mundi.

Miranda Feinstein
Edward Nathan Sonnenbergs Inc.

Hennie Geldenhuys
Department of Land Affairs

Sean Gilmour
PricewaterhouseCoopers

Tim Gordon-Grant
Bowman Gilfillan, member of Lex Mundi

Igno Gouws
Webber Wentzel

Roelof Grové
Adams & Adams

King Impex

Unathi Kondile
Bowman Gilfillan, member of Lex Mundi

Erle Koomets
PricewaterhouseCoopers

Renee Kruger
Webber Wentzel

Irvin Lawrence
Garlicke & Bousfield Inc

Sam Lefafa
Department of Land Affairs

João Martins
PricewaterhouseCoopers

Joey Mathekga
CIPRO (Companies & IPR Registration Office)

Gabriel Meyer
Deneys Reitz / Africa Legal

Amit Parekh
Bowman Gilfillan, member of Lex Mundi

Q & N West Export Trading House

Eamonn Quinn
Eamonn David Quinn Attorney

Antoinette Reynolds
Department of Land Affairs

Malaika Ribeiro
PricewaterhouseCoopers

Nyasha Samuriwo
Bowman Gilfillan, member of Lex Mundi

Peter Sands
SDV Ltd

Richard Shein
Bowman Gilfillan, member of Lex Mundi

Rob Smorfitt
Chamber of Commerce & Industries

Chris Todd
Bowman Gilfillan, member of Lex Mundi

TransUnion ITC

Jacques van Wyk
Cliffe Dekker

Llewellyn van Wyk
CSIR

Claire Van Zuylen
Bowman Gilfillan, member of Lex Mundi

Allen West
Department of Land Affairs

St Elmo Wilken
Deneys Reitz / Africa Legal

Rozalynne Wright
Webber Wentzel

SPAIN

Allen & Overy LLP

Ana Armijo
Ashurst

Cristina Ayo Ferrándiz
Uría & Menéndez, member of Lex Mundi

Arancha Badillo
Garrigues

Vicente Bootello
Garrigues

Agustín Bou
Jausas

James Bryant
Orrick, Herrington & Sutcliffe

Cristina Calvo
Ashurst

Ariadna Cambronero Ginés
Uría & Menéndez, member of Lex Mundi

Francisco Conde Viñuelas
Cuatrecasas

Jaume Cornudella Marquès
Landwell, Abogados y Asesores Fiscales

Miguel Cruz
Landwell, Abogados y Asesores Fiscales

Fernando de la Puente Alfaro
Colegio de Resgitradores de la Propiedad y Mercantiles de España

Agustín Del Río Galeote
Gómez-Acebo & Pombo Abogados

Iván Delgado González
Pérez - Llorca

Miguel Díez de los Ríos
Baker & McKenzie

Rossanna D'Onza
Baker & McKenzie

Ronald Ferlazzo
Orrick, Herrington & Sutcliffe LLP

Antonio Fernández
Garrigues

Juan Carlos Fernández Fernández-Avilés
Sagardoy Abogados

Alicia Gamez
Orrick, Herrington & Sutcliffe LLP

Valentín García González
Cuatrecasas

Borja García-Alamán
Garrigues

Ana Gómez
Monereo Meyer Marinel-lo Abogados

Juan Ignacio Gomeza Villa
Notario de Bilbao

Igor Kokorev
Pérez - Llorca

Alfonso Maíllo del Valle
Sánchez Pintado, Núñez & Asociados

Daniel Marín
Gómez-Acebo & Pombo Abogados

Jorge Martín - Fernández
Clifford Chance

José Manuel Mateo
Garrigues

Andrés Monereo Velasco
Monereo, Meyer & Marinel-Lo

Nicolás Nogueroles Peiró
Colegio de Registradores de la Propiedad y Mercantiles de España

Alberto Núñez-Lagos Burguera
Uría & Menéndez, member of Lex Mundi

Jose Palacios
Garrigues

Juan Manuel Pardiñas Aranda
Equifax Iberica

Daniel Parejo Ballesteros
Garrigues Abogados y Asesores Tributarios

Pedro Pérez-Llorca Zamora
Pérez - Llorca

Juan Ramon-Ramos
Landwell, Abogados y Asesores Fiscales

Enrique Rodriguez
Alitus S.A.

Iñigo Sagardoy
Sagardoy Abogados, member of Ius Laboris

Pilar Salinas Rincón
Sánchez Pintado, Núñez & Asociados

Pablo Santos
Gómez-Acebo & Pombo Abogados

Sönke Schlaich
Monereo, Meyer & Marinel-Lo

Rafael Sebastián
Uría & Menéndez, member of Lex Mundi

Lindsay Simmons
Orrick, Herrington & Sutcliffe LLP

Javier Simón
Baker & McKenzie

Cristina Soler
Gómez-Acebo & Pombo Abogados

Gabriel Solís
Garrigues

Juan Soravilla
Monereo Meyer Marinel-lo Abogados

Raimon Tagliavini
Uría & Menéndez, member of Lex Mundi

Francisco Téllez
Garrigues Abogados y Asesores Tributarios

Adrián Thery
Garrigues

Alejandro Valls
Baker & McKenzie

Juan Verdugo
Garrigues

Fernando Vives
Garrigues Abogados y Asesores Tributarios

SRI LANKA

APL

N.P.H. Amarasena
Credit Information Bureau

Chiranga Amirthiah
F.J. & G. De Saram, member of Lex Mundi

Manoj Bandara
F.J. & G. De Saram, member of Lex Mundi

Savantha De Saram
D.L. & F. De Saram

Chamari de Silva
F.J. & G. De Saram, member of Lex Mundi

Sharmela de Silva
Tiruchelvam Associates

Sadhini Edirisinghe
F.J. & G. De Saram, member of Lex Mundi

Champika Fernando
Tiruchelvam Associates

Samadh Gajaweera
Nithya Partners

Naomal Goonewardena
Nithya Partners

Priyanthi Guneratne
F.J. & G. De Saram, member of Lex Mundi

Ruwanthi Herat-Gunaratne
Nithya Partners

Vindya Hettige
Nithya Partners

Dhanushke Jayarathne
Hayleys Agro Biotech

Kishani Jayasooriya
Julius & Creasy

Tudor Jayasuriya
F.J. & G. De Saram, member of Lex Mundi

Inoka Jayawardhana
F.J. & G. De Saram, member of Lex Mundi

Mahes Jeyadevan
PricewaterhouseCoopers

Husni Jiffry
Lanka ORIX Securities Pvt Ltd

Julius & Creasy

LAN Management Development Service

Ruvindu Manathunga
HIF Logistics (PVT) Ltd.

Dian Nanayakkara
Tiruchelvam Associates

Asiri Perera
MIT Cargo (Pvt) Ltd.

Lakshana Perera
Sudath Perera Associates

Hiranthi Ratnayake
PricewaterhouseCoopers

Paul Ratnayeke
Paul Ratnayeke Associates

Tiruchelvam Associates

Harini Udugampola
F.J. & G. De Saram, member of Lex Mundi

Shehara Varia
F.J. & G. De Saram, member of Lex Mundi

Charmalie Weerasekera
Sudath Perera Associates

Shashi Weththasinghe
Julius & Creasy

ST. KITTS AND NEVIS

Trilla
Daniel Brantley & Associates

Department of Labour

Michella Adrien
Michella Adrien Law Office

Nicholas Brisbane
N. Brisbane & Associates

Bertill Browne
St. Kitts Electricity Department

Scott Caines
Frank B. Armstrong Ltd.

Idris Fidela Clarke
Financial Services Department

Neil Coates
PricewaterhouseCoopers

Kennedy de Silva
Customs and Excise Department

Kamesha Graham
WalwynLaw

Renee Gumbs
Financial Services Department

Rodney Harris
Customs and Excise Department

Dollrita Jack-Cato
Webster Dyrud Mitchell

Dahlia Joseph
Daniel Brantley & Associates

L. Everette Martin
Eastern Caribbean Central Bank

Ayoub Morancie
Royal Bank of Canada

Patrick Patterson
Caribbean Associated Attorneys

Randy Prentice
Frank B. Armstrong Ltd.

Marscha Prince
PricewaterhouseCoopers

Warren Thompson
Constsves

Vernon S. Veira
Vernon S. Veira & Associates

Charles Walwyn
PricewaterhouseCoopers

ST. LUCIA

Thaddeus M. Antoine
FRANCIS & ANTOINE

Aisha Baptiste
HIGH COURT REGISTRY

Gerard Bergasse
TROPICAL SHIPPING

Desma F. Charles
*REGISTRY OF COMPANIES AND
INTELLECTUAL PROPERTY*

Peter I. Foster
*PETER I. FOSTER &
ASSOCIATES*

Peterson D. Francis
*PETERSON D. FRANCIS
WORLDWIDE SHIPPING &
CUSTOMS SERVICES LTD.*

Carol J. Gedeon
CHANCERY CHAMBERS

GORDON & GORDON CO

Anderson Lake
BANK OF ST LUCIA LTD

Brian Louisy
*THE ST. LUCIA CHAMBER OF
COMMERCE INDUSTRY AND
AGRICULTURE*

Duane C. Marquis
NLBA ARCHITECTS

Stephen Mcnamara
MCNAMARA & CO.

Richard Peterkin
PRICEWATERHOUSECOOPERS

Eldris Pierre-Mauricette
TROPICAL SHIPPING

Paul Popo
LAND REGISTRY

Gilroy Pultie
*ST. LUCIA ELECTRICITY
SERVICES LIMITED (LUCELEC)*

Margaret Anne St. Louis
*MINISTRY OF PLANNING,
DEVELOPMENT, ENVIRONMENT
AND HOUSING*

Gillian Vidal-Jules
MINISTRY OF JUSTICE

Brenda M. Williams
CHASE, SKEETE & BOLAND

ST. VINCENT AND
THE GRENADINES

Kay R.A. Bacchus-Browne
*KAY BACCHUS - BROWNE
CHAMBERS*

Aurin Bennett
AURIN BENNETT ARCHITECTS

Graham Bollers
REGAL CHAMBERS

Evelyn Cambridge
*DOUGIE'S CUSTOMS &
SHIPPING AGENCY*

Parnel R. Campbell
CAMPBELL'S CHAMBERS

Mira E. Commissiong
EQUITY CHAMBERS

Paula E. David
SAUNDERS & HUGGINS

Stanley DeFreitas
DEFREITAS & ASSOCIATES

Bernadine Dublin
LABOUR DEPARTMENT

Marlene Edwards
CAMPBELL'S CHAMBERS

Theona R. Elizee-Stapleton
*COMMERCE & INTELLECTUAL
PROPERTY OFFICE (CIPO)*

Tamara Gibson-Marks
HIGH COURT REGISTRY

Venessa Gibson
*NATIONAL COMMERCIAL BANK
(SVG) LTD.*

Stanley Harris
*ST. VINCENT ELECTRICITY
SERVICES LIMITED VINLEC*

Charleston H. Jackson
DR. LEWIS LAW CHAMBERS

Leroy James
CUSTOMS AUTHORITY

Sean Joachim
CARIBTRANS

Brenan B. King
*EQUINOX MARINE SURVEYING
& CONSULTING*

Rosann N.D. Knights
REGAL CHAMBERS

Errol E. Layne
ERROL E. LAYNE CHAMBERS

Linton A. Lewis
DR. LEWIS LAW CHAMBERS

Andrea Young Lewis
*COMMERCE & INTELLECTUAL
PROPERTY OFFICE (CIPO)*

Clairmonte Lynch
CUSTOMS AUTHORITY

Moulton Mayers
*MOULTON MAYERS
ARCHITECTS*

Sabrina Neehall
SCOTIABANK

Kathy-Ann Noel
SAUNDERS & HUGGINS

Floyd A. Patterson
PANNELL KERR FORSTER

Richard Peterkin
PRICEWATERHOUSECOOPERS

Maria Reece
SCOTIABANK

Nicole O.M. Sylvester
*CARIBBEAN INTERNATIONAL
LAW FIRM*

Gertel Thom
HIGH COURT KINGSTOWN

L.A. Douglas Williams
*LAW FIRM OF PHILLIPS &
WILLIAMS*

Arthur F. Williams
WILLIAMS & WILLIAMS

Steve J. Wyllie
*ST. VINCENT ELECTRICITY
SERVICES LIMITED VINLEC*

SUDAN

Omer Abdel Ati
OMER ABDEL ATI SOLICITORS

Abdullah Abozaid
*LAW OFFICE OF ABDULLAH A.
ABOZAID*

Mohamed Ibrahim Adam
DR. ADAM & ASSOCIATES

Jamal Ibrahim Ahmed
ATTORNEY-AT-LAW

Ashraf A.H. El Neil
*MAHMOUD ELSHEIKH OMER &
ASSOCIATES ADVOCATES*

Tariq Mohmoud Elsheikh
Omer
*MAHMOUD ELSHEIKH OMER &
ASSOCIATES ADVOCATES*

Yassir Elsiddig
*MARWACO FOR MEDICAL &
CHEMICAL IMPORTS LTD.*

Kastaki S. Ganbert
K.S. GANBERT & SONS LTD.

Osman Mekki Abdurrahman
HLCS

Mekki Osman
HLCS

Osman Osman
HLCS

Amal Sharif
*MAHMOUD ELSHEIKH OMER &
ASSOCIATES ADVOCATES*

Abdel Gadir Warsama
*DR. ABDEL GADIR WARSAMA
GHALIB & ASSOCIATES LEGAL
FIRM*

Tag Eldin Yamani Sadig
*MONTAG TRADING &
ENGINEERING CO. LTD.*

SURINAME

G. Clide Cambridge
*PARAMARIBO CUSTOM BROKER
& PACKER*

Anoeschka Debipersad
*A.E. DEBIPERSAD &
ASSOCIATES*

Marcel K. Eyndhoven
*N.V. ENERGIEBEDRIJVEN
SURINAME*

Carel van Hest
ARCHITECT

HAKRINBANK N.V.

Johan Kastelein
KDV ARCHITECTS

Stanley Marica
*ADVOKATENKANTOOR MARICA
LAW FIRM MARICA*

Anouschka Nabibaks
*BDO ABRAHAMSRAIJMANN &
PARTNERS*

B.M. Oemraw
N.V. GLOBAL EXPEDITION

Angèle J. Ramsaransing-Karg
*BDO ABRAHAMSRAIJMANN &
PARTNERS*

Adiel Sakoer
N.V. GLOBAL EXPEDITION

Inder Sardjoe
N.V. EASY ELECTRIC

Albert D. Soedamah
SOEDAMAH & ASSOCIATES

Radjen A. Soerdjbalie
NOTARIAAT R.A. SOERDJBALIE

Jennifer van Dijk-Silos
LAW FIRM VAN DIJK-SILOS

M.E. van Genderen-Relyveld
HIGH COURT OF JUSTICE

J.R. von Niesewand
HIGH COURT OF JUSTICE

Perry D. Wolfram
BROCAD N.V.

SWAZILAND

Vincent Galeromeloe
TransUNION ITC

Tina Phumlile Khoza
*MUNICIPAL COUNCIL OF
MANZINI*

Paul Lewis
PRICEWATERHOUSECOOPERS

Andrew Linsey
PRICEWATERHOUSECOOPERS

C.J. Littler
C.J. LITTLER & CO.

Jerome Ndzimandze
SPEED LIMIT CONSTRUCTION

José Rodrigues
RODRIGUES & ASSOCIATES

P.M. Shilubane
*P.M. SHILUBANE &
ASSOCIATES*

Mahene Thwala
THLWAWA ATTORNEYS

Bradford Mark Walker
BRAD WALKER ARCHITECTS

SWEDEN

Mats Berter
MAQS LAW FIRM

Linda Broström-Cabrera
PRICEWATERHOUSECOOPERS

Roger Gavelin
PRICEWATERHOUSECOOPERS

Olof Hallberg
ADVOKATFIRMAN LINDAHL

Emil Hedberg
*ADVOKATFIRMAN VINGE KB,
MEMBER OF LEX MUNDI*

Petter Holm
*GÄRDE WESSLAU
ADVOKATBYRÅ*

Bengt Kjellson
LANTMÄTERIET

Christoffer Monell
*MANNHEIMER SWARTLING
ADVOKATBYRÅ*

Karl-Arne Olsson
*GÄRDE WESSLAU
ADVOKATBYRÅ*

Mattias Örnulf
*HÖKERBERG & SÖDERQVIST
ADVOKATBYRÅ KB*

Carl Östring
MAGNUSSON

Patrik Ottoson
MAQS LAW FIRM

PANALPINA AB

Jesper Schönbeck
*ADVOKATFIRMAN VINGE KB,
MEMBER OF LEX MUNDI*

Odd Swarting
SETTERWALLS ADVOKATBYRÅ

SWITZERLAND

Peter R. Altenburger
ALTENBURGER

Rashid Bahar
BÄR & KARRER AG

Beat M. Barthold
FRORIEP RENGGLI

Marc Bernheim
STAIGER SCHWALD & PARTNER

Bernhard G. Burkard
*NOTARIAT BERNHARD
BURKARD*

Mauro Cavadini
*BRUNONI MOLINO MOTTIS
ADAMI*

Robert P. Desax
PRICEWATERHOUSECOOPERS

Cyrill Diem

Suzanne Eckert
WENGER PLATTNER

Olivier Hari
SCHELLENBERG WITTMER

Jakob Hoehn
*PESTALOZZI LACHENAL PATRY,
MEMBER OF LEX MUNDI*

Ueli Huber
HOMBURGER

David Hürlimann
*CMS VON ERLACH HENRICI
AG*

Vincent Jeanneret
SCHELLENBERG WITTMER

Hanspeter Klaey

Wassilos Lytras
*APM GLOBAL LOGISTICS
SWITZERLAND LTD.*

Christian P. Meister
NIEDERER KRAFT & FREY

Valerie Meyer
NIEDERER KRAFT & FREY

Andrea Molino
*BRUNONI MOLINO MOTTIS
ADAMI*

Georg Naegeli
HOMBURGER

Gema Olivar

Elena Sampedro
SCHELLENBERG WITTMER

Daniel Schmitz
PRICEWATERHOUSECOOPERS

Daniel Steudler
*SWISSTOPO, DIRECTORATE FOR
CADASTRAL SURVEYING*

Barbara Stöckli-Klaus
FRORIEP RENGGLI

Andrin Waldburger
PRICEWATERHOUSECOOPERS

ZEK SWITZERLAND

SYRIA

Mazen Abo Nasr
YASER HMEDAN LAW OFFICE.

Sulafah Akili
*MINISTRY OF ECONOMY &
TRADE*

Mouazza Al Ashhab
*AUDITING CONSULTING
ACCOUNTING CENTER*

Hani Al Jaza'ri
*SYRIAN ARAB CONSULTANTS
LAW OFFICE*

Rawaa Al Midani
*MINISTRY OF TRADE &
ECONOMY*

Abd Anaser Al Saleh
SBANEH

Alissar Al-Ahmar
AL-AHMAR & PARTNERS

Nabih Alhafez
*SFS (SPEED FORWARD
SHIPPING)*

Bisher Al-Houssami
*AL-ISRAA INT'L FREIGHT
FORWARDER*

Rasem Al-Ikhwan
HOME TEXTILE COMPANY

Wasim Anan
YASER HMEDAN LAW OFFICE.

Nasim Awad
*LEGALITY - LAWYERS &
CONSULTANTS*

Karam I. Bechara
BANK AUDI

Hani Bitar
*SYRIAN ARAB CONSULTANTS
LAW OFFICE*

Riad Daoudi
*SYRIAN ARAB CONSULTANTS
LAW OFFICE*

Lina El-Hakim
HAKIM LAW FIRM

Youssef El-Hakim
HAKIM LAW FIRM

Wael Hamed
YASER HMEDAN LAW OFFICE.

Abdul Raouf Hamwi
CIVIL ENGINEERING OFFICE

Bashir Haza
*MINISTRY OF TRADE &
ECONOMY*

Yaser Hmedan
YASER HMEDAN LAW OFFICE.

Ibrahim Ibrahim
*MINISTRY OF TRADE &
ECONOMY*

Joumana Jabbour
ATTORNEY-AT-LAW

Antoun Joubran
*SYRIAN ARAB CONSULTANTS
LAW OFFICE*

Osama Karawani
KARAWANI LAW OFFICE

Raed Karawani
KARAWANI LAW OFFICE

Fadi Kardous
KARDOUS LAW OFFICE

Mazen N. Khaddour
*LAW OFFICE OF M.
KHADDOUR & ASSOCIATES*

Salah Kurdy
YASER HMEDAN LAW OFFICE.

Moussa Mitry
*UNIVERSITY OF DAMASCUS /
LOUKA & MITRY LAW OFFICE*

Gabriel Oussi
*SYRIAN ARAB CONSULTANTS
LAW OFFICE*

Housam Safadi
SAFADI BUREAU

Maya Saleh
YASER HMEDAN LAW OFFICE.

Samer Sultan
SULTANS LAW

TAIWAN, CHINA

Victor Chang
LCS & PARTNERS

John Chen
FORMOSA TRANSNATIONAL

Nicholas V. Chen
PAMIR LAW GROUP

Din Shin Chen
*SUPERTECH CONSULTANTS
INTERNATIONAL*

Paul F. Chen
*SUPERTECH CONSULTANTS
INTERNATIONAL*

Frances F.Y. Chen
*TAI E INTERNATIONAL PATENT
& LAW OFFICE*

Yu-Li Chen
*TAIWAN SHIHLIN DISTRICT
COURT*

Edgar Y. Chen
TSAR & TSAI LAW FIRM

Tina Chen
WINKLER PARTNERS

Chun-Yih Cheng
FORMOSA TRANSNATIONAL

Abraham Cheng
LEXCEL PARTNERS

Yu-Chung Chiu
MINISTRY OF THE INTERIOR

Julie C. Chu
JONES DAY

Steven Go
PRICEWATERHOUSECOOPERS

May Han
*TAI E INTERNATIONAL PATENT
& LAW OFFICE*

Yuling Hsu
FORMOSA TRANSNATIONAL

Tony Hsu
PAMIR LAW GROUP

Barbara Hsu
SDV LTD.

Robert Hsu
SDV LTD.

Inu Hsu
TAIPOWER

T.C. Huang
HUANG & PARTNERS

Margaret Huang
LCS & PARTNERS

Joanne Hung
YANGMING PARTNERS

Zue Min Hwang
*ASIA WORLD ENGINEERING &
CONSTRUCTION CO.*

Charles Hwang
YANGMING PARTNERS

Nathan Kaiser
WENFEI LAW

Wen-Horng Kao
PRICEWATERHOUSECOOPERS

Lawrence Lee
HUANG & PARTNERS

Michael D. Lee
PAMIR LAW GROUP

Poching Lee
WENFEI LAW

Chih-Shan Lee
WINKLER PARTNERS

Hung-Lieh Liang
PRICEWATERHOUSECOOPERS

Tory C.T. Liao
*TAI E INTERNATIONAL PATENT
& LAW OFFICE*

Perkin T.Y. Liaw
*TAI E INTERNATIONAL PATENT
& LAW OFFICE*

Ming-Yen Lin
*DEEP & FAR, ATTORNEYS-
AT-LAW*

Jeffrey Lin
*JOINT CREDIT INFORMATION
CENTER*

Rich Lin
LCS & PARTNERS

Emily Lin
PAMIR LAW GROUP

Yishian Lin
PRICEWATERHOUSECOOPERS

Frank Lin
REXMED INDUSTRIES CO., LTD.

Youlanda Liu
PAMIR LAW GROUP

Charlotte Liu
PRICEWATERHOUSECOOPERS

Catherine Liu
SDV LTD.

Julia Liu
SDV LTD.

Jennifer Lo
PRICEWATERHOUSECOOPERS

Mike Lu
LEXCEL PARTNERS

Lloyd G. Roberts III
WINKLER PARTNERS

Michael Schreiber
YANGMING PARTNERS

Jasmine C. Shen
PAMIR LAW GROUP

Tanya Y. Teng
HUANG & PARTNERS

Bee Leay Teo
BAKER & MCKENZIE

C.F. Tsai
*DEEP & FAR, ATTORNEYS-
AT-LAW*

Eric Tsai
*PUHUA & ASSOCIATES,
PRICEWATERHOUSECOOPERS
LEGAL SERVICES*

Rita Tsai
APL

Joe Tseng
LCS & PARTNERS

Richard Watanabe
PRICEWATERHOUSECOOPERS

Robin J. Winkler
WINKLER PARTNERS

Main-Main Wu
*ASIA WORLD ENGINEERING &
CONSTRUCTION CO.*

Pei-Yu Wu
BAKER & MCKENZIE

Quiao-ling Wu
*DEEP & FAR, ATTORNEYS-
AT-LAW*

Shin Mei Wu
*JOINT CREDIT INFORMATION
CENTER*

Echo Yeh
LEXCEL PARTNERS

Andrew Yeh
PANALPINA

Shih-Ming You
MINISTRY OF THE INTERIOR

TAJIKISTAN

Bakhtiyor Abdulhamidov
*AKHMEDOV, AZIZOV &
ABDULHAMIDOV ATTORNEYS*

Ardak Aiyekeyeva
PRICEWATERHOUSECOOPERS

Shavkat Akhmedov
*AKHMEDOV, AZIZOV &
ABDULHAMIDOV ATTORNEYS*

Dilshod Alimov
*USAID/BEI, PRAGMA
CORPORATION*

Abdulbori Baybayev
LEX LAW FIRM

Faridun Boboev
*GOLDEN LION GROUP
COMPANIES*

Sergey Chetverikov
PRICEWATERHOUSECOOPERS

Adkham Ergashev
IFC

Courtney Fowler
PRICEWATERHOUSECOOPERS

Elena Kaeva
PRICEWATERHOUSECOOPERS

Abdulkhamid Muminov
PRICEWATERHOUSECOOPERS

Mizrobiddin Nugmanov
GLOBALINK LOGISTICS GROUP

Madina Nurmatova
*TAJIKISTAN BEE - SME POLICY
PROJECT*

Zarina Odinaeva
IFC

Manuchehr Rakhmonov
USAID/BEI, PRAGMA CORP

Nurali Shukurov
USAID/BEI, PRAGMA CORP

Djasurbek Teshaev
*GOLDEN LION GROUP
COMPANIES*

Victoria Victorova
IFC

Wendy Jo Werner
IFC

TANZANIA

Patrick Ache
MKONO & CO.

Krista Bates van Winkelhof
FK LAW CHAMBERS

Steven de Backer
MKONO & CO.

Santosh Gajjar
SUMAR VARMA ASSOCIATES

Farija Ghikas
REX ATTORNEYS

Christopher Giattas
REX ATTORNEYS

Eve Hawa Sinare
REX ATTORNEYS

Johnson Jasson
*JOHNSON JASSON &
ASSOCIATES ADVOCATES*

Ngwaru Maghembe
MKONO & CO.

Victoria Lyimo Makani
REX ATTORNEYS

Bruno Marilhet
SHARBATHO

Tabitha Maro
REX ATTORNEYS

Ken Mkondya
REX ATTORNEYS

Nimrod Mkono
MKONO & CO.

Angela Mndolwa
FK LAW CHAMBERS

Arafa Mohamed
REX ATTORNEYS

Chris Msuya
HORWARTH TANZANIA

Lugano J.S. Mwandambo
REX ATTORNEYS

Shabani Mwatawala
PSM ARCHITECTS CO. LTD.

Alex Thomas Nguluma
REX ATTORNEYS

Gilbert Nyantanyi
MKONO & CO.

Conrad Nyukuri
*PRICEWATERHOUSECOOPERS
LEGAL SERVICES*

Adalbert Rusagara
BREAKTHROUGH HOLDINGS

Charles R.B. Rwechungura
REX ATTORNEYS

Rishit Shah
PRICEWATERHOUSECOOPERS

Geoffrey Sikira
TANGANYIKA LAW SOCIETY

Eve Hawa Sinare
REX ATTORNEYS

Mohamed H. Sumar
SUMAR VARMA ASSOCIATES

David Tarimo
PRICEWATERHOUSECOOPERS

Mustafa Tharoo
*RINGO & ASSOCIATES,
MEMBER OF THE AFRICA
LEGAL NETWORK*

THAILAND

ALLEN & OVERY

Khunying Natthika
Wattanavekin Angubolkul
*EASTERN SUGAR AND CANE
COMPANY LIMITED*

Janist Aphornratana
PRICEWATERHOUSECOOPERS

Angsurus Areekul
*THAI CONTRACTORS
ASSOCIATION UNDER H.M. THE
KING'S PATRONAGE*

Chalee Chantanayingyong
*SECURITIES & EXCHANGE
COMMISSION*

Phadet Charoensivakorn
*NATIONAL CREDIT BUREAU
CO., LTD.*

Thunyaporn Chartisathian
*SIAM PREMIER INTERNATIONAL
LAW OFFICE LTD.*

Chinnavat Chinsangaram
WHITE & CASE

John Fotiadis
*TILLEKE & GIBBINS
INTERNATIONAL LTD., MEMBER
OF LEX MUNDI*

Seetha Gopalakrishnan
PRICEWATERHOUSECOOPERS

Vira Kammee
SIAM CITY LAW OFFICES LTD.

Yingyong Karnchanapayap
*TILLEKE & GIBBINS
INTERNATIONAL LTD., MEMBER
OF LEX MUNDI*

Sakares Khamwalee

Komkrit Kietduriyakul

Chaiyut Kumkun
Customs Standard Procedure and Valuation Division

LawPlus Ltd.

William Lehane

Sakchai Limsiripothong
White & Case

Pratchayapa Mahamontree
Siam City Law Offices Ltd.

Anawat Malawan
Vickery& Worachai Ltd.

Douglas D. Mancill
Deacons

Pauline A. Manzano
PricewaterhouseCoopers

Steven Miller
Mayer Brown JSM, member of Lex Mundi

Kulachet Nanakorn
White & Case

Thawatchai Pittayasophon
Securities and Exchange Commission

Viro Piyawattanameth

Sompong Pongsakulrangsee
Metropolitan Electricity Authority

Cynthia M. Pornavalai
Tilleke & Gibbins International Ltd., member of Lex Mundi

Supan Poshyananda
Securities and Exchange Commission

Chanet Precharonaset
APL Logistics Services Ltd.

Sudthana Puntheeranurak
National Credit Bureau Co., Ltd.

Michael Ramirez
Tilleke & Gibbins International Ltd., member of Lex Mundi

Piyanuj Ratprasatporn
Tilleke & Gibbins International Ltd., member of Lex Mundi

Dussadee Rattanopas

Thavorn Rujivanarom
PricewaterhouseCoopers

Maythawee Sarathai
Mayer Brown JSM, member of Lex Mundi

Kowit Somwaiya
LawPlus Ltd.

Rachamarn Suchitchon
Securities and Exchange Commission

Picharn Sukparangsee
Siam City Law Offices Ltd.

Chusert Supasitthumrong
Tilleke & Gibbins International Ltd., member of Lex Mundi

Ornjira Tangwongyodying
PricewaterhouseCoopers

Krisada Thamviriyarak
Chodthanawat Co., Ltd

Alongkorn Tongmee
Tilleke & Gibbins International Ltd., member of Lex Mundi

Paisan Tulapornpipat
Blue Ocean Logistics Co., Ltd.

Pattara Vasinwatanapong
Vickery& Worachai Ltd.

Harold K. Vickery Jr.
Vickery & Worachai Ltd.

Pimvimol Vipamaneerut
Tilleke & Gibbins International Ltd., member of Lex Mundi

Avoot Wannvong
Office of the Public Sector Development Commission

Kobkarn Wattanavrangkul
Toshiba Co. Ltd

Somsak Witnalakorn
Metropolitan Electricity Authority

TIMOR-LESTE

Candido da Conceição
USAID

Roberto Monteiro
SDV

Cornelio Pacheco
JVK International Movers

Tjia Soh Siang
Tjia & Tchai Associates

Francisco Soares
Serviço do Imposto de Timor Leste

TOGO

Bolloré DTI - SDV

Jean-Marie Adenka
Cabinet Adenka

Da-Blece Afoda-Sebou
Ordre National des Architectes du Togo,(ONAT)

Kokou Gadémon Agbessi
Cabinet Lucreatif

Kafoui Agboyibor
Cabiet Me Yawovi Agboyibo

Martial Akakpo
SCP Martial Akakpo

Adzewoda Ametsiagbe
Direction Générale de l'Urbanisme et de l'Habitat

Kokou Darius Atsoo
SCP Martial Akakpo

Philippe Attoh
SCP Martial Akakpo

Sylvanus Dodzi Awutey
Cabinet Lucreatif

Jonathan Darboux
BCEAO

Fatimatou Zahra Diop
BCEAO

Foli Doe-Bruce
A.U.D.E.P. International

Koffi Joseph Dogbevi
Cabinet LUCREATIF

Firmin Kwami Dzonoukou
Notaire

Sonhaye Gbati
Fondation Heinrich Klose

Franklin Koffi Gbedey
Engineer

Jean Claude Gnamien
FIDAFRICA / PricewaterhouseCoopers

Hermann Gnango
FIDAFRICA / PricewaterhouseCoopers

Evelyne M'Bassidgé
FIDAFRICA / PricewaterhouseCoopers

Adeline Messou
FIDAFRICA / PricewaterhouseCoopers

Tiburce Monnou
SCP Martial Akakpo

Olivier Pedanou
Cabinet Lucreatif

Galolo Soedjede
Avocat à la Cour

Dominique Taty
FIDAFRICA / PricewaterhouseCoopers

Inès Mazalo Tekpa
Cabinet Lucreatif

Fousséni Traoré
FIDAFRICA / PricewaterhouseCoopers

Adjé Prince Wilsom Adjete
Avocat à la Cour

Prince Zacharie Adjé Wilson-Adjete
Cabinet de Maître Galolo Soedjede, avocat au Barreau du Togo

TONGA

Inoke Afu
Dateline Shipping & Travel Ltd.

Ramsay R. Dalgety
Tonga Electric Power Board

Fine Tohi
Dateline Shipping & Travel Ltd.

William Clive Edwards
Law Office

Aisake Eke
Ministry of Finance

Sione Etika
Etika Law Office

Anthony Ford
Supreme Court

Salesi Fotu
Land Registry

L. Aloma Johansson
R. Albin Johansson & Co. Public Accountants and Business Consultants

Lusio Lausi'i
Ministry of Labor, Commerce and Industries

Maliu Mafi
Island Enterprises Ltd.

Mele Mafi Otuafi

Lee Miller
Waste Management Ltd.

Laki M. Niu
Laki Niu Offices

Samiuela M. Palu
Magistrate's Court

Siaosi Peleki Moala
Ministry of Works

Sipiloni Raas
Jaimi Associates - Architects

David Reesby
Fletcher Royco Joint Venture

Ian Skelton
Shoreline Distribution Ltd.

Dana Stephenson
Law Office

Ralph Stephenson
Law Office

Maliu Taione

Sione Havea Taione
Supreme Court of Justice

Hiva Tatila
Tonga Development Bank

Christine Uta'atu
Uta'atu & Associates

Isileli Vea
Jaimi Associates - Architects

Diana Warner
Skip's Custom Joinery Ltd.

TRINIDAD AND TOBAGO

Andre Bass
The Fast Freight Group

Steve Beckles
R.D. Rampersad & Co.

Tiffanny Castillo
M. Hamel-Smith & Co., member of Lex Mundi.

Terry Curtis
TransUnion

Rachael Cyrus
M. Hamel-Smith & Co., member of Lex Mundi

Gary Edwards
T & K Engineering Limited

Nicole Ferreira-Aaron
M. Hamel-Smith & Co., member of Lex Mundi

Larry Hackshaw
Caribbean Shipping & Consolidating Corp

Peter Inglefield
PricewaterhouseCoopers

Colin Laird
Colin Laird Associates

Marcia Leonard
The Fast Freight Group

Keomi Lourenco
M. Hamel-Smith & Co., member of Lex Mundi

Ramesh Lutchman
TransUnion

Marjorie Nunez
Lex Caribbean

Gregory Pantin
M. Hamel-Smith & Co., member of Lex Mundi

Sonji Pierre Chase
Lex Caribbean

Deborah Ragoonath
PricewaterhouseCoopers

Mark Ramkerrysingh
Fitzwilliam Stone Furness-Smith & Morgan

Ramdath Dave Rampersad
R.D. Rampersad & Co.

Danzel Reid
Trinidad & Tobago Electricity Commission

Bryan Rooplal
Employers' Consultative Association of Trinidad and Tobago

Winston R. Simmonds
Caribbean Shipping & Consolidating Corp

Stephen A. Singh
Lex Caribbean

Patricia Thomas
World Freight s.a.r.l.

Jonathan Walker
M. Hamel-Smith & Co., member of Lex Mundi

Grantley Wiltshire
M. Hamel-Smith & Co., member of Lex Mundi

TUNISIA

Samir Abdelly
Abdelly & Associes

Monêm Achour
Achour & Associates

Mokhtar Amor
Société Tunisienne de l'Electricité et du Gaz

Mohamed Moncef Barouni
ACR

Adly Bellagha
Adly Bellagha & Associates

Mohamed Ben Abdallah
Agence de Promotion de l'Industrie

Hend Ben Achour
Adly Bellagha & Associates

Rafika Ben Aissa Bouslama
Ministère de la Justice

Othman Ben Arfa
Société Tunisienne de l'Elecricite et du Gaz

Ismail Ben Farhat
Adly Bellagha & Associates

Béatrice Ben Hassen
SLTC Graveleau, Dachser Group

Elyès Ben Mansour
Avocats Conseils Associés

Miriam Ben Rejeb
PricewaterhouseCoopers Legal Services

Kamel Ben Salah
Gide Loyrette Nouel, member of Lex Mundi

Abdelfattah Benahji
Ferchiou & Associés Meziou Knani

Belkacem Berrah
Tribunal de 1ère Instance de Tunis

Manel Bondi
PricewaterhouseCoopers

Salaheddine Caid Essebsi
CE&P Law Firm

Salma Chaari
Abdelly & Associes

Faouzi Cheikh
Banque Centrale

Abdelmalek Dahmani
Dahmani Transit International

Eric Douay
SDV

Mohamed Lotfi El Ajeri
Avocat a la Cour et Mediateur agree par le B.B.MC

Mourad El Aroui
Amen Bank

Yassine El Hafi
Adly Bellagha & Associates

Faïza Feki
Banque Centrale

Abderrahmen Fendri
PricewaterhouseCoopers

Yessine Ferah
CE&P Law Firm

Amel Ferchichi
Gide Loyrette Nouel, member of Lex Mundi

Noureddine Ferchiou
Ferchiou & associés Meziou Knani

Afif Gaigi
Avocats Conseils Associés

Lamia Harguem
Gide Loyrette Nouel, member of Lex Mundi

Institut d'Economie Quantitative

Badis Jedidi
Gide Loyrette Nouel, member of Lex Mundi

Najla Jezi
ACR

Sami Kallel
Kallel & Associates

Adlene Kooli
Comete Engineering

Ministère du Développement et de la Coopération Internationale

Amina Larbi
Gide Loyrette Nouel, member of Lex Mundi

Mohamed Louzir
Cabinet M.S. Louzir

Mabrouk Maalaoui
PricewaterhouseCoopers

Slim Malouche
Malouche law firm

Khaled Marzouk
République Tunisienne Centre Informatique du Ministere des Finances

Mohamed Ali Masmoudi
PricewaterhouseCoopers Legal Services

Sarah Mebezaa
Comete Engineering

Radhi Meddeb
Comete Engineering

Faouzi Mili
Mili and Associates

Hedidar Moufida
Agence de Promotion de L'Industrie

Mohamed Taieb Mrabet
Banque Centrale

Ahmed Ouerfelli
Legal and Judicial research Centre

Imed Tanazefti
Gide Loyrette Nouel, member of Lex Mundi

Rachid Tmar
PricewaterhouseCoopers Legal Services

Amine Turki
Ordre des Architectes de Tunisie

Anis Wahabi
AWT Audit & Conseil

Sebai Youssef
République Tunisienne, Ministère de l'Intérieur et du développement local

Mohamed Ali Masmoudi
PricewaterhouseCoopers Legal Services

TURKEY

Melike Akan
Mehmet Gün & Co.

Ceyda Akbal
Turunç Law Office

Melis Akkurt
Bener Law Office, member of Ius Laboris

Miray Akovalıgil
Pekin & Pekin, member of Lex Mundi, member of SEE Legal

Ceren Aktaş
PricewaterhouseCoopers

Bora Aktürk
Aktürk & Çetiner AB

Mehmet Alakas
Alacloth

Duygu Alkan
Alkan Deniz Mavio⊠lu Dilmen Law Office

Mustafa Alper
YASED - International Investors Association

Arda Alposkay
Devres Law office

Uğur Amasya
Amasya Law Office

Melsa Ararat
Corporate Governance Forum of Turkey, Sabanci University

Şeref Can Arat
Mehmet Gün & Co.

Naci Arkan
Ministry of Finance

Özen Atihan
Pekin & Pekin, member of Lex Mundi, member of SEE Legal

Pınar Aybek
Bener Law Office, member of Ius Laboris

Levent Aydaş
Ayda⊠ Liman Kurman

Yasemin Aydoğmuş
Mehmet Gün & Co.

Elvan Aziz Bikmen
Paksoy & Co. Law Firm

Derya Baksı Pekyalçın
Tarlan & Pekyalç⊠n Law Office

Selin Barlak
Paksoy & Co. Law Firm

Burçin Barlas
Alkan Deniz Mavio⊠lu Dilmen Law Office

Cansel Baydinç
Herguner Bilgen Ozeke

Erim Bener
Bener Law Office, member of Ius Laboris

Yvonne Bensason
Mehmet Gün & Co.

Sinan Borovalı
Pekin & Pekin, member of Lex Mundi, member of SEE Legal

Tuba Burcu Senel
Turkish Confederation of Employer Associations

Gulnur Camcı
Somay Hukuk Burosu

Esin Çamlıbel
Turunç Law Office

Can Canko
Pekin & Pekin, member of Lex Mundi, member of SEE Legal

M. Fadlullah Cerrahoğlu
Cerraho⊠lu Law Firm

F. Şebnem Çetiner
Aktürk & Çetiner AB

Fikret Çetinkaya
KPMG Yetkin Ymm A.⊠

Gulnisa Coşkun
Pekin & Pekin, member of Lex Mundi, member of SEE Legal

Ebru Dabbagh
Turunç Law Office

Kürşat Demirezen
ICT International Trading

Orkun Deniz
Kredit Kayit Bureau

Eda Denize
Alkan Deniz Mavio⊠lu Dilmen Law Office

Rüçhan Derici
⊠e Dan⊠manl⊠k Ltd. ⊠ti.

Emine Devres
Devres Law office

Başak Diclehan
KPMG Yetkin Ymm A.⊠

Onur Dönmez
Orhaner Law Office

Dilara Duman
Sar⊠brahimo⊠lu Law Office

Erdem Egemen
PricewaterhouseCoopers

Murat Emirhanoğlu
KPMG Yetkin Ymm A.⊠

Sedat Eratalar
Deloitte & Touche

Gökben Erdem Dirican
Pekin & Pekin, member of Lex Mundi, member of SEE Legal

Esin Ertek
PricewaterhouseCoopers

Luc Fourcade
SDV - Horoz Logistics

Hakkı Gedik
Herguner Bilgen Ozeke

Arman Gezer
Deloitte & Touche

Sait Gözüm
Deloitte & Touche

Ali Gözütok
Pekin & Pekin, member of Lex Mundi, member of SEE Legal

Hakan Güleçyuz
Ultrasonik Ltd.

Onur Gülsaran
Cerraho⊠lu Law Firm

Rıfat Günay
Central Bank

A. Feridun Güngör
Ernst & Young

Hande Hamevi
Pekin & Pekin, member of Lex Mundi, member of SEE Legal

Şebnem Işık
Mehmet Gün & Partners

Oğuz Kain
Pekin & Pekin, member of Lex Mundi, member of SEE Legal

Egemen Karaduman
Ernst & Young

Ozan Karaduman
Mehmet Gün & Co.

Ekin Kavukçuoğlu
Deloitte & Touche

Gözde Kayacık
Pekin & Bayar Law Firm

Betül Kencebay
YASED - International Investors Association

Özlem Kızıl
Çakmak Avukatl⊠k Bürosu

Özcan Koç
Gulhan Marble

Sertak Kokenek
Bener Law Office, member of Ius Laboris

Cumhur Köseoğlu
Kentsel Machinery Co. Ltd.

Cengiz Koyuncu
Tektron D⊠⊠ Tic. Ltd. ⊠ti.

Kürşat Kunter
Central Bank

Burcak Kurt
Somay Hukuk Burosu

Alpaslan Hamdi Kuzucuoğlu
Istanbul Metropolitan Municipality

Altan Liman
Ayda⊠ Liman Kurman

Koshy Mathai
IMF

Orhan Yavuz Mavioğlu
Alkan Deniz Mavio⊠lu Dilmen Law Office

Rana Mazlum Yılmaz
Yilmaz Law Offices

Lerzan Nalbantoğlu
Turunç Law Office

Yılmaz Nalçakar
Med Shipping Logistics Transport & Trade Ltd. Corporation

Jacques Naudin
SDV - Horoz Logistics

Zeynephan Oğuz
Cerraho⊠lu Law Firm

Fahri Okumuş
Central Bank

Şebnem Önder
Çakmak Avukatl⊠k Bürosu

Ertaç Öner
The Chamber of Architects of Turkey

Çağlayan Orhaner Dündar
Orhaner Law Office

Selin Özbek
Ozbek Attorneys at Law

Selin Özdoğan
Cerraho⊠lu Law Firm

Ekin Vukçuoğlu Özgülsen
Deloitte & Touche

Funda Özsel
Bener Law Office, member of Ius Laboris

Tuba Özsezen
YASED - International Investors Association

Alaattin Özyürek
Investment Support and Promotion Agency of Turkey

Ferhat Pekin
Pekin & Bayar Law Firm

Çağıl Şahin Biber
PricewaterhouseCoopers

Bilge Saltan
Dülger Law Firm

Hasan Sarıçiçek
KPMG Yetkin Ymm A.⊠

Selim Sarıibrahimoğlu
Sar⊠brahimo⊠lu Law Office

Mustafa Serdaroğlu
Pekin & Pekin, member of Lex Mundi, member of SEE Legal

Ayşe Sert
Çakmak Avukatlık Bürosu

Ufuk Soğütlüoğlu
Deloitte & Touche

Sera Somay
Somay Hukuk Burosu

Emine Sönmez
PricewaterhouseCoopers Legal Department

Naz Tamer
Mehmet Gün & Co.

Aylin Tarlan
Tarlan & Pekyalç⊠n Law Office

Bülent Taş
Ministry of Finance

Güzel Toker
PricewaterhouseCoopers

Filiz Toprak
Mehmet Gün & Partners

Şule Tunalı
*SALKIM TARIM ÜRÜNLERI SAN.
VE TIC. LTD. ŞTI.*

*TURKISH INDUSTRIALISTS' AND
BUSINESSMEN'S ASSOCIATION
(TUSIAD)*

Noyan Turunç
TURUNÇ LAW OFFICE

Ibrahim Tutar
*PENETRA CONSULTING AND
AUDITING*

Ebru Tuygun
DELOITTE & TOUCHE

Gökçe Ucuzal
*BENER LAW OFFICE, MEMBER
OF IUS LABORIS*

Tuğçe Uğurlu
HERGUNER BILGEN OZEKE

Arzu Uluç
CENTRAL BANK

Hilal Ünal
GOKSER MACHINE LTD

Furkan Ünal
*PGLOBAL ADVISORY SERVICES
LTD.*

Begüm Yavuzdoğan
MEHMET GÜN & PARTNERS

Banyu Yılmaz
*UNION OF CHAMBERS AND
COMMODITY EXCHANGES*

Asım Serdar Yılmaz
ÇAKMAK AVUKATLIK BÜROSU

Hülya Yılmaz
DELOITTE & TOUCHE

Cağatay Yılmaz
YILMAZ LAW OFFICES

Aylin Yontar
CERRAHOĞLU LAW FIRM

Murat Yülek
*PGLOBAL ADVISORY SERVICES
LTD.*

Serap Zuvin
SERAP ZUVIN LAW OFFICES

UGANDA

Joachim Alinaitwe
*SHONUBI, MUSOKE & CO.
ADVOCATES*

Joseph Baliddawa
PRICEWATERHOUSECOOPERS

Walugembe Christopher
MMAKS ADVOCATES

Frederick M.S Egonda-Ntende
HIGH COURT

Moses Jurua Adriko
MMAKS ADVOCATES

Francis Kamulegeya
PRICEWATERHOUSECOOPERS

John Fisher Kanyemibwa
*KATEERA & KAGUMIRE
ADVOCATES*

Phillip Karugaba
MMAKS ADVOCATES

Edwin Karugire
*KIWANUKA & KARUGIRE
ADVOCATES*

Jim Kasigwa
PRICEWATERHOUSECOOPERS

Vincent Katutsi
*KATEERA & KAGUMIRE
ADVOCATES*

Peter Kauma
*KIWANUKA & KARUGIRE
ADVOCATES*

Sophie Kayemba
PRICEWATERHOUSECOOPERS

Robert Kiggundu
ARCH FORUM LTD.

Geoffrey Kiryabwire
JUSTICE

Kiryowa Kiwanuka
*KIWANUKA & KARUGIRE
ADVOCATES*

Robert Komakec
ARCH FORUM LTD.

Eeshi Kutugu
PRICEWATERHOUSECOOPERS

James Kyazze
*SHONUBI, MUSOKE & CO.
ADVOCATES*

Joseph Luswata
*SEBALU & LULE ADVOCATES
AND LEGAL CONSULTANTS*

Robinah Lutaaya
PRICEWATERHOUSECOOPERS

Ben Luwum
BVL & CO.

John Mpambala
KAMPALA CITY COUNCIL

Paul Frobisher Mugambwa
PRICEWATERHOUSECOOPERS

Simon Muhumuza
KAMPALA CITY COUNCIL

Cornelius Mukiibi
C. MUKIIBI SENTAMU & CO.

Fatuma Nabulime
SDV TRANSAMI LTD.

Plaxeda Namirimu
PRICEWATERHOUSECOOPERS

Rachel Nansikombi
PRICEWATERHOUSECOOPERS

Diana Ninsiima
MMAKS ADVOCATES

Alex Rezida
*NANGWALA, REZIDA & CO.
ADVOCATES*

Kenneth Rutaremwa
*KATEERA & KAGUMIRE
ADVOCATES*

Ali Sengendo
MWEBE, SEBAGGALA & CO.

Stephen Serunjogi
*KATEERA & KAGUMIRE
ADVOCATES*

Alan Shonubi
*SHONUBI, MUSOKE & CO.
ADVOCATES*

Manish Siyani
*SEYANI BROTHERS & CO. (U)
LTD*

Parbat Siyani
*SEYANI BROTHERS & CO. (U)
LTD*

Sebadduka Swaibu
SHABA MOTORS LTD.

Godfrey Zziwa
*MUWANGUZI, ZZIWA & MUSISI
ADVOCATES*

UKRAINE

Oleg Y. Alyoshin
VASYL KISIL & PARTNERS

Sasha Androschuk
GRISCHENKO & PARTNERS

Aleksandra Androschyk
GRISCHENKO & PARTNERS

Andrey Astapov
*ASTAPOV LAWYERS
INTERNATIONAL LAW GROUP*

Olga Balytska
DLA PIPER

Ron J. Barden
PRICEWATERHOUSECOOPERS

Igor Bessonov
IFC

Florentin Blanc
IFC

Timur Bondaryev
*ARZINGER & PARTNERS
INTERNATIONAL LAW FIRM*

Tatiana Buchko
*SHEVCHENKO DIDKOVSKIY &
PARTNERS*

Igor Dankov
PRICEWATERHOUSECOOPERS

Vladimir Didenko
PRICEWATERHOUSECOOPERS

Eugene Freyuk
ILYASHEV & PARTNERS

Karyna Gorovaya
INTERNATIONAL LAW OFFICES

Kseniya Guretskaya
INTERNATIONAL LAW OFFICES

Lesia Iakovenko
IFC

Sanjar Ibragimov
IFC

Nataliya Khutoryanets
ZAMORSKA & PARTNERS LLC

Andriy Kirmach
CHADBOURNE & PARKE LLP

Kateryna Kokot
THE SILECKY FIRM

Sergei Konnov
KONNOV & SOZANOVSKY

Maksym Kopeychykov
ILYASHEV & PARTNERS

Kseniya Koryukalova
KONNOV & SOZANOVSKY

Tatyana Kuzmenko
*ASTAPOV LAWYERS
INTERNATIONAL LAW GROUP*

Borys Lobovyk
KONNOV & SOZANOVSKY

Valeriy Lukinov
VENISSA LTD.

Mikhail Malkov

Dmitry Maximov
REM SHIPPING LTD.

Vadym Mizyakov
*SHEVCHENKO DIDKOVSKIY &
PARTNERSAGH*

Natalya Myroshnychenko
INTERNATIONAL LAW OFFICES

Sergiy Onishchenko
CHADBOURNE & PARKE LLP

Kateryna Onul
IFC

Dmytro Orendarets
*ARZINGER & PARTNERS
INTERNATIONAL LAW FIRM*

Oleksandr Padalka
*SHEVCHENKO DIDKOVSKIY &
PARTNERS*

Magdalena Patrzyk
PRICEWATERHOUSECOOPERS

Olexiy V. Pokotylo
*HANNES SNELLMAN,
ATTORNEYS-AT-LAW LTD.*

Sava P. Poliakov
GRISCHENKO & PARTNERS

Vitaliy Pravdyuk
KONNOV & SOZANOVSKY

Anna Putintseva
CHADBOURNE & PARKE LLP

Dmitry Pyatachenko
IFC

Marina Savchenko
*ASTAPOV LAWYERS
INTERNATIONAL LAW GROUP*

Olga Serbul
*LAW FIRM IP & C. CONSULT
LLC*

Mykhailo Shchitka
VASYL KISIL & PARTNERS

Olga Shumikhina
GRISCHENKO & PARTNERS

Markian B. Silecky
THE SILECKY FIRM

Svitlana Silecky
THE SILECKY FIRM

Anna Sisetska
VASIL KISIL & PARTNERS

Artem Skorobogatov
INTERNATIONAL LAW OFFICES

Oleksander Subbotin
*ARZINGER & PARTNERS
INTERNATIONAL LAW FIRM*

Iryna Telychko
GRISCHENKO & PARTNERS

Oleg Vusochinskiy
GRISCHENKO & PARTNERS

Tetyana Vydoborets
KONNOV & SOZANOVSKY

Anna Yakubenko
PRICEWATERHOUSECOOPERS

Olexiy Yanov
*LAW FIRM IP & C. CONSULT,
LLC*

Tatiana Zamorska
ZAMORSKA & PARTNERS LLC

Sergiy Zheka
CHADBOURNE & PARKE LLP

UNITED ARAB
EMIRATES

ALLEN & OVERY LLP

Taleb Abdel Karim Jafar
DUBAI MUNICIPALITY

Daoud Abdel Rahman
Al-Hajri
DUBAI MUNICIPALITY

Mohamed Ahmed Saleh
DUBAI MUNICIPALITY

Mahmood Al Bastaki
DUBAI TRADE

Rasha Al Saeed
BAKER BOTTS LLP

Saeed Al-Hamiz
CENTRAL BANK

Ashraf Ali
*GOLDEN BUILDING MATERIALS
TRADING*

Saaran Alshammari
JUBAIL PEARL

Khaled Amin
*SHALAKANY LAW OFFICE,
MEMBER OF LEX MUNDI*

Ali Awais
BAKER BOTTS LLP

Jennifer Bibbings
TROWERS & HAMLINS

Salmeen Dahi Bin Salmeen
DUBAI MUNICIPALITY

Lisa Dale
AL TAMIMI & CO.

Precilla D'Souza
AL TAMIMI & CO.

Sydene Helwick
AL TAMIMI & CO.

Zaid Kamhawi
EMCREDIT

Manijeh Khan
*SHALAKANY LAW OFFICE,
MEMBER OF LEX MUNDI*

Suneer Kumar
AL SUWAIDI & CO.

Ravi Kumar
DUBAI TRADE

John Kunjappan
MAERSK LINE

Mohamed Mahmood
Mashroom
DUBAI MUNICIPALITY

Khulood Obaid

Yasser Omar
*SHALAKANY LAW OFFICE,
MEMBER OF LEX MUNDI*

Iqbal Pedhiwala
SILK BRIDGE TRADING EST

Henrik Petersen
MAERSK KANOO LLC

Dean Rolfe
PRICEWATERHOUSECOOPERS

Luke Sajan
DAMCO

Munir Suboh
ABU-GHAZALEH LEGAL

Neil Taylor

Mariel Yard
PRICEWATERHOUSECOOPERS

Natasha Zahid
BAKER BOTTS LLP

UNITED KINGDOM

ALLEN & OVERY LLP

Kon Asimacopoulos
KIRKLAND & ELLIS LLP

Jon Atkey
*HER MAJESTY'S LAND
REGISTRY*

Nick Benwell
SIMMONS & SIMMONS

Georgie Blyth
*PRICEWATERHOUSECOOPERS
LEGAL SERVICES LLP*

Becky Borman
PRICEWATERHOUSECOOPERS

Techia Braveboy
*CLEARY GOTTLIEB STEEN &
HAMILTON LLP*

Penny Bruce
PricewaterhouseCoopers Legal LLP

Richard Collier-Keywood
PricewaterhouseCoopers

Simon Cookson
Ashurst

Laura Cram
Ashurst

David Crosthwaite
Davis Langdon LLP

Shreya Damodaran
Cleary Gottlieb Steen & Hamilton LLP

Kirsten Dettmanl
Simmons & Simmons

Aaron Espin
Cleary Gottlieb Steen & Hamilton LLP

Nick Francis
PricewaterhouseCoopers

Paul Gilbert
Finers Stephens Innocent LLP

Helen Gorty
Simmons & Simmons

Lynn Hiestand
Skadden, Arps, Slate, Meagher & Flom

Neville Howlett
PricewaterhouseCoopers

Stefano Iacomelli
Iosto International Services Ltd

Simon Jay
Cleary Gottlieb Steen & Hamilton LLP

Nistha Jeram-Dave
PricewaterhouseCoopers Legal LLP

Tam John
Addison Technology Ltd

Gillian Key-Vice
Experian Ltd.

Shinoj Koshy
Cleary Gottlieb Steen & Hamilton LLP

Kwame Asamoah
HW Chartered Accountants

Kristi Lehtis
Simmons & Simmons

Emma Malkin
Weil, Gotshal & Manges

Christopher Mallon
Skadden, Arps, Slate, Meagher & Flom

Charles Mayo
Simmons & Simmons

David McCullogh
TPS Consultancy

John Meadows
HM Land Registry, England & Wales

Alison Murrin
Ashurst

Lyndon Norley
Kirkland & Ellis LLP

Oludare Omoyayi
Conjor Investment Ltd.

Fiona Patterson
Simmons & Simmons

Christian Pilkington
Skadden, Arps, Slate, Meagher & Flom

Security Foiling Limited

Andrew Shutter
Cleary Gottlieb Steen & Hamilton LLP

Katherine Stones
Weil, Gotshal & Manges

Lance Terry
Glanvilles Solicitors

Paul Timmins
Approved Inspector Services Limited

Andrew van der Lem
Better Regulation Executive

Maria-Eleni Vlachakou
PricewaterhouseCoopers

Sally Willcock
Weil, Gotshal & Manges

UNITED STATES

Stephen Anderson
PricewaterhouseCoopers

Birute Awasthi
Competent Amerinde Consolidated

Asheet Awasthi
Fortune Law Group

Luke A. Barefoot
Cleary Gottlieb Steen & Hamilton LLP

Donald Bernstein

Walter Bobadilla
Agouti Construction Consulting, LLC.

Agne Ceskeviciute
Fortune Law Group

Victor Chiu
Cleary Gottlieb Steen & Hamilton LLP

Richard Conza
Cleary Gottlieb Steen & Hamilton LLP

Jean Pierre de Nes
Bollore – SDV

Joshua L. Ditelberg
Seyfarth Shaw LLP

Lindsay Dunn

Craig Eisele
Trans-African Development Strategies, L.L.C.

Julija Gecaite
Competent Amerinde Consolidated

Benjamin E. Gehrt
Seyfarth Shaw LLP

Lindsee P. Granfield
Cleary Gottlieb Steen & Hamilton LLP

Steven Horowitz
Cleary Gottlieb Steen & Hamilton LLP

Monika Knyzelyte
Fortune Law Group

Arthur Kohn
Cleary Gottlieb Steen & Hamilton LLP

Azniv Ksachikyan
Orrick, Herrington & Sutcliffe LLP

Fiana Kwasnik
Cleary Gottlieb Steen & Hamilton LLP

Michael Lazerwitz
Cleary Gottlieb Steen & Hamilton LLP

Bradford L. Livingston
Seyfarth Shaw LLP

Colin Lloyd
Cleary Gottlieb Steen & Hamilton LLP

Paul Marquardt
Cleary Gottlieb Steen & Hamilton LLP

Karen Monroe
Siller Wilk LLP

Robert Morris
PricewaterhouseCoopers

Kelly J. Murray
PricewaterhouseCoopers

Philippe A. Naudin
SDV

Samuel Nolen
Richards, Layton & Finger, P.A., member of Lex Mundi

Sean O'Neal
Cleary Gottlieb Steen & Hamilton LLP

Jeffrey Penn
Cleary Gottlieb Steen & Hamilton LLP

Maria Priezzheva
Orrick Herrington & Sutcliffe LLP

Stephen Raslavich
United States Bankruptcy Court

Sandra Rocks
Cleary Gottlieb Steen & Hamilton LLP

Olga Sirodoeva
Orrick Herrington & Sutcliffe LLP

Catharine Slack

David Snyder
Snyder & Snyder, LLP

My Chi To
Debevoise & Plimpton LLP

Frederick Turner
Snyder & Snyder, LLP

Mikhail Usubyan
Orrick, Herrington & Sutcliffe LLP

Penny Vaughn
PricewaterhouseCoopers

Karen Wagner

URUGUAY

Bernardo Amorín
Olivera & Delpiazzo

Jonás Bergstein
Estudio Bergstein

Corina Bove
Guyer & Regules, member of Lex Mundi

Carlos Brandes
Guyer & Regules, member of Lex Mundi

Nicolas Brause
Jiménez de Aréchaga, Viana & Brause

Virginia Brause
Jiménez de Aréchaga, Viana & Brause

Jorge De Vita
Jorge de Vita Studio

Leonardo Decarlini
PricewaterhouseCoopers

María Durán
Hughes & Hughes

Noelia Eiras
Hughes & Hughes

Gabriel Ejgenberg
Estudio Bergstein

Fabrizio Fava
Panalpina World Transport Ltd

Marcelo Femenías Vidal
Bado, Kuster, Zerbino & Rachetti

Agustina Fernádez Giambruno
Guyer & Regules, member of Lex Mundi

Javier Fernández Zerbino
Bado, Kuster, Zerbino & Rachetti

Juan Federico Fischer
LVM Attorneys at Law

Federico Formen
LVM Attorneys at Law

Sergio Franco
PricewaterhouseCoopers

Nelson Alfredo Gonzales
SDV S.A.

Gabriela Gutierrez
Estudio Bergstein

Ariel Imken
Superintendencia de Instituciones de Intermediación Financiera - Banco Central del Uruguay

Alfredo Inciarte Blanco
Estudio Pérez del Castillo, Inciarte, Gari Abogados

Alma Kubachek
Estudio Juridico Notarial de Alma Kubachek

Ricardo Mezzera
Estudio Dr. Mezzera

Alejandro Miller Artola
Guyer & Regules, member of Lex Mundi

Matias Morgare
SDV S.A.

Luis Muxi
LVM Attorneys at Law

Juan Martín Olivera
Olivera & Delpiazzo

María Concepción Olivera
Olivera & Delpiazzo

Ricardo Olivera-García
Olivera & Delpiazzo

Gabriel Pedro
PricewaterhouseCoopers

Juan Pablo Pesce
Conatel S.A.

Ismael Pignatta Sánchez
Guyer & Regules, member of Lex Mundi

María José Poey
Guyer & Regules, member of Lex Mundi

Verónica Raffo
Ferrere Attorneys

Aejandro Rey Jiménez de Aréchaga
Guyer & Regules, member of Lex Mundi

María Noel Riotorto
Guyer & Regules, member of Lex Mundi

Analía Rodríguez
Banco Central

Agustina Rodríguez
Ferrere Attorneys

Monica Santos
Olivera & Delpiazzo

Juan Troccoli
LVM Attorneys-at-Law

Gerardo Viñoles
Vinoles Studio

Alexandra Weisz
Dovat, Carriquiry & Asociados

UZBEKISTAN

Jakhongir Abdurazaqov
Avent Advocat

Rimat Achmedshin
Fides

Mels Akhmedov
BAS

Dildar M. Alimbekova
Business Women's Association of Uzbekistan

Umid Aripdjanov
Grata Law Firm

Nelly Djurabaeva
M&M

Khalid Farooq
Globalink Logistics Group

Irina Gosteva
Denton Wilde Sapte

Nail Hassanov
Law Firm Leges Advokat

Rustam Ikramov
Himoya Law Office

Mansurkhon Kamalov
Foreign Enterprise of Huawei Tech Investment of Tashkent

Mouborak Kambarova
Denton Wilde Sapte

Babur Karimov
Grata Law Firm

Khurshid Kasimdzhanov
M&M Logistics

Nurali Eshibaevich Khalmuratov
Central Bank

Zafar Khashimov
Anglesey Food

Arif Nasibov
IFC

Vera Ni
Anglesey Food

Malika Norova
Grata Law Firm

Vsevolod Payevskiy
IFC

PricewaterhouseCoopers

Laziza Rakhimova
Grata Law Firm

Valeria Samborskaya
*NATIONAL CENTRE OF
GEODESY & CARTOGRAPHY*

Alexander Samborsky
*NATIONAL CENTRE OF
GEODESY & CARTOGRAPHY*

Sofiya Shaikhraziyeva
GRATA LAW FIRM

Nizomiddin Shakhabutdinov
LAW FIRM LEGES ADVOKAT

Alisher Shaykhov
*CHAMBER OF COMMERCE AND
INDUSTRY*

Alishev Shurkurlaev
BERAD GROUP CO.

Petros Tsakanyan
AZIZOV & PARTNERS

Ihtiyorjon Turaboyev
IFC

Rafael Valyulin
GENERAL MOTORS

VANUATU

Christopher Dawson
DAWSON BUILDERS

*EXPRESS CUSTOMS SERVICES
LTD.*

David Hudson
HUDSON & SUGDEN

Mark Stafford
BDO BARRETT & PARTNERS

Dani Yawa
PACIFIC LAWYERS

VENEZUELA

Jorge Acedo-Prato
*HOET PELAEZ CASTILLO &
DUQUE, MEMBER OF LEX
MUNDI*

Juan Enrique Aigster
*HOET PELAEZ CASTILLO &
DUQUE, MEMBER OF LEX
MUNDI*

Servio T. Altuve Jr.
*SERVIO T. ALTUVE R. &
ASOCIADOS*

Carlos Bachrich Nagy
*DE SOLA PATE & BROWN,
ABOGADOS - CONSULTORES*

Mercedes Briceño
CONAPRI

Diego Castagnino
*HOET PELAEZ CASTILLO &
DUQUE, MEMBER OF LEX
MUNDI*

Lubín Chacón
*BENSON, PEREZ MATOS,
ANTAKLY & WATTS*

María Paola D´Onghia
*HOET PELAEZ CASTILLO &
DUQUE, MEMBER OF LEX
MUNDI*

Arturo De Sola Lander
*DE SOLA PATE & BROWN,
ABOGADOS - CONSULTORES*

Carlos Domínguez Hernández
*HOET PELAEZ CASTILLO &
DUQUE, MEMBER OF LEX
MUNDI*

Jose Fereira
RODRIGUEZ & MENDOZA

Francisco Gámez Arcaya
GÁMEZ & VERA ABOGADOS

Alejandro Giolito
PRICEWATERHOUSECOOPERS

Ruben Gottberg
PRICEWATERHOUSECOOPERS

Jose Guerra
PRICEWATERHOUSECOOPERS

Maigualida Ifill
PRICEWATERHOUSECOOPERS

Enrique Itriago
RODRIGUEZ & MENDOZA

Lorena Mingarelli Lozzi
*DE SOLA PATE & BROWN,
ABOGADOS - CONSULTORES*

Fernando Miranda
PRICEWATERHOUSECOOPERS

Fernando Miranda
*PRICEWATERHOUSECOOPERS
LEGAL SERVICES*

Bruno Paredes
LOGISTIKA TSM

John R. Pate
*DE SOLA PATE & BROWN,
ABOGADOS - CONSULTORES*

Bernardo Pisani
RODRIGUEZ & MENDOZA

Eduardo Porcarelli
CONAPRI

Melissa Puga Santaella
CONAPRI

Laura Silva Aparicio
*HOET PELAEZ CASTILLO &
DUQUE, MEMBER OF LEX
MUNDI*

John Tucker
*HOET PELAEZ CASTILLO &
DUQUE, MEMBER OF LEX
MUNDI*

VIETNAM

Vuong Kim Anh
*HOA BINH CHINH PHUC DINH
CAO*

A.T.A ARCHITECTS CO. LTD

Nicolas Audier
GIDE LOYRETTE NOUEL

Nguyen Xuan Bang
*DESCON CONSTRUCTION
CORPORATION*

Tam Bu
*ORRICK, HERRINGTON &
SUTCLIFFE LLP*

Anne-Lise Chatelain
GIDE LOYRETTE NOUEL

Daniel Chernov
DFDL MEKONG

Giles Thomas Cooper
DUANE MORRIS LLC

Anna Craven
*FRESHFIELDS BRUCKHAUS
DERINGER*

Trong Hieu Dang
VISION & ASSOCIATES

Nguyen Dang Viet
BIZCONSULT

Minh Day
*ORRICK, HERRINGTON &
SUTCLIFFE LLP*

Dang The Duc
INDOCHINE COUNSEL

Minh Duong
ALLENS ARTHUR ROBINSON

Tieng Thu Duong
VISION & ASSOCIATES

John Farmer
*ORRICK, HERRINGTON &
SUTCLIFFE, LLP*

David Fitzgerald
PRICEWATERHOUSECOOPERS

Albert Franceskinj
DS AVOCATS

Giang Ha Thi Phuong
PRICEWATERHOUSECOOPERS

Pham Hanh
DUANE MORRIS LLC

Le Hong Phong
BIZCONSULT

Lê Thj Hônh Hai
*HOA BINH CHINH PHUC DINH
CAO*

Konrad Hull
LUCY WAYNE & ASSOCIATES

Tuong Long Huynh
GIDE LOYRETTE NOUEL

Etienne Laumonier
GIDE LOYRETTE NOUEL

Kevin Le
*CITY OCEAN LOGISTICS CO.,
LTD.*

Cong Dinh Le
DC LAW

Viet Hai Le
*HOA BINH CHINH PHUC DINH
CAO*

Nguyen Huy Thuy Le
INDOCHINE COUNSEL

Truan Chien Le
NOVAPRO & ASSOCIATES

Thi Loc Le
YKVN LAWYERS

Thuy Anh Le Phan

Kevin Lê Viêt Há
*CITY OCEAN LOGISTICS CO.,
LTD.*

Tien Ngoc Luu
VISION & ASSOCIATES

Hoang Minh Duc
DUANE MORRIS LLC

Michelle Mobley
*FRESHFIELDS BRUCKHAUS
DERINGER*

Hoang Kim Oanh Nguyen
BAKER & MCKENZIE

Linh Chi Nguyen
BAKER & MCKENZIE

Tran Van Quynh Nguyen
BAKER & MCKENZIE

Ngoc Bich Nguyen
DC LAW

Cong To Nguyen
GIDE LOYRETTE NOUEL

Bien Nguyen
HOAI TRUNG TEA COMPANY

Phan Manh Long Nguyen
HUNG & PARTNERS

Thi Xuan Trinh Nguyen
LUCY WAYNE & ASSOCIATES

Dao Nguyen
MAYER BROWN JSM

Van Anh Nguyen
VIETBID LAW FIRM

Linh D. Nguyen
VILAF - HONG DUC LAW FIRM

Tram Nguyen – Huyen
GIDE LOYRETTE NOUEL

Tuan Nguyen Anh
DP CONSULTING LTD

PANALPINA

Bac Pham Nghiem Xuan
VISION & ASSOCIATES

Anh Vu Phan
INDOCHINE COUNSEL

Dinh Thi Quynh Van
PRICEWATERHOUSECOOPERS

Isabelle Robineau
DFDL MEKONG LAW GROUP

Nguyen Thang
*VIETCOMBANK (BANK OF
FOREIGN TRADE OF VIETNAM)*

Pham Thi Thanh Huyen
INDOCHINE COUNSEL

Nguyen Thi Thu Huyen
GIDE LOYRETTE NOUEL

Nhung Thieu Hong
PRICEWATERHOUSECOOPERS

Ngo Quanc Thuy
DUANE MORRIS LLC

Tan Heng Thye
CHEN SHAN & PARTNERS

Trung Tran
MAYER BROWN JSM

Lan Tran
*ORRICK, HERRINGTON &
SUTCLIFFE LLP*

Hai Tran Thanh
PBC PARTNERS

Nam Hoai Truong
INDOCHINE COUNSEL

Robert Vernon
VIETNAM CONSULTANTS LTD

Nguyen Thu Thuy Vo
SDV LTD.

Tuyêt Hanh Võ Thi
CHEN SHAN & PARTNERS

Thu Hang Vu
BAKER & MCKENZIE

Trang Vu
*CREDIT INFORMATION CENTRE
- STATE BANK OF VIETNAM*

Dzung Vu
YKVN LAWYERS

Benjamin Yap
KELVIN CHIA PARTNERSHIP

**WEST BANK AND
GAZA**

Nidal Abu Lawi
*PALESTINE REAL ESTATE
INVESTMENT CO.*

Amal Abujaber
*PALESTINIAN MONETARY
AUTHORITY*

Safwan Al-Nather
*GERMAN TECHNICAL
COOPERATION*

Sharhabeel Al-Zaeem
*SHARHABEEL AL-ZAEEM AND
ASSOCIATES*

Haytham L. Al-Zu'bi
*AL-ZU'BI LAW OFFICE,
ADVOCATES & LEGAL
CONSULTANTS*

Mohammed Amarneh
*LEGAL AID& HUMAN RIGHTS
COORDINATOR*

Moyad Amouri
PRICEWATERHOUSECOOPERS

Khalil Ansara
CATHOLIC RELIEF SERVICES

Nizam Ayoob
*MINISTRY OF NATIONAL
ECONOMY*

Ali Faroun
*PALESTINIAN MONETARY
AUTHORITY*

Ali Hamoudeh
*JERUSALEM DISTRICT
ELECTRICITY CO. LTD.*

Samir Huleileh
PADICO

Hiba Husseini
HUSSEINI & HUSSEINI

Fadi Kattan
*TRANSJORDANIAN
ENGINEERING LTD.*

Mohamed Khader
*LAUSANNE TRADING
CONSULTANTS*

Wadee Nofal
NOFAL LAW FIRM

Samer Odeh
LAND REGISTRATION

Michael F. Orfaly
PRICEWATERHOUSECOOPERS

Ali Saffarini
SAFFARININ LAW FIRM

Maha Sbeih
*MINISTRY OF NATIONAL
ECONOMY*

Karim Fuad Shehadeh
*A.F. & R. SHEHADEH LAW
OFFICE*

Ramzi Skakini
SKAKINI FIRM

Samer Tammam
TAMMAM TRADE

Hisham Ziad
*PALESTINIAN MONETARY
AUTHORITY*

YEMEN

Abdulalah A. Al karraz
*LANDS & SURVEYING
AUTHORITY*

Qusai Abdalla
*ABDALLA AL-MEQBELI &
ASSOCIATES*

Walaa Abdalla
*ABDALLA AL-MEQBELI &
ASSOCIATES*

Mohamed Taha Hamood
Al-Hashimi
*MOHAMED TAHA HAMOOD
& CO.*

Louai Al-Meqbeli
*ABDALLA AL-MEQBALI &
ASSOCIATES*

Abdalla Al-Meqbeli
*ABDALLA AL-MEQBALI &
ASSOCIATES*

Alaa Al-Meqbeli
*ABDALLA AL-MEQBALI &
ASSOCIATES*

Mohamed Hamoud Baider
IFC

Randall Cameron
*MEJANNI, HAZEM HASSAN &
CO. KPMG*

Nowar M. Mejanni
*MEJANNI, HAZEM HASSAN &
CO. KPMG*

Zayed Mohammed Budier
*LANDS & SURVEYING
AUTHORITY*

Sanjay Prajapapi
*RATCO FOR TRADING &
SERVICES*

Mayad Saeed Abdullah Yafai
IFC

ZAMBIA

Shaira Adamali
PRICEWATERHOUSECOOPERS

Peter Armond
*CREDIT REFERENCE BUREAU
AFRICA LIMITED*

Candice Arnold
GLOBAL LOGISTICS

Jim Barnhart
USAID

Deborah Bwalya
CORPUS GLOBE ADVOCATES

Chewe K. Bwalya
D.H. KEMP & CO.

Anthony Bwembya
PACRO

Felix Chabala
*ENVIRONMENTAL COUNCIL OF
ZAMBIA*

Bonaventure Chibamba
Mutale
ELLIS & CO.

Mwelwa Chibesakunda
*CHIBESAKUNDA & CO./ DLA
PIPER*

Elias Chipimo
CORPUS GLOBE ADVOCATES

Steven Chisenga
CORPUS GLOBE ADVOCATES

Emmanuel Chulu
PRICEWATERHOUSECOOPERS

David Doyle
MANICA LTD

Arshad A Dudhia
MUSA DUDHIA

Robin Durairajah
*CHIBESAKUNDA & CO./ DLA
PIPER*

Karl Frick
SDV

Allan Garraway
*ZAMBIA CUSTOMS AND
FORWARDING AGENTS
ASSOCIATION*

Passmore Hamukoma
ZAMBIA BUSINESS FORUM

James Harley
PRICEWATERHOUSECOOPERS

Edgar Hamuwele
GRANT THORNTON

Grant Henderson
*CHIBESAKUNDA & CO./ DLA
PIPER*

Andrew Howard
SHARPE HOWARD & MWENYE

Jacqueline Jhata
CORPUS GLOBE ADVOCATES

Chance Kaonga
*NATIONAL COUNCIL FOR
CONSTRUCTION*

Harriet Kapampa Kapekele
CORPUS GLOBE ADVOCATES

Calvin Kasanda
*MINISTRY OF COMMERCE,
TRADE AND INDUSTRY*

Mutale Kasonde

Pixie Kasonde-Yangailo
P.H. YANGAILO & CO.

Chipepo Kasumpa
ZAMBIA BUSINESS FORUM

Anila Kuntawala
CELTIC FREIGHT

Yogesh Kuntawala
CELTIC FREIGHT

Kim Leneveu
AGS FRASERS

Walusiku Lisulo
LISULO + BWALYA

Alexander Lwatula
BARCLAYS BANK

Clyde Mbazima
*CHIBESAKUNDA & CO./ DLA
PIPER*

Bonaventure Mbewe
BARCLAYS BANK

Jyoti Mistry
PRICEWATERHOUSECOOPERS

Mwape Mondoloka
BARCLAYS BANK

Priscilla Moyo
GLOBAL LOGISTICS

Barnaby B. Mulenga
MINISTRY OF LAND

Chipo Munkombwe
PRICEWATERHOUSECOOPERS

Henry Musonda
*KIRAN & MUSONDA
ASSOCIATES*

Makungo Muyembe
MINISTRY OF LABOR

Teddie Mwale
ZESCO LTD

Francis Mwape
*NATIONAL COUNCIL FOR
CONSTRUCTION*

Shupi Mweene
*MINISTRY OF COMMERCE,
TRADE AND INDUSTRY*

Marjorie Grace Mwenda
*M.G. JOHNSON-MWENDA
& CO.*

Kanti Patel
*CHRISTOPHER, RUSSELL COOK
& CO.*

Solly Patel
*CHRISTOPHER, RUSSELL COOK
& CO.*

Aleksandar Perunicic
SDV

Miriam Sabi
*ZRA- CUSTOMER SERVICE
CENTER*

Mabvuto Sakala
CORPUS GLOBE ADVOCATES

Valerie Sesia
*CUSTOMIZED CLEARING AND
FORWARDING LTD.*

Nicole Sharpe-Phiri
SHARPE HOWARD & MWENYE

Kim Shelsby
ZAMBIA THRESHOLD PROJECT

Kayula Siame
*MINISTRY OF COMMERCE,
TRADE AND INDUSTRY*

Jason Villar
USAID

Albert M. Wood
ALBERT M WOOD & CO.

ZIMBABWE

Gulshen Afridi
SDV

Mark Badenhorst
PRICEWATERHOUSECOOPERS

Richard Beattie
THE STONE/ BEATTIE STUDIO

Innocent Chagonda
ATHERSTONE & COOK

Paul De Chalain
PRICEWATERHOUSECOOPERS

Beloved Dhlakama
BYRON VENTURAS & PARTNERS

Harry Kantor
KANTOR & IMMERMAN

Peter Lloyd
GILL, GODLONTON & GERRANS

Manuel Lopes
PRICEWATERHOUSECOOPERS

João Martins
PRICEWATERHOUSECOOPERS

Jim McComish
*PEARCE MCCOMISH
ARCHITECTS*

Sternford Moyo
SCANLEN & HOLDERNESS

Ostern Mutero
SAWYER & MKUSHI

Vanani Nyangulu
V.S. NYANGULU & ASSOCIATES

Malaika Ribeiro
PRICEWATERHOUSECOOPERS

Unity Sakhe
KANTOR & IMMERMAN

STANDING ORDER FORM

Standing orders are available to institutional customers only.

If you or your organization would like to automatically receive each new edition of Doing Business *as it is published, please check the box below, complete your address details, and mail or fax this order form to us. This will establish a standing order for your organization, and you will be invoiced each year upon publication. You may also e-mail books@ worldbank.org requesting your standing order for* Doing Business. *At any time you can cancel the standing order by sending an e-mail to books@worldbank.org.*

☐ *I would like to automatically receive each new edition of* Doing Business. *I understand that I will be invoiced each year upon publication.*

Name

Title

Organization

Address

City

State   *Zip/Postal code*

Country

Phone

Fax

E-mail

Institutional customers in the U.S. only: Please include purchase order

By mail
World Bank Publications
P.O. Box 960, Herndon
VA 20172-0960, USA

Online
www.worldbank.org/publications

By fax
+ 1-703-661-1501

Questions?
E-mail us at books@worldbank.org

By phone
+ 1-703-661-1580 or 800-645-7247

Available for US customers only, international customers please contact your local distributor to establish a standing order.

Individuals interested in receiving future editions of Doing Business *may ask to be added to our mailing list at books@worldbank.org.*

Please indicate in your e-mail that you would like to be added to the Doing Business *e-mail list.*

DDBSO6